Magazine Markets for Children's Writers™ 2007

Writer's Institute
Publications

Acknowledgments

The editors of this directory appreciate the generous contributions of our instructors and students and the cooperation of the magazine editors who made clear their policies and practices.

MARNI MCNIFF, Editor

SUSAN TIERNEY, Articles Editor

CLAIRE BROWN, Assistant Editor

BARBARA COLE, Assistant Editor

SHERRI KEEFE, Assistant Editor

Contributing Writers: EILEEN BYRNE, LAURA CLARK. BARBARA COLE, CAROLINE LAFLEUR, NOREEN GUMAN, KATHY VARDA

Cover Art: KAREN STORMER BROOKS

International Standard Book Number 1-889715-33-6

1-800-443-6078. www.writersbookstore.com
email: services@writersbookstore.com
Printed in Canada.

Contents

Submissions Guide   5

This section offers tips and step-by-step instructions for researching the market; writing query letters; preparing manuscript packages and bibliographies; initiating follow-up; and understanding copyrights, permissions, and other common publishing terms.

Gateway to the Markets   31

Contents (cont.)

Step-by-Step through the Submissions Process

The Perfect Pitch

You've just come up with a brilliant idea for a magazine article while taking your dog for a walk. Do you a) pitch it to the next person who passes you on the street; b) write a letter to *Highlights* as soon as you get home; or c) research the topic—and possible markets—over the next few weeks?

Ideas are all around us. As writers, it's hard to contain our excitement when new ideas take hold. We tend to share them with everyone, which can sometimes be beneficial, providing valuable feedback and constructive criticism. But there's more to making a sale than just the germ of an idea. Usually, the success of any new idea requires some degree of nurturing, starting with a great sales pitch. Creating the perfect pitch requires time, research—and a plan. (In other words, the answer is 'c'!)

In the world of magazine writing, the plan focuses on creating a perfect match between your idea and a target publication. You'll want to offer that publication's editor an irresistible match of quality, topic, and reader interest. Your goal is to identify the subjects those readers enjoy and then create material that engages them. Such information gathering will help support and complete your idea, so don't make your pitch until it is ready. Following are some tips to launch your research.

What Captivates Young Readers?

You'll increase your publication odds if you know what topics interest children. Consider how a child views the world. What kinds of things are they interested in? What is their typical day like? Researching current publications also goes a long way toward understanding your target audience.

Researching potential subjects can begin by surveying the categories of magazines in *Magazine Markets for Children's Writers*. Start with the Category Index on pages 372–376, an excellent guide to finding magazines that publish the types of articles or stories you write on the subjects that interest you.

You'll find general interest publications, like *Highlights for Children* or *Spider*, and also special interest periodicals on topics such as health, sports, science, fiction, college, religion, history, and so on. Continue your research online or at libraries. Do Internet searches, and check the library or bookstores. What magazines are out there, for what ages, and what subjects do they cover? Along with magazines targeted specifically to children, be sure to check parenting, educational, and regional magazines.

You'll find that each magazine covers numerous subjects from month to month or year to year, even special interest publications that cover a niche more deeply than widely. Read several issues of each magazine to research which subjects a potential target magazine has covered recently and how it has approached particular subjects in the past. Begin to make a list of the magazines that cover subjects of interest to you. Use the Magazine Match List on page 7.

Roll Call: Who Are Your Readers?

Researching readers is intricately tied to subjects, but a magazine's target age and how the publication speaks to that age—voice and purpose—are important factors in the market research you perform. Select subjects and slants based on age-appropriateness. If you'd like to take on the subject of animals' sleep habits, for example, you'd write an article or story for early readers with less specific information than you would for a middle-grader, and with a different tone.

Once again, go to the Internet and other media, as well as to schools and children's activities, to get a feel for the interests and developmental levels of the readership that is drawing you. For example, go to www.google.com and select the directory. Click Kids and Teens. Look at the websites under preschool, school time, teen life, and other categories. The arts section has many interesting sites that can give you additional insights into every age group.

Look Deeper: Magazine Specifications

Create a magazine market file that seems to be a match with your interests. Use index cards, a notebook, or your computer to develop a file for each magazine for your initial list of publications. Request sample issues for the magazines and read them. Listings in *Magazine Markets for Children's Writers* will tell you if writers' guidelines, an editorial calendar, or a theme list are available, as well as the cost of a sample copy and the size of the envelope to send with your request. (See page 55 for a sample listing.)

You may find the magazines you're targeting at your local library or newsstand, which will save you time and postage. Or, go to their websites—Web addresses are included in the listings.

Review each of the magazines in more detail for subjects related, or comparable, to yours. You should also check the Reader's Guide to Periodical Literature in your library to see if a target magazine has printed a piece similar to yours within the past two years. You may want to find another magazine or, depending on the publication, develop a new slant if you find that your topic is already well covered.

Study the Magazine and Its Guidelines

Sample issues. Use the Magazine Description Form (see example on page 8) to continue your detailed analysis of the publications, especially those you're beginning to hone in on as good matches. Record what you learn about each magazine. Evaluate how you could shape or present your manuscript to improve your chances of getting it published. If a particular idea or target magazine doesn't work out now, it may in the future—or it may lead to other ideas, angles, or possible markets. Review your market files periodically to generate ideas.

Writers' Guidelines. If the listing notes that a magazine offers writers' guidelines, you should send a letter requesting them with an SASE (see sample on page 9). Many magazines also list their writers' guidelines on their websites. This is specified in the listing. Read writers' guidelines, editorial calendars, and theme lists carefully. They may give you specific topics to write about, but even if you're creating your own, take the guidelines seriously. They are key to the needs of publications and often new writers give them too little weight.

Some guidelines are more detailed and helpful than others, but virtually all will tell you something about the readership, philosophy, and voice, as well as word length requirements, submissions format, and payment. More than that, some guidelines can give writers specific insights into the immediate needs of a magazine. For example, *The Magazine of Science Fiction and Fantasy* guidelines say, "We prefer character-driven stories; we receive a lot of fantasy fiction, but never enough science fiction or humor," while *Junior Baseball* guidelines are directive in another way: "A well-detailed story, full of supporting facts, figures, and anecdotes, makes for a better feature."

Magazine Match List: Subjects

Idea Topic: _____

	Magazine	Audience Age	Similar/Related Subject	Slant	Date Published
1.					
2.					

The guidelines will also indicate the rights a publication purchases, payment policies, and many more specifics—factors you'll consider as you get closer to submission. Many experienced writers do not sell all rights, unless the fee is high enough to be worth it; reselling articles or stories for reprint rights can be an additional source of income. (See the discussion of rights on page 24.)

Read with a Writer's Eye

Your review of sample magazines and guidelines should include:

• **Editorial objective.** Turn to the issue masthead, where the names of the editors are listed. Sometimes the magazine's editorial objective is also stated here. Does your story or article fit its purpose?

• **Audience.** What is the age range of the readers and the characters or children portrayed? For fiction, is your main character at the upper end of that range? Kids want to read about characters their own age or older.

• **Table of contents.** Study the table of contents. Usually, the stories and articles with bylines were written by freelancers like you. Compare the author names there with the editors and staff listed in the masthead to make sure that the publication is not primarily staff-written.

• **Article and story types.** Examine the types of articles and stories in the issue. Does one theme tie the articles and stories together? For example, does every article in a science magazine focus on plants, or do the articles cover a broader range of subjects? If the magazine issues a theme list, review it to see the range of topics. Think about the presentation as well: Is the magazine highly visual or does it rely primarily on text? Will photographs or illustrations be a consideration for you? Are there sidebars, and are you willing to provide those?

• **Style.** How is the writing impacted by the age of the audience? Read each story and

---

Magazine Description Form

Name of Magazine: *Calliope*   **Editor:** Rosalie F. Baker
Address: Cobblestone Publishing, 30 Grove Street, Suite C, Peterborough, NH 03458

Freelance Percentage: 95%   **Percentage of Authors Who Are New to the Magazine:** 30–40%

Description
What subjects does this magazine cover? *Calliope* features articles, interviews, fiction, and hands-on projects that focus on various aspects of world history.

Readership
Who are the magazine's typical readers? Middle-grade readers ages 9 to 14

Articles and Stories
What particular slants or distinctive characteristics do its articles or stories emphasize? Articles take a lively, original approach to historical subjects. Each issue is theme-based.

Potential Market
Is this magazine a potential market? Yes. I have an article that matches an upcoming theme.

Ideas for Articles or Stories
What article, story, or department idea could be submitted? Submit biographical fiction on Napoleon Bonaparte and the French Revolution, including excerpts from Napoleon's own letters.

article to get an idea of the style and tone the magazine prefers. Are there numerous three-syllable words, or mostly simple words? Are most sentences simple or complex, or a mixture of both? Is the tone upbeat and casual, or informative and educational? Do the writers speak directly to readers in a conversational way, or is the voice appropriately authoritative?

• **Editor's comments.** Note in the writers' guidelines particularly what *feel* for the magazine the editors provide. *Ladybug*'s guidelines include this important request: "(We) look for beauty of language and a sense of joy or wonder." *Magazine Markets for Children's Writers* includes a section called Editor's Comments in each listing. Study this section carefully as well. The editors give you tips on what they most want to see, or don't need.

Refine Your Magazine List

After you analyze your selected magazines, rank them by how well they match your idea, article or story's subject, style, and target age. Then return to the listings to examine other factors, such as the magazine's freelance potential, its receptivity to new or unpublished writers, rights purchased, and payment.

These facts reveal significant details about the magazine that you can use to your advantage as a freelance writer. For example, many published writers prefer magazines that:

- Publish a high percentage of authors who are new to the magazine;
- Respond in one month as opposed to three;
- Pay on acceptance rather than on publication.

If you're not yet published, however, writing for a nonpaying market may be worth the effort to earn the clips to build published credits. Once you've acquired credentials in these markets, you can list these published pieces in your queries to paying markets.

Ever written for a school or church newsletter, or a volunteer organization? If you don't have published 'clips,' writing samples such as these can also serve to showcase your writing skills and style.

Sample Guidelines Request

Name
Address
City, State ZIP

Date

Dear (Name of Current Editor):

I would like to request a copy of your writers' guidelines and editorial calendar. I have provided a self-addressed, stamped envelope for your convenience.

Sincerely,

Your name

Submitting Your Work to an Editor

Your market study will prepare you to draft a query or cover letter that convinces the right editor of why your idea is suitable for the magazine and why you are the person to write it. When do you send a query, and when should you send a cover letter and manuscript? Should a query be accompanied by an outline or synopsis or other materials? Is a query ever appropriate for fiction?

In your research, you should already have begun to see the variety of submission possibilities. Let's sort them out.

Know What Editors Want

Some editors want the query alone; it's efficient and provides them with enough information to make a decision about the article's appeal to their readers. Others want queries accompanied by a synopsis, outline, or other information for an article. Yet other editors prefer to have a complete article or story to get a full sense of the work you do and whether the subject is a match for them. Expect that the editor who accepts a complete, unsolicited manuscript may require even more revisions or rewrites than if you had queried first.

In reality, queries for magazine fiction are rare, although they've become somewhat more common for book-length fiction. Magazine stories are short enough without being too much for an editor to review.

If the editor asks for a:	Send:
Query (nonfiction)	• One-page letter indicating article topic, slant, target readership, word count • Bibliography of research sources • One-page résumé (if requested) • SASE
Query (fiction)	• One-page letter containing a brief synopsis of the plot, indicating target readership and word count • SASE
Complete manuscript (nonfiction)	• Brief cover letter • Manuscript • Bibliography of research sources • List of people interviewed • SASE
Complete manuscript (fiction)	• Brief cover letter • Manuscript • SASE

Keys to Writing a Query Letter

Imagine you're at a writing conference and you step onto an elevator with the editor of a major children's magazine. The editor smiles and asks if you're a writer, and you find yourself in the perfect position to make a pitch for your latest article. The problem: You've only got fifteen seconds, about the time it takes for the elevator to go up one floor.

Just as an "elevator speech" is a key concept in the marketing world, a query letter is the writer's equivalent. Editors look at hundreds of submissions, and a query is your chance to get his or her attention and make a positive impression. In the space of a page, a query tells the editor why your article will benefit that particular magazine and why you are the best person to write it. A good query is not about you; instead, it should focus on the needs of the magazine and how your article addresses those needs.

You may have already written an article and want to sell it to a magazine that only reviews query letters. Or, you may be writing a query in advance of writing an article. Either way, there are several advantages to using a query letter:

- Editors generally respond faster to queries than manuscripts.

- Your chances for a sale increase because, at this early stage, the editor is still able to help mold your manuscript to fit the magazine.

- You save research and writing time by knowing exactly what the editor wants.

Do Your Homework

Before you write your query letter, know the magazine inside and out. Review several sample issues and the guidelines, then tailor your idea to work specifically for that publication. Know the word limit the magazine prefers and whether or not it requires a bibliography of sources. Most editors like articles with quotes from experts in the field you're writing about. Be prepared to tell the editor who you'll interview for the piece. For example, if you want to write an article about robots, you might plan to interview robot designers and include their names in your query letter. Or, if the magazine uses primarily articles from a kid's point of view, track down members of a science club or other youth organization who have experience making robots of their own. It may also help to name an expert who can vet the final manuscript and vouch for its accuracy. Lastly, know whether you can obtain photos—this can often swing a sale.

What Makes a Good Query Letter

A good query letter is short and to the point. If you can't get your idea across in one page or less, your article may not be as tightly focused as it should be.

Below are the basic steps in writing a query (see the examples on pages 13–16):

- Direct your query to a specific editor.

- Begin with a lead paragraph that grabs the editor's interest and conveys your slant. Attention-grabbing techniques like statistics or an unusual "twist" on a topic make an editor want to keep reading.

- Include a brief description of your article that conveys your central idea. This should be very narrow in focus.

- Show how your idea meets the editorial goals of the targeted magazine.

- Indicate approximate word length.

- Provide specific details as to what will be in the article—anecdotes, case histories, statistics, etc.

- Cite sources, research resources, and planned interviews.

- Indicate number and type of photographs or illustrations available. If you can't provide any, don't mention them at all.

- List your publishing credits briefly and, if enclosed, refer to your resume, clips, or writing samples. If you are unpublished, don't draw attention to it. Instead, emphasize relevant or unique experience you may have in regard to the subject.

- Close by asking if the magazine is interested; mention whether your query represents a simultaneous submission.

• Include other information if requested, such as an outline or bibliography.

A Good First Impression

Your query is the first impression the editor will have of you and your work, so take a few extra minutes to make sure it's ready to send.

• Use good quality bond paper.

• The font should be close to Times Roman 12 point.

• Use a letter-quality printout, with crisp, dark type.

• Leave 1 to 1¼-inch margins on all four sides. Single spacing is preferred.

• A query is meant to showcase your writing skills, so proofread for grammar, spelling, typos, etc.

• Make sure your contact information is included in the query in case the editor wants to contact you, along with a self-addressed, stamped envelope or postcard for the editor's reply.

Submitting kid-friendly photos with your manuscript can increase the likelihood of a sale. If you don't have a knack for photography, look for images from trade associations, PR departments, or government organizations—whatever is appropriate for your article.

Email or Snail Mail?

If your target magazine accepts both hard copy and email queries, which should you choose? Email does not always mean faster response times, but it does cut down on the time and cost involved in preparing and mailing a traditional submission package.

It also presents new challenges. Email has changed the style of queries somewhat because it is less formal than print. While this is a welcome change in most cases, be watchful that the tone of your email remains professional at all times. Also, avoid using cutesy email addresses and a too-familiar tone, which turns off editors.

If you do submit via email, check each publisher's guidelines to determine their preferences for the following:

• **File attachments.** Most publishers prefer that submissions be included in the main body of the email, not as an attachment. Once an editor gets to know you, attachments may then be preferable.

• **Electronic format.** Rich text format (RTF), Microsoft Word, and HTML are most commonly used for sending documents electronically; postscript and PDF files are also sometimes accepted.

• **Contact information.** Don't forget to include your contact information in the body of your email, as well as the full title of your work.

• **Subject line.** Unless a publisher has specific directions for the subject line, make yours as informative as possible, i.e., "Submission—How to Write Children's Books."

Query Letter—Checklist

Your query letter will make the difference between a sale and a rejection in today's magazine market. The following checklist and sample query letter offer tips on how to avoid simple mistakes that can cost you a sale.

• Verify that you are writing to the current editor and correct address; double-check the spelling of the name and address.

• Phrase the letter as if the article is in the planning stage. Editors prefer pieces written specifically for their publication, not generic articles.

• Give enough examples of what you will cover to allow the editor to get a feel for the article. Include any unique material, interviews, or primary sources that you will use.

• Note any background or experience you have that gives you credibility in writing this piece for this particular audience. **Include publishing credits if available.** No need to tell the editor if you are unpublished; let your work speak for you. If you have been published, briefly give the editor your publishing history.

• Keep the closing brief and professional; remember to include an SASE.

Address
Phone Number
Email
Date

Kim Griswell
Highlights for Children
803 Church Street
Honesdale, PA 18431

Dear Ms. Griswell,

Wherever Cuddles goes, she attracts attention. It's not every day you see a horse that stands only 24 inches tall and wears sneakers on her hooves! Nor does one often spot a tiny horse peering out of the backseat of a taxi or riding down a department store escalator. People are even more surprised when they notice that Cuddles is guiding a blind person. Cuddles really is a very unusual horse—she is the first horse to work as a trained guide to a blind person.

I propose to write an article telling about the Guide Horse Foundation, where Don and Janet Burleson are successfully training pygmy horses to guide the blind. This article, tentatively titled "Is that Horse Wearing Sneakers?" would describe the tasks guide horses are trained to do, from following simple verbal commands to using "intelligent disobedience." It would also delve into the special talents horses possess that enable them to be good guides, like 350-degree range of vision. In addition, the article will describe the activities of guide horses in their off hours. Guide horses work hard all week, so who could begrudge them a rewarding game of bobbing for apples, or blame them as they snore and drool in their sleep.

"Is that Horse Wearing Sneakers?" would target readers from 9 to 12 and run about 1,600 words. Photos of pygmy guide horses at work, at rest, and in uniform are available upon request.

If you would be interested in seeing the finished article, I would be happy to submit it for your consideration. I have enclosed a self-addressed, stamped envelope and I look forward to your reply.

Best regards,

Shannon Teper

Sample Query & Article Outline

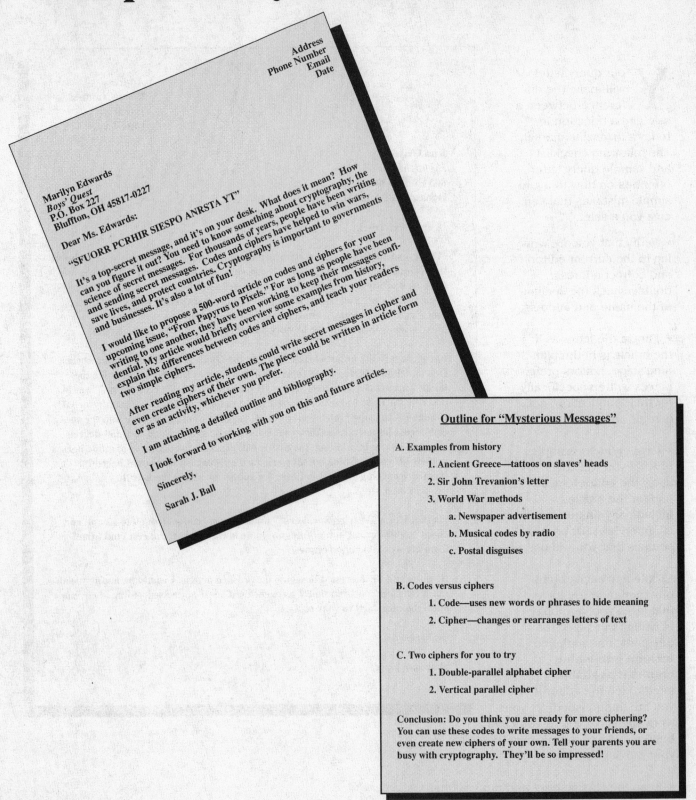

Address
Phone Number
Email
Date

Marilyn Edwards
Boys' Quest
P.O. Box 227
Bluffton, OH 45817-0227

Dear Ms. Edwards:

"SFUORR PCRHIR SIESPO ANRSTA YT"

It's a top-secret message, and it's on your desk. What does it mean? How can you figure it out? You need to know something about cryptography, the science of secret messages. For thousands of years, people have been writing and sending secret messages. Codes and ciphers have helped to win wars, save lives, and protect countries. Cryptography is important to governments and businesses. It's also a lot of fun!

I would like to propose a 500-word article on codes and ciphers for your upcoming issue, "From Papyrus to Pixels." For as long as people have been writing to one another, they have been working to keep their messages confidential. My article would briefly overview some examples from history, explain the differences between codes and ciphers, and teach your readers two simple ciphers.

After reading my article, students could write secret messages in cipher and even create ciphers of their own. The piece could be written in article form or as an activity, whichever you prefer.

I am attaching a detailed outline and bibliography.

I look forward to working with you on this and future articles.

Sincerely,

Sarah J. Ball

Outline for "Mysterious Messages"

A. Examples from history
  1. Ancient Greece—tattoos on slaves' heads
  2. Sir John Trevanion's letter
  3. World War methods
     a. Newspaper advertisement
     b. Musical codes by radio
     c. Postal disguises

B. Codes versus ciphers
  1. Code—uses new words or phrases to hide meaning
  2. Cipher—changes or rearranges letters of text

C. Two ciphers for you to try
  1. Double-parallel alphabet cipher
  2. Vertical parallel cipher

Conclusion: Do you think you are ready for more ciphering? You can use these codes to write messages to your friends, or even create new ciphers of your own. Tell your parents you are busy with cryptography. They'll be so impressed!

Sample Query Letters

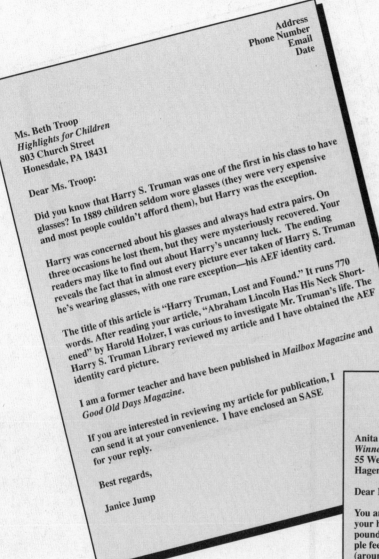

Address
Phone Number
Email
Date

Ms. Beth Troop
Highlights for Children
803 Church Street
Honesdale, PA 18431

Dear Ms. Troop:

Did you know that Harry S. Truman was one of the first in his class to have glasses? In 1889 children seldom wore glasses (they were very expensive and most people couldn't afford them), but Harry was the exception.

Harry was concerned about his glasses and always had extra pairs. On three occasions he lost them, but they were mysteriously recovered. Your readers may like to find out about Harry's uncanny luck. The ending reveals the fact that in almost every picture ever taken of Harry S. Truman he's wearing glasses, with one rare exception—his AEF identity card.

The title of this article is "Harry Truman, Lost and Found." It runs 770 words. After reading your article, "Abraham Lincoln Has His Neck Shortened" by Harold Holzer, I was curious to investigate Mr. Truman's life. The Harry S. Truman Library reviewed my article and I have obtained the AEF identity card picture.

I am a former teacher and have been published in *Mailbox Magazine* and *Good Old Days Magazine.*

If you are interested in reviewing my article for publication, I can send it at your convenience. I have enclosed an SASE for your reply.

Best regards,

Janice Jump

Address
Phone Number
Email
Date

Anita Jacobs, Editor
Winner Magazine
55 West Oak Ridge Drive
Hagerstown, MD 21740

Dear Ms. Jacobs:

You are about to make a presentation when suddenly your legs are spaghetti, your hands feel clammy, your stomach turns somersaults and your heart pounds loudly. You have stage fright! This is a sensation that millions of people feel, kids included. As young people begin to feel more self-conscious (around 9 or 10 years old) they can develop stage fright. This is a difficult problem when they are constantly asked to present work in front of the class, read out loud, or even ask a teacher a question. Kids might feel even worse because they think they are alone in their fears. They don't realize that even the most experienced actors can feel stage fright.

I would like to write a 600-word article that shows students they are not alone in their fear. I would include a quote from a famous actor (Ian McKellen) showing that everyone can feel stage fright. The article would list several strategies for coping with stage fright, both during the preparation period and at the presentation itself.

As a Theatre of Youth specialist, I have worked with people of all ages. I've seen the transition from young children who are willing to go anywhere their imagination takes them, to adolescents who are afraid of embarrassment. With some practical skills, all young people can learn to control their fears.

Thank you for your time. I am enclosing an SASE for your reply.

Sincerely,

Lisa A. Kramer

Sample Query Letters

Kim Griswell
Highlights for Children
803 Church Street
Honesdale, PA 18431

Address
Phone Number
Email
Date

Dear Ms. Griswell:

Working with clay is fun! You can smush it, squeeze it, and shape it. It feels cool in your hands. Have you ever made a mobile? Did you know that you can make a clay mobile?

I am proposing a how-to article for 3- to 12-year-old children. This article would be tentatively called "Let's Make a Clay Mobile." The length of the article would be about 200 words. The article would provide step-by-step instructions that children must follow to make a clay mobile.

I have a BS in education with a minor in art. I have created craft ideas and used them in my work with children.

I am recently published in *Kids Holiday Craft Magazine* and will have an article in an upcoming issue of *Wee Ones.* I am also a member of the Society of Children's Book Writers and Illustrators.

If you are interested in seeing the article, I would be happy to submit it for your consideration. I can furnish photographs of work in progress and the finished product.

Sincerely,

Suzanne Miles

Address
Phone Number
Email
Date

Heather A. Delabre, Associate Editor
Spider
Cricket Magazine Group
P.O. Box 300
315 Fifth Street
Peru, IL 61354-0300

Dear Ms. Delabre:

Did you know some spiders' silk is so strong it can stop a bird in flight? That a thread of spider silk as big as a pencil could stop an airplane?

My proposed article titled "Web Masters" is a craft and science article of about 400 words. It shows children how to build a web like a spider, and shares some amazing spider facts.

I believe "Web Masters" would be a perfect fit for *Spider* (no pun intended).

My story "Just Luka and Me," was published in *Simple Pleasures of Friendship* (Conari/Red Wheel/Weiser, January 2004). My activity article, "Snowflake Shake" is forthcoming in *Spider*.

If you are interested in seeing this article, I would be happy to submit it for consideration. I have enclosed an SASE for your convenience.

Yours truly,

Keely Parrack

Enc.: SASE

Preparing a Manuscript Package

The following guide shows how to prepare and mail a professional-looking manuscript package. However, you should always adhere to an individual magazine's submission requirements as detailed in its writers' guidelines and its listing in this directory.

Cover Letter Tips

Always keep your cover letter concise and to the point. Provide essential information only.

If the letter accompanies an unsolicited manuscript submission (see below), indicate that your manuscript is enclosed and mention its title and word length. If you're sending the manuscript after the editor responded favorably to your query letter, indicate that the editor requested to see the enclosed manuscript.

Provide a brief description of the piece and a short explanation of how it fits the editor's needs. List any publishing credits or other pertinent qualifications. If requested in the guidelines or listing, note any material or sources you can provide. Indicate if the manuscript is being sent to other magazines as well (a simultaneous submission). Mention that you have enclosed a self-addressed, stamped envelope for return of the manuscript.

Address
Phone Number
Email
Date

Sample Cover Letter

Mr. Marvin Wengerd, Editor
Nature Friend
2673 Township Road 421
Sugarcreek, OH 44681

Dear Mr. Wengerd:

What can fly but would rather not run, lives in the wild in almost every area of the United States, was once thought to be noble enough to be our national bird, and is the staple of Thanksgiving dinners throughout the nation?

You have most likely guessed the turkey and you are correct. Enclosed is an article of about 800 words tentatively titled "My Neighbors Are a Bunch of Turkeys," as well as a sidebar titled "Ten Strange Turkey Facts" of about 370 words.

Wild turkeys are the only domesticated animal native to North America and thus quite an important part of our history and environment. Living on this farm, I have seen all sorts of wildlife roaming the meadows, fields, and woods. This is the first time I was able to observe a species so close and so often as to be able to research my field notes. I think your young readers will be as intrigued as I have been about this bird that can be found in their backyards.

Thank you for your time and I look forward to hearing from you.

Sincerely,

Jan E. Fetherolf-Shick

Enc.: Manuscript, SASE

Subject/
Specifications:
A brief description of the topic and its potential interest to the magazine's readers. Word lengths, age range, availability of photos, and other submission details.

Publishing
Credits or
Relevant
Experience

Closing:
Be formal and direct.

Standard Manuscript Format

The format for preparing manuscripts is fairly standard—an example is shown below. Double-space manuscript text, leaving 1- to 1½-inch margins on the top, bottom, and sides. Indent 5 spaces for paragraphs.

In the upper left corner of the first page (also known as the title page), single space your name, address, phone number, and email address. In the upper right corner of that page, place your word count.

Center the title with your byline below it halfway down the page, approximately 5 inches. Then begin the manuscript text 4 lines below your byline.

In the upper left corner of the following pages, type your last name, the page number, and a word or two of your title. Then, space down 4 lines and continue the text of the manuscript.

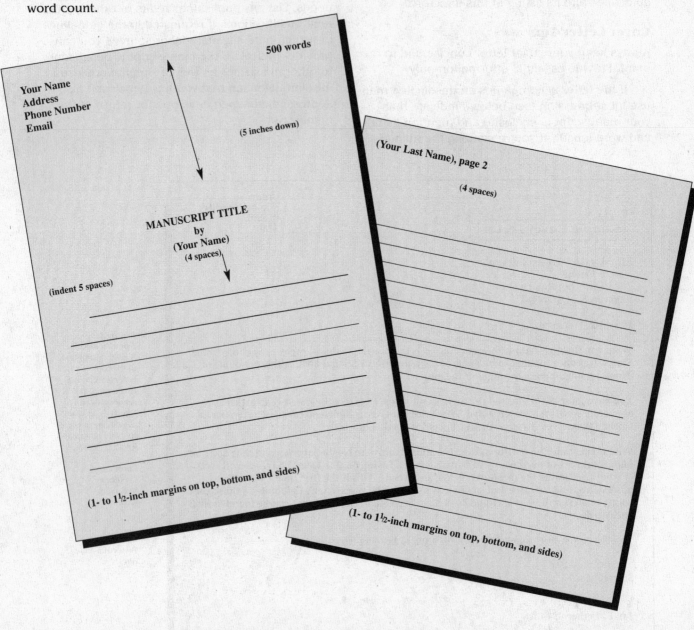

500 words

Your Name
Address
Phone Number
Email

(5 inches down)

MANUSCRIPT TITLE
by
(Your Name)
(4 spaces)

(indent 5 spaces)

(1- to 1½-inch margins on top, bottom, and sides)

(Your Last Name), page 2

(4 spaces)

(1- to 1½-inch margins on top, bottom, and sides)

Sample Cover Letters

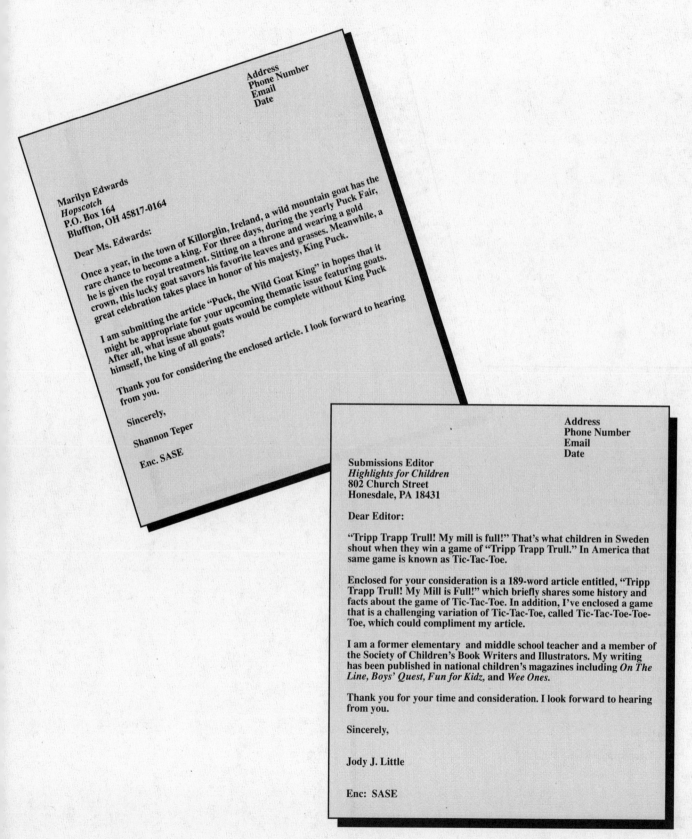

Address
Phone Number
Email
Date

Marilyn Edwards
Hopscotch
P.O. Box 164
Bluffton, OH 45817-0164

Dear Ms. Edwards:

Once a year, in the town of Killorglin, Ireland, a wild mountain goat has the rare chance to become a king. For three days, during the yearly Puck Fair, he is given the royal treatment. Sitting on a throne and wearing a gold crown, this lucky goat savors his favorite leaves and grasses. Meanwhile, a great celebration takes place in honor of his majesty, King Puck.

I am submitting the article "Puck, the Wild Goat King" in hopes that it might be appropriate for your upcoming thematic issue featuring goats. After all, what issue about goats would be complete without King Puck himself, the king of all goats?

Thank you for considering the enclosed article. I look forward to hearing from you.

Sincerely,

Shannon Teper

Enc. SASE

Address
Phone Number
Email
Date

Submissions Editor
Highlights for Children
802 Church Street
Honesdale, PA 18431

Dear Editor:

"Tripp Trapp Trull! My mill is full!" That's what children in Sweden shout when they win a game of "Tripp Trapp Trull." In America that same game is known as Tic-Tac-Toe.

Enclosed for your consideration is a 189-word article entitled, "Tripp Trapp Trull! My Mill is Full!" which briefly shares some history and facts about the game of Tic-Tac-Toe. In addition, I've enclosed a game that is a challenging variation of Tic-Tac-Toe, called Tic-Tac-Toe-Toe-Toe, which could compliment my article.

I am a former elementary and middle school teacher and a member of the Society of Children's Book Writers and Illustrators. My writing has been published in national children's magazines including *On The Line, Boys' Quest, Fun for Kidz,* and *Wee Ones.*

Thank you for your time and consideration. I look forward to hearing from you.

Sincerely,

Jody J. Little

Enc: SASE

Sample Cover Letters

Submissions Editor
Highlights for Children
803 Church Street
Honesdale, PA 18431

Address
Phone Number
Email
Date

Dear Editor:

A spider, thirty feet tall, is luring children into downtown Ottawa, Canada! It's perched outside the National Gallery of Canada right now, inviting children to walk underneath the spider's body and touch its giant bronze legs.

"Mommy, A Giant Spider" is an article for children ages 3 to 7. The enclosed article runs 255 words. Included are a bibliography, reference material, and suggestions for a picture and graphic.

I'm a full-time freelance writer living in Ottawa. I have one book published, as well as several articles published in *Odyssey, YES Mag,* and even *Highlights for Children* a few years back.

Thank you for your consideration.

Sincerely,

Diana Thistle Tremblay

Virginia Edwards, Editor
Boys' Quest
P.O. Box 227
Bluffton, OH 45817-0227

Dear Ms. Edwards:

Have you ever wondered who could eat a bee without getting stung? Enclosed is a lively article for children ages six to nine entitled "Who Eats Bees?" It explains the many different types of animals that eat bees to survive. It also explains the process by which they catch the bees and how they devenomize them in order to eat them.

Although there have been numerous articles written on bees and bee stings, I thought it would be interesting to see it from a different perspective—this time focusing on who is getting the bee instead of the bee getting us!

I've enclosed a copy of the manuscript, along with a sidebar detailing some interesting facts. Thank you for your time and I look forward to hearing from you.

Sincerely,

Beth Lucas

Enc.: Manuscript, sidebar, SASE

Sample Cover Letter & Bibliography

Address
Phone Number
Email
Date

Jonathan Shaw, Editor
The School Magazine
NSW Department of Education and Training
P.O. Box 1928
Macquarie Centre, NSW 2113 Australia

Dear Mr. Shaw:

I'm sure you've heard of Winnie-the-Pooh! Who hasn't? Do you know that Winnie was a real, live bear? *She* was born in 1914 near the town of White Water in the Canadian province of Manitoba. A trapper shot her mother while Winnie was still a cub. Normally, cubs don't survive in the wilderness when they lose their mother, but Winnie's case was different. The trapper caught Winnie and brought her to the train station in White River on a leash. A Canadian Army veterinary officer saw Winnie there and purchased her from the trapper. That began her rise from orphaned cub to international star.

Children of all ages know and love Winnie-the-Pooh, but how many of them know her origin? The enclosed article "Winnie-the-Who?" tells the story of Winnie's beginnings as an orphaned bear cub and of her benefactor, Lieutenant Harry Colebourn. I hope "Winnie" can find a place in the pages of *The School Magazine* where she will once again entertain and delight young readers who may have thought themselves too old for teddy bear stories.

I've enclosed a bibliography, a disposable manuscript, and an SAE/IRC for your reply. I look forward to hearing from you.

Sincerely,

Jim Slater

Enc: bibliography/ms/SAE/IRC

Bibliography

Colebourn, Fred, "Lt. Harry Colebourn and Winnie-the-Bear," original biographical sketch written by Harry Colebourn's son, Fred Colebourn, May 1988. Corrected and edited by CWO Gordon Crossley, Fort Garry Horse Museum and Archives, May 1999 to August 2000. www.fortgarryhorse.ca/HTML/winnie-the-bear.html

"Pooh Corner Biographies: A. A. Milne." www.pooh-corner.com/biomilne.html

Shushkewich, Val. The Real Winnie, A One-of-A-Kind Bear, Toronto, Ontario: Natural Heritage/Natural History Inc. 2003.

Snell, Gordon. Oh, no! More Canadians!: Hysterically Historical Rhymes, Toronto, McArthur & Company, 1998.

"Disney and Pooh" www.just-pooh.com/disney.html

"Winnie-the-Pooh FAQ" www.lavasurfer.com/pooh-faq3.html#18

"Winnie the Pooh—History of Pooh" www.just-pooh.com/history

"Winnie the Pooh—Real Toys" www.just-pooh.com/toys.html

Bibliography

Nothing inspires more confidence in you as a writer than a thorough bibliography. More than just a list of materials you plan on using (or have already used) to prepare your article, a well-rounded, diverse bibliography can be an important tool to help sell your writing. Not only does it show that you've properly acknowledged and credited your sources of information, but also that the finished piece is likely to be supported by strong evidence found in a variety of credible sources. For many editors, extensive research often indicates originality in a manuscript.

Some magazines require a bibliography as part of a submission package for nonfiction articles. (Bibliographies are rarely required for fiction, with the possible exception of historical fiction.) Unique research methods are required for every project but, in general, the bibliography should be made up of resources that are both historical and current, target adults and children, and cover primary and secondary sources. It should also show that you plan on culling information from other sources, such as interviews with experts or other relevant individuals (a profile subject and those who know him or her, for example), websites, and museums. And don't hesitate to think outside the box when it comes to information gathering: maps, court documents, diaries, old photographs, song lyrics, census data, and other sources offer a wealth of information that can make your work shine.

Citation styles vary greatly, but several references are available and generally accepted for bibliographic format. Among these are: *The Chicago Manual of Style*; *Modern Language Association (MLA) Handbook*; or handbooks by news organizations such as the *New York Times*.

Need an expert interview to enhance your bibliography? Professional member associations, consumer advocacy organizations, and large corporations offer a host of potential interview subjects.

Sample Bibliography

**Bibliography for "The Doctor is In:
Cleaner Fish on the Coral Reef"**

Copley, Jon. "Coral Reefs Operate Free Market Economy." *New Scientist,* April 2002.

Dr. James D. Franklin, Scientist, National Coral Reef Institute, interview.

Murphy, Richard C. *Coral Reefs: Cities Under the Sea.* Princeton, NJ: Darwin Press, 2002.

Natural History Museum, "Life on the Reef."
http://www.nhm.ac.uk/nature-online/life.html

Sale, Peter F. *Coral Reef Fishes: Dynamics and Diversity in a Complex Ecosystem.* Burlington, MA: Academic Press, 2002.

Preparing a Résumé

Several publications in this directory request that prospective writers send a list of publishing credits or enclose a résumé with their submission. As you read through the listings, you will notice that some editors want to see a résumé only, while others may request a résumé with a query letter, writing samples, or a complete manuscript.

By reviewing a résumé, an editor can determine if a prospective writer has the necessary experience to research and write material for that publication.

A résumé that you submit to a magazine is different from one you would submit when applying for a job, because it emphasizes writing experience, memberships in writing associations, and education. This type of résumé does not list all of your work experience or every association to which you belong, but should include only those credentials that demonstrate experience related to the magazine's editorial requirements. In the case of educational or special interest publications, be sure to include pertinent work experience.

No one style is preferred, but make sure your name and email address (if you have one) appear at the top of the page. Keep your résumé short and concise—it should not be more than one page long.

Sample Résumés

Joanna Coates
Address
Phone
Email

EDUCATION:

University of Missouri, Columbia, MO
1980   M.Ed. Reading
1975   B.A. English Education

Missouri Certified Teacher of English and Reading Specialist

TEACHING EXPERIENCE:
1997–present   Instructor
Adult Continuing Education ESL Classes
Springfield College, Springfield, MO

1981-1995   Classroom Teacher
Middle School English and Reading
John Jay Middle School, Thornfield, MO

EDUCATIONAL MATERIAL PUBLISHED:
Educational Insights
1995   FUN WITH READING II
Story/activity kit
1993   FUN WITH READING I
Story/activity kit

MEMBERSHIP:
Society of Children's Book Writers and Illustrators

Maria Lital
Address
Phone
Email

EDUCATION:
1989   Bachelor of Arts
History/Journalism
University of North Carolina,
Chapel Hill, North Carolina

WORK EXPERIENCE:
1998–present   Media Sales Representative,
Clarkson Ledger, Ripley, Tennessee

1996-1998   Researcher/Librarian, Station WBXI,
Danville, Kentucky

1993–1996   Researcher, *Family News*, Raleigh, North Carolina

1990–1993   Assistant Librarian, Public Library; Edenton, North Carolina

RELATED ACTIVITIES:
1998–present   Newsletter Editor, St. James Church, Ripley, Tennessee

1998–present   Historical Tour Guide, Ripley, Tennessee, Historical Association

1996–present   Active in Civil War Reenactments

MEMBERSHIP:
1996–present   American Library Association

Copyright and Permissions

Just like the movie you watched last night and the CD you listened to on the way to work this morning, your magazine article is one of many creative works that is afforded the protection of copyright. As one of the nation's "copyright-based industries," publishing relies heavily on the concept of obtaining legal ownership of written works. When you write an article, you own the legal rights to the manuscript, as well as the right to decide how it is reproduced and, for certain works, how it is performed or displayed.

As of 1998, your heirs can also enjoy the fruits of your labor: That's when Congress passed the Copyright Term Extension Act, which offers you copyright protection for your work created during or after 1978 for your lifetime plus 70 years, until you choose to sell all or part of the copyright for this work.

Do You Need to Register Your Work?

Thanks to copyright law, your work is protected from the moment it is recorded in a tangible medium, such as a computer file or on paper, without any need for legal action or counsel. You don't even need to register your work with the United States Copyright Office; in fact, most editors view an author's copyright notice on manuscripts as the sign of an amateur, or a signal that the author doesn't trust the publication. A copy of the manuscript and a dated record of your submission will provide proof of creation, should the need arise.

If you do decide to register your work, obtain an application form and directions on the correct way to file your copyright application. Write to the Library of Congress, Copyright Office, 101 Independence Ave. S. E., Washington, DC 20559-6000. These forms and directions are also available online in Adobe Acrobat format at: www.copyright.gov/forms. Copyright registration fees are currently $30.

If you have registered your unpublished manuscript with the Library of Congress, notify your editor of that fact once it is accepted for publication.

Rights Purchased by Magazines

As a writer and copyright holder, you have the right to decide how your work should be shared with the world. By agreeing to publication in a magazine, you also agree to transfer some of your rights over to the magazine so that your article can be printed and distributed as part of that publication. A publisher is restricted, however, on when, how, and where he or she may publish your manuscript—terms that are set down in a publishing contract. Below is a list of common rights that are purchased by magazines:

All World Rights: The publisher purchases all rights to publish your work anywhere in the world any number of times. This includes all forms of media (both current and those which may be developed later). The publisher also has the right to all future use of the work, including reprints, syndication, creation of derivative works, and use in databases. You no longer have the right to sell or reproduce the work, unless you can negotiate for the return of certain rights (for example, book rights).

All World Serial Rights: The publisher purchases all rights to publish your work in newspapers, magazines, and other serial publications throughout the world any number of times. You retain all other rights, such as the right to use it as a chapter in a book.

First Rights: A publisher acquires the right to publish your work for the first time in any specified media. Electronic and nontraditional markets often seek these rights. All other rights, including reprint rights, belong to you.

Electronic Rights: Publishers use this as a catch-all for inclusion in any type of electronic publication, such as CD-ROM, websites, ezines, or in an electronic database.

First North American Serial Rights: The publisher can publish your work for the first time in a U.S. or Canadian periodical. You retain the book and North American reprint rights, as well as first rights to a foreign market.

Second or Reprint Rights: This allows a publication non-exclusive rights to print the material for the second time. You may not authorize second publication to occur until after the work has appeared in print by the publisher who bought first rights.

One-time Rights: Often bought by regional publications, this means the publication has bought the right to use the material once. You may continue to sell the material elsewhere; however, you should inform the publisher if this work is being simultaneously considered for publication in a competing magazine.

You should be aware that an agreement may limit a publisher to the right to publish your work in certain media (e.g., magazines and other periodicals only) or the agreement may include wider-ranging rights (e.g., the right to publish the manuscript in a book or an audiocassette). The right may be limited to publishing within a specific geographic region or in a specific language. Any rights you retain allow you to resell the manuscript within the parameters of your agreement.

It is becoming increasingly common for magazines to purchase all rights, especially those who host Internet sites and make archives of previously published articles available to readers. Unless you have extensive publishing credentials, you may not want to jeopardize the opportunity to be published by insisting on selling limited rights.

E-zines typically purchase both exclusive and non-exclusive electronic rights. They may want to publish your article exclusively for a particular period of time (usually one year). After that you may be free to sell it elsewhere or place it on your own website, while the original e-zine continues to display or archive the article.

Contracts and Agreements

Typically, when a publisher indicates an interest in your manuscript, he or she specifies what rights the publication will acquire. Then usually, but not always, a publisher will send you a letter of agreement or a standard written contract spelling out the terms of the agreement.

If a publisher does not send you a written contract or agreement and appears to be relying on oral consent, you need to consider your options. While an oral agreement may be legally binding, it is not as easy to enforce as a written one. To protect your interests, draft a letter outlining the terms as you understand them (e.g., a 500-word article without photos, first North American serial rights, paying on acceptance at $.05 a word). Send two copies of the letter to the editor (with a self-addressed, stamped envelope), asking him or her to sign one and return it to you if the terms are correct.

Work Made for Hire

Another term that is appearing more frequently in contracts is work made for hire. As a freelance writer, most editors treat you as an independent contractor (not an employee) who writes articles for their publication. Magazine editors can assign or commission articles to freelancers as works-made-for-hire, making the finished article property of the publisher.

Under current copyright laws, only certain types of commissioned works are considered works-made-for-hire, and only when both the publisher and the commissioned writer agree in writing. These works typically include items such as contributions to "collective works" such as magazines. A contract or agreement clearly stating that the material is a work-made-for-hire must be signed by both parties and be in place before the material is written. Once a writer agrees to these terms, he or she no longer has any rights to the work.

Note that a pre-existing piece, such as an unsolicited manuscript that is accepted for publication, is not considered a commissioned work.

Guidelines for Permission to Quote

When you want to quote another writer's words in a manuscript you're preparing, you must get that writer's permission. If you don't, you could be sued for copyright infringement. Here are some guidelines:

- Any writing published in the U.S. prior to 1923 is in the public domain, as are works created by the U.S. government. Such material may be quoted without permission, but the source should be cited.

- No specific limits are set as to the length of permitted quotations in your articles: different publishers have various requirements. Generally, if you quote more than a handful of words, you should seek permission. Always remember to credit your sources.

- The doctrine of "fair use" allows quoting portions of a copyrighted work for certain purposes, as in a review, news reporting, nonprofit educational uses, or research. Contrary to popular belief, there is no absolute word limit on fair use. But as a general rule, never quote more than a few successive paragraphs from a book or article and credit the source.

- If you're submitting a manuscript that contains quoted material, you'll need to obtain permission from the source to quote the material before it is published. If you're uncertain about what to do, your editor should be able to advise you.

Resources

Interested in finding out more about writers and their rights under the law? Check these sources for further information:

The Publishing Law Center
www.publaw.com/legal.html
The Copyright Handbook: How to Protect and Use Written Works, 8th Edition by Attorney Stephen Fishman. Nolo, 2005.
The Writer's Legal Guide, 3rd Edition by Tad Crawford. Allworth Press, 2002.

It's important for freelance writers to be as knowledgeable about selling their work as they are about creating it. For real-world advice, check out writers' groups (such as the Authors Guild), which sometimes offer contract advice, sample contracts, and tips on contract negotiation.

Last Steps and Follow Up

Before mailing your manuscript, check the pages for neatness, readability, and proper page order. Proofread for typographical errors. Redo pages if necessary. Keep a copy of the manuscript for your records.

Mailing Requirements

Assemble the pages (unstapled) and place your cover letter on top of the first page.

Send manuscripts over 5 pages in length in a 9x12 or 10x13 manila envelope. Include a same-size SASE marked "First Class." If submitting to a foreign magazine, enclose the proper amount of International Reply Coupons (IRC) for return postage. Mail manuscripts under 5 pages in a large business-size envelope with a same-size SASE folded inside.

Package your material carefully and address the outer envelope to the magazine editor. Send your submission via first-class or priority mail. Don't use certified or registered mail. (See Postage Information, page 30.)

Follow Up with the Editor

Some writers contend that waiting for an editor to respond is the hardest part of writing. But wait you must. Editors usually respond within the time period specified in the listings.

If you don't receive a response by the stated response time, allow at least three weeks to pass before you contact the editor. At that time, send a letter with a self-addressed, stamped envelope requesting to know the status of your submission.

The exception to this general rule is when you send a return postcard with a manuscript. In that case, look for your postcard about three weeks after mailing the manuscript. If you don't receive it by then, write to the editor requesting confirmation that it was received.

If more than two months pass after the stated response time and you don't receive any response, send a letter withdrawing your work from consideration. At that point, you can send your query or manuscript to the next publication on your list.

What You Can Expect

The most common responses to a submission are an impersonal rejection letter, a personalized rejection letter, an offer to look at your material "on speculation," or an assignment.

If you receive an impersonal rejection note, revise your manuscript if necessary, and send your work to the next editor on your list. If you receive a personal note, send a thank-you note. If you receive either of the last two responses, you know what to do!

Set Up a Tracking System

To help you keep track of the status of your submissions, you may want to establish a system in a notebook, in a computer file, or on file cards (see below).

This will keep you organized and up-to-date on the status of your queries and manuscripts and on the need to follow up with certain editors.

SENT QUERIES TO THE FOLLOWING PUBLICATIONS

Editor	Publication	Topic	Date Sent	Postage	Accepted/ Rejected	Rights Offered

SENT MANUSCRIPTS TO THE FOLLOWING PUBLICATIONS

Editor	Publication	Title	Date Sent	Postage	Accepted/ Rejected	Rights Offered

Frequently Asked Questions

How do I request a sample copy and writers' guidelines?

Write a brief note to the magazine: "Please send me a recent sample copy and writers' guidelines. If there is any charge, please enclose an invoice and I will pay upon receipt." The magazine's website, if it has one, offers a faster and less expensive alternative. Many companies put a part of the magazine, writers' guidelines, and sometimes a theme list or editorial calendar on the Internet.

How do I calculate the amount of postage for a sample copy?

Check the listing in this directory. In some cases the amount of postage will be listed. If the number of pages is given, use that to estimate the amount of postage by using the postage chart at the end of this section. For more information on postage and how to obtain stamps, see page 30.

Should my email submission 'package' be different than a submission via snail mail?

In general, an email submission should contain the same elements as a mailed one—i.e. a solid article description, sources, etc. In all cases, writers' guidelines should be followed to the letter when it comes to sending writing samples, bibliographies, and other requirements, either as separate file attachments or embedded in the email text.

What do I put in a cover letter if I have no publishing credits or relevant personal experience?

In this case, you may want to forego a formal cover letter and send your manuscript with a brief letter stating: "Enclosed is my manuscript, (Insert Title), for your review." For more information on cover letters, see pages 17–20.

How long should I wait before contacting an editor after I have submitted my manuscript?

The response time given in the listings can vary, and it's a good idea to wait three to four weeks after the stated response time before sending a brief note to the editor asking about the status of your manuscript. You might use this opportunity to add a new sales pitch or include additional material to show that the topic is continuing to generate interest. If you do not get a satisfactory response or you want to send your manuscript elsewhere, send a certified letter to the editor withdrawing the work from consideration and requesting its return. You are then free to submit the work to another magazine.

I don't need my manuscript returned. How do I indicate that to an editor?

With the capability to store manuscripts electronically and print out additional copies easily, some writers keep postage costs down by enclosing a self-addressed, stamped postcard (SASP) saying, "No need to return my manuscript. Please use this postcard to advise me of the status of my manuscript. Thank you."

Common Publishing Terms

All rights: Contractual agreement by which a publisher acquires the copyright and all use of author's material (see page 24).

Anthology: A collection of selected literary pieces.

Anthropomorphization: Attributing human form or personality to things not human (i.e., animals).

Assignment: Manuscript commissioned by an editor for a stated fee.

Bimonthly: A publication that appears every two months.

Biweekly: A publication issued every two weeks.

Byline: Author's name credited at the heading of an article.

Caption: Description or text accompanying an illustration or photograph.

CD-ROM (compact disc read-only-memory)**:** Non-erasable compact disc containing data that can be read by a computer.

Clip: Sample of a published work.

Contributor's copies: Copies of the publication issue in which the writer's work appears.

Copyedit: To edit with close attention to style and mechanics.

Copyright: Legal rights that protect an author's work (see page 24).

Cover letter: Brief letter sent with a manuscript introducing the writer and presenting the materials enclosed (see page 17).

Disk submission: Manuscript that is submitted on a computer disk.

Early readers: Children 4 to 7 years.

Editorial calendar: List of topics, themes, or special sections that are planned for upcoming issues for a specific time period.

Electronic submission: Manuscript transmitted to an editor from one computer to another through a modem.

Email (electronic mail)**:** Messages sent from one computer to another via computer network or modem.

English-language rights: The right to publish a manuscript in any English-speaking country.

Filler: Short item that fills out a page (e.g., joke, light verse, or fun fact).

First serial rights: The right to publish a work for the first time in a periodical; often limited to a specific geographical region (e.g., North America or Canada) (see page 24).

Genre: Category of fiction characterized by a particular style, form, or content, such as mystery or fantasy.

Glossy: Photo printed on shiny rather than matte-finish paper.

Guidelines: See **Writers' guidelines.**

In-house: See **Staff written.**

International Reply Coupon (IRC): Coupon exchangeable in any foreign country for postage on a single-rate, surface-mailed letter.

Kill fee: Percentage of the agreed-upon fee paid to a writer if an editor decides not to use a purchased manuscript.

Layout: Plan for the arrangement of text and artwork on a printed page.

Lead: Beginning of an article.

Lead time: Length of time between assembling and printing an issue.

Libel: Any false published statement intended to expose another to public ridicule or personal loss.

Manuscript: A typewritten or computer-printed version of a document (as opposed to a published version).

Masthead: The printed matter in a newspaper or periodical that gives the title and pertinent details of ownership, advertising rates, and subscription rates.

Middle-grade readers: Children 8 to 12 years.

Modem: An internal device or a small electrical box that plugs into a computer; used to transmit data between computers, often via telephone lines.

Ms/mss: Manuscript/manuscripts.

One-time rights: The right to publish a piece once, often not the first time (see page 25).

On spec: Refers to writing "on speculation," without an editor's commitment to purchase the manuscript.

Outline: Summary of a manuscript's contents, usually nonfiction, organized under subheadings with descriptive sentences under each.

Payment on acceptance: Author is paid following an editor's decision to accept a manuscript.

Payment on publication: Author is paid following the publication of the manuscript.

Pen name/pseudonym: Fictitious name used by an author.

Pre-K: Children under 5 years of age; also known as *preschool*.

Proofread: To read and mark errors, usually in printed text.

Query: Letter to an editor to promote interest in a manuscript or an idea.

Rebus story: A "see and say" story form, using pictures followed by the written words; often written for pre-readers.

Refereed journal: Publication that requires all manuscripts be reviewed by an editorial or advisory board.

Reprint: Another printing of an article or story; can be in a different magazine format, such as an anthology.

Reprint rights: See **Second serial rights.**

Response time: Average length of time for an editor to accept or reject a submission and contact the writer with his or her decision.

Résumé: Account of one's qualifications, including educational and professional background, as well as publishing credits.

SAE: Self-addressed envelope (no postage).

SASE: Self-addressed, stamped envelope.

SASP: Self-addressed stamped postcard.

Second serial rights: The right to publish a manuscript that has appeared in another publication; also known as *Reprint rights* (see page 24).

Semiannual: Occurring every six months or twice a year.

Semimonthly: Occurring twice a month.

Semiweekly: Occurring twice a week.

Serial: A publication issued as one of a consecutively numbered and indefinitely continued series.

Serial rights: See **First serial rights.**

Sidebar: A short article that accompanies a feature article and highlights one aspect of the feature's subject.

Simultaneous submission: Manuscript submitted to more than one publisher at the same time; also known as multiple submission.

Slant: Specific approach to a subject to appeal to a certain readership.

Slush pile: Term used within the publishing industry to describe unsolicited manuscripts.

Solicited manuscript: Manuscript that an editor has requested or agreed to consider.

Staff written: Prepared by members of the magazine's staff; also known as *in-house.*

Syndication rights: The right to distribute serial rights to a given work through a syndicate of periodicals.

Synopsis: Condensed description or summary of a manuscript.

Tabloid: Publication printed on an ordinary newspaper page, turned sideways and folded in half.

Tearsheet: A page from a newspaper or magazine (periodical) containing a printed story or article.

Theme list: See **Editorial calendar.**

Transparencies: Color slides, not color prints.

Unsolicited manuscript: Any manuscript not specifically requested by an editor.

Work-made-for-hire: Work specifically ordered, commissioned, and owned by a publisher for its exclusive use (see page 25).

World rights: Contractual agreement whereby the publisher acquires the right to reproduce the work throughout the world (see page 24); also known as *all rights.*

Writers' guidelines: Publisher's editorial objectives or specifications, which usually include word lengths, readership level, and subject matter.

Writing sample: Example of your writing style, tone, and skills; may be a published or unpublished piece.

Young adult: Readers 12 to 18 years.

Postage Information

How Much Postage?

When you're sending a manuscript to a magazine, enclose a self-addressed, stamped envelope with sufficient postage; this way, if the editor does not want to use your manuscript, it can be returned to you. To help you calculate the proper amount of postage for your SASE, here are the U.S. postal rates for first-class mailings in the U.S. and from the U.S. to Canada based on the latest increase (2006). Rates are expected to increase again, so please check with your local Post Office, or check the U.S. Postal Service website at usps.com.

Ounces	9x12 Envelope (Approx. no. of pages)	U.S. First-Class Postage Rate	Rate from U.S. to Canada
1	1–5	$ 0.39	$ 0.63
2	6–10	0.63	0.90
3	11–15	0.87	1.15
4	16–20	1.11	1.40
5	21–25	1.35	1.70
6	26–30	1.59	1.95
7	31–35	1.83	2.20
8	36–40	2.07	2.50

The amount of postage and size of envelope necessary to receive a sample copy and writers' guidelines are usually stated in the magazine listing. If this information is not provided, use the chart above to help gauge the proper amount of postage.

How to Obtain Stamps

People living in the U.S., Canada, or overseas can acquire U.S. stamps through the mail from the Philately Fulfillment Service Center. Call 800-STAMP-24 (800-782-6724) to request a catalogue or place an order. For overseas, the telephone number is 816-545-1100. You pay the cost of the stamps plus a postage and handling fee based on the value of the stamps ordered, and the stamps are shipped to you. Credit card information (MasterCard, Visa, and Discover cards only) is required for fax orders. The fax number is 816-545-1212. If you order through the catalogue, you can pay with a U.S. check or an American Money Order. Allow 3–4 weeks for delivery.

Gateway to the Markets

Funny Business: A Serious Look at Middle-Grade Humor

By Lisa Harkrader

Laughter, said author, cartoonist, and humorist James Thurber, need not be cut out of anything, since it improves everything. If you don't believe Thurber, ask a middle-grade reader. While middle-graders' tastes vary wildly—from science fiction to sports to everything in between—one element almost everyone loves is humor. For reluctant readers, humor can be the hook they need to start reading. For strong readers, humor is another delectable treat in an activity they already enjoy.

For magazine editors, well-written humor is something always welcome. "*Cricket* just needs more humor, period," says Deborah Vetter, Contributing Editor for the Cricket Magazine Group.

The Appeal

Readers of all ages love humor, but middle-graders are especially drawn to it. "It helps to make reading fun," says Judy Burke, Senior Editor at *Highlights for Children*. "If reading is a struggle for a middle-grade reader, then humor in a story is a nice incentive and reward."

"It is empowering," says Timothy Tocher, author of hilarious short stories and poems, as well as novels such as *Chief Sunrise, John McGraw, and Me*. "They are at the mercy of parents and teachers, as well as older, bigger kids. Humor can ease the pain of a reprimand, defuse anger, or create a bond."

Lynea Bowdish, who has written short stories and books such as *How To Be Nice—And Other Lessons I Didn't Learn*, agrees. "They're just beginning to find out all sorts of embarrassing and painful things about themselves, their families, and the world outside them. Everything's uncertain—their bodies, their minds, the day to day stuff. What can they do to survive those years? Laugh!"

When we think of humorous stories, fiction immediately springs to mind, but humor can energize other magazine pieces, too. "We can always use more humorous stories and poems," says Burke. "When appropriate, it's certainly welcome in nonfiction, too, but it should never feel forced."

The Audience

Middle-graders range in age from 8 to about 12, but what tickles a child entering third grade is vastly different from what makes a preteen laugh. "The older a reader becomes, the more sophisticated—and subtle—the humor can become," says Burke.

In her four-decade career, Jane Yolen has published stories, poems, and more than 250 books, including *Wizard's Hall* and *How Do Dinosaurs Say Goodnight?* "Puns are tough for the youngest to understand," she says. "Sarcasm and irony don't make sense to anyone under the age of eight or nine."

Subject matter and voice also vary from the youngest middle-grade stories to the oldest. Look at three humorous stories published for this age range in the same month, June 2006. "The Tax Collector's Cow" (*Spider*), Eugie Foster's story about sisters outwitting a tax collector, is a folktale aimed at younger middle-graders. Shift to *Girls' Life* and Emilie Le Beau's "Miss Quit," which uses a present-tense, chick-lit voice and the problems of a reluctant beauty contestant to hook older middle-grade girls. "Weighing Winchester," written by Linda Opp for *Pockets*—a devotional middle-grade publication—is a funny story involving queasy stomachs and a dog on a diet, but like many stories in religious magazines, the message is front and center.

The Surprise

Writers employ many tools to infuse their stories with humor. In "Michael MacGregor Sure Can Snore" (*Highlights*, July 2006), Barbara S. Garriel uses the time-honored humor technique of exaggeration to describe Michael's snores: "Michael's parents just shook their heads when the snores rattled things off the shelves in Michael's room. They felt sorry for the hamsters when they started running in their hamster wheel—backward. Mom couldn't even hear herself practicing her saxophone."

In Eva Schlesinger's poem, "Would You Like to Elope, Antelope?" (*Cricket*, February 2006), the humor rests in wordplay, with three words that are funny in and of themselves (*elope, antelope, cantaloupe*) made funnier when used together in a rhyme.

In "The Skipped-Lunch Disaster" (*U.S. Kids*, March/April 2006), Mary Wesa Kramer uses slapstick humor in a snowballing series of events that starts with Butch the Bully sitting by Andrew at lunch and ends with the police captain clearing a traffic jam caused by a gushing water hydrant.

Underlying each humor technique is the element of surprise. Funny stories turn readers' expectations on end in ways that are surprising but satisfying.

In Ethel Pochocki's poem, "Mouse in the House" (*Cricket*, June 2006), the narrator arms herself with a broom to chase a terrified mouse past her dozing "embarrassment of cats." The poem leads readers to believe the narrator is horrified at seeing a mouse and disgusted with her cats for not helping. But in the end, we are surprised (and delighted) to find that the narrator is trying to catch the mouse and set it free before the cats wake up and harm it.

The surprise in Janni Lee Simner's "Frog Princes" is a new twist on an old fairy tale. Simner is the author of many short stories and novels, including *Secret of the Three Treasures*, says, "Every reader out there knows that princes become frogs, and mostly we consider this a good thing," says Simner. "But where the reader sees a noble prince, the story's protagonist, Kim, sees only that her frog had disappeared—and she liked that frog. Her reactions are quite serious to her, but they're not the reactions the reader expects, so we laugh."

> *Laughter need not be cut out of anything since it improves everything.*
> — **James Thurber**

Giggle Triggers

Certain subjects seem inherently funny to middle-graders: noses, bad smells, underwear. As George Orwell said, "Every joke is a tiny revolution." Humor about odors and underwear is irreverent and subversive.

"For kids it's called bathroom humor," says Vetter. "We find humor in our body functions; it's a weird human trait. Part of it's the grossness factor, especially popular with middle-graders."

Bathroom humor doesn't have to be offensive. In Timothy Tocher's "Sweat Sock Switch" (*Cricket*, February 2006), stinky socks play a starring role, but the story is more about the perils of making assumptions than about bad odors. "Unlocking the Secrets of Dung" (*Cricket*, March 2006) shows how scientists study fossilized dung to find out more about dinosaurs. Author Connie Goldsmith "uses humor as bait to lure her readers into a substantive scientific article," says Vetter.

Writers should study each magazine to find out whether gross humor is appropriate. "We don't use a lot of that type of humor in *Highlights*," says Burke. "We don't have any set rules; we just go by what feels right for us, and bathroom humor usually doesn't."

The Springboard

Although entire books have been written dissecting successful humor techniques, most writers agree that funny stories arise more naturally.

"No author I know thinks, 'Ah, time for

some exaggeration or hyperbole,'" says Yolen. "That's the stuff teachers and critics look for, but it's just part of the organic bag of tricks writers use without forethought or hindthought or sometimes any kind of thought at all."

Like Yolen, most writers focus on the story rather than the humor. "I think of it more as a by-product of other things I'm doing," says Bowdish. "The humor is never the main point with me. I'm not exactly sure how to be funny just to be funny!"

"I follow the voice," says Simner, "and I follow the character, just as I do when I write things that aren't funny. For me, humor happens when story elements collide."

Tocher also mixes story elements as a springboard for humor. "It often starts with placing a character in a situation. In the story I consider my funniest, 'Sgt. Monday and the Enchanted Kingdom Police' (*Cricket*, April 2002), I juxtaposed a hard-boiled, by-the-book policeman with nursery rhyme and fairy tale characters." The story won a Society of Children's Book Writers & Illustrators Magazine Merit Award.

Many funny stories use a first-person narrator. "First person helps me find and maintain a distinctive voice for my main character," says Tocher. "I try to make my character speak to the reader with all the quirks of language particular to his or her personality."

As popular as funny stories are with readers and editors, writers must be careful not to force the humor. "One common mistake is when writers set up a whole story for a punchline ending," says Burke. "Those stories usually feel thin and unsatisfying." Vetter agrees: "We see slapstick humor that's slapped onto a poem or story with a trowel, instead of arising naturally from a situation or a character's personality traits."

Beneath the Humor

"The secret source of Humor itself is not joy but sorrow," said Mark Twain. Much humor, even for kids, is built on serious subjects.

A boy who seeks revenge on the guy who stole his girlfriend and ends up learning painful truths about himself sounds like the

---

What works: Editors weigh in

- **Judy Burke, Senior Editor,** *Highlights for Children:* "We like all kinds of humor, and I think that authors are sometimes surprised at some of the stories we accept. They'll say, 'I thought it might be too zany/quirky/offbeat for you, and I almost didn't send it in.' We know that kids have varying tastes when it comes to humor, so we try to mix it up. If a story is well written and funny and we think that a reader will connect with it, then we'll buy it. So don't be afraid to try us!"

- **Deborah Vetter, Contributing Editor, Cricket Magazine Group:** Among the kinds of humor that play well to middle-grade audiences are "tongue-in-cheek humor, role reversal (as in *Freaky Friday*), and situational humor (as in *I Love Lucy*). For tongue-in-cheek, think of the light touch some authors bring to their retellings of folktales, such as Elisabeth Greenberg's 'How the Merry Minstrel Found His Beauty' (*Cricket*, May 2006). Timothy Tocher's story 'Spring Fever' (*Cricket*, March 2007) revolves around role reversal. The grown-ups squabble and act like kids instead of authority figures. For situational humor, think of 'The Necktie,' by Iranian author Hooshang Moradi Kermani (*Cricket*, April 2006), in which Majid wants to appear grown-up for an engagement ceremony, so he appropriates a tie, and the situation goes from bad to worse. Finally, *Cicada*, our magazine for teens, is also in desperate need of humor, which can include satire."

---

makings of a pretty heavy story. But in "Sweat Sock Switch," that story is hilarious. The protagonist, and the reader, still learns an important lesson about blaming others for your own shortcomings, but humor makes that lesson easier to swallow.

Humor makes stories easier to read, but it doesn't make them easier to write. "It's really easy to make a reader cry—yes, the dog dies. Or the mother. Or the baby sister," says Yolen. "Much harder to make the reader laugh."

Writers who can make readers laugh will find middle-graders and editors delighted by their stories and clamoring for more. Because, as Tocher points out, "If you share a laugh with someone, don't you look forward to being with that person again?"

The Magic of Retelling Fairy Tales and Folklore

By Mark Haverstock

Over the centuries, fairy tales and folktales have exercised a spell over listeners and readers. "I love these old stories because they are wonderful, colorful, always exciting tales, and they also have lots of food for thought in them," says author Robert D. San Souci, who might be cast as King of the Folk for his many writings in the genre. "You can enjoy the story as simply a great story, but you'll come away from them with ideas about how to live as a better person. And you may come away with a better appreciation of what it is like to live in another part of the world or maybe at a very different time in history."

Editors love them too. "They have so much meaning distilled into them," says Alice Letvin, Editorial Director of the Cricket Magazine Group and Editor of *Babybug* and *Ladybug*. "They show basic patterns of human experience and kids relate strongly to universal characters—either facing danger or on a quest of some sort, facing a contest of good and evil, or facing up to their fears and overcoming them." Letvin thinks fairy and folktales "often have more meaning than the stories of everyday life. They have a different dimension, and I think kids are interested in both."

Retelling and adapting these tales can be a welcome and creative change of pace for fiction writers, but the process involves more than just restating a tale with a few twists. Editors demand cultural authenticity. Authors must truly know the stories, what came before, how to remain true to the past, and how to be original, all at the same time.

Tracking Down a Tale

When it comes to traditional fairy tales and folktales, there is really nothing new under the sun. Similar motifs run through stories found in very different parts of the world. Variations of the Cinderella story, for example, appear in many cultures. "But once in a while, an author unearths a fairy tale that is new to us and may come from a different culture," says Deborah Vetter, Contributing Editor of Cricket Magazine Group. "They're still out there; we don't have them all."

Folktales suitable for adaptation come from many sources. You might start by exploring a nearby university library, where you're likely to find older books or specialized collections. Another rich source of tales is the Folklore Project, sponsored by the Work Projects Administration (WPA) during the 1930s. The Library of Congress collection includes 2,900 documents representing the work of more than 300 WPA writers from 24 states. (See the sidebar on page 35 for additional sources.)

San Souci does formal research, but he also picks up leads during his travels across the country. "*The Secret of the Stones* came to me as a result of an invitation to visit the remarkable Tutwiler Collection of Southern History and Literature at the Birmingham Public Library while I was presenting at a local college," he explains. "I heard 'The Talking Eggs' at an informal gathering of storytellers during a visit to a library convention in New Orleans years ago. The moment I heard it, I thought it might have a possibility of being turned into a picture book."

Look to family and friends for folktales. You may also know someone who can share oral stories from their culture, or you may remember tales told by a parent or grandparent. When it comes to your own culture, you'll have the advantage of being able to add necessary details for authenticity.

Finding little-known gems among folk and

fairy tales may be a challenge, since many that seem to be originals are retold in translations from other languages. "The originals often aren't written in English and even those that were may have been in stories told in earlier forms of English, such as Anglo-Saxon (also

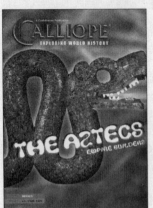

known as Old English) or Middle English," says Rosalie Baker, Co-Editor of *Calliope*. "Many of these retold tales have been retold so many times and there are so many versions that it's sometimes difficult to find the original." Baker suggests that authors rely on reputable sources and dig deeply to see if they're consistent with accepted traditions.

To stay on the right side of copyright law, stories you retell must be in the public domain, which generally means they were published before 1923. Editors expect that you will do the necessary research to comply, and also that you provide at least two published sources to establish a tale's authenticity. If the story is from a particular culture in which you grew up, this may be a moot point if you're collecting the information firsthand and transcribing it to paper.

New Life in Old Tales

Once you've found a suitable tale, where do you begin with your retelling? Some of the tales from the nineteenth or early twentieth century are written in language that can be difficult and dated. "It's nice to make the language accessible to modern children, though you still want to maintain the flavor of the original period or story," says Vetter. "Sometimes authors add new twists. If a story is really sexist or violent (something we don't feel is appropriate for our audiences) we encourage writers to tweak it a bit."

Characters might also be recast, especially since tales tend to stress narrative and cleverness of plot. Today's readers are accustomed to seeing more fully rounded characters. "You've got the basic plot, but if you're going to bring it to life in your own way, you've got to put yourself in the skin of that character and make that character come alive," says Letvin. "This can be done through little reactions: what he says, what he notices, how he interacts with the other characters. It often doesn't take much, but it makes all the difference in the tale when somebody's paying attention to the details."

Though Vetter doesn't think there's anything wrong with adhering to the traditional character types often found in these tales, it can be fun to change them. "We have a piece in an upcoming issue that's a retelling of the Cinderella tale. Instead of Cinderella wanting to go to the ball, she decides she'd rather stay home and read a good book while her frivolous stepsisters are off chasing the prince," says Vetter. "That gives the story a different take. The author made Cinderella a little more self-sufficient and secure in whom she was. We thought that the author had taken such a modern look at her character, which we liked."

Cultural context is needed for authenticity.

San Souci has taken the Cinderella tale one step further in *Cinderella Skeleton,* a fractured fairy tale in rhyme. "I've always loved Cinderella tales—retelling them from many cultural backgrounds, but always trying to put a fresh spin on things," he says. "A scary Cinderella seemed like fun. The more I said the phrase, the more I realized it had a bit of internal rhyme to it, ella Skele. A full narrative poem seemed like an interesting challenge and a new way to give a spin to a time-honored tale."

The amount of modification to a time-honored tale often determines the billing. "I think Eric Kimmel does a great job of explaining how he handles his fairy tales and folktales," explains Vetter. "He says that if he doesn't change it very much, he'll say *retold by*; if he changes a little bit, he'll say, *adapted by*; and if he really changes it, he'll say *by Eric Kimmel*." One example of a significant change was when Kimmel once took a Russian fairy tale and set it in the American Wild West. "Four Dollars and Fifty Cents" appeared in *Cricket* in September-October 1989, and won the 1990 Paul A. Witty Short Story Award.

Politically Correct

Retelling and adapting a plot or characters is only part of the story. Cultural context is needed to maintain authenticity. "I have a personal feeling about this: Take time to understand the culture from which the tale originates," says Marileta Robinson, Senior Editor of *Highlights for Children.* "Show respect for that culture."

Research into Native American folktales has been problematic for some stories *Cricket* has received. "Sometimes you'll find these tales in old books that just say 'an American Indian story,'" says Vetter. "You're left wondering which culture. We know there are many different Native American cultures, so we would like authors to do more digging." Once an author has found a source, Vetter in some cases has recommended contacting a member of the relevant tribe to factcheck the story for any cultural inaccuracies.

Author Aaron Shepard notes that the Internet is a good place to find people who can supply information on customs, traditions, and other helpful facts. "I needed to name the heroine of a folktale from the Chagga tribe of Mount Kilimanjaro," he says. "I managed to find the home page of a Chagga tribesman teaching at Pennsylvania State University. By e-mail, he suggested several names, one of which was perfect." Shepard has also used Internet newsgroups and e-mail discussion lists, many dedicated to specific countries, cultures, or religions.

Fairy tales weren't originally written specifically for children. The historical collections of fairy and folktales in Italy, France, and Germany from the sixteenth to the nineteenth century—most notably by the Brothers Grimm—included many tales that involved violence, death, and sometimes even sex. It wasn't until later that fairy tales took a literary turn into children stories, and today's most modern tales are even less edgy.

"With the *Ladybug* audience ages two to six, we're searching for more folk retellings, fables, or stories with a mythic resonance to balance out stories of everyday life," says Letvin. "They can't be too scary, which doesn't always mean that creatures don't get eaten, but they do have to be more sensitive and have a gentler edge. With *Spider,* you can have a troll under the bridge, and it can be fearsome to walk over the bridge."

Adding Some Drama

One spin on fairy and folktales often overlooked by authors is to present them as plays. These productions are typically adapted for elementary school audiences, and teachers often incorporate them into their language arts and social studies curriculum as a fun way to learn. "Our folk and fairy tale plays work especially well for third- to fifth-grade classes," says Elizabeth Preston, Editor of *Plays.* "At this level, students are better able to appreciate the folktale traditions and the cultural aspects."

Dramatic adaptations of fairy tales and folktales are very straightforward. Playwrights appreciate that most tales are well-written and can be adapted without significant changes to the original story. "The nice thing about adapting these stories is that most have interesting characters that can be played broadly," says

---

Folktale and legend links

Want to find out more about folklore from around the world? Try these links:

- **Folklore and Mythology Electronic Texts:** A collection compiled by D. L. Ashliman, folklore researcher and professor emeritus, University of Pittsburgh. www.pitt.edu/~dash/folktexts.html
- **Folklore, Myth and Legend:** A collection of stories and folktale links compiled by David K. Brown, University of Calgary. www.ucalgary.ca/%7Edkbrown/storfolk.html
- **Internet Sacred Text Archive:** Electronic texts from many religions, mythologies, legends, folklore, and on occult and related topics. www.sacred-texts.com/index.htm. Examples include a collection of sixty Slavonic folktales, www.sacred-texts.com/neu/sfs/index.htm
- **Library of Congress American Folklife Center:** Includes text and audio recordings. www.loc.gov/folklife
- **Myths and Legends:** An extensive collection of links for research. http://home.comcast.net/~chris.s/myth.html

Folktale under construction: A master writer's process

When it comes to retelling a folktale, what original elements ultimately should stay? Which should you reshape and why? Author Robert D. San Souci offers personal insights into the process of adapting "The Talking Eggs."

Sourcing: "I first heard the tale during a visit to a library convention in New Orleans. I'm always looking for that element of perceived value—a story that is fun, exciting, but also has a lesson to share without hitting young readers over the head. In *The Talking Eggs,* underpinning the magical tale is the reinforcement of such values as treating people appropriately, keeping promises, thinking carefully before making choices, and not being selfish and greedy."

Verification: "This covers two areas. First, make sure that what you're hearing is a true folktale, not simply a family tale created by a single teller or a story told in the manner of a folktale but not the genuine article. A primary source here is Stith Thompson's *Motif-Index of Folk-Literature.* In the case of 'The Talking Eggs,' I found a number of variants, including numerous versions from Africa including the same elements, that reveal this folktale has roots going back hundreds of years. In the U.S., the earliest published source was Alcee Fortier's *Louisiana Folktales,* published in 1895. Most editors require an absolute minimum of two independently sourced versions of a folktale to establish its authenticity. This also establishes that the source is not protected by copyright, as a genuine folktale. However, one needs to be careful here: The story of 'The Talking Eggs,' for example, is in the public domain as a 'tale of the people.' My text, not the story, is protected by copyright. Other authors could use my tale as part of background research, but would have to come up with their own version that does not use my words."

Compositing: "When I have a variety of sources available, I begin the winnowing process, looking for those elements that are key to the majority of tellings and to keep the substance of the original intact. In the case of "The Talking Eggs," these elements are pretty straightforward: a good sister and a selfish sister in tension, à la Cinderella stories; encounters with an old woman on a magical farm, where each will be tested; the consequences of the testing process (here choosing either the plain eggs that say 'Take me!' or the gold, silver, bejeweled eggs that warn 'Don't take me!')."

Editing: "This was fairly minimal with *The Talking Eggs* since the storyline was really straightforward and concise: a brief cautionary tale with magical elements that give it great kid appeal. With longer, more complex tales, such as *Sukey and the Mermaid,* this may involve removing redundant passages, editing out elements that distract from the main story line, and blending characters who serve the same function in the story. The only major change in *The Talking Eggs* was turning the two grotesque floating heads and hands holding axes that guard the old woman's farm to a two-headed cow—an image inherently laughable to children. I did not change the later image of the old woman removing her head (though the editor strongly suggested it) because this is essential to establish the good sister's courage and wisdom in recognizing that a strange event is not necessarily a threatening one."

Texturing: "This is the part of the rewriting process where I try to put as much into dialogue as possible. Often, folktales are blocks of narrative. Breaking one up into passages of dialogue serves the double purpose of making the text look less intimidating to younger or reluctant readers. It also adds appeal for readalouds. Here is also where I cull from my notebooks unique words, phrases, sayings, gathered on previous trips to a given region. In *The Talking Eggs,* I used such notebook descriptions as a farm that 'looked like the tail end of bad luck' or a little girl who is 'sharp as forty crickets.' This gives a flavor of the area to the story. Characterization also is a consideration—fleshing out characters who, in folktales, often have no more dimension than generic descriptions of 'that girl,' 'that boy,' 'the Prince,' or 'the maiden.'"

Rewriting: "Here's the key to preparing any manuscript, as all writers know. I do many rewrites getting the material ready to present to the editor. Of course, once the editor has purchased the text, there comes more rewriting. And, once the illustrator is on board, there is probably going to be final tweaking to bring text and illustrations into sync."

Preston, "and the dialogue found in the adapted play versions is often as good as the prose in the original tales."

When writing a play, keep in mind that teachers and students are the primary audience, and that many plays will be performed by classes often numbering from 20 to 30. Look for ways to get an entire class involved. "You don't want clumps of kids standing on stage serving no useful purpose," says Preston. "It's great for kids to be in a play, but it's also good for them to help work on the play behind the scenes as well." Plan to have something going on at all times or the kids and the audience will get restless. The forward movement of the play should be continual.

Keep sets and props as simple as possible, taking into consideration that most teachers have budget issues. Everyday objects from around the house are preferable to elaborate scenery and construction. Production notes for plays should be kept as simple as possible.

The most crucial element is good dialogue. "That's what really gets my attention," says Preston. "Obviously, if you have a good story, that's important, but the essence of the story comes out in the dialogue." Once you've written a play, Preston suggests that you get someone to read the finished piece aloud with you to help polish your writing.

Editor Needs

Magazines in the Carus Publishing Group are by far the largest market for fairy tales, folktales, and related genres. "It is a favorite and it is a tradition among the Cricket Magazine Group, though it's not the only thing we like to do," says Vetter. "But we get so many of them and they're so good. That's why we publish them." Vetter notes that they don't get enough tales from South America or Africa.

Carus's Cobblestone Publishing division works from yearly editorial calendars that can be found at each magazine's website. "If we're doing something in *Faces*, which examines different places and cultures, we generally have a folktale that represents that culture in each issue," says Lou Warnycia, Managing Editor. Since the material is strictly theme-based, it's important to query only on topics listed in the editorial calendar.

Baker routinely includes folktales in the magazines she edits, because she feels it will help readers better understand the civilization being described in a particular issue. The October 2006 *Calliope* about Mesopotamia includes three retold tales: "The Great Flood," "The Story of Creation," and "The Goddess Inanna." Baker says, "In every issue, I try to bring in some retold legend or myth or some tradition that is related to the theme. Historical accounts and records provide all the facts and the details that happened on a given day, but the retold stories give you a broader insight into how the people felt, how they lived, and how they conducted their lives."

Plays sometimes receives folktales of England, Ireland, and China, but Preston would like to see more submissions from other cultures, especially lesser-known stories. "One example we had in our April issue was 'Anansi and the King's Drum,' one of the Anansi tales that are popular in Africa," says Preston. "It's a whole group of folktales that feature a wily spider named Anansi who comes up with creative solutions for various problems."

"I'm looking for tales that are easily understood by kids and appeal to kids," says Robinson. "Humor, natural sounding dialogue, action, and cultural details should be worked into the story so well that they don't stand out or trip up a reader. We prefer a positive message in the story and a bit of wisdom you can take away."

Retelling and adapting folklore really isn't much different from doing a makeover on a room in your house or apartment: painting on updated language, rearranging some plot items, and adding art to add character. The look is quite different, but the basic framework of the story stays in tact. Just remember not to discard those valued items that have made the story withstand the test of time.

Not Your Mother's Teen Magazine

By Christina Hamlett

The best part about receiving my first subscription to *Seventeen* was that I was only 15 at the time and felt as if I were getting juicy insider tips on how to behave in two years. The bad news was that the subscription came with the caveat that my mother would preview each issue to make sure I didn't get any "wild" ideas. Although it was the late 1960s, the content was dominated by mini-skirts, cute little boots, Mary Quant cosmetics, and lip gloss in trippy neon tubes—the product of editors

who had grown up under the direction of mothers who believed nice girls never call boys and college is the place to meet suitable husbands. *Seventeen* reinforced a pre-liberation mantra that being pretty and adored carried more weight than being empowered to go for the gold, with or without a beau.

Within its white bread, middle-class context were no problems that couldn't be resolved by going to a movie with friends, buying a new nail polish, or listening to the Beatles. *Seventeen* offered true stories with perky endings. It explored other cultures only through the discerning lens of high fashion, foreign pen pals, or tasty cuisines replicated in the suburbs.

In teen magazines today, the models are still cute, the cover stories still promise quick-fix solutions to bad hair and boring wardrobes, and there's no shortage of tips for meeting Mr. Right. The big difference is the voice. It's no longer your mother talking but an older sister or best friend. Two such

voices—best-selling author and *Girls' Life* columnist Carol Weston and lifestyle consultant and *Seventeen* shuistrologer Ellen Whitehurst—share the scoop on what it takes to tap into the *'tudes* of today's female teens.

Then and Now

"My generation," says Whitehurst, "was so much more naive and focused on much more immature events and happenings. We worried more about if our mothers would let us wear lip gloss than if a hurricane heading straight for the mainland would wipe out an entire state. We were not so stressed and not nearly so knowing regarding current events, nor did we ever worry about what have now become devastating, yet all too common, disasters in the daily fabric of today's girls' lives."

Tragedies and serious issues visit every generation, but Whitehurst continues, "The difference in content from then, the 70s, until now directly reflects the differences in evolutionary cultural considerations. The evidence lies in some of the preoccupations of these young girls and what they tell us their stressors are. Not that my readers today still don't worry about lip gloss and the right colors for them; it's just that they have to worry if that gloss will get blown up in some random terrorist attack."

Weston agrees. "I've been answering female mail since (my book) *Girltalk: All the*

Voices

- Carol Weston: www.carolweston.com. *Girls' Life*, www.girlslife.com
- Ellen Whitehurst: www.ellenwhitehurst.com. *Seventeen*, www.seventeen.com

Stuff Your Sister Never Told You (now in its fourth edition) first came out in 1985, and I've been *Girls' Life*'s 'Dear Carol' since the magazine's first issue. Many things have not changed over the years. Girls in the 10 to 15 age bracket still want to know how to get a guy to notice them, how to get over shyness, how to deal with overprotective moms, changing friendships, school stress, and also if I have any tips for losing weight or using tampons! But many subjects have indeed changed. When I started writing for girls, eating disorders were just beginning to be talked about. I also remember the first time a girl wrote about *cutting*. I didn't know what she meant. I remember when a girl, speaking about sex, wrote about being *orally active*. Now there's a term! Today, girls write me about issues involving Internet romance, MySpace.com, etc. I think my challenge as an advice columnist is to make my column a mix of both new and perennial queries, and soft and hard-hitting questions."

Behavioral boundaries—the rules once laid down as law by mom and dad—have blurred significantly, compounding the complications of adult-to-teen advice. This stems in large part from mom and dad struggling to redefine themselves in the wake of divorce, single parenthood, and remarriage, and often trying to be a cool pal more than a stodgy authority figure. Once a parent could say, "Just because your friends want to wear

> ## *Iconography strongly influences teen decision-making.*

turquoise eye shadow doesn't mean you can, too." Now parents defensively contend, "Just because movie stars are having babies out of wedlock doesn't mean it's okay."

YA writers must avoid the same misstep. The current marriage of media, politics, and culture has relativized the definition of propriety, making it incumbent upon writers for this audience above all to stay focused on facts, not fantasy. They may then stand to become positive role models who are close enough to offer more grounding in reality

than an idolized celebrity, yet are also far enough removed from the readers to offer an unbiased viewpoint.

Whitehurst praises *Seventeen*'s Editor in Chief Atoosa Rubenstein as "a genius at ferreting as well as intuiting what girls need to keep them interested and empowered at the same time."

Weston, who had her first byline with *Seventeen* when she was 19, says that much of the core angst underscored in the questions she receives for her *Girls' Life* advice column is timeless, part of every generation's mindset. "It's great that girls today feel more empowered than they used to. On the other hand, sometimes girls write to say they've phoned a boy 10 times and he still won't go out with them. It's my job to say, 'Just because you're allowed to phone a guy does not mean you have a green light to keep calling and calling. If the writing is on the wall, read it. You have to be sensitive, not just assertive.'"

Substance and Symbols

Iconography strongly influences teen decision-making: "Hollister jeans make him cool; those bracelets are so Goth; I have to have that Jeep, not a Volvo, Dad!" Sadly, this often translates to teens and tweens attaching higher importance to what is worn on the outside than defining what exists on the inside. The need to be part of the right crowd by sporting popular labels often prompts them to purchase items out of want, not need, and to act out of thoughtlessness rather than make decisions.

Skilled and truthful writers can reverse this thinking. Show that behind those $200 must-have shoes is a story about the Third World worker who was paid less than $10 for the labor. Connect a story to worthy causes in the community that could have used the $200 to feed a family, help an accident victim, or contribute to cleaning a local environmental hazard.

The summer issues of the teen magazines suggest that girls can accomplish more on their summer break than lying on the beach and getting a tan. *Seventeen*'s Real Life section, for example, includes links to opportunities for volunteerism, environmental activism, and raising money for worthy causes at home and abroad.

Justine introduces its 13- to 19-year-old readers to summer internships to learn about local government, and suggests girls donate

their long tresses to Locks of Love to aid children suffering the effects of chemotherapy or strap on tool belts for Habitat for Humanity. *American Girl* and *New Moon* encourage philanthropic thought at an even earlier age (8 to 14) through articles that promote respect for global diversity and appreciation for freedoms enjoyed on American soil.

With this in mind, submissions showcasing the generous works of contemporary young women are often welcome at these magazines and others directed to teen girls. So are those that profile contemporary or historical figures who changed the lives all women live.

The Age Line

We're living in an "instant-now" world where so many messages clamor to be heard that only the sharpest tend to get through.

"The biggest challenge I find writing for this demographic is that these girls are so smart and so savvy and hungry for information that empowers them and yet they're so used to an expedited culture that it's imperative to attract and keep their attention in a very short span of time," observes Whitehurst. Her "girl Shui" for *Seventeen* offers

Celebrity circuit

Once upon a time there were stars who had lives. Private lives. Between the combination of a less intrusive media and icons who were more discreet, fans could only fantasize that their idols' glamorous worlds were perfect. In a naive time decades ago, such ideas set up unrealistic expectations that if you, too, were rich, famous, stunning, and thin, your existence would be blissfully carefree.

Although today's YA magazines have no shortage of interviews with hottie boy bands, actors, and insider scoops on new and emerging talents, they're also shedding cautionary light on the dark side of glam. For example, in the June/July 2006 issue of *Cosmo Girl*, Mary J. Blige discussed the struggle she endured as a result of dropping out of school, becoming hooked on drugs, and tolerating abusive relationships. In the same issue, Scarlett Pomers, who played Reba McEntire's daughter on the television show *Reba*, disclosed how her obsession with losing weight had career consequences she never anticipated.

Is it lonely at the top? The June/July 2006 issue of *Elle Girl* profiles *The O.C.*'s heartthrob Adam Brody, who confesses to the relatable teen angst of feeling unloved. Musician Teddy Geiger (June/July 2006 *Justine*) goes geeky in social situations. *American Idol* winner Carrie Underwood, who graces the cover of June/July 2006 *Girls' Life*, reminds readers that fame can vanish as quickly as it arrives. In the same issue, *Girls' Life* weighs in on how teen celebrities' unhealthy habits are not only hurting their reputations but encouraging their impressionable fans to engage in risky behavior.

Not every true life story in these magazines is about Hollywood. Girls and young women whose lives were once much like those of the readers have taken the spotlight as a result of date rape, brutal murders, medical maladies and, in the case of *Seventeen*'s feature on Florida State University student Suzanne Gonzales, acts of suicide motivated by "friends" in Internet chatrooms.

While articles on celebrities may be more difficult for some writers to carry off, the subjects—positive and negative—are worth pursuing, with all the freshness and honesty of youth: health of mind and body, self-knowledge, hard work, confronting failure and success, family, true friendship. All the realities and joys of growing up.

insights and advice that stems from a meld of astrology and Feng Shui.

"I tread a razor-thin line of readers being incredibly mature—yet not quite adults—and recognizing that they're acculturated to getting information in brief and cogent bites," Whitehurst says. "The challenge lies in writing to them in a quick, fully informational way. They don't need or want to spend much time digesting what I'm offering but they still want the full nutritional value and the full results that Feng Shui can render in terms of making their lives less cluttered and more power-filled."

It is one of the challenges in writing for tween and teen girls that the line between childhood and adulthood is so vitally important and yet so variable. Writing for this audience is about universals, and about individuality too. For instance, as Weston says, "I never want it to sound as if all girls are in trouble because I believe most 11-year-olds, deep down, aren't fundamentally different from how 11-year-olds used to be. In fact, I'm offended when the media makes it sound like (oral sex) is akin to a casual kiss. A girl who's servicing a boy in the school hallway isn't a typical teen: She's a girl crying out for attention in all the wrong ways. There have always been and always will be some girls desperately in need of sensible advice. The sobering reality for me is that I can't save them all!"

Reaching the ears of this audience also means speaking to their reading abilities. Girls do tend to be better readers than boys, but they're also living in a sound byte world. They have their own idiom, but don't really want to hear adult writers mimicking them or sounding foolish. Study tween and teen girl magazines, websites, television shows, and movies; listen to girls at the mall or on athletic fields. Find the vocabulary and voice that will reach them, while staying true to your own voice.

They do speak of the same things you spoke of as a teen, and they speak of more.

"Even though the commonality of family and guys and getting good grades are still the overriding themes of any day and age," says Whitehurst, "the difference that 30 years and a lot of informational technology have made can be likened to the difference between crawling and taking a supersonic jet."

As rapidly as things have accelerated, however, YA magazines are a remarkable opportunity to encourage today's young women to enjoy the adventure, and to realize that each generation has broadened the playing field of opportunity in education, sports, and leadership. At the same time, these publications, especially those geared to tweens, reinforce the value and nurturing of peer friendships. If young people, parents, teachers, and writers are to succeed on all fronts, the message is clear: We're all in this together.

The difference that a generation and information technology have made is like the difference between crawling and taking a supersonic jet.

Beyond the Material: Writing Religious Nonfiction

By Katherine Swarts

If you want to write articles, but wonder if you have a prayer of selling anything, a good place to start is with religious magazines. While Sunday school papers and even teen religious *glossies* are rarely high-paying markets, they are often highly receptive to new writers. Especially if your own faith is important to you, selling such articles can be personally fulfilling as well as a source of income and clips.

Categorizing Your Writing

Religious periodicals address readers of all ages and present opportunities for writers of all interests and skills.

Bible or other scriptural exposition. An expository religious article might be a commentary on a passage of scripture, a story from a holy book, or a principle of belief. Exposition is explanatory or interpretive, but not argumentative or critical. An article of this type may cover a passage verse by verse, or it may focus on larger sections of writings or teachings. It is informative and usually discusses relevant history, culture, and theology. With the Bible story of David and Goliath, for example, a writer might explain battle customs and military strategies of the time period, weigh the evidence for the story being actual history or a legend, or compare it with stories from elsewhere in the Bible, from other religious traditions, or from real life.

Life application. This category overlaps with exposition (with many articles a combination of both), but the distinguishing mark of a life application article is a focus on what the reader can learn, rather than on the hows and whys of a text. Using the David and Goliath example again, a life application article might explain how to trust God in the face of over-whelming odds—school bullies, peer pressure, or a tense situation with a teacher. Life application articles nearly always include contemporary examples (true or theoretical) of how a principle can be applied.

Apologetics. An apologetics article argues the merits of a particular belief or doctrine, and responds to critics and detractors. *Apologetics* carries on the meaning of the Latin word *apologia*, which means a defense or justification. Do not confuse the word with *apologetic*, in the sense of regretful. An apologetic article may be intense, but it should never devolve into blind raving; every point made must have some rational backup.

Evangelistic. This can be a subgenre of apologetics, or of personal experience articles. The goal of an evangelistic article is to win converts, from any other religion or from none. It is more likely to be published in an open-forum magazine than in a specifically religious one whose readers are already converts or being raised in a given faith. It may be geared toward a specific group or a general audience. This kind of writing is a job for a skillful and tactful writer—and one with a reasonably thick skin, as there is usually backlash from people who consider "I'm right and you're wrong" an unpardonable attitude in even its mildest manifestations.

Contemporary issues. Pieces on contemporary issues are most popular with magazines for high school readers, as they deal with difficulties such as hate crimes and the morality surrounding teen pregnancy. But even younger children can understand the dynamics of concerns such as poverty and divorce. An article discussing contemporary issues from a religious perspective has three distinguishing marks: (1) it takes a distinct moral stand (unless it's a point/counterpoint article designed to present two points of view); (2) it includes some note of optimism or hope; and (3) it tries to look at matters from a "how does God feel about this?" perspective rather than simply airing the writer's opinion.

Religious history. Writing on the history of religion is frequently objective and as such may appear in non-religious magazines, or ones sponsored by religions other than the one discussed. With a magazine that does represent the relevant religion, journalistic objectivity is less crucial, but such articles are still oriented more toward information than toward opinion. The history covered may be recent or ancient. The topic may even be about ancient traditions of uncertain historicity.

Religious news. This is the most objective category, regardless of the writer's or publisher's own beliefs. A religious news article, which is a form of journalism, may focus on religious debate within a church denomination, on disagreements between different religions, on missionary or social work, or on events sponsored by one or several religious groups.

Outside of these specifically religious subgenres, nearly any nonfiction article—whether the topic is a building project or a collection of science trivia—can be adapted for religious magazines, either by including religious references or simply by being wholesome reading.

About Friends and Foes

Now, a few hints for deciding what type of article you should write:

Are you a dedicated follower of any religion? If so, you might want to focus on writing for publications for that religious community. On the other hand, if you are gifted in tact and persuasion, you might prefer writing evangelistic articles. If you do send an article to a publication read by members of another religion—or of none—be extra careful to avoid insulting or bigoted insinuations. Be honest about your own faults, not just the other person's, and don't automatically take the most visible elements of a religion as its most accurate representatives. Give other faiths the benefit of the doubt wherever possible.

Are you prone to diatribes and defensiveness? If so (be honest here!), think twice before proposing an article on comparative religion or contemporary issues. You may not have the tact to pull it off. If you must say your piece, do everything possible to avoid loaded words and to acknowledge the more reasonable elements of the other side.

What are your primary interests? If you love history in any shape or form, religious history will be easy to add to the mix. If you're a journalist at heart, religious news may be perfect for you. If you were on your school debating team, you may be suited to write apologetics; and if you love scriptural study for its own sake, consider an expository article.

Do you have a pet cause such as helping the homeless? If so, you may be suited to write a contemporary issue article on the subject, or a life application article encouraging youngsters to get involved.

The Ten Writing Commandments

Now on to the *hows* of religious writing.

Thou shalt remember the human. Even if you consider your religion the one true faith, followers of other religions are still human beings—and individuals. Avoid blanket criticisms of other faiths and of secularists. Any statement or implication that "atheists have no morals" or "Sunis are intolerant and violent" at best offends readers who have friends or relatives in that group, and at worst encourages the same bigotry that starts religious wars.

Even when speaking kindly of others, "Be careful with the names of 'denominations,'" says Yael Resnick, Publisher/Editor of *Natural Jewish Parenting,* "since such labels have often been imposed from outside and can have negative connotations. Don't call a group of Torah-observant or Hassidic Jews 'ultra-Orthodox,' because few use this label to describe themselves. If you must

Articles to read

The following offer a brief illustration of the range of articles possible in religious magazine writing for children, parents, and educators.

- Bianchi, Tracey, "Should I Keep Going? Going the Extra Mile in Leadership." *MOPS International, Mothers of Preschoolers*. www.mops.org
- Chasnoff, Joel, "Peter Himmelman: Jamming with a Jewish Soul." *BabagaNewz* (September 2002). www.babaganewz.com
- Copland, Ralph M., "A Challenge for the New Teacher." *Journal of Adventist Education* (October/November 2002, p. 40).
- Jones, Jeremy V., "Bethany Hamilton Rides the Wave." *Breakaway* (July 2005). www.breakawaymag.com
- "The Borrowed Motorcycle," as told to Juliana Marin. *Guide* (March 18, 2006). www.guidemagazine.org
- Mills, Charles, "The Escape Artist." *Guide Magazine Online*. www.guidemagazine.org
- Ntihemuka, Patty Froese, "The Knock-Knock Disaster." *Guide* (April 22, 2006). www.guidemagazine.org
- Rosenbaum, Stanley Ned, "Angel in the House? Women's Roles in Interfaith Marriages." *Dovetail* (September/October 2004).
- Ryder, Susan, "A Muslim/Christian Couple: The Wedding and After." *Dovetail* (January/February 2006).
- Shellenberger, Susie, "Going Deeper: Would Jesus Church-Hop?" *Brio and Beyond* (2004). www.briomag.com/briomagazine/briobeyond

identify a specific person using a label, ask that person for his or her preference."

Remember that thou art only human. Even if the scriptures of your religion are infallible, you aren't. True, there are many points on which devotees can agree. There are also many points on which the greatest theologians differ. So try not to state your interpretations as though you were the Prophet Mohammed receiving the Qur'an by angelic dictation. "Be careful of words like *always, never,* or *shouldn't,*" says Resnick. "Give your readers something to think about, but don't do their thinking for them. You don't have to answer every question or solve the mysteries of life."

Thou shalt not preach. Virtually every reli-gious editor raises this point. No religious writer should forget it. No "I say unto you" implications! If writing for an audience of another faith, never slip into a "turn or burn" approach, especially for young readers. It may have worked in an age when nearly everyone shared the same basic theological ideas, but it won't scare anyone straight in the modern, multicultural era.

Thou shalt mind thy market research. Another pet peeve of editors is the writer who sends in a submission without even glancing at the guidelines, let alone the magazine. Wit-ness the how-to article sent to a magazine whose guidelines explic-itly state, "We publish only devotionals for chil-dren." The only thing worse is the writer who has read the guidelines and sends an inappro-priate piece anyway, asking the editor flat out to make an exception. "One of the biggest mis-takes writers make is

not knowing the mission statement, doctrinal position, or core values of the publisher," says Dana Wilkerson, Senior Editor of Group Pub-lishing's Hands-On Bible Curriculum, which publishes *Children's Ministry, Group,* and *Rev!* "Another big mistake is not following the edi-tor's specifications."

Thou shalt avoid religious jargon. "There is a fine line between being inspirational and being clichéd, sentimental, or corny," says Resnick. Don't toss in phrasing just because you heard it in church. *Saved by the blood* is bewildering; *born again* is a cliché; *jihad* and *crusade* are loaded words.

Thou shalt not quote scripture for the sake of quoting, nor load thy article with unquoted citations. No young reader wants to spoil the flow of reading by stopping every two sen-tences to look up a verse! If you must send your readers to the original source, at least put the references in a sidebar.

Thou shalt do thy research. A surprising number of people know little about the history and scriptures of their own religions, much less anyone else's. Attending weekly services is not research! Read scripture; read commentaries; research the other matters affecting your article. "If you are not well-versed in the tenets and practices of your own religion," says Resnick, "or if you are not a member of the religion you are writing about, have several knowledgeable representatives of that faith read your article and correct any inaccuracies. Do not rely on one person for feedback; interview people across a spectrum, to synthesize their religious perspectives into a coherent understanding of the range of lifestyles and beliefs." Wilkerson adds, "Always verify your facts—biblical, historical, statistical. Include references with your manuscript."

Thou shalt not get uppity with editors. Pride goeth before a fall. Never say, "God gave me this message for the world." Most religious editors have heard that from more untalented-but-egotistical types than they care to remember. No matter how vital a message you have, don't complain to the editor who fails to appreciate your proposal. Editors, like umpires, stick religiously to their original calls.

Thou shalt give inspired work the thorough treatment it deserves. A surprising number of writers think *inspiration* equals *divine dictation* and expect the first draft to be perfect. Treat religious articles with the same careful editing and rewriting due any manuscript. "Read over what you have written," says Resnick, "and ask yourself whether you have given the reader something new and original, something based on your unique perspective, or whether you're covering territory that has been done many times before." Then read it over once more—preferably after a week's rest—to purge the manuscript of typos and grammatical errors!

Thou shalt pray for skill and humility as much as for success. "You can tell the world," as one book for Christian writers put it. Whatever you tell them, be sure you tell it right!

The Reading Classroom: Write for Today's Educational Markets

By Christina Hamlett

For generations of elementary school children, one event could be counted on like clockwork from week to week and year to year: the appearance on our desks every Monday of *Weekly Reader*, a kid-friendly newspaper that summarized current events, increased our vocabularies, and pushed our mental margins to explore global viewpoints. The newsy materials from outside sources seemed a welcome bonus to the curriculum for our teachers and were a fun, informative break from textbooks for us. Like many of my peers, however, I had no idea where these publications originated, much less that freelance writers—including librarians and teachers like our own—were penning much of the content.

Today, opportunities for writers to contribute to the classroom scene through articles that educate, enlighten, and entertain are plentiful. Many kinds of educational materials assist educators day to day, reach children on subjects relevant to contemporary culture, encourage creative thinking, and help different kinds of learners acquire new skills at their own paces.

ABCs

While you need not be a teacher to write for classroom and other educational magazines, knowledge of educational principles, the way children learn, and of course, subject matter are all essential. Many of the ongoing contributors to publications such as *Weekly Reader*, *School Arts*, and *Scholastic Classroom* are current or former teachers. From an editor's point of view, those with jobs in educational settings grasp the way young minds work and already have access to the periodicals read by students at specific ages. Educators have an intimate knowledge of classroom needs, learning stages, and the curriculum. They know about budgets and broader educational needs.

Whether your goal is to gear material toward students or to the adults teaching them, if you're a topical expert outside the educational network, you've got homework to do. Here's the assignment: (1) initiate conversations with actual teachers; (2) read relevant publications and participate in chatrooms such as those found at Teachers.Net (http://teachers.net/mentors); (3) google *classroom magazines* and *teacher resources*; and (4) review state curriculum websites.

Don't forget the needs of private and home schools, so for extra credit, research those as well. Both are on the rise, as are adult continuing education and distance learning. For freelancers, these trends all translate to openings in online forums and workshops, specialized newsletters, multimedia packages, and a diverse range of classroom publications.

Learn from Mistakes

Let's move to a lesson in what not to do, to what's wrong with many writers' submissions.

Susan Thurman was founder and editor for 11 years of *Class Act*, a grammar and writing magazine, and is the author of the book *The Only Grammar Book You'll Ever Need: A One-Stop Source for Every Writing Assignment*. "We always got far too many submissions that were not geared to our audience," says Thurman. "We were specifically for classroom teachers of English, and our guidelines clearly stated this, but we'd get submissions giving us 'terrific ideas about how to teach math' or something else that was equally irrelevant. We also saw too many elementary topics that would not fit with the age group we targeted. Often we knew right away that the writer was totally unfamiliar with the needs and interests of the middle school or high school student."

Weekly Reader Senior Managing Editor Anne Flounders cites an ongoing problem with contributors who simply don't know when to stop talking. "We have writers who submit stories to us that are hundreds of words past the assigned word limit. My advice to writers: There is always a way to tell a story well within the assigned word limit: Find it! It might involve making tough choices, but that's all part of the process."

More bluntly, imagine an editor who has a space to fill that takes 1,000 words and a writer who gives them 1,500 or even 2,000 words. Why would an editor be pleased with the extra work of cutting and trimming—a revision that you know as a writer yourself is time-consuming? An editor has other articles to edit and assign, and may work on layout, budget, supervise staff, and so on. He or she wants to work with you one on one, but can't teach you. That is one fact every writer of educational articles should know. You are teaching, not being taught. Give the editor what they need, with the least amount of work for them, and you've learned a very valuable lesson.

Brian Willoughby, Managing Editor of *Teaching Tolerance* from the Southern Poverty Law Center, has seen more than his share of rambling manuscripts. "Too many people are too wordy and lack the ability to edit themselves or to find a colleague, friend, or mentor who's willing to give them constructive feedback."

Because his publication addresses contemporary issues regarding respect for and understanding of cultural diversity for students, many of the manuscripts he receives confuse the magazine's message with expression of their own agendas. "The result," Willoughby says, "are unfocused stories. This is especially true of people submitting personal or political essays. You can't cover everything in a magazine article, so don't even try! Choose a focused idea, then stay within that framework. If you feel compelled to step outside that focus, write that material down for another story."

Sloppiness is another no-no. Some students with learning disabilities or weak academic skills need room for their intelligence and creativity to bloom, without formal strictures such

"There is always a way to tell a story within an assigned word limit: Find it!"

as spelling rules or paragraphing. That is not the case for adult writers for educational publications. "I don't mind catching a few little errors now and then," admits Willoughby. "As an editor, it's part of my job. But don't shoot yourself in the foot by leaving in misspelled words or typos that a simple spellcheck would have caught."

Thurman has a strong stance on errors. "Submissions that contain too many spelling, grammatical, or usage mistakes," she says, cast suspicion on the credibility of the content. "If they weren't careful enough in their presentation, how could I trust their methods of research?"

Topically Speaking

Writers who have no sense of topics that have been done to death are also frustrating to editors. "I can't tell you," says Willoughby, "how many pitches have we've seen on the effects of 9/11 or stories that bash No Child

WEEKLY WR READER

Winter Olympics

The Olympics are events in which athletes from around the world compete in different sports. This February, the Winter Olympics will be held in Turin, Italy. One of the newest Winter Olympic sports is snowboarding.

Left Behind but offer no new thinking or alternative ideas or plans."

Here's another major assignment for you: As a writer, be steps ahead. Publishers work months ahead because of the practical time needed for editing, factchecking, copyediting, proofreading, production, printing, and mailing. Time takes its toll on topics. Perhaps even more important, writers and the ideas they present to children should be forward thinking and lively, not tired. The more creative and active and connected you are—and the more you can write in that way for children—the more you will find success in writing for the educational and every other market.

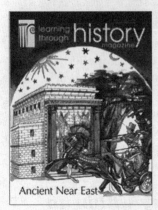
Ancient Near East

From Flounders's viewpoint at *Weekly Reader,* "Certain topics we've covered a number of times, and will again—obesity, nutrition, exercise, depression, drug abuse. If writers want to pitch stories about these topics, they need to give us a new, unexpected, newsworthy angle, not just a general overview of the problem."

Fresh and *forward thinking* apply no less to topics based in the past. The bimonthly magazine *Learning Through History* invites freelancers to explain life in the past lane through its 64-page themed issues, study guides, discussion questions, and school crafts projects. Its signature tone takes readers beyond generic timelines found in most textbooks with references to supplemental books, films, and websites. The goal is to encourage enthusiasm for lifelong learning. Insider note: Taking the website's virtual tour is a must prior to pitching ideas.

For history in the making, writers with journalism credentials should check out *The New York Times Upfront,* a teen-friendly newspaper published by Scholastic that has as much need for cutting-edge features as it does teacher guidelines. Recent articles such as "The Great Immigration Debate," by Patricia Smith, and "Are There Civil Rights in Cyberspace?" by Adam Liptak are reflective of content that spurs classroom discussion.

To score high marks with educational publications, study their most recent issues as judiciously as you review their submissions requirements. For policies, standards, and proven classroom strategies, read online and print resources such as those of the National Education Association, Editorial Projects in Education, or associations like the National Council of Teachers of English. The *Times Education Supplement* (www.tes.co.uk) is one of the world's leading education newspapers, and can be a unique aid in staying abreast of educational news and views. See the sidebar for similar associations that can keep you informed, most of which have their own publications in need of freelance writers.

Talking the Talk

Writing for young readers, of course, is also a delicate balancing act between trying to pretend you're their age and constantly reminding them that you're not. "At *Positive Teens,*" says Publisher and Editor in Chief Susan Manning, too many submissions "have a tendency to preach or give advice. Some articles have included terms such as *you should* and *you need to,* or *don't* and *do.* Quite a few queries, stories, and interviews we receive are also written by authors who have more experience as younger children's writers.

Educational associations

- Editorial Projects in Education: www.edweek.org
- National Council for the Social Studies: www.ncss.org
- National Council of Teachers of English: www.ncte.org
- National Council of Teachers of Mathematics: www.nctm.org
- National Education Association: www.nea.org
- National Science Teachers Association: www.nsta.org

Homeschooling
- *Homefires:* www.homefires.com
- *Homeschooling Parent:* www.homeschoolingparent.com
- *Home Education Magazine:* www.homeedmag.com

Our demographics are ages 12 to 21, which is a completely different audience. That said, certain words can really turn them off."

Manning also says that when adults try to speak in the voice of a contemporary teenager, it can be problematic. "One writer, in an attempt to sound cool, used outdated slang terms and referenced celebrity sports figures who were popular more than 20 years ago." The range of topics *Positive Teens* publishes is reflected in "What's the Hype about Ballroom Dancing?" by Erikka J. Adams; "Mathematical Mysteries," by Carolyn Richard; and "How About a Drink of Water? Yeah, Right!" by Rebecca Norris. In the case of ESL students, take additional care to minimize colloquialisms. Provide easy frames of reference for concepts that may not have a counterpart within their own culture.

Homeroom

The proliferation of moms and dads assuming a new role as home educators has generated a major need for lesson plans that can be integrated into family life—math skills applied to measuring recipes; geography and history examined in the context of planning a road trip to national parks and monuments; language and cultural arts prevalent in ethnic community festivals.

If the development of homeschooling materials excites you, jumpstart your brain with a Google search of *free lesson plans*. Familiarize yourself with organizations such as the American Homeschool Association and the National African American Homeschoolers Alliance, both of which have numerous links to lesson plan writing opportunities. *Homefires*, *Homeschooling Parent*, and *Home Education Magazine* have an ongoing need for innovative lesson plans, interactive games, and also for how-to advice for novice homeschoolers.

Carol Narigon, Articles Editor for *Home*

Electronic aids

Just because you know a topic well doesn't always mean you can explain it to someone else. The ability to tailor an effective message requires awareness of the target audience's reading and comprehension levels. This especially applies to classroom materials used by ESL students whose vocabularies may not correspond to the standards of their assigned grade level.

If you use Microsoft Word, you have an ally in this challenge. Select *Tools* in the menu bar, click *Options*, then *Spelling and grammar*. In addition to selecting *Check grammar with spelling,* click on *Show readability statistics*. At the end of the check, the spelling and grammar box displays a report with the number of passive sentences in your document, the Flesch reading ease score (percentage of the population who could read your text without difficulty) and the Flesch-Kincaid grade level.

Let's say you've written:

Henry VIII, vehement in his quest to usurp the power and authority of the Pope by declaring matrimony to his beloved Anne Boleyn, decided to abolish the existing religious order and establish the Church of England.

The assessment score reveals that (1) only 19.8 percent of the population would understand it and (2) it has been written for twelfth grade or higher. Contrast this to:

Henry VIII wants to marry Anne Boleyn. The Pope, however, won't approve it. Henry starts his own church.

This revision changes the stats to 64.4 percent and a fifth-grade reading level.

Such electronic wizardry is a derivation of the Fog Index often used by politicians to frame campaign messages. The Fog formula takes the average sentence length plus the number of 3-syllable words in a 100-word passage and multiplies that sum by 0.4 to determine a reading grade level. (Test this yourself on the first 100 words of any published children's book or classroom magazine.) If results are higher than desired, the text can be revised with shorter sentences, shorter words, or a combination of both.

Education Magazine, says she is always receptive to homeschooling articles that touch the heart, are informative, or make her laugh out loud. "In our July/August 2006 edition, Sue Zelie wrote a poignant personal interest article about her daughter growing up, 'Moose in the Mist.' Karen Kirkwood's article 'The GED

Option' gives readers information on a topic many are interested in even if their kids are too young for a GED yet. One of our most popular articles was 'Messy Homeschoolers,' by Mary Kenyon, a confessional article about what life as a homeschooler is really like."

For the truly entrepreneurial, why not start your own newsletter or blog? While the pay may be nonexistent, establishing a following (and a portfolio!) is advantageous for expanding into larger markets.

Technology has brought the world closer to the schoolhouse doorstep, although the downside is that cyber distractions up the challenge of keeping students engaged. Success will come to the classroom wordsmith who can promote active learning through materials that ask as many questions as they answer, and who strives to attach relevance to the learner's personal journey, regardless of age and whether the classroom is real or virtual.

Listings

How to Use the Listings

The pages that follow feature profiles of 632 magazines that publish articles and stories for, about, or of interest to children and young adults. Throughout the year, we stay on top of the latest happenings in children's magazines to bring you new and different publishing outlets. This year, our research yielded over 60 additional markets for your writing. They are easy to find; look for the listings with a star in the upper right corner.

A Variety of Freelance Opportunities

This year's new listings reflect the interests of today's magazine audience. You'll find magazines targeted to readers interested in nature, the environment, computers, mysteries, child care, careers, different cultures, family activities, and many other topics.

Along with many entertaining and educational magazines aimed at young readers, we list related publications such as national and regional magazines for parents and teachers. Hobby and special interest magazines generally thought of as adult fare but read by many teenagers are listed too.

In the market listings, the Freelance Potential section helps you judge each magazine's receptivity to freelance writers. This section offers information about the number of freelance submissions published each year.

Further opportunities for selling your writing appear in the Additional Listings section on page 287. This section profiles a range of magazines that publish a limited amount of material targeted to children, young adults, parents, or teachers. Other outlets for your writing can be found in the Selected Contests and Awards section, beginning on page 331.

Using Other Sections of the Directory

If you are planning to write for a specific publication, turn to the Magazine and Contest Index beginning on page 372 to locate the listing page. The Category Index, beginning on page 347, will guide you to magazines that publish in your areas of interest. This year, the Category Index also gives the age range of each publication's readership. To find the magazines most open to freelance submissions, turn to the Fifty+ Freelance index on page 346, which lists magazines that rely on freelance writers for over 50% of the material they publish.

Check the Market News, beginning on page 344, to find out what's newly listed, what's not listed and why, and to identify changes in the market that have occurred during the past year.

About the Listings

We revisited last year's listings and, through a series of mailed surveys and phone interviews, verified editors' names, mailing addresses, submissions and payment policies, and current editorial needs. All entries are accurate and up-to-date when we send this market directory to press. Magazine publishing is a fast-moving industry, though, and it is not unusual for facts to change before or shortly after this guide reaches your hands. Magazines close, are sold to new owners, or move; they hire new editors or change their editorial focus. Keep up to date by requesting sample copies and writers' guidelines.

Note that we do *not* list:

- Magazines that did not respond to our questionnaires or phone queries. Know that we make every effort to contact each editor before press date.

- Magazines that *never* accept freelance submissions or work with freelance writers.

To get a real sense of a magazine and its editorial slant, we recommend that you read several recent sample issues cover to cover. This is the best way to be certain a magazine is right for you.

Chess Life for Kids

New listing ——

P.O. Box 3967
Crossville, TN 38577

Who to contact —— Editor: Glenn Petersen

Profiles the publication, its interests, and readers ——

Description and Interests
Targeted to scholastic members of the U.S. Chess Federation only, this magazine includes articles on chess instruction and tips, tournament participation and upcoming tournament information, chess camps, and related activities.
- **Audience:** 12 years and under
- **Frequency:** 6 times each year
- **Distribution:** 100% controlled
- **Circulation:** 14,200
- **Website: www.uschess.org**

Freelance Potential
58% written by nonstaff writers. Publishes 45 freelance submissions yearly; 10% by unpublished writers, 10% by authors who are new to the magazine. Receives several queries yearly.

Designates the amount and type of freelance submissions published each year; highlights the publication's receptivity to unpublished writers ——

Provides guidelines for submitting material; lists word lengths and types of material accepted from freelance writers ——

Submissions
Query or send complete ms. Accepts email submissions to gpetersen@uschess.org and simultaneous submissions if identified. Responds in 2 weeks.
Articles: To 1,000 words. Informational and instructional articles; and profiles. Topics include chess instruction and tips, tournaments, and chess camps and lessons.

Sample Issue
24 pages: 12 articles.
- "Our Heritage." Article profiles Harry Nelson Pillsbury, one of the five greatest chess players in American history.
- "The Art of Chess." Article outlines several tactical tricks to add to a player's arsenal of skills.
- "Queen City Classic." Article recounts the events surrounding the Fifth Annual Cris Collinsworth ProScan Foundation Queen City Classic tournament, which took place April 1, 2006.

Analyzes a recent sample copy of the publication; briefly describes selected articles, stories, departments, etc. ——

Lists types of rights acquired, payment rate, and number of copies provided to freelance writers ——

Rights and Payment
First North American serial rights. Written material, $75 per page. Pays on publication.

Editor's Comments
We are looking for more articles on chess instruction and tournament participation and information, but there is also room for articles on chess camps and similar activities. Remember, our readers are 12 and under, so please use words appropriate and understandable for this age group. It is advisable to read an issue of our magazine to get a sense of our style.

Offers advice from the editor about the publication's writing style, freelance needs, audience, etc. ——

Icon Key

☆ New Listing　　🖱 Epublisher　　⊗ Not currently accepting submissions

Abilities

340 College Street, Suite 401
Toronto, Ontario M5T 3A9
Canada

Managing Editor: Jaclyn Law

Description and Interests
This magazine is a cross-disability lifestyle magazine that inspires readers to participate in organizations, events, and services dedicated to people with disabilities.
- **Audience:** Families with disabled members
- **Frequency:** Quarterly
- **Distribution:** 80% controlled; 10% newsstand; 10% other
- **Circulation:** 45,000
- **Website: www.abilities.ca**

Freelance Potential
50% written by nonstaff writers. Publishes 30–40 freelance submissions yearly; 5–10% by unpublished writers, 75% by authors who are new to the magazine. Receives 120 queries, 504 unsolicited mss yearly.

Submissions
Query with writing samples; or send complete ms. Accepts hard copy and email submissions to jaclyn@abilities.ca. SAE/IRC. Responds in 2–3 months.
Articles: 1,500–2,000 words. Informational, self-help, and how-to articles; personal experience and opinion pieces; profiles; interviews; and humor. Topics include travel, health, sports, recreation, employment, education, transportation, housing, social policy, sexuality, reviews, and special events of relevance to Canadians.
Depts/columns: 500–1,200 words. Crafts, cooking, and accessibility issues.

Sample Issue
60 pages (50% advertising): 13 articles; 9 depts/columns. Guidelines available.
- "The Joy of Yoga." Article describes how yoga can be enjoyed by people with disabilities.
- "Persons with Disabilities in Television Programming." Article tells how Canada's broadcasters are including more of the disadvantaged in their ranks.
- Sample dept/column: "For Your Information" details a self-employment program to help the disabled.

Rights and Payment
First and electronic rights. Written material, $25–$350. Kill fee, 50%. Pays 60 days after publication. Provides 2 contributor's copies.

Editor's Comments
We encourage material that shed light on a particular area of interest or provides a personal perspective on any aspect of life pertinent to people with disabilities.

Above & Beyond

P.O. Box 408
Fort Madison, IA 52627

Editor: Donna Borst

Description and Interests
Gifted students and bright learners who are looking for creative, challenging enrichment activities are the audience for *Above & Beyond*. Its materials are tailored toward middle school students and relate to the core curriculum.
- **Audience:** Grades 5–8
- **Frequency:** 5 times each year
- **Distribution:** Subscription; other
- **Circulation:** 1,200
- **Website: www.menageriepublishing.com**

Freelance Potential
99% written by nonstaff writers. Publishes 60–100 freelance submissions yearly.

Submissions
Prefers complete ms; accepts query. Prefers email submissions to donna@menageriepublishing.com. Accepts hard copy. SASE. Responds in 2–3 months.
Other: Story starters, logic puzzles, creative writing exercises, problem-solving scenarios, school projects, and other enrichment activities.

Sample Issue
62 pages: 22 activities. Sample copy, $5.25 with SASE. Guidelines available.
- "The Seven Wonders of the Ancient World." Lesson unit includes ideas that connect vocabulary, pictures, and videos to timelines, collages, and a model-building activity on the Seven Wonders.
- "*Beyond the Burning Time*: A Literature Study." Activity features ideas for learning about the Salem witch hunt through a novel by Kathryn Lasky.
- "Conversing in Code." Activity teaches about cryptology, ciphers, symbols, and other codes.

Rights and Payment
First rights. Written material, payment rates vary. Payment policy varies. Provides 1 contributor's copy.

Editor's Comments
Ours is not a typical classroom magazine—we do not want the usual submissions, such as short stories, bulletin boards, and crafts. We're looking for material that will provide exceptional challenges for gifted and talented students. Submissions should include an introduction, activities, references, and an answer key if necessary. Specify the grade level the material is suitable for. Materials are chosen based on merit and the other submissions we have on hand.

Ad Astra

ADDitude Magazine

1620 I Street NW, Suite 615
Washington, DC 20006

Membership Services Manager: Katherine Brick

Description and Interests
This journal's objective is to educate the public about space. Readers are space enthusiasts and technologists furthering their involvement with all aspects of the space industry, from economic needs to global ideas and perspectives.
• **Audience:** Adults and college students
• **Frequency:** Quarterly
• **Distribution:** 100% subscription
• **Circulation:** 20,000
• **Website:** www.nss.org

Freelance Potential
95% written by nonstaff writers. Publishes 50 freelance submissions yearly. Receives 65 queries and unsolicited mss yearly.

Submissions
Query or send ms with résumé. Accepts disk submissions and email to nsshq@nss.org. Artwork improves chance of acceptance. SASE. Response time varies.
Articles: Word lengths vary. Topics include science and technology in exploration and development organizations and the aerospace industry.
Depts/columns: Word lengths vary. Opinion pieces and reviews.
Artwork: Electronic images.

Sample Issue
48 pages (14% advertising): 7 articles; 6 depts/columns. Sample copy, $11.25 ($4 postage).
• "Salute to Salyut 1." Article pays tribute to Russian cosmonauts whose bravery ended in disaster upon reentry of the Soyuz in 1971.
• "Making Sun-Shades from Moon Dust." Article previews a visionary proposal and the technology needed for erecting a super shield in space to counteract global warming.
• Sample dept/column: "A Quarter-Century of Space Advocacy" presents a memoir and overview of the International Space Development Conferences and a discussion of space advocacy and the space entrepreneurial movement.

Rights and Payment
First North American serial rights. No payment.

Editor's Comments
Writers with expertise in space and technology are welcome to submit articles. Material about children related to space is published occasionally.

39 West 37th Street, 15th Floor
New York, NY 10018

Editor: David Freeman

Description and Interests
ADDitude Magazine is published for parents of children with Attention Deficit Disorder. Each issue of this self-help publication features articles on treatment, as well as profiles of and interviews with individuals who have personal experience with ADD.
• **Audience:** Adults
• **Frequency:** 6 times each year
• **Distribution:** Subscription; other
• **Circulation:** 40,000
• **Website:** www.additudemag.com

Freelance Potential
80% written by nonstaff writers. Publishes 15–20 freelance submissions yearly; 30% by unpublished writers, 30% by authors who are new to the magazine. Receives 96 queries yearly.

Submissions
Query. No unsolicited mss. Accepts email queries to submissions@additudemag.com. Response time varies.
Articles: To 2,000 words. Informational articles and personal experience pieces. Topics include Attention Deficit Disorder, education, recreation, and child development.
Depts/columns: Word lengths vary. Profiles of schools and teachers; first-person experiences from parents; and AD/HD news and notes.

Sample Issue
62 pages (33% advertising): 3 articles; 16 depts/columns. Sample copy, $6.95. Guidelines available.
• "12 Chances to Be a Better Parent." Article explains how to avoid common mistakes when raising a child with ADD.
• "Nothing Can Stop Us." Article shares the stories of three athletes who reveal how ADD helped them.
• Sample dept/column: "Success at School" offers tips teachers can use to help students with ADD make good use of their time.

Rights and Payment
First rights. All material, payment rates vary. Kill fee, $75. Pays on publication.

Editor's Comments
We'd like to review first-person articles by individuals whose stories might be helpful to others. We encourage you to share your insights and experiences with other adults and families living with ADD.

Adoptalk

North American Council on Adoptable Children
970 Raymond Street, Suite 106
St. Paul, MN 55114-1149

Editor: Diane Riggs

Description and Interests
This newsletter features factual articles that cover issues and concerns surrounding adoption and foster care. It is published by the North American Council on Adoptable Children.
- **Audience:** Adults
- **Frequency:** Quarterly
- **Distribution:** 100% controlled
- **Circulation:** 3,700
- **Website:** www.nacac.org

Freelance Potential
65% written by nonstaff writers. Publishes 3 freelance submissions yearly; 10% by unpublished writers, 60% by authors who are new to the magazine. Receives 5 queries and unsolicited mss yearly.

Submissions
Query or send complete ms with bibliography. Accepts hard copy and and email to dianeriggs@ nacac.org. Responds in 2–3 weeks.
Articles: To 2,000 words. Informational articles; personal experience pieces; profiles; and interviews. Topics include adoptive and foster care, parenting, recruitment, adoption news, conference updates, and NACAC membership news.
Depts/columns: Word lengths vary. Book reviews and first-person essays.

Sample Issue
20 pages (no advertising): 4 articles; 6 depts/ columns. Sample copy, free with 9x12 SASE ($.87 postage). Guidelines available.
- "Self-Care: Barriers and Basics for Foster/Adoptive Parents." Article discusses how to balance the physical and emotional needs of traumatized children with personal self-care.
- "Families Can Prepare for and Address Adoption Dynamics." Article explains how to successfully integrate adoptees into a family.
- Sample dept/column: "Speak Out Corner" presents short news items.

Rights and Payment
Rights policy varies. No payment. Provides 5 contributor's copies.

Editor's Comments
At this time, we are looking for material on issues related to adoption and diversity, such as race, background, and lifestyles.

Adoptive Families

39 West 37th Street, 15th Floor
New York, NY 10018

Submissions: Susan Coughman

Description and Interests
Advice and support for families who plan to adopt or have recently adopted children are found in this magazine. It offers a mix of practical information, humor, and personal experiences.
- **Audience:** Adoptive families
- **Frequency:** 6 times each year
- **Distribution:** 90% subscription; 10% other
- **Circulation:** 40,000
- **Website:** www.adoptivefamilies.com

Freelance Potential
75% written by nonstaff writers. Publishes 100 freelance submissions yearly; 20% by unpublished writers, 50% by authors who are new to the magazine. Receives 500–600 unsolicited mss yearly.

Submissions
Query or send complete ms. Accepts hard copy, Macintosh disk submissions (Microsoft Word), and email to letters@adoptivefamilies.com. SASE. Responds in 4–6 weeks.
Articles: 500–1,800 words. Self-help and how-to articles; personal experience pieces; humor; and interviews. Topics include family issues, child development, health, teen topics, education, learning disabilities, careers, and multicultural topics.
Depts/columns: To 1,200 words. Opinion and personal experience pieces focusing on adoption, single parenting, and birth-parent issues; book and media reviews.
Other: Seasonal material on ethnic holidays, National Adoption Month, and Martin Luther King, Jr., Day.

Sample Issue
70 pages (40% advertising): 3 articles; 16 depts/ columns. Sample copy, $6.95. Guidelines available.
- "New Family Values." Article explains how nontraditional adoptive families can thrive in today's world.
- Sample dept/column: "And So It Begins" is a personal experience piece by a mother who has learned how to cope with attachment disorder.

Rights and Payment
All rights. All material, payment rates vary. Provides 2 contributor's copies.

Editor's Comments
Personal experience pieces that offer compelling, unique insights on adoption will always receive our full consideration.

African American Family

22041 Woodward Avenue
Ferndale, MI 48220

Editor: Denise Crittendon

Description and Interests
Serving African American parents in the metropolitan Detroit area, this lifestyle magazine focuses on family and parenting issues, family health, family entertainment and travel, education, fatherhood, developmental and behavioral issues, and community projects. It also contains profiles of local individuals and regional current events.
- **Audience:** Parents
- **Frequency:** Monthly
- **Distribution:** Subscription; other
- **Circulation:** Unavailable
- **Website:** www.metroparent.com

Freelance Potential
20% written by nonstaff writers. Publishes 20 freelance submissions yearly.

Submissions
Query through website only. Accepts simultaneous submissions if identified. Response time varies.
Articles: Word lengths vary. Informational articles; profiles; interviews; personal experience and self-help pieces; and reviews. Topics include current events, education, history, nature, the environment, recreation, social issues, sports, and travel.
Depts/columns: Word lengths vary. Profiles community issues, health and fitness, regional resources and events.

Sample Issue
46 pages: 2 articles; 7 depts/columns. Guidelines available at website.
- "A Father's Influence." A local firefighter, a physician, and a television anchor each discuss the trials and triumphs of parenting.
- "Unexpected Journey." Article takes a look at how some local teenage boys are dealing with their new roles as fathers.
- Sample dept/column: "Health and Healing" talks about the Northland Mall walking club, which promotes health, fitness, and community outreach.

Rights and Payment
Rights vary. Written material, payment rates vary. Pays on publication.

Editor's Comments
We welcome queries from qualified journalists with professional, solid reporting skills. Metro Detroit area ideas and sources are preferred.

AIM Magazine

P.O. Box 1174
Maywood, IL 60153

Editor: Myron Apilado

Description and Interests
Self-described as "America's intercultural magazine," this publication examines racism and how it affects mankind. Each issue includes stories, essays, articles, and opinion pieces related to ethnic and intercultural concerns.
- **Audience:** Educators
- **Frequency:** Quarterly
- **Distribution:** Subscription
- **Circulation:** 2,000
- **Website:** www.aimmagazine.org

Freelance Potential
95% written by nonstaff writers. Publishes 50 freelance submissions yearly; 50% by unpublished writers, 80% by authors who are new to the magazine. Receives 98 unsolicited mss yearly.

Submissions
Send complete ms. Accepts hard copy and simultaneous submissions. SASE. Responds in 1 month.
Articles: 2,000 words. Informational articles; personal experience and opinion pieces; essays, profiles; and interviews. Topics include social issues, racial issues, bigotry, culture, ethnic holidays, politics, humor, and feminism.
Fiction: 4,000 words. Genres include inspirational, historical, ethnic, humorous, contemporary, and literary fiction and humor.

Sample Issue
48 pages: 11 articles; 3 stories; 7 poems. Sample copy, $5 with 9x12 SASE (5 first-class stamps). Writers' guidelines, editorial calendar, and theme list available.
- "Black History or Mental Slavery?" Article discusses why African Americans need to celebrate what needs to be celebrated, not what they are told to celebrate.
- "Snakebite." Short story explores the effects of war on one U.S. Marine.

Rights and Payment
First rights. Articles, $15–$25. Short stories, $100. Pays on publication. Provides 1 contributor's copy.

Editor's Comments
We seek compelling, well-written stories that have social significance, proving that people from different racial or ethnic backgrounds are more alike than they are different. Our goal is to purge racism from our bloodstream by way of the written word.

Alateen Talk

Al-Anon Family Group
1600 Corporate Landing Parkway
Virginia Beach, VA 23454-5617

Associate Director, Member Services: Barbara Older

Description and Interests
This newsletter is written by and for members of Alateen, a fellowship of young Al-Anon members, usually teenagers, whose lives have been affected by someone's drinking. Each issue includes articles and letters to encourage members to share their experiences, strengths, and hopes.
• **Audience:** 6–18 years
• **Frequency:** Quarterly
• **Distribution:** 100% subscription
• **Circulation:** 4,000
• **Website:** www.al-anon.alateen.org

Freelance Potential
90% written by nonstaff writers. Publishes 85–120 freelance submissions yearly; 90% by unpublished writers. Receives 100–150 unsolicited mss yearly.

Submissions
Accepts complete ms from Alateen members only. Accepts hard copy. SASE. Responds in 2 weeks.
Articles: Word lengths vary. Self-help and personal experience pieces. Topics include alcoholism and its effects on relationships, social issues, and family life.
Depts/columns: Staff written.
Artwork: B/W line art.
Other: Poetry.

Sample Issue
8 pages (no advertising): 3 articles; 13 letters; 12 activities. Sample copy, free with 9x12 SASE ($.87 postage). Guidelines available to Alateen members.
• "New Hope Alateen." First-person piece from a young member explains that he began the Alateen program when his family became uncontrollable.
• "Just for Today." Short letter by a member reveals how she discovered that a Higher Power could help her cope with her alcoholic parent.
• "Discussion and Sharing." Activity helps readers share humor and laughter to aid their recovery.

Rights and Payment
All rights. No payment.

Editor's Comments
Our membership magazine publishes material written by members of Alateen. We seek articles that can help members learn effective ways to cope with their problems, help one another understand the principles of the Alateen program, and share ways to overcome personal difficulties.

Amazing Journeys Magazine

3205 Highway 431
Spring Hill, TN 37174

Editor: Edward Knight

Description and Interests
Science fiction and fantasy stories that appeal to teens and adults appear in this digest-sized publication. It looks for fiction written in the style of the "golden age" of this genre.
• **Audience:** YA–Adult
• **Frequency:** Quarterly
• **Distribution:** 50% subscription; 50% newsstand
• **Circulation:** Unavailable
• **Website:** www.journeybookspublishing.com

Freelance Potential
95% written by nonstaff writers. Publishes 36–40 freelance submissions yearly; 40% by unpublished writers, 50% by authors who are new to the magazine. Receives 800 unsolicited mss yearly.

Submissions
Send complete ms. Accepts hard copy and email submissions to journey@journeybookspublishing.com (Microsoft Word or rich text attachments). No simultaneous submissions. SASE. Responds in 2 months.
Fiction: 3,000–7,000 words. Genres include science fiction and fantasy.
Other: Poetry, 20–40 lines.

Sample Issue
104 pages (3% advertising): 10 stories; 2 poems. Sample copy, $6.99 with 9x12 SASE ($1.52 postage). Guidelines available at website.
• "Noncompliance." Story portrays a future police state in which government regulation has gotten completely out of control.
• "The Lucky Son." Story features a classroom in which students are eliminated based on their appearance and genes.

Rights and Payment
First North American serial rights. Written material, $.005 per word to a maximum of $25. Poetry, $5 per poem. Pays on acceptance. Provides 1 contributor's copy.

Editor's Comments
This year, we would like to see more "near future" science fiction stories. We're seeing too much time travel fiction. We'll consider writing in most fantasy or science fiction genres, but we tend to avoid publishing very dark pieces. Please remember that we only publish G- or PG-rated material. Stories should never have sexual content.

American Baby

375 Lexington Avenue, 9th Floor
New York, NY 10017

Editorial Assistant: Colleen Dowd

Description and Interests
Targeting expectant and new parents, this magazine includes articles and tips on caring for children under the age of two. It covers topics such as health and nutrition, fashion, baby gear, baby care and development, and other pregnancy related issues.
• **Audience:** Parents
• **Frequency:** Monthly
• **Distribution:** 50% subscription; 50% controlled
• **Circulation:** 2.1 million
• **Website:** www.americanbaby.com

Freelance Potential
55% written by nonstaff writers. Publishes 24 freelance submissions yearly; 20% by unpublished writers. Receives 996 unsolicited mss yearly.

Submissions
Query with clips or writing samples; or send complete ms. Accepts hard copy and simultaneous submissions if identified. SASE. Responds in 2 months.
Articles: 1,000–2,000 words. Informational and how-to articles; profiles; interviews; humor; and personal experience pieces. Topics include pregnancy, pre-conception, infants, child care, child development, and adoption.
Depts/columns: 1,000 words. Medical updates, relationships, new product information, and fashion.
Other: Submit seasonal material 3 months in advance.

Sample Issue
96 pages (50% advertising): 14 articles; 4 depts/columns. Sample copy, free with 9x12 SASE ($2 postage). Guidelines available.
• "For Crying Out Loud." Article discusses why babies cry and explains how to soothe them.
• "Emergency First Aid." Article offers a guide for treating childhood injuries calmly and confidently.
• Sample dept/column: "Crib Notes" includes potty training tips, information on snow cone machines, and safety tips.

Rights and Payment
First serial rights. Articles, to $2,000. Depts/columns, to $1,000. Pays on acceptance. Provides 5 contributor's copies.

Editor's Comments
While we prefer to work with published writers, we do work with a small number of new writers each year.

American Careers

6701 West 64th Street
Overland Park, KS 66202

Editor: Mary Pitchford

Description and Interests
Published in two editions, one for middle school students and one for high school students, this magazine features up-to-date career information designed to promote career development and career education.
• **Audience:** 12–18 years
• **Frequency:** Annually
• **Distribution:** 99% schools; 1% other
• **Circulation:** 400,000
• **Website:** www.carcom.com

Freelance Potential
90% written by nonstaff writers. Publishes 15 freelance submissions yearly; 20% by unpublished writers, 40% by authors who are new to the magazine. Receives 240+ queries yearly.

Submissions
Query with résumé and clips. Accepts hard copy. SASE. Responds in 2 months.
Articles: 300–750 words. Informational and how-to articles; personal experience pieces; and profiles. Topics include career planning, employability skills, self-evaluation, career development, career clusters, and entrepreneurs.
Artwork: Color prints or digital photos.
Other: Quizzes and self-assessments.

Sample Issue
64 pages (no advertising): 26 articles. Sample copy, $4 with 9x12 SASE (5 first-class stamps). Writer's guidelines available.
• "Teaching Outside the Box." Article describes the novel approaches one teacher uses when working with children with special needs.
• "Machine Shop Flair." Article reports that a knack for sheet metal work led one man to a career designing orthotics and prosthetics.
• "Product Managers." Article highlights the workday and professional responsibilities of marketing product managers.

Rights and Payment
All rights. All material, payment rates vary. Pays on publication. Provides 2 contributor's copies.

Editor's Comments
We're looking for material on the hot new jobs in the health, information technology, and business fields that will help students discover what they need to know about employment opportunities.

American Cheerleader

110 William Street, 23rd Floor
New York, NY 10038

Editorial Director: Sheila Noone

Description and Interests
This colorful magazine features intriguing stories about cheering and articles about issues that surround the world of cheerleading, including health, nutrition, team bonding, competition, and tryouts.
- **Audience:** 13–18 years
- **Frequency:** 6 times each year
- **Distribution:** Subscription; newsstand
- **Circulation:** 200,000
- **Website: www.americancheerleader.com**

Freelance Potential
50% written by nonstaff writers. Publishes 15 freelance submissions yearly; 20% by unpublished writers, 20% by authors who are new to the magazine. Receives 12–24 queries and unsolicited mss yearly.

Submissions
Query with clips; or send complete ms. Prefers email submissions to snoone@lifestylemedia.com. Responds in 3 months.
Articles: To 1,000 words. Informational and how-to articles; profiles; personal experience pieces; and photo-essays. Topics include cheerleading, workouts, competitions, scholarships, fitness, college, careers, and popular culture.
Depts/columns: Word lengths vary. Product news, safety issues, health, nutrition, fundraising, beauty, and fashion.
Artwork: High resolution digital images; 35mm color slides.

Sample Issue
144 pages (40% advertising): 9 articles; 24 depts/columns. Sample copy, $3.99 with 9x12 SASE ($1.70 postage). Editorial calendar available.
- "If You Were on My Team." Article offers insight on what it would be like to be a member of the California Allstars.
- "Dream Big!" Article describes how some cheerleaders are achieving success in life.
- Sample dept/column: "Coach's Clinic" takes a look at a sequence performed by a varsity squad.

Rights and Payment
All rights. All material, payment rates vary. Pays 2 months after acceptance. Provides 1 author's copy.

Editor's Comments
We look for upbeat and "sporty" writing to catch the attention of our teenaged readers.

American Cheerleader Junior

110 William Street, 23rd Floor
New York, NY 10038

Editorial Director: Sheila Noone

Description and Interests
Celebrating the spirit of cheerleading, this magazine offers cheerleading tips and techniques, profiles of cheerleaders, and competition coverage. Its readers include elementary school and pre-teen girls who enjoy cheerleading.
- **Audience:** 7–12 years
- **Frequency:** Annually
- **Distribution:** Subscription; newsstand
- **Circulation:** 65,000
- **Website: www.americancheerleader.com**

Freelance Potential
35% written by nonstaff writers. Publishes 5 freelance submissions yearly; 20% by unpublished writers, 30% by authors who are new to the magazine. Receives 72 queries, 24 unsolicited mss yearly.

Submissions
Query with clips; or send complete ms. Prefers email submissions to snoone@lifestylemedia.com. Responds in 3 months.
Articles: To 1,000 words. Informational and how-to articles; profiles; photo-essays; and personal experience pieces. Topics include cheerleading, fitness, health, and popular culture.
Depts/columns: Word lengths vary. Cooking, information for parents, fundraising.
Artwork: High resolution digital images; 35mm color slides.
Other: Activity, games, crafts, and poetry.

Sample Issue
64 pages (40% advertising): 9 articles; 16 depts/columns. Sample copy, $4.99 with 9x12 SASE ($.77 postage). Guidelines available.
- "Um, Excuse Me." Article provides sample questions parents should ask their kid's cheerleading coach.
- "Top 5 Things To Do." Article takes a look at fun activities to do while traveling to competitions.
- Sample dept/column: "Stunting 101" offers instructions on how to do the Scorpion move.

Rights and Payment
All rights. All material, payment rates vary. Pays 2 months after acceptance. Provides 1 author's copy.

Editor's Comments
We are interested in tips and strategies for ways to perfect a tryout, step-by-step stunts, and articles covering nutrition and the latest trends in cheer fashion.

American Girl

Pleasant Company Publications
8400 Fairway Place
Middleton, WI 53562

Editorial Assistant

Description and Interests
American Girl educates and entertains girls ages eight and up with articles, crafts, and letters of interest to readers in their formative years. The goal of this publication is to reinforce the self-confidence, self-esteem, and curiosity of each reader.
- **Audience:** 8–12 years
- **Frequency:** 6 times each year
- **Distribution:** Subscription; newsstand; schools
- **Circulation:** 700,000
- **Website:** www.americangirl.com

Freelance Potential
10% written by nonstaff writers. Publishes 5 freelance submissions yearly; 5% by unpublished writers, 5% by authors who are new to the magazine. Receives 648 unsolicited mss yearly.

Submissions
Query for nonfiction. Send complete ms for fiction. Accepts hard copy and simultaneous submissions if identified. SASE. Responds in 4 months.
Articles: 500–1,000 words. Informational articles; profiles; and interviews. Topics include nature, food, hobbies, the arts, crafts, sports, and culture.
Fiction: To 2,300 words. Contemporary, historical, and multicultural fiction; and mystery.
Depts/columns: 175 words. Profiles, how-to pieces, and craft ideas.
Other: Word games and puzzles.

Sample Issue
48 pages (no advertising): Sample copy, $4.50 at newsstands. Guidelines available.
- "Confessions of a Former Only Child." Story shares the feelings of a young girl who becomes a big sister after being an only child for 11 years.
- "Heart to Heart." Article shares the experiences of young girls who stood up for themselves.
- Sample dept/column: "Friendship Matters" offers tips to tame the green-eyed monster for girls who may be too jealous of their friends.

Rights and Payment
First North American serial rights. Written material, payment rates vary. Pays on acceptance. Provides 1 contributor's copy.

Editor's Comments
We currently seek true stories about girls who have had unusual experiences for our "Girls Express" section.

American Libraries

American Library Association
50 East Huron Street
Chicago, IL 60611

Acquisitions Editor: Beverly Goldberg

Description and Interests
All aspects of library programming and management are addressed in this publication from the American Library Association. Librarians working in public, private, and school libraries use it as a resource for news and information about their field.
- **Audience:** Librarians and library media specialists
- **Frequency:** 11 times each year
- **Distribution:** 100% membership
- **Circulation:** 56,000
- **Website:** www.ala.org/alonline

Freelance Potential
60% written by nonstaff writers. Publishes 50 freelance submissions yearly; 50% by authors who are new to the magazine. Receives 492 mss yearly.

Submissions
Send complete ms. Accepts hard copy, IBM disk submissions (Microsoft Word), and email to americanlibraries@ala.org. No simultaneous submissions. SASE. Responds in 8–10 weeks.
Articles: 600–2,500 words. Informational articles; profiles; and interviews. Topics include modern libraries, new technologies, and intellectual freedom.
Depts/columns: Word lengths vary. Opinion, events, professional development, and Internet updates.

Sample Issue
80 pages (27% advertising): 7 articles; 17 depts/columns. Sample copy, $6. Guidelines available.
- "The Subtle Approach." Personal experience piece describes how one high school librarian entices teens to read by setting up unusual book displays.
- "Opening New Worlds." Article investigates how librarians can play a role in serving the literature needs of Latinos.
- Sample dept/column: "Professional Literature" examines resources for continuing education.

Rights and Payment
First North American serial rights. Written material, $50–$400. Pays on acceptance. Provides 1+ contributor's copies.

Editor's Comments
Ours is a professional journal, but the writing is inviting and readable—don't send scholarly articles with excessive footnotes. You must, however, base your writing on facts and research. Most articles are written by our readers.

American School & University

9800 Metcalf Avenue
Overland Park, KS 66212

Executive Editor: Susan Lustig

Description and Interests
School administrators and other professionals who plan, design, build, and maintain education facilities read this publication. It includes news, industry reports, and how-to articles related to buildings that house elementary through college classrooms.
- **Audience:** School administrators
- **Frequency:** Monthly
- **Distribution:** 100% controlled
- **Circulation:** 63,000
- **Website:** www.asumag.com

Freelance Potential
35% written by nonstaff writers. Publishes 40 freelance submissions yearly; 30% by authors who are new to the magazine. Receives 180 queries yearly.

Submissions
Query with outline. Prefers email queries to slustig@prismb2b.com. Will accept hard copy and disk submissions (Microsoft Word or ASCII). SASE. Responds in 2 weeks.
Articles: 1,200 words. Informational and how-to articles. Topics include facilities management, maintenance, technology, energy, furnishings, and security.
Depts/columns: 250–350 words. Opinion, new product information, new technologies, and case histories.

Sample Issue
62 pages (55% advertising): 5 articles; 5 depts/columns. Sample copy, $10. Guidelines and editorial calendar available.
- "Lasting Impression." Article reports on how schools and universities can use life-cycle costing to provide sustainable facilities that will endure generations.
- "On Film." Article tells how the right window film can improve indoor air quality in schools.
- Sample dept/column: "Inside" discusses issues associated with the Americans with Disabilities Act.

Rights and Payment
All rights. Written material, payment rates and payment policy vary. Provides 2 contributor's copies.

Editor's Comments
Feature articles should inform the reader about a process, trend, general category of product, or service of interest to educational administrators. We primarily run articles that correspond to our editorial calendar. Please be aware that we do not publish articles aimed at teachers or students.

American Secondary Education

Ashland University, Weltmer Center
401 College Avenue
Ashland, OH 44805

Editor: James A. Rycik

Description and Interests
Administrators, researchers, and classroom teachers make up the readership of this publication. It offers information on the serious issues that currently confront secondary educational systems. Topics include administration issues, teaching techniques, and education theories.
- **Audience:** Secondary school educators and researchers
- **Frequency:** 3 times each year
- **Distribution:** 70% colleges and universities; 30% subscription
- **Circulation:** 450
- **Website:** www.ashland.edu/ase.html

Freelance Potential
95% written by nonstaff writers. Publishes 20 freelance submissions yearly; 10% by unpublished writers, 80% by authors who are new to the magazine. Receives 40–50 unsolicited mss yearly.

Submissions
Send 3 copies of complete ms with disk and 100-word abstract. No simultaneous submissions. SASE. Response time varies.
Articles: 10–30 double-spaced manuscript pages. Informational articles. Topics include secondary education research and practice.
Depts/columns: Book reviews, word lengths vary. "In the Schools" provides a personal look at innovative programs unique to a particular school district.

Sample Issue
93 pages (no advertising): 5 articles; 1 book review. Sample copy, free. Guidelines available.
- "Making Change at a Junior High School: One Principal's Sense of It." Article describes the experiences of one urban junior high school principal who was part of a grant targeting schools with at-risk youth.
- "The Importance of Principals: Site Administrators' Roles in Novice Teacher Induction." Article studies principals' roles in a large, urban, standards-based induction program using five case study schools.

Rights and Payment
All rights. No payment. Provides 1 contributor's copy.

Editor's Comments
We look for articles that address current theory research, and practice that has a clear relevance to secondary education.

American String Teacher

4153 Chain Bridge Road
Fairfax, VA 22030

Editor: Tami O'Brien

Description and Interests
This magazine of the American String Teachers Association promotes excellence in string and orchestra teaching and playing. The purpose of this journal is to further the professional growth of its members.
- **Audience:** String teachers and performers
- **Frequency:** Quarterly
- **Distribution:** 100% subscription
- **Circulation:** 11,500
- **Website:** www.astaweb.com

Freelance Potential
75% written by nonstaff writers. Publishes 30 freelance submissions yearly; 5% by unpublished writers, 50% by authors who are new to the magazine. Receives 24–36 queries yearly.

Submissions
Prefers query; accepts 5 copies of complete ms. Prefers email submissions to dlitmus@ksu.edu. Accepts hard copy. No simultaneous submissions. SASE. Responds in 3 months.
Articles: 1,000–3,000 words. Informational and factual articles; profiles; and association news. Topics include teaching, methodology, techniques, competitions, and auditions.
Depts/columns: Word lengths vary. Teaching tips, opinion pieces, and industry news.

Sample Issue
92 pages (45% advertising): 5 articles; 12 depts/columns. Sample copy, free with 9x12 SASE ($3.25 postage). Guidelines available.
- "Exploring Musical Fiction for the String Player and Teacher." Article explores the joy and excitement reading musical fiction can bring to students as well as teachers.
- Sample dept/column: "My Turn" offers a string musician's views on playing Bach's solo cello suites.

Rights and Payment
All rights. No payment. Provides 5 contributor's copies.

Editor's Comments
We accept articles from members of our association only. We look for articles that present a thorough treatment of a narrow topic rather than a superficial treatment of a broad topic. Articles should be based on research rather than opinion or experience. Please note that we would much prefer to see query letters over completed manuscripts.

Analog Science Fiction and Fact

Dell Magazine Fiction Group
475 Park Avenue South
New York, NY 10016

Editor: Stanley Schmidt

Description and Interests
Science and technology serve as the foundation of all the stories that appear in this magazine, and also as the subjects of factual articles about current research findings that will have a major impact on the future.
- **Audience:** YA–Adult
- **Frequency:** 10 times each year
- **Distribution:** 80% subscription; 20% newsstand
- **Circulation:** 40,000
- **Website:** www.analogsf.com

Freelance Potential
100% written by nonstaff writers. Publishes 80–90 freelance submissions yearly; 10% by unpublished writers, 10% by authors who are new to the magazine. Receives 6.000 unsolicited mss yearly.

Submissions
Query for serials. Send complete ms for shorter works. Accepts hard copy. SASE. Responds in 6 weeks.
Articles: To 6,000 words. Informational articles. Topics include science and technology.
Fiction: Serials, 40,000–80,000 words. Novellas and novelettes, 10,000–20,000 words. Short stories, 2,000–7,000 words. Physical, sociological, and psychological science fiction; technological and biogenetic fiction.
Depts/columns: Staff written.

Sample Issue
144 pages (7% advertising): 1 article; 4 stories; 1 novella; 2 novelettes; 6 depts/columns. Sample copy, $5 with 6x9 SASE. Guidelines available.
- "The Shape of Wings to Come." Article looks at the history and the future of flight.
- "Lighthouse." Story revolves around a graduate student's discovery of a new type of astronomical body.
- "Numismatist." Novelette follows an investigator as he tries to discover what sent a quiet coin collector on a killing spree.

Rights and Payment
First North American serial and non-exclusive rights. Serials, $.04 per word; other written material, $.05–$.08 per word. Pays on acceptance. Provides 2 copies.

Editor's Comments
Our readers are intelligent and technically knowledgeable, but come from diverse backgrounds. Keep specialized jargon and mathematical detail to a minimum.

Anime

Beckett Media
15850 Dallas Parkway
Dallas, TX 75248

Editor: Doug Kale

Description and Interests
Fans of Anime and Manga read this magazine for information on the latest games, cards, videos, and collectibles. It includes special sections on Naruto, InuYasha, and FullMetal Alchemist.
• **Audience:** YA–Adults
• **Frequency:** Monthly
• **Distribution:** 80% newsstand; 20% subscription
• **Circulation:** 100,000
• **Website:** www.beckettanime.com

Freelance Potential
50% written by nonstaff writers. Publishes 20 freelance submissions yearly; 10% by unpublished writers, 1% by authors who are new to the magazine.

Submissions
Prefers query with outline and clips. Accepts complete ms. Accepts hard copy and email submissions to anime@beckett.com. SASE. Responds in 1–2 months.
Articles: 500–2,000 words. Informational articles; profiles; and reviews. Topics relating to InuYasha, Yu-Gi-Oh, Pokémon, DragonBall, Duel Masters, Chobits, and FullMetal Alchemist games, cards, and memorabilia collecting.
Fiction: Word lengths vary. Adventure stories.
Depts/columns: 500–750 words. News, fan art, and price guides.

Sample Issue
80 pages: 20 articles; 3 depts/columns; 2 contests; 1 event calendar. Sample copy, $6.99. Writers' guidelines available.
• "Interview with an Alchemist." Article interviews Scott McNeil, the voice behind Hohenheim in FullMetal Alchemist, Koga in InuYasha, and many other characters.
• "Drawn by Destiny." Article investigates the relationship between Kira and Lacus in Gundam Seed.
• Sample dept/column: "Cards" looks at cards for the number-one animated cartoon series for teens.

Rights and Payment
First North American serial rights. Articles and fiction, $100–$200. Depts/columns, $50–$200. Pays on acceptance. Provides 2 contributor's copies.

Editor's Comments
If you have up-to-date information about the world of anime entertainment or can provide a well-written review, we'd like to hear from you.

AppleSeeds

Cobblestone Publishing Company
30 Grove Street
Peterborough, NH 03458

Editor: Susan Buckley

Description and Interests
Elementary school students read this multidisciplinary social studies magazine. Its pages are filled with historically accurate articles, stories, and activities designed to teach young readers about the past and present. Each issue is theme-based.
• **Audience:** 7–10 years
• **Frequency:** 9 times each year
• **Distribution:** 100% subscription
• **Circulation:** 10,000
• **Website:** www.cobblestonepub.com

Freelance Potential
90% written by nonstaff writers. Publishes 90–100 freelance submissions yearly; 20% by unpublished writers, 35% by authors who are new to the magazine. Receives 600+ queries yearly.

Submissions
Query. All queries must be theme-related. Prefers email queries to swbuc@aol.com. Accepts hard copy. SASE. Responds in 2–3 months if interested.
Articles: 200–700 words. Informational articles; personal experience pieces; profiles; and interviews. Topics include history, biography, geography, the arts, multicultural and ethnic issues, social issues, science, travel, health, fitness, and hobbies.
Fiction: Word lengths vary. Genres include folklore and biographical stories.
Depts/columns: 150–300 words. Theme-related activities and profiles.
Other: Poetry.

Sample Issue
34 pages (no advertising): 14 articles; 2 depts/columns; 1 activity. Guidelines and theme list available at website.
• "A Different Childhood." Article examines what life was like in the era of Laura Ingalls Wilder.
• Sample dept/column: "Where in the World?" features maps and facts about the life and writing of Laura Ingalls Wilder.

Rights and Payment
All rights. Written material, $50 per page. Pays on publication. Provides 2 contributor's copies.

Editor's Comments
Each issue of our magazine is strictly theme-based; we will review no queries that are not theme-related. You'll find theme lists posted at our website.

Aquila

Freepost BR 1158
Eastbourne BN21 2BR
United Kingdom

Editor: Jackie Berry

Description and Interests
This British publication is read by bright children with inquiring minds. Each issue takes readers on a journey of discovery to investigate new topics.
- **Audience:** 8–13 years
- **Frequency:** Monthly
- **Distribution:** 100% subscription
- **Circulation:** 8,000
- **Website:** www.aquila.co.uk

Freelance Potential
80% written by nonstaff writers. Publishes 100 freelance submissions yearly; 25% by unpublished writers, 25% by authors who are new to the magazine. Receives 492 queries yearly.

Submissions
Query with résumé. Accepts hard copy and email to info@aquila.co.uk (Microsoft Word). SAE/IRC. Responds in 2–4 months.
Articles: 750–800 words. Informational and how-to articles; profiles; and interviews. Topics include pets, animals, the arts, crafts, hobbies, history, mathematics, nature, the environment, science, and technology.
Fiction: To 1,000 words. Genres include historical and contemporary fiction, science fiction, folklore, folktales, mystery, and adventure.
Artwork: Color prints and transparencies. JPEG digital images.
Other: Arts and crafts activities. Submit seasonal material 3 months in advance.

Sample Issue
20 pages (no advertising): 3 articles; 1 story; 1 activity; 8 book reviews; 11 quizzes. Sample copy, £5.00 with 9x12 SAE/IRC; also available at website. Writers' guidelines available.
- "In Tune with Mozart." Article highlights the life and musical talents of Wolfgang Amadeus Mozart.
- "Can Billy Play?" Short story about a mysterious ginger-haired boy who haunts a small village.

Rights and Payment
First rights. Articles and fiction, £60–£80. Artwork, payment rates vary. Pays on publication. Provides up to 6 contributor's copies.

Editor's Comments
We want educational and entertaining articles and stories that encourage readers to explore facts and discover things for themselves.

Arizona Parenting

2432 West Peoria Avenue, Suite 1185
Phoenix, AZ 85029

Editor: Lyn Wolford

Description and Interests
The pages of this regional glossy are filled with articles and tips on topics related to parenting, education, finances, and family issues. It also makes readers aware of resources and services available in the state.
- **Audience:** Parents
- **Frequency:** Monthly
- **Distribution:** 100% other
- **Circulation:** 80,000
- **Website:** www.azparenting.com

Freelance Potential
50% written by nonstaff writers. Publishes 20 freelance submissions yearly; 5% by unpublished writers, 25% by authors who are new to the magazine. Receives 520 queries, 300 unsolicited mss yearly.

Submissions
Query or send complete ms. Prefers email to lyn.wolford@azparenting.com. Accepts hard copy. SASE. Responds in 2–3 months.
Articles: 850–2,400 words. Informational articles; profiles; interviews; and humor. Topics include parenting, family issues, education, finances, health, travel, sports, computers, recreation, and fitness.
Depts/columns: 400–850 words. Child development, short news items, and family forums.
Artwork: B/W prints and transparencies.

Sample Issue
66 pages (50% advertising): 9 articles; 2 depts/columns; 1 events calendar. Sample copy, free with 9x12 SASE ($2 postage). Editorial calendar available.
- "Understanding Eating Disorders." Article discusses the dangers of eating disorders in teens.
- "Her Money, Her Investments." Article offers advice and strategies for planning a financial future.
- Sample dept/column: "Family F.Y.I." includes information on a backyard brunch, edible blooms, and summer movie fun.

Rights and Payment
First North American serial and electronic rights. All material, payment rates vary. Pays on publication. Provides 2–3 contributor's copies.

Editor's Comments
We continue to look for fresh, well-written articles that cover parenting issues as well as other topics of interest to families living in Arizona.

Art Education

Virginia Commonwealth University
Department of Art Education
P.O. Box 843084
Richmond, VA 23284

Editor: Dr. Pam Taylor

Description and Interests
Art educators working with kindergarten through high school students use this magazine to keep up to date in their field and to find innovative instructional resources. It is the official publication of the National Art Education Association.
• **Audience:** Art educators
• **Frequency:** 6 times each year
• **Distribution:** 70% subscription; 30% newsstand
• **Circulation:** 20,000
• **Website:** www.naea-reston.org/publications.html

Freelance Potential
100% written by nonstaff writers. Publishes 36 freelance submissions yearly; 25% by unpublished writers, 5% by authors who are new to the magazine. Receives 120 unsolicited mss yearly.

Submissions
Send 3 copies of complete ms. Accepts hard copy, disk submissions, and simultaneous submissions if identified. SASE. Responds in 8–10 weeks.
Articles: To 3,000 words. Informational articles; personal experience pieces; interviews; and profiles. Topics include the visual arts, curriculum planning, art history, and art criticism.
Depts/columns: To 2,750 words. "Instructional Resources" features lesson plan ideas.
Artwork: 8x10 or 5x7 B/W prints, slides, or digital images.

Sample Issue
54 pages (3% advertising): 7 articles; 1 dept/column. Sample copy, $1.25 with 9x12 SASE ($.87 postage). Guidelines available.
• "Invitations to Understanding: Explorations in the Teaching of Arts to Children." Article examines why art teacher education must combine theoretical knowledge and real world experience.
• "Nurturing Aesthetic Awareness in Young Children." Article explores developmentally appropriate art viewing experiences.

Rights and Payment
All rights. No payment. Provides 2 author's copies.

Editor's Comments
Please note that we deal with issues of professional interest to art educators, and all articles are reviewed by an editorial board. Each issue of our magazine addresses a theme or topic.

Arts & Activities

12345 World Trade Drive
San Diego, CA 92128

Editor-in-Chief: Maryellen Bridge

Description and Interests
Art teachers share their experiences and expertise in *Arts & Activities*, including classroom teaching ideas, successful methods, and information on activities.
• **Audience:** Art educators, grades K–12
• **Frequency:** 10 times each year
• **Distribution:** 100% subscription
• **Circulation:** 20,000
• **Website:** www.artsandactivities.com

Freelance Potential
90% written by nonstaff writers. Publishes 60–90 freelance submissions yearly; 30% by unpublished writers, 30% by authors who are new to the magazine. Receives 144 unsolicited mss yearly.

Submissions
Send complete ms. Accepts disk submissions with hard copy. No simultaneous submissions. SASE. Responds in 4–8 months.
Articles: Word lengths vary. Informational, how-to, and practical application articles; and personal experience pieces. Topics include art education, program development, collage, printmaking, art appreciation, and composition.
Depts/columns: Word lengths vary. New product information, short news items, and book reviews.
Artwork: Color photos; digital images, minimum 2550 x 3400 pixel resolution.
Other: Lesson plans for classroom projects.

Sample Issue
50 pages (29% advertising): 11 articles; 6 depts/columns. Sample copy, $3 with 9x12 SASE ($2 postage). Guidelines and theme list available.
• "Feeling Like Frida." Article depicts how one teacher introduced her class to the art of Frida Kahlo.
• "Drawing with Glue." Article details an art class project using glue and watercolors.
• Sample dept/column: "Shop Talk" reviews new art products and books.

Rights and Payment
First North American serial rights. All material, payment rates vary. Pays on publication. Provides 3 contributor's copies.

Editor's Comments
All submissions must include visuals, either photos or original children's art. We need lesson plans in all media, and high school level art projects.

Asimov's Science Fiction

Dell Magazine Group
475 Park Avenue, 11th Floor
New York, NY 10016

Editor: Sheila Williams

Description and Interests
A leading publisher of science fiction and fantasy stories, *Asimov's Science Fiction* includes character-driven novelettes and short stories, as well as book reviews, commentaries, and information on upcoming events.
- **Audience:** YA–Adult
- **Frequency:** 10 times each year
- **Distribution:** 87% subscription; 13% newsstand
- **Circulation:** 60,000
- **Website: www.asimovs.com**

Freelance Potential
97% written by nonstaff writers. Publishes 85 freelance submissions yearly; 10% by unpublished writers, 30% by authors who are new to the magazine. Receives 8,400 unsolicited mss yearly.

Submissions
Send complete ms. No queries. Accepts hard copy. SASE. Responds in 6–8 weeks.
Fiction: To 20,000 words. Genres include science fiction and fantasy.
Depts/columns: Word lengths vary. Book and website reviews.
Other: Poetry, to 40 lines.

Sample Issue
144 pages (10% advertising): 2 novelettes; 6 stories; 6 depts/columns. Sample copy, $5 with 9x12 SASE ($.77 postage). Guidelines available.
- "The World and Alice." Sad tale tells of a woman who never feels part of the world around her.
- "Fireflies." Story depicts a couple who comes to terms with their future as they sit and watch the fireflies one evening.

Rights and Payment
First worldwide English language serial rights. Fiction, $.06–$.08 per word. Poetry, $1 per line. Depts/columns, payment rates vary. Pays on acceptance. Provides 2 contributor's copies.

Editor's Comments
We publish serious, thoughtful, accessible works of science fiction. Borderline fantasy is fine, but no swords or sorcery. We are not interested in any works that contain explicit sex or violence. We will consider material submitted by any writer, previously published or not. Some of our best stories have come from unpublished writers.

ASK

Carus Publishing
140 South Dearborn Street, Suite 1450
Chicago, IL 60603

Editor

Description and Interests
ASK tackles topics about life and our environment that intrigue young readers. Material delves into questions that lead to understanding the bigger pictures found all around us in life. Formats include activities, cartoon strips, contests, and lots of illustrations.
- **Audience:** 7–10 years
- **Frequency:** 9 times each year
- **Distribution:** Subscription; newsstand
- **Circulation:** 32,000
- **Website: www.cricketmag.com**

Freelance Potential
10% written by nonstaff writers. Of the freelance submissions published yearly, 10% are by authors who are new to the magazine.

Submissions
All material is commissioned from experienced authors. Send résumé and clips.
Articles: To 1,500 words. Informational articles; interviews; and photo-essays. Topics include animals, pets, science, the environment, nature, computers, technology, history, math, and the arts.
Depts/columns: Word lengths vary. News items.

Sample Issue
34 pages (no advertising): 4 articles; 5 depts/columns. Sample copy available at website.
- "Our Weird Neighborhood." Article explores the sun and planets in our solar system and how they came to be formed.
- "Discovering Planet Earth." Article uses a cartoon format to relate the methods used by ancient astronomers to discover Earth.
- "Ride a Comet." Article looks at the composition and activities of comets in space, and early speculations about them.

Rights and Payment
Rights vary. Written material, payment rates and payment policy vary.

Editor's Comments
Material submitted should challenge readers to explore new ideas about the real world. Articles should go beyond simple facts and use drama and interesting language to draw readers into the information. We encourage children to learn about everything in their world, from sleep to Egyptian hieroglyphics. All material is assigned to experienced writers.

Atlanta Baby

2346 Perimeter Park, Suite 101
Atlanta, GA 30341

Editor: Liz White

Description and Interests
This magazine provides articles on pregnancy and childrearing, as well as family resources in the Atlanta area for expectant parents and parents of children up to age two.
• **Audience:** Parents
• **Frequency:** Quarterly
• **Distribution:** 100% controlled
• **Circulation:** 25,000
• **Website:** www.atlantaparent.com

Freelance Potential
25% written by nonstaff writers. Publishes 50 freelance submissions yearly; 5% by unpublished writers, 30% by authors who are new to the magazine. Receives 2,400 unsolicited mss yearly.

Submissions
Send complete ms. Prefers email submissions to lwhite@atlantaparent.com. Accepts hard copy. SASE. Responds in 2 months.
Articles: 600–1,200 words. Informational and how-to articles; and humor. Topics include pregnancy, childbirth, child development, early education, health and fitness, and parenting.
Depts/columns: Word length varies. Short essays and resource guides.
Other: Submit seasonal material 6 months in advance.

Sample Issue
28 pages (50% advertising): 5 articles; 3 depts/columns. Sample copy, $2 with 9x12 SASE. Guidelines available.
• "Pregnancy Cravings." Article examines why women crave unusual foods during pregnancy.
• "Best Baby Advice." Article provides a listing of useful websites for new parents.
• Sample dept/column: "Nursery Giggles" is an essay on the unexpected things new moms find themselves doing for their children.

Rights and Payment
One-time rights. Written material, $35–$50. Pays on publication. Provides 1 tearsheet.

Editor's Comments
We are interested in down-to-earth advice for expectant parents and parents of children up to age two. All articles should be in the third person, except for humor pieces. Please refer to local experts or support groups.

Atlanta Parent

2346 Perimeter Park Drive, Suite 101
Atlanta, GA 30341

Publisher: Liz White

Description and Interests
This award-winning magazine fills its pages with information for parents of children up to the age of 16 residing in the Atlanta metropolitan area. Articles on educational issues, health, family recreation, and parenting are included. It also covers family-friendly events and parenting resources.
• **Audience:** Parents
• **Frequency:** Monthly
• **Distribution:** 100% controlled
• **Circulation:** 110,000
• **Website:** www.atlantaparent.com

Freelance Potential
40% written by nonstaff writers.

Submissions
Send complete ms. Accepts hard copy, disk submissions, and email submissions to lwhite@ atlantaparent.com. SASE. Response time varies.
Articles: 600–1,200 words. Informational and how-to articles and humor. Topics include education, child care, child development, health, fitness, and parenting issues.
Depts/columns: Word lengths vary. Resource guides.
Other: Submit secular holiday material 6 months in advance.

Sample Issue
106 pages (55% advertising): 8 articles; 7 depts/columns. Sample copy, $3 with 9x12 SASE. Guidelines available.
• "Video Game Overload." Article discusses the risks of children overusing portable game devices and how parents can stay involved in monitoring them.
• "Keeping Teens Safe Behind the Wheel." Article explores strategies for educating new teen drivers.
• Sample dept/column: "Learning 101" offers tips for flying and making kites.

Rights and Payment
One-time print and web rights. Written material, $35–$50. Pays on publication. Provides 1 tearsheet.

Editor's Comments
We look for entertaining and informative articles on topics related to parenting. If you are writing about a problem, give parents the symptoms or signs of the problem and the solution or information on where they can turn for help. Include phone numbers for national resources and support groups if possible.

Atlanta Sporting Family

240 Prospect Place
Alpharetta, GA 30005

Editor: Michael J. Pallerino

Description and Interests
Atlanta Sporting Family is read by families in the Atlanta area of Georgia. Each issue informs its readers of local events and resources and features articles relating to healthful living, sports, and recreation.
- **Audience:** Parents
- **Frequency:** 8 times each year
- **Distribution:** Schools; subscription
- **Circulation:** 100,000
- **Website:** www.sportingfamily.com

Freelance Potential
30% written by nonstaff writers. Publishes 10 freelance submissions yearly; 10% by authors who are new to the magazine. Receives 600 queries, 120 unsolicited mss yearly.

Submissions
Query or send complete ms. Accepts email queries (no attachments) and email submissions (complete ms as a Microsoft Word attachment) to editor@sportingfamily.com. Responds in 1 month.
Articles: Word lengths vary. Informational and how-to articles; profiles; and personal experience pieces. Topics include health, fitness, recreation, social issues, and sports.
Depts/columns: Word lengths vary. News, health and wellness, and recreation ideas.

Sample Issue
48 pages: 4 articles; 6 depts/columns. Writers' guidelines available.
- "Getting Fit." Article tells of the winning experience of a single mom who participated in the *Atlanta Sporting Family* Fitness Challenge.
- "When Time Matters." Article explores the Roswell Emergency Care Center and its community benefits.
- Sample dept/column: "Health & Wellness" discusses research testing a new concept that helps kids learn while staying healthy in classrooms of the future.

Rights and Payment
First and electronic rights. Written material, payment rates vary. Pays on publication.

Editor's Comments
We seek articles and news covering regional sports, social issues, and healthful living. Our readers, active families living in the Atlanta area, read this magazine for its articles, resources, and up-to-date information on sports, recreation, and local events.

Austin Family

P.O. Box 7559
Round Rock, TX 78683-7559

Editor: Barbara Cooper

Description and Interests
Promoting "smart parenting and healthy homes" is the goal of *Austin Family*. This regional magazine includes events calendars, reviews of family books and movies, and articles on health and child rearing.
- **Audience:** Parents
- **Frequency:** Monthly
- **Distribution:** 80% controlled; 10% schools; 5% subscription; 5% other
- **Circulation:** 35,000
- **Website:** www.austinfamily.com

Freelance Potential
70% written by nonstaff writers. Publishes 15 freelance submissions yearly; 10% by unpublished writers, 50% by authors who are new to the magazine. Receives 804 queries and unsolicited mss yearly.

Submissions
Query or send complete ms. Accepts hard copy, simultaneous submissions if identified, and email submissions to 2003@austinfamily.com. Availability of artwork improves chance of acceptance. SASE. Responds in 3 months.
Articles: 800 words. Informational, practical application, and how-to articles. Topics include parenting, the family, environment, recreation, ethnic and multicultural issues, hobbies, crafts, computers, careers, college, pets, current events, and health.
Depts/columns: 800 words. Humor; book and film reviews; health and safety.
Artwork: B/W prints.
Other: Submit seasonal material 6 months in advance.

Sample Issue
64 pages (50% advertising): 5 articles; 11 depts/columns; 1 readers' poll; 1 contest; 1 camp guide; 4 calendars. Sample copy, free.
- "Preparing Your Teen for a First Job." Article tells how to help teens get and keep a summer job.
- Sample dept/column: "Health & Safety" reports on the potential dangers of storing water in plastic.

Rights and Payment
First and second serial rights. All material, payment rates vary. Payment policy varies.

Editor's Comments
We still need more articles on education and advice about parenting teens.

BabagaNewz

90 Oak Street
Newton, MA 02464

Production Editor: Aviva Werner

Description and Interests
This news magazine for Jewish pre-teens offers analysis of current events and youth trends while also covering religious holidays and cultural events. Designed for classroom use, each issue is accompanied by a teachers' guide.
• **Audience:** 9–13 years
• **Frequency:** 8 times each year
• **Distribution:** Schools; subscription
• **Circulation:** 41,029
• **Website:** www.babaganewz.com

Freelance Potential
40% written by nonstaff writers. Publishes 20 freelance submissions yearly.

Submissions
Query. All material is written on assignment. Accepts hard copy. SASE. Response time varies.
Articles: Word lengths vary. Informational and how-to articles; profiles; and interviews. Topics include renewal, friendship, personal satisfaction, peace, caring for the environment, truth, responsibility, heroism, health, seder, the Torah, Jewish holidays, history, political science, social studies, language, and sports.
Depts/columns: Word lengths vary. World news, short profiles, and science news.

Sample Issue
22 pages (no advertising): 5 articles; 1 play; 2 depts/columns; 5 activities; 1 contest. Sample copy and guidelines available by email request to aviva@babaganewz.com.
• "Ricky Ullman: Jewish a 'Phil' iation." Article profiles a teen from Israel who is starring in a new Disney Channel sitcom.
• "Zionism without Zion?" Play recounts how there was once a movement to create a Jewish state in Uganda.
• Sample dept/column: "Nuggetz" features short news items and profiles.

Rights and Payment
All rights. Written material, payment rates vary. Pays on acceptance. Provides contributor's copies upon request.

Editor's Comments
Everything is written on assignment, but we'll consider queries for articles related to an upcoming theme.

Babybug

Cricket Magazine Group
315 5th Street
P.O. Box 300
Peru, IL 61354

Submissions Editor

Description and Interests
Published by the well-known Cricket Magazine Group, this magazine features simple stories and poems, words, and concepts that parents can read aloud to young children.
• **Audience:** 6 months–2 years
• **Frequency:** 10 times each year
• **Distribution:** 90% subscription; 10% newsstand
• **Circulation:** 50,000
• **Website:** www.cricketmag.com

Freelance Potential
100% written by nonstaff writers. Publishes 30–40 freelance submissions yearly; 50% by authors who are new to the magazine. Receives 2,400 unsolicited mss yearly.

Submissions
Send complete ms. Accepts hard copy and simultaneous submissions if identified. SASE. Responds in 3–4 months.
Articles: 10 words. Topics include simple concepts and ideas.
Fiction: 3–6 short sentences. Age-appropriate humor and short stories.
Other: Rhyming and rhythmic poetry, to 8 lines. Parent/child activities, to 8 lines.

Sample Issue
22 pages (no advertising): 4 stories; 2 poems. Sample copy, $5. Guidelines available.
• "Kim and Carrots." This ongoing short story takes a little girl, her stuffed bunny, and her mother on a game of hide and seek.
• "Kitchen Fun." Short story depicts a toddler playing and cleaning up in the kitchen.
• "My Ball." Short poem shows what a little red ball can do.

Rights and Payment
Rights vary. Written material, $25 minimum. Pays on publication. Provides 6 contributor's copies.

Editor's Comments
We would like to publish as many original contributions from children's authors and artists as we can. Our standards are very high, and we will accept only top-quality material. Before attempting to write for us, please be sure to familiarize yourself with our requirements and with the interests and abilities of our audience. We do not accept queries.

Baby Dallas

Lauren Publications
4275 Kellway Circle, Suite 146
Addison, TX 75001

Editorial Director: Shelley Hawes Pate

Description and Interests
Baby Dallas serves as a resource for expectant and new parents. Dallas-area residents read the free publication for guidelines, advice, humor, and up-to-date information on health and safety issues.
• **Audience:** Parents
• **Frequency:** Twice each year
• **Distribution:** 90% controlled; 10% subscription
• **Circulation:** 120,000
• **Website:** www.babydallas.com

Freelance Potential
25% written by nonstaff writers. Publishes 12–15 freelance submissions yearly; 20% by authors who are new to the magazine. Receives 240 queries yearly.

Submissions
Query with résumé. Accepts hard copy, simultaneous submissions if identified, and email queries to editorial@dallaschild.com. SASE. Responds in 2–3 months.
Articles: 1,000–2,500 words. Informational, self-help, and how-to articles; profiles; interviews; humor; and personal experience pieces. Topics include parenting, education, current events, social issues, multicultural and ethnic issues, health and fitness, crafts, and computers.
Depts/columns: 800 words. Health updates, safety issues, baby care, and parent resources.

Sample Issue
38 pages (14% advertising): 2 articles; 6 depts/columns. Sample copy, free with 9x12 SASE. Writers' guidelines available.
• "Breastfeeding Through Bottle." Article shares one mother's story and offers tips on long-term pumping.
• "The Birth Gift: With Love from Him to You." Article discusses the growing custom of fathers giving gifts after mom gives birth.
• Sample dept/column: "Health" reports on plagiocephaly correction and early detection.

Rights and Payment
First rights. Written material, payment rates vary. Pays on publication. Provides contributor's copies upon request.

Editor's Comments
We seek practical articles written with a sense of humor and comforting style for first-time parents. We are dedicated to preparing parents for baby's birth.

Baby Talk

The Parenting Group
135 West 50th Street, 3rd Floor
New York, NY 10020

Senior Editor: Patty Onderko

Description and Interests
Offering a wealth of information for expectant mothers and parents of toddlers up to the age of 18 months, this magazine includes articles on topics such as baby care, child development, and health.
• **Audience:** Parents
• **Frequency:** 10 times each year
• **Distribution:** 100% controlled
• **Circulation:** 2 million
• **Website:** www.babytalk.com

Freelance Potential
50% written by nonstaff writers. Publishes 40 freelance submissions yearly; 20% by authors who are new to the magazine. Receives 504 queries yearly.

Submissions
Query with clips or writing samples. No simultaneous submissions. SASE. Responds in 2 months.
Articles: 1,500–2,000 words. Informational and how-to articles; and personal experience pieces. Topics include pregnancy, baby care, infant health, juvenile equipment and toys, day care, marriage, and relationships.
Depts/columns: 500–1,200 words. News, advice, women's and infant health, and personal experiences from new parents.

Sample Issue
104 pages (50% advertising): 6 articles; 15 depts/columns. Sample copy, free with 9x12 SASE ($1.60 postage). Guidelines and theme list available.
• "Life After Adoption." Article offers advice on making a smooth transition after bringing an adopted child home.
• "Little Ego Boosters." Article discusses how to raise a confident child.
• Sample dept/column: "Dad's Side" offers a father's humorous thoughts on dads and childcare.

Rights and Payment
First rights. Articles, $1,000–$2,000. Depts/columns, $300–$1,200. Pays on acceptance. Provides 2–4 contributor's copies.

Editor's Comments
Our readers turn to us to provide them with the basics of baby care. We tell them what they need to know (and why) in a reassuring tone, adding a touch of humor when appropriate. Freelance writers have the best chance at publication with an article.

Baltimore's Child

11 Dutton Court
Baltimore, MD 21228

Editor: Dianne R. McCann

Description and Interests
Billed as a news magazine for families, this tabloid serves parents in the Baltimore, Maryland, area by reporting on local events, resources, child development issues, and education.
- **Audience:** Parents
- **Frequency:** Monthly
- **Distribution:** Unavailable
- **Circulation:** 52,000
- **Website:** www.baltimoreschild.com

Freelance Potential
95% written by nonstaff writers. Publishes 250 freelance submissions yearly; 5% by unpublished writers, 10% by authors who are new to the magazine.

Submissions
Prefers query; accepts complete ms. Accepts hard copy and email submissions to dianne@ baltimoreschild.com. SASE. Response time varies.
Articles: 1,000–1,500 words. Informational articles. Topics include parenting issues, education, health, fitness, child care, social issues, and regional news.
Depts/columns: Word lengths vary. Music; family cooking; pet care; baby and toddler issues; parenting children with special needs; parenting teens; and family finances.

Sample Issue
82 pages: 8 articles; 1 story; 12 depts/columns; 4 calendars. Writers' guidelines and sample copy available at website.
- "Ohmmmmmmmm. Feel Good at Any Age with Yoga." Article reports on how both children and parents can benefit from this exercise form.
- "Cheap Thrills for the Summertime." Article presents last-minute, inexpensive ideas for keeping kids busy over the summer.
- Sample dept/column: "Teen" analyzes the risks and rewards of graduation season.

Rights and Payment
One-time rights. Written material, payment rates vary. Payment policy varies.

Editor's Comments
Our typical reader is looking for suggestions on where to go or what to do with children or how to solve a common problem. Stories should have a local angle and offer specific resources and information. Positive and practical are key words.

Baseball Youth

P.O. Box 983
Morehead, KY 40351

President: Scott Hacker

Description and Interests
Self-described as "The Nation's Baseball Magazine for Kids," this publication offers fun articles and photos about baseball. Video game news and reviews, training tips, ballpark features, and Major and Minor League Baseball information are also part of the mix.
- **Audience:** YA
- **Frequency:** Quarterly
- **Distribution:** Subscription; newsstand
- **Circulation:** Unavailable
- **Website:** www.baseballyouth.com

Freelance Potential
50% written by nonstaff writers. Publishes 25–30 freelance submissions yearly.

Submissions
Query or send complete ms. Accepts email submissions to mailbox@baseballyouth.com. Response time varies.
Articles: Word lengths vary. Informational and how-to articles; profiles; interviews; photo-essays; and personal experience pieces. Topics include youth baseball, Major League and Minor League Baseball, video games, baseball equipment and fashion, ballparks, and baseball players and personalities.
Depts/columns: Word lengths vary. Baseball cards, drills, new product information, player and stadium profiles.
Other: Puzzles and games.

Sample Issue
66 pages: 4 articles; 12 depts/columns; 1 poster; 1 quiz. Sample copy, $3.95 at newsstands. Writers' guidelines available.
- "Learn from the Best." Article features advice from Bill and Cal Ripken about helping young players understand the concept of generating momentum.
- "Dreams Do Come True." Article tells about Little League players who made it to the big leagues.
- Sample dept/column: "Youth Field Profile" visits a ballpark for kids built by John Grisham.

Rights and Payment
All rights. Written material, payment rates and payment policy vary.

Editor's Comments
We welcome new writers who feel that they can add to the excitement of our magazine. Our primary goal is to re-energize youth baseball.

Bay Area Baby

1660 South Amphlett Boulevard, Suite 335
San Mateo, CA 94402

Special Sections Editor

Description and Interests
Targeting expectant and new parents residing in the
San Francisco Bay area, this magazine features articles
and tips on topics related to pregnancy and child care
and development. In addition, it offers information on
local resources and baby events.
- **Audience:** Parents
- **Frequency:** Twice each year
- **Distribution:** 100% controlled
- **Circulation:** 80,000
- **Website:** www.bayareaparent.com

Freelance Potential
50% written by nonstaff writers. Publishes 21 freelance submissions yearly; 50% by authors who are
new to the magazine. Receives 96 queries yearly.

Submissions
All work is assigned. Query. Accepts hard copy. SASE.
Responds in 1–2 months.
Articles: 1,200–1,400 words. Informational, self-
help, and how-to articles; personal experience pieces;
profiles; interviews; and humor. Topics include preg-
nancy, prenatal care, childbirth, and infant care.
Depts/columns: 800 words. Parenting updates.
Artwork: 8x10 B/W or color prints. No slides.
Other: Submit seasonal material 6 months in
advance.

Sample Issue
58 pages: 10 articles; 6 depts/columns. Sample copy,
free with 9x12 SASE (5 first-class stamps). Guidelines
and theme list available.
- "6 Tips to Starting Your Pregnancy Off Right." Article
  offers tips for having a healthy pregnancy and a
  healthy baby.
- "How Your Baby Grows." Article outlines basic milestones of infant development.
- Sample dept/column: "Baby Bits" offers information
  on two new centers for expectant parents.

Rights and Payment
Regional rights. Written material, payment rates vary.
Pays on publication. Provides 1 contributor's copy.

Editor's Comments
All of our work is done by assignment. If you have
an idea for a topic relating to pregnancy or baby
care, send us a query. We prefer information that is
local, well-researched, and geared toward our target
audience—expectant and new parents.

Bay State Parent

800 Main Street
Holden, MA 05120

Editor: Susan S. Petroni

Description and Interests
Local, national, and family issues are presented in this
publication for parents. While there is some local
Massachusetts Bay area focus, there is also general
interest material geared to family life.
- **Audience:** Parents
- **Frequency:** Monthly
- **Distribution:** Newsstand: subscription; other
- **Circulation:** 45,000
- **Website:** www.baystateparent.com

Freelance Potential
90% written by nonstaff writers. Publishes 12–15 freelance submissions yearly; 5% by unpublished writers,
50% by authors who are new to the magazine.
Receives 120 queries yearly.

Submissions
Query. Accepts email queries to editor@
baystateparent.com (Microsoft Word). Artwork improves
chance of acceptance. Responds in 1 month.
Articles: To 2,000 words. Informational and how-to
articles; and humor. Topics include regional and local
events, travel, books, arts and crafts, family finance,
and computers.
Fiction: To 1,000 words. Contemporary, mainstream,
and literary fiction.
Depts/columns: To 1,500 words. Accepts seasonal
material 4 months in advance.
Artwork: B/W and color prints. JPEGs at 200 dpi.

Sample Issue
86 pages (15% advertising): 14 articles; 12 depts/
columns. Sample copy, free. Guidelines available.
- "Cruising with Babies, Toddlers, and Teens." Article
  provides practical tips for making family travel
  easier and more fun.
- "Travel to Family-Friendly St. Petersburg, Florida."
  Article extols the various activities of the area.
- Sample dept/column: "Adoption Insights" probes
  how adoption affects children.

Rights and Payment
Massachusetts exclusive rights. All material, payment
rates vary. Pays on publication.

Editor's Comments
We would like to receive more multi-sourced,
researched articles with a news-type concept. At
this time, we are not looking for personal essays or
how-to articles on children's crafts.

BC Parent News Magazine

Sasamat RPO 72086
Vancouver, British Columbia V6R 4P2
Canada

Editor: Elizabeth Shaffer

Description and Interests

For almost 15 years, this independent parenting magazine has been providing parents, expectant parents, and caregivers with trustworthy information that addresses their concerns. Targeting residents of the Lower Mainland region, it also informs readers of local resources available to them.
- **Audience:** Parents
- **Frequency:** 8 times each year
- **Distribution:** 100% newsstand
- **Circulation:** 40,000
- **Website:** www.bcparent.ca

Freelance Potential

80% written by nonstaff writers. Publishes 25 freelance submissions yearly; 10–30% by authors who are new to the magazine.

Submissions

Send complete ms. Accepts email submissions to editor@bcparent.ca (attach RTF file) and IBM disk submissions. SAE/IRC. No simultaneous submissions. Responds in 2 months.
Articles: 500–1,000 words. Informational articles. Topics include health care, education, pregnancy and childbirth, adoption, computers, sports, money matters, the arts, community events, teen issues, baby and child care, and family issues.
Depts/columns: Word lengths vary. Parent news, family health, media reviews.

Sample Issue

32 pages: 3 articles; 1 summer fun guide; 1 summer camp guide; 4 depts/columns. Writers' guidelines and editorial calendar available.
- "Aquarium Turns 50!" Article reports on the Vancouver Aquarium's plans to continue its legacy of community education, conservation, and research.
- "Make a Splash." Article offers advice on swimming lessons and water safety for kids.
- Sample dept/column: "Family Health" discusses the types of rashes babies and children can develop.

Rights and Payment

First rights. Articles, $85; reprints, $50. Depts/columns, payment rates vary. Pays on acceptance.

Editor's Comments

We provide our readers with in-depth, cutting-edge articles about today's parenting issues. Check our editorial calendar for upcoming topics.

Better Homes and Gardens

Meredith Corporation
1716 Locust Street
Des Moines, IA 50309-3023

Department Editor

Description and Interests

Better Homes and Gardens is a well-known family magazine featuring articles on just about everything related to gardening, decorating, cooking, and entertaining. It also includes articles on health and nutrition, family issues, travel, and the environment. Each issue of this publication has a special section for kids.
- **Audience:** Adults
- **Frequency:** Monthly
- **Distribution:** Subscription; newsstand
- **Circulation:** 7.6 million
- **Website:** www.bhg.com

Freelance Potential

10% written by nonstaff writers. Publishes 25–30 freelance submissions yearly; 25% by authors who are new to the magazine. Receives 240 queries yearly.

Submissions

Query with résumé and clips or writing samples. No unsolicited mss. Accepts hard copy. SASE. Responds in 1 month.
Articles: Word lengths vary. Informational and how-to articles; personal experience pieces; and profiles. Topics include food and nutrition, home design, gardening, outdoor living, travel, the environment, health, fitness, holidays, education, parenting, and child development.

Sample Issue

280 pages: 41 articles. Sample copy, $2.99 at newsstands. Guidelines available.
- "Raising Kids." Article shares ideas on making birthdays memorable while teaching kids about giving and receiving.
- "Eating Well." Article tells how to create home-made pizza that is healthy, delicious, and includes all of the major food groups.
- "Savvy Gardener." Article provides easy-to-do ideas for growing and pruning roses.

Rights and Payment

All rights. Written material, payment rates vary. Pays on acceptance. Provides 1 contributor's copy.

Editor's Comments

New writers have the best chance of being published with submissions on health, travel, parenting, or education. Our focus is on house and home related topics, including gardening. Please do not send articles on beauty, poetry, or fictional pieces.

Big Apple Parent

350 Fifth Avenue, Suite 2420
New York, NY 10118

Editor: Helen Freedman

Description and Interests
For 21 years, this tabloid has been providing New York City parents with articles on topics related to raising children, such as health, family issues, sports, current events, and education.
- **Audience:** Parents
- **Frequency:** Monthly
- **Distribution:** 100% controlled
- **Circulation:** 70,000
- **Website:** www.parentsknow.com

Freelance Potential
10% written by nonstaff writers. Publishes 20 freelance submissions yearly; 10% by unpublished writers, 20% by authors who are new to the magazine. Receives 300 queries, 100 unsolicited mss yearly.

Submissions
Query or send complete ms. Accepts hard copy and email submissions to hfreedman@davlermedia.com. Responds in 1 month.
Articles: 800–1,000 words. Informational and how-to articles; profiles; interviews; and personal experience pieces. Topics include family issues, health, nutrition, fitness, crafts, current events, gifted and special education, nature, sports, and regional news.
Depts/columns: 750 words. News and reviews.
Other: Submit seasonal material 4 months in advance.

Sample Issue
74 pages: 7 articles; 12 depts/columns; 1 calendar of events. Sample copy, free with 10x13 SASE. Guidelines available at website.
- "Play Ball!" Article offers suggestions for getting your children through Little League season with the right attitude.
- "Who's in Charge?" Article discusses problems that may come up when a nanny is hired.
- Sample dept/column: "Business of Parenting" takes a look at a spray alternative to baby wipes.

Rights and Payment
First serial rights. No payment. Provides 2 contributor's copies.

Editor's Comments
We look for fresh material on topics that New York City parents want to know about. Keep in mind that we never publish memoir, fiction, or poetry. We are also not reading travel pieces right now.

Birmingham Christian Family

P.O. Box 382724
Birmingham, AL 35238

President: Laurie Stroud

Description and Interests
This free tabloid puts a positive, Christian perspective on parenting issues while also spotlighting the work of individuals and organizations that are working to address the needs of Birmingham-area families.
- **Audience:** Families
- **Frequency:** Monthly
- **Distribution:** 95% newsstand; 5% subscription
- **Circulation:** 35,000
- **Website:** www.christianfamilypublications.com

Freelance Potential
30% written by nonstaff writers. Publishes 100 freelance submissions yearly; 5% by unpublished writers, 2–3% by authors who are new to the magazine. Receives 240 queries, 72 unsolicited mss yearly.

Submissions
Query with photos if applicable. Accepts email submissions to laurie@birminghamchristian.com. Availability of artwork improves chance of acceptance. SASE. Responds in 1 month.
Articles: To 500 words. Informational, self-help, and how-to articles; profiles; and personal experience pieces. Topics include animals, pets, the arts, crafts, hobbies, current events, fitness, music, recreation, religion, travel, and sports.
Fiction: To 500 words. Inspirational and humorous fiction.
Depts/columns: To 500 words. Book and movie reviews, family finances, restaurant reviews, family health.

Sample Issue
34 pages (25% advertising): 2 articles; 23 depts/columns; 1 calendar. Sample copy, free with 9x12 SASE ($3 postage). Editorial calendar available.
- "Beth Twitty, A Beacon of Hope." Article profiles the mother of a missing teen who is working to educate families about travel safety.
- Sample dept/column: "Mission Makers" describes the work of the Oak Mountain Missions group.

Rights and Payment
Rights vary. No payment.

Editor's Comments
We're looking for writers who can provide our readers with positive, Christian articles with a strong local focus. We try to present ways to grow and develop as part of Birmingham's Christian community.

The Black Collegian

140 Carondelet Street
New Orleans, LA 70130

Vice President: Pres Edwards, Jr.

Description and Interests
Celebrating 35 years in print, this magazine for African American college students features inspiring and motivating articles on self-development and preparing for a professional career. It also reports on industry trends and includes profiles of successful African Americans.
- **Audience:** African Americans, 18–30 years
- **Frequency:** Twice each year
- **Distribution:** Internet; college campuses
- **Circulation:** 125,000
- **Website: www.blackcollegian.com**

Freelance Potential
95% written by nonstaff writers. Publishes 20 freelance submissions yearly; 33% by authors who are new to the magazine. Receives 24 queries yearly.

Submissions
Query. Prefers email queries to pres@imdiversity.com. Accepts hard copy. SASE. Responds in 3 months.
Articles: 1,500–2,000 words. Informational, self-help, and how-to articles; profiles; and personal experience pieces. Topics include careers, personal development, job hunting, colleges, financial aid, history, technology, and multicultural and ethnic issues.
Depts/columns: Word lengths vary. Health issues and African American book and art reviews.
Artwork: 5x7 and 11x14 B/W and color transparencies. B/W and color line art.

Sample Issue
104 pages: 6 articles; 1 dept/column. Writers' guidelines available.
- "Tip: Making Your Own Success." Article profiles Craig Hill, a vice president at BNSF Railway.
- "The African American Student as a Consumer." Article reports on the findings of a survey of college undergraduates throughout the country.
- "Today's Black Collegians." Article explores what some college students say about life and concerns on campus today.

Rights and Payment
One-time rights. Written material, payment rates vary. Pays after publication. Provides 1 contributor's copy.

Editor's Comments
We look for timely information that will benefit students as they plan their chosen careers.

The Blue Review

Submissions Editor: Kathy Greer

Description and Interests
The Blue Review is a monthly, theme-based e-zine aimed at children's writers of all experience levels, offering helpful, informative articles about the craft of writing. Published online only, it features regular columns that include children's market news, Q&As, writing nonfiction, a contest corner, and book talk.
- **Audience:** Children's writers
- **Frequency:** Monthly
- **Distribution:** 100% Internet
- **Hits per month:** Unavailable
- **Website: www.boost4writers.com**

Freelance Potential
25% written by nonstaff writers. Publishes 48 freelance submissions yearly.

Submissions
Send complete ms. Accepts email submissions to eringobraugh5@juno.com (no attachments) and simultaneous submissions if identified. Responds in 2–4 weeks.
Articles: 1,000–1,200 words. Informational articles.
Depts/columns: Staff written.
Other: Filler, 500–700 words. Topics of interest to children's writers.

Sample Issue
Sample copy, writers' guidelines, and theme list available at website.
- "Add a Bit of Salt and Pepper to Taste." Article shares the thoughts of an author as she creates a story and characters while people-watching on the Montreal subway.
- "Continuing Your Education: The Low-Residency Model." Article discusses several choices for individuals interested in graduate programs in creative writing.
- "12 Elements of Revision." Article explains how to strengthen a story by eliminating wordiness, repetition, and unnecessary phrases.

Rights and Payment
One-time exclusive electronic rights. Articles, $25. Filler, $10. Pays on publication. Provides 1 contributor's copy.

Editor's Comments
We seek articles that are well researched, well written, theme-based, and focused toward children's writers. Works from new and established writers are welcome.

Book Links

American Library Association
50 East Huron Street
Chicago, IL 60611

Editor: Laura Tillotson

Description and Interests
The mission of *Book Links* is to connect books, libraries, and classrooms. Published by the American Library Association, it is read by teachers, librarians, media specialists, and parents.
- **Audience:** Adults
- **Frequency:** 6 times each year
- **Distribution:** 98% subscription; 2% controlled
- **Circulation:** 20,577
- **Website:** www.ala.org/booklinks

Freelance Potential
90% written by nonstaff writers. Publishes 60 freelance submissions yearly; 20% by unpublished writers, 30% by authors who are new to the magazine. Receives 96 queries yearly.

Submissions
Query. No unsolicited mss. SASE. Response time varies.
Articles: Word lengths vary. Informational articles; profiles; interviews; and personal experience pieces. Topics include children's books, current and historical events, nature, the environment, and ethnic and multicultural subjects.
Depts/columns: Classroom ideas for curriculum enrichment, 800–1,200 words. Book lists for specific countries or themes, 250–300 words. Interviews with authors and illustrators, word lengths vary.

Sample Issue
64 pages (28% advertising): 10 articles; 3 depts/columns. Sample copy, $6. Writers' guidelines and theme list available.
- "A Quest for Land During Reconstruction." Article discusses a book set in the American South during the era of Reconstruction.
- "Arab Children's Literature." Article provides an update on books about Arabs and Islam.
- Sample dept/column: "Author Focus" examines the work of author and artist Jeanette Winter.

Rights and Payment
All rights. Articles, $100. Pays on publication. Provides 2 contributor's copies.

Editor's Comments
We primarily need bibliographies, essays that link books on a similar theme, retrospective reviews, and other features targeted to educators working at the preschool through eighth-grade levels.

Bop

6430 Sunset Boulevard, Suite 700
Hollywood, CA 90028

Editor-in-Chief: Leesa Coble

Description and Interests
This Hollywood magazine delivers the latest gossip, interviews, celebrity profiles, photos, and posters, as well as fun quizzes for teen fans. Fashion ideas and contest information are also a part of its mix.
- **Audience:** 10–16 years
- **Frequency:** Monthly
- **Distribution:** 90% newsstand; 10% subscription
- **Circulation:** 200,000
- **Website:** www.bopmag.com

Freelance Potential
1% written by nonstaff writers. Publishes 2 freelance submissions yearly; 50% by authors who are new to the magazine. Receives 24 queries yearly.

Submissions
Query with résumé and clips for celebrity-related pieces only. Accepts hard copy and simultaneous submissions if identified. SASE. Responds in 2 months.
Articles: To 700 words. Celebrity interviews; profiles of film and television personalities and recording stars; and behind-the-scenes reports on the entertainment industry.
Depts/columns: Staff written.
Other: Quizzes and puzzles. Submit seasonal material 3–5 months in advance.

Sample Issue
100 pages (15% advertising): 17 articles; 18 depts/columns; 18 posters; 6 quizzes. Sample copy, $3.99 at newsstands.
- "Hop on the Bus with Simple Plan." Article offers a view inside Simple Plan's tour bus and an idea of the band's activities during travel time.
- "Get to Know Green Day from A to Z." Article provides facts, fun quotes, and secrets about this popular band.
- "Is Jesse Fearless?" Article tells fans about singer Jesse McCartney's thrill-seeking activities.

Rights and Payment
All rights. Written material, payment rates vary. Pays on publication. Provides 2 contributor's copies.

Editor's Comments
We are looking for interviews and insider items that connect fans with the personal lives of their favorite young rockers and television and film personalities. We look for authentic and fresh topics that will pique the interest of our readers.

The Boston Parents' Paper

670 Centre Street
Jamaica Plain, MA 02130

Editor: Alison O'Leary Murray

Description and Interests
This regional magazine strives to present the most comprehensive, up-to-date, and relevant information available on issues of concern to parents and those interested in families and children.
- **Audience:** Parents
- **Frequency:** Monthly
- **Distribution:** 98% controlled; 2% subscription
- **Circulation:** 70,000
- **Website:** www.bostonparentspaper.com

Freelance Potential
50% written by nonstaff writers. Publishes 36 freelance submissions yearly; 10% by unpublished writers, 50% by authors who are new to the magazine. Receives 36 queries yearly.

Submissions
Query with clips or writing samples. Accepts hard copy. SASE. Availability of artwork improves chance of acceptance. Response time varies.
Articles: Word lengths vary. Informational articles; profiles; and interviews. Topics include child development, education, parenting, family issues, and health.
Depts/columns: To 1,800 words. Short news items, parenting tips, and profiles.
Artwork: B/W prints. Line art.
Other: Submit seasonal material 6 months in advance.

Sample Issue
76 pages (45% advertising): 3 articles; 12 depts/columns; 1 calendar of events. Guidelines and theme list available.
- "Still Fighting Fat." Article explains why we're losing the war on childhood obesity.
- "'N' is for Nutrition." Article examines school food programs and explains how to make school lunches more nutritious.
- Sample dept/column: "The 10 Talents of Parenting" suggests being silly as an alternative to nagging.

Rights and Payment
First North American serial and electronic rights. All material, payment rates vary. Pays within 30 days of publication. Provides 5 contributor's copies.

Editor's Comments
We want to give parents basic information on the day-to-day challenges and joys of child-rearing, as well as the opportunity to explore the complex issues that confront families today.

Boys' Life

Boy Scouts of America
1325 West Walnut Hill Lane
P.O. Box 152079
Irving, TX 75015-2079

Senior Editor: Michael Goldman

Description and Interests
This general interest magazine from the Boy Scouts covers everything from professional sports to American history to how to pack a canoe. It also publishes short stories that feature boys.
- **Audience:** 6–18 years
- **Frequency:** Monthly
- **Distribution:** 95% subscription; 5% other
- **Circulation:** 1.3 million
- **Website:** www.boyslife.org

Freelance Potential
80% written by nonstaff writers. Publishes 50 freelance submissions yearly; 1% by unpublished writers, 2% by authors who are new to the magazine. Receives 96+ queries yearly.

Submissions
Query for articles and depts/columns. Query or send complete ms for fiction. Accepts hard copy. SASE. Responds to queries in 4–6 weeks, to mss in 6–8 weeks.
Articles: 500–1,500 words. Informational and how-to articles; profiles; and humor. Topics include sports, science, American history, geography, animals, nature, and the environment.
Fiction: 1,000–1,500 words. Genres include mystery, adventure, humor, and science fiction.
Depts/columns: 300–750 words. Cars, music, collecting, space and aviation, computers, and pets.
Other: Puzzles and cartoons.

Sample Issue
58 pages (18% advertising): 7 articles; 13 depts/columns; 5 cartoons; 4 activities. Sample copy, $3.60 with 9x12 SASE. Guidelines available.
- "Lightning!" Article explains the science of lightning and how to keep safe in a storm.
- "Just Plain Batty." Article tells how some big-league baseball players take superstitions to the extreme.
- Sample dept/column: "Outdoors" explains the science of tree rings.

Rights and Payment
First rights. Articles, $400–$1,500. Fiction, $750+. Depts/columns, $150–$400. Pays on acceptance. Provides 2 contributor's copies.

Editor's Comments
We rarely use unsolicited nonfiction submissions. Try submitting a story or something for a department.

Boys' Quest

P.O. Box 227
Bluffton, OH 45817-0227

Editor: Marilyn Edwards

Description and Interests
A companion publication to *Hopscotch*, this magazine features articles, fiction, and poetry written to engage the minds of young boys.
- **Audience:** 5–14 years
- **Frequency:** 6 times each year
- **Distribution:** 60% school libraries; 30% subscription; 10% newsstand
- **Circulation:** 12,000
- **Website:** www.boysquest.com

Freelance Potential
80% written by nonstaff writers. Publishes 30–40 freelance submissions yearly; 20% by unpublished writers, 20% by authors who are new to the magazine. Receives 1,000–1,200 queries and mss yearly.

Submissions
Prefers complete ms. Accepts queries. Accepts hard copy and simultaneous submissions. SASE. Responds to queries in 1–2 weeks, to mss in 2–3 months.
Articles: 500 words. Informational and how-to articles; profiles; personal experience pieces; and humor. Topics include pets, nature, hobbies, science, games, sports, careers, family, culture and customs, and cars.
Fiction: 500 words. Genres include adventure and sports stories; mysteries; multicultural fiction; and stories about animals, sports, and nature.
Depts/columns: 300–500 words. Science projects.
Artwork: Prefers B/W prints; accepts color prints.
Other: Puzzles, activities, riddles, and poetry.

Sample Issue
50 pages (no advertising): 5 articles; 5 stories; 5 activities; 2 depts/columns; 2 poems; 1 comic. Sample copy, $5 with 9x12 SASE. Guidelines and theme list available with #10 SASE.
- "Coin Collecting for Two." Article offers tips for starting a coin collection with your grandfather.
- Sample dept/column: "Science" describes the balloon in the bottle trick.

Rights and Payment
First and second rights. Articles and fiction, $.05 per word. Depts/columns, $35. Poems and activities, $10+. Photos, $5–$10. Pays on publication. Provides 1 contributor's copy.

Editor's Comments
We need more good nonfiction with photo support. We're seeing too much fiction.

Bread for God's Children

P.O. Box 1017
Arcadia, FL 34265-1017

Editorial Secretary: Donna Wade

Description and Interests
The articles and stories in this publication are written from a child's viewpoint and help Christian families learn to apply the Word of God in their daily lives.
- **Audience:** Families
- **Frequency:** 6–8 times each year
- **Distribution:** 100% subscription
- **Circulation:** 10,000
- **Website:** www.breadministries.com

Freelance Potential
30% written by nonstaff writers. Publishes 25 freelance submissions yearly; 50% by authors who are new to the magazine. Receives 12,000+ unsolicited mss yearly.

Submissions
Send complete ms. Accepts hard copy and simultaneous submissions if identified. No email submissions. SASE. Responds to mss in 2–3 months.
Articles: 600–800 words. Informational and personal experiences that inspire readers to grow in their spiritual lives.
Fiction: Christian theme-based stories for younger children, 500–800 words. Stories for middle-grade and young adult readers, 800–1,000 words.
Depts/columns: To 800 words. Parenting issues, family activities, and issues of interest to teens.
Other: Filler and crafts.

Sample Issue
28 pages (no advertising): 5 stories; 8 depts/columns; 1 Bible study. Sample copy, free with 9x12 SASE (5 first-class stamps). Guidelines available at website.
- "Baby Brother." Story tells how a young boy turns to Jesus when he needs help babysitting his two-year-old brother.
- "Let's Chat I'm Bored." Article offers creative ideas for keeping your mind stimulated instead of playing video games.
- Sample dept/column: "Please Hold" explains the importance of patience and waiting for your prayers to be answered.

Rights and Payment
First rights. Pays on publication. Articles, $30. Fiction, $40–$50. Short filler, $10. Provides 3 copies.

Editor's Comments
We would like to see more stories that help children learn to trust God to be with them and guide them.

Breakaway

Focus on the Family
8605 Explorer Drive
Colorado Springs, CO 80920

Editor: Mike Ross

Description and Interests
This fast-paced magazine is designed to teach, entertain, and inspire teenage boys. It seeks to strengthen their self-esteem and provide healthy role models while making the Bible relevant in today's world.
- **Audience:** 12–18 years
- **Frequency:** Monthly
- **Distribution:** 97% subscription; 3% other
- **Circulation:** 95,000
- **Website:** www.breakawaymag.com

Freelance Potential
20% written by nonstaff writers. Publishes 5 freelance submissions yearly; 1% by unpublished writers, 1% by authors who are new to the magazine. Receives 600 unsolicited mss yearly.

Submissions
Send complete ms. Accepts hard copy and electronic submissions through website. SASE. Responds in 8–10 weeks.
Articles: 600–1,200 words. How-to and self-help articles; personal experience pieces; profiles; interviews; and humor. Topics include religion, sports, and multicultural issues.
Fiction: 1,500–2,200 words. Contemporary, religious and inspirational fiction; suspense; adventure; humor; and stories about sports.
Depts/columns: Word lengths vary. Advice. Scripture readings, and Bible facts.
Other: Filler. Submit seasonal material about religious holidays 6–8 months in advance.

Sample Issue
32 pages (9% advertising): 6 articles; 5 depts/columns. Sample copy, $2 with 9x12 SASE (2 first-class stamps). Guidelines available.
- "Rock It!" Article examines rock climbing and how to tackle this challenging sport.
- "Dollars and Sense." Article provides advice on earning money and spending it wisely.

Rights and Payment
First or one-time rights. Written material, $.15 per word. Pays on acceptance. Provides 5 author's copies.

Editor's Comments.
We rarely publish unsolicited material since the content of each issue is determined far in advance and most features are generated by our ministry. If you have material to submit please follow our guidelines.

Brilliant Star

1233 Central Street
Evanston, IL 60201

Associate Editor: Susan Engle

Description and Interests
This magazine teaches Bahá'í precepts to help young readers learn about their spiritual identity.
- **Audience:** 8–12 years
- **Frequency:** 6 times each year
- **Distribution:** 75% subscription; 25% other
- **Circulation:** 7,000
- **Website: www.brilliantstarmagazine.org**

Freelance Potential
15% written by nonstaff writers. Publishes 5 freelance submissions yearly; 5% by unpublished writers, 80% by authors who are new to the magazine. Receives 100 unsolicited mss yearly.

Submissions
Query with clips for nonfiction. Send complete ms for fiction. Accepts hard copy, email to brilliantstar@usbnc.org, and simultaneous submissions if identified. SASE. Responds in 6–8 weeks.
Articles: To 700 words. Informational and how-to articles; personal experience pieces; profiles; and biographies. Topics include the Bahá'í Faith, historical Bahá'í figures, religion, history, ethnic and social issues, travel, music, nature, and the environment.
Fiction: To 700 words. Early reader fiction. Genres include ethnic, multicultural, historical, contemporary, and problem-solving fiction.
Depts/columns: To 600 words. Religion, nature, health, and ethics.
Other: Puzzles, activities, games, and recipes.

Sample Issue
30 pages: 1 article; 1 story; 1 comic; 10 activities; 10 depts/columns. Sample copy, $3 with 9x12 SASE (5 first-class stamps). Guidelines, theme list, and editorial calendar available.
- "Riley's Rainforest." Article proposes ideas and skills for developing friendships.
- "Reach for the Top." Story depicts a boy's victory over his fear.
- Sample dept/column: "Shining Lamp" profiles a Bahá'í whose heritage, education, and courage shaped her vision and conviction.

Rights and Payment
All or one-time rights. No payment. Provides 2 copies.

Editor's Comments
Please send for our theme list before submitting. Note that poetry written by adults is not accepted.

Brio

Focus on the Family
8605 Explorer Drive
Colorado Springs, CO 80920

Editor: Susie Shellenberger

Description and Interests
This Christian magazine for teenage girls is designed to help them develop spiritually and to foster a healthy image of themselves. These twin goals are addressed through timely and entertaining articles with a positive spin.
- **Audience:** 12–15 years
- **Frequency:** Monthly
- **Distribution:** Subscription; newsstand
- **Circulation:** 200,000
- **Website:** www.briomag.com

Freelance Potential
65% written by nonstaff writers. Publishes 75 freelance submissions yearly; 1% by unpublished writers, 5% by authors who are new to the magazine. Receives 300 queries, 300 unsolicited mss yearly.

Submissions
Query or send complete ms. Accepts hard copy. SASE. Responds in 4–6 weeks.
Articles: To 2,000 words. Informational and how-to articles; profiles; interviews; and personal experience pieces. Topics include Christian living, peer relationships, family life, and contemporary issues.
Fiction: To 2,000 words. Genres include contemporary fiction, romance, and humor with Christian themes.
Depts/columns: Staff written.
Other: Cartoons, anecdotes, and quizzes.

Sample Issue
40 pages (6% advertising): 10 articles; 1 poem; 9 depts/columns. Sample copy, $2. with 9x12 SASE ($.52 postage). Guidelines available.
- "Running Low on Joy." Article outlines four steps to find joy in your life.
- "The Purity Test." Article provides advice on how to filter your media choices.
- Sample dept/column: "Our Hero" profiles an individual who has made an important contribution to the world.

Rights and Payment
First rights. Written material, $.08–$.15 per word. Pays on acceptance. Provides 3 contributor's copies.

Editor's Comments
We are looking for upbeat articles on subjects important to young women. All of the material we publish features a Christian emphasis.

Brio and Beyond

Focus on the Family
8605 Explorer Drive
Colorado Springs, CO 80920

Editor: Susie Shellenberger

Description and Interests
This Focus on the Family magazine targets older teen girls with its articles about relationships, entertainment, beauty, health, and spiritual health. All material is designed to bring readers closer to God.
- **Audience:** 16–19 years
- **Frequency:** Monthly
- **Distribution:** 100% subscription
- **Circulation:** 50,000
- **Website:** www.briomag.com

Freelance Potential
65% written by nonstaff writers. Publishes 75 freelance submissions yearly; 70% by unpublished writers, 50% by authors who are new to the magazine. Receives 800 queries yearly.

Submissions
Send complete ms. Accepts hard copy and disk submissions. Availability of artwork improves chance of acceptance. SASE. Responds in 1 month.
Articles: Word lengths vary. Informational and how-to articles; profiles; interviews; reviews; personal experience pieces; and humor. Topics include religion, multicultural and social issues, college, careers, crafts, hobbies, health, fitness, music, popular culture, sports, and travel.
Fiction: Word lengths vary.
Depts/columns: Staff written.
Artwork: Color prints or transparencies. Line art.
Other: Submit seasonal material 6 months in advance.

Sample Issue
38 pages (no advertising): 15 articles; 3 depts/columns. Sample copy, free. Guidelines available.
- "P-s-st . . . Your Mom's a Girl, Too." Article written by a mom explains why moms can offer teenage girls a lot of guidance.
- "She's Got a Reason." Article profiles teenage worship leader, Jaime Jamgochian.

Rights and Payment
First or second rights. All material, payment rates vary. Pays on acceptance. Provides 2 author's copies.

Editor's Comments
We address contemporary issues that are relevant to older teen girls. The purpose of all of our content is to support Christian faith and values.

Brooklyn Parent

350 Fifth Avenue, Suite 2420
New York, NY 10118

Editor: Judy Antell

Description and Interests
Brooklyn Parent features articles of interest to parents and families. Topics include child development, family issues, raising children, pregnancy, and local news and services. This parenting tabloid also features the latest information on health care and education.
• **Audience:** Parents
• **Frequency:** Monthly
• **Distribution:** 100% controlled
• **Circulation:** 50,000
• **Website:** www.parentsknow.com

Freelance Potential
10% written by nonstaff writers. Publishes 20 freelance submissions yearly; 25% by authors who are new to the magazine. Receives 300 queries and unsolicited mss yearly.

Submissions
Query or send complete ms. Accepts hard copy and email to hellonwheels@parentsknow.com or judy@parentsknow.com. SASE. Responds in 1 week.
Articles: 800–1,000 words. Informational articles; profiles; interviews; and personal experience pieces. Topics include family issues, health, nutrition, fitness, crafts, current events, gifted education, humor, nature, and regional news.
Depts/columns: 750 words. News and reviews.
Other: Submit seasonal material 4 months in advance.

Sample Issue
64 pages: 8 depts/columns; 7 articles; 1 calendar of events. Sample copy, free with 10x13 SASE. Guidelines available.
• "Be-Bop Babies." Article discusses the benefits of exposing children to music and gives a brief overview of some music classes available.
• "Treating Ear Infections: Less Is More." Article discusses different treatments for ear infections and recommends not using antibiotics.
• Sample dept/column: "What's in a Chicken Nugget?" reveals the hidden ingredients in this popular food.

Rights and Payment
First New York area rights. No payment.

Editor's Comments
We look for material with a new twist on a traditional topic. Controversial issues in the field of parenting are always of interest. We seek submissions with up-to-date information on local services and regional events.

ByLine

P.O. Box 5240
Edmond, OK 73083-5240

Articles Editor: Marcia Preston
Fiction Editor: Carolyn Wall
Poetry Editor: Sandra Soli

Description and Interests
Articles on the craft and business of writing fiction, nonfiction, and poetry, as well as regular columns on writing and children's literature, are featured in each issue of this publication.
• **Audience:** Writers
• **Frequency:** 11 times each year
• **Distribution:** 100% subscription
• **Circulation:** 3,500
• **Website:** www.bylinemag.com

Freelance Potential
80% written by nonstaff writers. Publishes 198 freelance submissions yearly. Receives 3,600 queries and unsolicited mss yearly.

Submissions
Query or send complete ms. Accepts hard copy and simultaneous submissions if identified. SASE. Responds in 1–2 months.
Articles: 1,500–1,800 words. Informational and how-to articles. Topics include writing and marketing fiction, nonfiction, and poetry; finding an agent; grammar; and writing humor.
Depts/columns: 200–400 words. Humor, marketing tips, and contest information.

Sample Issue
36 pages (8% advertising): 3 articles; 1 story; 12 depts/columns. Sample copy, $5 with 9x12 SASE. Guidelines available.
• "This Little Writer Had a Website . . ." Feature article discusses the benefits of maintaining a professional author's website.
• "Double-Dip to Sell More Articles." Article explains how to spin off the idea for an article into more specialized pieces to sell to other publications.
• Sample dept/column: "Ode to Hank the Ficus" is a short humorous piece about a writer with a not-so-green thumb.

Rights and Payment
All rights. Articles, $75. Fiction, $100. Depts/columns, $15–$35. Pays on acceptance. Provides 1–3 copies.

Editor's Comments
Our goal is to encourage and advise both novice and published writers; we buy the work of beginners and veterans alike. We also sponsor monthly contests to motivate writers by providing deadlines and competition against other writers.

BYU Magazine

218 UPB
Provo, UT 84602

Editor: Jeff McClellan

Description and Interests
This magazine, read by students and friends of Brigham Young University, includes information on campus life, alumni news, and thought-provoking articles that are intended to inspire spiritual growth.
- **Audience:** YA–Adult
- **Frequency:** Quarterly
- **Distribution:** 98% controlled; 2% schools
- **Circulation:** 190,000
- **Website:** www.magazine.byu.com

Freelance Potential
45% written by nonstaff writers. Publishes 10 freelance submissions yearly; 5% by authors who are new to the magazine. Receives 120 queries yearly.

Submissions
Query with writing samples. Accepts hard copy. SASE. Responds in 6–12 months.
Articles: 2,000–4,000 words. Informational, factual, and how-to articles; self-help and personal experience pieces; and humor. Topics include college life, careers, computers, current events, health, fitness, religion, science, technology, sports, and family issues.
Depts/columns: To 1,500 words. Campus news, book reviews, commentary, and alumni updates.
Artwork: 35mm color prints or transparencies.
Other: Word lengths vary. BYU trivia.

Sample Issue
56 pages (15% advertising): 4 articles; 4 depts/columns. Sample copy, free. Guidelines available.
- "My Dear Young Friends." Article presents excerpts from speeches given by BYU president Gordon B. Hinckley over his 50 years as a member of the Board of Trustees.
- "A Welcoming Campus Home." Article provides a look at the new alumni and visitor's center at BYU.
- Sample dept/column: "BYU Today" looks at the obstacles a former BYU student overcame to win an Olympic medal.

Rights and Payment
First North American serial rights. Articles, $.35 per word. Pays on publication. Provides 10 contributor's copies.

Editor's Comments
Our goal is to inspire our graduates and friends to remain connected to our university through articles that inform and motivate.

Cadet Quest

Calvinist Cadet Corps
P.O. Box 7259
Grand Rapids, MI 49510

Editor: G. Richard Broene

Description and Interests
Middle-grade and young adult readers who have joined the Calvinist Cadet Corps youth organization turn to this magazine for articles, stories, and activities based on Christian principles.
- **Audience:** 9–14 years
- **Frequency:** 7 times each year
- **Distribution:** 100% subscription
- **Circulation:** 8,000
- **Website:** www.calvinistcadets.org

Freelance Potential
58% written by nonstaff writers. Publishes 25 freelance submissions yearly; 3% by unpublished writers, 5% by new authors. Receives 400 mss yearly.

Submissions
Send complete ms. Accepts hard copy, email submissions to submissions@calvinistcadets.org (no attachments), and simultaneous submissions if identified. SASE. Responds in 1 month.
Articles: 400–1,000 words. Informational and factual articles; profiles; and interviews. Topics include religion, spirituality, camping skills, crafts, hobbies, sports, nature study, the environment, stewardship, and serving God.
Fiction: 900–1,600 words. Adventure and sports stories with a Christian perspective.
Depts/columns: Word lengths vary. Cadet Corps news and Bible stories.
Other: Puzzles and cartoons.

Sample Issue
24 pages (2% advertising): 1 article; 2 stories; 2 depts/columns; 2 activities; 6 Bible lessons; 1 comic.
Sample copy, free with 9x12 SASE ($1.01 postage). Guidelines and theme list available with SASE or at website.
- "Matched Pairs." Story features twin boys who get "new" skates at a skate and ski swap.
- "Eagles: The Bald and the Beautiful." Article provides facts about the North American bald eagle.

Rights and Payment
First and second serial rights. Written material, $.04–$.05 per word. Other material, payment rates vary. Pays on acceptance. Provides 1 contributor's copy.

Editor's Comments
Articles that profile real Christian role models are especially welcome this year.

Calliope

Cobblestone Publishing
30 Grove Street, Suite C
Peterborough, NH 03458

Editor: Rosalie Baker

Description and Interests
Each issue of this lively magazine focuses on a specific theme of world history to enhance readers' understanding of other cultures.
- **Audience:** 9–14 years
- **Frequency:** 9 times each year
- **Distribution:** 100% subscription
- **Circulation:** 12,000
- **Website:** www.cobblestonepub.com

Freelance Potential
95% written by nonstaff writers. Publishes 75 freelance submissions yearly; 25% by unpublished writers, 30–40% by authors who are new to the magazine. Receives 300 queries yearly.

Submissions
Query with outline, bibliography, and clips or writing samples. All material must relate to upcoming themes. SASE. Responds in 4 months.
Articles: Features, 700–800 words. Sidebars, 300–600 words. Informational articles and profiles. Topics include Western and Eastern world history.
Fiction: To 800 words. Genres include historical and biographical fiction, adventure, retold legends, and historical plays.
Depts/columns: 300–600 words. Current events, archaeology, languages, and book reviews.
Artwork: B/W or color prints or slides. B/W or color line art.
Other: Puzzles, games, activities, crafts, and recipes; to 700 words.

Sample Issue
48 pages (no advertising): 16 articles; 8 depts/columns; 2 activities. Sample copy, $4.95 with 9x12 SASE ($2 postage). Guidelines and theme list available.
- "Legend of the Suns." Article explains the Aztec beliefs about the sun and the moon.
- Sample dept/column: "Fun with Words" offers a number of English words that can be traced to original Aztec terms.

Rights and Payment
All rights. Articles and fiction, $.20–$.25 per word. Other material, payment rates vary. Pays on publication. Provides 2 contributor's copies.

Editor's Comments
We're looking for historical material that includes maps, timelines, illustrations, and art references.

Camping Magazine

American Camping Association
5000 State Road 67 North
Martinsville, IN 46151-7902

Editor-in-Chief: Harriet Gamble

Description and Interests
Managers and staff members who work at recreational camps for children rely on this magazine for ideas about camp operations and keeping children active, involved, and healthy.
- **Audience:** Camp managers and educators
- **Frequency:** 6 times each year
- **Distribution:** 100% subscription
- **Circulation:** 7,000
- **Website:** www.ACAcamps.com

Freelance Potential
98% written by nonstaff writers. Publishes 20 freelance submissions yearly; 50% by unpublished writers, 50% by authors who are new to the magazine. Receives 96 queries yearly.

Submissions
Query with outline. Prefers email queries to magazine@acacamps.org. Accepts hard copy. SASE. Response time varies.
Articles: 1,500–4,000 words. Informational and how-to articles. Topics include camp management, special education, social issues, careers, health, recreation, crafts, and hobbies.
Depts/columns: 800–1,000 words. Opinion pieces, health issues related to camping, marketing ideas, and building and construction information.
Artwork: B/W and color prints and slides.

Sample Issue
72 pages (20% advertising): 7 articles; 9 depts/columns. Sample copy, $4.50 with 9x12 SASE. Guidelines and editorial calendar available.
- "Essentials of Homesickness Prevention." Article explains that the intensity of homesickness in campers can be reduced by doing a little work before opening day.
- "Excellence in Staff Training to Reduce Bullying." Article tells how both campers and staff engage in bullying behavior and how to stop it.

Rights and Payment
All rights. No payment. Provides 3 author's copies.

Editor's Comments
We're always interested in articles that present innovative programming ideas and management strategies written by people who have lots of hands-on experience working in children's camps. Articles that include research are very desirable.

Canadian Children's Literature

Department of English, University of Winnipeg
515 Portage Avenue
Winnipeg, Manitoba R3B 2E9 Canada

Editor: Perry Nodelman

Description and Interests
The purpose of this bilingual, refereed journal is to promote knowledge and understanding of books produced for children in Canada. It also covers other media, including film, drama, and television.
- **Audience:** Educators, scholars, and librarians
- **Frequency:** Quarterly
- **Distribution:** 70% subscription; 3% newsstand; 27% other
- **Circulation:** 900
- **Website:** http://ccl.uwinnipeg.ca

Freelance Potential
99% written by nonstaff writers. Publishes 100 freelance submissions yearly; 10% by unpublished writers, 40% by authors who are new to the magazine. Receives 120 unsolicited mss yearly.

Submissions
Query with summary; or send 3 copies of complete ms. Accepts hard copy and email submissions to ccl@uwinnipeg.ca. SAE/IRC. Responds to queries in 6 weeks, to mss in 6 months.
Articles: 2,000–6,000 words. Informational articles; reviews; profiles; and interviews. Topics include children's literature; film, videos, and drama for children; and children's authors.

Sample Issue
178 pages (2% advertising): 9 articles. Sample copy, $10. Writers' guidelines and theme list/editorial calendar available.
- "Canadian Young People and Their Reading Worlds: Conditions of Literature in Contemporary Canada." Article offers an overview of the children's publishing industry and charts trends in book distribution.
- "Snow Angels and Monarch Butterflies: Margaret Laurence's Children's Fiction." Article examines four children's books written by an author more famous for her adult novels.

Rights and Payment
First serial rights. No payment. Provides 1 contributor's copy.

Editor's Comments
We focus on texts for and about children of all ethnic and cultural backgrounds in Canada. Our publication is a venue for research and writing about how these texts function culturally and ideologically in the lives of children and adults.

Canadian Guider

50 Merton Street
Toronto, Ontario M4S 1A3
Canada

Editor: Sharon Pruner

Description and Interests
As the official publication of the Girl Guides of Canada, this magazine combines thought-provoking articles, resources for helping members, and practical ideas for hands-on programs.
- **Audience:** Girl Guide leaders
- **Frequency:** 3 times each year
- **Distribution:** 100% controlled
- **Circulation:** 40,000
- **Website:** www.girlguides.ca

Freelance Potential
5% written by nonstaff writers. Publishes 2 freelance submissions yearly; 50% by unpublished writers, 50% by authors who are new to the magazine. Receives 1 query monthly.

Submissions
Query with résumé. SAE/IRC. Responds in 1 month.
Articles: To 200 words. Informational and how-to articles; personal experience pieces; profiles; and interviews. Topics include leadership and life skills, fitness, health, camping, adventure, the outdoors, nature, the environment, the arts, social issues, and contemporary concerns.
Depts/columns: Word lengths vary. Activity ideas and leadership tips.
Artwork: B/W and color prints; digital images. See submission information at website.

Sample Issue
56 pages (12% advertising): 17 articles; 9 depts/columns. Sample copy, $3 with 9x12 SAE/IRC. Guidelines, editorial calendar, and theme list available.
- "By Girls, for Girls." Article highlights a new program for Pathfinders that offers choice and flexibility.
- "Sharing Knowledge and Skills." Article explains what to expect during training to be a Girl Guide adult leader.
- Sample dept/column: "Outdoor Guider" looks at camping in the winter months and how it can be challenging, exciting, and educational.

Rights and Payment
All rights. No payment. Provides 2 author's copies.

Editor's Comments
We promote Guiding as being full of adventure and we want to help girls stay connected to our organization. We're looking for material that Girl Guide leaders can use to become better leaders.

Capper's

1503 SW 42nd Street
Topeka, KS 66609

Editor-in-Chief: Katherine Compton

Description and Interests
This home-and-family tabloid promotes American values to a readership that primarily consists of residents of the rural, midwestern U.S.
- **Audience:** Families
- **Frequency:** Monthly
- **Distribution:** 100% subscription
- **Circulation:** 240,000
- **Website: www.cappers.com**

Freelance Potential
90% written by nonstaff writers. Publishes 40–50 freelance submissions yearly; 50% by unpublished writers, 70% by authors who are new to the magazine. Receives 480 unsolicited mss yearly.

Submissions
Send complete ms with photos for articles; query for fiction. Accepts hard copy. SASE. Responds to queries in 1 month, to mss in 3–4 months.
Articles: 700 words. General interest, historical, inspirational, and nostalgic articles. Topics include family life, travel, hobbies, and occupations.
Fiction: To 25,000 words. Serialized novels.
Depts/columns: 300 words. Personal experience pieces, humor, and essays.
Artwork: 35mm color slides, transparencies, or prints.
Other: Jokes; 5–6 per submission.

Sample Issue
48 pages (3% advertising): 24 articles; 1 serialized novel; 2 poems; 12 depts/columns. Sample copy, $1.95. Guidelines available.
- "Statue of Liberty Harbors Some Secrets." Article reveals little-known facts about this national symbol.
- "The Cold Facts about Ice Cream." Article traces the history of this popular frozen treat.
- Sample dept/column: "Garden Clippings" describes landscaping with non-plant material.

Rights and Payment
Shared rights. Articles, $2.50 per column inch; serialized novels, $75–$300. Pays on publication for nonfiction, on acceptance for fiction. Provides up to 5 contributor's copies.

Editor's Comments
Our publication emphasizes the positive aspects of life. Articles should be written in journalistic style; for fiction, avoid profanity, violence, sex, and alcohol use.

Careers and Colleges

2 LAN Drive, Suite 100
Westford, MA 01886

Managing Director: Jayne Pennington

Description and Interests
This magazine strives to provide a balanced approach to exploring career and higher education options. Written for high school students, it offers articles on time and money management and campus life, as well as profiles of students.
- **Audience:** 15–18 years
- **Frequency:** 5 times each year
- **Distribution:** 99% schools; 1% subscription
- **Circulation:** 752,000
- **Website: www.careersandcolleges.com**

Freelance Potential
80% written by nonstaff writers. Publishes 4 freelance submissions yearly; 10% by authors who are new to the magazine. Receives 96 queries yearly.

Submissions
Query with clips or writing samples. No unsolicited mss. Accepts hard copy. SASE. Responds in 2 months.
Articles: 800–2,400 words. Informational and how-to articles; profiles; interviews; and personal experience pieces. Topics include career choices, post-secondary education, independent living, social issues, and personal growth.
Depts/columns: Staff written.

Sample Issue
48 pages (29% advertising): 10 articles; 3 depts/columns. Sample copy, $6.95 with 10x13 SASE ($1.75 postage). Guidelines available.
- "Becoming a Well-Rounded Person." Article explains why it is important to get involved in a variety of activities and take courses outside of your major.
- "20 Tempting Tech Tools." Article offers an overview of the latest electronic gadgets.
- "A Natural Born Leader." Article profiles a teen who is passionate about her studies, her country, and her community.

Rights and Payment
First North American serial and electronic rights. Articles, $300–$800. Pays 2 months after acceptance. Provides 2 contributor's copies.

Editor's Comments
Please remember that our primary purpose is to help students achieve their academic, career, and financial goals. We like articles to be accompanied by lists of relevant websites and other resources.

Carolina Parent

5716 Fayetteville Road, Suite 201
Durham, NC 27713

Editor: Cathy Ashby

Description and Interests
Targeted to Carolina-triangle parents, teachers, child care providers, and other advocates of children up to the age of 18, this magazine provides information on family-related issues and child care.
- **Audience:** Parents and teachers
- **Frequency:** Monthly
- **Distribution:** Subscription; newsstand; other
- **Circulation:** 58,000
- **Website: www.carolinaparent.com**

Freelance Potential
50% written by nonstaff writers. Publishes 40 freelance submissions yearly; 20% by unpublished writers, 30% by authors who are new to the magazine.

Submissions
Accepts queries from established writers. New writers, send complete ms. Accepts hard copy and email submissions to editorial@carolinaparent.com (Microsoft Word attachments). SASE. Response time varies.
Articles: Word lengths vary. Informational and how-to articles; profiles; and personal experience pieces. Topics include college, careers, computers, crafts, hobbies, gifted education, health, fitness, humor, music, nature, the environment, recreation, regional news, science, technology, self-help, social issues, sports, and travel.
Depts/columns: Word lengths vary. Family finances, family issues, news, events, and health.

Sample Issue
72 pages: 6 articles; 17 depts/columns; 1 special section. Guidelines and editorial calendar available.
- "But I Really Wanted a Girl." Article discusses how new mothers can cope with the disappointment of not having the gender they had hoped for.
- "All Mothers Work." Article maintains that all mothers work hard to be the best parents they can be, whether they bring home a paycheck or not.
- Sample dept/column: "Ages 0–5" examines the latest medical information about circumcision to help parents make this decision.

Rights and Payment
First and electronic rights. Written material, $50–$75. Pays on publication.

Editor's Comments
We welcome submissions from freelancers with regionally oriented information and resources.

Catholic Digest

1 Montauk Avenue, Suite 200
New London, CT 06320

Assistant Editor: Kerry Weber

Description and Interests
This information-filled digest runs the article gamut from family life and praying, to global social situations and personal experiences. Its emphasis is on how spirituality can positively affect every aspect of a person's life and why it is needed.
- **Audience:** Adults
- **Frequency:** Monthly
- **Distribution:** 92% subscription; 8% other
- **Circulation:** 350,000
- **Website: www.catholicdigest.com**

Freelance Potential
44% written by nonstaff writers. Publishes 100–200 freelance submissions yearly; 12% by new authors. Receives 4,800 unsolicited mss monthly.

Submissions
Send complete ms. Accepts hard copy, disk submissions, and email submissions to cdsubmissions@bayard-inc.com. No simultaneous submissions. SASE. Responds in 6–8 weeks.
Articles: 1,000–3,500 words. Informational articles; profiles; and personal experience pieces. Topics include religion, prayer, spirituality, relationships, family issues, history, science, and nostalgia.
Depts/columns: 50–500 words. True stories about faith, spotlights of community organizations, and profiles of volunteers.
Other: Filler, to 500 words.

Sample Issue
128 pages (13% advertising): 6 articles; 15 depts/columns. Sample copy, free with 6x9 SASE ($1 postage). Guidelines available.
- "I Don't Take Care of Myself." Article offers tips for caregivers seeking time for themselves.
- "Medicine for Humanity." Article reports on how this organization improves women's health worldwide.
- Sample dept/column: "Excursions" takes the reader to find Quebec's romantic spirit.

Rights and Payment
One-time rights. Articles, $100–$400. Depts/columns, $2 per published line. Pays on publication. Provides 2 contributor's copies.

Editor's Comments
We would like to see more narrative journalism-style articles that tell engaging and uplifting stories about real people, real struggles, and real life choices.

Catholic Forester

P.O. Box 3012
335 Shuman Boulevard
Naperville, IL 60566-7012

Associate Editor: Patricia Baron

Description and Interests
Published for members of the Catholic Order of
Foresters, this magazine includes articles that inform,
educate, and entertain its readers, as well as informa-
tion about the organization and its members. The
audience ranges from teenagers to seniors.
• **Audience:** Catholic Forester members
• **Frequency:** Quarterly
• **Distribution:** 100% controlled
• **Circulation:** 100,000
• **Website:** www.catholicforester.com

Freelance Potential
20% written by nonstaff writers. Publishes 4–8 freelance submissions yearly; 5% by unpublished writers,
20% by authors who are new to the magazine.
Receives 240 unsolicited mss yearly.

Submissions
Send complete ms. Accepts hard copy. SASE.
Responds in 3–4 months.
Articles: 1,000 words. Informational and inspirational
articles. Topics include money management,
fitness, health, family life, investing, senior issues,
careers, parenting, and nostalgia.
Fiction: 1,000 words. Topics include inspirational,
humorous, and light fiction.
Other: Cartoons.

Sample Issue
39 pages (no advertising): 8 articles; 2 activities;
5 depts/columns. Sample copy, free with 9x12 SASE
(3 first-class stamps). Guidelines available.
• "Members Aid Hurricane Katrina Victims." Article profiles Forester groups around the country that helped
  after Katrina hit the Gulf Coast.
• "Nourishing Messages." Article connects how young
  girls see themselves with their behavior.
• Sample dept/column: "Spiritual" relates a bishop's
  most valued experiences.

Rights and Payment
First North American serial rights. Written material,
$.30 per word. Reprints, $50. Cartoons, one-time
rights, $30. Pays on acceptance. Provides 3 contribu-
tor's copies.

Editor's Comments
We would like to see more articles on health and
finance, and also like to include humor, light fiction,
or a good children's story.

Catholic Library World

100 North Street, Suite 224
Pittsfield, MA 01201-5109

Editor: Mary E. Gallagher, SSJ

Description and Interests
Anyone interested in books and library science will
find a wealth of book reviews in this magazine, the
official publication of the Catholic Library Association.
Material also includes information pertinent to librari-
ans and Catholic researchers.
• **Audience:** Adults
• **Frequency:** Quarterly
• **Distribution:** 99% subscription; 1% other
• **Circulation:** 1,100
• **Website:** www.cathla.org

Freelance Potential
25% written by nonstaff writers. Publishes 12 freelance submissions yearly. Receives 12 queries and
unsolicited mss yearly.

Submissions
Query or send complete ms. Accepts hard copy and
email submissions to cla@cathla.org (Microsoft Word
attachments). SASE. Response time varies.
Articles: Word lengths vary. Informational articles and
reviews. Topics include books, reading, library science, and Catholic Library Association news.
Reviews: 150–300 words. Topics include theology,
spirituality, pastoral issues, church history, education,
history, literature, library science, philosophy, and reference; children's and young adult topics include biography, fiction, multicultural issues, picture books, reference, science, social studies, and values.
Artwork: B/W and color prints and transparencies.
Line art.

Sample Issue
186 pages (2% advertising): 4 articles; 154 book
reviews; 1 media review; 4 depts/columns. Sample
copy, $15. Reviewers' guidelines available.
• "A Journey Through the World of Happy Middle
  School Literature." Article discusses how middle
  school literature deals with teenage problems.
• "Navigating the Labyrinth: Understanding and Getting
  the Most from Catholic Archives." Article shows how
  historians can best use religious records.

Rights and Payment
Rights vary. No payment. Provides 1 author's copy.

Editor's Comments
Submitted articles can pertain to libraries, librarianship, literature genres, and how to use libraries efficiently. Reviews of all books follow our guidelines.

Celebrate

6401 The Paseo
Kansas City, MO 64131

Submissions: Denise Willemin

Description and Interests
The uplifting Bible-influenced material in *Celebrate* ties together stories, activities, and poetry to provide an in-depth message for its young readers. The information also shows how the lessons apply to contemporary life.
- **Audience:** 3–6 years
- **Frequency:** Weekly
- **Distribution:** 100% subscription
- **Circulation:** 40,000
- **Website:** www.wordaction.com

Freelance Potential
40% written by nonstaff writers. Publishes 50 freelance submissions yearly; 30% by unpublished writers, 35% by authors who are new to the magazine. Receives 120 queries yearly.

Submissions
Query. Accepts hard copy and email queries to dwillemin@nazerene.org (Microsoft Word attachments). SASE. Responds in 2–4 weeks.
Other: Poetry, 4–8 lines. Bible stories, songs, finger plays, action rhymes, crafts, activities, and recipes.

Sample Issue
4 pages (no advertising): 2 Bible stories; 1 poem; 1 recipe; 2 activities. Sample copy, free with #10 SASE (1 first-class stamp). Writers' guidelines and theme list available.
- "God's Power When It Didn't Rain." Bible story retells the story of Elijah, whom God used as a messenger to King Ahab.
- "Food and Water for Elijah." Bible story demonstrates to the reader how God took care of Elijah while he was punishing others for neglecting God.
- "Orange Cup Bird Feeders." Activity explains how to make a bird feeder out of an orange, and ties the activity to the story of Elijah.

Rights and Payment
Rights vary. All material, payment rates and payment policy vary.

Editor's Comments
Writers should base all of their submissions on our theme lists, which correspond to the Sunday school curriculum published by WordAction. Use simple language appropriate for preschoolers, and show how character is developed by applying scriptural lessons.

Central Penn Parent

101 North Second Street, 2nd Floor
Harrisburg, PA 17101

Editor: Karren Johnson

Description and Interests
This tabloid recently celebrated its 10-year anniversary. Targeting parents in Pennsylvania's Cumberland, Dawson, Lancaster, and York counties, it covers regional activities and resources, while also addressing contemporary parenting concerns.
- **Audience:** Parents
- **Frequency:** Monthly
- **Distribution:** 100% controlled
- **Circulation:** 35,000
- **Website:** www.centralpennparent.com

Freelance Potential
50% written by nonstaff writers. Publishes 10 freelance submissions yearly; 20% by unpublished writers, 10% by authors who are new to the magazine. Receives 96 queries yearly.

Submissions
All articles are assigned to local writers. Query for reprints only. Accepts email queries to karrenm@journalpub.com. Availability of artwork improves chance of acceptance. Responds in 2 weeks.
Articles: 1,200–1,500 words. Informational articles and reviews. Topics include local family events and activities, health, nutrition, discipline, education, home life, technology, literature, parenting issues, and travel.
Depts/columns: 700 words. Family finances, health, infant issues, news, and education.
Artwork: Color prints and transparencies. Line art.
Other: Submit seasonal material at least 2 months in advance.

Sample Issue
48 pages (50% advertising): 2 articles; 12 depts/columns; 1 calendar; 1 resource list. Sample copy, free. Guidelines available.
- "Come One, Come All." Article features a list of do's and don'ts for planning children's parties.
- Sample dept/column: "House & Home" provides important information on trampoline safety.

Rights and Payment
All rights. Reprints, $35–$50. Pays on publication. Provides contributor's copies upon request.

Editor's Comments
We strongly prefer writing by people who live in the counties we serve. Otherwise, we will consider queries for reprints.

Characters

Kids' Short Story Outlet

P.O. Box 708
Newport, NH 03773

Editor: Cindy Davis

Description and Interests
This colorful magazine provides a variety of fantastic and realistic short stories to stimulate young readers' imaginations. Fiction from writers of all ages is welcome, but preference is given to work created by children and teens.
• **Audience:** 8–18 years
• **Frequency:** Quarterly
• **Distribution:** 100% subscription
• **Circulation:** Unavailable
• **Website: www.cdavisnh.com**

Freelance Potential
100% written by nonstaff writers. Publishes 44 freelance submissions yearly; 75% by unpublished writers, 50% by authors who are new to the magazine. Receives 420 unsolicited mss yearly.

Submissions
Send complete ms with short biography. Accepts email submissions to hotdog@nhvt.net (no attachments) and simultaneous submissions if identified. Responds in 2–4 weeks.
Fiction: To 2,000 words. Contemporary and historical fiction, mystery, humor, adventure, Westerns, romance, fantasy, nature and animal stories, and science fiction.

Sample Issue
44 pages: 11 stories. Sample copy, $5.75. Writers' guidelines available.
• "The Search." Story tells of a child's optimistic hunt for a helpful dinosaur when the teacher suggests that he use a thesaurus.
• "Of Porcupines and Pincushions." Story depicts a lesson revealed to a mischievous boy by animals in the wild.
• "Professor Knowsall." Story creates a whimsical dialogue between a lazy student and a computer with a mind of its own.

Rights and Payment
One-time and electronic rights. Written material, $5. Pays on publication. Provides 1 contributor's copy.

Editor's Comments
We welcome submissions from kids and from adults writing from the point of view and with the vocabulary of a child. We receive many talking-animal stories, but we rarely publish them. We would like to see more adventure and fantasy instead.

Charlotte Parent

2125 South End Drive, Suite 253
Charlotte, NC 28230

Editor: Eve White

Description and Interests
Serving a seven-county area around Charlotte, North Carolina, this magazine targets parents, teachers, child-care providers, and other child advocates.
• **Audience:** Parents
• **Frequency:** Monthly
• **Distribution:** 54% controlled; 35% schools; 10% libraries; 1% subscription
• **Circulation:** 55,000
• **Website: www.charlotteparent.com**

Freelance Potential
75% written by nonstaff writers. Publishes 60 freelance submissions yearly; 15% by unpublished writers, 25% by authors who are new to the magazine. Receives 300 queries, 600 unsolicited mss yearly.

Submissions
Query or send complete ms with résumé and bibliography. Prefers email to editor@charlotteparent.com. Accepts hard copy, Macintosh disk submissions, and simultaneous submissions if identified. SASE. Responds if interested.
Articles: 500–1,000 words. Informational and how-to articles. Topics include parenting, family life, finances, education, health, fitness, vacations, entertainment, regional activities, and the environment.
Depts/columns: Word lengths vary. Restaurant and media reviews; children's health; ages and stages.
Artwork: High-density Macintosh format artwork.
Other: Activities. Submit seasonal material 2–3 months in advance.

Sample Issue
96 pages (35% advertising): 8 articles; 13 depts/columns; 1 calendar; 1 directory. Sample copy, free with 9x12 SASE (5 first-class stamps). Guidelines and editorial calendar available.
• "Welcome to Holland!" Article explains how parents of children with special needs learn to accept and adjust to their children's disabilities.
• Sample dept/column: "Changing Families" deals with the challenges of finding summer child care.

Rights and Payment
First and Internet rights. Written material, payment rates vary. Pays on publication. Provides 1 copy.

Editor's Comments
Each issue includes several articles related to a theme. Submissions from freelancers are welcome.

Cheat Codes Magazine

15850 Dallas Parkway
Dallas, TX 75248

Editor: Doug Kale

Description and Interests
Cheat Codes Magazine is devoted to video game and cheat code tips, tricks, and reviews. Fantasy, Ninja, Grand Theft Auto, Super Mario Bros., Tomb Raider, The Godfather, and crime-related video games and cheat codes are covered.
- **Audience:** YA–Adult
- **Frequency:** 6 times each year
- **Distribution:** Unavailable
- **Circulation:** 75,000
- **Website:** www.beckettspotlight.com

Freelance Potential
25% written by nonstaff writers. Publishes 20 freelance submissions yearly; 20% by unpublished writers, 75% by authors who are new to the magazine.

Submissions
Query with résumé and related experience. Accepts hard copy. SASE.
Articles: Word lengths vary. Informational and how-to articles; personal experience pieces; and reviews. Topics include tips and tricks for cheat codes and video games, and game reviews.
Depts/columns: Word lengths vary. Contests, reader surveys, and video game price guides.

Sample Issue
80 pages: 11 articles; 4 depts/columns. Guidelines available via email to spotlight@beckett.com.
- "The Elder Scrolls IV: Oblivion." Article offers cheats and tips for this hot new game for PC and X360.
- "The Year of Final Fantasy." Article features reviews and previews of Dirge of Cerebrus, FFXII, and FFXIII, and FFIII---the hottest final fantasy games of 2006 and 2007.
- "New Super Mario Bros." Article discusses the new-fangled version of this classic game as well as the best cheats to use for this revised version.

Rights and Payment
All rights. Written material, payment rates vary. Pays 45 days after publication. Provides 2 contributor's copies.

Editor's Comments
Writers who have a great deal of video game and cheat code experience and knowledge are welcome to query. Writing needs to appeal to the young adult to adult age groups. Please take a look at an issue of *Cheat Codes* to get a feel for our style and focus.

ChemMatters

American Chemical Society
1155 16th Street NW
Washington, DC 20036

Editor: Kevin McCue

Description and Interests
This magazine from the Education Division of the American Chemical Society presents interesting, informative, and accurate information for teens who are taking introductory chemistry courses in high school.
- **Audience:** 14–18 years
- **Frequency:** 5 times each year
- **Distribution:** 80% schools; 20% subscription
- **Circulation:** 40,000
- **Website:** www.chemistry.org/education/chemmatters.html

Freelance Potential
90% written by nonstaff writers. Publishes 2 freelance submissions yearly; 10% by unpublished writers, 90% by authors who are new to the magazine. Receives 10–12 queries yearly.

Submissions
Query with abstract, outline, or related material that conveys the scientific content, and a writing sample. Prefers email queries to chemmatters@acs.org. Accepts hard copy. SASE. Responds in 5 days.
Articles: 1,400–2,100 words. Informational articles. Topics include chemistry, the human body, current events, food, and history.
Depts/columns: 1,400–2,100 words. "ChemSumer" reports on new products for teens and explains their chemistry. "Mystery Matters" explains how forensic chemistry solves crimes.
Artwork: JPEG or GIF line art.
Other: Chemistry oriented puzzles and activities.

Sample Issue
18 pages (no advertising): 3 articles; 3 depts/columns. Sample copy available at website. Guidelines and theme list available by email to chemmatters@acs.org.
- "Einstein's Miraculous Year." Article describes the scientist's work on the photoelectric effect.
- "Secrets of the Samurai Sword Revealed." Article discusses the chemical processes involved in making samurai swords.

Rights and Payment
All rights. Articles, $500–$1,000. Pays on acceptance. Provides 5 contributor's copies.

Editor's Comments
We try to meet students on their own terms with articles that are relevant to their interests.

Chesapeake Family

929 West Street, Suite 307
Annapolis, MD 21401

Editor: Susan Jenkins

Description and Interests
A mix of articles and information on parenting topics, resources, and events can be found in this regional publication. It is distributed free to parents of school-aged children residing in the Chesapeake Bay area.
- **Audience:** Parents
- **Frequency:** Monthly
- **Distribution:** 55% schools; 15% newsstand; 5% subscription; 25% other
- **Circulation:** 40,000
- **Website:** www.chesapeakefamily.com

Freelance Potential
80% written by nonstaff writers. Publishes 20 freelance submissions yearly; 10% by new authors. Receives 240 unsolicited mss yearly.

Submissions
Send complete ms. Accepts hard copy. SASE. Response time varies.
Articles: 1,000–1,200 words. Informational and how-to articles; and profiles. Topics include parenting, the environment, music, regional news, current events, education, entertainment, health, and family travel destinations.
Fiction: "Just for Kids" features stories and poems by local 4- to 17-year-old children.
Depts/columns: 700–900 words. Education, child development, and health.
Other: Submit seasonal material 3–6 months in advance.

Sample Issue
56 pages (45% advertising): 3 articles; 9 depts/columns. Guidelines and editorial calendar available.
- "Balti*MORE* Hot Spots for Families." Article takes a look at family-friendly locations in Baltimore.
- "Your Child's First Dentist Visit." Article offers suggestions for making a child's debut at the dentist a successful one.
- Sample dept/column: "Children's Health" offers information on life jackets and swaddling and sleep.

Rights and Payment
Geographic print rights; electronic rights negotiable. Features, $75–$110. Depts/columns, $50. Reprints, $35. Payment policy varies.

Editor's Comments
We accept material from published writers only, and we prefer that they be local.

Chess Life

P.O. Box 3967
Crossville, TN 38557-3967

Editor: Daniel Lucas

Description and Interests
Chess enthusiasts of all levels subscribe to this magazine, which describes itself as "the world's most widely read chess magazine." Its articles cover tournaments and other chess events, strategies, players, and the history of the game.
- **Audience:** YA–Adult
- **Frequency:** Monthly
- **Distribution:** 90% subscription; 10% newsstand
- **Circulation:** 60,000–80,000
- **Website:** www.uschess.org

Freelance Potential
75% written by nonstaff writers. Publishes 30 freelance submissions yearly; 30% by unpublished writers. Receives 180–420 queries yearly.

Submissions
Query with clips or writing samples. Accepts hard copy and email queries to dlucas@uschess.org. SASE. Responds in 1–3 months.
Articles: 800–3,000 words. Informational, how-to, and historical articles; personal experience and opinion pieces; profiles; and humor. Topics include chess games and strategies, tournaments and events, and personalities.
Depts/columns: To 1,000 words. Book and product reviews, short how-to's, and player profiles.
Other: Chess oriented cartoons, contests, and games.

Sample Issue
80 pages (16% advertising): 5 articles; 10 depts/columns. Sample copy, free with 9x12 SASE. Writers' guidelines available.
- "The Morphy of the North." Article profiles Harry Nelson Pillsbury, a chess genius who died at the age of 33 in the year 1906.
- "Alex the Invincible." Article interviews Alexander Onischuk, who became a grandmaster at 18 and recently moved to the U.S. from Russia.
- Sample dept/column: "Back to Basics" describes strategies for setting up an attack.

Rights and Payment
All rights. Written material, $100 per page. Kill fee, 30%. Pays on publication. Provides 2 author's copies.

Editor's Comments
The best opportunity for freelancers is to submit an article about "chess in everyday life" or a piece about a relatively unknown chess player.

Chess Life for Kids   Chicago Parent

P.O. Box 3967
Crossville, TN 38577

Editor: Glenn Petersen

Description and Interests
Targeted to scholastic members of the U.S. Chess Federation only, this magazine includes articles on chess instruction, tournament participation and upcoming tournament information, chess camps, and related activities.
- **Audience:** 12 years and under
- **Frequency:** 6 times each year
- **Distribution:** 100% controlled
- **Circulation:** 14,200
- **Website:** www.uschess.org

Freelance Potential
58% written by nonstaff writers. Publishes 45 freelance submissions yearly; 10% by unpublished writers, 10% by authors who are new to the magazine. Receives several queries and unsolicited mss yearly.

Submissions
Query or send complete ms. Accepts email submissions to gpetersen@uschess.org and simultaneous submission if identified. Responds in 2 weeks.
Articles: To 1,000 words. Informational and instructional articles; and profiles. Topics include chess instruction and tips, tournaments, and chess camps and lessons.

Sample Issue
24 pages: 12 articles.
- "Our Heritage." Article profiles Harry Nelson Pillsbury, one of the five greatest chess players in American history.
- "The Art of Chess." Article outlines several tactical tricks to add to a player's arsenal of skills.
- "Queen City Classic." Article recounts the events surrounding the Fifth Annual Cris Collinsworth ProScan Foundation Queen City Classic tournament, which took place April 1, 2006.

Rights and Payment
First North American serial rights. Written material, $75 per page. Pays on publication.

Editor's Comments
We are looking for more articles on chess instruction and tournament participation and information, but there is also room for articles on chess camps and similar activities. Remember, our readers are 12 and under, so please use words appropriate and understandable for this age group. It is advisable to read an issue of our magazine to get a sense of our style.

141 South Oak Park Avenue
Chicago, IL 60302

Editor: Susy Schultz

Description and Interests
Issues important to all aspects of family life are found in this publication that focuses on local people and events. The tone is one of "we're all in this together."
- **Audience:** Parents
- **Frequency:** Monthly
- **Distribution:** 90% controlled; 10% subscription
- **Circulation:** 138,000
- **Website:** www.chicagoparent.com

Freelance Potential
75% written by nonstaff writers. Publishes 50 freelance submissions yearly; 20% by unpublished writers, 20% by authors who are new to the magazine. Receives 480–540 queries yearly.

Submissions
Query with résumé and clips. Accepts hard copy and email queries to chiparent@chicagoparent.com. SASE. Responds in 6 weeks.
Articles: 1,500–2,500 words. Informational articles and profiles. Topics include local resources, regional events, parenting, grandparenting, maternity, foster care, child development, adoption, day care, careers, education, and family issues.
Depts/columns: 850 words. Opinion pieces, children's health, media reviews, travel, and fathering.
Other: Submit seasonal material 2 months in advance.

Sample Issue
108 pages (60% advertising): 14 articles; 16 depts/columns. Sample copy, $3.95. Guidelines and editorial calendar available.
- "The Kindergarten Crush." Article assures parents they don't need to worry about this innocent situation.
- "Can You Still Be Romantic After Kids?" Article offers tips to help parents become a couple again.
- Sample dept/column: "Spotlight" looks at special needs resources available.

Rights and Payment
One-time and Illinois exclusive rights. Articles, $125–$350. Depts/columns, $25–$100. Kill fee, 10%. Pays on publication. Provides contributor's copies upon request.

Editor's Comments
We like to include new voices in our publication and ask first-time writers to pitch an idea for our department "Short Stuff," our point of entry for new authors.

Child

Meredith Corporation
375 Lexington Avenue, 9th Floor
New York, NY 10017-4024

Submissions Editor

Description and Interests
Child helps readers meet the challenges of parenthood by presenting the latest information on topics such as health, safety, education, and nutrition. Articles also address the needs of moms by providing beauty and fashion advice and tips for staying healthy and fit.
• **Audience:** Parents
• **Frequency:** 10 times each year
• **Distribution:** 92% subscription; 8% newsstand
• **Circulation:** 825,000
• **Website: www.child.com**

Freelance Potential
70% written by nonstaff writers. Publishes 50 freelance submissions yearly; 10% by unpublished writers, 30% by authors who are new to the magazine. Receives 1,800 queries yearly.

Submissions
Query with published clips. Accepts hard copy. SASE. Responds in 2 months.
Articles: Word lengths vary. Informational and how-to articles; profiles; interviews; and personal experience pieces. Topics include pets, computers, crafts, hobbies, current events, gifted and special education, health, fitness, popular culture, science, sports, travel, fashion, and lifestyles.
Depts/columns: Word lengths vary. Food, nutrition, media reviews, safety, beauty, and dining out.
Other: Submit seasonal material 6–8 months in advance.

Sample Issue
160 pages (47% advertising): 12 articles; 18 depts/columns. Sample copy, $3.50 at newsstands. Guidelines and editorial calendar available.
• "How to Raise an Adventurous Eater." Article offers tips for getting kids to enjoy a variety of tastes.
• Sample dept/column: "Learning" reports on the innovative methods schools are using to teach young children to be active in their communities.

Rights and Payment
First rights for features; all rights for columns. Written material, payment rates vary. Pays on acceptance. Provides contributor's copies.

Editor's Comments
We will consider queries from published writers only on parenting, marital relationships, and children's health, behavior, and development.

Child Care Information Exchange

P.O. Box 3249
Redmond, WA 98073-3249

Editor: Bonnie Neugebauer

Description and Interests
Practical articles focusing on managing child-care centers, solutions to problems, social issues, and events related to the industry fill the pages of this publication for early childhood care professionals.
• **Audience:** Child-care professionals
• **Frequency:** 6 times each year
• **Distribution:** 100% subscription
• **Circulation:** 26,000
• **Website: www.childcareexchange.com**

Freelance Potential
65–75% written by nonstaff writers. Publishes 75 freelance submissions yearly; 50% by unpublished writers, 60% by authors who are new to the magazine. Receives 144 queries yearly.

Submissions
Query with outline and writing samples. Accepts hard copy. SASE. Responds in 1 week.
Articles: 1,500 words. Informational, practical application, how-to, and self-help articles. Topics include education, current events, multicultural and ethnic subjects, and social issues.
Depts/columns: Word lengths vary. Infant and toddler care, staff training and development, and parent perspectives.

Sample Issue
96 pages: 16 articles; 8 depts/columns. Sample copy, $8. Guidelines and theme list available.
• "State Standards for Children's Learning." Article explains what early learning standards are and what they mean for child-care providers.
• "Making Sense of Germ Control to Stay Healthy." Article offers tips to prevent and control infectious diseases and suggests ways to stay healthy.
• Sample dept/column: "Untangling the Tentacles of Commercialism" offers ideas for resisting commercialism and teaching children to think about what they really want.

Rights and Payment
All rights. Articles, $300. Other material, payment rates vary. Pays on publication. Provides 2 contributor's copies.

Editor's Comments
Articles informing child-care professionals of positive management techniques, social issues and solutions, and current trends in the field are always of interest.

Childhood Education

Association for Childhood Education International

17904 Georgia Avenue, Suite 215
Olney, MD 20832

Editor: Anne W. Bauer

Description and Interests
Professional educators and parents who are concerned with the education of children from infancy through adolescence are the target audience of this magazine.
- **Audience:** Educators; child-care professionals; parents
- **Frequency:** 6 times each year
- **Distribution:** 100% controlled
- **Circulation:** 10,000
- **Website:** www.acei.org

Freelance Potential
98% written by nonstaff writers. Publishes 40 freelance submissions yearly; 75% by authors who are new to the magazine. Receives 120 unsolicited mss each year.

Submissions
Send 4 copies of complete ms. Accepts hard copy and Macintosh or IBM disk submissions. SASE. Responds in 3 months.
Articles: 1,400–3,500 words. Informational articles. Topics include innovative teaching strategies, the teaching profession, research findings, parenting and family issues, communities, drug education, and safe environments for children.
Depts/columns: 1,000 words. Reviews of books for children, Spanish books; discussions of issues in education; topics for parents.

Sample Issue
62 pages (15% advertising): 5 articles; 10 depts/columns. Sample copy, free with 9x12 SASE (3 first-class stamps). Writers' guidelines and editorial calendar available.
- "Healing Words, Healing Hearts." Article explores how children's literature can be used to cope with the loss of a pet.
- Sample dept/column: "For Parents Particularly" discusses using music and movement to stimulate young children's interest in learning.

Rights and Payment
All rights. No payment. Provides 5 author's copies.

Editor's Comments
Ours is a professional journal that seeks to stimulate thinking rather than advocate fixed practice. We explore emerging ideas and present conflicting opinions that are supported by research.

Children and Families

1651 Prince Street
Alexandria, VA 22310

Editor: Julie Konieczny

Description and Interests
The goal of this magazine from the National Head Start Association is to provide expert advice to early childhood professionals. Topics covered include early childhood development, health and safety, parental involvement, classroom management, and leadership.
- **Audience:** Early childhood professionals
- **Frequency:** Quarterly
- **Distribution:** 90% subscription; 10% other
- **Circulation:** 15,000
- **Website:** www.nhsa.org

Freelance Potential
90% written by nonstaff writers. Publishes 25 freelance submissions yearly; 70% by unpublished writers, 70% by authors who are new to the magazine. Receives 24 queries yearly.

Submissions
Query with outline and possible sidebar information. Accepts email queries to julie@nhsa.org. Responds in 1–12 weeks.
Articles: 1,600–4,000 words. Informational and how-to articles. Topics include computers, gifted and special education, health, fitness, mathematics, multicultural issues, music, science, and technology.
Depts/columns: Word lengths vary. News, science lessons, learning styles and development.
Artwork: Color prints or transparencies.
Other: Jokes about young children. Submit seasonal material 4 months in advance.

Sample Issue
76 pages (25% advertising): 5 articles; 7 depts/columns. Guidelines and theme list available.
- "The Heart of Quality Care." Article serves as a reminder to administrators that their staff of child-care workers should be valued and nurtured.
- "College Coursework Is Only the Beginning." Article explores ways teachers can put the skills they learn in training classes into everyday practice.
- Sample dept/column: "How Children Learn" reviews early childhood programs in Brazil.

Rights and Payment
First rights. No payment. Provides 2+ author's copies.

Editor's Comments
In your query letter, clearly state what you are trying to teach or convey to early childhood professionals, and tell us how they will benefit from your article.

Children's Advocate Newsmagazine

Action Alliance for Children
1201 Martin Luther King Jr. Way
Oakland, CA 94612-1217

Editor: Jean Tepperman

Description and Interests

Readers of this magazine seek to influence public policy in the state of California on issues that affect young children. It targets parents and professionals involved in legislative advocacy and community organizing. It appears in both English and Spanish.
- **Audience:** Children's advocates
- **Frequency:** 6 times each year
- **Distribution:** 50% newsstand; 30% subscription; 20% controlled
- **Circulation:** 15,000
- **Website:** www.4children.org

Freelance Potential

40% written by nonstaff writers. Publishes 18 freelance submissions yearly. Receives few queries yearly.

Submissions

All articles are assigned. Send résumé with clips or writing samples. Accepts hard copy. SASE. Responds in 1 month.
Articles: 500–1,500 words. Informational articles; program descriptions; policy analysis pieces; and how-to articles. Topics include families, foster care, child care, education, child welfare, violence prevention, health, nutrition, poverty, and mental health.
Depts/columns: Short news items, 300–500 words. Public policy analysis, 500–1,100 words. Book reviews, word lengths vary.

Sample Issue

16 pages (4% advertising): 7 articles; 3 depts/columns. Sample copy, $3. Guidelines available.
- "An Environment Where Parents Feel Comfortable." Article showcases preschool programs that welcome immigrant parent involvement.
- "It's OK to Talk About It." Article tells how open communication can help kids develop healthy attitudes toward race.
- Sample dept/column: "Children's Advocates Roundtable" features updates on legislative issues.

Rights and Payment

First North American serial rights. Written material, to $.25 per word. Pays on acceptance. Provides 3 contributor's copies.

Editor's Comments

While we prefer to use our own group of writers, we will consider submissions from writers who are up to date on the issues we cover.

Children's Digest

Children's Better Health Institute
1100 Waterway Boulevard
Indianapolis, IN 46202

Editor: Patrick Perry

Description and Interests

This magazine for pre-teens offers information on science, fitness, and safety in a fun and colorful format. Activities and puzzles are included in each issue.
- **Audience:** 10–12 years
- **Frequency:** 6 times each year
- **Distribution:** 100% subscription
- **Circulation:** 60,000
- **Website:** www.childrensdigestmag.org

Freelance Potential

10% written by nonstaff writers. Publishes 30 freelance submissions yearly; 70% by unpublished writers. Receives 1,200 queries yearly.

Submissions

Query only. No unsolicited mss. Accepts hard copy and email queries to p.rasdall@chdl.org. SASE. Responds in 3 months.
Articles: To 1,200 words. Informational and how-to articles; profiles; interviews; and personal experience pieces. Topics include health, exercise, safety, hygiene, drug education, and nutrition.
Fiction: To 1,500 words. Genres include multicultural and ethnic fiction, science fiction, fantasy, adventure, mystery, humor, and stories about animals and sports.
Depts/columns: To 1,200 words. Book reviews, recipes, and information about personal health.
Other: Puzzles, games, and activities. Poetry, to 25 lines. Submit seasonal material 8 months in advance.

Sample Issue

36 pages (6% advertising): 1 article; 1 story; 3 depts/columns; 7 activities; 7 book reviews. Sample copy, $1.25 with 9x12 SASE. Guidelines available.
- "Book Your Flight." Article tells how books can take readers to exotic destinations and experiences.
- "Vile Verses." Article reviews a book of poems written by Roald Dahl.
- "What's My Number?" Activity asks readers to answer number questions.

Rights and Payment

All rights. Written material, $.12 per word. Pays prior to publication. Provides 10 contributor's copies.

Editor's Comments

We have a constant need for high-quality stories, articles, and activities with health-related themes. Profiles of athletes are of special interest.

Children's Ministry

1515 Cascade Avenue
Loveland, CO 80538

Associate Editor: Carmen Kamrath

Description and Interests
Success stories, problem solving articles, and personal growth aids fill this publication with resource material for people who serve children in the church.
- **Audience:** Children's ministry leaders; volunteers
- **Frequency:** 6 times each year
- **Distribution:** Subscription; other
- **Circulation:** 90,000
- **Website:** www.cmmag.com

Freelance Potential
60–65% written by nonstaff writers. Publishes 150 freelance submissions yearly; 30% by unpublished writers, 30% by authors who are new to the magazine. Receives 2,400 queries and unsolicited mss each year.

Submissions
Query or send complete ms. Prefers email submissions to ckamrath@cmmag.com. Accepts hard copy. SASE. Responds in 2–3 months.
Articles: 500–1,700 words. Informational and how-to articles; and personal experience pieces. Topics include Christian education, family issues, child development, and faith.
Depts/columns: 50–300 words. Educational issues, activities, devotionals, family ministry, parenting, crafts, and resources.
Other: Activities, games, and tips. Submit seasonal material 6–8 months in advance.

Sample Issue
170 pages (50% advertising): 11 articles; 17 depts/columns. Sample copy, $2 with 9x12 SASE. Writers' guidelines available.
- "Why Johnny Won't Come to Sunday School." Article examines how to help include children that struggle with reading.
- "Media-Driven Ministry." Article explores how high-tech media can create high-touch ministry.
- Sample dept/column: "Age-Level Insights" provides tips for helping different aged children cope in life.

Rights and Payment
All rights. Articles, to $350. Depts/columns, $40–$75. Pays on acceptance. Provides 1 contributor's copy.

Editor's Comments
We are seeking practical articles that cover topics such as working with volunteers, disciplining children, and communicating with children about faith and morals.

Children's Playmate

Children's Better Health Institute
1100 Waterway Boulevard
P.O. Box 567
Indianapolis, IN 46206-0567

Editor: Terry Harshman

Description and Interests
Children's Playmate features entertaining and educational stories, poems, activities, and articles for young readers. Published by the Children's Better Health Institute, this magazine emphasizes healthful living.
- **Audience:** 6–8 years
- **Frequency:** 6 times each year
- **Distribution:** 100% subscription
- **Circulation:** 80,000
- **Website:** www.childrensplaymatemag.org

Freelance Potential
25% written by nonstaff writers. Publishes 30 freelance submissions yearly; 10% by unpublished writers, 50% by authors who are new to the magazine. Receives 900 unsolicited mss yearly.

Submissions
Send complete ms. Accepts hard copy. SASE. Responds in 2–3 months.
Articles: To 500 words. Humorous and how-to articles. Topics include health, nature, fitness, the environment, science, hobbies, crafts, multicultural and ethnic issues, and sports.
Fiction: To 100 words. Rebus stories.
Other: Puzzles, activities, games, and recipes. Poetry, to 20 lines. Submit seasonal material about unusual holidays 8 months in advance.

Sample Issue
36 pages (no advertising): 3 stories; 2 depts/columns; 5 poems; 12 activities; 1 recipe. Sample copy, $1.75 with 9x12 SASE. Guidelines available.
- "Just Right." Story tells of a big bear that learns about friendship and sharing from a little bear.
- "The Tidal Pool." Article describes different sea creatures that live in a tidal pool.
- "One Silver Drop." Rebus follows a dew drop as it awakens bugs and insects on its pre-dawn journey.

Rights and Payment
All rights; returns book rights upon request. Written material, $.17 per word. Pays on publication. Provides up to 10 contributor's copies.

Editor's Comments
We seek material that is informative and fun for children ages six to eight. Articles, stories, and activities that relate to healthful living and safety are of interest to us. We also seek age-appropriate crafts, jokes, and recipes.

Children's Voice

440 First Street NE, 3rd Floor
Washington, DC 20001-2085

Managing Editor: Jennifer Michael

Description and Interests
This professional publication of the Child Welfare
League of America covers national, state, and local
events and trends that affect children, youth, and fam-
ilies. Its readers include child welfare agency execu-
tives, administrators, line workers, board members,
lay advocates, and volunteers.
• **Audience:** Child welfare professionals
• **Frequency:** 6 times each year
• **Distribution:** Subscription; membership
• **Circulation:** 25,000
• **Website: www.cwla.org/voice**

Freelance Potential
30% written by nonstaff writers. Publishes 10 freelance submissions yearly; 5% by unpublished writers,
10% by authors who are new to the magazine.
Receives 10 queries yearly.

Submissions
Query. Accepts email to voice@cwla.org (text only).
Availability of artwork improves chance of acceptance.
Responds in 1 week.
Articles: 1,500–3,000 words. Informational and how-
to articles; personal experience pieces; profiles; and
interviews. Topics include child welfare issues and
events, and agency programs.
Depts/columns: 200–500 words. Legislative updates;
agency and organization news.

Sample Issue
40 pages (20% advertising): 5 articles; 7 depts/
columns. Sample copy, $10. Guidelines available.
• "Calmness in an Age of Anxiety." Article suggests
  reassessing personal goals to achieve a better life.
• "Children Missing from Care." Article discusses how
  agencies respond to missing children.
• Sample dept/column: "Other Voices" offers an opinion on how to develop a truly equal education program for preschool children.

Rights and Payment
All rights. No payment. Provides contributor's copies
and a 1-year subscription.

Editor's Comments
We're looking for in-depth, timely information on
current child welfare issues. Although most of our
material is written by CWLA members, experts, and
professionals, we will consider material from freelance
sources.

Children's Writer

Institute of Children's Literature
95 Long Ridge Road
West Redding, CT 06896-1124

Editor: Susan Tierney

Description and Interests
Published professionals and aspiring children's writers
alike consult this newsletter for its information and
industry sources. Each issue offers articles on the
writing process and publishing trends, as well as mar-
ket reports.
• **Audience:** Children's writers
• **Frequency:** Monthly
• **Distribution:** 100% subscription
• **Circulation:** 14,000
• **Website: www.childrenswriter.com**

Freelance Potential
100% written by nonstaff writers. Publishes 75 freelance submissions yearly; 10% by unpublished writers,
15% by authors who are new to the magazine.
Receives 60+ queries yearly.

Submissions
Query with outline, synopsis, and résumé. Prefers
email queries through website. Accepts hard copy.
SASE. Responds in 2 months.
Articles: 1,500–2,000 words. Reports on children's
book and magazine publishing trends that feature
interviews with editors and writers. Topics include
industry trends, new markets, and publishers. Also
publishes features on writing technique, research,
motivation, and business issues.
Depts/columns: To 750 words, plus 125-word sidebar. Practical pieces about writing technique and
careers, insider tips, and children's publishing.

Sample Issue
12 pages (no advertising): 2 articles; 4 depts/
columns. Sample copy, free with #10 SASE (1 first-
class stamp). Writers' guidelines available with SASE
and at website.
• "Inner Journeys: Coming-of-Age Novels." Article discusses different definitions of coming-of-age novels
  and the common thread among them.
• Sample dept/column: "Commentary" discusses the
  sexual content in books for teenagers.

Rights and Payment
First North American serial rights. Articles, $135–
$350. Pays on acceptance.

Editor's Comments
We seek practical articles, helpful tips, and up-to-date
information that will guide writers in the writing
process and help them find places to sell their work.

Child Welfare Report

1439 Church Hill Street, Unit 302
Crystal Plaza
Waupaca, IL 54981

Editor: Mike Jacquart

Description and Interests
Published for professionals working with children and teenagers, this newsletter features practical and informative articles. Topics include special education, social issues, family life, and more.
- **Audience:** Child welfare professionals
- **Frequency:** Monthly
- **Distribution:** 100% subscription
- **Circulation:** 500
- **Website:** www.impact-publications.com

Freelance Potential
40% written by nonstaff writers. Publishes several freelance submissions yearly; 90% by authors who are new to the magazine. Receives 120+ queries each year.

Submissions
Query with outline. Accepts hard copy and IBM disk submissions (Microsoft Word). Availability of artwork improves chance of acceptance. SASE. Responds in 1 month.
Articles: Word lengths vary. Informational and how-to articles; personal experience and opinion pieces; interviews; and new product information. Topics include gifted and special education, disabilities, government programs, foster care, career choices, family life, parenting, psychology, mentoring, and multicultural and ethnic issues.

Sample Issue
8 pages (no advertising): 5 articles; 3 inserts; 1 resource page. Sample copy, $6.95 with #10 SASE (1 first-class stamp). Guidelines available.
- "Ten Tips for New Dads." Article lists ten tips for being a great dad.
- "Fetal Alcohol Children." Article explores the physical and behavioral characteristics of fetal alcohol syndrome and fetal alcohol effects.
- "Improving Children's Behavior." Article discusses two important phases for creating positive changes in children's behavior.

Rights and Payment
First rights. Written material, payment rates vary. Pays on publication. Provides 5 contributor's copies.

Editor's Comments
We currently seek material dealing with the mental health of children and teens. We look for submissions from professionals in the field of child welfare.

Christian Home & School

3350 East Paris Avenue SE
Grand Rapids, MI 48512-3054

Senior Editor: Roger Schmurr

Description and Interests
This magazine promotes Christian education and addresses a variety of parenting topics and issues that affect Christian parents.
- **Audience:** Parents
- **Frequency:** 6 times each year
- **Distribution:** 95% schools; 5% subscription
- **Circulation:** 66,000
- **Website:** www.csionline.org

Freelance Potential
75% written by nonstaff writers. Publishes 40–45 freelance submissions yearly; 10% by unpublished writers, 30% by authors who are new to the magazine. Receives 60 queries, 300 unsolicited mss yearly.

Submissions
Query or send complete ms. Accepts hard copy, email to rogers@csionline.org, and simultaneous submissions if identified. SASE. Responds in 7–10 days.
Articles: 1,000–2,000 words. Informational and how-to articles; and self-help and personal experience pieces. Topics include education, parenting, life skills, decision-making, self-control, discipline, family travel, faith, and social issues.
Fiction: Word lengths vary. Genres include fiction with Christian themes and Christmas stories.
Depts/columns: "Parentstuff," 100–250 words. Reviews and parenting tips, word lengths vary.

Sample Issue
32 pages (15% advertising): 5 articles; 10 stories; 17 book reviews. Sample copy, free with 9x12 SASE ($.87 postage). Guidelines available.
- "Catsup Isn't a Vegetable." Article offers ideas for getting kids to eat veggies.
- "Middle School Survival Guide." Article notes that starting middle school often requires a great adjustment on the part of students.
- Sample dept/column: "Profile" looks at a new school program that combines homeschooling with a traditional classroom experience.

Rights and Payment
First rights. Written material, $175–$250. "Parentstuff," $25–$40. Pays on publication. Provides 5 copies.

Editor's Comments
We are interested in articles about Christian schooling and the relationship of parents to Christian schools, as well as seasonal material.

The Christian Science Monitor

1 Norway Street
Boston, MA 02115

Kidspace and Home Forum Editor: Judy Lowe

Description and Interests
This newspaper includes "Home Forum," a section that publishes upbeat personal essays on varied topics and poetry that celebrates life. Its weekly "Kidspace" section offers high interest stories that entertain, empower, and educate kids.
- **Audience:** Adults and children, 7–12 years
- **Frequency:** Daily
- **Distribution:** 95% subscription; 5% newsstand
- **Circulation:** 80,000
- **Website:** www.csmonitor.com

Freelance Potential
90% written by nonstaff writers. Publishes 800 freelance submissions yearly; 20% by unpublished writers, 40% by authors who are new to the magazine. Receives 5,000 queries yearly.

Submissions
Query with résumé and clips. Send complete ms for "Home Forum." Accepts email to homeforum@csmonitor.com. Responds in 3 weeks if interested.
Articles: 700–900 words. Personal experience pieces and humor. Topics include gardening, travel, home and family, parenting, and food.
Artwork: Color negatives and slides; JPEG or PDF images.

Sample Issue
20 pages (15% advertising): 13 articles; 14 depts/columns. Guidelines available.
- "Can a Dad Ever Be the Epitome of 'Cool'?" Article shows how a father unwittingly becomes "cool" to his kids, without receiving proper credit.
- "I'd Like to Thank . . . Everyone." Article spoofs Academy Award acceptance speeches.
- "Hussein Admits Responsibility, Not Guilt." Article previews Saddam Hussein's probable trial defense strategy.

Rights and Payment
Exclusive rights. All material, payment rates vary. Pays on publication. Provides 1 contributor's copy.

Editor's Comments
We are interested in material that explores fresh individual solutions to a situation involving children, a unique personal slant on travel experiences, and poetry with global or cultural insights. We also want short pieces of 150–400 words for kids. Seasonal material is also welcome.

Christian Work at Home Moms

14607 Willow Creek Drive
Omaha, NE 68138

Editor: Jill Hart

Description and Interests
This is a privately owned and operated website designed to help visitors find and request information. It provides informative articles, job listings, business listings, resources, and encouragement for Christian parents who desire to work from home.
- **Audience:** Parents, ages 20–65
- **Frequency:** Weekly
- **Distribution:** 100% Internet
- **Hits per month:** 3,000+
- **Website:** www.cwahm.com

Freelance Potential
90% written by nonstaff writers. Publishes 30 freelance submissions yearly; 40% by unpublished writers, 10% by authors who are new to the magazine. Receives 50 unsolicited mss yearly.

Submissions
Send complete ms. Accepts submissions through website only. Response time varies.
Articles: Word lengths vary. Informational and how-to articles; personal experience pieces; profiles; and interviews. Topics include telecommuting, home business, marriage, parenting, spiritual growth, and homeschooling.

Sample Issue
Sample copy and guidelines available at website.
- "Become a Stay-at-Home Parent." Article details how to determine if working from home is a financial possibility.
- "How to Sell Your Crafts on eBay." Article tells how to successfully, and profitably, sell your projects over the Internet.
- "Organizing Your Home Office." Article addresses the challenge of maintaining an uncluttered office in order to work efficiently.

Rights and Payment
Electronic rights. No payment.

Editor's Comments
Our goal is to provide a network of Christian parents who work from home and who can help others achieve that goal. To that end, we are looking for articles and information on the resources available for our readers. Submissions can cover creative parenting articles, material that can deepen our readers' relationship with the Lord, and original ideas for homeschooling Christian students.

Church Educator

165 Plaza Drive
Prescott, AZ 86303

Editor: Linda Davidson

Description and Interests
The purpose of *Church Educator* is to offer Christian teachers and worship leaders practical, creative ideas for developing successful programs in mainline Protestant churches. Each issue includes sections that concentrate on ministry, worship, and leadership.
- **Audience:** Christian educators
- **Frequency:** Monthly
- **Distribution:** 100% subscription
- **Circulation:** 1,500
- **Website:** www.educationalministries.com

Freelance Potential
90% written by nonstaff writers. Publishes 85 free-lance submissions yearly; 10% by unpublished writers, 5% by authors who are new to the magazine. Receives 300 unsolicited mss yearly.

Submissions
Send complete ms. Accepts hard copy. SASE. Responds in 1 month.
Articles: 500–1,500 words. How-to articles. Topics include faith education, spirituality, and religion.
Depts/columns: Staff written.
Artwork: B/W prints and illustrations.
Other: Submit seasonal material about Advent, Christmas, Lent, Easter, and Pentecost 4 months in advance.

Sample Issue
40 pages (no advertising): 16 articles; 3 depts/columns. Sample copy, free with 9x12 SASE ($.83 postage). Guidelines and theme list available.
- "Noah Obeyed God." Article offers a plan for teaching the story of Noah's Ark to young children; includes ideas for props and follow-up activities.
- "Taking Time." Article discusses the unique rewards of summer youth programs.
- "Stop Lecturing, Start Talking." Article suggests several strategies teachers can use to stimulate class participation.

Rights and Payment
One-time rights. Written material, $.03 per word. Pays on publication. Provides 2 contributor's copies.

Editor's Comments
Our children's ministry section is most open to submissions from new writers. Send us your ideas for children's programs, especially those that include simple craft projects, games, or activities.

Cicada

Carus Publishing
140 South Dearborn Street, Suite 1450
Chicago, IL 60603

Submissions Editor

Description and Interests
Young adults ages 14 and older are the target audience of this literary magazine filled with high-quality, original short stories, poetry, and first-person essays. *Cicada* also features "Expressions," a section that presents readers' opinions and observations on everything from school life to concerns about social and cultural issues.
- **Audience:** 14–21 years
- **Frequency:** 6 times each year
- **Distribution:** 95% subscription; 5% newsstand
- **Circulation:** 18,500
- **Website:** www.cricketmag.com

Freelance Potential
98% written by nonstaff writers.

Submissions
Send complete ms. Accepts hard copy and simultaneous submissions if identified. SASE. Responds in 2–3 months.
Articles: To 5,000 words. Essays and personal experience pieces.
Fiction: To 5,000 words. Genres include adventure; fantasy; humor; and historical, contemporary, and science fiction. Plays and stories presented in a sophisticated cartoon format. Novellas, to 15,000 words.
Depts/columns: 300–500 words. Book reviews. "Expressions," 350–1,000 words.
Other: Cartoons. Poetry, to 25 lines.

Sample Issue
128 pages (no advertising): 5 stories; 5 poems; 4 depts/columns. Sample copy, $8.50. Writers' guidelines available.
- "The Wednesday Club." Story features a teenage girl who learns about serendipity and circumstance when she befriends a cancer patient.
- "Like Juggling Water." Story tells of the yearning for normalcy by 16-year-old Newton, who wants to leave his circus family and go to college.

Rights and Payment
All rights. Pays on publication. Fiction and articles, to $.25 per word. Poetry, to $3 per line.

Editor's Comments
We have very high standards and accept only top-quality material. Writers should review our guidelines and send only their best material. Please note that we will review complete manuscripts only.

Circle K

Circle K International
3636 Woodview Trace
Indianapolis, IN 46268-3196

Executive Editor: Kasey Jackson

Description and Interests
Circle K features a broad range of topics of interest to all college students, but specifically to service-minded individuals. Features include leadership and career development, self-help, and community involvement.
- **Audience:** YA–Adult
- **Frequency:** 6 times each year
- **Distribution:** Subscription; schools; controlled
- **Circulation:** 10,000
- **Website: www.circlek.org**

Freelance Potential
50% written by nonstaff writers. Publishes 12 freelance submissions yearly; 50% by unpublished writers, 50% by authors who are new to the magazine. Receives 48+ unsolicited mss yearly.

Submissions
Prefers query with clips or writing samples. Accepts complete ms. Accepts hard copy. SASE. Responds in 2 weeks.
Articles: 1,500–2,000 words. Informational and self-help articles. Topics include social issues, collegiate trends, community involvement, leadership, and career development.
Depts/columns: Word lengths vary. News and information about Circle K activities.
Artwork: 5x7 or 8x10 glossy prints; TIFF or JPEG files at 300 dpi or better.

Sample Issue
20 pages (no advertising): 6 articles; 5 depts/columns. Sample copy, $.75 with 9x12 SASE ($.75 postage). Guidelines available.
- "Bountiful Boston." Article offers suggestions for what to do while in Boston for the 2006 Circle K International convention.
- "Career Volunteers." Article shares some experiences from Peace Corps volunteers.
- Sample dept/column: "Service Initiative Aims to Get Kids Away from TV" explains the Circle K's campaign to "Turn off TV, Turn on Life."

Rights and Payment
First North American serial rights. Written material, $150–$400. Artwork, payment rates vary. Pays on acceptance. Provides 3 contributor's copies.

Editor's Comments
Members of the Circle K International, a collegiate community service organization, are our primary audience.

The Claremont Review

4980 Wesley Road
Victoria, British Columbia V8Y 1Y9
Canada

Business Editor: Lucy Bashford

Description and Interests
This literary journal provides a venue to display the works of young Canadian authors. Each issue includes a mix of fiction, short plays, poetry, interviews, and artwork.
- **Audience:** 13–19 years
- **Frequency:** Twice each year
- **Distribution:** 20% newsstand; 20% schools; 15% subscription; 45% other
- **Circulation:** 1,500
- **Website: www.theclaremontreview.ca**

Freelance Potential
99% written by nonstaff writers. Publishes 150 freelance submissions yearly; 90% by unpublished writers, 90% by authors who are new to the magazine. Receives 540 unsolicited mss yearly.

Submissions
Send complete ms with biography. Accepts hard copy. SAE/IRC. Responds in 1 month.
Articles: Word lengths vary. Interviews with contemporary authors and editors.
Fiction: To 5,000 words. Traditional, literary, experimental, and contemporary fiction. Also publishes adventure and sports stories.
Artwork: B/W and color prints and transparencies.
Other: Poetry, no line limit.

Sample Issue
136 pages (2% advertising): 15 stories; 1 interview; 40 poems. Sample copy, $10 with 9x12 SASE. Guidelines available at website.
- "Just Chew It." Story shares a father and son's experience at a baseball game, where the son learns a lesson about his father's past as a ball player.
- "Gravity." Story features a boy dangling from a bungee cord by one leg from a bridge while his friend comes to terms with events in his life.

Rights and Payment
Rights vary. All material, payment rates and payment policy vary. Provides 1 contributor's copy.

Editor's Comments
We love to tell stories, and welcome works from authors who are successful as well as those working toward success. While we mostly use Canadian writers, we will consider work from other writers ages 13 to 19. Send us a unique story that reveals something about the human condition.

The Clearing House

Heldref Publications
1319 18th Street
Washington, DC 20036

Managing Editor: Sarah Erdreich

Description and Interests
The Clearing House is a peer-reviewed journal that offers material of interest to middle-grade and high school teachers and administrators. Each issue includes articles that report on useful practices, research findings, and experiments.
- **Audience:** Educators
- **Frequency:** 6 times each year
- **Distribution:** Subscription; other
- **Circulation:** 1,500
- **Website:** www.heldref.org/tch.php

Freelance Potential
100% written by nonstaff writers. Publishes 25 freelance submissions yearly; 60% by authors who are new to the magazine. Receives 60–72 unsolicited mss yearly.

Submissions
Send complete ms. Accepts online submissions at http://mc.manuscriptcentral.com/tch. Responds in 3–4 months.
Articles: To 2,500 words. Informational and how-to articles. Topics include educational trends and philosophy, pre-service and in-service education, curriculum, learning styles, discipline, guidance and counseling, community involvement, gifted and special education, teaching techniques, educational testing and measurement, and technology.
Depts/columns: Word lengths vary. Educational news and opinion pieces.

Sample Issue
34 pages (no advertising): 8 articles. Sample copy, $17.50. Guidelines available in each issue.
- "Electronic Writing, Research, and Teaching." Article discusses how new technologies have changed the way many people write.
- "A Grading System for Composition Papers." Article explains a grading system that is objective yet allows room for personal judgment.

Rights and Payment
All rights. No payment. Provides 2 author's copies.

Editor's Comments
Consideration is given to articles that focus on educational strategies, issues, and ideas concerning middle-grade and high school educators. We also publish a limited number of articles that present the writer's opinion on controversial educational issues.

Cleveland Family

35475 Vine Street, Suite 224
Eastlake, OH 44095-3147

Editor: Frances Richards

Description and Interests
Self-described as "Your No. 1 parenting resource for tots to teens," this magazine provides information on child health and development, and regional family events and activities. It also includes calendars and school and camp directories.
- **Audience:** Parents
- **Frequency:** Monthly
- **Distribution:** 100% controlled
- **Circulation:** 70,000
- **Website:** www.clevelandakronfamily.com

Freelance Potential
50% written by nonstaff writers. Publishes 40–50 freelance submissions yearly; 33% by authors who are new to the magazine. Receives 9,000+ queries yearly.

Submissions
Query. Accepts email to editor@tntpublications.com. Responds only if interested.
Articles: 500+ words. Informational, self-help, and how-to articles; profiles; and reviews. Topics include the arts, animals, computers, crafts, health, fitness, education, popular culture, sports, the environment, religion, family travel, and regional issues.
Depts/columns: Word lengths vary. Facts for families, teen topics, and education issues.
Artwork: High resolution JPEG and TIFF files.

Sample Issue
46 pages (50% advertising): 8 articles; 9 depts/columns; 1 calendar. Editorial calendar available.
- "Don't Let Bed Rest Get You Down." Article explains the four different forms of bed rest for pregnant women and offers advice for expectant mothers.
- "Hot Shots." Article presents important immunization information for parents.
- Sample dept/column: "Classroom Corner" features tips for keeping math skills sharp over the summer.

Rights and Payment
Exclusive rights. Written material, payment rates vary. Pays on publication. Provides 1 contributor's copy.

Editor's Comments
Most of the writers who work with us live in northern Ohio and are familiar with the issues that interest our families. We cover a broad range of parenting issues related to raising children of all ages. We prefer fact-filled articles that provide practical information over first-person reflection pieces.

Click

Carus Publishing
140 South Dearborn Street, Suite 1450
Chicago, IL 60603

Editor

Description and Interests
Click provides information to young children about the everyday world, using a format that is colorful, fun, and intriguing. Each issue explores several aspects of a particular theme, from practical facts to relationships recognized in our familiar world.
• **Audience:** 3–7 years
• **Frequency:** 9 times each year
• **Distribution:** Newsstand; subscription
• **Circulation:** 54,000
• **Website:** www.cricketmag.com

Freelance Potential
90% written by nonstaff writers. Of the freelance submissions published yearly, 10% are by authors who are new to the magazine. Receives 48–60 queries each year.

Submissions
All material is commissioned from experienced authors. Send résumé and clips.
Articles: To 1,000 words. Informational articles; interviews; and photo-essays. Topics include the natural, physical, and social sciences; the arts; technology; math; and history.
Depts/columns: Word lengths vary. News items.

Sample Issue
34 pages (no advertising): 2 articles; 3 stories; 3 activities; 1 cartoon; 1 recipe. Sample copy available for ordering at website.
• "How T. J. Grew." Article follows a Siberian tiger from its birth at the Denver Zoo through adulthood.
• "The Best Apple Crisp in the World." Story turns a recipe into a lesson on how to measure.
• "Better Measure!" Activity provides information on how to measure different things such as height, a waist, windows, and containers.

Rights and Payment
Rights vary. Written material, payment rates and payment policy vary.

Editor's Comments
Our magazine wants to "open windows for young minds," and it tries to do that by presenting various aspects of our world at a level that young children can easily understand. Discovery, observation, investigation, and association are all methods that we encourage our young readers to use as they learn through our publication.

Club Connection

Assemblies of God
1445 North Boonville Avenue
Springfield, MO 65802-1894

Associate Editor: Sherrie Batty

Description and Interests
Club Connection is the official publication of Missionettes, a Christian club for girls. Each issue includes devotionals, Missionettes facts, and articles that discuss common reader interests.
• **Audience:** 6–12 years
• **Frequency:** Quarterly
• **Distribution:** 100% subscription
• **Circulation:** 9,000
• **Website:** www.clubconnection.ag.org

Freelance Potential
50% written by nonstaff writers. Publishes 30 freelance submissions yearly; 70% by authors who are new to the magazine. Receives 180–204 unsolicited mss yearly.

Submissions
Send complete ms. Accepts hard copy and simultaneous submissions. SASE. Responds in 1–2 months.
Articles: 300–700 words. Informational articles; personal experience pieces; profiles; interviews; and biographical pieces. Topics include religion, missions, hobbies, health, fitness, music, nature, the environment, multicultural and ethnic subjects, camping, pets, sports, recreation, science, and technology.
Depts/columns: Word lengths vary. Book and music reviews, club news, science, and advice.
Other: Puzzles, games, trivia, and recipes; word lengths vary.

Sample Issue
32 pages (5% advertising): 4 articles; 1 dept/column; 5 activity pages; 1 quiz. Sample copy, $2 with 9x12 SASE ($.77 postage). Guidelines and editorial calendar available.
• "Gabriella's Adventure." Article takes readers to the Republic of the Congo and presents information on the language, people, and faith of the region.
• "Remembering Dad." How-to article offers ideas for remembering lost and loved family members through scrapbook pages.

Rights and Payment
First or one-time rights. Articles, $10–$50. Pays on publication. Provides 2 contributor's copies.

Editor's Comments
This year, we need true stories about successful girls or groups, as well as how-to articles on engaging crafts or healthy snacks.

Cobblestone

Discover American History

Cobblestone Publishing
30 Grove Street, Suite 30
Peterborough, NH 03458

Editor: Meg Chorlian

Description and Interests
Each thematic issue of this magazine examines a different aspect of American history through in-depth articles, profiles, and stories.
- **Audience:** 8–14 years
- **Frequency:** 9 times each year
- **Distribution:** 100% subscription
- **Circulation:** 29,000
- **Website:** www.cobblestonepub.com

Freelance Potential
85% written by nonstaff writers. Publishes 180 freelance submissions yearly; 20% by unpublished writers, 25% by authors who are new to the magazine. Receives 350 queries yearly.

Submissions
Query with outline, bibliography, and clips or writing samples. All queries must relate to upcoming themes. Accepts hard copy. SASE. Responds in 5 months.
Articles: Features, 700–800 words. Sidebars, 300–400 words. Informational articles; profiles; and interviews. Topics include American history and historical figures and personalities.
Fiction: To 800 words. Genres include historical, multicultural, and biographical fiction; adventure; and retold legends.
Artwork: Color prints or slides. Line art.
Other: Puzzles, activities, games, and poetry.

Sample Issue
50 pages (no advertising): 11 articles; 12 depts/columns; 1 activity; 1 cartoon. Sample copy, $4.95 with 9x12 SASE ($1.24 postage). Guidelines and theme list available.
- "Crisis of Government." Article explains the history of the U.S. Constitutional Congress.
- "Pages on Patrol." Article looks at the role of pages in the U.S. Congress.
- Sample dept/column: "Going Global" explains how the British and Israeli Parliaments work, and how they differ from American democratic government.

Rights and Payment
All rights. Written material, $.20–$.25 per word. Artwork, payment rates vary. Pays on publication. Provides 2 contributor's copies.

Editor's Comments
Our feature articles include in-depth nonfiction, plays, first-person accounts, and biographies.

CollegeBound Teen Magazine

1200 South Avenue, Suite 202
Staten Island, NY 10314

Editor-in-Chief: Gina LaGuardia

Description and Interests
Teenagers preparing for college read this magazine for its informational articles. Topics cover social, lifestyle, and academic interests.
- **Audience:** 14–18 years
- **Frequency:** 9 times each year
- **Distribution:** 100% schools
- **Circulation:** 400,000–750,000 national; 100,000 regional
- **Website:** www.collegebound.net

Freelance Potential
25% written by nonstaff writers. Of the freelance submissions published yearly, 50% are by unpublished writers, 50% are by authors who are new to the magazine. Receives 300–400 queries yearly.

Submissions
Query with detailed outline. Accepts hard copy and email to editorial@collegebound.net. SASE. Responds in 3–5 weeks.
Articles: 800–1,500 words. Informational and how-to articles; profiles; interviews; reviews; and personal experience pieces. Topics include health and fitness, music, popular culture, college and careers, current events, and regional news.
Depts/columns: 150–450 words. Reviews of college guides, financial aid, lifestyle issues, and athletics.
Other: Submit seasonal material for back to school, Christmas, and prom season 4 months in advance.

Sample Issue
80 pages (30% advertising): Sample copy, $3.85 with 9x12 SASE. Guidelines and theme list/editorial calendar available.
- "Plastic Perfection." Article discusses the rise in the number of teens seeking plastic surgery.
- "Be Credit Card Savvy." Article gives the lowdown on credit card usage statistics, the fine print, and how to refrain from using them.

Rights and Payment
First rights; all rights if featured online. Articles, $70–$150. Pays on publication. Provides 1–2 copies.

Editor's Comments
We look for well-researched articles with real-life student experiences and expert advice. Topics of interest include dorm life, choosing the right college, fraternities and sororities, college happenings, and scholastic issues.

College Outlook

20 East Gregory Boulevard
Kansas City, MO 64114-1145

Editor: Brooke Pearl

Description and Interests
Since 1976, *College Outlook* has been guiding high school juniors and seniors preparing for college life. Articles that educate readers on issues related to the college application and selection process appear along with career profiles and career planning advice.
• **Audience:** College-bound students
• **Frequency:** Twice each year
• **Distribution:** 100% controlled
• **Circulation:** Spring, 440,000; Fall, 710,000
• **Website:** www.collegeoutlook.net

Freelance Potential
60% written by nonstaff writers. Publishes 5–10 freelance submissions yearly; 95% by unpublished writers, 95% by authors who are new to the magazine. Receives 96 queries and unsolicited mss yearly.

Submissions
Query with clips or writing samples; or send complete ms. Accepts hard copy. SASE. Responds in 1 month.
Articles: To 1,500 words. Informational and how-to articles; personal experience pieces; and humor. Topics include school selection, financial aid, scholarships, student life, extracurricular activities, money management, and college admissions procedures.
Artwork: 5x7 B/W and color transparencies.
Other: Gazette items on campus subjects, including fads, politics, classroom news, current events, leisure activities, and careers.

Sample Issue
48 pages (15% advertising): 11 articles. Sample copy, free. Guidelines available.
• "From Old School to New School." Article highlights some of the major differences between high school and college environments.
• "All In." Personal essay relates the experiences of a recent college grad who relocates to New York City and pounds the pavement in search of a job.
• "Ready, Set, Go to Grow!" Article discusses the life-altering experience of studying abroad.

Rights and Payment
All rights. No payment. Provides 2 contributor's copies.

Editor's Comments
We look for student-centered articles that provide solid college and career information for our readers. We'd like to make them more aware of the Internet resources available to them as well.

Columbus Parent

5300 Crosswinds Drive
Columbus, OH 43228

Editor: Donna Willis

Description and Interests
Parents in the Columbus, Ohio, area receive timely and interesting articles from this free tabloid magazine. Articles focus on raising happy, healthy children and on the needs and concerns of parents.
• **Audience:** Parents
• **Frequency:** Monthly
• **Distribution:** 90% newsstand; 10% subscription
• **Circulation:** 125,000
• **Website:** www.columbusparent.com

Freelance Potential
50% written by nonstaff writers. Publishes 15 freelance submissions yearly; 40% by authors who are new to the magazine. Receives 500 queries yearly.

Submissions
Query. Accepts email queries to dwillis@ thisweeknews.com. Response time varies.
Articles: 700 words. Informational, self-help, and how-to articles; profiles; interviews; and reviews. Topics include the arts, current events, health and fitness, humor, music, recreation, and travel.
Fiction: 300 words. Humorous stories.
Depts/columns: 300 words. Local events, food, health, book reviews, travel, and local personalities.
Artwork: Color prints and transparencies.
Other: Submit seasonal material 2 months in advance.

Sample Issue
64 pages (50% advertising): 4 articles; 20 depts/columns; 1 directory. Sample copy, free at local newsstands. Guidelines and theme list available.
• "Padding the Nest." Article looks at what expectant fathers can do to prepare for a new baby.
• "A Father's World." Article shares the experiences of three fathers with busy careers and how they make time for their families.
• Sample dept/column: "Feeding Hungry Minds and Bodies" offers ideas on how dads can encourage healthy nutrition and lifestyles for the whole family.

Rights and Payment
Rights vary. Written material, $.10 per word. Pays on publication.

Editor's Comments
We need well-researched features that use local sources. We are not interested in humor submissions, personal stories, or essays.

Complete Woman

875 North Michigan Avenue, Suite 3434
Chicago, IL 60611-1901

Executive Editor: Lora Wintz

Description and Interests
Articles about love, sex, and relationship issues
appear in *Complete Woman*, along with self-help
pieces, career advice, celebrity profiles, and health
and fitness tips.
- **Audience:** Adults
- **Frequency:** 6 times each year
- **Distribution:** Subscription; newsstand
- **Circulation:** 875,000

Freelance Potential
90% written by nonstaff writers. Publishes 75 freelance submissions yearly; 20% by unpublished
writers, 30% by authors who are new to the magazine.
Receives 720 queries yearly.

Submissions
Query or send complete ms with clips and résumé.
Accepts hard copy and simultaneous submissions if
identified. SASE. Responds in 3 months.
Articles: 800–1,200 words. Informational articles
and personal experience pieces. Topics include
health, exercise, beauty, skin care, fashion, relationships, romance, business, sex, and self-improvement.
Depts/columns: Word lengths vary. Careers, new
products, beauty, and news.

Sample Issue
106 pages: 35 articles; 7 depts/columns. Sample
copy, $3.99 at newsstands.
- "Five Ways to Make Competition Work for You."
  Article explores ways to turn the negative aspects
  of competition into self-improvement tools.
- "The Long-Distance Relationship Survival Guide."
  Article offers advice for working through the challenges of long-distance dating.
- Sample dept/column: "Closing Thoughts" shares
  a woman's true story of reconnecting with and
  marrying her long-lost boyfriend.

Rights and Payment
Rights vary. Written material, payment rates vary. Pays
on publication. Provides 1 contributor's copy.

Editor's Comments
We could use more well-researched self-help articles
from writers who have been previously published in
other national magazines. Beauty advice is needed
as well. We look for writing that addresses issues of
interest to today's woman in a fresh, entertaining,
and informative manner.

Connect for Kids

1625 K Street NW
Washington, DC 20006

Editor: Susan Phillips

Description and Interests
As an online publication, *Connect for Kids* uses com-
munications technologies to keep readers up to date
on the latest issues related to all aspects of child-
rearing in America.
- **Audience:** Parents and others who work
  with children
- **Frequency:** Weekly
- **Distribution:** 100% Internet
- **Hits per month:** Unavailable
- **Website: www.connectforkids.com**

Freelance Potential
40% written by nonstaff writers. Publishes 24 freelance submissions yearly; 25% by authors who are
new to the magazine. Receives 150 queries yearly.

Submissions
Query. Accepts hard copy and email to susan@
connectforkids.org. SASE. Response time varies.
Articles: 900–1,500 words. Informational articles;
profiles; reviews; and photo-essays. Topics include
adoption, foster care, the arts, child abuse and
neglect, health, child care and early development, kids
and politics, community building, learning
disabilities, crime and violence prevention, parent
involvement in education, development, out of
school time, diversity and awareness, parenting,
education, family income and poverty, volunteering,
and mentoring.

Sample Issue
Guidelines available at website.
- "How-To Advice for Parents on Picking a Great
  School." Article describes a new book on choosing
  your child's school, and promotes an upcoming
  author appearance on an online book chat.
- "Experts Tackle the Big Questions—Poverty, Race,
  and Children's Lives—in Online Chat." Article previews the facts of poverty in America and intoduces
  the online chat participant and hosts.

Rights and Payment
All rights. Payment rates and payment policy vary.

Editor's Comments
We are looking for more material on early childhood
development, children's youth activism, and solutions-
oriented coverage of critical issues affecting children.
We have enough on school reform.

Connecticut Parent

420 East Main Street, Suite 18
Branford, CT 06405

Editor & Publisher: Joel MacClaren

Description and Interests
Articles of interest to Connecticut parents can be
found in this magazine. Topics such as education,
health, personal improvement, and parenting are
covered. In addition, it provides information on local
resources and events.
- **Audience:** Parents
- **Frequency:** Monthly
- **Distribution:** 95% controlled; 5% subscription
- **Circulation:** 60,000
- **Website: www.ctparent.com**

Freelance Potential
20% written by nonstaff writers. Publishes 36 freelance submissions yearly; 25% by unpublished
writers. Receives 600 unsolicited mss yearly.

Submissions
Send complete ms. Prefers email to ctparent@aol.com.
Accepts hard copy. SASE. Response time varies.
Articles: 500–1,000 words. Self-help articles; profiles;
and interviews. Topics include parenting, regional
news, family relationships, social issues, education,
special education, health, fitness, entertainment,
and travel.
Depts/columns: 600 words. Family news, new product information, and media reviews.

Sample Issue
90 pages (60% advertising): 8 articles; 4 depts/
columns. Sample copy, $5 with 9x12 SASE.
Guidelines available.
- "Family Health." Article discusses the connection
  between a good diet and fitness, and tells how to
  feed a picky eater.
- "The Education Journey." Article explores ways to
  make the right education choices for children.
- Sample dept/column: "Family Travel" offers information on vacationing in Vermont.

Rights and Payment
One-time rights. All material, payment rates vary. Pays
on publication. Provides 1 contributor's tearsheet.

Editor's Comments
We continue to look for fresh articles that cover topics
such as parenting, health and fitness, marriage, childbirth, and family-friendly travel spots. Children's activities and crafts are welcome. We do not publish poetry
or fiction. Keep in mind that articles must be exclusive
to Connecticut.

Connecticut's County Kids

1175 Post Road East
Westport, CT 06880

Editor: Linda Greco

Description and Interests
Striving to help parents raise their children in
Connecticut, this publication touches on issues such
as education, health, parenting skills, nutrition, read-
ing, crafts, and cooking with kids.
- **Audience:** Parents
- **Frequency:** Monthly
- **Distribution:** 99% controlled; 1% subscription
- **Circulation:** 32,000
- **Website: www.countykids.com**

Freelance Potential
90% written by nonstaff writers. Publishes 60 freelance submissions yearly; 2% by unpublished writers,
20% by authors who are new to the magazine.
Receives 1,000+ queries, 500 unsolicited mss yearly.

Submissions
Query or send complete ms. Prefers email submissions to countykids@ctcentral.com. Accepts hard
copy. SASE. Responds only if interested.
Articles: 600–1,200 words. Informational articles;
profiles; and personal experience pieces. Topics
include nature, animals, crafts, ethnic subjects,
and sports.
Depts/columns: 500–800 words. Parenting, pediatric
health issues, growth and development, and family
issues.

Sample Issue
40 pages (50% advertising): 8 articles; 14 depts/
columns. Sample copy, free with 10x13 SASE.
Guidelines and editorial calendar available.
- "Kids and Gardening." Article discusses the benefits
  of letting children have their own small garden.
- "Do Day Campers Get Homesick, Too?" Article offers
  tips to help stop homesickness before it starts.
- Sample dept/column: "Mom's View" offers a mom's
  thoughts on being an "uncool" mother.

Rights and Payment
First rights. Written material, $.05 per word. Artwork,
payment rate varies. Pays on publication. Provides
2 contributor's copies.

Editor's Comments
We continue to need articles on parenting and family
issues. Be sure to include resources and other ways
for parents to put your tips to practical use or get
more information. Also, we like good photos. Include
them with your article whenever possible.

The Conqueror

United Pentecostal Church International
8855 Dunn Road
Hazelwood, MO 63042-2299

Administrative Secretary: Cindy Sorrels

Description and Interests
Striving to encourage spiritual growth and inspire faith in God, this magazine features stories and articles for young adults. It is published by the United Pentecostal Church International.
- **Audience:** 12–18 years
- **Frequency:** 6 times each year
- **Distribution:** 80% churches; 20% subscription
- **Circulation:** 5,200
- **Website:** http://pentecostalyouth.org

Freelance Potential
80% written by nonstaff writers. Publishes 20–25 freelance submissions yearly; 25% by unpublished writers, 20% by authors who are new to the magazine. Receives 150–200 unsolicited mss yearly.

Submissions
Send complete ms. Prefers email submissions to csorrels@upci.org. Accepts hard copy and simultaneous submissions if identified. SASE. Responds in 3 months.
Articles: Features, 1,200–1,800 words. Shorter articles, 600–800 words. Personal experience pieces and profiles. Topics include religion, missionary-related subjects, spiritual growth, social issues, and current events.
Fiction: 600–900 words. Real-life fiction with Christian themes. Genres include humor and romance.
Depts/columns: Word lengths vary. Book and music reviews; opinion and first-person pieces by teens; and reports on church events.

Sample Issue
16 pages (11% advertising): 4 articles; 1 story; 2 depts/columns. Sample copy, free with 9x12 SASE (2 first-class stamps). Guidelines available.
- "Shy No More." Essay shares how a high school girl uses her faith in God to overcome her shyness.
- "True North." Story tells of a teen who finds comfort in fitting in during a youth group camping trip
- Sample dept/column: "Zero Hour" discusses the importance of making a commitment to Jesus.

Rights and Payment
All rights. All material, $15–$50. Pays on publication. Provides 1 contributor's copy.

Editor's Comments
We are interested in seeing articles on youth culture and trends, and community awareness.

Countdown for Kids

Juvenile Diabetes Research Foundation
120 Wall Street, 19th Floor
New York, NY 10005

Editor: Rachael Lewinson

Description and Interests
Targeting children with Type I diabetes and their families, this magazine offers kid-friendly information on diabetes, treatments, diet, and health.
- **Audience:** 10+ years
- **Frequency:** Quarterly
- **Distribution:** Subscription; other
- **Circulation:** Unavailable
- **Website:** www.jdrf.org

Freelance Potential
50% written by nonstaff writers. Publishes 3 freelance submissions yearly; 10% by authors who are new to the magazine. Receives 120 queries and unsolicited mss yearly.

Submissions
Query or send complete ms. Accepts hard copy. SASE. Response time varies.
Articles: Word lengths vary. Informational, factual, and self-help articles; personal experience pieces; profiles; and interviews. Topics include coping with Type I diabetes, health, fitness, careers, college, popular culture, social issues, and diabetes research.
Depts/columns: Word lengths vary. Diabetes news and information; career profiles; and advice.

Sample Issue
16 pages (1% advertising): 5 articles; 1 dept/column. Sample copy available.
- "The Inside Story." Article explains how the right combination of food and insulin mean better health for the whole body.
- "Fantastic Food Facts." Article discusses the relationship between good food choices and balancing insulin, food, and activity.
- "Control Is an Attitude." Article looks at why diabetes is more than just a matter of numbers.

Rights and Payment
First North American serial rights. All material, payment rates vary. Pays on publication. Provides 1 contributor's copy.

Editor's Comments
The goal of our magazine is to educate young readers about coping with their diabetes. We're interested in articles that help readers deal with various social and personal issues concerning diabetes, make good choices, and make a difference in their communities. We also need information on current diabetes research.

Cousteau Kids

Weekly Reader
200 First Stamford Place
P.O. Box 120023
Stamford, CT 06912

Editor: Melissa Norkin

Description and Interests
Cousteau Kids is an educational publication encompassing all areas of science, natural history, marine biology, ecology, and the environment as they relate to our global water system.
- **Audience:** 8–12 years
- **Frequency:** 6 times each year
- **Distribution:** 100% membership
- **Circulation:** 80,000
- **Website:** www.cousteaukids.org

Freelance Potential
10% written by nonstaff writers. Publishes 4 freelance submissions yearly; 50% by authors who are new to the magazine. Receives 48 queries yearly.

Submissions
Query. Accepts hard copy and simultaneous submissions if identified. SASE. Responds only if interested.
Articles: 400–600 words. Shorter pieces, to 250 words. Informational articles. Topics include unique aquatic organisms, underwater habitats, ocean phenomena, the environment, and the physical properties of water.
Depts/columns: Staff written.
Artwork: Color slides.
Other: Games based on scientific fact, original science experiments, and art projects related to an ocean theme.

Sample Issue
24 pages (no advertising): 7 articles; 7 depts/columns. Sample copy, $2 with 9x12 SASE (3 first-class stamps). Guidelines available.
- "Protecting Our Rain Forests." Article offers interesting facts about our rain forest resources.
- "Planet Earth: It's a Greenhouse." Article discusses the effects of Earth's greenhouse gases.

Rights and Payment
One-time reprint rights; worldwide translation rights for use in other Cousteau Society publications. Articles, $100–$300. Shorter pieces, $15–$100. Pays on publication. Provides 3 contributor's copies.

Editor's Comments
We are not a good market for beginning or unpublished writers, as our content is primarily staff written. We're always looking for fresh ideas and a variety of perspectives, though, so if you have written for children, we will review your query.

Creative Kids

Prufrock Press
P.O. Box 8813
Waco, TX 76714

Submissions Editor

Description and Interests
Subtitled "The National Voice for Kids," this magazine features original writing and artwork by students between the ages of 8 and 14. It publishes stories, songs, cartoons, articles, and other creative work.
- **Audience:** 8–14 years
- **Frequency:** Quarterly
- **Distribution:** Subscription; schools
- **Circulation:** 3,600
- **Website:** www.prufrock.com

Freelance Potential
97% written by nonstaff writers. Publishes 150 freelance submissions yearly; 95% by unpublished writers, 80% by authors who are new to the magazine. Receives 6,000 unsolicited mss yearly.

Submissions
Send complete ms. Accepts hard copy. Availability of artwork improves chance of acceptance. SASE. Responds in 4–6 weeks.
Articles: 800–900 words. Informational, self-help, and how-to articles; humor; photo-essays; and personal experience pieces. Topics include animals, pets, sports, social issues, travel, and gifted education.
Fiction: 800–900 words. Genres include real-life and problem-solving stories; inspirational, historical, and multicultural fiction; mystery; suspense; folktales; humor; and stories about sports and animals.
Artwork: B/W and color prints and transparencies. Line art on 8½x11 white paper.
Other: Poetry, songs, word puzzles, games, and cartoons. Submit seasonal material 1 year in advance.

Sample Issue
34 pages (no advertising): 3 articles; 5 stories; 18 poems; 3 cartoons; 4 activities; 1 review. Guidelines available.
- "Diverella." Story features a beautiful girl who loves to dive but has trouble with her stepsisters.
- "The Perfect Setting." Essay describes the author's wonder at being in a beautiful place.
- "Write On." Essay discusses whether there is too much violence in video games.

Rights and Payment
Rights vary. No payment. Provides 3–4 author's copies.

Editor's Comments
We're seeing too much formulaic poetry. Students must follow our guidelines carefully.

Cricket

Carus Publishing
140 South Dearborn Street, Suite 1450
Chicago, IL 60603

Submissions Editor

Description and Interests
This literary magazine brings high-quality fiction and nonfiction to its readers. *Cricket* also contains a mix of poetry, puzzles, science experiments, and cultural activities, games, and music.
- **Audience:** 9–14 years
- **Frequency:** Monthly
- **Distribution:** 92% subscription; 8% newsstand
- **Circulation:** 70,000
- **Website:** www.cricketmag.com

Freelance Potential
100% written by nonstaff writers. Publishes 150 freelance submissions yearly; 30% by unpublished writers, 50% by new authors. Receives 12,000 mss yearly.

Submissions
Send complete ms; include bibliography for nonfiction. Accepts hard copy and simultaneous submissions. SASE. Responds in 2–3 months.
Articles: 200–1,500 words. Informational and how-to articles; biographies; and profiles. Topics include science, technology, history, archaeology, architecture, geography, foreign culture, adventure, and sports.
Fiction: 200–2,000 words. Genres include humor, mystery, fantasy, science fiction, folktales, fairy tales, mythology, and historical and contemporary fiction.
Depts/columns: Staff written.
Other: Poetry, to 25 lines. Puzzles, games, crafts, recipes, and science experiments, word lengths vary.

Sample Issue
64 pages (no advertising): 8 stories; 1 serial; 4 poems; 1 puzzle. Sample copy, $5 with 9x12 SASE. Writers' guidelines available.
- "Tiyoro and the Kissing Bird." Story tells of how a magic bird tricks a very stubborn African woman into falling in love with a man who loves her.
- "Getting There Is Half the Fun." Interview with a professional pilot answers questions about training, flying, and on-the-job adventures.

Rights and Payment
Rights vary. Articles and fiction, to $.25 per word. Poetry, to $3 per line. Pays on publication. Provides 6 contributor's copies.

Editor's Comments
Our standards are very high. Send only top-quality manuscripts for consideration.

Crinkles

Libraries Unlimited
88 Post Road West
Westport, CT 06881-9962

Managing Editor: Deborah Levitov

Description and Interests
This magazine for children is designed to stimulate their curiosity and encourage the development of problem-solving skills through fun and interactive articles and activities.
- **Audience:** 7–11 years
- **Frequency:** 6 times each year
- **Distribution:** 100% subscription
- **Circulation:** 6,000
- **Website:** www.crinkles.com

Freelance Potential
70% written by nonstaff writers. Publishes 2–3 freelance submissions yearly; 30% by authors who are new to the magazine. Receives 36 queries yearly.

Submissions
Query with résumé. Accepts email queries only to deborah.levitov@lu.com. Responds in 1 month.
Articles: Word lengths vary. Informational, factual, and how-to articles. Topics include history, culture, multicultural and ethnic subjects, social issues, science, animals, nature, the environment, the arts, and sports.
Other: Puzzles, games, and crafts.

Sample Issue
48 pages (no advertising): 13 articles; 13 activities. Guidelines available.
- "Kachina Dolls." Article explains the origins and uses of these Native American religious icons and provides instructions to create your own Kachina doll.
- "Anasazi: Ancient Cliff Dwellers—Vanished!" Article reveals the mystery surrounding these ancient stone dwellings and explains how to build your own adobe house with traditionally dressed Hopi and Navajo paper dolls.
- "Starry Starry Night at Kitt Peak Observatory." Article examines how telescopes work, what they can see in the night sky, provides a tour of this renowned observatory, and encourages children to write their own lyrics to "Twinkle Twinkle."

Rights and Payment
All rights. Written material, $150. Payment policy varies. Provides contributor's copies upon request.

Editor's Comments
We solicit manuscripts for our publication from leaders and experts in the field of education who are skilled in crafting articles and activities that challenge children.

Curious Parents

301 North Church Street
Moorestown, NJ 08057

Editor: Matt Stringer

Description and Interests
This magazine's primary audience is comprised of mothers, ages 25 to 54, who live in Philadelphia, the Delaware Valley, southern and central New Jersey, and the Lehigh Valley. They are committed to improving their parenting abilities and providing their children with the best possible growing-up experience. *Curious Parents* provides local resource information and covers all topics related to children and parenting.
- **Audience:** Parents
- **Frequency:** Monthly
- **Distribution:** Unavailable
- **Circulation:** 155,000
- **Website: www.curiousparents.com**

Freelance Potential
50% written by nonstaff writers. Publishes 70–100 freelance submissions yearly; many by unpublished writers and authors who are new to the magazine.

Submissions
Send complete ms. Accepts email submissions to editor@curiousparents.com. Response time varies.
Articles: Word lengths vary. Informational, how-to, and self-help articles. Topics include crafts, hobbies, current events, recreation, special education, safety, health, entertainment, networking, parenting, and travel.
Depts/columns: Word lengths vary. Health, book reviews, automobiles.

Sample Issue
40 pages: 12 articles; 3 depts/columns; 1 calendar of events.
- "Safety First, Fun Second." Article outlines simple precautions to take before riding on amusement park attractions.
- "Smarter by the Mile." Article offers brain-boosting activities for young travelers on long road trips.
- Sample dept/column: "Family Health" gives six safety tips for avoiding food-related illnesses during the summer months.

Rights and Payment
All rights. Written material, to $100. Pays on publication.

Editor's Comments
All articles submitted must by accompanied by a brief description of content. Since *Curious Parents* is a regional magazine, authors need to be extremely familiar with the area we serve and its resources.

Current Health 1

Weekly Reader Publishing
P.O. Box 120023
200 First Stamford Place
Stamford, CT 06912-0023

Editor: Jennifer Magid

Description and Interests
Students in the middle grades find information about nutrition, fitness, drug and alcohol prevention, and emotional well-being in this publication, distributed exclusively through schools.
- **Audience:** Grades 5–7
- **Frequency:** 8 times each year
- **Distribution:** 100% schools
- **Circulation:** 163,973
- **Website: www.weeklyreader.com/ch1**

Freelance Potential
50% written by nonstaff writers. Publishes 50 freelance submissions yearly; 30% by authors who are new to the magazine.

Submissions
All articles are assigned. Query with letter of introduction, list of areas of expertise, publishing credits, and clips. Accepts email queries to currenthealth@weeklyreader.com. No unsolicited mss. Responds in 1–4 months.
Articles: 850–2,000 words. Informational articles about subjects that relate to the middle-grade health curriculum. Topics include health, fitness, safety, first aid, nutrition, disease, drug education, psychology, and relationships.
Depts/columns: Word lengths vary. Health news, Q&As, medical investigations.

Sample Issue
30 pages (no advertising): 5 articles; 8 depts/columns. Sample copy available. Guidelines provided upon agreement.
- "It Feels Good to Laugh." Article explains why laughing is good for your health.
- "Energy Control." Article reports on the functions of the thyroid gland.
- Sample dept/column: "Dr. Detective" details how the work of Dr. Charles Nicolle led to the development of a vaccine against typhus in the 1930s.

Rights and Payment
All rights. Articles, $150+. Provides 2 author's copies.

Editor's Comments
We seek to provide students with information on the most current ideas, events, and issues they might otherwise miss. We also want to help our middle-grade readers make the right health choices and resist peer pressure.

Current Health 2

Weekly Reader Publishing
P.O. Box 120023
200 First Stamford Place
Stamford, CT 06912-0023

Editor: Anne Flounders

Description and Interests
Pre-teens and teens are the audience for this publication, which addresses general health issues. It focuses on nutrition, fitness, psychology, relationships, substance abuse, and human sexuality. Distributed through schools, it correlates with the middle school and high school health curricula.
- **Audience:** Grades 7–12
- **Frequency:** 8 times each year
- **Distribution:** 100% schools
- **Circulation:** 195,000
- **Website:** www.weeklyreader.com/ch2

Freelance Potential
90% written by nonstaff writers. Publishes 50 freelance submissions yearly; 30% by authors who are new to the magazine. Receives 60 queries yearly.

Submissions
Query with letter of introduction listing areas of expertise, publishing credits, and clips. Accepts email queries to currenthealth@weeklyreader.com. No unsolicited mss. Responds in 1–4 months.
Articles: 900–2,500 words. Informational articles on subjects related to the middle school and high school curricula. Topics include fitness, exercise, nutrition, disease, psychology, first aid, safety, human sexuality, and drug education.
Depts/columns: Word lengths vary. Health news, safety issues, and Q&As.

Sample Issue
32 pages (1% advertising): 5 articles; 6 depts/columns. Sample copy available. Guidelines provided on assignment.
- "Not Buying It." Article talks about new technologies that have changed advertising and how teens can be savvy consumers.
- "Food for Thought." Article examines whether good food can increase your brain power.
- Sample dept/column: "You Said It!" looks at the effects of performing random acts of kindness.

Rights and Payment
All rights. Articles, $150+. Pays on publication. Provides 2 contributor's copies.

Editor's Comments
Remember to tailor your writing to our audience of pre-teens and teens. All of our articles are designed to help readers make good choices.

Current Science

Weekly Reader Corporation
200 First Stamford Place
P.O. Box 120023
Stamford, CT 06912-0023

Managing Editor: Hugh Westrup

Description and Interests
Written for students in grades six through ten, *Current Science* covers all aspects of the science curriculum while relating topics to current news events. This publication is distributed in classrooms around the country. Topics covered include health, life science, physical science, and technology.
- **Audience:** 11–17 years
- **Frequency:** 16 times each year
- **Distribution:** 100% schools
- **Circulation:** 1 million
- **Website:** www.weeklyreader.com/features.cs.html

Freelance Potential
40% written by nonstaff writers. Publishes 30 freelance submissions yearly; 10% by authors who are new to the magazine. Receives 24 queries yearly.

Submissions
Query with résumé. No unsolicited mss. Availability of artwork improves chance of acceptance. SASE. Response time varies.
Articles: Word lengths vary. Informational articles. Topics include nature, science, the environment, technology, animals, physics, and earth science.
Depts/columns: Word lengths vary. Science-related news and Q&As.
Artwork: Color prints.
Other: Science-related photos, trivia, and puzzles.

Sample Issue
14 pages (no advertising): 4 articles; 3 depts/columns. Sample copy, free with 9x12 SASE.
- "Din in the Depths." Article discusses the harmful effects of underwater noise on marine life.
- "Being Green." Article shares the many ways students across the country are conserving energy and saving their schools thousands of dollars.
- Sample dept/column: "Dogs Smell Cancer" shares the results of an experiment conducted where canines showed an ability to detect cancer.

Rights and Payment
All rights. Written material, payment rates vary. Pays on acceptance. Provides contributor's copies.

Editor's Comments
We are interested in material that relates to the science curriculum and appeals to a variety of students. Our goal is to inspire children and stimulate critical thinking through real-world events related to science.

The Dabbling Mum

508 West Main Street
Beresford, SD 57004

Editor: Alyice Edrich

Description and Interests
Using educational how-to pieces and essay-style
stories, this online publication seeks to help parents
understand that dreams are worth fighting for and
going after. Topics range from parenting to climbing
the corporate ladder.
• **Audience:** Parents
• **Frequency:** Monthly
• **Hits per month:** 40,000
• **Website: www.thedabblingmum.com**

Freelance Potential
75% written by nonstaff writers. Publishes 60–200
freelance submissions yearly; 40% by unpublished
writers, 60% by authors who are new to the magazine.
Receives 120–480 queries yearly.

Submissions
Query with writing samples. Accepts online submissions only. Responds in 4–8 weeks.
Articles: 500–1,500 words. Informational and how-to
articles; and personal experience pieces. Topics
include family life, parenting, women's issues, home
businesses, Christian living, marriage, entertainment,
education, child development, teen issues, and contemporary social concerns.

Sample Issue
Guidelines available at website.
• "Start a Personal Trainer Business." Article gives
  specifics on how to start a business from home.
• "Host Your Own Event: Breakfast with an Author."
  Article offers several unique ways to sell books or
  author services.
• "Three Red Xs." Personal essay provides a lesson in
  good sportsmanship that becomes a family evening
  worth repeating.

Rights and Payment
One month exclusive online rights; indefinite archival
rights. Written material, $20–$40; reprints, $5. Pays
on publication.

Editor's Comments
We would like to see more ideas about specific home
businesses; stories centered around family recipes;
and essays about family travel and hometown missions. Please don't send us articles that contain
preachy Christian views, list articles filled with fluff,
or personal essays with "too much telling and not
enough showing."

Dallas Child

Lauren Publications
4275 Kellway Circle, Suite 146
Addison, TX 75001

Editorial Director: Shelley Hawes Pate

Description and Interests
Parents in the Dallas area read this free publication
for informative and inspirational articles that focus
on children from prenatal through adolescence. *Dallas
Child* is self-described as "the ultimate city guide
for parents."
• **Audience:** Parents
• **Frequency:** Monthly
• **Distribution:** 90% controlled; 10% subscription
• **Circulation:** 80,000
• **Website: www.dallaschild.com**

Freelance Potential
50% written by nonstaff writers. Publishes 10–20 freelance submissions yearly; 20% by authors who are
new to the magazine. Receives 396 queries yearly.

Submissions
Query with résumé. Accepts hard copy and simultaneous submissions if identified. SASE. Responds in
2–3 months.
Articles: 1,000–2,000 words. Informational and how-
to articles; personal experience and self-help pieces;
profiles; interviews; and humor. Topics include parenting, education, child development, family travel,
regional news, recreation, entertainment, current
events, social issues, multicultural and ethnic subjects,
health, fitness, and crafts.
Depts/columns: 800 words. Local events, travel, and
health news.

Sample Issue
94 pages (14% advertising): 9 articles; 10 depts/
columns. Sample copy, free with 9x12 SASE. Writers'
guidelines available.
• "The Mom Next Door." Article profiles a Dallas mother
  of three and shares her secrets of success.
• "A Candid Conversation: Bonnie Blair Speaks Out
  About SUI." Article discusses this Olympic gold-
  medal speed skater's problem with stress urinary
  incontinence.
• Sample dept/column: "Take Note" reports on the
  common yet misunderstood Celiac Disease.

Rights and Payment
First rights. Written material, payment rates vary. Pays
on publication. Provides author's copies on request.

Editor's Comments
We seek well-researched articles and ideas related to
raising a family from writers in the Metroplex area.

Dance Magazine

333 7th Avenue, 11th Floor
New York, NY 10001

Editor-in-Chief: Wendy Perron

Description and Interests
Dance enthusiasts read this publication for articles on dance, interviews with dancers, and up-to-date industry news. *Dance Magazine* covers all aspects of the dance world including current events, and also offers profiles of dance companies.
• **Audience:** YA–Adult
• **Frequency:** Monthly
• **Distribution:** Subscription; newsstand
• **Circulation:** 50,000
• **Website:** www.dancemagazine.com

Freelance Potential
65% written by nonstaff writers. Publishes 25 freelance submissions yearly; 20% by unpublished writers, 5% by authors who are new to the magazine. Receives 996 queries and unsolicited mss yearly.

Submissions
Query or send complete ms. Accepts hard copy. SASE. Response time varies.
Articles: Word lengths vary. Informational articles; profiles; and interviews. Topics include dance, dance instruction, choreography, the arts, family, and health concerns.
Fiction: To 4,000 words. Ethnic and multicultural fiction related to dance.
Depts/columns: Word lengths vary. New product information, reviews, dance news, and instruction.

Sample Issue
90 pages (33% advertising): 9 articles; 7 depts/columns. Sample copy, $4.95 with 9x12 SASE. Guidelines available.
• "Mind Your Body." Article discusses the benefits of yoga and describes three popular poses.
• "All in the Family." Article tells the story of two tap dancing siblings, Josette and Joseph Wiggan.
• Sample dept/column: "More Labor Strife in D.C." discusses problems between unionized dancers and the dance companies that fired them.

Rights and Payment
Rights negotiable. Written material, $.30 per word. Payment policy varies.

Editor's Comments
Writers must be knowledgeable about the dance world. We seek material on current events related to dance, articles on strategies for success in the dance community, and information on dance education.

Dance Teacher

Lifestyle Media, Inc.
110 William Street, Floor 23
New York, NY 10038

Managing Editor: Jeni Tu

Description and Interests
This magazine for and about dance education provides a forum for communication among experienced dance educators.
• **Audience:** Dance teachers and students
• **Frequency:** Monthly
• **Distribution:** 100% subscription
• **Circulation:** 20,000
• **Website:** www.dance-teacher.com

Freelance Potential
67% written by nonstaff writers. Publishes 10 freelance submissions yearly; 10% by unpublished writers, 10–15% by authors who are new to the magazine. Receives 100 queries yearly.

Submissions
Query. Accepts hard copy and email to jtu@ lifestylemedia.com. SASE. Responds in 2 months.
Articles: 1,000–2,000 words. Informational and how-to articles; and personal experience pieces. Topics include dance education, business, nutrition, injuries, health, performance, production, competition, and personalities.
Depts/columns: 700–1,200 words. Media reviews and industry news.
Artwork: Prefers color, accepts B/W slides, transparencies, and prints.

Sample Issue
164 pages (50% advertising): 6 articles; 20 depts/columns. Sample copy, free with 9x12 SASE ($1.37 postage). Guidelines and theme list available.
• "The Briansky Touch." Article profiles a teaching team at the Pennsylvania Youth Ballet who nurture their students with sensitivity and care.
• "Summer Study Success." Article explains how to make sure your students get the most out of a summer program.
• Sample dept/column: "Competition" offers helpful suggestions teachers can use when choosing members of a competition team.

Rights and Payment
All rights. Articles, $200–$300. Depts/columns, $100–$150. Pays on acceptance. Provides 1 author's copy.

Editor's Comments
This year, we are looking for practical pieces with a how-to angle on business management, teaching, and student health.

Dane County Kids

2001 Fish Hatchery Road
P.O. Box 8457
Madison, WI 53708-8457

Editor: Teresa Peneguy Paprock

Description and Interests
Dane County Kids is a resourceful tabloid read by parents, grandparents, and other child-care providers living in the Madison area of Wisconsin. Each issue features articles, tips, and information related to child rearing. Local events and services are also listed in each issue.
• **Audience:** Parents
• **Frequency:** Monthly
• **Distribution:** 100% controlled
• **Circulation:** 32,000
• **Website:** www.danecountykids.com

Freelance Potential
50% written by nonstaff writers. Publishes 30 freelance submissions yearly. Receives 12–24 queries and unsolicited mss yearly.

Submissions
Query or send ms. Accepts hard copy and disk submissions (RTF files). SASE. Response time varies.
Articles: To 1,000 words. Informational articles; personal experience pieces; profiles; and interviews. Topics include parenting, family issues, gifted and special education, multicultural issues, hobbies and crafts, animals, computers, and careers.
Depts/columns: To 750 words. Personal experience pieces, local school news, health and safety issues, and book reviews.

Sample Issue
28 pages (50% advertising): 17 articles; 6 depts/columns. Sample copy, $2. Guidelines and theme list/editorial calendar available.
• "You, Too, Can Survive National TV Turnoff Week." Article shares statistics and alternative ideas for children who watch too much television.
• "Young Cadets Learn Leadership." Article discusses the opportunities offered to youths ages 11 to 17 through the U.S. Naval Sea Cadet Corps program.

Rights and Payment
Rights negotiable. All material, payment rates vary. Pays on publication.

Editor's Comments
We only use submissions from local Madison area residents. Material must be reader-friendly and relate to children and families. We also seek submissions on local resources and creative tips on solving problems. Monthly topics can be found in our editorial calendar.

Daughters

34 East Superior Street, Suite 200
Duluth, MN 55802

Editor: Helen Cordes

Description and Interests
This newsletter strives to deliver effective parenting and communication techniques to parents of girls in all stages of adolescence. It features informational and self-help articles, essays, profiles, and interviews.
• **Audience:** Parents
• **Frequency:** 6 times each year
• **Distribution:** 100% subscription
• **Circulation:** 25,000
• **Website:** www.daughters.com

Freelance Potential
65% written by nonstaff writers. Publishes 10 freelance submissions yearly; 25% by unpublished writers, 25% by authors who are new to the magazine. Receives 24–36 queries yearly.

Submissions
Send complete ms for "Mothering Journey" and "Fathering Journey." Query for all other material. Prefers email queries to editor@daughters.com (Microsoft Word attachments). SASE. Responds in 1–2 months.
Articles: 700 words. Informational and self-help articles; personal experience pieces; profiles; and interviews. Topics include adolescent girls, health, fitness, social issues, body image, sexuality, education, communication, and parenting.
Depts/columns: "Mothering/Fathering Journey," first-person pieces that describe the emotional journey of parenting daughters; 650 words. "Let's Talk," essays that discuss ways to better communicate; 1,300 words.

Sample Issue
16 pages (no advertising): 7 articles; 1 dept/column. Guidelines and sample issue available at website.
• "Putting Perfectionism in Its Place." Article discusses strategies for helping girls let go of their need to be perfect.
• Sample dept/column: "Fathering Journey" shares how a father integrates his passion and parenting.

Rights and Payment
All rights. Written material, $.10–$.25 per word. Artwork, payment rates vary. Pays on publication. Provides 3 contributor's copies.

Editor's Comments
We typically use freelance writers for our 700-word departments. Material should focus on topics such as education, sports, or the media.

Davey and Goliath

Devotions for Families on the Go

Augsburg Fortress Publishers
P.O. Box 1209
Minneapolis, MN 55440-1209

Development Editor: Pamela Foster

Description and Interests
This digest-sized publication targets Christian parents who want to share Bible stories, family prayers, religious activities, and devotions with their elementary-school aged children.
- **Audience:** Families
- **Frequency:** Quarterly
- **Distribution:** Subscription
- **Circulation:** 50,000
- **Website:** www.augsburgfortress.org/dg/devotions

Freelance Potential
100% written by nonstaff writers. Publishes 30 freelance submissions yearly; 25% by unpublished writers, 75% by authors who are new to the magazine. Receives 60 queries yearly.

Submissions
Query with 6x9 SASE (2 first-class stamps). All work assigned on a contract basis. Accepts email to dg@augsburgfortress.org. Responds in 1 month.
Articles: 100–125 words. Bible stories; how-to articles on sharing and celebrating the Word of God.
Fiction: 100–125 words. Bible stories.
Depts/columns: 500 words. Bible facts, prayers, and activities.
Other: Puzzles, games, and mazes.

Sample Issue
64 pages (15% advertising): 26 devotions; 21 activities. Sample copy and guidelines provided free to prospective writers.
- "Giving All You Have." Devotional features a Bible story, prayer, and Bible facts about the importance of giving to others.
- "The Lost Man in the Tree." Devotional focuses on the story of Zacchaeus the tax collector and how salvation came to his house.

Rights and Payment
All rights. Written material, payment rates vary. Pays on acceptance. Provides 2 contributor's copies.

Editor's Comments
We assign the devotionals and other materials that appear in our magazine on a contract basis. If you can write meaningful retellings of Bible stories that are accompanied by family-friendly activities and fun Bible facts, contact us. All material is geared toward families with young children.

Devo'Zine

1908 Grand Avenue
P.O. Box 340004
Nashville, TN 37203-0004

Editor: Sandy Miller

Description and Interests
This devotional magazine was launched in 1996 to help teens develop a lifelong practice of spending time with God and to encourage them to reflect on what God is doing in their lives.
- **Audience:** YA
- **Frequency:** 6 times each year
- **Distribution:** 100% subscription
- **Circulation:** 105,000
- **Website:** www.devozine.org

Freelance Potential
100% written by nonstaff writers. Publishes 378 freelance submissions yearly; 50% by authors who are new to the magazine.

Submissions
Query. Accepts hard copy and email queries to devozine@upperroom.org. SASE. Responds in 4 months.
Articles: 150–500 words. Daily meditations, 150–250 words. Informational articles; personal experience pieces; and profiles. Topics include Christian faith, mentoring, independence, courage, teen parenting, creativity, social issues, and relationships.
Fiction: 150–250 words. Genres include contemporary and inspirational fiction.
Other: Prayers and poetry, 10–20 lines. Submit seasonal material 6–8 months in advance.

Sample Issue
64 pages (no advertising): 61 devotionals. Sample copy, $3.50. Guidelines and theme list available.
- "For Singer/Songwriter Shawn McDonald, God Makes All the Difference." Article profiles this former drug dealer, now a recording star, who turned his life over to Christ.
- "Grow." Devotional points out the many different ways of growing and the importance of growing as God directs us to.
- "Tame Your Tongue." Devotional offers tips for kicking the cursing habit.

Rights and Payment
First and second rights. Features, $100. Meditations, $25. Pays on acceptance.

Editor's Comments
Our meditations are grouped by weekly themes, so be sure to check our theme list before querying. Tell us which theme you'd like to write for.

Dig

Cobblestone Publishing
30 Grove Street, Suite C
Peterborough, NH 03458

Editor: Rosalie F. Baker

Description and Interests
Each issue of *Dig* focuses on a specific topic related to archaeology and investigates several aspects of it. Geared to middle school students, the information is presented in an interesting and intriguing format that makes learning fun.
- **Audience:** 9–14 years
- **Frequency:** 9 times each year
- **Distribution:** Subscription; newsstand
- **Circulation:** 19,000
- **Website:** www.cobblestonepub.com;
  www.digonsite.com

Freelance Potential
80% written by nonstaff writers. Publishes 40 freelance submissions yearly; 40% by unpublished writers, 60% by authors who are new to the magazine. Receives 96+ queries yearly.

Submissions
All submissions must relate to an upcoming theme. Query with outline, bibliography, and clips or writing samples. SASE. Responds in 4 months.
Articles: Word lengths vary. Informational articles and photo-essays. Topics include nature, animals, science, and technology.
Fiction: Word lengths vary. Stories related to the theme of each issue.
Depts/columns: Word lengths vary. Art, archaeology facts, quizzes, and projects.

Sample Issue
34 pages (no advertising): 10 articles; 6 depts/columns; 3 games. Sample copy, $5.95 at newsstands. Guidelines available.
- "Rediscovered!" Article relates the fascinating events leading up to the discovery of Machu Picchu.
- "Who Built Machu Picchu?" Article explains some of the culture, background, and history of the Incas.
- Sample dept/column: "All That Remains" tells how to look outdoors for information about the past.

Rights and Payment
All rights. Written material, $.20–$.25 per word. Pays on publication. Provides 2 contributor's copies.

Editor's Comments
Writers can check our upcoming themes, which are posted a year in advance. Please send for a theme list if you are interested. In each issue the material covers many interrelated aspects of the main topic.

Dimensions

1908 Association Drive
Reston, VA 20191

Editor: Traci Molnar

Description and Interests
As the official publication of DECA, an international association of marketing education students, this magazine focuses on readers' interests in marketing, management, and entrepreneurship.
- **Audience:** 14–18 years
- **Frequency:** Quarterly
- **Distribution:** Subscription; membership
- **Circulation:** 180,000
- **Website:** www.deca.org

Freelance Potential
60% written by nonstaff writers. Publishes 9 freelance submissions yearly; 50% by unpublished writers, 50% by authors who are new to the magazine.

Submissions
Query or send complete ms with short author biography. Accepts hard copy, Macintosh disk submissions (RTF files), email to traci-molnar@deca.org, and simultaneous submissions if identified. SASE. Response time varies.
Articles: 800–1,200 words. Informational and how-to articles; personal experience pieces; profiles; and interviews. Topics include general business, domestic and international management, marketing trends, sales, leadership development, franchising, personal finance, advertising, and business technology.
Depts/columns: 400–600 words. DECA chapter news and short business news items.

Sample Issue
24 pages (45% advertising): 9 articles; 5 depts/columns. Sample copy, free with 9x12 SASE. Writers' guidelines available.
- "What to Expect from Investing." Article explains how expectations play a critical role in finances.
- "The Promise and Perils of Blogging." Article discusses how the perceived anonymity of blogging gives way to cyber bullying and slander.
- Sample dept/column: "Short Stuff" reports on new business ideas, websites, and finance.

Rights and Payment
First North American serial rights. Written material, payment rates vary. Pays on publication.

Editor's Comments
Our journal has the appeal of a commercial magazine for young adults. Our approach to material is direct and conversational, rather than academic.

Dimensions of Early Childhood

Southern Early Childhood Association
P.O. Box 55930
Little Rock, AR 72215-5930

Dimensions Manager: Jennifer Bean

Description and Interests

Early childhood professionals read this publication for the latest information relevant to their field. *Dimensions of Early Childhood* is a refereed journal featuring a variety of articles on critical, timely topics.
- **Audience:** Early childhood professionals
- **Frequency:** 3 times each year
- **Distribution:** 100% subscription
- **Circulation:** 19,000
- **Website:** www.southernearlychildhood.org

Freelance Potential

99% written by nonstaff writers. Publishes 40 freelance submissions yearly; 90% by unpublished writers, 80% by authors who are new to the magazine. Receives 84 unsolicited mss yearly.

Submissions

Send complete ms. Prefers email submissions to editor@southernearlychildhood.org. Accepts hard copy and disk submissions. SASE. Responds in 3–4 months.
Articles: Word lengths vary. Informational articles. Topics include emergent curriculum for children, effective classroom practices, theory and research, program administration, family relationships, and resource systems.
Depts/columns: Word lengths vary. Book reviews, support strategies, and SECA updates.

Sample Issue

40 pages (20% advertising): 5 articles; 3 depts/columns. Sample copy, $5. Guidelines available.
- "Physically Active for Life: Eight Essential Motor Skills for All Children." Article discusses the importance of physical activity for young children.
- "Rethinking the Dynamics of Young Children's Social Play." Article discusses the findings of a recent study of young children in free-play situations.
- Sample dept/column: "Books for Early Childhood Educators" offers reviews of recommended books.

Rights and Payment

All rights. No payment. Provides 1 contributor's copy.

Editor's Comments

This journal seeks to enhance the quality of children's lives through early care and education. We seek material that is of interest to early childhood professionals, including social workers, child-care providers, teachers and researchers.

Dogs for Kids

BowTie, Inc.
P.O. Box 6050
Mission Viejo, CA 92690-6050

Editor: Jackie Franza

Description and Interests

Published by the editors of *DogFancy*, this magazine provides entertaining, informative articles of interest to young dog owners and enthusiasts. Its well-illustrated articles cover topics such as health care, breeding, training, and traveling with dogs.
- **Audience:** 10–15 years
- **Frequency:** 6 times each year
- **Distribution:** Subscription; newsstand
- **Circulation:** 20,000
- **Website:** www.dogsforkids.com

Freelance Potential

50% written by nonstaff writers. Publishes 15–25 freelance submissions yearly; 20% by authors who are new to the magazine. Receives 1,200 queries yearly.

Submissions

Query with writing samples. Accepts hard copy. SASE. Responds in 8–10 weeks.
Articles: 1,200–1,800 words. Informational and how-to articles; profiles; photo-essays; and personal experience pieces. Topics include animals and pets.
Depts/columns: To 650 words. Tips on dog behavior, health, breeds, nutrition, and new products.
Other: Puzzles, activities, and games.

Sample Issue

64 pages (10% advertising): 7 articles; 6 depts/columns; 4 activities; 5 breed reviews. Sample copy, $2.99 with 9x12 SASE. Guidelines available.
- "Character Counts." Article explores the possibility that dogs have the ability to judge good character in people.
- "Shall We Dance?" Article takes a look at the relatively new sport of canine freestyle, also known as dancing with your dog.
- Sample dept/column: "Nose for the News" offers short reports on dog events and happenings.

Rights and Payment

First rights. All material, payment rates vary. Pays on publication. Provides 2 contributor's copies.

Editor's Comments

If you want to be published in our magazine, you must be able write in a style that will appeal to kids between the ages of 10 and 15. Our readers know a lot about dogs, so it's important that you do, too. We are still interested in training tips, volunteering opportunities, nutrition, and profiles of working dogs.

Dovetail

A Journal By and For Jewish/Christian Families

775 Simon Greenwell Lane
Boston, KY 40107

Editor: Mary Rosenbaum

Description and Interests
Concerns and issues related to interfaith childrearing and family life are addressed in this online journal. Each issue revolves around a particular theme.
- **Audience:** Interfaith families
- **Frequency:** 6 times each year
- **Distribution:** 100% Internet
- **Hits per month:** Unavailable
- **Website:** www.dovetailinstitute.org

Freelance Potential
95% written by nonstaff writers. Publishes 10 freelance submissions yearly; 90% by unpublished writers, 90% by authors who are new to the magazine. Receives 192 queries and unsolicited mss yearly.

Submissions
Query or send complete ms. Accepts hard copy, Macintosh and text file submissions, email submissions to DI-IFR@Bardstown.com, and simultaneous submissions if identified. SASE. Responds in 1–2 months.
Articles: 800–1,000 words. Informational articles; profiles; interviews; reviews; and personal experience pieces. Topics include the interfaith community, parenting, anti-semitism, gender roles, religious holidays, family issues, social concerns, and education.
Other: Poetry, line lengths vary.

Sample Issue
Sample issue, guidelines, and theme list available at website.
- "Bar Mitzvah, Interfaith Style." Article describes an interfaith coming-of-age ceremony.
- "A Wedding Our Way—Finally." Article recounts a couple's wedding memories as they celebrate 50 years of marriage.
- "A Muslim/Christian Couple: The Wedding and After." Article considers the public perception of a religion that is different from the cultural norm.

Rights and Payment
One-time rights. Articles, $25; reviews, $15. Pays on publication. Provides download access to copies.

Editor's Comments
We are seeking articles in particular that provide substantive material dealing with interfaith childrearing. Personal experiences and research submissions must directly relate to interfaith marriage situations. Our publication does not accept material that proselytizes or has a vague "feel good" tone.

Dragon

2700 Richards Road, Suite 201
Bellevue, WA 98005

Editor-in-Chief: Erik Mona

Description and Interests
This magazine is devoted exclusively to the game of Dungeons and Dragons. It provides information on spells, magic items, new feats, races, and rule systems for game players, masters, and fans.
- **Audience:** YA–Adult
- **Frequency:** Monthly
- **Distribution:** Subscription; newsstand
- **Circulation:** 50,000
- **Website:** www.paizo.com/dragon

Freelance Potential
80% written by nonstaff writers. Publishes 350 freelance submissions yearly; 20% by unpublished writers, 20% by authors who are new to the magazine.

Submissions
Query with clips. Prefers email queries to dragon@paizo.com. Accepts hard copy. No simultaneous submissions. SASE. Responds in 3 months.
Articles: Word lengths vary. Informational articles. Topics include new feats, weapons, spells, magic items, equipment, and prestige classes.
Depts/columns: Word lengths vary. News and gear for gamers, game previews, and answers to rules questions.
Other: Comics.

Sample Issue
130 pages: 7 articles; 1 story; 7 depts/columns; 2 comics. Sample copy, $6.99 at newsstands. Guidelines available at website.
- "The Ecology of the Dracolich." Article includes complete information about the history, physiology, and psychology of Dracoliches.
- "Planar Dragons: Wyrms of Another World." Article features facts about the chromatic and metallic dragons of the Material Plane.
- Sample dept/column: "Age of Worms" explains how to survive the Age of Worms Adventure Path.

Rights and Payment
All rights. Written material, $.05 per word. Pays on publication.

Editor's Comments
The best articles appeal to both experts and non-experts. Our advice to freelancers is to write about a subject that interests you and follow the guidelines posted at our website. We don't publish pieces written in the first person.

Dramatics

Educational Theatre Association
2343 Auburn Avenue
Cincinnati, OH 45219

Editor: Donald Corathers

Description and Interests
This educational theater magazine is published by the International Thespian Society and provides serious young theater students and their teachers with the tools to be better performers, information on pursuing an acting career, and creating a lifelong appreciation of the theater.
- **Audience:** High school students and teachers
- **Frequency:** 9 times each year
- **Distribution:** 100% subscription
- **Circulation:** 37,000
- **Website:** www.edta.org

Freelance Potential
80% written by nonstaff writers. Publishes 41 freelance submissions yearly; 25% by unpublished writers, 50% by authors who are new to the magazine. Receives 480 unsolicited mss yearly.

Submissions
Send complete ms. Accepts hard copy and email submissions to dcorathers@edta.org. SASE. Responds 2–4 months.
Articles: 750–4,000 words. Informational articles; interviews; and book reviews. Topics include playwriting, musical theater, acting, auditions, stage makeup, set design, and production.
Fiction: 500–3,500 words. Full-length and one-act plays suitable for high school audiences.
Artwork: 5x7 or larger B/W prints or 35mm or larger color transparencies. B/W line art. High resolution JPGs or TIFFs.

Sample Issue
50 pages (40% advertising): 6 articles; 1 play; 1 dept/column. Sample copy, $3 with 9x12 SASE. Guidelines available.
- "Earnest and Clueless." Article reviews several new plays.
- "Dressing the Show: Inside the Costume Shop." Article looks at the job of a theatrical costume designer.
- "Honour." Play depicts the life of Joan of Arc.

Rights and Payment
First rights. Written material, $50–$400. Pays on publication. Provides 5 contributor's copies.

Editor's Comments
We are looking for articles that provide students and teachers with the resources for making better theater.

Earlychildhood News

2 Lower Ragsdale, Suite 125
Monterey, CA 93940

Director of Publishing: Megan Shaw

Description and Interests
Readers find research-based and experience-based articles for teachers of children from infants to age eight, ideas for appropriate age-related activities, and general educational material in this publication.
- **Audience:** Early childhood professionals and parents
- **Frequency:** 6 times each year
- **Distribution:** Subscription; controlled
- **Circulation:** 50,000
- **Website:** www.earlychildhoodnews.com

Freelance Potential
90% written by nonstaff writers. Publishes 10 freelance submissions yearly; 5% by unpublished writers, 15% by authors who are new to the magazine. Receives 96 queries and unsolicited mss yearly.

Submissions
Query with clips and writing samples; or send complete ms. Accepts email submissions to mshaw@ excelligencemail.com. SASE. Responds in 2 months.
Articles: 600–1,200 words. Informational and self-help articles; success stories; and interviews. Topics include early childhood education; health and safety; advocacy; testing; multicultural subjects; family, social, and emotional issues; and professional development.
Depts/columns: 500 words. Topics vary.

Sample Issue
46 pages (50% advertising): 8 articles; 5 depts/ columns; 1 activity. Sample copy available. Guidelines and editorial calendar available.
- "Using Assessment Data to Promote Inclusion of Young Children." Article looks at transitioning children with disabilities into a classroom.
- "Let's Find Out About It!" Article examines how to incorporate science into preschool learning.
- Sample dept/column: "Tips and Tidbits" offers ideas for making bird feeders and birdfeeder biscuits.

Rights and Payment
All rights. Written material, $75–$300. Depts/ columns, payment rates vary. Pays on acceptance. Provides 1 contributor's copy.

Editor's Comments
Although our writing style is non-academic, the content of an article should be grounded in solid research. Include charts, graphs, and illustrations.

Early Childhood Today

Scholastic Inc.
557 Broadway, 5th Floor
New York, NY 10012-3999

Editor-in-Chief: Diane Ohanesian

Description and Interests
Teachers, directors, and child-care providers turn to this professional publication for information in the field of early childhood care and education.
- **Audience:** Early childhood professionals
- **Frequency:** 8 times each year
- **Distribution:** Subscription; schools
- **Circulation:** 55,000
- **Website:** http://teachers.scholastic.com/ products/ect

Freelance Potential
100% written by nonstaff writers. Publishes 5 freelance submissions yearly; 10% by unpublished writers, 50% by authors who are new to the magazine. Receives 10–15 queries yearly.

Submissions
Query. No unsolicited mss. Accepts hard copy. SASE. Responds in 1 month.
Articles: Word lengths vary. Informational, educational, and how-to articles. Topics include child advocacy, child development, special needs, communication, physical development, family issues, health, technology, and multicultural issues.
Depts/columns: Word lengths vary. Ideas and resources, leadership, behavior and development, and hands-on activities.

Sample Issue
64 pages (8% advertising): 1 article; 14 depts/ columns. Sample copy available.
- "Why Children Need to Play." Opinion piece discusses the link between play and the development of cognitive and social skills that are prerequisites for learning complex concepts.
- "Open the Door!" Article explains how to prepare a classroom that is ready to welcome children and invites families in a nonthreatening, accommodating way.

Rights and Payment
All rights. Written material, payment rates vary. Pays on acceptance. Provides 3 contributor's copies.

Editor's Comments
We welcome queries for material that involves children in developmentally appropriate experiences and encourages educators to interact with their students. Articles should offer readers practical information and tips that can be put to use in the classroom.

East of the Web

361 Manhattan Building
Fairfield Road
London E32UL
England

Editor: Alex Patterson

Description and Interests
This website's purpose is to showcase the work of short story writers. It features both children's and adult fiction in a variety of genres, including romance, humor, science fiction, horror, and hyperfiction. *East of the Web* gives emerging writers the chance to be read by agents, the press, film makers, and other publishers.
- **Audience:** All ages
- **Frequency:** Unavailable
- **Distribution:** 100% Internet
- **Hits per month:** 40,000+
- **Website: www.eastoftheweb.com**

Freelance Potential
96% written by nonstaff writers. Publishes 150 freelance submissions yearly; 50% by unpublished writers, 85% by authors who are new to the magazine. Receives 6,000 unsolicited mss yearly.

Submissions
Send complete ms. Accepts email submissions to submissions@eastoftheweb (TEXT, RTF files, or Microsoft Word attachments). SASE. Responds in 3–4 months.
Fiction: Word lengths vary. Genres include contemporary fiction, mystery, folktales, fairy tales, humor, science fiction, and stories about animals.

Sample Issue
Guidelines available at website.
- "The Hare Who Would Not Be King." Story set on the African plains tells of a lion who misuses his power as king of the animals.
- "Mr. Sticky." Story features a young girl and her fascination with a small water snail living in her aquarium tank.
- "The Tidy Drawer." Story tells about a daughter and her mother who find treasures in a "catch-all" drawer in the kitchen.

Rights and Payment
Non-exclusive rights. No payment.

Editor's Comments
We receive thousands of submissions, so it is crucial that you follow the submissions guidelines at our website if you wish to be considered for publication. We select stories based solely on the quality of the writing, regardless of the author's experience. New, fresh voices are welcome.

Educational Horizons

Pi Lambda Theta
P.O. Box 6626,
4101 East Third Street
Bloomington, IN 47407-6626

Managing Editor

Description and Interests
Published by an international honor society for educators, this digest-sized publication features scholarly articles, research findings, and essays on educational issues of national and international significance.
- **Audience:** Pi Lambda Theta members
- **Frequency:** Quarterly
- **Distribution:** 90% controlled; 10% subscription
- **Circulation:** 17,000
- **Website: www.pilambda.org**

Freelance Potential
95% written by nonstaff writers. Publishes 10–15 freelance submissions yearly; 75% by authors who are new to the magazine. Receives 60 queries, 12 unsolicited mss yearly.

Submissions
Query with outline/synopsis; or send complete ms with biography. Accepts hard copy and simultaneous submissions if identified. Availability of artwork improves chance of acceptance. SASE. Responds to queries in 1 month, to mss in 3–4 months.
Articles: 3,500–5,000 words. Informational articles; research reports; and scholarly essays. Topics include educational, social, and cultural issues.
Depts/columns: 500–750 words. Education topics in the news; multicultural education; legal issues; and book reviews.
Artwork: B/W prints and camera-ready illustrations.

Sample Issue
64 pages (4% advertising): 11 articles; 2 depts/columns. Sample copy, $5 with 9x12 SASE ($.87 postage). Writers' guidelines and theme list available at website.
- "Learning to See with a Third Eye." Article offers a teacher's personal experiences with addressing educational inequities.
- "Taking Time to Tend to the 'Good.'" Article discusses the need to take a strengths-based approach to educational reform.

Rights and Payment
First rights. No payment. Provides 5 author's copies.

Editor's Comments
We look for articles that interest the reflective, inquiring educator. While most published submissions have been invited, we occasionally use non-invited submissions. We also accept unsolicited book reviews.

Educational Leadership

1703 North Beauregard Street
Alexandria, VA 22311-1714

Editor: Margaret Scherer

Description and Interests
Written for professionals interested in curriculum, instruction, supervision, and leadership in education, this magazine is published by the Association for Supervision and Curriculum Development. Each issue addresses a theme.
- **Audience:** Educators
- **Frequency:** 8 times each year
- **Distribution:** 90% subscription; 10% schools
- **Circulation:** 170,000
- **Website: www.ascd.org**

Freelance Potential
95% written by nonstaff writers. Publishes 130 freelance submissions yearly; 50% by unpublished writers, 50% by authors who are new to the magazine. Receives 1,000 unsolicited mss yearly.

Submissions
Send complete ms. Accepts hard copy. Does not return mss. Responds in 1–2 months.
Articles: 1,500–2,500 words. How-to articles and personal experience pieces. Topics include reading, assessment, instructional strategies, student achievement, gifted and special education, science, technology, and multicultural and ethnic subjects.
Depts/columns: Word lengths vary. Education news and opinion pieces. Also includes policy, book, and website reviews.

Sample Issue
96 pages (25% advertising): 15 articles; 6 depts/columns. Sample copy, $6. Guidelines and theme list available.
- "Tools for the Mind." Article talks about how schools are using computers primarily to teach low-level skills rather than to deepen student learning.
- "Listen to the Natives." Article discusses how students often surpass teachers in digital knowledge.
- Sample dept/column: "Web Wonders" talks about online research and "blogs."

Rights and Payment
All or first rights. No payment. Provides 5 contributor's copies.

Editor's Comments
The more appropriate an article is for a theme issue, the more likely we will publish it. Features usually describe research-based solutions to current problems in education.

Education Forum

60 Mobile Drive
Toronto, Ontario M4A 2P3
Canada

Managing Editor: Marianne Clayton

Description and Interests
Educators who work in the Canadian province of Ontario turn to this magazine for discussions of national and international issues, teaching strategies, and media reviews.
- **Audience:** Teachers
- **Frequency:** 3 times each year
- **Distribution:** 90% membership; 10% subscription
- **Circulation:** 50,000
- **Website:** www.osstf.on.ca

Freelance Potential
90% written by nonstaff writers. Publishes 35 freelance submissions yearly; 20% by unpublished writers, 80% by authors who are new to the magazine. Receives 48 queries and unsolicited mss yearly.

Submissions
Query with clips or writing samples; or send complete ms. Accepts hard copy. No simultaneous submissions. SAE/IRC. Responds to queries in 1–2 months.
Articles: To 2,500 words. How-to and practical application articles on education trends; discussions of controversial issues; and teaching techniques for use in secondary school classrooms.
Depts/columns: "Openers" features news and opinion pieces, to 300 words. "Forum Picks" uses media and software reviews.
Artwork: B/W prints and line art. Color prints and transparencies.
Other: Classroom activities, puzzles, and games. Submit seasonal material 8 months in advance.

Sample Issue
42 pages (18% advertising): 7 articles; 1 story; 8 depts/columns. Sample copy, free with 9x12 SAE/IRC. Guidelines available.
- "From Humble Beginnings." Article chronicles 200 years of secondary education in Ontario.
- Sample dept/column: "International Perspectives" reports on how protesters helped to block the Free Trade Area of the Americas.

Rights and Payment
First North American serial rights. No payment. Provides 5 contributor's copies.

Editor's Comments
Our audience includes public high school teachers, continuing education teachers, social workers, and psychologists. We welcome work from new writers.

Education Week

6935 Arlington Road, Suite 100
Bethesda, MD 20814-5233

Executive Editor: Greg Chronister

Description and Interests
Elementary and secondary school educators have been reading this newspaper for more than 20 years to keep up with the events, trends, and programs that affect schools and the people who staff them. *Education Week* is published by Editorial Projects in Education, a nonprofit organization.
- **Audience:** Educators
- **Frequency:** 44 times each year
- **Distribution:** Subscription; schools; newsstand
- **Circulation:** 50,000
- **Website:** www.edweek.org

Freelance Potential
8% written by nonstaff writers. Publishes 125 freelance submissions yearly; 80% by unpublished writers, 75% by authors who are new to the magazine. Receives 600 unsolicited mss yearly.

Submissions
Send complete ms. Accepts IBM disk submissions (WordPerfect or Microsoft Word) and Macintosh disk submissions (plain text). SASE. Responds in 6–8 weeks.
Articles: 1,200–1,500 words. Essays about child development and education related to grades K–12 for use in "Commentary" section.
Depts/columns: Staff written.

Sample Issue
44 pages (25% advertising): 24 articles; 14 depts/columns. Sample copy, $3 with 9x12 SASE ($1 postage). Guidelines available.
- "Californians Set to Vote on Universal PreK Plan." Article reports on Proposition 82, which would make all of California's 4-year-olds eligible for free preschool.
- "The Heart of the Matter." Article explains how a school district in Kentucky is successfully dealing with the poor reading skills of its high school students.
- "Bridging Differences." Commentary features a dialogue between two renowned educators who often hold opposing viewpoints.

Rights and Payment
First rights. "Commentary," $200. Pays on publication. Provides 2 contributor's copies.

Editor's Comments
Freelance writers involved in elementary or secondary education are welcome to submit opinion pieces for our "Commentary" section.

EduGuide

321 North Pine
Lansing, MI 48933

Editor: Sheryl James

Description and Interests
This magazine is offered in four editions for elementary school, middle school, high school, and college students. The publications are designed to help parents and other caregivers increase their children's odds for success from birth through college.
- **Audience:** Parents
- **Frequency:** 3 times each year
- **Distribution:** 50% subscription; 50% schools
- **Circulation:** 300,000
- **Website:** www.partnershipforlearning.org

Freelance Potential
85% written by nonstaff writers. Publishes 25–30 freelance submissions yearly; 10% by unpublished writers, 60% by new authors. Receives 48 mss yearly.

Submissions
Send complete ms. Accepts hard copy and email submissions to jan@partnershipforlearning.org. SASE. Responds in 4–6 weeks.
Articles: 500–1,000 words. Informational and how-to articles; profiles; interviews; and personal experience pieces. Topics include the arts, college, careers, computers, gifted education, health, fitness, history, humor, mathematics, music, science, technology, special education, and issues related to elementary and secondary education.
Depts/columns: Word lengths vary. Advice and opinion pieces.
Artwork: Color prints and transparencies. Line art.
Other: Reviews, 200 words. Submit seasonal material 3 months in advance.

Sample Issue
40 pages: 4 articles; 2 depts/columns. Sample copy, $3 with 9x12 SASE ($1 postage). Guidelines and theme list/editorial calendar available.
- "What I Wish We Had Known When We Started High School." Article offers ways parents can make sure their children get the most out of high school.
- Sample dept/column: "Parent Primer" provides tips on saving time and money for college.

Rights and Payment
First or second rights. All material, payment rates vary. Pays on acceptance. Provides 5 author's copies.

Editor's Comments
We need articles that help parents understand topics and trends in education.

Edutopia

P.O. Box 3494
San Rafael, CA 94912

Senior Editor: Jennifer Sweeney

Description and Interests
Public school environments constantly change to meet new mandates and theories, and *Edutopia* keeps parents and professionals on top of those shifts and the resulting effects on teachers and students. Its range of topics extends from teaching techniques and fitness to technology and monetary concerns.
- **Audience:** Educators; parents; policy makers
- **Frequency:** 8 times each year
- **Distribution:** 90% subscription; 10% newsstand
- **Circulation:** 100,000
- **Website:** www.edutopia.org

Freelance Potential
70% written by nonstaff writers. Publishes 20 freelance submissions yearly; 30% by authors who are new to the magazine. Receives 36–60 queries yearly.

Submissions
Query with résumé and clips. Prefers email queries to edit@edutopia.org. Response time varies.
Articles: 300–2,500 words. Informational and how-to articles; and personal experience pieces. Topics include computers, education, current events, health and fitness, nature, the environment, popular culture, recreation, science, technology, social issues, and travel.
Depts/columns: 700 words. Health, education, and ethnic and multicultural issues.

Sample Issue
56 pages (35% advertising): 3 articles; 13 depts/columns. Sample copy, $4.95. Guidelines available.
- "Fighting for Fitness." Article shows what schools are doing to counter childhood obesity.
- "Adopt and Adapt." Article illustrates why it's not enough for schools just to use technology—they also have to shape it to their individual needs.
- Sample dept/column: "Going Green" examines a Chicago school that is environmentally friendly.

Rights and Payment
First North American serial rights. Written material, payment rates vary. Pays on acceptance. Provides 2 copies.

Editor's Comments
Our feature articles and lifestyle sections are the best entrée for writers new to our publication. We focus on new directions in education and teaching methods, and present the information in a no-nonsense, snappy style with witty overtones.

Elementary School Writer

Writer Publications
P.O. Box 718
Grand Rapids, MN 55744-0718

Editor: Emily Benes

Description and Interests
Elementary School Writer is a newspaper featuring the works of students in elementary school. Throughout the country, students of subscribing teachers submit their stories, poems, articles, and essays to be read by their peers. Topics include school experiences, memories, imaginative stories, and social issues.
• **Audience:** Elementary school students
• **Frequency:** 6 times each year
• **Distribution:** 100% schools
• **Circulation:** Unavailable

Freelance Potential
100% written by nonstaff writers. Publishes 300 freelance submissions yearly; 95% by unpublished writers, 75% by authors who are new to the magazine. Receives 36,000 unsolicited mss yearly.

Submissions
Accepts submissions from students of subscribing teachers in elementary school only. Accepts hard copy, email submissions to writer@mx3.com (ASCII text only), and simultaneous submissions if identified. SASE. Response time varies.
Articles: To 1,000 words. Informational and how-to articles; profiles; and personal experience pieces. Topics include current events, humor, multicultural and ethnic issues, nature, the environment, popular culture, recreation, sports, and travel.
Fiction: To 1,000 words. Genres include humor, science fiction, and stories about nature, the environment, and sports.
Other: Poetry, no line limit. Seasonal material.

Sample Issue
8 pages (no advertising): 27 stories; 19 poems. Sample copy, free. Guidelines available in each issue.
• "Hurricane Rita." Story shares a young girl's feelings about being evacuated from her home during Hurricane Rita.
• "5 Times Faster." Story tells of an adventure a young boy has with his cousin who can run and climb faster than he can, but he never gives up.

Rights and Payment
One-time rights. No payment.

Editor's Comments
We are devoted to publishing the original works of elementary school students. Our newspaper is used as a teaching tool in classrooms around the country.

Ellery Queen's Mystery Magazine

475 Park Avenue South, 11th Floor
New York, NY 10016

Editor: Janet Hutchings

Description and Interests
Self-described as the "world's leading mystery magazine," this publication features a gamut of crime and detection stories, hard-boiled detective stories, and imaginative "impossible" crimes.
• **Audience:** YA–Adult
• **Frequency:** 10 times each year
• **Distribution:** 90% subscription; 10% newsstand
• **Circulation:** 180,780
• **Website:** www.themysteryplace.com

Freelance Potential
100% written by nonstaff writers. Publishes 125 freelance submissions yearly; 7% by unpublished writers, 25% by authors who are new to the magazine. Receives 2,600 unsolicited mss yearly.

Submissions
Send complete ms. Accepts hard copy and and simultaneous submissions if identified. SASE. Responds in 3 months.
Fiction: Feature length, 2,000–12,000 words. Minute mysteries, 250 words. Novellas by established authors, to 20,000 words. Genres include contemporary and historical crime fiction, psychological thrillers, mystery, suspense, and detective and private-eye stories.
Other: Poetry, line length varies.

Sample Issue
144 pages (6% advertising): 9 stories; 7 book reviews. Sample copy, $5. Guidelines available.
• "Once Upon a Time." Short story delves into the investigation that ensues when a human bone is discovered in the woods.
• "The Frog that Croaked in the Night." Surprising story tells of a man who is killed when a dead frog hits him in the head.
• "The Spare Key." Story focuses on a landlady who has a unique way of keeping track of her renters.

Rights and Payment
First and anthology rights. All material, $.05–$.08 per word. Pays on acceptance. Provides 3 author's copies.

Editor's Comments
As always, we are looking for classical whodunits. We are especially happy to review first stories by authors who have never before published fiction professionally. First-story submissions should be addressed to our Department of First Stories.

eSchoolNews

7920 Norfolk Avenue, Suite 900
Bethesda, MD 20814

Editor: Greg Downey

Description and Interests
Technology in kindergarten through college class-rooms is the focus of this tabloid. It appears both online and in print, providing coverage of school technology news, events, key players, products, services, and strategies.
- **Audience:** Educators
- **Frequency:** Monthly
- **Distribution:** 100% subscription
- **Circulation:** Unavailable
- **Website:** www.eschoolnews.com

Freelance Potential
20% written by nonstaff writers. Publishes 6–8 freelance submissions yearly. Receives 12 unsolicited mss yearly.

Submissions
Prefers query. Accepts complete ms. Accepts hard copy and email to GDowney@eschoolnews.com. SASE. Response time varies.
Articles: Word lengths vary. Informational and how-to articles; profiles; and reviews. Topics include gifted and special education, science, technology, and social issues.
Depts/columns: Word lengths vary. News, reviews, new product information, grants and funding, best practices, opinion pieces.

Sample Issue
38 pages (45% advertising): 15 articles; 11 depts/columns. Sample copy available at website.
- "65% Rule Threatens School IT." Article reports on new rules adopted recently in Texas and Georgia that could force cutbacks in IT staffing and infrastructure needs.
- "School Buses to Go Hybrid." Article describes the manufacture of new fuel-efficient buses.
- Sample dept/column: "Grants & Funding" tells why anticipating future grant programs now can pay off later.

Rights and Payment
Rights vary. Written material, payment rates vary. Pays on acceptance.

Editor's Comments
Our purpose is to provide school administrators, educators, and technology professionals with the information they need to make good decisions. We want relevant, cutting-edge reporting.

Exceptional Parent

551 Main Street
Johnstown, PA 15901

Editor-in-Chief: Dr. Rick Rader

Description and Interests
This award-winning magazine is dedicated to providing information to parents, educators, and health care professionals who care for children and young adults with special needs.
- **Audience:** Parents, teachers, and professionals
- **Frequency:** Monthly
- **Distribution:** Subscription; controlled
- **Circulation:** 70,000
- **Website:** www.eparent.com

Freelance Potential
95% written by nonstaff writers. Publishes 50–60 freelance submissions yearly; 50% by unpublished writers, 50% by authors who are new to the magazine. Receives 96+ queries yearly.

Submissions
Query. Prefers email queries to jkatarski@eparent.com. Accepts hard copy. SASE. Responds in 3–4 weeks.
Articles: To 2,000 words. Informational articles; personal experience pieces; profiles; and interviews. Topics include the social, psychological, legal, political, technological, financial, and educational concerns faced by individuals with disabilities.
Depts/columns: Word lengths vary. Opinion and personal experience pieces, news items, new product information, and media reviews.

Sample Issue
84 pages (50% advertising): 12 articles; 11 depts/columns. Sample copy, $4.99 with 9x12 SASE ($2 postage). Guidelines and editorial calendar available.
- "Thinking Outside the Box." Article describes how a girl with cerebral palsy uses assistive technology to make her life better.
- "A Life Without Boundaries." Article discusses how a mobility system helped a teen with Muscular Dystrophy become more independent.
- Sample dept/column: "Research Reflections" discusses how Tourette Syndrome can be treated.

Rights and Payment
First North American serial rights. No payment. Provides 2 contributor's copies.

Editor's Comments
We look for practical information and advice that readers can use to make life easier and happier when caring for a person with special needs.

Faces

Cobblestone Publishing Company
Division of Carus Publishing
30 Grove Street, Suite C
Peterborough, NH 03458

Editor: Elizabeth Carpentiere

Description and Interests
Faces devotes each issue to a different country. It covers topics including culture, geography, people, cuisine, special events, and history of the area.
- **Audience:** 9–14 years
- **Frequency:** 9 times each year
- **Distribution:** 100% subscription
- **Circulation:** 15,000
- **Website:** www.cobblestonepub.com

Freelance Potential
80% written by nonstaff writers. Publishes 80 freelance submissions yearly; 10% by unpublished writers, 25% by authors who are new to the magazine. Receives 360 queries yearly.

Submissions
Query with outline, bibliography, and clips or writing samples. Accepts email queries to facemag@yahoo.com. Responds in 5 months.
Articles: 800 words. Informational articles and personal experience pieces related to the theme of each issue. Supplemental articles, 300–600 words.
Fiction: To 800 words. Stories, legends, and folktales from countries around the world—all related to the theme of each issue.
Depts/columns: Staff written.
Artwork: Color prints and transparencies.
Other: Games, crafts, puzzles, and activities, to 700 words. Poetry, to 100 lines.

Sample Issue
48 pages (no advertising): 10 articles; 1 story; 8 depts/columns; 3 activities. Sample copy, $4.95 with 9x12 SASE ($2 postage). Guidelines and theme list available at website.
- "The Sinking City." Article illustrates why Venice is having a serious problem with water damage.
- "The One-Legged Crane." Story retells a popular tale from Italy.
- "Mangia!" Article explores some of the myths and realities of Italian food.

Rights and Payment
All rights. Articles and fiction, $.20–$.25 per word. Pays on publication. Provides 2 contributor's copies.

Editor's Comments
We would like to receive articles featuring authentic voices from a specific culture, and interviews with children or young adults about life in a specific culture.

Face Up

75 Orwell Road
Rathgar, Dublin 6
Ireland

Editor: Gerard Moloney

Description and Interests
Subtitled "For Teens Who Want Something Deeper," this magazine focuses on issues that affect today's young adults. Much of the material published in *Face Up* focuses on spreading the Word of God.
- **Audience:** 14–18 years
- **Frequency:** 10 times each year
- **Distribution:** 80% school; 15% subscription; 5% newsstand
- **Circulation:** 12,000
- **Website:** www.faceup.ie

Freelance Potential
100% written by nonstaff writers. Publishes 60 freelance submissions yearly; 30% by unpublished writers, 70% by authors who are new to the magazine. Receives 500 unsolicited mss yearly.

Submissions
Send complete ms. Accepts email submissions to info@faceup.ie. Availability of artwork improves chance of acceptance. Responds in 1 month.
Articles: 900 words. Informational and how-to articles; personal experience pieces; profiles; and interviews. Topics include college, careers, current events, health, fitness, music, popular culture, and sports.
Depts/columns: 500 words. Opinion pieces, advice, health issues, the Internet, and reviews.
Artwork: Color prints and transparencies.
Other: Submit seasonal material on Christmas, Easter, and final exams 3 months in advance.

Sample Issue
38 pages (5% advertising): 6 articles; 12 depts/columns. Sample copy, guidelines, theme list, and editorial calendar available.
- "These Girls Bought Illegal Weapons on the Net . . . How?" True story provides insight into how easy it can be to purchase illegal material over the Internet.
- "It's Depressing and Uplifting Too!" Profile of the band Snow Patrol describes the band's journey making their second album.

Rights and Payment
Rights and payment rates vary. Pays on publication. Provides 2 contributor's copies.

Editor's Comments
We look for articles with an active voice that are direct and to the point.

Faith & Family

432 Washington Avenue
North Haven, CT 06473

Editorial Assistant: Robyn Lee

Description and Interests
This magazine is for Catholic parents who want to build faithful, integrated families. It offers a Catholic perspective on education, child raising, and social and political issues. *Faith & Family* is distributed through churches and to individual subscribers.
• **Audience:** Catholic families
• **Frequency:** Quarterly
• **Distribution:** 90% subscription; 10% other
• **Circulation:** 32,000
• **Website:** www.faithandfamilymag.com

Freelance Potential
90% written by nonstaff writers. Publishes 35 freelance submissions yearly; 15% by unpublished writers, 10% by authors who are new to the magazine. Receives 300 queries yearly.

Submissions
Query. Prefers email queries to editor@ faithandfamilymag.com. Responds in 2–3 months.
Articles: 600–2,000 words. Informational, how-to, and self-help articles; profiles; interviews; personal experience pieces; and media reviews. Topics include family life, parenting, marriage, religion, and social and political issues.
Depts/columns: Word lengths vary. Tips for home, garden, and food; entertainment reviews; spirituality.
Artwork: Prefers color photos or slides.

Sample Issue
96 pages (30% advertising): 7 articles; 14 depts/columns. Sample copy, $4.50. Guidelines available.
• "Mother-in-Law and Daughter-in-Law Relationships." Article offers advice for women on both sides of this delicate family relationship.
• "Benedict and the Children." Article reports on a meeting between Pope Benedict and 10,000 children in St. Peter's Square.
• Sample dept/column: "Family Matters" features a first-person piece about a troubled marriage.

Rights and Payment
First North American serial rights. Written material, $.33 per word. Pays on publication.

Editor's Comments
We're looking for queries that give a good idea of the angle and content of the article or column. Proposals should target a specific section of our magazine and reflect familiarity with that section.

Family Circle

Meredith Corporation
375 Lexington Avenue, 9th Floor
New York, NY 10017

Senior Editor: Jonna Gallo

Description and Interests
This well-known magazine strives to celebrate today's family and champions the woman at its center. Each page provides smart, practical solutions to help mothers raise happy, healthy families.
• **Audience:** Families
• **Frequency:** 15 times each year
• **Distribution:** 60% subscription; 40% newsstand
• **Circulation:** 3.8 million
• **Website:** www.familycircle.com

Freelance Potential
80% written by nonstaff writers. Publishes 50 freelance submissions yearly; 50% by unpublished writers, 20% by authors who are new to the magazine. Receives 300 queries yearly.

Submissions
Query with outline and 2 clips or writing samples. No simultaneous submissions. SASE. Responds in 6–8 weeks.
Articles: 2,000–2,500 words. Profiles of women who make a difference; reports on contemporary family issues; real-life inspirational issues.
Depts/columns: 750–1,500 words. Beauty, fashion, health, legal issues, parenting, relationships, home decorating, food, and fitness.

Sample Issue
188 pages (48% advertising): 21 articles; 11 depts/columns. Sample copy, $1.99 at newsstands. Guidelines available.
• "Easy Money." Article profiles three families that learned how to earn more, spend less, and save for the future.
• "Better to Forgive." Article explains why letting go of grudges is good for your health.
• Sample dept/column: "My Hometown" visits the village of Solving, California.

Rights and Payment
Rights negotiable. Written material, $1 per word. Kill fee, 10%. Pays on acceptance. Provides 1 contributor's copy.

Editor's Comments
Our magazine delivers essential advice for tough parenting challenges; provides fun suggestions for family activities; offers healthy and delicious recipes; and showcases projects to create a comfortable home while helping readers look and feel their best.

The Family Digest

P.O. Box 40137
Fort Wayne, IN 46804

Manuscript Editor: Corine B. Erlandson

Description and Interests
Articles on topics such as family life, parish life, spirituality, saints' lives, prayer, and church traditions are featured in this magazine for Catholic families. It also includes anecdotes and cartoons.
- **Audience:** Catholic families
- **Frequency:** 6 times each year
- **Distribution:** 100% controlled
- **Circulation:** 150,000

Freelance Potential
95% written by nonstaff writers. Publishes 60 freelance submissions yearly; 30% by authors who are new to the magazine. Receives 100 unsolicited mss each year.

Submissions
Send complete ms. Accepts hard copy and disk submissions. No simultaneous submissions; previously published material will be considered. SASE. Responds in 1–2 months.
Articles: 750–1,300 words. Informational, how-to, self-help, and inspirational articles; and personal experience pieces. Topics include family and parish life, spiritual living, church traditions, prayer, saints' lives, and seasonal material.
Depts/columns: Staff written.
Other: Humorous anecdotes, 25–100 words. Cartoons. Submit seasonal material 7 months in advance.

Sample Issue
48 pages (no advertising): 10 articles; 5 depts/columns. Sample copy, free with 6x9 SASE (2 first-class stamps). Guidelines available.
- "On Losing My Father." First-person essay tells how one woman deals with grieving her father's death.
- "Loving My Cat in Life and Death." Essay shares the author's comfort found in a poem after her cat dies.
- "How to Relate to a Dying Friend." Article offers suggestions for visiting with a terminally ill friend.

Rights and Payment
First North American serial rights. Articles, $40–$60. Anecdotes, $25. Pays 1–2 months after acceptance. Provides 2 contributor's copies.

Editor's Comments
We are interested in positive articles that focus on families' relationships with the Catholic parish. We're also interested in stories about Catholic youth.

FamilyFun

47 Pleasant Street
Northampton, MA 01060

Features Editor

Description and Interests
As the name implies, this publication contains a wealth of ideas for helping families have fun together. Activities, travel finds, family situations, meals, traditions, relationships, and entertainment are all here.
- **Audience:** Parents
- **Frequency:** 10 times each year
- **Distribution:** Subscription; newsstand
- **Circulation:** 2 million
- **Website: www.familyfun.com**

Freelance Potential
50% written by nonstaff writers. Publishes 100+ freelance submissions yearly; 1% by unpublished writers, 2% by authors who are new to the magazine. Receives thousands of unsolicited mss yearly.

Submissions
Query or send complete ms with clips or writing samples. Accepts hard copy. SASE. Responds in 2–3 months.
Articles: 750–3,000 words. Informational and how-to articles. Topics include cooking, games, crafts, activities, educational projects, sports, holiday parties, travel, and creative solutions to household problems.
Depts/columns: 50–1,500 words. News items about family travel, media reviews, and inspirational or humorous pieces focusing on family life.
Other: Submit seasonal material 6 months in advance.

Sample Issue
120 pages (47% advertising): 6 articles; 14 depts/columns. Sample copy, $3.95 at newsstands. Guidelines available at website.
- "Sibling Revelry!" Article lists several ideas to help siblings get along with each other.
- "Coming to a Museum Near You." Article details several traveling exhibits geared to children and the museum schedules where they can be seen.
- Sample dept/column: "My Great Idea" features methods that worked to solve a particular problem.

Rights and Payment
All rights. Articles, $1.25 per word. Other material, payment rates vary. Pays on acceptance.

Editor's Comments
We feature information that provides ideas for building strong, healthy families. Our emphasis is on activities that are fun, family-tested, and affordable.

Family Works Magazine

4 Joseph Court
San Rafael, CA 94903

Editor: Lew Tremaine

Description and Interests
This tabloid magazine is available at no charge to families in the San Francisco area. It includes articles on parenting, education, health, and finances, and community news reports.
- **Audience:** Parents, caregivers, and professionals
- **Frequency:** Monthly
- **Distribution:** 50% newsstand; 40% schools; 10% subscription
- **Circulation:** 30,000
- **Website:** www.familyworks.org

Freelance Potential
80% written by nonstaff writers. Publishes 75 freelance submissions yearly; 25% by unpublished writers, 25% by authors who are new to the magazine. Receives over 100 queries and unsolicited mss yearly.

Submissions
Send complete ms. Accepts hard copy, disk submissions, and email submissions to familynews@ familyworks.org. Availability of artwork improves chance of acceptance. SASE. Responds in 1 month.
Articles: 1,000 words. Informational articles; profiles; and interviews. Topics include parenting, family issues, recreation, education, finance, crafts, hobbies, sports, health, fitness, nature, and the environment.
Depts/columns: Word lengths vary. Reviews, recipes, and organizational news.
Artwork: B/W and color prints.

Sample Issue
24 pages (46% advertising): 7 articles; 2 depts/columns. Sample copy, free. Guidelines available.
- "Violence Today? Violence Tomorrow." Article examines the effects of domestic violence on children's futures.
- "Playing the Sports Game." Article provides 12 tips for parents of children who play team sports.
- "Bye, Bye Bills." Article provides useful advice on paying down your debt.

Rights and Payment
One-time rights. No payment. Provides 3 copies.

Editor's Comments
We welcome submissions from established and first-time writers. We prefer articles that entertain, inform and encourage our readers in their roles as parents and caregivers. We are especially interested in material on managing the complexities of the teenage years.

Faze Teen

4936 Yonge Street, Suite 2400
Toronto, Ontario M2N 6S3
Canada

Editor: Lorraine Zander

Description and Interests
Popular culture and celebrities are featured prominently in this magazine for Canadian teens. Appearing in print and online, it also includes pieces on contemporary issues, social issues, health, careers, fashion, and beauty.
- **Audience:** 13–18 years
- **Frequency:** 5 times each year
- **Distribution:** Subscription; newsstand; school libraries; Internet
- **Circulation:** 200,000
- **Website:** www.fazeteen.com

Freelance Potential
80% written by nonstaff writers. Publishes 100+ freelance submissions yearly; 50% by authors who are new to the magazine. Receives 96 queries each year.

Submissions
Query. Accepts email queries to editor@fazeteen.com. Response time varies.
Articles: Word lengths vary. Informational and factual articles; profiles; interviews; and personal experience pieces. Topics include current affairs, real-life issues, famous people, entertainment, science, travel, business, technology, and health.
Depts/columns: Word lengths vary. Updates on world events; career explorations; new products.

Sample Issue
66 pages (3% advertising): 9 articles; 11 depts/columns. Sample copy, $3.50 Canadian. Guidelines available at website.
- "Life with Rock Stars." Article looks at the high-pressure life of a music publicist.
- "Playing with Death." Article warns teens of the dangers of a fainting game that is harmful to their bodies and potentially fatal.
- Sample dept/column: "Global Issues" features short news items from around the world.

Rights and Payment
All rights. Written material, $50–$300. Payment policy varies. Provides 1 contributor's copy.

Editor's Comments
We prefer to receive submissions from writers who are close in age to our teen readers. Submissions from college journalism students are always welcome. Travel, social issues, and technology are hot topics.

FitPregnancy

21100 Erwin Street
Woodland Hills, CA 91367

Executive Editor: Sharon Cohen

Description and Interests
This magazine for expectant mothers provides informative articles on health, nutrition, exercise, psychology, food, fashion, and beauty during pregnancy. It also includes articles for parents of babies up to the age of two.
- **Audience:** Adults
- **Frequency:** 6 times each year
- **Distribution:** 60% subscription; 40% newsstand
- **Circulation:** 500,000
- **Website: www.fitpregnancy.com**

Freelance Potential
40% written by nonstaff writers. Publishes 50 freelance submissions yearly; 3% by unpublished writers, 5% by authors who are new to the magazine. Receives 360 queries yearly.

Submissions
Query with clips. Prefers email queries to scohen@ fitpregnancy.com. Responds in 1 month.
Articles: 1,200–2,400 words. Informational articles and personal experience pieces. Topics include health, fitness, family issues, psychology, postpartum issues, and breastfeeding.
Fiction: Word lengths vary. Humorous stories.
Depts/columns: 600 words. Nutrition, baby care, food, fashion, beauty, news items, and new product information.

Sample Issue
134 pages (42% advertising): 14 articles; 17 depts/ columns. Sample copy, $4.95 at newsstands. Guidelines available.
- "Detox Your Diet." Article provides healthful eating tips for expectant moms.
- "Class Action." Article suggests moms use stroller walks to make new friends and get back into shape.
- Sample dept/column: "Labor & Delivery" provides information for expectant moms from a longtime labor nurse.

Rights and Payment
Rights vary. Written material, payment rates vary. Pays on publication. Provides 2 contributor's copies.

Editor's Comments
Feature articles cover broad, timely topics. We welcome queries from writers who have new or important ideas to share with our readers. Queries should include information about experts you plan to interview.

FLW Outdoor Magazine ☆

30 Gamble Lane
Benton, KY 42054

Managing Editor: Chris Eubanks

Description and Interests
This fishing and outdoors magazine concentrates on several varieties of fish, with a focus on fishing techniques as well as entertaining fishing-related topics. It also features a regular section for kids.
- **Audience:** Adults and children ages 5–12
- **Frequency:** 8 times each year
- **Distribution:** 85% subscription; 15% newsstand
- **Circulation:** 50,000
- **Website: www.flwoutdoors.com**

Freelance Potential
60% written by nonstaff writers. Of the freelance submissions published yearly, 20% are by authors who are new to the magazine. Receives 300 queries yearly.

Submissions
Query or submit writing sample. Accepts email queries to ceubanks@flwoutdoors.com. Responds in 1 week.
Articles: 200 words. Factual, informational, and how-to articles; and profiles. Topics include nature, the environment, recreation, fishing, and humor.
Fiction: To 500 words. Genres include adventure fiction and nature stories.
Depts/columns: Word lengths vary. Seasonal fishing, tournaments, and conservation.
Other: Puzzles.

Sample Issue
120 pages: 7 articles; 12 depts/columns. Writers' guidelines available.
- "What Fish Can You Catch in the Winter?" Article for children highlights techniques used by ice anglers for catching wintering game fish.
- "Piranha!" Article demonstrates that the 17 species of this bloodthirsty fish deserve their reputation for ferocity.
- Sample dept/column: "King for a Day" relates how a boy fishing in a junior event bested competitors in adult tournaments held the same day.

Rights and Payment
First North American serial rights. Written material, $200–$500. Payment policy varies.

Editor's Comments
We are currently seeking true stories of young anglers and articles on different fishing techniques. Please note that we offer three editions of the magazine: bass edition, walleye edition, and saltwater edition.

Focus on the Family Clubhouse

8605 Explorer Drive
Colorado Springs, CO 80902

Associate Editor: Suzanne Hadley

Description and Interests
Stories and articles in *Focus on the Family* reflect a Judeo-Christian viewpoint without making numerous references to Scripture. The material has a broad appeal for parents using it to teach values to children.
- **Audience:** 8–12 years
- **Frequency:** Monthly
- **Distribution:** 100% subscription
- **Circulation:** 115,000
- **Website:** www.clubhousemagazine.com

Freelance Potential
20% written by nonstaff writers. Publishes 12–15 freelance submissions yearly; 50% by unpublished writers, 5% by authors who are new to the magazine. Receives 1,140 unsolicited mss yearly.

Submissions
Send complete ms. Accepts hard copy. SASE. Responds in 4–6 weeks.
Articles: 800–1,000 words. Informational, how-to, and factual articles; interviews; personal experience pieces; and humor. Topics include sports, nature, history, fantasy, religion, current events, and multicultural issues.
Fiction: 500–1,500 words. Genres include historical, contemporary, and religious fiction; parables; humor; and mystery.
Other: Activities and Bible-related comics. Submit Christian holiday material 7 months in advance.

Sample Issue
24 pages (5% advertising): 2 articles; 4 stories; 5 depts/columns. Sample copy, $1.50 with 9x12 SASE (2 first-class stamps). Guidelines available.
- "Creator or Chance?" Article tackles the confusion concerning the creation-versus-evolution debate.
- "The Room." Story shows how a young immigrant girl moves from anger to acceptance for her life.
- Sample dept/column: "Clean Slate" provides a math puzzle that reveals a Bible passage when solved.

Rights and Payment
First rights. Written material, to $150. Pays on acceptance. Provides 5 contributor's copies.

Editor's Comments
We look for submissions that relate to matters concerning marriage and the family, and encourage the inclusion of anecdotes and illustrations. Stories should bring abstract concepts to life.

Focus on the Family Clubhouse Jr.

8605 Explorer Drive
Colorado Springs, CO 80920

Associate Editor: Suzanne Hadley

Description and Interests
With its gentle emphasis on Christian values, this publication teaches children positive attitudes and outlooks. Its guidance comes from stories and articles that portray realistic situations.
- **Audience:** 4–8 years
- **Frequency:** Monthly
- **Distribution:** 98% subscription; 2% newsstand
- **Circulation:** 105,000
- **Website:** www.clubhousemagazine.com

Freelance Potential
20% written by nonstaff writers. Publishes 6–12 freelance submissions yearly; 1% by unpublished writers, 5% by authors who are new to the magazine. Receives 720 unsolicited mss yearly.

Submissions
Send complete ms. Accepts hard copy. No simultaneous submissions. SASE. Responds in 4–6 weeks.
Articles: To 600 words. Informational articles. Topics include the environment, nature, hobbies, health, and fitness.
Fiction: 250–1,000 words. Genres include Bible stories; humor; folktales; and religious, contemporary, and historical fiction.
Other: Puzzles, activities, games, cartoons, and poetry with biblical themes. Submit seasonal material 6 months in advance.

Sample Issue
24 pages (no advertising): 2 articles; 2 stories; 3 depts/columns; 5 activities; 1 comic. Sample copy, $1.50 with 9x12 SASE (2 first-class stamps). Guidelines available.
- "Joyful Noise." Article reports on young children attending the Saddleback School of Music and Arts.
- "A Family Tree for Tyler." Story emphasizes the importance of recognizing that we are all related.
- Sample dept/column: "You Make It" shows how to make table decorations for Thanksgiving.

Rights and Payment
First North American serial rights. Written material, to $150. Pays on acceptance. Provides 2 copies.

Editor's Comments
While we encourage material that focuses on Christian values, we want it to be implicit rather than using explicit scriptural references. Try to open your article with an anecdote between a parent and child.

Fort Myers Magazine

15880 Summerlin Road, Suite 189
Ft. Myers, FL 33908

Publisher: Andrew Elias

Description and Interests
Covering events in southwest Florida, this tabloid provides information on local cultural events and entertainment, and national arts and lifestyles.
- **Audience:** Adults
- **Frequency:** 6 times each year
- **Distribution:** 2% controlled; 1% subscription; 97% other;
- **Circulation:** 20,000
- **Website:** www.ftmyersmagazine.com

Freelance Potential
95% written by nonstaff writers. Publishes 10–15 freelance submissions yearly; 75% by unpublished writers, 50% by authors who are new to the magazine. Receives 2,400–3,000 unsolicited mss yearly.

Submissions
Query or send complete ms. Accepts hard copy, Macintosh disk submissions, and email submissions to ftmyers@optonline.net. SASE. Responds in 1–6 weeks.
Articles: 500–2,000 words. Informational articles; profiles; interviews; reviews; and local news. Topics include the arts, media, entertainment, travel, computers, crafts, current events, health and fitness, history, popular culture, recreation, social and environmental issues, and parenting.
Depts/columns: Word lengths vary. Sports, recreation, and book reviews.
Artwork: JPG, TIFF, or PDF images.

Sample Issue
30 pages (40% advertising): 2 articles; 2 reviews; 1 dept/column; 1 calendar. Sample copy, $3 with 9x12 SASE ($.77 postage). Guidelines and editorial calendar available.
- "The Veranda's Lasting Charms." Article describes a restaurant and its outdoor surroundings.
- "Making it Real." Article profiles artist Greg Biolchini, a local legend.
- "Reviving an American Classic." Article reviews a current play, *To Kill a Mockingbird.*

Rights and Payment
One-time rights. Pays 30 days from publication. Written material, $.10 per word. Provides 2 copies.

Editor's Comments
Submissions should reflect the tone of our readers, who are educated and active residents, 20 to 75 years old,

Fort Worth Child

Lauren Publications
4275 Kellway Circle, Suite 146
Addison, TX 75001

Editorial Director: Shelley Hawes Pate

Description and Interests
With a special focus on children from prenatal through adolescence, this magazine publishes informative articles for parents and families. Each issue also includes information on local resources, services, and events for residents of Fort Worth, Texas.
- **Audience:** Parents
- **Frequency:** Monthly
- **Distribution:** 90% controlled; 10% subscription
- **Circulation:** 40,000
- **Website: www.fortworthchild.com**

Freelance Potential
25% written by nonstaff writers. Publishes 12–15 freelance submissions yearly; 20% by authors who are new to the magazine. Receives 240 queries yearly.

Submissions
Query with résumé. Accepts hard copy and simultaneous submissions if identified. SASE. Responds in 2–3 months.
Articles: 1,000–2,500 words. Informational, self-help, and how-to articles; humor; profiles; and personal experience pieces. Topics include family, parenting, education, health, nutrition, exercise, travel, crafts, hobbies, computers, regional news, and multicultural and ethnic issues.
Depts/columns: 800 words. Health news and reviews.

Sample Issue
64 pages (14% advertising): 2 articles; 7 depts/columns. Sample copy, free with 9x12 SASE. Writers' guidelines available.
- "Beyond Dyslexia." Article discusses language-learning differences, including dyslexia.
- "The Politics of Mothering." Article reports on the many organizations for today's mother.
- Sample dept/column: "Take Note" looks at the do's and don'ts of bribing a child.

Rights and Payment
First rights. Written material, payment rates vary. Pays on publication. Provides contributor's copies upon request.

Editor's Comments
We seek articles that offer a well-informed, local perspective on issues affecting families in the Fort Worth area. Our goal is to educate, inspire, inform, and entertain our readers with up-to-date information.

Fostering Families Today

541 East Garden Drive, Unit N
Windsor, CO 80550

Editor: Richard Fischer

Description and Interests
This entertaining and educational resource is primarily read by parents and professionals involved in the child welfare system. It features articles related to adoption and foster care internationally, nationally, and domestically.
- **Audience:** Parents
- **Frequency:** 6 times each year
- **Distribution:** Subscription
- **Circulation:** 26,000
- **Website:** www.fosteringfamiliestoday.com

Freelance Potential
75% written by nonstaff writers. Publishes several freelance submissions yearly.

Submissions
Send complete ms. Accepts hard copy, IBM disk submissions (Microsoft Word or ASCII), and email to louis@adoptinfo.net. SASE. Response time varies.
Articles: 500–1,200 words. Informational and how-to articles; profiles; and personal experience pieces. Topics include parenting, pertinent research, health and family, adoption, single parenting, adolescence, special-needs children, foster parenting, multicultural families, issues in education, and legal issues.
Depts/columns: Word lengths vary, Parenting topics, events, cultural information, identity formation, legal issues, and reviews.

Sample Issue
62 pages (no advertising): 17 articles; 10 depts/columns. Guidelines available.
- "Bonding Is a Vital Issue: Appellate Courts Agree." Article defines bonding and gives specific examples of court cases that have considered its importance.
- "Treating Tough Guise." Article discusses the importance of positive male role models for boys.
- Sample dept/column: "Crossing the Line" shares the experiences of a "car pool" mom.

Rights and Payment
One-time rights. No payment. Provides 2 contributor's copies and a 1-year subscription.

Editor's Comments
We look for material related to adoption and foster care. Personal experience pieces that deal with issues such as multicultural families, children with special needs, and health issues are of interest to us. Submissions should be concise and reader-friendly.

The Friend

The Church of Jesus Christ of Latter-day Saints
50 East North Temple, 24th Floor
Salt Lake City, UT 84150

Managing Editor: Vivian Paulsen

Description and Readership
A publication for young Mormons, *The Friend* features articles, poems, comics, and stories that illustrate biblical teachings. Its goal is to help readers understand how the Gospel of Jesus Christ relates to their lives.
- **Audience:** 3–11 years
- **Frequency:** Monthly
- **Distribution:** 100% subscription
- **Circulation:** 252,000
- **Website:** www.lds.org

Freelance Potential
60% written by nonstaff writers.

Submissions
Send complete ms. Accepts hard copy. SASE. Responds in 2 months.
Articles: To 1,200 words. Informational and factual articles; profiles; personal experience pieces; and true stories. Topics include spirituality, the Mormon church, personal faith, and conflict resolution.
Depts/columns: Word lengths vary. Profiles of children from different countries.
Other: Poetry, word lengths vary. Puzzles, activities, crafts, and cartoons. Submit seasonal material 8 months in advance.

Sample Issue
50 pages: 7 articles; 8 stories; 4 depts/columns; 7 activities; 2 poems. Sample copy, $1.50 with 9x12 SASE (4 first-class stamps). Guidelines available.
- "Abuela's Answer." Story portrays a wise grandmother who responds to insults by setting an example.
- "Fortune Cookies." Story shows how a young girl learns compassion and kindness after acting wrongly toward a fellow student.
- Sample dept/column: "Making Friends" profiles a young chess tournament winner, athlete, and honor student who is an all-around "nice guy."

Rights and Payment
All rights. Pays on acceptance. Articles 200–400 words, $100; 400+ words, $250. Poems, $50. Other material, $15+. Provides 2 contributor's copies.

Editor's Comments
We look for fictionalized, detailed stories based on childhood experience, from a child's point of view. We also need very short stories and poems that convey a sense of joy and reflect Gospel teachings. Simple recipes and crafts projects are also welcome.

Fuel

401 Richmond Street West, Suite 245
Toronto, Ontario M5V 1X3
Canada

Editorial Assistant: Mandy Ng

Description and Interests
Distributed free to schools across Canada, this magazine focuses on relationships, fitness, computers, technology, fashion, cars, and music for Canadian teenage boys.
- **Audience:** 14–18 years
- **Frequency:** Monthly
- **Distribution:** Unavailable
- **Circulation:** 100,000
- **Website:** www.fuelpowered.com

Freelance Potential
100% written by nonstaff writers. Publishes 10 freelance submissions yearly; 100% by authors who are new to the magazine. Receives 55 queries each year.

Submissions
Query. Accepts hard copy and email queries to mandy@youthculture.com. SASE. Response time varies.
Articles: 1,200–2,000 words. Informational and how-to articles; profiles; interviews; personal experience pieces; and reviews. Topics include health and fitness, college and career, social and personal issues, gaming, sports, and technology.
Depts/columns: Word lengths vary. Film, music, health, cars, relationships, and fashion.

Sample Issue
22 pages: 5 articles; 5 depts/columns. Writers' guidelines available.
- "OK Computer." Article takes a look at the gear necessary to make great computer-based recordings and discusses artists who are taking laptop music to new heights.
- "TXT Generation." Article discusses the importance of text messaging in today's society.
- Sample dept/column: "Pulse" offers tips on looking your best for prom night through strength training and eating right.

Rights and Payment
Rights vary. Written material, payment rates vary. Pays on publication.

Editor's Comments
We have recently made some changes to our magazine to make it more innovative and interactive for teens, so it is best to take a look at an issue before querying us.

Fun For Kidz

P.O. Box 227
Bluffton, OH 48517-0227

Editor: Marilyn Edwards

Description and Interests
Each issue of *Fun For Kidz* is filled with activities targeting both boys and girls. Activities relate to pets, nature, hobbies, sports, and science, and each issue revolves around a theme.
- **Audience:** 6–13 years
- **Frequency:** 6 times each year
- **Distribution:** 80% subscription; 20% newsstand
- **Circulation:** 6,000
- **Website:** www.funforkidz.com

Freelance Potential
100% written by nonstaff writers. Publishes 100 freelance submissions yearly; 15% by unpublished writers, 15% by authors who are new to the magazine. Receives 1,000 unsolicited mss yearly.

Submissions
Send complete ms. Accepts hard copy and simultaneous submissions if identified. Availability of artwork improves chance of acceptance. SASE. Responds in 4–6 weeks.
Articles: 500 words. Informational and how-to articles. Topics include nature, animals, pets, careers, cooking, and sports.
Fiction: 500 words. Animal stories, humorous fiction, and adventure.
Depts/columns: Word lengths vary. Puzzles, science, and collecting.
Artwork: B/W and color prints or transparencies. Line art.
Other: Activities, filler, games, jokes, and puzzles. Submit seasonal material 6–12 months in advance.

Sample Issue
50 pages (no advertising): 2 articles; 7 depts/columns; 8 activities; 1 cartoon. Sample copy, $5. Guidelines and theme list available.
- "Magical Number Nine." Article explains how you can read the nine times table on your hands.
- Sample dept/column: "Workshop" tells how to build a snow fort block maker.

Rights and Payment
First or reprint rights. Written material, $.05 per word. Artwork, payment rates vary. Pays on publication. Provides 1 contributor's copy.

Editor's Comments
We need more cooking and craft-based activity pieces, as well as nonfiction with photos.

Games

6198 Butler Pike, Suite 200
Blue Bell, PA 19422-2600

Editor-in-Chief: R. Wayne Schmittberger

Description and Interests
In addition to feature articles about games, this maga-zine offers visual and verbal puzzles, quizzes, game reviews, and contests. It targets an audience of young adults and adults who enjoy exercising their brains in new and different ways.
• **Audience:** YA–Adult
• **Frequency:** 10 times each year
• **Distribution:** 70% subscription; 30% newsstand
• **Circulation:** 75,000
• **Website:** www.gamesmagazine-online.com

Freelance Potential
86% written by nonstaff writers. Publishes 200+ free-lance submissions yearly; 10% by unpublished writers, 20% by authors who are new to the magazine. Receives 960 queries and unsolicited mss yearly.

Submissions
Query with outline for articles. Send complete ms for shorter pieces. Accepts hard copy. SASE. Responds in 6–8 weeks.
Articles: 1,500–3,000 words. Informational articles; profiles; and humor. Topics include game-related events and people, wordplay, and human ingenuity. Game reviews by assignment only.
Depts/columns: Staff written except for "Gamebits."
Other: Visual and verbal puzzles, quizzes, contests, two-play games, and adventures.

Sample Issue
80 pages (8% advertising): 1 article; 6 depts/columns; 19 puzzles and games. Sample copy, $4.50 with 9x12 SASE ($1.24 postage). Guidelines available.
• "High-Tech War Games." Article describes how sophisticated computer simulations help prepare the U.S. military for almost any scenario.
• "Well-Connected Celebrities." Game connects celebrity last names to objects to create new words.

Rights and Payment
All North American serial rights. Articles, $500–$1,200. "Gamebits," $100–$250. Pays on publication. Provides 1 contributor's copy.

Editor's Comments
For puzzles and games, we look for fresh, lively ideas, carefully worked out for solvability. Visual appeal, a sense of humor, and the incorporation of pictures or objects from popular culture and everyday life are big pluses.

Genesee Valley Parent

1 Grove Street, Suite 204
Pittsford, NY 14534

Managing Editor: Margo Perine

Description and Interests
Articles about general parenting issues appear along with departments focusing on health, regional news, and teen issues in this publication for families in the Rochester, New York, area.
• **Audience:** Parents
• **Frequency:** Monthly
• **Distribution:** 65% controlled; 30% schools; 5% other
• **Circulation:** 37,000
• **Website:** www.gvparent.com

Freelance Potential
75% written by nonstaff writers. Publishes 50 free-lance submissions yearly; 5% by authors who are new to the magazine. Receives 240 queries yearly.

Submissions
Query with clips or writing samples. Accepts hard copy and simultaneous submissions if identified. SASE. Responds in 1–3 months.
Articles: 700–1,200 words. Informational and how-to articles; personal experience pieces; interviews; reviews; and humor. Topics include regional family events and concerns, special and gifted education, social issues, family problems, health and fitness, and parenting issues.
Depts/columns: 500–600 words. News, teen issues, and family health.
Other: Submit seasonal material 4 months in advance.

Sample Issue
46 pages (50% advertising): 4 articles; 6 depts/columns; 1 calendar. Writers' guidelines and editorial calendar available.
• "Teaching Your Tot: How Much Is Too Much?" Article discusses the negative aspects of teaching preschool children too much, too soon.
• "Making Memories." Article explores the growing pop-ularity of scrapbooking.
• Sample dept/column: "Healthy Family" provides important information about peanut allergies.

Rights and Payment
Second rights. Articles, $30–$45. Depts/columns, $25–$30. Pays on publication. Provides 1 tearsheet.

Editor's Comments
We look for accurate articles that cite local resources of value to Greater Rochester parents.

GeoParent

7944 East Beck Lane
Scottsdale, AZ 85260

Editors: Betsy Bailey & Nancy Price

Description and Interests
This website provides support and information for parents raising children of all ages. In addition to factual articles, it features interactive tools and practical resources on a broad range of family topics.
- **Audience:** Parents
- **Frequency:** Weekly
- **Distribution:** 100% Internet
- **Hits per month:** Unavailable
- **Website:** www.geoparent.com

Freelance Potential
90% written by nonstaff writers. Publishes 50 freelance submissions yearly. Receives 50 queries and unsolicited mss yearly.

Submissions
Prefers query. Accepts complete ms. Accepts hard copy, email submissions to content@coincide.com, and submissions through the website. SASE. Response time varies.
Articles: 500–2,500 words. Informational articles and advice. Topics include parenting, child development, family issues, child care, education, and gifted and special education.
Depts/columns: Word lengths vary. Parenting advice.

Sample Issue
Sample copy and guidelines available at website.
- "How to Talk to Kids About Hurricane Katrina." Article advises parents on how to limit media coverage of tragic events and how to address the concerns of children who are upset by the images they see.
- "Raising Truthful Kids." Article discusses what to do when kids lie and explains how to get them to take responsibilty for their actions.

Rights and Payment
Rights vary. Written material, $25–$50; $10 for reprints. Pays on publication.

Editor's Comments
We try to bring parents with children of all ages the resources they need and want. Our website offers thousands of informational articles, interactive tools, and an active and expansive support community. Articles should be based on research and interviews with experts and be written in a friendly, personal style. We are in constant need of short notes/blurbs to run on health, fitness, and lifestyle issues, as well as product introductions and reviews.

Gifted Education Press Quarterly

10201 Yuma Court
P.O. Box 1586
Manassas, VA 20109

Editor & Publisher: Maurice D. Fisher

Description and Interests
The education of gifted minority children is the focus of this newsletter. It includes articles on programs that can be applied to gifted education.
- **Audience:** Educators, administrators, and parents
- **Frequency:** Quarterly
- **Distribution:** 100% subscription
- **Circulation:** 7,000
- **Website:** www.giftedpress.com

Freelance Potential
90% written by nonstaff writers. Publishes 15 freelance submissions yearly; 20% by unpublished writers, 80% by authors who are new to the magazine. Receives 30 queries yearly.

Submissions
Query. Accepts hard copy. SASE. Responds in 2 weeks.
Articles: 3,000–5,000 words. Informational and how-to articles; personal experience pieces; profiles; and interviews. Topics include gifted education, homeschooling, multiple intelligence, parent advocates, social issues, science, history, the environment, and popular culture.

Sample Issue
14 pages (no advertising): 4 articles; 2 book reviews. Sample copy, $4 with 9x12 SASE.
- "Identification of Young Culturally Diverse Students for Gifted Education Programs." Article stresses that as gifted students are identified earlier, the demographics will change in gifted education programs.
- "Effective Pedagogical Strategies and Philosophies for Gifted Students of Color." Article discusses the challenges in meeting the needs of students with differences in learning styles, abilities, and interests.
- "A Measured Look at the Double Challenge to the Standardized I.Q. Test." Article challenges this test as a way to identify the gifted and talented.

Rights and Payment
All rights. No payment. Provides 5 contributor's copies.

Editor's Comments
We are committed to publishing material concerning gifted students in inner cities and urban areas. Our editors are also interested in rigorous mathematic and science programs for gifted students, as well as the impact of legislation on gifted and special education programs. Please visit our website for current information about our editorial needs.

Girls' Life

4517 Harford Road
Baltimore, MD 21214

Executive Editor: Kelly White

Description and Interests
This upbeat magazine for teens and tweens includes all the articles you would expect on fashion, beauty, health, fitness, school, dating, and self-esteem. It also includes celebrity news and information on young women making a difference in the world.
- **Audience:** 10–14 years
- **Frequency:** 6 times each year
- **Distribution:** Subscription; newsstand
- **Circulation:** 400,000
- **Website:** www.girlslife.com

Freelance Potential
40–50% written by nonstaff writers. Publishes 100+ freelance submissions yearly; 10% by unpublished writers, 10% by authors who are new to the magazine. Receives 996 queries and unsolicited mss yearly.

Submissions
Query or send complete ms with résumé and 2 clips. SASE. Responds in 3 months.
Articles: 1,200–2,500 words. Informational, service-oriented articles. Topics include self-esteem, body image, friendship, relationships, sibling rivalry, school success, facing challenges, and setting goals.
Depts/columns: 300–800 words. Celebrity spotlights; newsworthy stories about real girls; service pieces about friends, guys, and life; decorating tips; easy-to-do crafts and activities; and media reviews.
Artwork: 8x10 B/W and color prints. Line art.
Other: Puzzles and games. Poetry, to 100 lines.

Sample Issue
98 pages (30% advertising): 8 articles; 3 quizzes; 21 depts/columns. Sample copy, $5. Guidelines and editorial calendar available at website or with SASE.
- "Wipe Out Guilt." Article offers real-life situations and ways to be happy without feeling guilty.
- "The Secret Life of an Overweight Teenager." True story tells of a young woman's struggle with her weight and society's perception of her.
- Sample dept/column: "GL Life" offers seven easy steps to improve your grades.

Rights and Payment
All or first rights. All material, payment rates vary. Pays on publication. Provides 1 contributor's copy.

Editor's Comments
We look for material that helps young women make smart choices during the difficult teen years.

Green Teacher

95 Robert Street
Toronto, Ontario M5S 2K5
Canada

Editor: Tim Grant

Description and Interests
This magazine is intended to help teachers, parents, and other educators promote environmental and global awareness among students.
- **Audience:** Teachers, grades K–12
- **Frequency:** Quarterly
- **Distribution:** 50% newsstand; 40% subscription; 10% other
- **Circulation:** 7,500
- **Website:** www.greenteacher.com

Freelance Potential
90% written by nonstaff writers. Publishes 30 freelance submissions yearly; 70–80% by unpublished writers. Receives 120 queries yearly.

Submissions
Query with summary or outline. Accepts hard copy, queries faxed to 416-925-3474, and email queries to tim@greenteacher.com. Availability of artwork improves chance of acceptance. SASE. Responds in 2 months.
Articles: 1,500–3,000 words. Informational and how-to articles. Topics include the environment, science, education, and mathematics.
Depts/columns: Word lengths vary. Resources, reviews, and announcements.
Artwork: B/W or color prints or transparencies. Line art.
Other: Submit material for Earth Day 6 months in advance.

Sample Issue
48 pages (12% advertising): 9 articles; 2 depts/columns. Sample copy, $7. Guidelines available.
- "The Dinner Game." Article suggests a math activity to increase student awareness of the real cost of food.
- "Food for Thought: Practicing Conservation at the Table." Article offers a student activity to raise awareness of the environmental impact of food systems.
- "Earth and Religion: Seeking a Common Ground." Article reports on an interfaith/environmental conference.

Rights and Payment
Rights negotiable. No payment. Provides 5 copies.

Editor's Comments
We're looking for perspective pieces on the role of environmental or global education in the curriculum and practical classroom-ready activities.

Grit

1503 SW 42nd Street
Topeka, KS 66609-1265

Editor-in-Chief: K. C. Compton

Description and Interests
This magazine celebrates the intergenerational bonds among those who live on the land with spirit and style. It features articles and personal experience pieces.
- **Audience:** Families
- **Frequency:** 6 times each year
- **Distribution:** Subscription; newsstand
- **Circulation:** 150,000
- **Website: www.grit.com**

Freelance Potential
60% written by nonstaff writers. Publishes 150–200 freelance submissions yearly; 50% by unpublished writers, 50% by authors who are new to the magazine. Receives 2,400 queries yearly.

Submissions
Query. No unsolicited mss. Prefers email queries to grit@grit.com (include "Query" in the subject line). Accepts hard copy. SASE. Response time varies.
Articles: 800–1,500 words. Factual and how-to articles; profiles; and personal experience pieces. Topics include American history, family lifestyles, parenting, pets, crafts, community involvement, and antiques.
Depts/columns: 500–1,500 words. Topics include farm economics, comfort food, recipes, technology, medical advice, and equipment.
Artwork: Color slides. B/W prints for nostalgia pieces.

Sample Issue
48 pages (50% advertising): 4 articles; 12 depts/columns. Sample copy, $4. Guidelines and editorial calendar available.
- "Civilian Conservation Corps Built Pride." Article takes a look at a national program that helped put young men to work after the Great Depression.
- "Wind Power Pumped Life into West Texas." Article explores the American Wind Power Center in Texas.
- Sample dept/column: "Recipe Box" shares the history of molasses and includes recipes that use this sweetener.

Rights and Payment
Shared rights. All material, payment rates vary. Pays on publication. Provides 1 contributor's copy.

Editor's Comments
To write for us you must know about rural life. We serve as an authoritative voice for rural lifestyle farmers. Please note we no longer accept fiction or poetry.

Group

Group Publishing, Inc.
P.O. Box 481
Loveland, CO 80539–0481

Associate Editor: Chris Roberts

Description and Interests
This interdenominational magazine for youth ministers provides articles on how to run a successful ministry, improve outreach, encourage volunteerism, and offer advice to young people.
- **Audience:** Adults
- **Frequency:** 6 times each year
- **Distribution:** 100% subscription
- **Circulation:** 55,000
- **Website: www.group.com**

Freelance Potential
60% written by nonstaff writers. Publishes 200 freelance submissions yearly; 50% by unpublished writers, 80% by authors who are new to the magazine. Receives 300 queries yearly.

Submissions
Query with outline/synopsis and clips or writing samples. Accepts hard copy. State if artwork is available. SASE. Responds in 8–10 weeks.
Articles: 500–1,700 words. Informational and how-to articles. Topics include youth ministry strategies, recruiting and training adult leaders, understanding youth culture, professionalism, time management, leadership skills, and the professional and spiritual growth of youth ministers.
Depts/columns: "Try This One," to 300 words. "Hands-On Help," to 175 words.
Artwork: B/W or color illustration samples. Send artwork to art department. No photographs.

Sample Issue
122 pages (30% advertising): 5 articles; 29 depts/columns. Sample copy, $2 with 9x12 SASE. Guidelines available.
- "Who's Following You?" Article by a veteran youth leader explains how he recruited others to join him by following Jesus' example.
- "How to Mind Your Head: A Plan for Getting Organized that Really Works." Article stresses the importance of setting goals and using time effectively, rather than efficiently.

Rights and Payment
All rights. Articles, $125–$225. Depts/columns, $40. Pays on acceptance.

Editor's Comments
Our readers are looking for practical tips and proven strategies for managing their youth ministries.

Guide

Review and Herald Publishing Association
55 West Oak Ridge Drive
Hagerstown, MD 21740

Editor: Randy Fishell

Description and Interests

True life experiences and articles that demonstrate a strong Christian faith are featured in this publication created by members of the Seventh-day Adventist Church.
- **Audience:** 10–14 years
- **Frequency:** Weekly
- **Distribution:** 100% subscription
- **Circulation:** 29,000
- **Website: www.guidemagazine.org**

Freelance Potential

100% written by nonstaff writers. Publishes 175 freelance submissions yearly; 15% by unpublished writers, 20% by authors who are new to the magazine. Receives 420 unsolicited mss yearly.

Submissions

Send complete ms. Prefers email submissions to guide@rhpa.org. Accepts hard copy and simultaneous submissions if identified. SASE. Responds in 4–6 weeks.
Articles: To 1,200 words. True stories with inspirational and personal growth themes; true adventure pieces; and humor. Nature articles with a religious emphasis, 750 words.
Other: Puzzles, activities, and games. Submit seasonal material about Thanksgiving, Christmas, Mother's Day, and Father's Day 8 months in advance.

Sample Issue

32 pages (no advertising): 4 articles; 1 story; 5 activities; 2 Bible lessons. Sample copy, free with 9x12 SASE (2 first-class stamps). Guidelines available.
- "My Father's Promise." Article recounts a young girl's feelings while she waits for her father to visit her in the hospital.
- "Freaky Fungi." Article explains the many types of fungi, from mushrooms to toadstools.
- "A Whisper and a Prayer." Article describes how one child's faith helped him overcome a group of bullies.

Rights and Payment

First and reprint rights. Written material, $.06–$.12 per word. Pays on acceptance. Provides 3 contributor's copies.

Editor's Comments

We are currently seeking Christian humor articles and true life stories with urban settings that offer insight into African American or ethnic cultures.

Guideposts Sweet 16

1050 Broadway, Suite 6
Chesterton, IN 46304

Managing Editor: Betsy Kohn

Description and Interests

Geared toward pre-teen and teen girls, this magazine focuses on upbeat topics and true stories that also relate to the reality of that audience. Topics such as relationships, difficult peer situations, teen celebrities, beauty, and fashion are covered.
- **Audience:** 11–17 years
- **Frequency:** 6 times each year
- **Distribution:** 100% subscription
- **Circulation:** 200,000
- **Website: www.sweet16mag.com**

Freelance Potential

60% written by nonstaff writers. Publishes 100 freelance submissions yearly; 17% by unpublished writers, 55% by authors who are new to the magazine. Receives 1,200 queries yearly.

Submissions

Query or send complete ms. Accepts hard copy and email submissions to writers@sweet16mag.com. SASE. Responds in 1 month.
Articles: 750–1,500 words. Real life and first-person stories; profiles; and interviews. Topics include adventure, relationships, dating, friendship, peer pressure, and celebrities.
Depts/columns: 300–500 words. Beauty, "miracle" stories, teen profiles, and quizzes.

Sample Issue

50 pages (no advertising): 37 articles; 7 stories; 4 depts/columns. Sample copy, $4.50. Writers' guidelines available.
- "Flower Power." Article profiles a girl whose painting and drawing helped her through chemotherapy.
- "My Miracle Rescue." Story features a young girl who was found eight days after crashing down a ravine.
- Sample dept/column: "Mysterious Moments" offers accounts of strange but true incidents.

Rights and Payment

All rights. Articles, $150–$500. Depts/columns, $175–$400. Pays on acceptance. Provides 2–5 contributor's copies.

Editor's Comments

While we don't want overt moralizing, we do like to see stories that show readers that even hard situations can be overcome and turned into positive experiences. The writing, language, and events should be teen-friendly and realistic.

Gumbo Magazine

1818 North Dr. Martin Luther King Drive
Milwaukee, WI 53212

Managing Editor: Carrie Trousil

Description and Interests

Delving into the teen world, this publication covers topics ranging from teen athletes, music, and fashions to careers, money management, and health. Poetry and book reviews are also included in the mix.
- **Audience:** 13–19 years
- **Frequency:** 6 times each year
- **Distribution:** 50% schools; 40% libraries; 10% subscription
- **Circulation:** 25,000
- **Website:** www.gumboteenmagazine.com

Freelance Potential

15% written by nonstaff writers. Publishes 15 freelance submissions yearly; 100% by unpublished writers. Receives 50 queries yearly.

Submissions

Query. Accepts email queries to carrie@ mygumbo.com. Responds in 2 weeks.
Articles: 700–1,000 words. Personal experience pieces; profiles; interviews; and reviews. Topics include college; career; computers; current events; health; fitness; music; popular culture; recreation; science; technology; sports; and self-help, multicultural, and social issues.
Depts/columns: Word lengths vary. Current events, technology, fashion, and book and music reviews.
Other: Poetry, to 500 words. Submit seasonal material 6 months in advance.

Sample Issue

58 pages (30% advertising): 16 articles; 10 depts/ columns; 1 poem. Sample copy, $3 with 8x10 SASE ($1.23 postage). Guidelines and theme list available.
- "Where Are All the Jobs?" Article shows why it's hard for teens to find jobs.
- "Adero Neely." Article spotlights the young singer and his bright future.
- Sample dept/column: "CD Review" details the music of The Pussycat Dolls, Kaci Brown, and others.

Rights and Payment

One-time rights. Written material, $25. Pays on publication. Provides 10 contributor's copies.

Editor's Comments

We are looking for writers between the ages of 13 and 19 to contribute to our publication. Topics that interest us currently are more serious issues facing teens in particular and the world in general.

Gwinnett Parents Magazine

3651 Peachtree Parkway, Suite 325
Suwanee, GA 30024

Editor: Terry Porter

Description and Interests

This magazine is exclusively published for parents residing in Gwinnett County, Georgia, and is available to them at no charge. It provides local information as well as broader themed articles on parenting, education, health, safety, recreation, children's activities, and family issues.
- **Audience:** Parents
- **Frequency:** Monthly
- **Distribution:** Subscription; newsstand
- **Circulation:** Unavailable
- **Website:** www.gwinnettparents.com

Freelance Potential

40% written by nonstaff writers. Publishes several freelance submissions yearly.

Submissions

Query or send complete ms. Accepts email submissions only to editor@gwinnettparents.com. Include "Editorial Submission" in the subject line or it will not be read. Responds in 3–4 weeks.
Articles: 500–1,000 words. Informational articles; profiles; and personal experience pieces. Topics include finances, homeschooling, recreation, health, after-school activities, and other parenting issues.
Depts/columns: Word lengths vary. Health, parenting, ages and stages, family fun time.

Sample Issue

60 pages (50% advertising): 5 articles; 1 calendar; 15 depts/columns. Sample copy, $4 with 9x12 SASE ($.77 postage). Guidelines available at website.
- "Planning Your Child's First Sleepover Party." Article provides helpful hints for a foolproof sleepover.
- "The Top Ten Life Lessons Your Child Can Learn from Playing Golf." Article outlines the ten important qualities for life that golf can teach children.
- Sample dept/column: "Health" offers ways to prevent stretch marks during pregnancy.

Rights and Payment

First and non-exclusive online archival rights. Articles, $75. Depts/columns, $50. Pays on publication.

Editor's Comments

Our readers are everyday parents, mainly stay-at-home and working moms. Our publication emphasizes the importance and pleasures of parenting. Well-written, professional articles are needed, particularly those that incorporate local sources and news.

Happiness

P.O. Box 388
Portland, TN 37148

Editor: Sue Fuller

Description and Interests
This magazine provides readers with a television schedule and family-oriented, uplifting articles and activities. In addition, it includes stories and poems.
- **Audience:** Families
- **Frequency:** Weekly
- **Distribution:** Subscription
- **Circulation:** 150,000
- **Website:** www.happiness.com

Freelance Potential
50% written by nonstaff writers.

Submissions
Send complete ms. Accepts hard copy. Availability of artwork improves chance of acceptance. SASE. Responds in 3 months.
Articles: 500 words. Informational, how-to, self-help, and inspirational articles; and personal experience pieces. Topics include education, health, fitness, crafts, hobbies, animals, pets, nature, the environment, recreation, and travel. Also publishes humor and biographical articles.
Fiction: 500 words. Inspirational fiction, real-life stories, and stories about animals.
Depts/columns: 25–75 words. Crafts, cooking, and tips from readers.
Artwork: Color prints.
Other: Puzzles, activities, and poetry. Submit seasonal material 4 months in advance.

Sample Issue
40 pages (no advertising): 3 articles; 7 depts/columns; 6 activities. Guidelines available.
- "What To Do When the Joy Is Gone." Article offers simple steps to take when experiencing difficult times in life.
- "Help For Hackers—Killing A Cough." Article takes a look at how to choose the right cough medicine.
- Sample dept/column: "Shared Memories" shares an author's reflection of her high school days learning the Greg Shorthand method.

Rights and Payment
First rights. All material, payment rates vary. Pays on publication.

Editor's Comments
We look for upbeat articles on topics readers can relate to. They should focus on a happy, healthy lifestyle. No negative material, please.

High Adventure

The General Council of the Assemblies of God
1445 North Boonville Avenue
Springfield, MO 65802-1894

Editor: John Hicks

Description and Interests
Stories, crafts, ideas, and personal experiences are used in this publication to provide readers with spiritual guidance to help them attain higher ideals.
- **Audience:** Boys, grades K–12
- **Frequency:** Quarterly
- **Distribution:** 95% charter; 5% subscription
- **Circulation:** 87,000
- **Website:** www.royalrangers.ag.org

Freelance Potential
70% written by nonstaff writers. Publishes 125 freelance submissions yearly; 5% by unpublished writers, 30% by authors who are new to the magazine. Receives 360–480 unsolicited mss yearly.

Submissions
Send complete ms. Accepts hard copy, IBM disk submissions, email submissions to ranger@ag.org, and simultaneous submissions if identified. SASE. Responds in 1–2 months.
Articles: To 1,000 words. Informational, how-to, and self-help articles; profiles; humor; personal experience pieces; and inspirational pieces. Topics include religion, geography, history, nature, travel, sports, college, and multicultural issues.
Fiction: 1,000 words. Genres include inspirational, historical, religious, adventure, and multicultural fiction. Also publishes problem-solving stories and humor.
Depts/columns: Word lengths vary. News items.
Artwork: Color prints.
Other: Puzzles, activities, games, and jokes. Submit seasonal material 6 months in advance.

Sample Issue
14 pages (no advertising): 3 articles; 1 comic; 2 depts/columns. Sample copy, free with 9x12 SASE. Guidelines available.
- "Calling All Worm Farmers." Article explains how to compost with worms.
- Sample dept/column: "The Value of Royal Rangers" spotlights personal stories of several members.

Rights and Payment
First or all rights. All material, payment rates vary. Pays on publication. Provides 2 contributor's copies.

Editor's Comments
We look for submissions with a Christian emphasis that address youth issues. Articles should provide enjoyment while challenging the reader.

Higher Things

Dare To Be Lutheran

P.O. Box 580111
Pleasant Prairie, WI 53158-8011

Executive Editor: Rev. Todd A. Peperkorn, STM

Description and Interests
A resource and personal reading for youth groups and confirmation classes, *Higher Things* covers topics such as doctrine, practice, and current social issues. It also features humor, fiction, a review of the small catechism, and Bible studies.
- **Audience:** 13–19 years
- **Frequency:** Quarterly
- **Distribution:** Subscription; other
- **Circulation:** Unavailable
- **Website:** www.higherthings.org

Freelance Potential
25% written by nonstaff writers. Publishes 20 freelance submissions yearly.

Submissions
Query or send complete ms. Accepts hard copy and email to peperkorn@higherthings.org. SASE. Response time varies.
Articles: 500–800 words. Informational and how-to articles; profiles; interviews; and personal experience pieces. Topics include religion, current events, recreation, social issues, and travel.
Depts/columns: Staff written.

Sample Issue
32 pages (10% advertising): 5 articles; 6 depts/columns. Sample copy, $3. Guidelines available.
- "Love Songs for Jesus?" Article looks into how God is portrayed in contemporary Christian music.
- "The Myths of Evolution." Article discusses four concepts of the theory of evolution and debates whether they are fact or not.
- "Life in the Blood." Article examines embryonic stem cell research and discusses searching for an alternative to destroying life when harvesting cells.

Rights and Payment
Rights vary. Articles, $50–$100. Pays on publication.

Editor's Comments
Christ and His work are the focus of *Higher Things*. We need writing that is fresh, lively, and focuses on God's work in Christ for salvation. They should appeal to our readers, which include young teens who are innocent in their interests and older teens who are testing the waters. Please take time to choose the correct subject matter and vocabulary for each particular age group. Also, articles should have a proper balance of law and Gospel, with the Gospel predominating.

Highlights for Children

803 Church Street
Honesdale, PA 18431

Manuscript Submissions

Description and Interests
This educational publication features fun activities, articles, stories, poetry, and art for children. The philosophy of this magazine is that "children are the world's most important people."
- **Audience:** 2–12 years
- **Frequency:** Monthly
- **Distribution:** 100% subscription
- **Circulation:** 2.5 million+
- **Website:** www.highlights.com

Freelance Potential
98% written by nonstaff writers. Publishes 200 freelance submissions yearly; 30% by unpublished writers, 40% by new authors. Receives 7,980 mss yearly.

Submissions
Send complete ms for fiction; query for nonfiction. Accepts hard copy. SASE. Responds to queries in 2–4 weeks, to mss in 4–6 weeks.
Articles: To 800 words. Informational articles; interviews; profiles; and personal experience pieces. Topics include nature, animals, science, crafts, hobbies, world culture, and sports.
Fiction: To 400 words for ages 3–7; to 800 words for ages 8–12. Rebuses, to 120 words. Genres include mystery, adventure, and multicultural fiction. Also features sports stories and retellings of traditional stories.
Depts/columns: Word lengths vary. Science, crafts, and pets.
Other: Puzzles and games. Poetry, to 100 lines.

Sample Issue
42 pages (no advertising): 4 articles; 7 stories; 9 depts/columns; 1 rebus; 10 activities; 11 poems. Sample copy, free with 9x12 SASE (4 first-class stamps). Guidelines available.
- "Hot Spot!" Article takes a look at the geysers, hot springs, and mud pots in Yellowstone National Park.
- "Dumplings on Sundays." Story features a young girl who shares with her family her desire to quit piano.
- Sample dept/column: "Nature Watch" offers information on earthworms.

Rights and Payment
All rights. Written material, payment rates vary. Pays on acceptance. Provides 2 contributor's copies.

Editor's Comments
Nonfiction articles and contemporary stories using lively language and strong characters are of interest.

The High School Journal

CB#3500 University of North Carolina
Editorial Office, School of Education
Chapel Hill, NC 27599

Submissions Editor

Description and Interests
This publication reports on research findings concerning secondary school teaching and teaching techniques. Articles also address adolescent growth, development, interests, and other issues as they affect academic performance.
- **Audience:** Secondary school educators and administrators
- **Frequency:** 4 times each school year
- **Distribution:** 100% subscription
- **Circulation:** 800
- **Website:** www.uncpress.unc.edu

Freelance Potential
100% written by nonstaff writers. Publishes 20–30 freelance submissions yearly; 25% by unpublished writers, 85% by authors who are new to the magazine. Receives 324 unsolicited mss yearly.

Submissions
Send 3 copies of complete ms. Accepts email submissions to daniellacook@gmail.com. Responds in 3–4 months.
Articles: 1,500–2,500 words. Informational articles on adolescent issues as they affect school practices; reports on successful teaching practices; and research reports on teacher, administrator, and student interaction in school settings.
Depts/columns: 300–400 words. Book reviews.
Artwork: Line art.

Sample Issue
80 pages (no advertising): 7 articles. Sample copy, $7.50 with 9x12 SASE. Guidelines available.
- "No Hard Feelings: Finding the Focus in a Teacher-Student Function." Article offers guidelines teachers can follow to create positive, productive relationships with their students.
- "High School Schedule Changes and the Effect of Lost Instructional Time on Achievement." Article reports that students who missed class time because they were changing their schedules had no loss of academic achievement.

Rights and Payment
All rights. No payment. Provides 3 contributor's copies.

Editor's Comments
If you're researching issues related to secondary school or to adolescent growth and development, we'd like to hear from you.

High School Writer
Junior High Edition

Writer Publications
P.O. Box 718
Grand Rapids, MN 55744-0718

Editor: Emily Benes

Description and Interests
High School Writer showcases the works of junior high students across the country. Teachers who subscribe to this newspaper submit the poems, articles, essays, stories, and artwork of their students.
- **Audience:** Junior high school students
- **Frequency:** 6 times each year
- **Distribution:** 100% schools
- **Circulation:** 44,000

Freelance Potential
100% written by nonstaff writers. Publishes 300 freelance submissions yearly; 95% by unpublished writers, 75% by authors who are new to the magazine. Receives 36,000 unsolicited mss yearly.

Submissions
Accepts submissions from students of subscribing teachers in junior high school only. Send complete ms. Accepts hard copy and simultaneous submissions if identified. SASE. Response time varies.
Articles: To 2,000 words. Informational and how-to articles; profiles; and personal experience pieces. Topics include family, religion, health, social issues, careers, college, multicultural issues, travel, nature, the environment, science, and computers.
Fiction: To 2,000 words. Genres include historical and contemporary fiction, science fiction, drama, adventure, suspense, mystery, humor, fantasy, and stories about sports and nature.
Artwork: B/W line art.
Other: Poetry, no line limit.

Sample Issue
8 pages (no advertising): 16 stories; 8 articles; 17 poems. Sample copy, free. Guidelines available in each issue.
- "Code Breakers." Article describes an eighth-grade boy's fascination with making and breaking codes.
- "The Move." Story shares the feelings of a young girl when she moves into a new house with her family.
- "Mystery Man." Article thanks a man who saved a boy's cousin when her car went off the road and into a freezing river.

Rights and Payment
One-time rights. No payment.

Editor's Comments
We provide a real audience for student writers. We seek original material that is of interest to our readers.

High School Writer Senior

Writer Publications
P.O. Box 718
Grand Rapids, MN 55477-0718

Editor: Emily Benes

Description and Interests
High school students from subscribing schools around the country submit their poems, articles, and stories to this newspaper. This publication highlights the literary talents of students for an audience of their peers.
- **Audience:** Senior high school students
- **Frequency:** 6 times each year
- **Distribution:** 100% schools
- **Circulation:** 44,000

Freelance Potential
100% written by nonstaff writers. Publishes 300 freelance submissions yearly; 95% by unpublished writers, 75% by authors who are new to the magazine. Receives 36,000 unsolicited mss yearly.

Submissions
Accepts submissions from students of subscribing teachers in senior high school only. Send complete ms. Accepts hard copy, email submissions to writer@mx3.com (ASCII text), and simultaneous submissions if identified. SASE. Response time varies.
Articles: To 2,000 words. Informational and how-to articles; profiles; and personal experience pieces. Topics include current events, humor, muticultural and ethnic issues, nature, environment, popular culture, recreation, sports, and travel.
Fiction: To 2,000 words. Genres include humor, science fiction, adventure, and stories about sports.
Other: Poetry, no line limit. Seasonal material.

Sample Issue
8 pages (no advertising): 22 stories; 15 poems. Sample copy, free. Guidelines available in each issue.
- "Family Dispute." Story shares the points of view of a father and son as they discuss the son's report card.
- "Heaven on Earth." Story describes a small garden that is reserved for only a select few, comparing it to the feeling of life inside a snow globe.
- "Deer Hunting." Story reveals the experience of a young hunter who learns a lesson about patience.

Rights and Payment
One-time rights. No payment.

Editor's Comments
Morally uplifting topics are always of interest to this newspaper. We seek original works from high school students of subscribing schools. Submissions on most subjects are accepted, as long as they are presented in good taste.

Alfred Hitchcock's Mystery Magazine

475 Park Avenue South
New York, NY 10016

Editor: Linda Landrigan

Description and Interests
Named after the master of movie mystery, this publication takes delight in printing nearly every type of that genre—suspense, courtroom dramas, stories of espionage and intrigue, and police procedurals. Crime is the essence of all material published, either as an outright act or an insinuated one.
- **Audience:** Adults
- **Frequency:** 10 times each year
- **Distribution:** Subscription; newsstand
- **Circulation:** 150,000
- **Website:** www.themysteryplace.com

Freelance Potential
99% written by nonstaff writers. Publishes 80–100 freelance submissions yearly; 10% by unpublished writers, 10% by authors who are new to the magazine. Receives 1,200–1,500 unsolicited mss yearly.

Submissions
Send complete ms. Accepts hard copy. No simultaneous submissions. SASE. Responds in 3 months.
Fiction: 12,000 words. Classic crime mysteries, detective stories, suspense, private-eye tales, courtroom drama, and espionage.
Depts/columns: Word lengths vary. Reviews, puzzles, and bookstore profiles.

Sample Issue
144 pages (2% advertising): 9 stories; 8 depts/columns. Sample copy, $5. Guidelines available.
- "The Master of Animals." Story uses a Costa Rican rainforest for its "whodunit" setting.
- "The Casanova Caper." Story puts a Venetian private eye at the service of the notorious Casanova.
- Sample dept/column: "Reel Crime" examines the work of writer René Balcer.

Rights and Payment
First serial, anthology, and foreign rights. Written material, payment rates vary. Pays on acceptance. Provides 3 contributor's copies.

Editor's Comments
All submissions must be pure fiction—we do not accept stories that are based on actual crimes or other real-life events. Submissions should be previously unpublished with story ideas that are fresh, well-told, and absorbing. We sometimes accept tales of the supernatural but only if a crime is an integral part of the story plot.

Hit Parader

210 Route 4 East, Suite 211
Paramus, NJ 07652

Editor

Description and Interests
Heavy metal, hard rock, and underground band fans keep up to date with industry news and personalities in *Hit Parader*. Included are profiles of and interviews with band members, articles about industry trends, and upcoming concert and group information.
- **Audience:** YA
- **Frequency:** Monthly
- **Distribution:** Subscription; newsstand
- **Circulation:** 150,000
- **Website:** www.hitparader.com

Freelance Potential
10% written by nonstaff writers. Publishes 10 freelance submissions yearly; 50% by authors who are new to the magazine.

Submissions
Query. Accepts hard copy. Availability of artwork improves chance of acceptance. SASE. Responds in 1–3 months.
Articles: 1,000 words. Lifestyle articles; profiles; and interviews. Topics include hard rock and heavy metal musicians and bands.
Depts/columns: Word lengths vary. Reports on instruments and sound equipment; profiles of new bands; and reviews of video games, music videos, and new music releases.
Artwork: 3x5 and 5x7 B/W prints and color transparencies.
Other: Submit seasonal material about anniversaries or notable events 4 months in advance.

Sample Issue
98 pages (50% advertising): 12 articles; 15 depts/columns. Sample copy, $4.99 at newsstands. Writers' guidelines available.
- "Red Tape: Out from Under." Article profiles the California-based, punk-metal-poet band, Red Tape.
- Sample dept/column: "Tech Talk with Staind" profiles the band Staind and their motivations behind writing and performing.

Rights and Payment
First rights. Articles, $100–$150. Other material, payment rates vary. Pays on publication. Provides 1 contributor's copy.

Editor's Comments
We need more interviews of up-and-coming, hot groups from writers connected to the industry.

Home Education Magazine

P.O. Box 1083
Tonasket, WA 98855

Editor: Carol Narigon

Description and Interests
Providing practical information and inspiration for parents who homeschool are two of the goals of this publication. It also explores serious issues surrounding successful homeschool training, such as financial aspects, college considerations, styles of teaching, the balance between education and socializing, parents' time allotments, and teaching ideas.
- **Audience:** Parents
- **Frequency:** 6 times each year
- **Distribution:** 50% subscription; 20% controlled; 30% other
- **Circulation:** 110,000
- **Website:** www.homeedmag.com

Freelance Potential
40% written by nonstaff writers. Publishes 35 freelance submissions yearly; 25% by unpublished writers, 40% by authors who are new to the magazine. Receives 720+ queries and unsolicited mss yearly.

Submissions
Query or send complete ms with résumé. Prefers email submissions to articles@homeedmag.com. Accepts hard copy. SASE. Responds in 1–2 months.
Articles: 1,000–1,500 words. Informational, how-to, and personal experience articles. Topics include homeschooling, education, and parenting.
Depts/columns: Staff written.

Sample Issue
58 pages (13% advertising): 6 articles; 12 depts/columns; 1 poem. Sample copy, $6.50 via email. Guidelines available.
- "Learning Logs." Article explores the benefits that learning logs provide to children and parents.
- "A Day in the Life: Home + Love = Learning." Article covers several teaching styles of homeschooling.
- "How to Join a New Home School Group." Article discusses ways to feel comfortable in a new group.

Rights and Payment
First North American serial and electronic rights. Articles, $50–$100. Pays on acceptance. Provides 1 contributor's copy.

Editor's Comments
Our magazine reaches a widely diverse readership and our content reflects that diversity. We would like to see more well-written humorous pieces relating to real homeschooling experiences.

Homeschooling Today

P.O. Box 436
Barker, TX 77413

Editor-in-Chief: Stacy McDonald

Description and Interests
Since 1992, *Homeschooling Today* has presented practical information and encouragement to parents who have chosen to teach their children at home. Ready-to-use study units and lessons appear along with articles offering advice and practical tips. Much of its material is written from a Christian perspective.
- **Audience:** Parents
- **Frequency:** 6 times each year
- **Distribution:** Subscription; newsstand
- **Circulation:** 30,000
- **Website:** www.homeschoolingtoday.com

Freelance Potential
90% written by nonstaff writers. Publishes 10–20 freelance submissions yearly; 10% by unpublished writers, 5% by authors who are new to the magazine. Receives 60–120 unsolicited mss yearly.

Submissions
Send complete ms. Accepts hard copy and email submissions to editor@homeschoolingtoday.com (Microsoft Word or RTF attachments). SASE. Responds in 3–6 months.
Articles: 1,000–2,500 words. Informational, self-help, and how-to articles; profiles; interviews; and personal experience pieces. Topics include education, music, technology, special education, the arts, history, mathematics, and science.
Depts/columns: Word lengths vary. New product information, reviews, music, the arts, literature.

Sample Issue
84 pages: 5 articles; 14 depts/columns. Sample copy, $5.95. Guidelines available.
- "What Is a Young Earth Worldview?" Article addresses issues associated with evolution and what the Bible says about the age of the Earth.
- "A Museum Guide for the Creation Minded." Article discusses what parents who are creationists should tell children before a museum visit.
- Sample dept/column: "Understanding the Arts" discusses Vincent van Gogh's passion for Christ.

Rights and Payment
First rights. Written material, $.08 per word. Pays on publication. Provides 1 contributor's copy.

Editor's Comments
Please note that most of the articles we publish are geared to Christian homeschooling parents.

Hopscotch

P.O. Box 164
Bluffton, OH 45817-0164

Editor: Marilyn Edwards

Description and Interests
Based on the idea that every girl deserves the right to be a young girl before becoming a young adult, *Hopscotch* covers timeless topics and leaves the cosmetics, fashion, and dating to other magazines.
- **Audience:** 6–13 years
- **Frequency:** 6 times each year
- **Distribution:** 70% subscription; 30% newsstand
- **Circulation:** 16,000
- **Website:** www.hopscotchmagazine.com

Freelance Potential
100% written by nonstaff writers. Publishes 150 freelance submissions yearly; 20% by unpublished writers, 30% by authors who are new to the magazine. Receives 1,500 queries and unsolicited mss yearly.

Submissions
Query or send complete ms. Include photographs with nonfiction. Accepts hard copy and simultaneous submissions. SASE. Responds to queries in 1–2 weeks, to mss in 2–3 months.
Articles: To 500 words. Informational articles; profiles; and personal experience pieces. Topics include pets, nature, hobbies, science, games, sports, simple cooking, and careers.
Fiction: To 1,000 words. Genres include mystery, adventure, and historical and multicultural fiction.
Depts/columns: 500 words. Crafts and cooking.
Artwork: Prefers B/W prints. Accepts color prints.
Other: Puzzles, activities, and poetry.

Sample Issue
50 pages (no advertising): 5 articles; 5 stories; 2 depts/columns; 7 activities; 2 comics; 3 poems. Sample copy, $5 with 9x12 SASE. Guidelines and theme list available with #10 SASE.
- "The Secret Journal of Beatrix Potter." Article recounts the young life of this famous author.
- "Snow Day." Story features a girl who spends a snow day playing with a homeschooled friend.

Rights and Payment
First and second rights. Written material, $.05 per word. Artwork, payment rates vary. Pays on publication. Provides 1 contributor's copy.

Editor's Comments
We are always in need of cute and clever recipes, well-written and illustrated crafts, riddles, and jokes. We have too much fiction at this time.

The Horn Book Magazine

56 Roland Street, Suite 200
Boston, MA 02129

Editor-in-Chief: Roger Sutton

Description and Interests
The Horn Book Magazine is a resourceful journal of children's literature, written to inform its audience with reviews of books achieving high standards. This publication also features articles and essays related to children's literature.
- **Audience:** Parents, teachers, and librarians
- **Frequency:** 6 times each year
- **Distribution:** 70% subscription; 10% newsstand; 20% other
- **Circulation:** 16,000
- **Website:** www.hbook.com

Freelance Potential
70% written by nonstaff writers. Publishes 12–15 freelance submissions yearly; 10% by unpublished writers, 30% by authors who are new to the magazine. Receives 240 queries, 120 unsolicited mss yearly.

Submissions
Query or send complete ms. Accepts hard copy. SASE. Responds in 4 months.
Articles: To 2,800 words. Interviews with children's authors, illustrators, and editors; critical articles about children's and young adult literature; and book reviews.
Depts/columns: Word lengths vary. Perspectives from illustrators; children's publishing updates; and special columns.

Sample Issue
122 pages (20% advertising): 5 articles; 3 reviews; 2 depts/columns. Sample copy, free with 9x12 SASE. Guidelines and editorial calendar available.
- "Graphic Novels 101." Article describes what a graphic novel is and answers some general questions about them.
- "Happy Centennial, Meindert DeJong!" Article highlights many books by one of the most celebrated children's book writers of the 1950s and 1960s.
- Sample dept/column: "Foreign Correspondence" tells of the novels written together by two authors from very different cultural backgrounds.

Rights and Payment
All rights. Written material, payment rates vary. Pays on publication. Provides 1 contributor's copy.

Editor's Comments
Parents, librarians, teachers, writers, and publishers read this journal for the latest information and critical reviews of young adult and children's books.

Horsemen's Yankee Pedlar

83 Leicester Street
North Oxford, MA 01537

Editor: Molly Johns

Description and Interests
Horse enthusiasts living in New England read this magazine for informational articles and in-depth coverage of the equine industry. Competitions, breeding, training, horse care, education, news, and events are covered in each issue of this tabloid.
- **Audience:** YA–Adult
- **Frequency:** Monthly
- **Distribution:** Newsstand; subscription; schools
- **Circulation:** 50,000
- **Website:** www.pedlar.com

Freelance Potential
50% written by nonstaff writers. Publishes 40 freelance submissions yearly; 5% by authors who are new to the magazine. Receives 360 queries, 240 unsolicited mss yearly.

Submissions
Query or send complete ms. Accepts hard copy and simultaneous submissions if identified. SASE. Responds to queries in 1–2 weeks, to mss in 2–3 months.
Articles: 500–800 words. Informational and how-to articles; personal experience pieces; interviews; and reviews. Topics include horse breeds, disciplines, training, health care, and equestrian equipment.
Depts/columns: Word lengths vary. News, book reviews, business issues, nutrition, and legal issues.
Artwork: B/W and color prints.

Sample Issue
234 pages (75% advertising): 64 articles; 18 depts/columns. Sample copy, $3.99 with 9x12 SASE (7 first-class stamps). Guidelines available.
- "A Portrait of Jo Hight." Article profiles a lifetime horse lover's passion for and contribution to the Saddlebred horse industry.
- Sample dept/column: "Stable Solutions" explains the different laws for shipping your horses safely.

Rights and Payment
First North American serial rights. Written material, $2 per published column inch. Show coverage, $75 per day. Pays 30 days after publication. Provides 1 tearsheet.

Editor's Comments
A knowledge of horsemanship in the New England region is required. Well-written submissions covering all facets of the equine industry will be considered.

Horsepower

P.O. Box 670
Aurora, Ontario L4G 4J9
Canada

Managing Editor: Susan Stafford

Description and Interests

This magazine for young horse lovers features educational and entertaining material related to horses. The underlying emphasis is always safety, especially in regard to instructional articles.
- **Audience:** 9–16 years
- **Frequency:** 6 times each year
- **Distribution:** 80% subscription; 10% schools; 10% controlled
- **Circulation:** 10,000
- **Website:** www.horse-canada.com

Freelance Potential

50% written by nonstaff writers. Publishes 15–20 freelance submissions yearly; 10% by unpublished writers, 10% by new authors. Receives 10–20 mss yearly.

Submissions

Query with outline or synopsis; or send complete ms with résumé. Accepts hard copy, IBM disk submissions (ASCII or WordPerfect), and email submissions to info@horse-canada.com. SAE/IRC. Responds to queries in 1–2 weeks, to mss in 2–3 months.
Articles: 500–1,000 words. Informational and how-to articles; profiles; and humor. Topics include breeds, training, stable skills, equine health, and tack.
Fiction: 500 words. Adventure, humorous stories, and sports stories related to horses.
Depts/columns: Staff written.
Artwork: B/W and color prints.
Other: Horse-themed activities, games, and puzzles.

Sample Issue

16 pages (20% advertising): 3 articles; 4 depts/columns; 2 activities; 2 puzzles; 1 poster. Sample copy, $3.95. Guidelines and theme list available.
- "Horse Health." Article offers advice for detecting and treating a lame horse.
- "Trainer's Corner." Article profiles the world-famous horse trainer, Linda Tellington-Jones.
- "Ride a Piece of History." Article reviews the history of the antique carousel at Lakeside Park in Ontario.

Rights and Payment

First North American serial rights. Written material, $50–$90. Artwork, $10–$75. Pays on publication. Provides 1 contributor's copy.

Editor's Comments

We seek informative articles on horse care and horse health, and how-to articles emphasizing safe riding.

Hudson Valley Parent

174 South Street
Newburgh, NY 12550

Editor: Leah Black

Description and Interests

Distributed free to parents living in the mid-Hudson Valley of New York, this resourceful magazine includes articles on topics related to parenting. It also covers regional events.
- **Audience:** Parents
- **Frequency:** Monthly
- **Distribution:** 100% other
- **Circulation:** 70,000
- **Website:** www.excitingread.com

Freelance Potential

95% written by nonstaff writers. Publishes 120 freelance submissions yearly; 60% by unpublished writers, 40% by authors who are new to the magazine. Receives 96 queries, 240 unsolicited mss yearly.

Submissions

Query with writing samples; or send complete ms. Prefers email to editor@excitingread.com. Accepts hard copy. SASE. Responds in 3–6 weeks.
Articles: 700–1,200 words. Informational and how-to articles; and practical application pieces. Topics include parenting, grandparenting, computers, technology, recreation, health, fitness, sports, hobbies, and the home.
Depts/columns: 700 words. Health, education, and adolescent issues.
Other: Submit seasonal material 6 months in advance. "Vida y Familia Hispana," Spanish section.

Sample Issue

62 pages (50% advertising): 8 articles; 4 depts/columns. Sample copy, free with 9x12 SASE. Guidelines and editorial calendar available.
- "Perfect Party Planning." Article offers ideas for hosting a birthday party that can be fun for everyone.
- "Communication Breakdown." Article takes a look at ways to improve communication with adolescents.
- Sample dept/column: "Child Behavior" discusses the benefits of yoga with children.

Rights and Payment

One-time rights. Written material, $25–$70. Pays on publication. Provides contributor's copies.

Editor's Comments

Feel free to submit manuscripts, or query with a few ideas you think might interest our readers. Describe any research you may have done and list other sources you plan to consult. Sell your idea to us.

Humpty Dumpty's Magazine

Children's Better Health Institute
1100 Waterway Boulevard, P.O. Box 567
Indianapolis, IN 46206–0567

Editor: Phyllis Lybarger

Description and Interests
One of the many publications from the Children's Better Health Institute, this magazine targets early readers and helps them learn good lifestyle habits through fun stories, articles, games, and activities.
- **Audience:** 4–6 years
- **Frequency:** 6 times each year
- **Distribution:** 100% subscription
- **Circulation:** 236,000
- **Website:** www.humptydumptymag.org

Freelance Potential
10% written by nonstaff writers. Publishes 10–12 freelance submissions yearly; 5% by unpublished writers, 12% by authors who are new to the magazine.

Submissions
Send complete ms. Accepts hard copy. SASE. Responds in 10–12 weeks.
Articles: To 250 words. Factual, observational, and how-to articles. Topics include health, fitness, sports, science, nature, the environment, animals, crafts, hobbies, and multicultural and ethnic subjects.
Fiction: To 300 words. Genres include early reader contemporary and multicultural fiction; stories about sports; fantasy; folktales; mystery; drama; and humor.
Depts/columns: Word lengths vary. Recipes and health and fitness news.
Other: Puzzles, activities, and games. Submit seasonal material 8 months in advance.

Sample Issue
36 pages (2% advertising): 3 articles; 1 story; 4 depts/columns; 9 games/activities; 1 recipe; 1 poem. Sample copy, $1.25. Guidelines available.
- "The Wiggle, Wobble Mystery." Story tells of a boy who is anxious for his loose tooth to fall out.
- "I Only Have Beats for You." Article teaches children about their heart, from the organ's point of view.
- Sample dept/column: "Humpty Dumpty's Choice" offers book reviews on subjects relevant to the issue's stories.

Rights and Payment
All rights. Written material, $.22 per word. Pays on publication. Provides 10 contributor's copies.

Editor's Comments
We look for stories, articles, and activities that promote good health. All material should reflect modern life and promote wholesome values.

Ignite Your Faith

Christianity Today
465 Gunderson Drive
Carol Stream, IL 60188

Editor: Chris Lutes

Description and Interests
Formerly known as *Campus Life*, this magazine empowers Christian teens to deepen their faith. It targets high school and early college youth with biblical applications and spiritually challenging questions, as well as articles on typical teen experiences.
- **Audience:** 13–19 years
- **Frequency:** 9 times each year
- **Distribution:** 100% subscription
- **Circulation:** 100,000
- **Website:** www.igniteyourfaith.com

Freelance Potential
60% written by nonstaff writers. Publishes 15–20 freelance submissions yearly; 10% by unpublished writers, 20% by authors who are new to the magazine. Receives 300 queries yearly.

Submissions
Query with one-page synopsis. No unsolicited mss. Accepts hard copy and simultaneous submissions if identified. SASE. Responds in 3–6 weeks.
Articles: 700–1,500 words. Personal experience pieces and humor. Topics include Christian values, beliefs, and Christian education.
Fiction: 1,000–1,500 words. Genres include contemporary fiction with religious themes.
Depts/columns: Staff written.

Sample Issue
64 pages (30% advertising): 4 articles; 27 depts/columns. Sample copy, $3 with 9x12 SASE. (3 first-class stamps). Guidelines available.
- "Party Girl?" Article tells of a college student who desires popularity but won't sacrifice her religious beliefs to fit in.
- "The Day God Died." Article meditates on the disciples' confusion before the Resurrection.
- Sample dept/column: "Don't Be a Prayer Robot" discusses the difference between responsible use of prayer for purposes of growth and requests for favors.

Rights and Payment
First rights. Written material, $.20–$.25 per word. Pays on acceptance. Provides 2 contributor's copies.

Editor's Comments
We look for fictional stories in a first-person format that highlight the positive effects of following faith. We also offer humor and material about Christian college experience. We discourage use of religious clichés.

The Illuminata

5624 Fairway Drive
Zachary, LA 70791

Editor-in-Chief: Bret Funk

Description and Interests
Science fiction, fantasy, horror, and other speculative fiction appear in this online magazine from Tyrannosaurus Press. In addition to short stories, it publishes reviews and articles about these literary genres.
- **Audience:** YA–Adult
- **Frequency:** Monthly
- **Distribution:** 100% Internet
- **Hits per month:** 400
- **Website:** www.tyrannosauruspress.com

Freelance Potential
25% written by nonstaff writers. Publishes 10–15 freelance submissions yearly; 95% by unpublished writers, 90% by authors who are new to the magazine. Receives 10 queries yearly.

Submissions
Query following guidelines at website. Accepts email queries to submissions@tyrannosauruspress.com (no attachments). Responds in 1–3 months.
Articles: 1–2 pages in length. Informational articles about science fiction, fantasy, and horror.
Fiction: Word lengths vary. Genres include fantasy, science fiction, and horror.
Depts/columns: Reviews of science fiction and fantasy books and stories, 500–1,000 words.

Sample Issue
12 pages. Sample copy and writers' guidelines available at website.
- "Firefly Me Away." Article discusses a short-lived but much-loved television show that was set 500 years in the future.
- "Reflecting on Fandom." Article explores the culture of science fiction fan groups and their different activities.
- Sample dept/column: "Reviews" offers analyses of books by Jane Lindskold, Christopher Paolini, and others.

Rights and Payment
Rights vary. No payment.

Editor's Comments
We are interested in reviewing queries only. Query letters should be straightforward and to the point; when writing them, keep brevity in mind. We do not want detailed synopses or large chunks of manuscripts pasted into the query. Remember, be creative. This is your chance to intrigue us.

Indy's Child

1901 Broad Ripple Avenue
Indianapolis, IN 46220

Editorial Assistant: Lynette Rowland

Description and Interests
Described as "central Indiana's only parenting publication," this tabloid has been serving families for more than 20 years. It features up-to-date information on parenting, education, family travel, home topics, and new products.
- **Audience:** Parents
- **Frequency:** Monthly
- **Distribution:** 50% newsstand; 30% controlled; 10% religious instruction; 10% schools
- **Circulation:** 144,000
- **Website:** www.indyschild.com

Freelance Potential
80% written by nonstaff writers. Publishes 75 freelance submissions yearly; 20% by authors who are new to the magazine. Receives 1,200+ mss yearly.

Submissions
Send complete ms. Accepts email submissions to editor@indyschild.com and Macintosh disk submissions. SASE. Responds in 3–4 months.
Articles: 1,000–2,000 words. Informational and self-help articles; profiles; and personal experience pieces. Topics include the arts, careers, hobbies, current events, education, health, multicultural and ethnic issues, music, popular culture, recreation, social issues, sports, and travel.
Depts/columns: To 1,000 words. Expert advice, women's health, movie and museum reviews, and teen and tween issues.
Artwork: Color prints, transparencies, or digital images.
Other: Puzzles, activities, filler, games, and jokes.

Sample Issue
46 pages (50% advertising): 6 articles; 11 depts/columns; 1 calendar. Sample copy, free. Guidelines and editorial calendar available.
- "Create Your Own Outdoor Retreat." Article offers tips on gardening and landscaping for families.
- Sample dept/column: "Profile" visits a new high school with an innovative job share program.

Rights and Payment
First or second rights. Written material, $100. Pays on publication. Provides 1–50 contributor's copies.

Editor's Comments
Features must be carefully researched and written clearly and concisely.

InQuest Gamer

151 Wells Avenue
Congers, NY 10920

Editor: Brent Fischdaugh

Description and Interests
InQuest Gamer was launched in 1995 to bring readers the best information on all types of games. It covers video games, computer games, collectible card games, role playing games, and board games. In addition to feature articles, it publishes product reviews and gaming industry news.
• **Audience:** YA–Adult
• **Frequency:** Monthly
• **Distribution:** Subscription
• **Circulation:** Unavailable
• **Website:** www.wizarduniverse.com

Freelance Potential
40% written by nonstaff writers. Publishes many freelance submissions yearly.

Submissions
Query or send complete ms. Accepts email submissions to bfischdaugh@wizarduniverse.com. Response time varies.
Articles: Word lengths vary. Informational articles; new product information; opinion pieces; and media reviews. Topics include audio, video, software, computers, entertainment, and games.
Depts/columns: Word lengths vary. Game updates, news, notes, previews, and computer information.

Sample Issue
104 pages: 7 articles; 8 depts/columns. Sample copy, $4 with 9x12 SASE ($.77 postage). Writers' guidelines available.
• "Top 100 Creatures." Article examines the nuts and bolts of all 3,679 creatures in the game *Magic* to settle which power cards tower over the field.
• "X-Men Classic." Article takes a nostalgic look back at the Silver Age of the X-Men comics.
• Sample dept/column: "Plugged In" looks at what's hot in electronic gaming.

Rights and Payment
Rights, payment rates, and payment policy vary.

Editor's Comments
For the past 10 years, we've been offering our readers the best gaming information available. We always need more news and updates that will interest gaming enthusiasts of all ages. Articles about up-and-coming game releases and articles that feature detailed overviews and strategies have the best chance of making it into the magazine.

Insight

55 West Oak Ridge Drive
Hagerstown, MD 21740-7390

Editor: Dwain Neilson Esmond

Description and Interests
This Christian magazine for teens includes articles and stories on topics related to living in today's challenging world. It is published by the Seventh-day Adventist Church.
• **Audience:** 14–21 years
• **Frequency:** Weekly
• **Distribution:** 10% subscription; 90% other
• **Circulation:** 21,000
• **Website:** www.insightmagazine.org

Freelance Potential
99% written by nonstaff writers. Publishes 150 freelance submissions yearly; 50% by unpublished writers, 70% by authors who are new to the magazine. Receives 996 unsolicited mss yearly.

Submissions
Send complete ms. Accepts hard copy, disk submissions (Microsoft Word), and email submissions to insight@rhpa.org. SASE. Responds in 1–3 months.
Articles: 500–1,500 words. Informational articles; profiles; biographies; reports on volunteer and mission trips; and humor. Topics include social issues, religion, music, and careers.
Depts/columns: Word lengths vary. True-to-life stories and personal experience pieces.
Other: Submit material about Christmas, Easter, Mother's Day, Father's Day, and Valentine's Day 6 months in advance.

Sample Issue
16 pages (2% advertising): 3 articles; 3 depts/columns. Sample copy, $2 with 9x12 SASE (2 first-class stamps). Guidelines available.
• "God Cried Too." Article tells how a boy finds comfort in God while coping with the suicidal death of his brother.
• "What Diabetes Taught Me." Article describes how a boy's faith in God increases when he finds out he is a diabetic.
• Sample dept/column: "Search the Word" discusses how goodness comes from God alone.

Rights and Payment
First rights. Written material, $50–$125. Pays on acceptance. Provides 3 contributor's copies.

Editor's Comments
We look for material that is Christ-centered and takes a positive approach to topics of teen interest.

InSite

P.O. Box 62189
Colorado Springs, CO 80962-2189

Editor: Alison Hayhoe

Description and Interests
InSite is a Christian journal published for individuals who serve at Christian camps, conferences, and retreat centers. The purpose of this publication is to motivate, inspire, and inform its readers of God's work.
- **Audience:** Adults
- **Frequency:** 6 times each year
- **Distribution:** 95% subscription; 5% other
- **Circulation:** 9,000
- **Website:** www.ccca-us.org

Freelance Potential
90% written by nonstaff writers. Publishes 80 freelance submissions yearly. Receives 12 queries each year.

Submissions
Query with résumé and writing samples. Accepts email queries to editor@ccca-us.org. Availability of artwork may improve chance of acceptance. SASE. Responds in 1 month.
Articles: 800–1,500 words. Informational and how-to articles; profiles; and interviews. Topics include biography, crafts, hobbies, health and fitness, multicultural and ethnic issues, nature, the environment, popular culture, recreation, religion, social issues, and sports.
Depts/columns: Staff written.
Artwork: B/W and color prints and transparencies.
Other: Submit seasonal material 6 months in advance.

Sample Issue
42 pages (25% advertising): 7 articles; 8 depts/columns. Sample copy, $4.95 with 9x12 SASE ($1.40 postage). Guidelines and theme list available at website.
- "This Is a Test." Article emphasizes the importance of health screening for campers and camp staff.
- "Let Us Pray." Article shares the personal prayer experiences of several camp leaders.
- "Kinship Connections." Article discusses the value of creating grandparent-grandchild camp programs.

Rights and Payment
First rights. Written material, $.16 per word. Artwork, $25–$250. Pays on publication. Provides 1 copy.

Editor's Comments
We seek articles that show (rather than tell) what God is doing through Christian camp and conference ministries. How-to pieces, profiles, and interviews are most open to freelance writers.

Instructor

Scholastic Inc.
557 Broadway
New York, NY 10016

Features Editor

Description and Interests
This resourceful magazine for educators of kindergarten through eighth-grade students includes useful articles on topics related to teaching practices and educational issues, as well as creative, hands-on activities.
- **Audience:** Teachers, grades K–8
- **Frequency:** 8 times each year
- **Distribution:** 40% subscription; 30% newsstand; 30% schools
- **Circulation:** 250,000
- **Website:** www.scholastic.com/instructor

Freelance Potential
60% written by nonstaff writers. Publishes 10 freelance submissions yearly; 20% by unpublished writers, 70% by authors who are new to the magazine. Receives 100 unsolicited mss yearly.

Submissions
Send complete ms. Accepts hard copy. Availability of artwork improves chance of acceptance. SASE. Responds in 3–4 months.
Articles: 1,200 words. Informational and how-to articles; and personal experience pieces. Topics include animals, pets, the arts, biography, college, career, computers, news, mathematics, science, music, nature, the environment, and special education.
Depts/columns: News items, Q&As, and computers; word lengths vary. Classroom activities; to 250 words. Humorous or poignant personal essays; to 400 words.
Artwork: Color prints or transparencies. Line art.
Other: Puzzles, games, and activities, 40–800 words. Submit seasonal material 6 weeks in advance.

Sample Issue
64 pages (40% advertising): 7 articles; 5 depts/columns; 7 activities. Sample copy, $3 with 9x12 SASE ($.77 postage). Guidelines and theme list available at website.
- "Worry Free Whiteboards." Article explores the use of new interactive whiteboards.
- Sample dept/column: "Classroom Tech" takes a look at kids on the web, and offers search engine tips.

Rights and Payment
All rights. Articles, $600. Depts/columns, $250–$300. Pays on publication. Provides 2 contributor's copies.

Editor's Comments
We look for well-written articles that are innovative and written in a "magazine voice."

InTeen

P.O. Box 436987
Chicago, IL 60643

Editor: Aja Carr

Description and Interests
Urban Ministries, an African American Christian publishing company, produces *InTeen* for use in religious education classes. Through lessons, puzzles, cartoons, and projects, *InTeen* strives to connect Bible teachings to the everyday world of black, urban teens.
- **Audience:** 15–17 years
- **Frequency:** Quarterly
- **Distribution:** 80% subscription; 20% newsstand
- **Circulation:** 75,000
- **Website:** www.inteen.net

Freelance Potential
95% written by nonstaff writers. Publishes 52 freelance submissions yearly; 60% by unpublished writers, 50% by authors who are new to the magazine. Receives 360 queries yearly.

Submissions
Send résumé with writing samples. All material is written on assignment. SASE. Responds in 3–6 months.
Articles: Word lengths vary. Bible study guides and Bible lessons; how-to articles; profiles; interviews; and reviews. Topics include religion, biography, college, careers, black history, multicultural and ethnic subjects, social issues, and music.
Fiction: Word lengths vary. Stories are sometimes included as part of study plans. Genres include inspirational, multicultural, and ethnic fiction; real-life stories; and problem-solving stories.
Other: Puzzles, activities, and poetry. Submit seasonal material 1 year in advance.

Sample Issue
48 pages (no advertising): 8 articles; 1 story; 1 poem; 1 Bible verse; 13 Bible study guides. Writers' guidelines available.
- "Laughter Therapy." Article profiles a woman who is a member of a clown ministry group.
- "Called to Share Your Gifts." Bible study teaches that our talents, skills, and abilities are gifts from God.

Rights and Payment
All rights for work-for-hire material. One-time rights for features and poetry. Written material, rates vary. Pays 2 months after acceptance. Provides 2 copies.

Editor's Comments
If your writing samples show that you can speak to the unique needs of teens—especially urban, African American teens—we may contact you for an assignment.

InTeen Teacher

P.O. Box 436987
Chicago, IL 60643

Editor: Aja Carr

Description and Interests
This magazine, the teacher's edition of *InTeen*, includes commentary, background, and lesson plans that build on the Bible studies presented in *InTeen*. Its purpose is to help teachers empower their African American students to overcome obstacles and successfully follow Jesus Christ.
- **Audience:** Religious educators
- **Frequency:** Quarterly
- **Distribution:** 80% subscription; 20% newsstand
- **Circulation:** 75,000
- **Website:** www.inteen.net

Freelance Potential
95% written by nonstaff writers. Publishes 52 freelance submissions yearly; 60% by unpublished writers, 50% by authors who are new to the magazine. Receives 360 queries yearly.

Submissions
Send résumé with writing samples. All material is written on assignment. SASE. Responds in 3–6 months.
Articles: Word lengths vary. Publishes Bible study plans and guides for teaching Christian values to African American teens.
Fiction: Word lengths vary. Stories are sometimes included as part of study plans. Genres include inspirational, multicultural, and ethnic fiction. Also publishes real-life and problem-solving stories.
Other: Puzzles, activities, and poetry. Submit seasonal material 1 year in advance.

Sample Issue
80 pages (no advertising): 13 teaching plans; 13 Bible study guides. Guidelines available.
- "One Special Person." Teaching plan outlines ways to convey the message that God wants married couples to persevere despite setbacks.
- "A Matter of Taste?" Teaching plan helps students understand that everyone they encounter has unique feelings and needs.

Rights and Payment
All rights for work-for-hire material. One-time rights for features and poetry. Written material, payment rates vary. Pays 2 months after acceptance. Provides 2 contributor's copies.

Editor's Comments
Our writers are experienced Christian teachers. Send us your résumé, and we'll consider you for an assignment.

International Gymnast

P.O. Box 721020
Norman, OK 73070

Editor: Dwight Normile

Description and Interests
International Gymnast is dedicated to serving the gymnastics community. New training ideas, competition reports, profiles of gymnasts, and humorous fiction make up each issue of this magazine.
- **Audience:** 10–16 years
- **Frequency:** 10 times each year
- **Distribution:** 95% subscription; 5% newsstand
- **Circulation:** 17,000
- **Website: www.intlgymnast.com**

Freelance Potential
10% written by nonstaff writers. Publishes 5 freelance submissions yearly; 50% by unpublished writers, 50% by authors who are new to the magazine. Receives fewer than 12 unsolicited mss yearly.

Submissions
Send complete ms. Accepts hard copy and simultaneous submissions if identified. SASE. Responds in 1 month.
Articles: 1,000–2,250 words. Informational articles; profiles; and interviews. Topics include gymnastics competitions and coaching, and personalities involved in the sport around the world.
Fiction: To 1,500 words. Stories about gymnastics.
Depts/columns: 700–1,000 words. News, training tips, and opinion pieces.
Artwork: B/W prints. 35mm color slides for cover.

Sample Issue
54 pages (14% advertising): 4 articles; 10 depts/columns. Sample copy, $5 with 9x12 SASE. Writers' guidelines available.
- "Honoring Excellence." Article highlights four gymnasts inducted into the International Gymnasts Hall of Fame in Oklahoma City on May 20, 2005.
- Sample dept/column: "IG Kids Club" profiles a young Canadian gymnast, 13-year-old Kelsey Hope.
- Sample dept/column: "Spotted" offers tidbits of information on gymnasts and coaches spotted in different locations around the world.

Rights and Payment
All rights. Written material, $15–$25. Artwork, $5–$50. Pays on publication. Provides 1 author's copy.

Editor's Comments
We are currently seeking in-depth interviews revealing unknown facts with top figures in artistic/rhythmic gymnastics and sports acrobatics.

Jack And Jill

Children's Better Health Institute
1100 Waterway Boulevard
P.O. Box 567
Indianapolis, IN 46206-0567

Editor: Daniel Lee

Description and Interests
The Children's Better Health Institute publishes this educational magazine for children in second and third grades. *Jack And Jill* features articles, stories, and activities promoting good health and nutrition.
- **Audience:** 7–10 years
- **Frequency:** 6 times each year
- **Distribution:** 100% subscription
- **Circulation:** 200,000
- **Website: www.jackandjillmag.org**

Freelance Potential
10% written by nonstaff writers. Publishes 10 freelance submissions yearly; 70% by authors who are new to the magazine. Receives 1,200 mss yearly.

Submissions
Send complete ms. Accepts hard copy. SASE. Responds in 3 months.
Articles: 500–600 words. Informational and how-to articles; humor; profiles; and biographies. Topics include sports, health, exercise, safety, nutrition, and hygiene.
Fiction: 500–900 words. Genres include mystery, fantasy, folktales, humor, science fiction, and stories about sports and animals.
Artwork: Submit sketches to Andrea O' Shea, art director; photos to Daniel Lee, editor.
Other: Poetry, games, puzzles, activities, and cartoons. Submit seasonal material 8 months in advance.

Sample Issue
36 pages (4% advertising): 4 articles; 1 story; 4 depts/columns; 5 activities; 3 poems. Sample copy, $6.50 ($2 postage). Guidelines available.
- "Betsy Brandon Meets the President." Story tells of a young girl in the year 1791, who meets George Washington at her home.
- "A Doctor for Her People." Article profiles the first female Native American doctor, Dr. Susan Picotte.
- Sample dept/column: "Your Body's Fire Department" explains how your body cools itself when overheated.

Rights and Payment
All rights. Articles and fiction, to $.17 per word. Other material, payment rates vary. Pays on publication. Provides 10 contributor's copies.

Editor's Comments
Humorous stories, fun activities, and interesting articles promoting a healthy lifestyle are always of interest.

Jakes Magazine

P.O. Box 530
Edgefield, SC 29824

Editor: Matt Lindler

Description and Interests
This magazine for young members of the National Wild Turkey Federation is dedicated to informing, educating, and involving youth in wildlife conservation and the wise stewardship of our natural resources.
- **Audience:** 10–17
- **Frequency:** Quarterly
- **Distribution:** 100% controlled
- **Circulation:** 200,000
- **Website: www.nwtf.org/jakes**

Freelance Potential
50% written by nonstaff writers. Publishes 15–20 freelance submissions yearly; 10% by unpublished writers, 70% by authors who are new to the magazine. Receives 100–150 queries yearly.

Submissions
Query or send complete ms. Accepts material between May and December only. Accepts hard copy, email to MLindler@nwtf.org, and simultaneous submissions if identified. SASE. Response time varies.
Articles: 600–1,200 words. Informational articles; profiles; and personal experience pieces. Topics include nature, the environment, animals, pets, hunting, fishing, and other outdoor sports.
Fiction: 800–1,200 words. Historical fiction.
Other: Trading cards, member showcase.

Sample Issue
32 pages: 3 articles; 1 story; 3 depts/columns. Guidelines available at website.
- "Bucksaw and Dan." Article profiles a hunter who travels with a puppet to teach young people about hunting, wildlife, and the outdoors.
- "Deserve a Turkey." Story tells of a boy and his grandfather who go turkey hunting.
- Sample dept/column: "Backyard Ecology" offers information about the California condor.

Rights and Payment
Rights vary. Written material, $100–$300. Pays on publication. Provides 2 contributor's copies.

Editor's Comments
We are looking for fun stories that are of interest to our young readers. Submitted material should emphasize the outdoors, conservation, hunting, hunter safety, hunting ethics, or heritage. Historical fiction must be accurate socially and culturally.

Journal of Adolescent & Adult Literacy

International Reading Association
800 Barksdale Road, P.O. Box 8139
Newark, DE 19714–8139

Editorial Assistant: Carol Nicholls

Description and Interests
This peer-reviewed journal of the International Reading Association provides information on current theories, research, and practices for teaching reading to young people and adults. Its target audience includes teachers, reading specialists, librarians, and parents.
- **Audience:** Reading education professionals
- **Frequency:** 8 times each year
- **Distribution:** 100% subscription
- **Circulation:** 16,000
- **Website: www.reading.org**

Freelance Potential
100% written by nonstaff writers. Publishes 50 freelance submissions yearly; 20% by unpublished writers, 10% by authors who are new to the magazine. Receives 252 unsolicited mss yearly.

Submissions
Send complete ms. Accepts electronic submissions through http://mc.manuscriptcentral.com/ira/jaal. SASE. Responds in 2–3 months.
Articles: 1,000–6,000 words. Informational and how-to articles; and personal experience pieces. Topics include reading theory, research, and practice; and trends in teaching literacy.
Depts/columns: Word lengths vary. Opinion pieces, reviews, and technology information.

Sample Issue
98 pages (7% advertising): 5 articles; 3 depts/columns. Sample copy, $10.
- "Recentering the Middle School Classroom as a Vibrant Learning Community." Article examines the role technology can play in encouraging students to participate in literary discussions.
- "There's a Better Word: Urban Youth Rewriting Their Social Worlds Through Poetry." Article relates how a poetry program helped students gain writing skills and confidence.

Rights and Payment
All rights. No payment. Provides 5 contributor's copies for articles; 2 copies for depts/columns.

Editor's Comments
We are dedicated to improving reading instruction worldwide and to promoting high levels of literacy. We seek articles that encourage professional development, advocate policies to improve reading instruction, and explore new research.

Journal of Adventist Education

12501 Old Columbia Pike
Silver Spring, MD 20904-6600

Editor: Beverly J. Rumble

Description and Interests
This professional publication for Seventh-day Adventist teachers and administrators provides both practical and theoretical material related to teaching at the kindergarten through college levels.
- **Audience:** Educators, school board members
- **Frequency:** 5 times each year
- **Distribution:** Subscription; religious instruction; controlled
- **Circulation:** 15,000
- **Website:** http://education.gc.adventist.org/JAE

Freelance Potential
90% written by nonstaff writers. Publishes 30 freelance submissions yearly. Receives 24–48 queries each year.

Submissions
Query. Accepts hard copy. Availability of artwork improves chance of acceptance. SASE. Responds in 3 weeks.
Articles: To 2,000 words. Informational and how-to articles. Topics include parochial, gifted, and special education; religion; mathematics; science; and technology.
Artwork: B/W and color prints and transparencies. Line art.

Sample Issue
46 pages (5% advertising): 8 articles; 1 book review. Sample copy, $3.50 with 9x12 SASE ($.68 postage). Guidelines available.
- "How to Liven Lethal Lectures." Article explains how to tell if a lecture is the best way to convey information, and if so, how to keep students' attention.
- "Are Adventist Nursing Schools Really Different?" Article outlines the advantages of attending a nursing school run by Seventh-day Adventists.

Rights and Payment
First North American serial rights. Articles, to $100. Artwork, payment rates vary. Pays on publication. Provides 2 contributor's copies.

Editor's Comments
We're always interested in articles that talk about creative and effective ways to enhance teaching skills and classroom learning. Include charts or graphs if appropriate. All writing, whether theoretical or practical, must skillfully integrate Seventh-day Adventist faith, values, and learning.

Journal of School Health

American School Health Association
7263 State Route 43
P.O. Box 708
Kent, OH 44240–0708

Editor: James H. Price

Description and Interests
This magazine is the official publication of the American School Health Association. It publishes research papers, position papers, and articles that promote the health of children and young people and inform their health-care providers.
- **Audience:** School health professionals
- **Frequency:** 10 times each year
- **Distribution:** Subscription
- **Circulation:** 5,000
- **Website:** www.ashaweb.org

Freelance Potential
95% written by nonstaff writers. Publishes 60 freelance submissions yearly; 90% by authors who are new to the magazine. Receives 120 queries yearly.

Submissions
Query or send complete ms. Accepts email only through www.manuscriptcentral.com/josh. Responds to queries in 2 weeks, to mss in 3–4 months.
Articles: 2,500 words. Informational articles; research papers; commentaries; and practical application pieces. Topics include teaching techniques, health services in the school system, nursing, medicine, substance abuse, nutrition, counseling, and ADD/AHD.

Sample Issue
48 pages (no advertising): 2 articles; 4 research papers; 1 commentary. Sample copy, $8.50 with 9x12 SASE. Guidelines available.
- "Sports Medicine and School Nurses: A Growing Need for Further Education and Appropriate Resources." Article addresses the specific areas in which school nurses need training in order to provide better care for injured athletes.
- "Asthma Status and Severity Affects Missed School Days." Article studies the correlation between students with asthma and absenteeism.

Rights and Payment
All rights. No payment. Provides 2 author's copies.

Editor's Comments
Please visit our website and review our detailed guidelines for submitting a manuscript. We are looking for original, data-based research papers, position papers, and analysis by health professionals on health-related topics, as well as innovative ideas concerning health instruction in kindergarten through grade 12.

Juco Review

1755 Telstar Drive, Suite 103
Colorado Springs, CO 80920

Submissions: Wayne Baker

Description and Interests
For almost 70 years, this magazine has been keeping members of the National Junior College Athletic Association up to date with articles covering college sporting events, athletes and coaches, health and fitness, and association news.
- **Audience:** YA–Adult
- **Frequency:** 9 times each year
- **Distribution:** 90% controlled; 10% subscription
- **Circulation:** 2,700
- **Website:** www.njcaa.org

Freelance Potential
10% written by nonstaff writers. Publishes 5–7 freelance submissions yearly; 90% by unpublished writers, 80% by authors who are new to the magazine. Receives up to 12 unsolicited mss yearly.

Submissions
Send complete ms. Accepts hard copy. Availability of artwork improves chance of acceptance. SASE. Responds 2 months.
Articles: 1,500–2,000 words. Informational articles. Topics include sports, college, careers, health, fitness, and NJCAA news.
Artwork: B/W prints and transparencies.

Sample Issue
24 pages (25% advertising): 7 articles. Sample copy, $4 for current issue; $3 for back issue with 9x12 SASE. Editorial calendar available.
- "Pepsi/NATYCAA Cup Standings." Article looks at Iowa City Central and Mohawk Valley Community Colleges' ratings in the Pepsi/NATYCAA Awards Program.
- "NJCAA College of the Month—Wallace State Community College." Article describes one of the premier two-year colleges in the southeastern U.S.
- "Reed K. Swenson Award." Article describes an award given to outstanding Americans who have contributed in general to the intercollegiate athletic scene.

Rights and Payment
All rights. No payment. Provides 3 author's copies.

Editor's Comments
The majority of our content is coverage of schools and their athletes and coaches who are members of our organization. We do, at times, include articles on health, fitness, and nutrition. Articles that cover football and women's athletics are of interest to us.

Junior Baseball

P.O. Box 9099
Canoga Park, CA 91309

Editor/Publisher: Dave Destler

Description and Interests
Junior Baseball addresses the needs and interests of youth baseball players, parents, coaches, and league officials. It caters to the players who consider baseball their major, or only, sport. Editorial content emphasizes family involvement and values such as sportsmanship, teamwork, pride, responsibility, and respect for others.
- **Audience:** 7–17 years; parents and coaches
- **Frequency:** 6 times each year
- **Distribution:** 60% subscription; 20% newsstand; 20% controlled
- **Circulation:** 32,000
- **Website:** www.juniorbaseball.com

Freelance Potential
50% written by nonstaff writers. Publishes 20 freelance submissions yearly; 10% by unpublished writers, 20% by authors who are new to the magazine. Receives 50 queries and unsolicited mss yearly.

Submissions
Query with writing samples; or send complete ms with photos. Accepts email submissions to dave@juniorbaseball.com. Availability of artwork improves chance of acceptance. Responds in 1–2 weeks.
Articles: 1,000–2,000 words. Informational and how-to articles; personal experiences; and profiles.
Depts/columns: 500 words. Product reviews.
Artwork: High resolution digital photos.

Sample Issue
42 pages (30% advertising): 8 articles; 10 depts/columns. Sample copy, $3.95 with 9x12 SASE ($1.35 postage). Guidelines available.
- "Dream Team." Article looks back at the 2005 Cooperstown Youth Hall of Fame Tournament, won by the Houston Heat 12U team.
- "Throwing the Curve." Article demonstrates with copy and pictures how to throw a great curve ball.
- Sample dept/column: "Rookie Club" describes the position of catcher and tells how to be a good one.

Rights and Payment
All rights. Written material, $.10–$.20 per word. Pays on publication. Provides 1 contributor's copy.

Editor's Comments
Whether written for younger or older readers, we look for submissions that are well-detailed and full of supporting facts, figures, and anecdotes.

JuniorWay

P.O. Box 436987
Chicago, IL 60643

Editor: Katherine Steward

Description and Interests
This magazine makes learning about the Word of God fun and interesting through its use of articles, Bible lessons, stories, and activities. It targets young Christian African Americans in urban areas, and is used by Sunday school teachers.
- **Audience:** 9–11 years
- **Frequency:** Quarterly
- **Distribution:** 100% religious education
- **Circulation:** 75,000
- **Website:** www.urbanministries.com

Freelance Potential
95% written by nonstaff writers. Publishes 52 freelance submissions yearly. Receives 240 queries yearly.

Submissions
Send résumé and writing samples. All material is written on assignment. Response time varies.
Articles: Word lengths vary. Personal experience pieces; photo-essays; and humor. Topics include religion, social issues, ethnic and multicultural subjects, hobbies, crafts, nature, the environment, pets, and African American studies.
Fiction: Word lengths vary. Inspirational stories with multicultural or ethnic themes; adventure stories; humor; and folktales.
Artwork: B/W and color prints and transparencies.
Other: Activities, games, puzzles, jokes, and filler. Accepts seasonal material for Vacation Bible School.

Sample Issue
34 pages (no advertising): 13 Bible lessons; 1 story; 8 activities; 1 prayer; 1 cartoon. Guidelines and theme list available.
- "A Second Chance." Bible lesson focuses on making mistakes and giving second chances and explores how God gave humankind another chance.
- "It's Not Fair." Bible lesson tells how a boy feels he is being treated unfairly, and how God's children should continue to Worship Him.
- "Word Up for Juniors." Activity asks readers to discover their purpose in life.

Rights and Payment
All rights. All material, payment rates vary. Pays on publication.

Editor's Comments
We look for stories and activities that will help children understand the Word of God.

JuniorWay Teacher

P.O. Box 436987
Chicago, IL 60643

Editor: Katherine Steward

Description and Interests
Teaching instructions, questions, and commentary appear with each lesson presented in this magazine, which is used in religious education classes for African American children ages nine to eleven. The contents of the magazine reflect the experience of kids who reside in urban areas.
- **Audience:** Religious educators
- **Frequency:** Quarterly
- **Distribution:** 100% religious instruction
- **Circulation:** Unavailable
- **Website:** www.urbanministries.com

Freelance Potential
95% written by nonstaff writers. Publishes 52 freelance submissions yearly. Receives 240 queries each year.

Submissions
Query with résumé. All material is written on assignment. Response time varies.
Articles: Word lengths vary. Informational and how-to articles; personal experience pieces; and teaching guides. Topics include religion, science, technology, social issues, crafts, hobbies, animals, pets, and African American history.
Artwork: B/W and color prints and transparencies.

Sample Issue
96 pages (no advertising): 1 article; 13 teaching plans; 13 Bible study guides. Sample copy, $1.90. Guidelines and theme list available.
- "Tips and Ideas: How Should Christians Live?" Article explains that Christians need God's Spirit in their hearts in order to live according to His will.
- "Who's Responsible?" Teaching plan explains how to present a lesson about faithful and responsible service to God.
- "Forgive and Be Forgiven." Teaching plan offers ideas for putting together a lesson about the importance of God's forgiveness of us and our forgiveness of others.

Rights and Payment
All rights. All material, payment rates vary. Pays on publication.

Editor's Comments
Our material is written to challenge middle-grade students and enrich their Sunday school experience. Ideas from talented teachers are welcome.

Justine Magazine

6263 Poplar Avenue, Suite 430
Memphis, TN 38119

Editorial Director/Publisher: Jana Pettey

Description and Interests
The editorial content of this teen magazine is tasteful, wholesome, and entertaining, setting it apart from the typical teen tabloid. Topics of interest include decorating ideas, craft projects, beauty tips, exercise and nutrition, self-confidence, and dealing with family issues. *Justine Magazine* also features fashion and make-up advice; reviews of books, movies, and music; and information about today's hottest stars.
- **Audience:** 13–18 years
- **Frequency:** 6 times each year
- **Distribution:** 70% subscription; 30% newsstand
- **Circulation:** 250,000
- **Website:** www.justinemagazine.com

Freelance Potential
20% written by nonstaff writers. Publishes 25 freelance submissions yearly; 25% by unpublished writers, 90% by authors new to the magazine. Receives 100 queries yearly.

Submissions
Query with résumé and clips. Accepts hard copy and disk submissions. SASE. Response time varies.
Articles: Word lengths vary. Informational articles; profiles; and personal experience pieces. Topics include room decorating, beauty, health, nutrition, family issues, recreation, travel, and fashion.
Depts/columns: Word lengths vary. Health, fashion, exercise, entertainment, and media and book reviews.

Sample Issue
96 pages: 6 articles; 31 depts/columns.
- "The Click Five." Article profiles the lead singer of this new Beatles-esque band.
- "My Life in the Movies." Article tells the story of how 24-year-old Molly made it from Tennessee to Hollywood, and is now pursuing a career in filmmaking.
- Sample dept/column: "Jump into Shape" shares a few quick, calorie burning, jump rope exercises.

Rights and Payment
Rights vary. Written material, payment rates vary. Pays 30 days after publication.

Editor's Comments
There hasn't been a magazine for teen girls, until now, that's entertaining, stylish, and wholesome. We look for material that relates to our readers without making them blush. Articles offering advice on a variety of topics are always of interest.

Kaleidoscope
Exploring the Experience of Disability Through Literature & the Fine Arts

701 South Main Street
Akron, OH 44311-1019

Editor-in-Chief: Gail Willmott

Description and Interests
Kaleidoscope has a creative focus of thought provoking material that examines the experience of disability from the perspective of individuals, families, healthcare professionals, and society as a whole.
- **Audience:** YA–Adults
- **Frequency:** Twice each year
- **Distribution:** 65% controlled; 35% subscription
- **Circulation:** 1,000
- **Website:** www.udsakron.org

Freelance Potential
90% written by nonstaff writers. Publishes 50 freelance submissions yearly; 10% by unpublished writers, 70% by authors who are new to the magazine. Receives 120 queries, 288 unsolicited mss yearly.

Submissions
Query or send complete ms with author bio. Accepts hard copy and email submissions to mshiplett@udsakron.org (Microsoft Word). SASE. Responds to queries in 2 weeks, to mss in 6 months.
Articles: 5,000 words. Informational articles; profiles; interviews; reviews; and personal experience pieces. Topics include art, literature, biography, and multicultural and social issues
Fiction: 5,000 words. Genres include folktales, humor, and problem-solving and multicultural fiction.
Other: Poetry.

Sample Issue
64 pages (no advertising): 3 articles; 5 stories; 1 personal essay; 10 poems. Sample copy, $6 with 9x12 SASE. Guidelines and editorial calendar available.
- "The Balm of Creative Endeavor." Article recounts how chemotherapy led to the author's first novel.
- "Past the Bone." Story conveys the mental tiredness of a woman overburdened with responsibilities.
- "If I Could Only Bring You Back." Poem touches on the agony of having a loved one who is disabled.

Rights and Payment
First rights. Written material, $25–$100. Poetry, $10. Pays on publication. Provides 2 contributor's copies.

Editor's Comments
Material in our publication is disability-related. We are particularly interested in personal essays, articles about family issues, and reviews. We definitely would like to see more humor and less stereotypical, patronizing, and sentimental attitudes toward disability.

Kansas School Naturalist

Department of Biological Sciences
Emporia State University
1200 Commercial Street
Emporia, KS 66801-5087

Editor: John Richard Schrock

Description and Interests
This digest-sized educational publication is comprised of one lengthy article per issue that pertains in some way to the natural ecology of Kansas. Topics cover the use and maintenance of natural resources, insects, nature, and the natural history of Kansas. The publication is used by educators and read by students, librarians, teachers, naturalists, conservationists, and other professionals interested in naturalist education and studies.
- **Audience:** Teachers, librarians, and conservationists
- **Frequency:** Irregular
- **Distribution:** 70% schools; 30% other
- **Circulation:** 9,800
- **Website: www.emporia.edu/ksn**

Freelance Potential
75% written by nonstaff writers. Of the freelance submissions published yearly, 20% are by unpublished writers and 75% are by authors who are new to the magazine.

Submissions
Query or send complete ms. Accepts hard copy and IBM disk submissions. SASE. Response time varies.
Articles: Word lengths vary. Informational and how-to articles. Topics include natural history, nature, science, technology, animals, health, and education—all with a Kansas focus.
Artwork: B/W and color prints and transparencies.
Other: Seasonal material.

Sample Issue
15 pages (no advertising): 1 article. Sample copy, free.
- "Stream Ecology." Article explains the natural cycles that occur in Earth's water supply, concentrating on the vital part that streams play in maintaining important ecological communities, contributing to our aesthetic values and leisure enjoyment, and providing sustenance to the aquatic life that teems within them.

Rights and Payment
All rights. No payment. Provides contributor's copies.

Editor's Comments
Although we maintain a relaxed writing style, our publication is scientific in nature and requires a high standard of research and scientific knowledge. Most of the articles are written by professionals, but we will review inquiries from qualified writers.

Keynoter

Key Club International
3636 Woodview Trace
Indianapolis, IN 46268-3196

Executive Editor: Shanna Mooney

Description and Interests
Members of Key Club read this magazine for articles about community service and leadership, as well as academic and general interest topics. It also includes information on club activities, members, and events.
- **Audience:** 14–18 years
- **Frequency:** 8 times each year
- **Distribution:** 100% membership
- **Circulation:** 240,000
- **Website: www.keyclub.org/magazine**

Freelance Potential
40% written by nonstaff writers. Publishes 16 freelance submissions yearly; 10% by unpublished writers, 30% by authors who are new to the magazine. Receives 100 queries yearly.

Submissions
Query with outline/synopsis and clips or writing samples. Accepts hard copy, email queries to keynoter@ kiwanis.org, and simultaneous submissions if identified. SASE. Responds in 1 month.
Articles: 1,000–1,500 words. Informational, self-help, and service-related articles. Topics include education, teen concerns, community service, leadership, school activities, social issues, and careers.
Depts/columns: Staff written.
Artwork: Color prints and illustrations.
Other: Submit seasonal material about back to school, college, and summer activities 3–7 months in advance.

Sample Issue
20 pages (5% advertising): 3 articles; 4 depts/columns. Sample copy, free with 9x12 SASE ($.83 postage). Guidelines available.
- "Out from the Shadows." Article discusses how to overcome shyness.
- "Boston Beckons." Article explores the city of Boston, where the Key Club held an International Convention.

Rights and Payment
First North American serial rights. All material, $150–$350. Pays on acceptance. Provides 3 contributor's copies.

Editor's Comments
We are looking for well-written articles that provide a high school take on social or cultural issues, such as hectic lives and obesity.

Keys for Kids

P.O. Box 1001
Grand Rapids, MI 49510

Editor: Hazel Marett

Description and Interests
This digest-sized publication includes daily devotionals for grade-school through young adult readers. Each devotional is based on a Scripture passage and includes a Bible verse to memorize.
- **Audience:** 6–12 years
- **Frequency:** 6 times each year
- **Distribution:** 100% controlled
- **Circulation:** 70,000
- **Website:** www.cbhministries.org

Freelance Potential
99% written by nonstaff writers. Publishes 50–60 freelance submissions yearly; 50% by authors who are new to the magazine. Receives 144 unsolicited mss each year.

Submissions
Send complete ms. Accepts hard copy and simultaneous submissions. SASE. Responds in 2 months.
Articles: 400 words. Devotionals. Topics include contemporary social issues, family life, trust, friendship, salvation, witnessing, prayer, marriage, and faith.

Sample Issue
80 pages: 59 devotionals. Sample copy, free with 9x12 SASE. Guidelines available.
- "A Hopeless Case." Devotional stresses that no one is hopeless, and that with God and prayer all things are possible.
- "Lesson on Listening." Devotional discusses personal responsibility and using parental experience and wisdom for guidance.
- "Keep in Practice." Devotional notes that practice is important to become good, even when becoming a strong Christian.

Rights and Payment
First and second rights. Written material, $25. Pays on acceptance. Provides 1 contributor's copy.

Editor's Comments
We're looking for stories with spiritual applications that feature ordinary kids facing contemporary dilemmas. Be sure to include something that illustrates a spiritual or biblical truth. Think about what questions you can include with each story; they should be something readers can share with parents and friends. Don't be afraid of controversial subjects: pornography, child abuse, prejudice, violence, and peer pressure can all be handled with Christian grace.

Kids Discover

149 Fifth Avenue, 12th Floor
New York, NY 10010-6801

Editor: Stella Sands

Description and Interests
This magazine is full of educational, fact-filled, and fun articles for children in the elementary grades. Each issue covers a theme on a topic related to science, history, nature, the environment, geography, ecology, weather, travel, architecture, and animals. It publishes no fiction.
- **Audience:** 6–12 years
- **Frequency:** Monthly
- **Distribution:** Subscription
- **Circulation:** 500,000
- **Website:** www.kidsdiscover.com

Freelance Potential
100% written by nonstaff writers. Receives 120 queries yearly.

Submissions
No unsolicited mss. All articles written on assignment.
Articles: Word lengths vary. Informational and general interest articles; and profiles. Topics include geology, lakes, ecology, the Mississippi River, World War I, ancient Egypt and China, Thomas Jefferson, weather, the solar system, earthquakes, knights and castles, the Industrial Revolution, Ellis Island, and George Washington.

Sample Issue
20 pages (no advertising): 6 articles; 1 chart; 3 activities. Sample copy available upon email request to editor@kidsdiscover.com.
- "Food, Glorious Food." Article talks about the different kinds of micro- and macro-nutrients and the role of calories.
- "Eating Your A, B, C's—and Iron, too." Article explains the value of vitamins and how you get them from the food you eat.
- "The Balancing Act." Article tells why eating healthfully is often a matter of balancing food groups.

Rights and Payment
Rights vary. All material, payment rates vary. Payment policy varies.

Editor's Comments
We have a reliable group of writers whom we work with, so it can be difficult to break into the pages of our magazine. If you have strong credentials, you may contact us and we might assign an article relating to an upcoming theme. You must be able to write in a way that will engage young readers in the subject.

The Kids Hall of Fame® News

3 Ibsen Court
Dix Hills, NY 11746

Publisher: Victoria Nesnick

Description and Interests
The Kids Hall of Fame News is an online publication that highlights the extraordinary achievements of individuals under the age of 20. The goal of this e-zine is to provide positive peer role models to motivate and inspire kids to reach their highest potential.
- **Audience:** 6–12 years
- **Frequency:** Unavailable
- **Distribution:** 100% Internet
- **Hits per month:** 8,000
- **Website:** www.thekidshalloffame.com

Freelance Potential
40% written by nonstaff writers. Publishes 300 freelance submissions yearly; 10% by unpublished writers, 20% by new authors. Receives 1,200 mss yearly.

Submissions
Send complete ms. Accepts hard copy. SASE. Responds in 1–2 months.
Articles: 1,000–2,000 words. Informational and self-help articles; personal experience pieces; photo-essays; profiles; and interviews. Topics include the arts, college, careers, hobbies, gifted and special education, music, sports, and multicultural issues.
Artwork: 8½ x11 B/W or color prints. Line art.
Other: Poetry, no line limit. Filler.

Sample Issue
Sample copy and guidelines available at website.
- "1- to 5-Year-Old Inductees." Article profiles several children with remarkable talents, including a 2-year-old jigsaw puzzle whiz and a political expert.
- "8-Year-Old Inductees." Article features four 8-year-olds, including the famous King Tut of Egypt.
- "13-Year-Old Inductees." Article profiles four teens with amazing accomplishments, two of whom were born with disabilities.

Rights and Payment
Rights vary. All material, payment rates vary. Pays on acceptance.

Editor's Comments
We accept true stories only about the positive achievements of young people under the age of 20. We do not publish fiction. Articles that inspire our readers are of special interest. We seek submissions of nomination stories and information on individuals who are champions, contest winners, life savers, web designers, environmentalists, or academic whizzes.

Kids Life

1426 22nd Avenue
Tuscaloosa, AL 35401

Publisher: Mary Jane Turner

Description and Interests
Kids Life presents a wealth of information for parents living in western Alabama. It is a guide to regional events, programs, and resources, and features articles on family and parenting issues, as well as religion and education.
- **Audience:** Parents
- **Frequency:** 6 times each year
- **Distribution:** Subscription; newsstand; schools
- **Circulation:** 30,000
- **Website:** www.kidslifemagazine.com

Freelance Potential
50% written by nonstaff writers. Publishes 15 freelance submissions yearly; 50% by unpublished writers, 10% by authors who are new to the magazine. Receives 600+ unsolicited mss yearly.

Submissions
Query or send complete ms. Accepts hard copy and email submissions to kidslife@comcast.net. SASE. Responds to email in 2 weeks.
Articles: 1,000 words. Informational articles; reviews; and personal experience pieces. Topics include parenting, education, child care, religion, cooking, crafts, health, and current events.
Artwork: Color prints or transparencies. Line art.
Other: Puzzles and games. Poetry, to 100 lines.

Sample Issue
50 pages (60% advertising): 8 articles; 6 depts/columns. Sample copy, free.
- "Are We There Yet?" Article outlines family enjoyments at Sea Island Resort, Georgia, including marsh kayaking and a sea turtle walk.
- "Reading Aloud." Article provides creative and valuable tips for enhancing this important activity.
- Sample dept/column: "*Kids Life* Shopping Cart" details the stimulations of two favorite resources for play: an age-appropriate LEGO collection or themed kit and BRIO's wooden blocks and toys.

Rights and Payment
Rights vary. Written material, to $30. Pays on publication. Provides 1 contributor's copy.

Editor's Comments
We're interested in articles on issues related to parenting, children, and families for our readership of busy moms and dads. Articles that spotlight local attractions and services are particularly welcome.

Kids' Ministry Ideas

55 West Oak Ridge Drive
Hagerstown, MD 21740

Editor: Ginger Church

Description and Interests
Targeting those who provide spiritual nurturing to children in local churches, this publication provides affirmation, pertinent and informative articles, program ideas, resource suggestions, and answers to questions from a Seventh-day Adventist Christian perspective.
- **Audience:** Teachers; youth leaders; parents
- **Frequency:** Quarterly
- **Distribution:** Subscription
- **Circulation:** 4,500
- **Website: www.reviewandherald.org**

Freelance Potential
100% written by nonstaff writers. Publishes 60 freelance submissions yearly.

Submissions
Send complete ms. Accepts hard copy and email submissions to kidsmin@rhpa.org. SASE. Response time varies.
Articles: 300–800 words. Informational articles. Topics include religious program ideas, resources, youth ministry, family, Vacation Bible School, spirituality, faith, and prayer.
Depts/columns: Word lengths vary. Crafts, leadership, and teaching ideas.

Sample Issue
32 pages: 4 articles; 8 depts/columns. Sample copy and guidelines available.
- "Burnout: A Preventable Phenomenon." Article discusses how to recognize when someone is approaching burnout and what to do about it.
- "What's Good for One . . . May Not Be Good for Another!" Article describes different learning styles and how to structure programs to reach everyone.
- Sample dept/column: "Capturing Curiosity" takes a look at the beauty of the monarch butterfly.

Rights and Payment
First North American serial rights. Written material, $20–$100. Pays 5–6 weeks after acceptance. Provides 1 contributor's copy.

Editor's Comments
We strive to provide resources for those leading children to Jesus. We look for practical ideas and easy-to-understand instructions that leaders can implement in their area of ministry. Use of sidebars, boxes, and lists of information are encouraged. Please include quotes and credible sources in your article.

Kids On Wheels

P.O. Box 1287
Wilmington, NC 28402

Editorial Director: Jean Dobbs

Description and Interests
Targeted to "young wheelers ahead of the curve," this magazine is dedicated to empowering young wheelchair users. It features articles that deal with school, friends, sports, and activities, and tips for handling disabilities. It also contains profiles of talented disabled people, contests, and event information.
- **Audience:** 8+ years
- **Frequency:** Quarterly
- **Distribution:** Subscription
- **Circulation:** Unavailable
- **Website: www.kidsonwheels.us**

Freelance Potential
20% written by nonstaff writers. Publishes 10–15 freelance submissions yearly.

Submissions
Query or send complete ms. Accepts hard copy and email submissions to jean@kidsonwheels.us. SASE. Response time varies.
Articles: Word lengths vary. Informational and self-help articles; and personal experience pieces. Topics include education, health and fitness, social issues, relationships, sports, activities, and travel.
Depts/columns: Word lengths vary. Profiles, contests, puzzles, and jokes.

Sample Issue
24 pages: 2 articles; 7 depts/columns.
- "Swimming with Dolphins." Article discusses children's encounters while swimming with dolphins as therapy for their disabilities.
- "Back to School." Article advises kids on how to balance their schoolwork and social lives.
- Sample dept/column: "Try This" focuses on cycling as an adaptive sports program for children with disabilities.
- Sample dept/column: "Spotlight" reports on the close friendship between two young American girls with cerebral palsy who met at a rehabilitation center in Poland.

Rights and Payment
First North American serial rights. Written material, payment rates vary. Pays on publication.

Editor's Comments
Activities, games, jokes, filler, and puzzles are among our current needs. Please take a look at several issues of our magazine to get to know our style.

Kids' Rooms Etc.

1716 Locust Street, Ln 208
Des Moines, IA 50309-3023

Editor: Suzanne Morrissey

Description and Interests
This *Better Homes and Gardens* special interest publication focuses on decorating children's bedrooms and playrooms. Information includes new products, decor, solutions to small spaces, storage, gender-specific ideas, furniture styles, theme- and age-related decorating, and color accents.
- **Audience:** Adults
- **Frequency:** Quarterly
- **Distribution:** 100% newsstand
- **Circulation:** 450,000

Freelance Potential
90% written by contract writers. Of the contract submissions published each year, 10% are by unpublished writers, 10% by authors who are new to the magazine.

Submissions
Send résumé only. Accepts email to suzanne.morrissey@meredith.com. Responds in 3 months.
Articles: 300–600 words. Informational and how-to articles. Topics include decor, travel, crafts, hobbies, and regional news.
Depts/columns: 150–250 words. New products.
Artwork: 8x10 B/W and color prints. Line art.
Other: Puzzles and games. Poetry, to 100 lines.

Sample Issue
120 pages (5% advertising): 14 articles; 5 depts/columns. Sample copy, $8.99.
- "Grid Work." Article describes how a small playroom can utilize a wall structure for storage.
- "Heavy Metal." Article pictures how to incorporate metal accent pieces for storage in a boy's room.
- Sample dept/column: "Kidbits" highlights new products for children.

Rights and Payment
Universal rights. All material, payment rates vary. Pays on completion of assignment. Provides 3 copies.

Editor's Comments
Our publication features writing that is snappy and fun underlined by knowledgeable expertise. We would like to see more material on storage for kids' items, small-space design ideas, and design on a budget. We rarely use completed manuscripts sent to us; instead we assign stories to freelance writers once the idea has been fleshed out by our staff.

Kids VT

10½ Alfred Street
Burlington, VT 05401

Editor: Susan Holson

Description and Interests
Self-described as a "light parenting publication," this tabloid reports on regional resources and events of interest to families living in the Burlington, Vermont, area. It focuses on happenings, attractions, parties, camps, and family health.
- **Audience:** Parents
- **Frequency:** 10 times each year
- **Distribution:** 100% other
- **Circulation:** 22,000
- **Website:** www.kidsvt.com

Freelance Potential
98% written by nonstaff writers. Publishes 50–75 freelance submissions yearly; 25–50% by authors who are new to the magazine. Receives 480–960 unsolicited mss yearly.

Submissions
Send complete ms. Accepts faxes to 802-865-0595, email to editorial@kidsvt.com, and simultaneous submissions if identified. Response time varies.
Articles: 500–1,500 words. Informational articles; profiles; interviews; and humor. Topics include the arts, education, recreation, nature, the environment, music, camps, maternity issues, and infancy.
Depts/columns: Word lengths vary. News and media reviews.
Other: Activities and games. Submit seasonal material 2 months in advance.

Sample Issue
32 pages (50% advertising): 8 articles; 5 depts/columns; 1 calendar; 1 poem. Theme list available.
- "Gardens Grow Children." Article describes the many ways children benefit from growing a garden.
- "Teen$: Mind Your Own Bu$ine$$." Article features ideas and resources for teens who are interested in earning extra spending money.
- Sample dept/column: "Healthy Families" talks about the latest treatments for ear infections.

Rights and Payment
Exclusive Vermont rights. Written material, $15–$40. Pays on publication. Provides 1–2 author's copies.

Editor's Comments
We're interested in positive parenting articles that will appeal to parents in the Burlington area. Our purpose is to help make parenting an enjoyable experience for our readers.

Know

The Science Magazine for Curious Kids

501-3960 Quadra Street
Victoria, British Columbia V8X 4A3
Canada

Managing Editor: Adrienne Mason

Description and Interests
This magazine targets Canadian children who are curious about the world around them. Launched in January of 2006, it fills its pages with fun, informative, interactive material on a myriad of science topics.
- **Audience:** 6–9 years
- **Frequency:** 6 times each year
- **Distribution:** 90% subscription; 5% newsstand; 5% schools
- **Circulation:** 7,500
- **Website:** www.knowmag.ca

Freelance Potential
55% written by nonstaff writers. Publishes 5 freelance submissions yearly; 5% by unpublished writers, 100% by authors who are new to the magazine. Receives 60 queries yearly.

Submissions
Query with résumé and clips. Send complete ms for poetry and fiction. Accepts hard copy and email submissions to adrienne@knowmag.ca. SAE/IRC. Responds to queries in 1 week, to mss in 2 months.
Articles: 250 words. Informational and how-to articles. Topics include science, technology, computers, math, nature, the environment, animals, pets, biography, and history.
Fiction: 400 words. Stories about science.
Depts/columns: 200–250 words. Science news and book and product reviews.
Other: Games, jokes, riddles, poetry, and science experiments.

Sample Issue
30 pages (6% advertising): 5 articles; 9 depts/columns. Sample copy, $3.95 Canadian. Guidelines and theme list available.
- "Life on the Beach." Article examines the lives of shore birds, moon snails, clams, sand dollars, and other sea creatures.
- Sample dept/column: "Know You" looks at the science behind freckles.

Rights and Payment
First North American serial rights. Written material, $.40 per word. Pays on publication. Provides 2 contributor's copies.

Editor's Comments
Please check our theme list before submitting. Use short sentences and a fun, clear writing style.

Know Your World Extra

200 First Stamford Place
Stamford, CT 06910

Associate Editor: Jeff Ives

Description and Interests
This entertaining and educational magazine is designed to get students interested in reading and to expand their language skills.
- **Audience:** 10–18 years
- **Frequency:** Monthly
- **Distribution:** 50% controlled; 50% schools
- **Circulation:** 97,000
- **Website:** www.weeklyreader.com/kyw

Freelance Potential
5% written by nonstaff writers. Publishes 2–3 freelance submissions yearly; 10% by unpublished writers, 30% by authors who are new to the magazine. Receives 10+ queries yearly.

Submissions
Query with writing samples. SASE. Response time varies.
Articles: 350–500 words. Informational and how-to articles; plays; profiles; and interviews. Topics include animals, current events, health and fitness, history, humor, music, popular culture, science, technology, and sports.
Depts/columns: 150–200 words. Current events, health, animals, and sports.
Other: Crosswords, riddles, and puzzles.

Sample Issue
16 pages (no advertising): 5 articles; 1 play. Sample copy, free with 9x12 SASE. Guidelines available.
- "A Football Hero Without Feet." Article profiles a 17-year-old high school student who plays football, even though he was born without legs.
- "Tara's Curfew Panic." A Reader's Theater play tells the story of a girl who misses her curfew but doesn't get in trouble, thanks to her brother.
- "All Aboard the French Fry Bus." Article reports on a new fuel derived from used restaurant grease and oil.

Rights and Payment
One-time rights. Written material, payment rates vary. Pays on approval. Provides 5 contributor's copies.

Editor's Comments
We like to use original plays and stories by freelance authors when we find a writer who fits our editorial focus. Our audience consists or readers who are struggling at their grade levels. A typical issue of our magazine includes stories about popular youth topics, a readers' theater play, and an in-depth cover story.

Ladies Home Journal

Meredith Corporation
125 Park Avenue
New York, NY 10017

Deputy Editor: Margot Gilman

Description and Interests
For more than 100 years, this women's magazine has provided its readers with advice and information about family matters, beauty, fashion, health, and home management.
- **Audience:** Women
- **Frequency:** Monthly
- **Distribution:** Subscription; newsstand
- **Circulation:** 4.1 million
- **Website:** www.lhj.com

Freelance Potential
85% written by nonstaff writers. Publishes 25 freelance submissions yearly; 1% by unpublished writers, 5% by authors who are new to the magazine. Receives 2,400 queries yearly.

Submissions
Query with résumé, outline, and clips or writing samples for nonfiction. Accepts fiction through literary agents only. SASE. Responds in 1–3 months.
Articles: 1,500–2,000 words. Informational, how-to, and personal experience articles; profiles; and interviews. Topics include family issues, parenting, social concerns, fashion, beauty, and women's health.
Fiction: Word lengths vary. Accepts agented submissions only.
Depts/columns: Word lengths vary. Marriage and relationship issues, fashion and beauty advice, short lifestyle items.

Sample Issue
168 pages (15% advertising): 12 articles; 8 depts/columns. Sample copy, $2.49 at newsstands.
- "The Duchess Diaries." Article presents interviews with Sarah Ferguson and her two daughters, Princesses Beatrice and Eugenie.
- "The Risks of Automatic Bill Paying." Article explains how to protect your money when making debit transactions.
- Sample dept/column: "My Life as a Mom" tells why it's sometimes better to let children face their fears.

Rights and Payment
All rights. All material, payment rates vary. Pays on publication. Provides 2 contributor's copies.

Editor's Comments
Dramatic first-person pieces about family challenges are welcome. We are also interested in up-to-date health pieces.

Ladybug
The Magazine for Young Children

Carus Publishing
140 South Dearborn Street, Suite 1450
Chicago, IL 60603

Submissions Editor

Description and Interests
This magazine features original stories and poems by the world's best children's authors. Each issue of *Ladybug* also includes activities, songs, and games for young children.
- **Audience:** 2–6 years
- **Frequency:** Monthly
- **Distribution:** 92% subscription; 8% other
- **Circulation:** 130,000
- **Website:** www.cricketmag.com

Freelance Potential
100% written by nonstaff writers. Publishes 100 freelance submissions yearly. Receives 2,400 unsolicited mss yearly.

Submissions
Send complete ms with exact word count. Accepts hard copy and simultaneous submissions. SASE. Responds in 3–4 months.
Articles: To 300 words. Informational, humorous, and how-to articles. Topics include nature, family, animals, the environment, and other age-appropriate topics.
Fiction: 100–800 words. Read-aloud, early reader, picture, and rebus stories. Genres include adventure, humor, mild suspense, folktales, and contemporary fiction.
Other: Puzzles, activities, games, crafts, finger plays, and songs. Poetry, to 20 lines.

Sample Issue
36 pages (no advertising): 5 stories; 1 rebus; 4 poems; 1 song; 2 activities. Sample copy, $5. Guidelines available.
- "Feathers Fall from Trees." Story tells of two children collecting feathers from a tree in their village to bring to the medicine man.
- "Rain Family." Story describes the adventures that a family has together when it rains.

Rights and Payment
Rights vary. Stories and articles, $.25 per word. Poems, $3 per line; $25 minimum. Other material, payment rates vary. Pays on publication. Provides 6 contributor's copies.

Editor's Comments
Contributors must be familiar with this age group. We look for manuscripts that convey a child's sense of joy and wonder.

The Lamp-Post

1106 West 16th Street
Santa Ana, CA 92706

Senior Editor: David G. Clark

Description and Interests
The Lamp-Post features articles, book reviews, essays, and fiction related to the author C. S. Lewis and his work. It is a publication of the C. S. Lewis Society of Southern California.
- **Audience:** Adults
- **Frequency:** Quarterly
- **Distribution:** 100% controlled
- **Circulation:** 100

Freelance Potential
90% written by nonstaff writers. Publishes 12 freelance submissions yearly; 20% by unpublished writers, 60% by authors who are new to the magazine. Receives 15 unsolicited mss yearly.

Submissions
Send complete ms. Accepts hard copy and email to dgclark@adelphia.net (Microsoft Word or RTF attachments). No simultaneous submissions. SASE.
Responds in 2 days.
Articles: 2,000 words. Informational articles and essays. Topics include C. S. Lewis and his works, and the mythopoeic tradition to which Lewis and J. R. R. Tolkien contributed.
Fiction: Word lengths vary. Stories in the style of the work of C. S. Lewis.
Depts/columns: Word lengths vary. Book reviews.
Other: Poetry, word lengths vary.

Sample Issue
40 pages (15% advertising): 5 articles; 3 poems; 2 depts/columns. Sample copy, $4. Guidelines available in each issue.
- "The Founding of Narnia: Allusions in *The Magician's Nephew.*" Article discusses what may be considered the most autobiographical book in The Chronicles of Narnia series.
- "C. S. Lewis and the Dragon." Article analyzes the author's use of this mythical creature.

Rights and Payment
Rights vary. No payment. Provides 2 contributor's copies.

Editor's Comments
We especially seek scholarly or informal articles that will enhance our understanding, appreciation, and experience of the person and works of C. S. Lewis. We do occasionally publish poetry, but we are receiving too much fiction.

Language Arts

Ohio State University
333 Arps Hall
1945 North High Street
Columbus, OH 43210

Language Arts Editorial Team

Description and Interests
This publication acts as a resource for literacy and language arts teachers working with students in preschool through eighth grade. Its major focus is on the transformations occurring in education, curricula, and literacy practices. Its goal is to shake up the establishment.
- **Audience:** Teachers
- **Frequency:** 6 times each year
- **Distribution:** 100% subscription
- **Circulation:** 22,000
- **Website:** www.ncte.org

Freelance Potential
95% written by nonstaff writers. Publishes 30 freelance submissions yearly; 15% by unpublished writers, 30% by authors who are new to the magazine. Receives 180 unsolicited mss yearly.

Submissions
Send 6 copies of complete ms; include electronic Microsoft Word or PDF file. Accepts hard copy and IBM or Macintosh disk submissions. 2 SASEs. Responds in 3–9 months.
Articles: 2,500–6,500 words. Research articles; position papers; personal experiences; and opinion pieces. Topics include language arts, linguistics, and literacy.
Depts/columns: Word lengths vary. Profiles of children's authors and illustrators; reviews of children's trade books and professional resources; and theme related research papers.

Sample Issue
80 pages (8% advertising): 6 articles; 4 depts/columns. Sample copy, $5 with 9x12 SASE. Guidelines and theme list available.
- "What I've Learned from Teachers of Writing." Article expresses the views of an experienced writing teacher regarding children's natural writing abilities.
- "The Zine Project: Writing with a Personal Perspective." Article discusses a college teaching method.
- Sample dept/column: "Reading Corner for Educators" looks at the fate of writing workshops.

Rights and Payment
All rights. No payment. Provides 2 author's copies.

Editor's Comments
We are especially interested in articles that question educational practices in order to gain new understandings. We are not interested in work that doesn't question standard teaching methods.

L.A. Parent

443 East Irving Drive, Suite A
Burbank, CA 91504

Editor: Carolyn Graham

Description and Interests
For over 27 years, this resourceful magazine has been providing parents living in Southern California with a mix of articles and news on topics such as education, child care, health, discipline, social issues, and other parenting topics.
- **Audience:** Parents
- **Frequency:** Monthly
- **Distribution:** Schools; subscription; other
- **Circulation:** 120,000
- **Website: www.laprent.com**

Freelance Potential
70% written by nonstaff writers. Publishes 20 freelance submissions yearly; 5% by unpublished writers, 10% by authors who are new to the magazine. Receives 120 queries yearly.

Submissions
Query with clips. Accepts hard copy. SASE. Responds in 6 months.
Articles: 400–1,500 words. Practical application and how-to articles; profiles; and interviews. Topics include parenting and family issues, health, fitness, social issues, travel, and gifted and special education.
Depts/columns: 1,000 words. Family life, technology, travel destinations, events.
Artwork: B/W and color prints and transparencies.

Sample Issue
90 pages (60% advertising): 2 articles; 7 depts/columns; 1 calendar. Sample copy, $3. Guidelines and theme list available.
- "Tuning in to Fatherhood." Article provides different views of fatherhood from a newsman, a co-anchor, and a group of musicians.
- "The Surgeon General on Raising Healthy Kids." Article describes the views of U.S. Surgeon General Richard Carmona regarding improving the health of children.
- Sample dept/column: "Family Man" offers a humorous essay by a dad on kids and candy.

Rights and Payment
First serial rights. Written material, payment rates vary. Pays on publication. Provides contributor's copies.

Editor's Comments
We are looking for locally oriented education stories as well as articles on health topics from local writers.

Launch Pad

Teen Missions International
885 East Hall Road
Merritt Island, FL 32953

Editor: Linda Maher

Description and Interests
The activities of and opportunities for teen mission work are highlighted in this tabloid by Teen Missions International. Contents include news of current Christian evangelical work by the organization's members, alumni news, essays, and personal accounts of field experiences.
- **Audience:** YA–Adult
- **Frequency:** Twice each year
- **Distribution:** Subscription; other
- **Circulation:** Unavailable
- **Website: www.teenmissions.org**

Freelance Potential
10% written by nonstaff writers. Publishes 10 freelance submissions yearly; 15% by unpublished writers, 10% by authors who are new to the magazine. Receives 12–24 queries yearly.

Submissions
Query. Accepts hard copy. SASE. Response time varies.
Articles: Word lengths vary. Informational and factual articles; personal experience pieces; profiles; interviews; and photo-essays. Topics include mission work and teen evangelism in different countries.
Fiction: Word lengths vary. Inspirational, ethnic, and multicultural fiction.
Depts/columns: Word lengths vary. Alumni news and teen mission opportunities.

Sample Issue
8 pages (5% advertising): 3 articles; 4 depts/columns. Sample copy available.
- "AOSC One-Year Volunteer Program." Article chronicles the difference that one young woman is making while working with children in Malawi.
- "Alumni News." Article covers weddings, anniversaries, deaths, births, ministries, and other milestones of alumni of Teen Mission International.
- Sample dept/column: "Overseas Boot Camps" describes various evangelistic global work projects.

Rights and Payment
Rights vary. No payment.

Editor's Comments
Our publication is an upbeat account of what teen missions are accomplishing around the world. Current needs include articles about North American youths who want to help people who are spiritually lost.

Leadership for Student Activities

National Association of Secondary School Principals
1904 Association Drive
Reston, VA 20191-1537

Editor: Lyn Fiscus

Description and Interests
High school and middle school advisors of student leadership groups look to this magazine for ideas and inspiration. It focuses on honor society and student council activities, as well as other aspects of youth volunteerism.
• **Audience:** Student leaders and advisors
• **Frequency:** 9 times each year
• **Distribution:** 95% subscription; 5% other
• **Circulation:** 30,000
• **Website:** www.nhs.us

Freelance Potential
67% written by nonstaff writers. Publishes 18–25 freelance submissions yearly; 75% by unpublished writers, 50% by authors who are new to the magazine. Receives 12–24 queries, 48 unsolicited mss yearly.

Submissions
Query with clips; or send complete ms. Accepts hard copy and email submissions to L4SA@att.net. SASE. Responds to queries in 2 weeks, to mss in 1 month.
Articles: 1,200–1,700 words. Informational and how-to articles; profiles; and interviews. Topics include student activities, leadership development, and careers.
Depts/columns: Reports on special events, 100–350 words; advice for and by activity advisors, 1,000–1,500 words; national and regional news, leadership plans, and opinion pieces, word lengths vary.
Artwork: B/W and color prints and transparencies.
Other: Submit seasonal material 4 months in advance.

Sample Issue
44 pages (21% advertising): 5 articles; 9 depts/columns. Sample copy, free with 9x12 SASE ($1.24 postage). Guidelines and theme list available.
• "Putting Learning into Service." Article explores ways to turn service projects into learning opportunities.
• Sample dept/column: "Project Showcase" features a welcome luncheon and sundae bar activity.

Rights and Payment
All rights. Written material, payment rates vary. Payment policy varies. Provides 5 contributor's copies.

Editor's Comments
We need descriptions of projects that others can replicate, reports on National Honor Society chapters and activities, and leadership lesson plans.

Leading Edge

4198 JFSB
Provo, UT 84602

Fiction Director

Description and Interests
Science fiction and fantasy short stories, novelettes, novellas, and poetry are the focus of this literary journal. Each issue also includes science fiction and fantasy related articles, book reviews, and interviews.
• **Audience:** YA–Adult
• **Frequency:** Twice each year
• **Distribution:** 30% subscription; 70% other
• **Circulation:** 500
• **Website:** www.leadingedgemagazine.com

Freelance Potential
90% written by nonstaff writers. Publishes 12 freelance submissions yearly; 90% by unpublished writers, 90% by authors who are new to the magazine. Receives 500 unsolicited mss yearly.

Submissions
Send complete ms. Accepts hard copy. No simultaneous submissions. SASE. Responds in 2–3 months.
Articles: 1,000–10,000 words. Informational articles; interviews; and book reviews. Topics include science fiction, fantasy, science, mythology, and speculative anthropology.
Fiction: To 17,000 words. Genres include science fiction and fantasy.
Depts/columns: Staff written.
Other: Poetry, no line limit.

Sample Issue
200 pages (no advertising): 1 article; 6 stories; 2 poems; 7 depts/columns. Sample copy, $4.95. Guidelines available.
• "Firstborn." Futuristic story tells of a commander-to-be who must learn war strategy and techniques from his hated brother.
• "The Covenant." Short story features a man who must find a cure for a new Earth plague.

Rights and Payment
First North American serial rights. Written material, $.01 per word. Artwork, payment rates vary. Pays on publication. Provides 2 contributor's copies.

Editor's Comments
In addition to our usual mix of fiction, we also publish nonfiction articles about science fiction, science, fantasy, and mythology. Note that our editors will not consider material with excessive sex, violence, or profanity, or stories that belittle traditional family values or religious beliefs.

Leading Student Ministry

One LifeWay Plaza
Nashville, TN 37234-0174

Editor-in-Chief: Paul Turner

Description and Interests
Professionals and volunteers who lead youth ministry programs affiliated with the Southern Baptist Convention look for practical and inspirational writing in this magazine. Published by LifeWay Christian Resources, it focuses on ministry to teens.
- **Audience:** Youth ministers and leaders
- **Frequency:** Quarterly
- **Distribution:** Unavailable
- **Circulation:** 10,000
- **Website:** www.lifeway.com

Freelance Potential
85% written by nonstaff writers.

Submissions
Query or send complete ms with résumé. Accepts email submissions to paul.turner@lifeway.com (Microsoft Word attachments). Responds to queries in 2–3 days, to mss in 2–3 weeks.
Articles: 1,000–1,800 words. How-to articles; profiles; interviews; and personal experience pieces. Topics include adolescent ministry, religion, college, careers, current events, health, fitness, music, popular culture, and parenting teens. Also publishes humorous articles.
Depts/columns: 500–1,000 words. Bible study, resource reviews, teaching tips, parent ministry, adolescent development and counseling, and college ministry.
Other: Jokes. Submit seasonal material 3 months in advance.

Sample Issue
62 pages (no advertising): 5 articles; 10 depts/columns. Sample copy, $3.95. Guidelines available.
- "Essentials of Small-Town Youth Ministry." Article weighs the advantages and challenges of ministering to youth in a small town.
- Sample dept/column: "Leading Bible Study" offers ideas for keeping teens inspired after a week of summer camp.

Rights and Payment
All rights. Written material, $.10 per word. Pays on acceptance. Provides 2 contributor's copies.

Editor's Comments
Familiarity with our magazine and our guidelines will greatly improve your chance of submitting a successful proposal to us.

Learning and Leading with Technology

International Society for Technology in Education
175 West Broadway, Suite 300
Eugene, OR 97401-3003

Editor: Davis N. Smith

Description and Interests
Educators and administrators read this publication for the latest information on classroom technology, curriculum development, and educational leadership and policy. Practical ideas on integrating technology in the classroom are included in each issue.
- **Audience:** Educators, K–12
- **Frequency:** 8 times each year
- **Distribution:** 90% subscription; 10% libraries
- **Circulation:** 12,000
- **Website:** www.iste.org/LL

Freelance Potential
90% written by nonstaff writers. Publishes 75 freelance submissions yearly; 50% by unpublished writers, 75% by authors who are new to the magazine. Receives 75 queries, 200 unsolicited mss yearly.

Submissions
Query. Accepts email queries to submission@iste.org and simultaneous submissions if identified. Response time varies.
Articles: 600–2,000 words. Informational and how-to articles; and personal experience pieces. Topics include computers, software, technology, media applications, teaching methods, and telecommunications.
Depts/columns: Word lengths vary. Research, software, reviews, and curriculum ideas.
Artwork: B/W prints. Line art.

Sample Issue
64 pages (20% advertising): 8 articles; 11 depts/columns. Sample copy, free with 9x12 SASE (3 first-class stamps). Guidelines and editorial calendar available at website.
- "Digesting a Story." Article discusses how a second-grade class uses multi-media in the classroom.
- "Making Biology Matter." Article tells of an attractive alternative to learning science from a textbook.
- Sample dept/column: "What Really Works" offers two resources for professional development.

Rights and Payment
All rights; returns limited rights to author upon request. No payment. Provides 3 contributor's copies.

Editor's Comments
We seek articles emphasizing the how-to aspects of integrating technology appropriately in kindergarten through twelfth-grade classrooms. Technology-using educators are our audience.

The Learning Edge

Clonlara School
1289 Jewett
Ann Arbor, MI 48104

Editor: Judy Gelner

Description and Interests
Families and students enrolled in the Clonlara School Home Based Education Program read this newsletter for its coverage of school news, educational resources, and event information.
- **Audience:** Clonlara School members
- **Frequency:** 6 times each year
- **Distribution:** 100% subscription
- **Circulation:** 1,000
- **Website:** www.clonlara.com

Freelance Potential
25% written by nonstaff writers. Of the freelance submissions published yearly, 10% are by unpublished writers, 1% are by authors who are new to the magazine. Receives 12 queries yearly.

Submissions
Query. Accepts hard copy. SASE. Responds in 2 months.
Articles: Word lengths vary. Informational and how-to articles; personal experience pieces; and profiles. Topics include homeschooling, education, technology, career choices, and college.
Depts/columns: Word lengths vary. School programs, membership news and information, and curriculum resources.
Other: Puzzles and activities.

Sample Issue
12 pages (no advertising): 2 articles; 5 depts/columns. Sample copy available upon request.
- "From the Secondary Program." Article discusses the changes in the new credit report form for high school students.
- "Experience Government from the Inside: The Presidential Classroom Program." Article outlines a program designed to introduce high school juniors and seniors to the nation's capital.
- Sample dept/column: "Summer At Clonlara" takes a look at the school's graduation ceremony and day and summer camp.

Rights and Payment
All rights. No payment.

Editor's Comments
We are interested in personal experience pieces from parents who are homeschooling that include successful tips and strategies. We continue to seek math and science articles with hands-on activities.

Learning Through History

P.O. Box 110129
Naples, FL 34108

Editor: Rebecca Thompson

Description and Interests
Each issue of this publication showcases a different historical theme, from ancient Egypt to the Great Depression and beyond. History, literature, science, and the arts are discussed as they relate to the theme.
- **Audience:** 9–16 years
- **Frequency:** 6 times each year
- **Distribution:** Subscription
- **Circulation:** 10,000
- **Website:** www.learningthroughhistory.com

Freelance Potential
100% written by nonstaff writers. Publishes 120 freelance submissions yearly; 8% by unpublished writers, 35–40% by authors who are new to the magazine.

Submissions
Accepts query with synopsis and clips from established writers. Other writers, send complete ms. Accepts email submissions to submissions@ LearningThroughHistory.com (Microsoft Word or plain text files). Responds in 2 weeks.
Articles: 1,000–1,400 words. Informational articles; biographies; and profiles. Topics include history, science, mathematics, geography, literature, and the arts.
Depts/columns: Staff written.
Artwork: JPEG, Photoshop, or Illustrator files; 300 dpi minimum.
Other: Arts and crafts accompanied by 2 or more digital photos.

Sample Issue
64 pages (no advertising): 17 articles; 2 depts/columns; 2 crafts; 2 literature study guides; 1 early learning unit. Guidelines available at website.
- "Life in the Trenches: A World Below Ground." Article digs into the use of trenches during WWI.
- Sample activity: "Arts & Crafts" reveals how to make a poppy wreath to commemorate fallen soldiers.

Rights and Payment
All print and electronic rights. Written material, $60. Arts and crafts projects, $30. Kill fee, 50%. Pays on publication. Provides 1 contributor's copy.

Editor's Comments
Rather than broad factual surveys, we are looking for focused and exciting articles that will engage our young readers. Include at least three meaningful discussion questions or activity suggestions.

Lexington Family Magazine

138 East Reynolds Road, Suite 201
Lexington, KY 40517

Publisher: Dana Tackett

Description and Interests
Parents who live in Lexington and other communities in central Kentucky use the practical advice and resource information found in this tabloid. It also covers women's health, home improvement, and consumer issues.
- **Audience:** Parents
- **Frequency:** Monthly
- **Distribution:** 50% schools; 50% other
- **Circulation:** 30,000
- **Website:** www.lexingtonfamily.com

Freelance Potential
50% written by nonstaff writers. Publishes 20 freelance submissions yearly; 20% by unpublished writers, 35% by authors who are new to the magazine. Receives 120 unsolicited mss yearly.

Submissions
Query or send complete ms. Accepts hard copy. SASE. Response time varies.
Articles: 500–1,500 words. Informational and how-to articles. Topics include the arts, hobbies, current events, education, health, fitness, regional history, multicultural issues, popular culture, recreation, science, technology, and family travel.
Depts/columns: 800 words. Pediatric medicine, short news items, child development issues.
Artwork: B/W and color prints. Line art.
Other: Puzzles, activities, and poetry.

Sample Issue
40 pages (50% advertising): 6 articles; 6 depts/columns; 1 calendar of events; 1 resource guide. Sample copy, free with 9x12 SASE ($1.50 postage). Guidelines and theme list available.
- "MySpace: Are Your Kids Safe?" Article explains the dangers that children may face when they log on to this popular website.
- "How to Talk to Aging Parents . . . And Still Remain Friends." Article offers advice for helping elderly parents through lifestyle changes.

Rights and Payment
All rights. Written material, payment rates vary. Pays on publication. Provides 25 contributor's copies.

Editor's Comments
We continue to look for well-written articles that deal with women's health issues and continuing education for adults.

Library Media Connection

480 East Wilson Bridge Road, Suite L
Worthington, OH 43085

Editor: Shelley Glantz

Description and Interests
Information that helps school library media and technology specialists appears in this magazine from Linworth Publishing, Inc. Its pages are filled with practical programming ideas, book and media reviews, and the latest research in this field.
- **Audience:** School librarians and media specialists
- **Frequency:** 7 times each year
- **Distribution:** 100% subscription
- **Circulation:** 15,000
- **Website:** www.linworth.com

Freelance Potential
100% written by nonstaff writers. Publishes 215 freelance submissions yearly; 75% by unpublished writers, 25% by authors who are new to the magazine. Receives 144 queries, 144 unsolicited mss yearly.

Submissions
Query or send complete ms with résumé. Accepts hard copy, disk submissions (Microsoft Word or ASCII), and email submissions to linworth@linworthpublishing.com. SASE. Responds 2 weeks.
Articles: Word lengths vary. Informational and how-to articles; personal experience pieces; and opinion. Topics include library science, research, technology, education, computers, and media services.
Depts/columns: Word lengths vary. Teaching tips, new products, and reviews.
Other: Submit seasonal material 6 months in advance.

Sample Issue
98 pages (15% advertising): 11 articles; 9 depts/columns. Sample copy, $11 with 9x12 SASE. Guidelines and theme list available.
- "Here, There, and Everywhere: Reading First in the Library." Article tells how librarians can work with basal reader-driven programs.
- "Reports without Copying." Article looks at the role media centers play in preventing plagiarism.
- Sample dept/column: "Reader's Advisory" answers a reader's question about historical picture books.

Rights and Payment
All rights. Written material, payment rates vary. Pays on publication. Provides 4 contributor's copies.

Editor's Comments
Contributors should be aware that many of our articles are theme-related. Inquire about our theme list.

Library Sparks

P.O. Box 800
W5527 State Road 106
Fort Atkinson, WI 53580

Managing Editor: Michelle McCardell

Description and Interests
This magazine is chock full of practical, ready-to-use lessons and activities for elementary teachers and librarians. It strives to provide resourceful information and engaging ideas to motivate students to read and use the library. Each issue centers on a theme.
• **Audience:** Librarians and teachers
• **Frequency:** 9 times each year
• **Distribution:** Subscription; other
• **Circulation:** Unavailable
• **Website:** www.librarysparks.com

Freelance Potential
95% written by nonstaff writers. Publishes 5 freelance submissions yearly; 25% by unpublished writers, 25% by authors who are new to the magazine. Receives 20 queries and unsolicited mss yearly.

Submissions
Query or send complete ms. Accepts hard copy and email submissions to librarysparks@highsmith.com. SASE. Response time varies.
Articles: Word lengths vary. Informational articles and profiles. Topics include connecting literature to the curriculum, lesson plans for librarians, library skills, children's authors and illustrators, and ideas for motivating students to read.
Depts/columns: Word lengths vary. Reading skills and book review activities, ready-made lessons, fingerplays and storytelling activities, booktalks, and reader's theater scripts.
Other: Reproducible games and activities, crafts.

Sample Issue
48 pages (no advertising): 1 article; 12 depts/columns. Sample copy available at website. Guidelines and editorial calendar available.
• "Art and Children's Illustrators." Article offers resources that explore children's book illustration.
• Sample dept/column: "Library Lessons" discusses research versus plagiarism.

Rights and Payment
Rights vary. Written material, payment rates vary. Pays on publication. Provides 1 contributor's copy.

Editor's Comments
We are looking for fresh, fun ideas that will encourage students to learn what the library has to offer, and help spark a love of reading. Lessons must be practical, ready-to-use, and target elementary age students.

Lifted Magazine

14781 Memorial Drive, Suite 1747
Houston, TX 77079

Editor: Tiffany Simpson

Description and Interests
Lifted Magazine targets young adults who are in tune with their faith and want an alternative to the mainstream magazine. Features include travel guides; articles about faith, cooking, college life, and careers; entertainment reviews; and short stories. It is available in print as well as online.
• **Audience:** 18–34 years
• **Frequency:** 6 times each year
• **Distribution:** Subscription; Internet
• **Circulation:** 10,000
• **Website:** www.liftedmag.com

Freelance Potential
95% written by nonstaff writers. Publishes 100 freelance submissions yearly; 80% by unpublished writers, 20% by authors who are new to the magazine.

Submissions
Send complete ms. Accepts email submissions to articles@liftedmag.com (Microsoft Word or text).
Articles: Word lengths vary. Informational articles; profiles; and personal experience pieces. Topics include faith, stories of inspiration, book reviews, dating and relationships, college and careers, food, and entertainment.
Fiction: Word lengths vary. Contemporary fiction.

Sample Issue
Sample copy and guidelines available at website.
• "Easier Said Than Done." Article shares the author's thoughts and suggestions about dating the way God wants us to date.
• "Open My Eyes, Father." Article tells of the life-changing prayer experienced by the author and relates it to the story of Abraham and Sarah.
• "Does God Really Care?" Article discusses different Bible stories, relating them to how some people might feel when it seems as though their prayers are never answered.

Rights and Payment
Rights vary. No payment.

Editor's Comments
We seek positive articles with a Christian undertone and will not publish anything with profanity or that refers to offensive subjects. We like fresh ideas that will appeal to our audience. Because we have a Christian readership, many of our writers express their faith in their writing, but this is not required.

The Lion

Lions Club International
300 West 22nd Street
Oak Brook, IL 60523-8842

Senior Editor: Robert Kleinfelder

Description and Interests
Articles and photos that spotlight the service goals and projects of Lions Clubs locally, nationally, and internationally can be found on the pages of this magazine. It also includes member profiles, club news, and general interest articles.
- **Audience:** Members of Lions Clubs
- **Frequency:** 10 times each year
- **Distribution:** 85% articles; 15% depts/columns
- **Circulation:** 490,000
- **Website:** www.lionsclub.org

Freelance Potential
40% written by nonstaff writers. Publishes 60 freelance submissions yearly; 10% by unpublished writers, 30% by authors who are new to the magazine. Receives 100 queries and unsolicited mss yearly.

Submissions
Prefers query; accepts complete ms. Accepts hard copy. SASE. Responds to queries in 10 days, to mss in 2 months.
Articles: 300–2,000 words. Informational articles; humor; and family-oriented photo-essays. Topics include Lions Club service projects, disabilities, social issues, and special education.
Depts/columns: Staff written.
Artwork: 5x7 glossy prints, slides, and digital images.

Sample Issue
56 pages (6% advertising): 18 articles; 9 depts/columns. Sample copy, free. Guidelines available.
- "How Not to Use Loser Language." Article examines ways to avoid using defensive language and how to discover the power of positive speech patterns.
- "Make Plans to Recycle for Sight." Article describes an eyeglass recycling campaign.
- "Choosing the Right Credit Card." Article takes a look at cash-back credit card options.

Rights and Payment
All rights. Written material, $100–$700. Pays on acceptance. Provides 4–10 contributor's copies.

Editor's Comments
We need more photo-essays of Lions Club service projects. Other submissions that would be of interest to us include family-oriented essays; articles about consumer issues, disabilities, and social issues; and humorous essays. Please note that we do not accept gags, filler, quizzes, or poems.

Listen Magazine

55 West Oak Ridge Drive
Hagerstown, MD 21740

Editor: Céleste Perrino-Walker

Description and Interests
Aimed at teenagers, *Listen Magazine* encourages the development of good habits and high ideals of physical, social, and mental health. Feature articles relate to the common concerns of today's teens.
- **Audience:** 12–18 years
- **Frequency:** 9 times each year
- **Distribution:** 60% subscription; 40% newsstand
- **Circulation:** 40,000
- **Website:** www.listenmagazine.org

Freelance Potential
90% written by nonstaff writers. Publishes 90 freelance submissions yearly; 15% by unpublished writers, 30% by authors who are new to the magazine. Receives 500 queries, 350 unsolicited mss yearly.

Submissions
Query or send complete ms. Accepts hard copy, email submissions to editor@listenmagazine.org, and simultaneous submissions if identified. SASE. Responds in 6 weeks.
Articles: 1,000–1,100 words. Informational articles; self-help pieces; and profiles. Topics include peer pressure, decision making, family conflict, suicide, self-esteem, self-discipline, and hobbies.
Fiction: 1,000–1,100 words. Contemporary fiction based on true events.
Depts/columns: Word lengths vary. Opinion pieces and short pieces on social issues.
Other: Poetry, line length varies.

Sample Issue
30 pages (no advertising): 12 articles; 6 depts/columns. Sample copy, $2 with 9x12 SASE (2 first-class stamps). Writer's guidelines and editorial calendar available.
- "Weed Out Weed." Article lists 10 reasons to avoid smoking marijuana.
- "The Run of My Life." Article tells the story of a 16-year-old girl who runs her very first marathon.
- Sample dept/column: "Good for You" highlights the dangers of tanning beds.

Rights and Payment
All rights. Written material, $.05–$.10 per word. Pays on acceptance. Provides 3 contributor's copies.

Editor's Comments
We seek professionally-written, teen-oriented articles and true stories of interest to our readers.

Live

The General Council of the Assemblies of God
1445 North Boonville Avenue
Springfield, MO 65802-1894

Editor: Richard Bennett

Description and Interests
True stories and fiction that present realistic characters who utilize biblical principals to resolve their problems scripturally can be found in this Sunday school class journal. It also includes poetry.
- **Audience:** 18+ years
- **Frequency:** Quarterly, in weekly sections
- **Distribution:** 100% religious instruction
- **Circulation:** 65,000
- **Website: www.radiantlife.org**

Freelance Potential
100% written by nonstaff writers. Publishes 110 freelance submissions yearly; 20% by unpublished writers, 100% by authors who are new to the magazine. Receives 2,100 queries and unsolicited mss yearly.

Submissions
Query or send complete ms. Accepts hard copy, email to rl-live@gph.org, and simultaneous submissions if identified. SASE. Responds in 6 weeks.
Articles: 800–1,200 words. Informational articles; humor; and personal experience pieces. Topics include family issues, parenting, and religious history.
Fiction: 800–1,200 words. Inspirational and historical fiction, adventure stories, and stories about family celebrations and traditions.
Other: Poetry, 12–25 lines. Filler, 200–600 words. Submit seasonal material 1 year in advance.

Sample Issue
8 pages (no advertising): 1 article; 1 story. Sample copy, free with #10 SASE ($.39 postage). Writers' guidelines available.
- "A Different Recipe." Story links a cake recipe to the experiences of life and the plans God has in store.
- "Certificate of Transport." Story relays the spiritual message of God offering a free gift to heaven.

Rights and Payment
First and second rights. Written material, $.10 per word for first rights; $.07 for second rights. Pays on acceptance. Provides 2 contributor's copies.

Editor's Comments
We are currently looking for more material on holidays, patriotic themes, discipleship, evangelism, and "gray area" issues. Make sure your stories have action and that the conflict and suspense increases to a climax. Characters should be active and confront conflict and change in believable ways.

Living

1251 Virginia Avenue
Harrisonburg, VA 22802

Editor: Melodie Davis

Description and Interests
This tabloid targets all family members with its positive articles about home, workplace, and community issues. It is read by residents of Harrisonburg, Virginia, and the surrounding towns.
- **Audience:** Families
- **Frequency:** Quarterly
- **Distribution:** 100% controlled
- **Circulation:** 150,000
- **Website: www.churchoutreach.com**

Freelance Potential
85% written by nonstaff writers. Publishes 55 freelance submissions yearly; 5% by unpublished writers, 30% by authors who are new to the magazine. Receives 600 unsolicited mss yearly.

Submissions
Send complete ms. Accepts email submissions to melodiemd@msn.com. Include name of magazine and title of article in the subject line; include your email address in the body of the email. Accepts hard copy and simultaneous submissions if identified. SASE. Responds in 3–4 months.
Articles: 500–1,000 words. Informational and how-to articles; and opinion and personal experience pieces. Topics include health and fitness, recreation, religion, social issues, education, and multicultural and ethnic issues.
Depts/columns: Staff written.

Sample Issue
32 pages (20% advertising): 13 articles; 5 depts/columns. Sample copy, free with 9x12 SASE (4 first-class stamps). Guidelines available at website.
- "Big Bill: A Family Man." Article profiles a common man who worked hard to help his children succeed.
- "Who's Afraid? Confronting Childhood Fears." Article explains how children can overcome fears by researching the things they are afraid of.

Rights and Payment
One-time and second rights. Articles, $30–$60. Pays on publication. Provides 2 contributor's copies.

Editor's Comments
Please remember that our magazine is written for families; we don't usually use pieces that are directed specifically to children. Our articles reflect Christian values. Your writing should offer hope and encouragement to healthy and positive relationships.

Living Safety

Canada Safety Council
1020 Thomas Spratt Place
Ottawa, Ontario K1G 5L5
Canada

General Manager: Jack Smith

Description and Interests
Published by the Canada Safety Council, an independent, not-for-profit organization, this magazine reaches an audience of adults, young adults, and children. Its purpose is to encourage public awareness of safety issues.
• **Audience:** All ages
• **Frequency:** Quarterly
• **Distribution:** 100% subscription
• **Circulation:** 80,000
• **Website:** www.safety-council.com

Freelance Potential
75% written by nonstaff writers. Publishes 25 freelance submissions yearly; 65% by unpublished writers, 10% by authors who are new to the magazine. Receives 12 queries yearly.

Submissions
Query with résumé and clips or writing samples. Accepts hard copy. SAE/IRC. Responds in 2 weeks.
Articles: 1,500–2,500 words. Informational articles. Topics include recreational, home, traffic, and school safety; and health issues.
Depts/columns: Word lengths vary. Safety news, research findings, opinions, and product recalls.
Other: Children's activities.

Sample Issue
32 pages (no advertising): 4 articles; 4 depts/columns; 1 kids' page. Sample copy, free with 9x12 SAE/IRC. Guidelines available.
• "From the Gate to Your Plate: How Safe Is Your Food?" Article addresses bacteria and other contaminants and explains what can be done to insure food safety.
• "Can't Throw It Away? You May Be a Hoarder." Article provides a thoughtful and detailed examination of why some people hoard, the causes, and the possible treatments.

Rights and Payment
All rights. Articles, to $500. Depts/columns, payment rates vary. Pays on acceptance. Provides 1–5 contributor's copies.

Editor's Comments
We strive to create 24-hour safety consciousness, reduce off-the-job accidents, and reinforce workplace safety. Acceptable topics include home, traffic, and recreational safety issues.

Living with Teenagers

One LifeWay Plaza
Nashville, TN 37234–0174

Editor: Bob Bunn

Description and Interests
This magazine for Christian families encourages and equips parents with biblically-based solutions for raising their teenagers and inspiring their families.
• **Audience:** Parents
• **Frequency:** Monthly
• **Distribution:** Subscription; religious instruction
• **Circulation:** 42,000
• **Website:** www.lifeway.com

Freelance Potential
90% written by nonstaff writers.

Submissions
No queries or unsolicited mss. Work done by assignment only. Submit writing samples if you wish to be considered for an assignment. SASE.
Articles: 600–2,000 words. Informational, self-help, and how-to articles; profiles; interviews; and reviews. Topics include parenting; colleges; current events; health; fitness; recreation; religion; and social, spiritual, multicultural, and ethnic issues.
Depts/columns: Staff written.

Sample Issue
34 pages (no advertising): 5 articles; 10 depts/columns. Sample copy, free.
• "The Good, the Bad, and the Holy." Article details how parents can raise media-savvy teenagers by shaping their child's worldview from a Christian perspective.
• "Game Planned." Article profiles John Croyle, a talented college football star who turned his back on the NFL and dedicated his life to helping disadvantaged teenagers.
• "Keeping Teens Plugged into Church." Article suggests ways to keep kids going to church as they grow into young adulthood.

Rights and Payment
All rights with non-exclusive license to the writer. Articles, $100–$300. Pays on acceptance. Provides 3 contributor's copies.

Editor's Comments
Articles for our magazine are developed in-house. We then contact highly qualified writers to further develop the story and craft the article. Anyone with an interest in writing for our publication should visit our website. Our editors will request specific writing samples to gauge the writer's compatibility with our needs.

Long Island Woman

P.O. Box 176
Malverne, NY 11565

Publisher: Arie Nadboy

Description and Interests
A mix of news and articles on topics that are of interest to women can be found in this tabloid that is distributed throughout Long Island. It covers health, lifestyles and family, sports, business, home decorating, gardening, and entertainment. Interviews with inspiring women and book reviews are also featured.
- **Audience:** Women
- **Frequency:** Monthly
- **Distribution:** 100% subscription
- **Circulation:** 40,000
- **Website:** www.liwomanonline.com

Freelance Potential
50% written by nonstaff writers. Publishes 30 freelance submissions yearly. Receives 844 unsolicited mss yearly.

Submissions
Send ms. Accepts email submissions to editor@liwomanonline.com. Availability of artwork improves chance of acceptance. SASE. Response time varies.
Articles: 350–2,000 words. Informational and how-to articles; profiles; and interviews. Topics include health, recreation, regional news, family, fashion, decorating, entertainment, and gardening.
Depts/columns: 500–1,000 words. Health, money, website information, local attractions and events.
Artwork: Electronic B/W and color prints. Line art.
Other: Submit seasonal material 90 days in advance.

Sample Issue
44 pages (60% advertising): 2 articles; 5 depts/columns. Sample copy, $5. Guidelines available.
- "Fran Drescher." Article offers an interview with this comic actress who also offers up a serious side as an advocate for gynecologic cancer education.
- "Robin Wagner." Article offers a profile of a figure skating coach whose student won the 2002 Olympic gold medal in women's figure skating.
- Sample dept/column: "Health" offers diet and exercise tips.

Rights and Payment
One-time and electronic rights. Written material, payment rates vary. Kill fee, 33%. Pays on publication. Provides 1 tearsheet.

Editor's Comments
We are looking for articles on health, fashion, and food. Currently, we have enough personal essays.

Look-Look Magazine

1201 West 5th Street, Suite T–850
Los Angeles, CA 90017

Editor: Amity

Description and Interests
This magazine provides an outlet for young people to showcase their talents by publishing their writings, drawings, photographs, and other forms of artistic expression.
- **Audience:** 12–30 years
- **Frequency:** Twice each year
- **Distribution:** 95% newsstand; 5% subscription
- **Circulation:** 55,000
- **Website:** www.look-lookmagazine.com

Freelance Potential
100% written by nonstaff writers. Publishes 120 freelance submissions yearly; 100% by unpublished writers, 100% by authors who are new to the magazine. Receives 8,000 queries yearly.

Submissions
Query. Accepts queries through website only. Response time varies.
Articles: To 2,000 words. How-to articles; profiles; interviews; and personal experience pieces. Topics include the arts and popular culture.
Fiction: To 2,000 words. Genres include contemporary, humorous, and multicultural fiction.
Artwork: B/W and color prints and transparencies. Line art.
Other: Poetry. Submit seasonal material 4 months in advance.

Sample Issue
98 pages (5% advertising): 1 article; 3 stories; 9 poems; 4 photo-essays. Sample copy, $5.95 with 9x12 SASE ($.77 postage). Guidelines and editorial calendar available at website.
- "Out and About: Southern Debutantes." Photo-essay documents four women frolicking in their debutante gowns.
- "Annapolis Mall." Poem observes the activity at a suburban shopping mall.
- "People I Like." Article shows a conversation between the author and her brother regarding their father's incarceration.

Rights and Payment
All rights. No payment. Provides 2 author's copies.

Editor's Comments
We accept a broad range of writing styles, but would like to see more pieces on political and environmental issues and fewer poems on relationship break-ups.

Loud Magazine

Lowcountry Parent

P.O. Box 50547
Palo Alto, CA 94303

Editor-in-Chief: Anne Schukat

Description and Interests
This magazine is devoted to youth with news just about them. Each issue provides reportage and insights on crucial issues facing young people as future leaders, pioneers, and mavericks in their chosen fields. It features articles covering youth rights, entrepreneurs, activists, careers, events, books, and music, and news briefs from around the world.
- **Audience:** 12–16 years
- **Frequency:** Quarterly
- **Distribution:** Subscription; newsstand; schools
- **Circulation:** Unavailable
- **Website: www.loudmagazine.com**

Freelance Potential
30% written by nonstaff writers. Publishes 30 freelance submissions yearly.

Submissions
Query with clips. Prefers email queries to submissions@loudmagazine.com. Accepts hard copy. SASE. Response time varies.
Articles: Word lengths vary. Informational and how-to articles; and profiles. Topics include youth rights, entrepreneurs, activists, politics, entertainment, technology, science, marketing, careers, and fashion.
Depts/columns: Word lengths vary. News and reviews. Music, technology, science, education, books, and travel.

Sample Issue
72 pages: 12 articles; 19 depts/columns. Sample copy, $3.95. Guidelines available.
- "Corporate Logo Tattoos." Article discusses companies using humans as billboards.
- "Where Are They Now?" Article describes what several reality show stars are doing now that the shows they were on have ended.
- Sample dept/column: "Sports & Health" reports on the benefits of using protective head gear while skating.

Rights and Payment
Rights vary. No payment for first-time authors; will pay for additional articles. Written material, payment rates vary. Pays on publication. Provides 1 author's copy.

Editor's Comments
We are looking for articles covering teen rights, teen entrepreneurs, and the entertainment industry. Please be concise; we don't have time to read lengthy ideas.

1277 Stiles Bee Avenue
Charleston, SC 29412

Submissions Editor: Christina Bean

Description and Interests
This free magazine for parents and families in the Charleston area of South Carolina features articles on parenting, child development, education, family issues, and health.
- **Audience:** Parents
- **Frequency:** Monthly
- **Distribution:** 80% subscription; 20% controlled
- **Circulation:** 38,000
- **Website: www.lowcountryparent.com**

Freelance Potential
25% written by nonstaff writers. Publishes many freelance submissions yearly; 10% by authors who are new to the magazine. Receives 100 mss monthly.

Submissions
Query with sample pages; or send complete ms with biography. Prefers email submissions to editor@lowcountryparent.com. Responds in 3 days.
Articles: Word lengths vary. Informational and factual articles; and personal experience pieces. Topics include parenting, child development, family issues, education, vacations, holidays, and pets.
Depts/columns: Word lengths vary. Infant, pre-teen, and teen development, health issues, and media reviews.
Artwork: B/W and color prints.
Other: Word lengths vary. Puzzles, jokes, and filler.

Sample Issue
30 pages (50% advertising): 3 articles; 7 depts/columns; 1 calendar of events. Sample copy, free. Guidelines available.
- "Let's Save!" Article offers easy-to-follow, common sense tips to stretch the family food budget.
- "Hitting the Wall." Article takes a humorous look at traveling with children during summer vacation.
- "Homework." Article reviews children's films, videos, and video games including *Akeelah and the Bee* (film); *Veggie Tales: LarryBoy and Bad Apple* (video); and *Over the Hedge* (video game).

Rights and Payment
One-time rights. Written material, $15–$100. Pays on publication. Provides 3 contributor's copies.

Editor's Comments
We need insightful and solutions-based articles that deal with the challenges of parenting. Also, we are seeking topics for parenting middle-school age kids.

The Magazine

643 Queen Street East
Toronto, Ontario M4M 1G4
Canada

Editor: Ed Conroy

Description and Interests
This entertainment digest for youth covers television, movies, the music scene, video games, and popular books. Each issue also includes contests, comics, and activities.
- **Audience:** 10–18 years
- **Frequency:** Monthly
- **Distribution:** Subscription; newsstand
- **Circulation:** 89,000
- **Website:** www.themagazine.ca

Freelance Potential
60% written by nonstaff writers. Publishes 100 freelance submissions yearly; 50% by unpublished writers, 50% by authors who are new to the magazine.

Submissions
Query or send complete ms. Accepts hard copy. SASE. Response time varies.
Articles: Word lengths vary. Informational articles; profiles; interviews; humor; and reviews. Topics include popular culture and entertainment, television, movies, video games, books, music, and lifestyles.
Depts/columns: Word lengths vary. Entertainment updates and gossip; reviews of DVDs, e-zines, and Internet sites.
Other: Puzzles, games, activities, and comics.

Sample Issue
112 pages: 7 articles; 15 depts/columns; 2 comics; 5 posters; 1 puzzle. Sample copy, $3.95. Writers' guidelines available.
- "Skye Sweetnam in a Barbie World." Article profiles the girl who is the singing voice of Barbie in *The Barbie Diaries*.
- "Billy Talent: Just Go Out There and Rock." Article interviews Billy Talent band members.
- Sample dept/column: "DVD Corner" provides reviews of a number of newly released DVDs.

Rights and Payment
All rights. Written material, payment rates vary. Payment policy varies.

Editor's Comments
Our publication cares about what youth think, and we shape each and every issue based on their advice and critiques. From *The Simpsons* to *The O.C.*, from Digimon to InuYasha, from Buffy to Batman, we raise the bar and tackle entertainment their way. Potential contributors must write in a way that appeals to youth.

Magazine of Fantasy & Science Fiction

P.O. Box 3447
Hoboken, NJ 07030

Editor: Gordon Van Gelder

Description and Interests
Science fiction and fantasy enthusiasts have been subscribing to this digest-sized publication for more than half a century. Each issue includes short stories, novellas, and novelettes, as well as staff-written reviews and essays.
- **Audience:** YA–Adult
- **Frequency:** Monthly
- **Distribution:** Subscription; newsstand
- **Circulation:** 45,000
- **Website:** www.sfsite.com/fsf

Freelance Potential
90% written by nonstaff writers. Publishes 60–90 freelance submissions yearly; 10% by unpublished writers, 15% by authors who are new to the magazine. Receives 500–650 unsolicited mss yearly.

Submissions
Send complete ms. Accepts hard copy and disk submissions. No simultaneous or electronic submissions. SASE. Responds in 1 month.
Fiction: 1,000–25,000 words. Features short stories, novellas, and novelettes. Genres include science fiction, fantasy, and humor.
Depts/columns: Staff written.

Sample Issue
162 pages (1% advertising): 4 stories; 1 novella; 2 novelettes; 5 depts/columns. Sample copy, $5. Guidelines available.
- "Planet of Mystery." Novella is a planetary romance that takes place on the second planet from the sun.
- "The Boy in Zaquitos." Story chronicles the career of an FBI agent who is hired because he is a chronic asymptomatic carrier of disease.
- "A Daze in the Life." Story features a man who is being paid to wear a cerebral appliance.

Rights and Payment
First world rights with option of anthology rights. Written material, $.06–$.09 per word. Pays on acceptance. Provides 2 contributor's copies.

Editor's Comments
What are we looking for? Upbeat visions of the future. We're tired of stories that depict gloomy futures, the return of the dead, and virus outbreaks. Try to be more original and inventive in your plot lines. And we never see enough humor. Remember, stories should be character-driven.

Magic the Gathering

Beckett Media
15850 Dallas Parkway
Dallas, TX 75248

Editorial Director: Doug Kale

Description and Interests
This Beckett publication is marketed to teens and adults who are enthusiasts of the Magic the Gathering game and are interested in collecting cards and other game memorabilia. Each issue also features an extensive price guide.
• **Audience:** YA–Adults
• **Frequency:** 6 times each year
• **Distribution:** 80% newsstand; 20% subscription
• **Circulation:** 80,000
• **Website:** www.beckettmagic.com

Freelance Potential
75% written by nonstaff writers. Publishes 30 freelance submissions yearly; 10% by unpublished writers, 10% by authors who are new to the magazine.

Submissions
Prefers query with outline and clips. Accepts complete ms. Accepts hard copy. SASE. Responds in 1–2 months.
Articles: 500–2,000 words. Informational articles; profiles; and reviews. Topics include card and memorabilia collecting.
Fiction: Word lengths vary. Adventure stories.
Depts/columns: 500–750 words. News related to Magic the Gathering, events, Q&As, and price guides.

Sample Issue
88 pages: 10 articles; 5 depts/columns; 1 poster; 1 reader survey. Sample copy, $5.99. Writers' guidelines available.
• "Deck Doctor." Article offers advice to a player about how to beef up his deck and improve his game-playing strategies.
• "Decks to Beat." Article features an overview of the top Pro Tour decks.
• Sample dept/column: "Magic News" updates readers on the next Magic set scheduled for release, Coldsnap, the third set in the Ice Age Block.

Rights and Payment
First North American serial rights. Articles and fiction, $150–$350. Depts/columns, $50–$200. Pays on acceptance. Provides 2 contributor's copies.

Editor's Comments
We're looking for articles that will help our readers play Magic the Gathering. Send us tips and ideas for new strategies. We also want well-written articles about tournaments.

Mahoning Valley Parent

100 DeBartolo Place, Suite 210
Youngstown, OH 44512

Editor & Publisher: Amy Leigh Wilson

Description and Interests
A mix of articles, personality profiles, and timely news can be found in this magazine for parents residing in Ohio's Mahoning Valley.
• **Audience:** Parents
• **Frequency:** Monthly
• **Distribution:** Subscription; newsstand; schools
• **Circulation:** 50,000
• **Website:** www.forparentsonline.com

Freelance Potential
99% written by nonstaff writers. Publishes 100 freelance submissions yearly; 5% by unpublished writers, 20% by authors who are new to the magazine. Receives 500 unsolicited mss yearly.

Submissions
Send ms. Accepts hard copy and email submissions to editor@mvparentmagazine.com. Retains all material on file for possible use; does not respond until publication. Include SASE if retaining ms is not acceptable.
Articles: 1,000–1,800 words. Informational and how-to articles; profiles; and reviews. Topics include regional news, current events, parenting, the environment, nature, crafts, travel, recreation, hobbies, and ethnic and multicultural subjects.
Depts/columns: Word lengths vary. Parenting issues, book reviews, events for kids.
Artwork: B/W and color prints.
Other: Seasonal material.

Sample Issue
50 pages (70% advertising): 5 articles; 8 depts/columns. Sample copy, free with 9x12 SASE. Guidelines and editorial calendar available.
• "Why Kids Need Water." Article discusses the health benefits of water and tells how to keep kids well hydrated during the summer.
• "Gardening Grows Healthy Kids." Article takes a look at how gardening has made a difference in the lives of young people.
• Sample dept/column: "Dad's Eye View" offers a humorous essay on the role of a father.

Rights and Payment
One-time rights. Articles, $20–$50. Pays on publication. Provides tearsheets.

Editor's Comments
We prefer well-written and researched pieces on topics of interest to parents living in northeastern Ohio.

The Majellan: Champion of the Family

P.O. Box 43
Brighton, Victoria 3186
Australia

Editor: Father Paul Bird, C. SS. R

Description and Interests

Holding up marriage as a sacred institution, this digest-sized publication contains articles that help couples build relationships and families based on Catholic values.
- **Audience:** Parents
- **Frequency:** Quarterly
- **Distribution:** 100% subscription
- **Circulation:** 23,000
- **Website:** www.majellan.org.au

Freelance Potential

60% written by nonstaff writers. Publishes 10 freelance submissions yearly; 10% by unpublished writers, 20% by authors who are new to the magazine. Receives 24–39 unsolicited mss yearly.

Submissions

Prefers complete ms; will accept query. Accepts hard copy and email submissions to majellan@hotkey.net.au (Microsoft Word or RTF attachments). SASE. Response time varies.
Articles: 750–1,500 words. Informational articles and personal experience pieces about marriage and family life situations.

Sample Issue

48 pages (15% advertising): 9 articles; 4 depts/columns.
- "Rites of Marriage." Article covers the new changes in the Catholic marriage rite that have been published in France and Italy.
- "Be an Anchor for Your Teen." Article emphasizes the importance of parents being available to listen to and interact with their teenagers.
- "God's Surprise Gift." Article points out the advantages of having a baby—even an unexpected one—after other children are grown.
- "The Family Table." Article points out that many family activities take place around a table, but the most important is when the family dines together.

Rights and Payment

Rights vary. Written material, $50–$80 Australian. Pays on acceptance.

Editor's Comments

Submissions should relate to our readers, who are people interested in issues relating to marriage and family life, particularly from a Catholic point of view. We also emphasize topics relating to teens.

Maryland Family

10750 Little Patuxent Parkway
Columbia, MD 21044

Editor: Betsy Stein

Description and Interests

Families residing in the greater Baltimore area read this parenting publication for its informative articles and reports on regional resources and events. Book reviews and articles on family issues are included.
- **Audience:** Maryland families
- **Frequency:** Monthly
- **Distribution:** Subscription; newsstand; other
- **Circulation:** 50,000
- **Website:** www.marylandfamilymagazine.com

Freelance Potential

75% written by nonstaff writers. Publishes 50 freelance submissions yearly; 10% by unpublished writers, 10% by authors who are new to the magazine. Receives 360–600 queries yearly.

Submissions

Query with description of your experience in proposed subject. Accepts hard copy. SASE. Responds in 1 month.
Articles: 800–1,000 words. Practical application pieces; how-to articles; and profiles. Topics include family issues, parenting, college, careers, summer camp, and national trends looked at from a local angle.
Artwork: Color prints and transparencies.
Other: News briefs on timely, local subjects and "Family Matters," 100–400 words. Submit seasonal material about holidays and events 2–3 months in advance.

Sample Issue

46 pages (50% advertising): 6 articles; 3 depts/columns; 1 calendar; 1 activity. Sample copy, free with 9x12 SASE.
- "Midnight Madness." Article offers tips from a local sleep expert on common toddler sleep issues.
- "An Amish Education." Article describes day trips that teach visitors about the Amish way of life.
- Sample dept/column: "Check Up" offers answers to medical questions.

Rights and Payment

First and electronic rights. Written material, payment rates vary. Pays on publication. Provides 1 copy.

Editor's Comments

We look for articles about current issues and stories that feature a local angle. As a regional publication, we provide resourceful information and reports on local events.

Massive Online Gamer Metro Parent Magazine

15850 Dallas Parkway
Dallas, TX 75248

Editor: Douglas Kale

Description and Interests
As the ultimate source for all MMO (massively multi-player online) games, this magazine features articles that reveal descriptions and experiences of MMO games as well as strategies and techniques for success at games related to war, adventure, science fiction, automobiles, pirates, and fantasy.
- **Audience:** YA–Adult
- **Frequency:** 6 times each year
- **Distribution:** Subscription; newsstand
- **Circulation:** 100,000
- **Website: www.beckettmog.com**

Freelance Potential
50% written by nonstaff writers. Publishes 60 freelance submissions yearly; 40% by unpublished writers, 40% by authors who are new to the magazine.

Submissions
Query with writing sample and list of MMO experience. Accepts hard copy. SASE. Guidelines available upon email request to mog@beckett.com.
Articles: Word lengths vary. Informational and how-to articles; personal experience pieces; and interviews. Topics include MMO game descriptions, strategies, and techniques.
Depts/columns: Word lengths vary. MMO etiquette, technology, contests, and news.

Sample Issue
88 pages: 24 articles; 10 depts/columns.
- "Beta Testing Basics." Article explains why beta tests, or playable demos, are good for both players and the companies who market the games.
- "Turning the Tides of War." Article describes the fantasy game, Warhammer WAR, in which the player must choose between good and order or chaos and destruction.
- Sample dept/column: "MOG News" recounts the first-ever dragon festival of the Guild Wars Factions held from June 30 to July 4, 2006.

Rights and Payment
All rights. Written material, payment rates varies. Pays 45 days after publication.

Editor's Comments
Please take the time to look at an issue of our magazine to get a feel for our style and content. We are looking for writers who have a great deal of MMO experience and knowledge.

22041 Woodward Avenue
Ferndale, MI 48220

Managing Editor: Julia Elliott

Description and Interests
Parents residing in southeastern Michigan turn to this tabloid for articles on topics such as parenting, education, finances, family travel, and health. It also reports on local resources and activities.
- **Audience:** Parents
- **Frequency:** Monthly
- **Distribution:** 75% newsstand; 25% subscription
- **Circulation:** 80,000
- **Website: www.metroparent.com**

Freelance Potential
75% written by nonstaff writers. Publishes 250 freelance submissions yearly; 5% by unpublished writers, 35% by authors who are new to the magazine. Receives 960+ unsolicited mss yearly.

Submissions
Send complete ms. Accepts email submissions to jelliott@metroparent.com. Responds in 1–2 days.
Articles: 1,500–2,500 words. Informational, self-help, and how-to articles; personal experience pieces; and interviews. Topics include parenting, family life, childbirth, education, social issues, child development, crafts, vacation travel, personal finance, fitness, health, and nature.
Depts/columns: 850–900 words. Family fun, media reviews, new product information, crafts, computers, and women's health.

Sample Issue
69 pages (60% advertising): 6 articles; 12 depts/columns. Sample copy, free. Guidelines available.
- "Pumped-Up Playsets." Article discusses the increase in the number of parents buying elaborate wooden play structures.
- "Father Knows Best." Article explores how a father's sense of play benefits kids.
- Sample dept/column: "Ages and Stages" discusses ways of baby proofing that will enhance a child's independence and confidence.

Rights and Payment
First rights. Articles, $150–$300. Depts/columns, $50–$100. Pays on publication. Provides 1 contributor's copy.

Editor's Comments
Articles covering kids' health issues and fun activities for families continue to be of interest to us. Please note that we no longer publish fiction.

Midwifery Today

P.O. Box 2672
Eugene, OR 97402

Managing Editor: Cheryl K. Smith

Description and Interests
This publication fosters communication about childbirth education and responsible midwifery conducted throughout the world.
- **Audience:** Childbirth practitioners
- **Frequency:** Quarterly
- **Distribution:** 80% subscription; 10% newsstand; 10% other
- **Circulation:** 4,000
- **Website: www.midwiferytoday.com**

Freelance Potential
95% written by nonstaff writers. Publishes 80–100 freelance submissions yearly; 50% by unpublished writers, 20% by authors who are new to the magazine. Receives 250 queries yearly.

Submissions
Query with author background; or send complete ms. Accepts email to editorial@midwiferytoday.com (Microsoft Word or RTF files). No simultaneous submissions. SASE. Responds in 1 month.
Articles: 800–1,500 words. Informational and instructional articles; profiles, interviews; personal experience pieces; and media reviews. Topics include feminism, health and fitness, medical care and services, diet and nutrition, and multicultural and ethnic issues—all as they relate to childbirth.
Artwork: B/W and color prints.

Sample Issue
72 pages (10% advertising): 25 articles; 9 depts/columns. Sample copy, $12.50. Guidelines and editorial calendar available.
- "Birth Crisis." Article criticizes intrusive medication and chemicals in birthing and maternity care.
- "Homebirth in Nigeria." Article reports on causes of high mortality rates and efforts for empowerment and education of women and midwives.
- Sample dept/column: "Tricks of the Trade" offers tips and techniques for pregnancy conditions.

Rights and Payment
Joint rights. No payment. Provides 2 author's copies and a 1-year subscription for articles over 800 words.

Editor's Comments
We seek technical and personal or philosophical articles, as well as birth-related art, humor, and poetry. We would like material about fathers as birth partners, and medical conditions of pregnancy and birth.

Minnesota Conservation ☆ Volunteer

500 Lafayette Road
St. Paul, MN 55155

Outreach Coordinator: Meredith McNab

Description and Interests
Natural resource conservation in Minnesota is the topic of this digest-sized publication. It appeals to wilderness paddlers, hunters, birders, anglers, and others, and its "Young Naturalist" section is written specifically for readers in grades five through nine.
- **Audience:** Children, 10–14 years; adults
- **Frequency:** Monthly
- **Distribution:** Schools; libraries; other
- **Circulation:** 150,000
- **Website: www.dnr.state.mn.us/magazine**

Freelance Potential
50% written by nonstaff writers. Receives 20 queries each year.

Submissions
Query with synopsis. Accepts hard copy and email submissions to cathy.mix@dnr.state.mn.us. SASE. Response time varies.
Articles: 1,200–1,800 words. Informational articles and essays. Topics include natural resources, conservation, nature, the environment, fishing, hiking, state parks, and outdoor recreation.
Depts/columns: Word lengths vary. "Young Naturalist" features information on Minnesota's natural resources and outdoor recreation for ages 10 to 14. "Field Notes," 200–500 words.

Sample Issue
64 pages: 6 articles; 9 depts/columns. Sample copy, free. Guidelines available at website.
- "Look Down in the Woods." Article for young readers showcases the different plants that can be found on the forest floor.
- "Mother's Day in Rattlesnake Country." First-person piece features one mother's thoughts about a May camping trip.
- Sample dept/column: "Minnesota Profile" presents facts about the American eel.

Rights and Payment
First North American serial and electronic rights. Written material, $.50 per word and $100 for electronic rights. Payment policy varies.

Editor's Comments
Briefly summarize your story and explain why it would be of interest to our readers. Keep the tone casual, use quotes and anecdotes liberally, and feel free to use first-person narration to engage readers.

Mission

223 Main Street
Ottawa, Ontario K1S 1C4
Canada

Editor: Peter Pandimakil

Description and Interests
Young adults and adults interested in theology and intercultural topics read *Mission* for information on interreligious topics and book reviews. This Christian journal also contains bilingual material and personal experience pieces.
- **Audience:** 14 years–Adult
- **Frequency:** Twice each year
- **Distribution:** 90% subscription; 10% other
- **Circulation:** 500
- **Website:** www.ustpaul.ca.com

Freelance Potential
95% written by nonstaff writers. Publishes 3–5 freelance submissions yearly; 60% by unpublished writers, 40% by authors who are new to the magazine. Receives 36 queries yearly.

Submissions
Send complete ms with résumé. Accepts disk submissions (RTF files), email submissions to ppandimakil@ustpaul.ca, and simultaneous submissions if identified. SAE/IRC. Responds in 1–2 months.
Articles: 8,000–10,000 words. Bilingual articles; reviews; and personal experience pieces. Topics include current events; history; religion; and multicultural, ethnic, and social issues.
Fiction: Word lengths vary. Historical, multicultural, ethnic, and problem-solving stories.
Artwork: 8x10 B/W and color prints.

Sample Issue
159 pages (no advertising): 6 articles; 10 book reviews. Sample copy, $12 U.S. with 8x6 SAE/IRC. Guidelines available.
- "Discussing the Trinity with African Traditionalists." Article examines the understanding of the Trinity through the African Traditionalist Religion.
- "Internet, Mission and Ecumenism." Article discusses the common ground between electronics and theology.

Rights and Payment
Rights vary. No payment. Provides 3 contributor's copies.

Editor's Comments
We seek scholarly material on topics of interest to our readers, which include interreligious and intercultural groups, Christian missions, and theological scholars. Personal experience pieces are welcome.

Momentum

National Catholic Educational Association
1077 30th Street NW, Suite 100
Washington, DC 20007-3852

Editor: Brian Gray

Description and Interests
Catholic educators and school administrators working at the preschool through college levels find practical writing in this magazine. It addresses issues of interest to parochial schools and parish religious education programs.
- **Audience:** Teachers, school administrators, parents
- **Frequency:** Quarterly
- **Distribution:** 100% controlled
- **Circulation:** 23,000
- **Website:** www.ncea.org

Freelance Potential
95% written by nonstaff writers. Publishes 90 freelance submissions yearly; 25% by unpublished writers, 80% by authors who are new to the magazine. Receives 96 queries and unsolicited mss yearly.

Submissions
Send complete ms with résumé and bibliography. Accepts hard copy, disk submissions (Microsoft Word), and email submissions to momentum@nea.org. SASE. Responds in 1–3 months.
Articles: 1,000–1,500 words. Informational and scholarly articles on catechetical education. Topics include teacher and in-service education, educational trends, technology, research, management, and public relations—all as they relate to Catholic education.
Depts/columns: Book reviews, 300 words. "Trends in Technology," 900 words. "From the Field," 700 words.

Sample Issue
80 pages (20% advertising): 15 articles; 6 depts/columns. Sample copy, free with 9x12 SASE ($1.05 postage). Guidelines and editorial calendar available.
- "See the World as Our Team." Article reports on a school tournament that celebrates youth, basketball, and faith.
- "From Pharoahs to Danny Phantom." Article analyzes the difficulties of forming faith in the midst of popular culture.

Rights and Payment
First rights. Articles, $75. Depts/columns, $50. Pays on publication. Provides 2 contributor's copies.

Editor's Comments
We always need professional ideas from the field that can be replicated in Catholic education settings. Try to keep articles short—anything more than 2,000 words is too long.

MOMSense

2370 South Trenton Way
Denver, CO 80231-3822

Editor: Mary Darr

Description and Interests
Moms of preschoolers read *MOMSense* for nurturing and practical support. Informative and inspiring articles written from a Christian perspective fill the pages of this magazine.
- **Audience:** Mothers
- **Frequency:** 7 times each year
- **Distribution:** 95% subscription; 5% other
- **Circulation:** 100,000
- **Website:** www.mops.org

Freelance Potential
70% written by nonstaff writers. Publishes 50 freelance submissions yearly; 40% by unpublished writers, 40% by authors who are new to the magazine. Receives 60 queries, 250 unsolicited mss yearly.

Submissions
Query or send complete ms. Prefers email submissions to MOMSense@mops.org (Mircrosoft Word attachments). Accepts hard copy. Availability of artwork improves chance of acceptance. SASE. Response time varies.
Articles: 500–1,000 words. Informational articles; profiles; and personal experience pieces. Topics include parenting, religion, and humor.
Depts/columns: Word lengths vary. Parenting and family life articles.
Artwork: B/W and color prints or transparencies.
Other: Accepts seasonal material 6–12 months in advance.

Sample Issue
32 pages (no advertising): 11 articles; 6 depts/columns. Sample copy, free. Guidelines available.
- "Nest or Cave?" Article offers affordable decorating ideas for creating a cozy nest in any home.
- "Running on Empty?" Article shares the story of two moms and their traditional, yearly get-away.
- Sample dept/column: "Raising Great Kids" stresses the balance between love and discipline.

Rights and Payment
First rights. Written material, $.15 per word. Payment policy varies. Provides contributor's copies.

Editor's Comments
We seek humorous or thought-provoking personal stories and well-researched, practical information that introduces moms to topics relevant to their lives. Submissions should be written with a biblical perspective.

MomsVoice.com

27909 NE 26th Street
Redmond, WA 98053

Editor: Krista Sweeney

Description and Interests
MomsVoice.com provides an online forum for mothers on issues that are relevant to their own well-being as well as that of their children. It includes personal experience pieces as well as information and advice from expert sources. Readers include moms of all categories—expectant, working, stay-at-home, single, and older mothers.
- **Audience:** Mothers
- **Frequency:** Monthly
- **Distribution:** 100% Internet
- **Hits per month:** 10,000
- **Website:** www.momsvoice.com

Freelance Potential
100% written by nonstaff writers. Publishes 100 freelance submissions yearly; 10% by unpublished writers, 20% by authors who are new to the magazine. Receives 120 queries yearly.

Submissions
Query with sample; or send complete ms. Accepts email to writers@momsvoice.com (Microsoft Word). Responds in 1 week.
Articles: 2,500 words. Informational and how-to articles; profiles; personal experience pieces; and reviews. Topics include parenting, pregnancy, health, fitness, regional news, social issues, education, gifted and special education, travel, and regional news.
Fiction: 2,500 words. Genres include real-life and inspirational fiction and humor.
Depts/columns: 2,500 words. Crafts, cooking, parenting tips, book reviews.
Other: Activities and filler.

Sample Issue
Sample copy and guidelines available at website.
- "Motherhood after the Storm." Personal experience piece describes how one mother has learned to cope with her bipolar disorder.
- "Obedience vs. Sacrifice." Article tells how one family helped another in a time of need.

Rights and Payment
First rights for 2 months. No payment.

Editor's Comments
In the coming year, we would like to see articles on mind, body, and spirit; tips for raising toddlers; and resources for parents of teens. Articles written on a professional and personal level are both encouraged.

Montessori Life

28 Park Avenue South
New York, NY 10010

Editor

Description and Interests
Articles pertinent to Montessori educators and parents can be found in this magazine. It covers child development and educational research, issues, trends, curricula, leadership, and policies.
- **Audience:** Educators; parents
- **Frequency:** Quarterly
- **Distribution:** 99% subscription; 1% other
- **Circulation:** 10,500
- **Website:** www.amshq.org

Freelance Potential
90% written by nonstaff writers. Publishes 40 freelance submissions yearly; 30% by unpublished writers, 30% by authors who are new to the magazine. Receives 120–240 unsolicited mss yearly.

Submissions
Send complete ms. Accepts email submissions to edmontessorilife@aol.com. Responds in 3 months.
Articles: 1,000–4,000 words. Informational, academic, and how-to articles; profiles; interviews; and humor. Topics include educational trends, social issues, gifted and special education, and family life—all with some connection to Montessori education.
Fiction: 1,000–1,500 words. Publishes allegorical fiction.
Depts/columns: 500–1,000 words. Montessori community news, events, media reviews, and parenting.

Sample Issue
66 pages (25% advertising): 11 articles; 6 depts/columns. Sample copy, $5 with 9x12 SASE. Guidelines available.
- "Montessori and One Teacher's Use of Technology." Article describes how a teacher integrates technology with the Montessori method.
- "Humor in the Hands of Seasoned Montessorians." Article discusses the benefits of using humor appropriately and effectively in the classroom.
- Sample dept/column: "Reviews" offers a review of the book and CD, *The Orchestra.*

Rights and Payment
All rights. Written material, payment rates vary. Pays on publication. Provides 1–5 contributor's copies.

Editor's Comments
We are looking for academic articles written by experts for Montessori educators, as well as articles that share the experiences of parents.

Moo-Cow Fan Club

P.O. Box 165
Peterborough, NH 03458

Editor: Becky Ances

Description and Interests
This magazine strives to make learning fun for children. Each issue includes nonfiction that is dedicated to one topic, as well as interviews and quizzes. It covers topics and features that may not be explored in school.
- **Audience:** 6–12 years
- **Frequency:** Quarterly
- **Distribution:** 80% newsstand; 10% subscription; 10% schools
- **Circulation:** 3,000
- **Website:** www.moocowfanclub.com

Freelance Potential
10% written by nonstaff writers. Publishes 10 freelance submissions yearly; 100% by authors who are new to the magazine. Receives 100+ queries yearly.

Submissions
Query with sample article. Accepts email queries to becky@moocowfanclub.com (no attachments), and hard copy. SASE. Responds in 3 weeks.
Articles: 300–550 words. Informational and how-to articles; profiles; and interviews. Topics include nature, animals, science, sports, and travel.
Fiction: 300–550 words. Genres include folktales and folklore.
Depts/columns: Staff written.

Sample Issue
48 pages (no advertising): 5 articles; 2 stories; 9 depts/columns; 2 cartoons. Sample copy, $6 with 9x12 SASE ($1.46 postage). Writers' guidelines and theme list available.
- "The Kingdoms." Article explores the different parts of Egyptian history.
- "The Heart of Kemet." Article takes a look at the Nile River and its importance to the ancient Egyptians.
- "The Sun God's Secret." Story tells how Ra became the sun god to the Egyptians.

Rights and Payment
All rights. Written material, $50. Pays on acceptance. Provides 3 contributor's copies.

Editor's Comments
We only publish articles that are related to our themes, and look for material that is interesting and fun, but not condescending. We steer away from dry, boring articles and pop culture references. Send us something that will motivate children to read.

Mothering

P.O. Box 1690
Santa Fe, NM 87504

Articles Editor: Candace Walsh

Description and Interests
Both the practical and inspirational sides of being a mother are explored in this magazine. It emphasizes natural childbirth and child rearing.
- **Audience:** Parents
- **Frequency:** 6 times each year
- **Distribution:** 70% subscription; 30% newsstand
- **Circulation:** 250,000
- **Website: www.mothering.com**

Freelance Potential
85% written by nonstaff writers. Publishes 100+ freelance submissions yearly; 20% by unpublished writers, 80% by authors who are new to the magazine. Receives 108 queries yearly.

Submissions
Query with outline/synopsis. Accepts hard copy. SASE. Responds in 2–4 weeks.
Articles: 2,000 words. Informational and factual articles; profiles; and personal experience pieces. Topics include pregnancy, childbirth, midwifery, health, homeopathy, teen issues, and organic foods.
Depts/columns: Word lengths vary. Cooking; book and product reviews; health news; parenting updates; and inspirational pieces.
Artwork: 5x7 B/W and color prints.
Other: Children's activities and arts and crafts. Poetry about motherhood and families. Submit seasonal material 6–8 months in advance.

Sample Issue
96 pages (35% advertising): 3 articles; 5 depts/columns. Sample copy, $5.95 with 9x12 SASE. Guidelines available.
- "Lessons in Public Breastfeeding." Article describes how the author became a proud advocate of nursing in public.
- Sample dept/column: "A Child's World" depicts easy-to-learn yoga postures that will help adolescents develop strong bodies and calm minds.

Rights and Payment
First rights. Written material, $100+. Artwork, payment rates vary. Pays on publication. Provides 2 contributor's copies and a 1-year subscription.

Editor's Comments
We choose articles based on how new the topic is to us and how unique the presentation is. Most of our articles are submitted by our readers.

Mother Verse Magazine

2663 Highway 3
Two Harbors, MN 55616

Editor: Melanie Mayo-Laakso

Description and Interests
This literary journal is dedicated to exploring and celebrating motherhood. It offers a mix of creative nonfiction, fiction, poetry, and visual art.
- **Audience:** Mothers
- **Frequency:** Quarterly
- **Distribution:** 50% subscription; 50% Internet
- **Circulation:** 15,000
- **Website: www.motherverse.com**

Freelance Potential
90% written by nonstaff writers. Publishes 80–90 freelance submissions yearly; 50% by unpublished writers, 75% by authors who are new to the magazine. Receives 30–40 queries, 300–400 unsolicited mss each year.

Submissions
Query or send complete ms. Prefers email submissions to submissions@motherverse.com (as RTF attachments or in the body of an email). Accepts hard copy and simultaneous submissions if identified. SASE. Responds in 2–4 weeks.
Articles: To 5,000 words. Essays and personal experience pieces. Topics include issues that affect modern-day mothers.
Fiction: 400 words. Stories related to motherhood.
Depts/columns: "Muddy Path," to 1,500 words; includes personal accounts of life. Book reviews, to a half page in length. "Literary Shorts," to 250 words.
Artwork: 8x10 B/W low resolution images.
Other: Poetry, to 4 poems per submission.

Sample Issue
50 pages: 2 articles; 1 story; 1 interview; 6 poems; 1 dept/column. Sample copy available online. Guidelines available at website.
- "Amazing Birth the Second Time Around." Personal experience piece describes a woman's desire to have natural childbirth following a cesarean delivery.
- "Mother Activist." Interview details a question and answer session with Jennifer Rogers, founder of Moms United.

Rights and Payment
One-time rights. No payment. Provides 2 contributor's copies or a 1-year subscription.

Editor's Comments
We are always open to reviewing material from both emerging and established writers.

Mr. Marquis' Museletter

Box 29556
Maple Ridge, British Columbia V2X 2V0
Canada

Editor: Kalen Marquis

Description and Interests
This literary newsletter features original short stories, poems, book reviews, and sketches to promote literacy and creativity in young writers.
- **Audience:** 2–21 years
- **Frequency:** Quarterly
- **Distribution:** 100% subscription
- **Circulation:** 150

Freelance Potential
90% written by nonstaff writers. Publishes 40 freelance submissions yearly; 90% by unpublished writers, 90% by authors who are new to the magazine. Receives 40 queries and unsolicited mss yearly.

Submissions
Query with writing samples; or send complete ms. Accepts hard copy, email to kmarquis@sd42.ca, and simultaneous submissions if identified. SAE/IRC. Responds in 4 months.
Articles: 300 words. Informational and factual articles; opinion and personal experience pieces; profiles; interviews; and book reviews. Topics include nature, the arts, current events, history, multicultural and ethnic issues, music, and popular culture. Also publishes biographies of painters, writers, and inventors.
Fiction: 300 words. Genres include adventure; contemporary, historical, multicultural, and inspirational fiction; and problem-solving stories.
Artwork: Line art.
Other: Poetry, 4–16 lines. Submit seasonal material 6 months in advance.

Sample Issue
10 pages (no advertising): 2 stories; 5 poems. Sample copy, $2 with #10 SASE. Guidelines available.
- "Milo the Detective Dog." Story tells of a dog who is dognapped by his own twin brother.
- "Winter Is Such a Blast." Story depicts the fun times a trio of friends have in the snow.

Rights and Payment
One-time rights. No payment. Provides 1 copy.

Editor's Comments
We publish many new writers. We love stories that encourage peace, love, joy, and a fresh, new understanding of life. Trust that your thoughts, feelings, and experiences are worthy of expression and that your craft will improve over time. The more you submit, the greater your chance of being published.

M: The Magazine for Montessori Families

3 Werner Way
Lebanon, NJ 08833

Editor-in-Chief: John Brady

Description and Interests
Serving families with children enrolled at Montessori schools, M features articles on Montessori teaching methods, benefits, and successes; family and ethical issues; motivating children; and parenting. It contains information for all age groups, not just preschoolers.
- **Audience:** Adults
- **Frequency:** 6 times each year
- **Distribution:** Subscription; other
- **Circulation:** Unavailable
- **Website: www.mthemagazine.com**

Freelance Potential
25% written by nonstaff writers. Publishes 20 freelance submissions yearly.

Submissions
Query with writing sample. Accepts hard copy. SASE.
Articles: Word lengths vary. Informational articles; profiles; personal experience pieces; photo-essays; interviews; and reviews. Topics include Montessori teaching methods and benefits, family issues, parenting, and student motivation.
Depts/columns: Word lengths vary. Ethical issues, parenting advice, cooking with children, news, and reading resources.

Sample Issue
40 pages: 9 articles; 7 depts/columns. Sample copy, $8.50.
- "Being a Montessori Parent." Article describes how parents can make every moment a learning experience for their child.
- "Fostering Peace." Article examines ways in which peace can take an active role in a child's life, and, in turn, have an important and inspiring impact.
- Sample dept/column: "Cooking with Kids" offers ideas for getting kids to eat a variety of vegetables and provides several kid-friendly recipes.

Rights and Payment
First North American serial rights. Written material, payment rates vary. Pays on publication.

Editor's Comments
We're looking for articles from writers who are very familiar with the Montessori methods and benefits. Also note that we like to include lots of important information, but we do not want our articles to read like a textbook, so be sure to read a copy of our magazine so you understand our goals and casual style.

MultiCultural Review

194 Lenox Avenue
Albany, NY 12208

Editor: Lyn Miller-Lachmann

Description and Interests
MultiCultural Review is a journal for educators and librarians at all levels. Topics covered include current issues related to multiculturalism in the U.S., ethnographic articles on specific groups, and nonprofit resources. It also includes bibliographic essays.
- **Audience:** Teachers and librarians
- **Frequency:** Quarterly
- **Distribution:** 80% subscription; 20% newsstand
- **Circulation:** 3,500+
- **Website:** www.mcreview.com

Freelance Potential
80% written by nonstaff writers. Publishes 16 freelance submissions yearly; 10% by unpublished writers, 20% by authors who are new to the magazine. Receives 80 unsolicited mss yearly.

Submissions
Send complete ms. Accepts hard copy and disk submissions. SASE. Responds in 3–4 months.
Articles: 2,000–6,000 words. Informational and how-to articles; profiles; and opinion pieces. Topics include the arts; education; writing; and social, multicultural, and ethnic issues.
Depts/columns: 1,500–2,000 words. News.
Other: Book and media reviews, 200–300 words.

Sample Issue
130 pages (10% advertising): 5 articles; 7 depts/columns; 161 reviews. Sample copy, $15. Guidelines and theme list available.
- "The Kindertransport." Article recounts efforts in the late 1930s to send children from Germany and German-occupied lands to England without their parents, to save them from the war.
- Sample dept/column: "Bridges on the I-Way: Multicultural Resources Online" provides a list of websites about Vietnam.

Rights and Payment
First serial rights. Articles, $50–$200. Depts/columns, $50. Reviews, no payment. Pays on publication. Provides 2 contributor's copies.

Editor's Comments
Article proposals rather than complete manuscripts may also be submitted; include writing samples. We are looking for interviews with and essays by notable multicultural children's writers. Keep in mind that we don't cover language or learning topics.

MultiMedia & Internet Schools

14508 NE 20th Avenue, Suite 102
Vancouver, WA 98646

Editor: David Hoffman

Description and Interests
This magazine gives educators, media specialists, and technology coordinators the information they need to put technology to work in kindergarten through twelfth-grade classrooms. It explores the educational uses of the Internet, computers, software, and other multimedia products.
- **Audience:** Librarians, teachers, and technology coordinators
- **Frequency:** 6 times each year
- **Distribution:** Subscription; other
- **Circulation:** 12,000
- **Website:** www.mmischools.com

Freelance Potential
90% written by nonstaff writers. Publishes 20–24 freelance submissions yearly; 20% by unpublished writers, 20% by authors who are new to the magazine. Receives 60 queries yearly.

Submissions
Query or send complete ms. Accepts email submissions to hoffmand@infotoday.com. Artwork improves chance of acceptance. Responds in 6–8 weeks.
Articles: 1,500 words. Informational and how-to articles. Topics include K–12 education, the Internet, multimedia and electronic resources, technology-based tools, and curriculum integration.
Depts/columns: Word lengths vary. Product reviews; ideas from educators.
Artwork: TIFF images at 300 dpi.

Sample Issue
48 pages (15% advertising): 4 articles; 5 depts/columns; 4 product reviews. Sample copy and guidelines, $7.95 with 9x12 SASE.
- "The Potential of Gaming on K–12 Education." Article tells how online gaming situations might be used to help students learn to think through real-life adventure plots and become successful in life.
- Sample dept/column: "The Pipeline" explores the educational uses of iPods.

Rights and Payment
First rights. Written material, $300–$350. Artwork, payment rates vary. Pays on publication. Provides 2 contributor's copies.

Editor's Comments
We strive to be a source of practical information about the educational technology of today and tomorrow.

Muse

Carus Publishing
140 South Dearborn Street, Suite 1450
Chicago, IL 60603

Editor: Virginia Edwards

Description and Interests
Muse tackles the challenging task of presenting serious material in a style and manner that will appeal to pre-teens and teens. Experiments, history, puzzles, science, and other topics guaranteed to stimulate thinking make up the contents of this eclectic collaboration between *Smithsonian* magazine and the Cricket Magazine Group.
- **Audience:** 10+ years
- **Frequency:** 9 times each year
- **Distribution:** 95% subscription; 5% newsstand
- **Circulation:** 51,000
- **Website:** www.cricketmag.com

Freelance Potential
100% written by nonstaff writers. Of the freelance submissions published yearly, 20% are by authors who are new to the magazine.

Submissions
Send résumé and clips. All material is commissioned from experienced authors.
Articles: To 1,500 words. Informational articles; interviews; and photo-essays. Topics include science, the environment, nature, computers, technology, history, math, and the arts.
Depts/columns: Word lengths vary. News items.

Sample Issue
48 pages (no advertising): 5 articles; 8 depts/columns. Sample copy and writers' guidelines available at website.
- "The Sentry-Box Experiments." Article elucidates the electricity experiments Benjamin Franklin proposed before he flew his "famous" kite.
- "Who Was Flo?" Article debates which species the 18,000-year-old remains of Flo belong to, after being found on the Polynesian island of Flores.
- Sample dept/column: "Hard Cash" explores puzzles designed by Bob Hearn.

Rights and Payment
Rights vary. Written material, payment rates and payment policy vary.

Editor's Comments
Articles should be a first-person account by a professional or by someone who has first-hand knowledge of a topic. Writing is conversational in tone, and topics are of current interest to kids about subjects they can understand without lengthy explanation.

Music Educators Journal

MENC
1806 Robert Fulton Drive
Reston, VA 20191

Managing Editor: Teresa Preston

Description and Interests
This journal covers all aspects of music education, including practical methods of instruction, professional philosophy, and current issues in learning and teaching music.
- **Audience:** Music teachers
- **Frequency:** 5 times each year
- **Distribution:** 100% membership
- **Circulation:** 80,000
- **Website:** www.menc.org

Freelance Potential
85% written by nonstaff writers. Publishes 30 freelance submissions yearly; 25% by unpublished writers. Receives 200 unsolicited mss yearly.

Submissions
Send 5 copies of complete ms. Accepts hard copy. SASE. Responds in 3 months.
Articles: 1,800–3,000 words. Instructional and informational articles; and historical studies of music education. Topics include teaching methods, professional philosophy, and current issues in music teaching and learning.
Depts/columns: Word lengths vary. Personal experience pieces, product reviews, commentary from music teachers, and MENC news.
Other: Submit seasonal material 8–12 months in advance.

Sample Issue
96 pages (40% advertising): 6 articles; 10 depts/columns. Sample copy, $6 with 9x12 SASE ($2 postage). Guidelines available.
- "Partnering with Music Therapists." Article shows how music therapists can be a valuable resource for students with disabilities.
- "Children with Disabilities Playing Musical Instruments." Article discusses strategies for teaching music to disabled students.
- Sample dept/column: "Idea Bank" suggests inviting staff to participate in school performances.

Rights and Payment
All rights. No payment. Provides 2 author's copies.

Editor's Comments
We select articles for their importance, timeliness, scope, and style. Writers should address the needs of a broad cross section of the more than 67,000 music educators who read the journal.

My Family Doctor

The Magazine That Makes House Calls

P.O. Box 38790
Colorado Springs, CO 80906

Managing Editor: Leigh Ann Hubbard

Description and Interests

Up-to-the-minute, reliable medical information and advice can be found in *My Family Doctor*. Focusing on mainstream medicine, it presents information in laymen's terms and with a positive tone.
• **Audience:** Adults
• **Frequency:** Quarterly
• **Distribution:** Unavailable
• **Circulation:** 100,000
• **Website:** www.familydoctormag.com

Freelance Potential

100% written by nonstaff writers. Publishes 70 freelance submissions yearly; 1% by unpublished writers, 1% by authors who are new to the magazine. Receives 144 queries yearly.

Submissions

Query with writing samples. Prefers email queries to managingeditor@familydoctormag.com. Accepts hard copy. SASE. Responds in 1 month.
Articles: 1,500 words. Informational articles and personal experience pieces. Topics include health, fitness, nutrition, and preventive medicine.
Depts/columns: 200–400 words. Medical studies and breakthroughs.
Other: Filler, 200–400 words.

Sample Issue

66 pages (2% advertising): 8 articles; 18 depts/columns. Sample copy, $4.95 at newsstands. Guidelines available.
• "Air Defense: How to Combat the Sneeze Siege." Article offers advice for coping with and treating seasonal allergies.
• "Diet Pills." Article tells why quick and easy weight-loss treatments don't work and may be dangerous.
• Sample dept/column: "Children's Health" presents the facts about ADHD.

Rights and Payment

First North American serial, exclusive syndication for one year, and nonexclusive rights. Written material, $.50 per word. Pays on publication.

Editor's Comments

To work with us, you must have the ability to engage readers with narrative, illustrative, positive writing. Strong research skills and an ability to write in a style a layperson can understand are also important. Most of our writers have medical degrees.

My Friend

Pauline Books & Media/Daughters of St. Paul
50 St. Pauls Avenue
Boston, MA 02130-3491

Editor: Sister Maria Grace Dateno, FSP

Description and Interests

My Friend, a magazine for Catholic children, features true and fictional stories, puzzles, crafts, comics, and contests that encourage faith and friendship with Jesus. It targets readers in the middle grades.
• **Audience:** 7–12 years
• **Frequency:** 10 times each year
• **Distribution:** 80% subscription; 20% newsstand
• **Circulation:** 8,000
• **Website:** www.myfriendmagazine.org

Freelance Potential

60% written by nonstaff writers. Publishes 30 freelance submissions yearly; 5% by unpublished writers, 50% by authors who are new to the magazine. Receives 1,000+ unsolicited mss yearly.

Submissions

Send complete ms. Accepts hard copy. No email submissions. SASE. Responds in 2 months.
Articles: 150–900 words. Informational, self-help, and how-to articles and biographies—all with some connection to the Catholic faith.
Fiction: 750–1,000 words. Genres include inspirational, contemporary, and multicultural fiction.
Depts/columns: Staff written.

Sample Issue

32 pages (no advertising): 2 articles; 3 stories; 4 depts/columns; 4 activities; 2 comics; 1 puzzle; 1 poem. Sample copy, $3.95 with 9x12 SASE ($1.29 postage). Guidelines and theme list available.
• "Stop and Think." Story features a girl who learns how to make a more meaningful Lenten sacrifice than just giving up candy.
• "Free the Children." Article talks about an organization founded by children to help children.
• "Rainbows without Rain." Article explains the rainbow effect seen on CDs and butterfly wings.

Rights and Payment

First worldwide rights. Written material, $80–$150. Pays on acceptance. Provides contributor's copies.

Editor's Comments

Although we use freelance material in virtually every issue of our magazine, we accept little, if any, of the fiction we receive. Avoid being preachy and predictable. We see too many stories about elderly neighbors or dead parents or grandparents.

Nashville Parent Magazine

2270 Metro Center Boulevard
Nashville, TN 37228

Editor: Susan B. Day

Description and Interests
This free publication is available to residents of the Nashville area. It is geared toward parents and families with young children and provides information on upcoming, regional, family-friendly events.
- **Audience:** Parents
- **Frequency:** Monthly
- **Distribution:** 50% newsstand; 10% subscription; 10% schools; 30% other
- **Circulation:** 85,000
- **Website: www.parentworld.com**

Freelance Potential
15–20% written by nonstaff writers. Publishes 400 freelance submissions yearly; 40% by authors who are new to the magazine. Receives 1,200 unsolicited mss each year.

Submissions
Send complete ms. Accepts hard copy, Macintosh disk submissions with hard copy, and email submissions to npinfo@nashvilleparent.com Availability of artwork improves chance of acceptance. SASE. Response time varies.
Articles: 800–1,000 words. Informational and how-to articles; profiles; interviews; photo-essays; and personal experience pieces. Topics include parenting, family issues, current events, social issues, health, music, travel, recreation, religion, the arts, crafts, computers, and multicultural and ethnic issues.
Depts/columns: Staff written.
Artwork: B/W prints.
Other: Submit seasonal material related to Christmas, Easter, and Halloween 2 months in advance.

Sample Issue
116 pages (50% advertising): 7 articles; 9 depts/columns. Sample copy, free with 9x12 SASE. Guidelines available.
- "Having a Baby Should Be Fun!" Article advises mothers-to-be to enjoy and savor their pregnancies.
- "Coddling." Article explains how overprotective parenting can sometimes become a hindrance.

Rights and Payment
One-time rights. Written material, $35. Pays on publication. Provides 3 contributor's copies on request.

Editor's Comments
We are looking for thoroughly researched, easy-to-read stories that cite local sources.

NASSP Bulletin

National Association of Secondary School Principals
1904 Association Drive
Reston, VA 20191-1537

Editor

Description and Interests
This peer-reviewed, scholarly journal presents research articles that emphasize effective administration and leadership in middle-level and secondary schools. It covers a wide range of topics of enduring interest to principals and educators.
- **Audience:** Secondary school educators and administrators
- **Frequency:** Quarterly
- **Distribution:** 100% subscription
- **Circulation:** 1,200
- **Website: www.principals.org**

Freelance Potential
98% written by nonstaff writers. Publishes 30 freelance submissions yearly; 2% by unpublished writers, 20% by authors who are new to the magazine. Receives 192 unsolicited mss yearly.

Submissions
Send complete ms with bibliography and abstract. Accepts hard copy and IBM disk submissions (Microsoft Word). SASE. Responds in 4–6 weeks.
Articles: 4,000 words. Informational articles. Topics include secondary school education, school administration, and leadership.
Depts/columns: Word lengths vary. "Resource Review" features book and product reviews.

Sample Issue
104 pages (1% advertising): 5 articles; 1 dept/column. Sample copy, free with 8x10 SASE. Guidelines available.
- "Academic Leadership in America's Public Schools." Article discusses the need for improved academic leadership and offers several models worth following.
- "An Administrator's Challenge: Encouraging Teachers to Be Leaders." Article maintains that high school administrators influence teacher leadership in both positive and negative ways.
- "The Value of Teacher Portfolios for Evaluation and Personal Growth." Article examines the advantages of portfolio-based teacher evaluations.

Rights and Payment
All North American serial rights. No payment. Provides 2 contributor's copies.

Editor's Comments
Topics we'd like to see covered include funding and equality, legal issues, safe schools, and literacy.

National Geographic Kids

National Geographic Society
1145 17th Street NW
Washington, DC 20036-4688

Editor: Julie Agnone

Description and Interests
"Dare to Explore" is the tagline for this publication that wants to provide new ways for kids to look at and learn about the world, and in the process become excited about it. The interactive magazine includes puzzles, games, contests, and activities.
- **Audience:** 6–14 years
- **Frequency:** 10 times each year
- **Distribution:** Subscription; newsstand
- **Circulation:** 1.3 million
- **Website:** www.nationalgeographic.com/ngkids

Freelance Potential
85% written by nonstaff writers. Publishes 20–25 freelance submissions yearly; 1% by unpublished writers, 30% by authors who are new to the magazine. Receives 360 queries yearly.

Submissions
Query with relevant clips. No unsolicited mss. SASE. Response time varies.
Articles: Word lengths vary. Informational articles. Topics include geography, archaeology, paleontology, history, science, technology, culture, natural history, engineering, entertainment, the environment, community service, diversity, and business.
Depts/columns: Word lengths vary. Fun facts, jokes, games, and amazing animals.
Other: Original games.

Sample Issue
46 pages (20% advertising): 6 articles; 1 story; 10 depts/columns. Sample copy, $3.95. Writers' guidelines available.
- "Sea Monsters." Article presents several prehistoric beasts that give T-Rex some serious competition.
- "Ice Hotel." Photo-essay displays hotels in Sweden, Quebec, and Alaska that are made of ice chunks.
- Sample dept/column: "Amazing Animals" provides accounts of surprising animal behaviors.

Rights and Payment
All rights. Written material, payment rates vary. Artwork, $100–$600. Pays on acceptance. Provides 3–5 contributor's copies.

Editor's Comments
We would like new writers to submit writing samples and résumés after becoming familiar with our format and content to make sure their idea will work. Story ideas should directly affect a child's life.

Natural Family Online

2413 West Algonquin Road, Suite 119
Algonquin, IL 60102-9402

Editor: Lisa Poisso

Description and Interests
This online publication serves those wishing to live more naturally, healthily, and peacefully in parenting and beyond. It features articles on a variety of topics related to parenting and family issues.
- **Audience:** Parents
- **Frequency:** Monthly
- **Distribution:** 100% Internet
- **Hits per month:** 60,000
- **Website:** www.naturalfamilyonline.com

Freelance Potential
60% written by nonstaff writers. Publishes 30–40 freelance submissions yearly.

Submissions
Query. Accepts email queries to editor@ naturalfamilyonline.com (no attachments).
Articles: 500–750 words. Informational articles; profiles; and personal experience pieces. Topics include attachment parenting, breastfeeding, ecological practices, family life, nutrition, vegan and vegetarian lifestyles, co-sleeping, holistic approaches, natural beauty and body care, yoga and pilates, natural pregnancy and childbirth, homeschooling, health care alternatives, cloth diapering, infant potty training, seasonal celebrations, and natural pet care.

Sample Issue
Sample copy and guidelines available at website.
- "Turn Your White Wedding Green." Article provides suggestions for an eco-friendly wedding, from choosing a hemp-made wedding gown to investing in a recycled gold ring.
- "'You're Fired!' When Doctors Fire Their Patients." Article shares the story of two families and their decision not to have their children vaccinated.
- "The Teen Years: Setting Limitlessness." Article offers suggestions for channeling your teens' energy.

Rights and Payment
First electronic and archival rights for 60 days. Articles, $15. Pays on publication.

Editor's Comments
We are currently seeking articles focusing on tips, tools, and strategies for implementing natural parenting on a daily basis. Our readers want to know what makes natural parenting practices beneficial, why they should use them, and how they can add natural parenting to their own family lives.

Nature Friend Magazine

4253 Woodrock Lane
Dayton, VA 22821

Editor: Kevin Shank

Description and Interests
The goal of this publication is to help children explore the wonders of God's creation through articles, stories, and activities.
• **Audience:** 6–12 years
• **Frequency:** Monthly
• **Distribution:** 100% subscription
• **Circulation:** 11,000
• **Website:** www.naturefriendmagazine.com

Freelance Potential
70% written by nonstaff writers. Publishes 50–90 freelance submissions yearly; 5% by unpublished writers, 10% by authors who are new to the magazine. Receives 480–720 unsolicited mss yearly.

Submissions
Send complete ms. Accepts hard copy. SASE. Response time varies.
Articles: 300–800 words. Informational and how-to articles. Topics include science, nature, and wildlife.
Fiction: 300–800 words. Genres include adventure stories, and stories about the outdoors, wildlife, the environment, and nature.
Artwork: 4x6 or larger prints.
Other: Puzzles and projects related to nature and science.

Sample Issue
24 pages (no advertising): 7 articles; 1 story; 1 dept/column; 3 activities. Sample copy and guidelines, $5 with 9x12 SASE ($1.11 postage).
• "No Bones About It." Short story teaches about sharks, their skeletons, and how they swim.
• "Shark Eggs Up Close." Article looks at the two types of shark embryos.
• Sample dept/column: "You Can Draw . . ." shows how to draw a clown fish and an anemone.

Rights and Payment
One-time rights. Written material, $.05 per word. Pays on publication. Artwork, payment rates and payment policy vary. Provides 1 contributor's tearsheet.

Editor's Comments
We are currently looking for how-to articles on nature projects and science experiments for children ages 6 to 12. Submissions should include step-by-step procedures. We encourage writers interested in contributing to *Nature Friend* to subscribe to the magazine, as there is no better way to become familiar with our style.

N.E.W. & Fox Valley Kids

P.O. Box 45050
Madison, WI 53713

Editorial Assistant: Kelsey Anderson

Description and Interests
This free parenting newspaper fills its pages with reports about local family activities and events, and articles of interest to families in Wisconsin.
• **Audience:** Parents
• **Frequency:** Monthly
• **Distribution:** Schools; libraries; other
• **Circulation:** 40,000
• **Website:** www.newandfoxvalleykids.com

Freelance Potential
80–90% written by nonstaff writers. Publishes many freelance submissions yearly; 5% by unpublished writers, 10% by authors who are new to the magazine. Receives 204 queries, 36 unsolicited mss yearly.

Submissions
Query or send complete ms. Accepts hard copy and disk submissions (RTF files). SASE. Response time varies.
Articles: To 750 words. Informational articles and humorous pieces. Topics include parenting, family issues, education, gifted and special education, regional and national news, crafts, hobbies, music, the arts, health, fitness, sports, animals, pets, travel, popular culture, and multicultural and ethnic issues.
Depts/columns: To 750 words. Women's and children's health, school news, and essays.
Other: Submit seasonal material 4 months in advance.

Sample Issue
12 pages (60% advertising): 2 articles; 10 depts/columns. Sample copy, free with 9x12 SASE. Guidelines and editorial calendar available.
• "Rockets for Schools Has the Right Stuff." Article highlights the rocket science program for schools in the city of Sheboygan.
• "Artistic and Wellness Center Helps Families Stay Centered." Article discusses the positive aspects of a community center in Appleton, where seven separate businesses reside in one building.
• Sample dept/column: "Rookie Dad" shares the story of a third-grader with a sore throat.

Rights and Payment
Rights negotiable. All material, payment rates vary. Pays on publication. Provides 2 contributor's copies.

Editor's Comments
All stories of interest to families should have a local angle. Contact us for our theme list and topic ideas.

New Expression

Columbia College
619 South Wabash, Suite 207
Chicago, IL 60605

Editorial Advisor: Wendell Hutson

Description and Interests
Sponsored by a number of nonprofit and educational institutions in the Chicago area, *New Expressions* is a tabloid written by teens, for teens. It covers current events and social and cultural issues that are important to young adults.
• **Audience:** YA–Adult
• **Frequency:** 9 times each year
• **Distribution:** 90% schools; 5% subscription; 5% other
• **Circulation:** 45,000
• **Website:** www.newexpressions.org

Freelance Potential
15% written by nonstaff writers. Publishes 40–50 freelance submissions yearly; 50% by unpublished writers, 50% by authors who are new to the magazine. Receives 36–48 unsolicited mss yearly.

Submissions
Send complete ms. Accepts email submissions only to nenewspaper@yahoo.com. Availability of artwork improves chance of acceptance. Response time varies.
Articles: No word limit. Informational articles; reviews; and personal experience pieces. Topics include current events, music, popular culture, and social issues.
Depts/columns: Word lengths vary. Book and entertainment reviews, teen business, school issues.
Artwork: B/W JPEG files.
Other: Poetry.

Sample Issue
24 pages (10% advertising): 3 articles; 8 depts/columns. Sample copy, $1. Guidelines and editorial calendar available.
• "College Out of Reach for Many Chicago Teens." Article examines why many Chicago high school graduates are not completing their college educations.
• "Budget Woes Could Affect Activities." Article reports that budget cuts may affect extracurricular programs in Chicago public schools.
• Sample dept/column: "Teens Mean Business" profiles an aspiring high school entrepreneur.

Rights and Payment
All rights. No payment.

Editor's Comments
Most pieces are staff written, but we will accept freelance work written by teens.

New Jersey Suburban Parent

Middlesex Publications
850 Route 1
North Brunswick, NJ 08902

Editor: Melodie Dhondt

Description and Interests
Formerly known as *Suburban Parent*, this central New Jersey tabloid is filled with articles of interest to parents of toddlers and teens. It also includes information on family-oriented events and activities.
• **Audience:** Parents
• **Frequency:** Monthly
• **Distribution:** 96% controlled; 4% other
• **Circulation:** 78,000
• **Website:** www.njparentweb.com

Freelance Potential
80% written by nonstaff writers. Publishes 12 freelance submissions yearly; 20% by unpublished writers, 40% by authors who are new to the magazine. Receives 1,440 queries yearly.

Submissions
Query with writing samples. Accepts hard copy and simultaneous submissions if identified. SASE. Responds in 2–8 weeks.
Articles: 700–1,000 words. Informational and how-to articles. Topics include parenting, family issues, cultural events, pregnancy, childbirth, sports, careers, financial concerns, and dining and media reviews.
Artwork: B/W or color prints.
Other: Submit seasonal material 4 months in advance.

Sample Issue
24 pages (60% advertising): 9 articles; 3 depts/columns; 1 calendar of events. Sample copy, free with 9x12 SASE. Writers' guidelines and editorial calendar available.
• "Helping Boys Succeed in School." Article offers expert advice on alternative teaching methods developed to help boys thrive academically.
• "Helping Your Child Cope with Homesickness." Article discusses ways parents can ease the loneliness most children initially feel at sleep-away camp.

Rights and Payment
Rights vary. Articles, $30. Artwork, payment rates vary. Pays on acceptance. Provides 1+ contributor's copies.

Editor's Comments
We publish timely and seasonal articles that are of interest to parents in central New Jersey. Please check our editorial calendar, which is available at our website, for upcoming themes.

New Moon

2 West First Street, Suite 101
Duluth, MN 55802

Editorial Department

Description and Interests

New Moon presents an image of girls and women as intelligent, active, and totally in charge. It strives to be an international and multicultural magazine that celebrates diversity and provides a place for girls to express themselves and communicate with others.

- **Audience:** Girls, 8–14 years
- **Frequency:** 6 times each year
- **Distribution:** 90% subscription; 10% newsstand
- **Circulation:** 25,000
- **Website:** www.newmoon.org

Freelance Potential

85% written by nonstaff writers. Publishes 50 freelance submissions yearly; 85% by unpublished writers, 20% by authors who are new to the magazine. Receives 720 queries and unsolicited mss yearly.

Submissions

Query or send complete ms. Accepts hard copy and email submissions to girl@newmoon.org. SASE for reply; does not return mss. Responds in 4–6 months.
Articles: 300–900 words. Profiles and interviews. Topics include careers, health, fitness, recreation, science, technology, and social issues.
Fiction: 900–1,600 words. Genres include contemporary, inspirational, multicultural, and ethnic fiction.
Depts/columns: Word lengths vary. Material about women and girls.
Other: Poetry from girls ages 8–14 only.

Sample Issue

48 pages (no advertising): 5 articles; 1 story; 19 depts/columns. Sample copy, $7. Guidelines available.
- "Out of this World." Article investigates the theory of parallel universes.
- "Grandma Crackers." Story features a grandmother who embarrasses her granddaughter.
- Sample dept/column: "Global Village: Bolivia" takes a closer look at Cochabamba, the author's home.

Rights and Payment

All rights. Written material, $.06–$.10 per word. Pays on publication. Provides 3 contributor's copies.

Editor's Comments

We would like to see more articles with multicultural themes about great women in history who are often overlooked. We do not publish moralistic material, or memoirs from adults. Our preference is for material from girls between the ages of eight and fourteen.

New York Family

63 West 38th Street, Suite 206
New York, NY 10018

Editor: Eric Messinger

Description and Interests

This magazine is dedicated to providing New York City parents with resources to meet their parenting needs. Each issue includes thought-provoking articles, information on resources, tips on parenting topics, and lifestyle pieces.

- **Audience:** Parents
- **Frequency:** Monthly
- **Distribution:** 96% controlled; 4% subscription
- **Circulation:** 25,000
- **Website:** www.manhattanmedia.com

Freelance Potential

50% written by nonstaff writers. Publishes 40 freelance submissions yearly; 40% by authors who are new to the magazine. Receives 600 queries yearly.

Submissions

Query with clips. Accepts hard copy. SASE. Response time varies.
Articles: 800–1,200 words. Informational articles; profiles; interviews; photo-essays; and personal experience pieces. Topics include gifted education, music, recreation, regional news, social issues, special education, travel, and women's issues.
Depts/columns: 400–800 words. News and reviews.

Sample Issue

78 pages: 4 articles; 15 depts/columns. Sample copy, free with 9x12 SASE. Guidelines available.
- "Private School Admissions." Article recommends taking a sensible and calm approach when searching for the right private school.
- "Brave New Baby." Article explores five high-tech options available for parents who want to conceive or know more about their babies' health.
- Sample dept/column: "Growing Up" discusses the importance of parents knowing their child's style of friendship.

Rights and Payment

First rights. Written material, $25–$300. Pays on publication. Provides 3 contributor's copies.

Editor's Comments

We are a family lifestyle magazine, which means we do traditional parenting stories as well as stories about education, real estate, vacation planning, financial planning, and a host of other subjects that impact New York families. If you have an idea for something that will fit our needs, send us a query.

New York Times Upfront 🖱

Scholastic Inc.
557 Broadway
New York, NY 10012-3999

Editor

Description and Interests
Published both in print and online, this magazine for high school students focuses on current events and topics related to school social studies curriculum. It is a collaboration between *The New York Times* and Scholastic Inc.
- **Audience:** 14–18 years
- **Frequency:** 18 times each year
- **Distribution:** 95% schools; 5% subscription
- **Circulation:** 250,000
- **Website:** www.upfrontmagazine.com

Freelance Potential
10% written by nonstaff writers. Publishes 2 freelance submissions yearly; 10% by authors who are new to the magazine. Receives 144 queries yearly.

Submissions
Query with résumé and published clips. Accepts hard copy. Availability of artwork improves chance of acceptance. SASE. Responds in 2–4 weeks only if interested.
Articles: 500–1,200 words. Informational articles; profiles; and interviews. Topics include popular culture, current events, social issues, history, careers, college, the arts, the environment, technology, science, politics, government, business, and multicultural and ethnic issues.
Depts/columns: Word lengths vary. First-person accounts from teens, news, and trends.
Artwork: High-resolution color prints or transparencies.

Sample Issue
14 pages (18% advertising): 6 articles; 2 depts/columns. Sample copy, $2.25. Writers' guidelines available.
- "Should the Driving Age Be Raised to 18?" Article presents opposing viewpoints on whether the driving age should be raised because of the number of car accidents involving teens.
- "Flu Fears." Article examines the spread of bird flu and the threat to humans.

Rights and Payment
All rights. All material, payment rates vary. Pays on publication.

Editor's Comments
Articles must be timely, interesting, and correlate to the high school curriculum. Remember that today's teens are sharp and aware of the world around them.

The Next Step Magazine

86 West Main Street
Victor, NY 14564

Editor-in-Chief: Laura Jeanne Hammond

Description and Interests
The Next Step Magazine is an objective, coast-to-coast teen publication distributed in high schools around the U.S. and in Ontario, Canada. Articles featured in this publication cover college and career planning as well as life skills, and target high school juniors and seniors.
- **Audience:** 14–21 years
- **Frequency:** 5 times each year
- **Distribution:** 100% controlled
- **Circulation:** 900,000
- **Website:** www.nextstepmag.com

Freelance Potential
50% written by nonstaff writers. Publishes 50 freelance submissions yearly.

Submissions
Query. Accepts email queries to laura@ nextSTEPmag.com. Response time varies.
Articles: 700–1,000 words. Informational, self-help, and how-to articles; profiles; interviews; personal experience pieces; humor; and essays. Topics include college planning, financial aid, campus tours, choosing a career, life skills, résumé writing, public speaking, personal finances, computers, multicultural and ethnic issues, social issues, sports, and special education.

Sample Issue
62 pages: 20 articles. Sample copy available at website. Guidelines available.
- "Over-Achievers, Take Note!" Article offers tips on balancing your life in college to avoid burning out.
- "9 College Myths (and Why They're Just Not True)." Article sets the record straight about nine common college myths.
- "Staying Safe at School." Article lists safety services available at most colleges and offers tips on staying safe and protecting your personal items.

Rights and Payment
All rights. Articles, payment rates vary. Pays within 30 days of acceptance.

Editor's Comments
Articles covering some aspect of the college-planning process are of interest. We look for up-to-date information and tips on preparing for college as well as choosing a career. Material should be concise, well-written, and entertaining.

Nick Jr. Family Magazine

1633 Broadway, 7th Floor
New York, NY 10019

Deputy Editor: Wendy Smolen

Description and Interests
Parents of children ages three to eleven read this publication for its practical parenting articles and stories. Topics of interest include health, vacations, family issues, recipes, activities, and crafts.
- **Audience:** Families
- **Frequency:** 9 times each year
- **Distribution:** 53% subscription; 46% controlled; 1% other
- **Circulation:** 1.1 million
- **Website:** www.nickjr.com

Freelance Potential
40% written by nonstaff writers. Publishes 10 freelance submissions yearly; 50% by authors who are new to the magazine. Receives 600 queries and unsolicited mss yearly.

Submissions
Query or send complete ms. Accepts hard copy. SASE. Responds in 3 months.
Articles: To 300 words. Informational and how-to articles. Topics include nature, the environment, music, social issues, popular culture, special education, animals, crafts, hobbies, pets, mathematics, current events, and multicultural and ethnic subjects.
Fiction: Word lengths vary. Genres include humor, adventure, and stories about nature, animals, and the environment.
Other: Activities and games.

Sample Issue
88 pages (45% advertising): 18 articles; 5 depts/columns; 1 pullout kids' magazine. Sample copy, $2.95 at newsstands.
- "Heads Up!" Article offers tips on fitting your child with the proper helmet, and the best way of getting them to wear a helmet.
- "Best Pets." Article shares suggestions for choosing the right pet for your family.
- Sample dept/column: "$100 Ideas" shares parenting tips from readers.

Rights and Payment
All rights. Written material, payment rates vary. Pays on publication. Provides 10 contributor's copies.

Editor's Comments
We are only interested in material relevant to children ages three to eleven. Creative activities and crafts that children and parents can do together are of interest.

No Crime

374 Fraser Street
North Bay, Ontario P1B 3W7
Canada

Managing Editor: Ken Sitter

Description and Interests
No Crime, published by Young People's Press, advocates that providing interesting activities and paying attention to youth can help keep them from committing crimes. Articles written by young people and by professionals highlight successful school and community programs that have reduced youth crimes.
- **Audience:** YA–Adult
- **Frequency:** 6 times each year
- **Distribution:** 100% Internet
- **Hits per month:** 24,000
- **Website:** www.nocrimetime.net

Freelance Potential
100% written by nonstaff writers. Publishes 150–200 freelance submissions yearly; 70% by unpublished writers, 75% by authors who are new to the magazine.

Submissions
Send complete ms. Accepts email submissions to media@ypp.net. Responds immediately.
Articles: Word lengths vary. Informational articles and personal experience pieces. Topics include youth justice, youth crime, and community-based programs in crime prevention.

Sample Issue
10 articles. Sample copy and guidelines available at website.
- "Defeating Boredom through Business." Article tells about a summer work program for pre-teens and teens in a small town that helps them earn money and teaches them about business.
- "Trekking the Arctic." Article recalls a tricky trek close to the Arctic Circle done by high school students who learned valuable lessons along the way.
- "Attending CSI: Senior High." Article looks at a high school course in Edmonton that teaches students how to become good citizens and prepares them for a career in law enforcement.

Rights and Payment
Rights, payment rates, and payment policy vary.

Editor's Comments
We encourage young writers to share their experiences, views on the issues facing young people today, information on media celebrities, reviews of new movies, CD releases, and television programs, or websites that are interesting to teens and young adults.

Northern Michigan Family Magazine

P.O. Box 579
Indian River, MI 49749

Editor: L. Scott Swanson

Description and Interests
Topics related to parenting, child development, education, and family life are covered in this magazine. It also lists regional resources and event information and is distributed free to parents in communities in northern Michigan.
- **Audience:** Parents
- **Frequency:** 6 times each year
- **Distribution:** 100% controlled
- **Circulation:** 6,000

Freelance Potential
50% written by nonstaff writers. Publishes 20 freelance submissions yearly; 25% by unpublished writers, 50% by authors who are new to the magazine. Receives 100 queries and unsolicited mss yearly.

Submissions
Query or send complete ms. Accepts hard copy, email to editor@resorter.com, and simultaneous submissions if identified. Availability of artwork improves chance of acceptance. SASE. Response time varies.
Articles: 200–1,500 words. Informational, self-help, and how-to articles; profiles; interviews; and personal experience pieces. Topics include parenting, family life, gifted and special education, current events, music, nature, the environment, regional news, recreation, and social issues.
Depts/columns: Word lengths vary. Family news and resources, health information, area events, and perspectives from parents.

Sample Issue
22 pages: 4 articles; 10 depts/columns. Sample copy, free with 9x12 SASE. Guidelines available.
- "Internet Leaves Kids More Vulnerable to Strangers." Article shares tips for keeping children safe from Internet predators.
- Sample dept/column: "The Craft Corner" offers easy directions for homemade milk paint and step-by-step instructions for making a kite.

Rights and Payment
All rights. Unsolicited articles and reprints, $10–$25; assigned articles, $25–$100. Payment policy varies.

Editor's Comments
We are looking for well-written, easy-to-read articles that include quotes from experts in the local community. We could also use more kid-friendly crafts, as well as recipes.

The Northland

P.O. Box 841
Schumacher, Ontario P0N 1G0
Canada

Submissions Editor

Description and Interests
This small family magazine is written for members of the Diocese of Moosonee of the Anglican Church of Canada. It focuses on church news and activities, while also featuring sermons, prayers, and other inspirational writing.
- **Audience:** Adults
- **Frequency:** Quarterly
- **Distribution:** 100% subscription
- **Circulation:** 500

Freelance Potential
100% written by nonstaff writers. Publishes several freelance submissions yearly. Receives few unsolicited mss yearly.

Submissions
Send complete ms. Accepts hard copy. SASE. Response time varies.
Articles: Word lengths vary. Informational and inspirational articles. Topics include the Anglican church, ministry, faith, prayer, church rites, baptism, confirmation, worship, and sermon ideas.
Depts/columns: Word lengths vary. Local church news and events.

Sample Issue
22 pages (no advertising): 13 articles; 2 depts/columns. Sample copy available.
- "Mission in Mistissini." Article describes the visit of the Archbishop of the Diocese of Moosonee to the Parish of St. John the Evangelist in Mistissini.
- "How Old Is Grandma?" Article offers perspectives from two grandmothers on the cultural and social changes that have taken place in their lifetimes.
- Sample dept/column: "Moose Notes" offers updates from different parishes in the diocese.

Rights and Payment
Rights vary. No payment.

Editor's Comments
Ours is a small, locally oriented magazine that provides information and some inspiration to the members of our diocese in Canada. We primarily print parish reports and news about what is happening in the diocese as a whole. Articles on current or upcoming religious celebrations and their relevance to our members are always appreciated. We also use some inspirational first-person essays about spiritual life and events.

North Texas Teens

Lauren Publications
4275 Kellway Circle, Suite 146
Addison, TX 75001

Editorial Director: Shelley Hawes Pate

Description and Interests

Targeting families with teenagers, *North Texas Teens* publishes articles related to parenting teens, family activities, education, health, effective communication, and media reviews. This publication is distributed free of charge throughout the Dallas area.
- **Audience:** Parents and teens
- **Frequency:** 9 times each year
- **Distribution:** Controlled; subscription
- **Circulation:** Unavailable
- **Website:** www.dallaschild.com

Freelance Potential

60% written by nonstaff writers. Publishes 12–15 freelance submissions yearly; 20% by authors who are new to the magazine. Receives 240 queries yearly.

Submissions

Query with résumé. Accepts hard copy. SASE. Responds in 2–3 months. Guidelines available.
Articles: 1,000–2,500 words. Informational articles; profiles; and personal experience pieces. Topics include gifted education, health and fitness, recreation, regional news, social issues, and sports.
Depts/columns: 800 words. Health news and reviews.

Sample Issue

46 pages (15% advertising): 2 articles; 9 depts/columns. Sample copy, free. Writers' guidelines available.
- "The Seven Habits of Highly Effective Teens." Article profiles author Sean Covey and discusses his national best seller.
- "77 Days of Summer." Article offers a list of boredom busters that will keep teens busy during the summer months.
- Sample dept/column: "Health & Safety" discusses the effects of insomnia and its link to health issues among teenagers.

Rights and Payment

First rights. Written material, payment rates vary. Pays on publication.

Editor's Comments

We seek articles of interest to teens and parents of teenagers living in the Dallas area. Topics related to health, education, and parenting issues are always of interest to our readers. We also seek media reviews and activity ideas that promote family relationships.

Northwest Baby & Child

4395 Rollinghill Road
Clinton, WA 98236

Editor: Betty Freeman

Description and Interests

This regional tabloid is read by expectant parents and parents of young children. Each issue covers topics of interest to parents and includes reports on local events and activities.
- **Audience:** Expectant and new parents
- **Frequency:** Monthly
- **Distribution:** 75% public distribution; 10% schools; 5% subscription; 10% other
- **Circulation:** 32,000
- **Website:** www.nwbaby.com

Freelance Potential

70% written by nonstaff writers. Publishes 75 freelance submissions yearly; 25% by unpublished writers, 25% by authors who are new to the magazine. Receives 792 queries yearly.

Submissions

Query. Accepts email queries to editor@nwbaby.com (no attachments). Responds in 2–3 months if interested.
Articles: 750 words. Informational and how-to articles; profiles; personal experience pieces; and interviews. Topics include early education, party ideas, home-based businesses, pregnancy and childbirth, family life, travel holidays, and traditions.
Depts/columns: Word lengths vary. Health, parenting tips, activities, and regional resources.

Sample Issue

12 pages (15% advertising): 6 articles; 2 depts/columns; 1 calendar of events. Sample copy, free with 9x12 SASE ($1.48 postage). Guidelines and editorial calendar available.
- "Give Your Kids Chores." Article reports on the positive outcome from allowing young children to help with the household chores.
- "The Joy of Cooking: Homemade Baby Food." Article explains how to make baby food.
- Sample dept/column: "Book Reviews" spotlights Easter board books for toddlers.

Rights and Payment

First rights. Written material, $10–$40. Pays on publication. Provides 1–2 contributor's copies.

Editor's Comments

We need articles that offer new ideas for balancing work and family, as well as articles on trends among today's parents. Material must relate to families living in the northwestern U.S.

OC Family

The News Magazine for Parents

1451 Quail Street, Suite 201
Newport Beach, CA 92660

Executive Editor: Craig Reem

Description and Interests
This magazine provides parents of infants through teenagers living in Orange County, California, with timely articles on area resources for families, health, parenting, and community events.
- **Audience:** Families
- **Frequency:** Monthly
- **Distribution:** Newsstand; subscription; controlled
- **Circulation:** 70,000
- **Website:** www.ocfamily.com

Freelance Potential
82% written by nonstaff writers. Publishes 50 freelance submissions yearly; 1% by unpublished writers, 1% by authors who are new to the magazine. Receives 144 queries yearly.

Submissions
Query. Accepts hard copy and email queries to OCFmag@aol.com. SASE. Responds in 1 month.
Articles: 800–2,500 words. Informational articles and profiles. Topics include education, the Internet, family activities, fine arts, regional food and dining, consumer interests, and grandparenting.
Depts/columns: Word lengths vary. Family life, personal finances, book and software reviews, and women's health.
Artwork: B/W and color prints.

Sample Issue
204 pages (60% advertising): 3 articles; 20 depts/columns; 2 directories. Sample copy, free. Editorial calendar available.
- "How to Teach Your Child Responsibility." Article discusses instilling a sense of pride and accomplishment in children.
- "Breathe Easy." Article describes the role of medication in managing asthma.
- Sample dept/column: "Your Family@Home" offers ideas for creating a successful work/life balance.

Rights and Payment
One-time rights. Articles, $100–$500. Artwork, $90. Kill fee, $50. Pays 45 days after publication. Provides 3 contributor's copies.

Editor's Comments
We are looking for articles about local family activities and experiences that are specific to Orange County. News-oriented feature articles with a local twist stand the best chance for publication.

Odyssey

Carus Publishing
30 Grove Street, Suite C
Peterborough, NH 03458

Senior Editor: Elizabeth E. Lindstrom

Description and Interests
Teens interested in science, math, and technology read *Odyssey*. It uses articles that incite readers' interest in the subjects, as well as hands-on activities that challenge students in middle school and high school.
- **Audience:** 10–16 years
- **Frequency:** 9 times each year
- **Distribution:** 100% subscription
- **Circulation:** 25,000
- **Website:** www.odysseymagazine.com

Freelance Potential
80% written by nonstaff writers. Publishes 50 freelance submissions yearly; 5% by unpublished writers, 25% by authors who are new to the magazine. Receives 144 queries yearly.

Submissions
Query with outline, biography, and clips or writing samples. Accepts hard copy. Availability of artwork improves chance of acceptance. Responds in 5 months only if interested.
Articles: 750–1,000 words. Informational articles; biographies; and interviews. Topics include mathematics, science, and technology.
Depts/columns: Word lengths vary. Short news items, brain teasers, items on animals.
Other: Activities, to 500 words. Seasonal material about notable astronomy or space events placed in current context, science projects, and experiments.

Sample Issue
48 pages (no advertising): 8 articles; 6 depts/columns; 3 activities. Sample copy, $4.50 with 9x12 SASE (4 first-class stamps). Writers' guidelines and theme list available.
- "Rip-Roarin' and Ready to Fly!" Article profiles a teen who is one of the best kiteboarders in the world.
- "Doing the Einstein Flip." Article reports on how a Cambridge physicist and teen BMX champion designed a wild bicycle stunt.

Rights and Payment
All rights. Written material, $.20–$.25 per word. Artwork, payment rates vary. Pays on publication. Provides 2 contributor's copies.

Editor's Comments
All material must relate to an upcoming theme to be considered for publication. We look for scientific accuracy and a lively approach to a subject.

The Old Schoolhouse

The Magazine for Homeschool Families

P.O. Box 1701
Dandridge, TN 37725

Editor

Description and Interests
Published for parents who homeschool their children, this magazine provides resources and materials that support and encourage homeschool families. The articles, written from a Christian perspective, address learning challenges, curricula, teaching styles, and current trends.
- **Audience:** Homeschool families
- **Frequency:** Quarterly
- **Distribution:** Unavailable
- **Circulation:** 22,000
- **Website:** www.thehomeschoolmagazine.com

Freelance Potential
20% written by nonstaff writers. Publishes 30–50 freelance submissions yearly; 75% by unpublished writers, 75% by authors who are new to the magazine. Receives 192 queries yearly.

Submissions
Query with outline, sample paragraphs, and brief author bio. Accepts email queries to publishers@tosmag.com. No simultaneous submissions. Response time varies.
Articles: 1,000–2,000 words. Informational and how-to articles and personal experience pieces. Topics include homeschooling, education, family life, art, music, spirituality, literature, child development, teen issues, science, history, and mathematics.
Depts/columns: Word lengths vary. Short news items, teaching styles, opinion pieces, children with special needs, and humor.

Sample Issue
192 pages (40% advertising): 3 articles; 17 depts/columns. Sample copy available. Guidelines available at website.
- "What Is a Blog?" Article explains what a blog is and how to find them on the Internet.
- "Making the Classics Live for Today's Student." Article shares a homeschooling mom's ideas for encouraging children to read and enjoy classic literature.

Rights and Payment
First rights. Written material, $.05 per word. Artwork, payment rates vary. Pays on publication. Provides 2 contributor's copies.

Editor's Comments
We don't accept complete manuscripts. Please check our guidelines if you have a prospective submission.

Once Upon a Time . . .

553 Winston Court
St. Paul, MN 55118

Editor/Publisher: Audrey B. Baird

Description and Interests
Real writers and illustrators write about their own experiences, success stories, work habits, ideas, and problem solving in this magazine. It serves as a support publication for children's writers and illustrators and offers concrete information and instruction.
- **Audience:** Children's writers and illustrators
- **Frequency:** Quarterly
- **Distribution:** 100% subscription
- **Circulation:** 1,000
- **Website:** www.onceuponatimemag.com

Freelance Potential
50% written by nonstaff writers. Publishes 160 freelance submissions yearly; 20% by unpublished writers, 20% by authors who are new to the magazine. Receives 204 unsolicited mss yearly.

Submissions
Send complete ms. No queries. Accepts hard copy. SASE. Responds in 2 months.
Articles: To 900 words. Informational, self-help, how-to articles; and personal experience pieces. Topics include writing and illustrating for children.
Depts/columns: Staff written.
Artwork: B/W line art.
Other: Poetry, to 24 lines.

Sample Issue
32 pages (2% advertising): 14 articles; 19 poems; 11 depts/columns. Sample copy, $5. Writers' guidelines available.
- "Recycling the Folks Inside Your Head." Article suggests ways to successfully move the characters that develop in a writer's mind to the written word.
- "10 Suggestions for Sticking with Writing." Article conveys practical ideas to consider if a writer feels like quitting after receiving a rejection letter.

Rights and Payment
One-time rights. No payment. Provides 2 contributor's copies; 6 copies for cover art.

Editor's Comments
We offer an opportunity for writers and illustrators to communicate with each other and share information. We do not publish poetry or fiction for children, but include many poems about writing or illustrating in each issue. At this time we would like to receive more articles on how to plot a story; we have enough material about rejection and comparing it to a baby's birth.

On Course

General Council of the Assemblies of God
1445 North Boonville Avenue
Springfield, MO 65802-1894

Assistant Editor

Description and Interests
Each issue of this Christian publication for teenagers is focused on a basic theme appealing to its readers. It features articles on real issues and emphasizes a biblical approach to facing these issues. Articles incorporating a Christian-based message with pop culture, trends, and entertainment are also included in each issue of On Course.
- **Audience:** 12–18 years
- **Frequency:** Quarterly
- **Distribution:** 100% controlled
- **Circulation:** 160,000
- **Website:** www.oncourse.ag.org

Freelance Potential
85% written by nonstaff writers. Publishes 32 freelance submissions yearly; 30% by unpublished writers, 40% by authors who are new to the magazine.

Submissions
Send résumé with clips or writing samples. All work is done by assignment only.
Articles: To 1,000 words. How-to articles; profiles; interviews; humor; and personal experience pieces. Topics include social issues, music, health, religion, sports, careers, college, and multicultural subjects.
Depts/columns: Word lengths vary. Profiles and brief news items.

Sample Issue
30 pages (33% advertising): 4 articles; 7 depts/columns. Sample copy, free. Guidelines available.
- "Beauty from Pain." Article shares Tricia Brock's painful learning experience and how it changed her spiritually and deepened her relationship with God.
- "Superman vs. Flash." Article features two friends in a fight and how the power of forgiveness helps them.
- Sample dept/column: "Truth" asks the question "How desperate are we for Jesus?" and shares a story from the New Testament Book of Luke.

Rights and Payment
First and electronic rights. Articles, $.10 per word. Provides 5 contributor's copies.

Editor's Comments
We currently seek articles on hard-hitting topics of interest to teenagers and lighter subject matters, both of which inspire or empower our readers to grow in their relationship with God. We welcome new and established writers for assigned material.

Organic Family Magazine

P.O. Box 1614
Wallingford, CT 06492-1214

Editor: Catherine Wong

Description and Interests
Families interested in organic living read this publication for articles on natural living and the environment. Topics include organic agriculture, nutrition, parenting, and progressive politics. Stories and poems related to nature are also part of the editorial mix.
- **Audience:** Families
- **Frequency:** Twice each year
- **Distribution:** Subscription
- **Circulation:** Unavailable
- **Website:** www.organicfamilymagazine.com

Freelance Potential
90% written by nonstaff writers. Publishes 40 freelance submissions yearly.

Submissions
Query or send complete ms. Prefers email submissions to sciencelibrarian@hotmail.com. Accepts hard copy. SASE. Response time varies.
Articles: Word lengths vary. Informational articles; interviews; and personal experience pieces. Topics include nature, organic agriculture, conservation, parenting, natural pet care, herbs, gardening, nutrition, progressive politics, health, wellness, and environmental issues.
Fiction: Word lengths vary. Stories about nature and the environment.
Depts/columns: Word lengths vary. New product reviews; recipes; profiles of conservation organizations; and book, movie, and website reviews.
Other: Poetry.

Sample Issue
28 pages: 8 articles; 11 depts/columns; 1 poem. Guidelines available at website.
- "Making Mealtimes Sacred." Article offers ideas for establishing a family mealtime tradition.
- "Homeschooling." Article shares the benefits of homeschooling from a homeschooling mom.
- Sample dept/column: "Reduce Trash" lists practical ways to help save the Earth.

Rights and Payment
One-time rights. No payment. Provides 1 author's copy.

Editor's Comments
We seek articles on organic alternatives and natural living. Intelligent political commentary and stories with an environmental theme are also of interest to us. We welcome submissions from new writers.

Our Children

National PTA
541 North Fairbanks Court, Suite 1300
Chicago, IL 60611-3396

Editor: Ted Villaire

Description and Interests
In addition to general parenting articles, *Our Children* includes discussions of parental involvement in education and ideas for running effective Parent Teacher Associations. The National PTA publishes this magazine for both members and non-members.
• **Audience:** Parents, educators, school administrators
• **Frequency:** 6 times each year
• **Distribution:** 90% membership; 10% subscription
• **Circulation:** 31,000
• **Website:** www.pta.org

Freelance Potential
50% written by nonstaff writers. Publishes 20–25 freelance submissions yearly; 75% by authors who are new to the magazine. Receives 180–240 queries and unsolicited mss yearly.

Submissions
Query or send complete ms. Accepts email submissions to tvillaire@pta.org. No simultaneous submissions. Final submissions must be sent on disk. SASE. Responds in 2 months.
Articles: 600–1,100 words. Informational and how-to articles. Topics include education, child welfare, and family life.
Depts/columns: Word lengths vary. Short updates on parenting and education issues.
Artwork: 3x5 or larger color prints and slides.
Other: Submit seasonal material 3 months in advance.

Sample Issue
20 pages (no advertising): 11 articles; 3 depts/columns. Sample copy, $2.50 with 9x12 SASE ($1 postage). Guidelines and theme list available.
• "When Adolescents Look for Love in Cyberspace." Article explains the many ways teens can meet online and how to keep kids safe on the Internet.
• Sample dept/column: "Good Ideas" tells how to plan a PTA-sponsored science event.

Rights and Payment
First rights. No payment. Provides 3 author's copies.

Editor's Comments
Our readers are typical American parents, many of whom are officers in their local PTAs. They want to know how they can help their children lead happier, healthier, more productive lives. We want direct, concrete articles written in conversational English.

Pack-O-Fun

2400 Devon, Suite 375
Des Plaines, IL 60018-4618

Managing Editor: Annie Niemiec

Description and Interests
Teachers and other adults working with elementary-age children read this resource for fun ideas and simple crafts. This magazine is designed to encourage creativity and make learning fun.
• **Audience:** 6–12 years; teachers; parents
• **Frequency:** 6 times each year
• **Distribution:** 67% subscription; 33% newsstand
• **Circulation:** 130,000
• **Website:** www.pack-o-fun.com

Freelance Potential
100% written by nonstaff writers. Receives 504 unsolicited mss yearly.

Submissions
Query or send complete ms with instructions and sketches if appropriate. Accepts hard copy. SASE. Responds in 4–6 weeks.
Articles: To 200 words. How-to's, craft projects, and party ideas.
Depts/columns: Word lengths vary. Art ideas; projects for children and adults to do together; ideas for vacation Bible school programs; and pictures of projects from readers.
Artwork: B/W line art.
Other: Puzzles, activities, games, and skits. Poetry.

Sample Issue
66 pages (10% advertising): 11 crafts and activities; 3 depts/columns. Sample copy, $4.99 with 9x12 SASE (2 first-class stamps). Guidelines available.
• "Gone Buggy Bulletin Board." Article provides instructions for creating an attractive and fact-filled bulletin board all about bugs.
• "Appreciation Cards." Article offers step-by-step directions for making mini book keepsakes.
• Sample dept/column: "The Bookcase" reviews fun and inspiring books to encourage kids creatively.

Rights and Payment
All rights. Written material, $10–$15. Artwork, payment rates vary. Pays 30 days after signed contract. Provides 3 contributor's copies.

Editor's Comments
Innovative projects that use inexpensive materials are always of interest to us. Our crafts range from simple and independent to more complicated ones meant for adults. If you would like to submit an original craft idea, review our complete guidelines first.

Parent and Preschooler Newsletter

North Shore Child & Family Guidance Center
480 Old Westbury Road
Roslyn Heights, NY 11577-2215

Editor: Neala S. Schwartzberg, Ph.D.

Description and Interests
Articles by experts that address a range of issues facing parents and child care professionals, such as early education, diversity, discipline, emotional development, and parenting concerns, can be found in this resourceful newsletter.
- **Audience:** Parents, caregivers, and early childhood professionals
- **Frequency:** 10 times each year
- **Distribution:** 100% subscription
- **Circulation:** Unavailable
- **Website:** www.northshorechildguidance.org

Freelance Potential
90% written by nonstaff writers. Publishes 10 freelance submissions yearly; 50% by authors who are new to the magazine. Receives 72 queries yearly.

Submissions
Query with outline. Accepts disk submissions and email queries to nealas@panix.com. SASE. Responds in 1 week.
Articles: 2,000 words. Practical information and how-to articles. Topics include education, self-esteem, discipline, children's health, parenting skills, fostering cooperation through play, and coping with death.
Depts/columns: Staff written.

Sample Issue
8 pages (no advertising): 3 articles; 4 depts/columns. Sample copy, $3 with #10 SASE (1 first-class stamp). Guidelines and editorial calendar available.
- "Free to Learn." Article discusses how to help children explore and learn from the world around them.
- "Making the Most of a Museum Visit." Article offers tips on how to make visiting a museum an enjoyable learning experience.
- "Your Toddler as Junior Scientist." Article explores learning strategies in toddlers.

Rights and Payment
First world rights. Articles, $200. Pays on publication. Provides 10 contributor's copies.

Editor's Comments
We are interested in information on universal child development topics that are important to parents and preschoolers. Articles must provide examples and offer strategies and practical activities parents and children can enjoy together. Keep in mind we are distributed to an international audience.

Parentguide News

419 Park Avenue South, 13th Floor
New York, NY 10016

Editor: Anne Marie Evola

Description and Interests
This tabloid newspaper for parents is distributed free of charge in the New York metropolitan area. Each issue spotlights upcoming events and activities for kids and provides articles on issues relevant to parents of young children.
- **Audience:** Parents
- **Frequency:** Monthly
- **Distribution:** Subscription; controlled
- **Circulation:** 280,000
- **Website:** www.parentguidenews.com

Freelance Potential
85% written by nonstaff writers. Publishes 45 freelance submissions yearly; 20% by unpublished writers, 80% by authors who are new to the magazine. Receives 12 queries and unsolicited mss yearly.

Submissions
Query or send complete ms with résumé. Accepts hard copy. SASE. Responds in 3–4 weeks.
Articles: 750–1,500 words. Informational and self-help articles; humor; and personal experience pieces. Topics include parenting, family issues, social issues, current events, regional issues, popular culture, health, careers, computers, and science.
Depts/columns: 500 words. News of local schools and businesses, travel, reviews, and women's health.

Sample Issue
100 pages (39% advertising): 13 articles; 8 depts/columns; 2 directories; 1 calendar of events. Sample copy, free with 10x13 SASE. Guidelines available.
- "No Party Poopers." Article provides suggestions for helping your shy child have fun at special occasions.
- "Old-Fashioned Parenting." Article lists five principles every family should follow.
- Sample dept/column: "Health" offers tips, up-to-date information, and new product information related to a family's healthcare needs.

Rights and Payment
Rights negotiable. No payment. Provides 1+ copies.

Editor's Comments
Submissions that examine all aspects of parenting, from the humorous to the challenging, are welcome here. Professional advice backed up by reputable sources and quotes from experts is needed as well, as are reports on new trends.

Parenting

135 West 50th Street, 3rd Floor
New York, NY 10026

Submissions Editor

Description and Interests
This magazine for parents with children under the age of 12 provides useful child-rearing information and updates on pediatric health and behavior. Pregnancy and birth information are also included in its mix.
- **Audience:** Parents
- **Frequency:** 11 times each year
- **Distribution:** 90% subscription; 10% newsstand
- **Circulation:** 2 million+
- **Website: www.parenting.com**

Freelance Potential
80% written by nonstaff writers. Publishes few freelance submissions yearly; 5% by unpublished writers, 10% by authors who are new to the magazine. Receives 1,000 queries yearly.

Submissions
Query with clips. Accepts hard copy. SASE. Responds in 1–2 months.
Articles: 1,000–2,500 words. Informational, how-to, and self-help articles; profiles; and personal experience pieces. Topics include child development, behavior, health, pregnancy, and family activities.
Depts/columns: 100–1,000 words. Parenting tips and advice; child development by age range; work and family; and health and beauty advice for moms.

Sample Issue
170 pages (50% advertising): 10 articles; 15 depts/columns. Sample copy, $5.95 (mark envelope Attn: Back Issues). Guidelines available.
- "Choose Your Battles." Article describes how and when parents should react to their child's bad behavior.
- "Build on Your Child's Learning Style." Article discusses the many different ways children learn and offers advice on discovering which style best fits your child.
- Sample dept/column: "Healthy Bites" discusses picky eaters, crackers, and caffeine.

Rights and Payment
First world rights with 2 months exclusivity. Written material, payment rates vary. Pays on acceptance. Provides 1 contributor's copy.

Editor's Comments
We're interested in material that will educate our readers. Parenting tips and reality-tested advice is always of interest to us.

Parenting New Hampshire

P.O. Box 1291
Nashua, NH 03061-1291

Editor: Beth Quarm Todgham

Description and Interests
This regional tabloid focuses on general parenting issues and concerns, as well as local family activities, news, and events.
- **Audience:** Parents
- **Frequency:** Monthly
- **Distribution:** 100% controlled
- **Circulation:** 27,500
- **Website: www.parentingnh.com**

Freelance Potential
90% written by nonstaff writers. Publishes 24–30 freelance submissions yearly; 20% by unpublished writers, 50% by authors who are new to the magazine. Receives 700+ queries and unsolicited mss yearly.

Submissions
Query or send complete ms. Accepts hard copy, disk submissions, and email to news@parentingnh.com. SASE. Response time varies.
Articles: Word lengths vary. Informational and how-to articles; profiles; and interviews. Topics include parenting, education, maternity, childbirth, special needs, gifted education, fathering, child development, summer fun, birthday parties and holidays, back to school, and health.
Depts/columns: Word lengths vary. Child development, parenting issues, and medicine.
Other: Submit seasonal material 2 months in advance.

Sample Issue
64 pages (42% advertising): 7 articles; 12 depts/columns; 1 summer camp directory. Sample copy, free. Guidelines available.
- "Should We Have Another Baby?" Article examines the pros and cons of another family addition.
- "Baby, Show Me a Sign." Article looks at the value of teaching babies sign language.
- Sample dept/column: "Ten Tips" offers ways to ease toddler tantrums in public.

Rights and Payment
All rights. Articles, $30. Other material, payment rates vary. Pays on acceptance. Provides 3 author's copies.

Editor's Comments
Our readers are always interested in articles on how their families can have fun together. Information on New Hampshire activities and resources will be considered, as will authoritative articles on early childhood education and development.

ParentingUniverse.com

Best Parenting Resources, LLC
546 Charing Cross Drive
Marietta, GA 30066

Editor: Alicia Hagan

Description and Interests
Articles on parenting and a variety of lifestyle subjects can be found in this online newsletter. Readers find information and tips on topics such as pregnancy, child development, health, nutrition, education, child care, family life, home business, finances, and recreation. It also includes crafts and activities.
- **Audience:** Women
- **Frequency:** Daily
- **Distribution:** 100% Internet
- **Hits per month:** 1 million+
- **Website:** www.parentinguniverse.com

Freelance Potential
90% written by nonstaff writers. Publishes 500+ freelance submissions yearly. Receives 5,000+ queries, 144 unsolicited mss yearly.

Submissions
Query or send complete ms. Prefers online submissions through website. Accepts hard copy and email submissions to alicia@parentinguniverse.com. SASE. Response time varies.
Articles: Word lengths vary. Informational and how-to articles; profiles; reviews; interviews; and personal experience pieces. Topics include gifted education, pregnancy, parenting, health, fitness, recreation, self-help, and special education.
Depts/columns: Word lengths vary. Parenting tips and guides.

Sample Issue
Sample issue and guidelines available at website.
- "Advantages of Getting Tutors." Article discusses different types of tutors and offers guidelines for finding the right one.
- "A New Pet For the Holidays? Say It Isn't So!" Article explains why the holidays aren't the right time to give a new pet, and offers alternatives to pet giving.
- Sample dept/column: "Health" offers an article about healthy food choices for children.

Rights and Payment
Electronic rights. Written material, payment rates vary. Pays on publication. Provides 2 contributor's copies.

Editor's Comments
We are not accepting articles on the following subjects: loans, affiliates, Internet marketing, debt, credit repair or credit cards, ecommerce, or online networking. Articles on parenting subjects are welcome.

Parent Life

1 LifeWay Plaza
Nashville, TN 37234-0172

Editor-in-Chief: William Summey

Description and Interests
This magazine encourages and equips parents with Christian-based articles on topics such as medical issues and child development.
- **Audience:** Parents
- **Frequency:** Monthly
- **Distribution:** 90% churches; 10% subscription
- **Circulation:** 100,000
- **Website:** www.lifeway.com/magazines

Freelance Potential
90% written by nonstaff writers. Publishes 12 freelance submissions yearly; 5% by unpublished writers, 5% by authors who are new to the magazine. Receives 240 queries and unsolicited mss yearly.

Submissions
Query or send complete ms. Accepts hard copy and email submissions to parentlife@lifeway.com. SASE. Response time varies.
Articles: 500–1,500 words. Informational and how-to articles; and personal experience pieces. Topics include family issues, religion, education, health, fitness, and hobbies.
Depts/columns: 500 words. Family stories, medical advice, and crafts.
Artwork: Color prints or transparencies.
Other: Accepts seasonal material for Christmas and Thanksgiving.

Sample Issue
50 pages: 8 articles; 13 depts/columns. Sample copy, $2.95 with 10x13 SASE. Guidelines available.
- "Life from a Wheelchair." Article explores the challenges faced by families with children in wheelchairs, and how churches can welcome and include them.
- "Cheat-Proofing Your Child." Article describes the opportunities to cheat and ways to teach honesty.
- Sample dept/column: "Media Life" offers a view of issues related to TV, video games, movies, books, and other entertainment sources.

Rights and Payment
Non-exclusive rights. All material, payment rates vary. Pays on publication. Provides 1 contributor's copy.

Editor's Comments
We encourage qualified Christian writers who can equip parents with biblical solutions to a variety of family issues to send their material to us.

Parents & Kids

2727 Old Canton Road, Suite 294
Jackson, MS 39216

Editor: Gretchen Cook

Description and Interests
Parents of children from newborns to teens find useful articles on childrearing and parenting in this regional publication that targets Jackson, Mississippi, and the Gulf Coast region.
- **Audience:** Parents
- **Frequency:** 9 times each year
- **Distribution:** 66% schools; 34% controlled
- **Circulation:** 35,000
- **Website: www.parents-kids.com**

Freelance Potential
80% written by nonstaff writers. Publishes 80 freelance submissions yearly; 50% by unpublished writers. Receives 396 unsolicited mss yearly.

Submissions
Send complete ms. Accepts email submissions to pkmg@mindspring.com (in text of message and as Microsoft Word attachment). Responds in 6 weeks.
Articles: 700 words. Informational, self-help, and how-to articles. Topics include the arts, computers, crafts and hobbies, health, fitness, multicultural and ethnic issues, recreation, regional news, social issues, special education, sports, and travel.
Depts/columns: 500 words. Travel, cooking, and computers.
Artwork: B/W prints or transparencies. Line art. Prefers electronic files; contact publisher for specifics.
Other: Submit seasonal material 3–6 months in advance.

Sample Issue
52 pages (54% advertising): 7 articles; 7 depts/columns; 1 event guide; 1 directory. Sample copy, free with 9x12 SASE ($1.06 postage). Guidelines available at website.
- "School's Out, Now What?" Article provides ideas for fighting summer boredom.
- "Birthday Gifts." Article debates whether children should open their presents at a birthday party.
- Sample dept/column: "Learning Together" discusses choosing which battles to fight with our children.

Rights and Payment
One-time rights. Articles and depts/columns, $25. Pays on publication. Provides tearsheet.

Editor's Comments
Parenting articles with local information using local sources and quotes are of interest to us.

Parents' Press

1454 Sixth Street
Berkeley, CA 94710

Editor: Dixie M. Jordan

Description and Interests
The mission of *Parents' Press* is to provide San Francisco Bay-area parents with information that will help them make informed choices for their families. It uses research-based, practical articles on parenting issues, most with a Bay-area focus.
- **Audience:** Parents
- **Frequency:** Monthly
- **Distribution:** 100% controlled
- **Circulation:** 75,000
- **Website: www.parentspress.com**

Freelance Potential
60% written by nonstaff writers. Publishes 12 freelance submissions yearly; 25% by authors who are new to the magazine. Receives 720 unsolicited mss each year.

Submissions
Send complete ms. Accepts hard copy. SASE. Responds in 2 months.
Articles: To 1,500 words. Informational and how-to articles. Topics include child development, education, health, safety, party planning, and regional family events and activities.
Depts/columns: Staff written.
Artwork: B/W prints and transparencies. Line art.
Other: Submit seasonal material 2 months in advance.

Sample Issue
32 pages (63% advertising): 14 articles; 5 depts/columns; 1 calendar. Sample copy, $3 with 9x12 SASE ($1.93 postage). Writers' guidelines and theme list/editorial calendar available.
- "Little Kid Raves and Faves." Article presents a round-up of parks that appeal to younger children.
- "Picky Eaters." Article offers advice for parents of toddlers who are only interested in eating snacks.

Rights and Payment
All or second rights. Articles, $50–$500. Pays 45 days after publication.

Editor's Comments
Our greatest need is for well-researched articles with a strong San Francisco Bay-area focus. Send us useful, down-to-earth pieces—no political material, fiction, poetry, or childbirth stories. We'll consider interviews with well-known Bay-area figures who have children and how-to pieces on everyday parenting issues.

Park & Pipe

Partners

03-212 Henderson Highway, Suite 328
Winnipeg, Manitoba R2L 1L8
Canada

Managing Editor: Twila Driedger

Description and Interests
Created exclusively for Canadian teens, this magazine packs its pages with everything active teens love about the snowboarding and skiing culture. Its mission is to promote an active lifestyle in teens.
- **Audience:** 13–19 years
- **Frequency:** Quarterly
- **Distribution:** 100% schools
- **Circulation:** 150,000
- **Website: www.parkandpipemagazine.com**

Freelance Potential
40% written by nonstaff writers. Publishes 16 freelance submissions yearly; 50% by unpublished writers, 50% by authors who are new to the magazine. Receives 10 queries yearly.

Submissions
Query with 3 sports-related writing samples. Accepts email submissions to info@ parkandpipemagazine.com. Responds in 3–6 months.
Articles: 200–1,200 words. Informational and how-to articles; profiles; interviews; personal experience pieces; and photo-essays. Topics include skiing and snowboarding equipment, techniques, and events; health; nutrition; fitness; nature; the environment; sports; current events; college; and careers.
Depts/columns: Word lengths vary. Fitness advice; media reviews; resort reviews.
Artwork: JPEG images at 300 dpi.

Sample Issue
22 pages (30% advertising): 4 articles; 6 depts/columns. Guidelines and editorial calendar available.
- "Natural Talent." Article profiles Natasza Zurek, a skier and snowboarder who came to Vancouver from Poland.
- "Ill Scarlett . . . Frankly." Article interviews members of a band that is gaining popularity with skiers and snowboarders.
- Sample dept/column: "Personal Trainer" talks about nutrition for winter athletes.

Rights and Payment
First rights. All material, payment rates vary. Pays 30 days after publication. Provides 2 author's copies.

Editor's Comments
Resort reviews and feature articles are most open to new writers. We would also like to see pieces on off-beat ways for teens to stay active during the winter.

Christian Light Publications
P.O. Box 1212
Harrisonburg, VA 22803-1212

Editor: Etta Martin

Description and Interests
Through stories and activities, this publication promotes the beliefs of the Mennonite religion. Related articles also strengthen religious values and gently show the way of positive living.
- **Audience:** 9–14 years
- **Frequency:** Monthly
- **Distribution:** Sunday schools; subscription
- **Circulation:** 6,542
- **Website: www.clp.org**

Freelance Potential
98% written by nonstaff writers. Publishes 200–500 freelance submissions yearly; 5% by unpublished writers, 5% by authors who are new to the magazine. Receives 720–960 unsolicited mss yearly.

Submissions
Send complete ms. Prefers email submissions to partners@clp.org. Accepts hard copy, disk submissions, and simultaneous submissions if identified. SASE. Responds in 6 weeks.
Articles: 200–800 words. Informational articles. Topics include nature, customs, and biblical history.
Fiction: 400–1,600 words. Stories that emphasize Mennonite beliefs and biblical interpretations.
Other: Puzzles and activities with Christian themes. Poetry, no line limits. Submit seasonal material 6 months in advance.

Sample Issue
16 pages (no advertising): 2 articles; 4 stories; 7 activities; 5 poems. Sample copy, free with 9x12 SASE ($.87 postage). Guidelines and theme list available.
- "Helping Your Grandparents." Article expands a real-life experience into an example of general respect.
- "Better than Gold." Story relates how early study of Bible verses can be a comfort when one is older.
- Sample poem: "Coming of the Holy Spirit" explains the meaning of Pentecost.

Rights and Payment
First, reprint, or multiple use rights. Articles and stories, $.03–$.05 per word. Poetry, $.35–$.75 per line. Other material, payment rates vary. Pays on acceptance. Provides 1 contributor's copy.

Editor's Comments
We need material relevant to our theme list that will inspire our young readers, portray a spiritual lesson, and build conviction and Christian character.

Pediatrics for Parents

P.O. Box 63716
Philadelphia, PA 19147

Editor: Richard J. Sagall, M.D.

Description and Interests
Pediatrics for Parents strives to present an informed, common-sense approach to childhood health care, with an emphasis on preventive action.
- **Audience:** Parents
- **Frequency:** Monthly
- **Distribution:** 100% subscription
- **Circulation:** 500
- **Website: www.pedsforparents.com**

Freelance Potential
50% written by nonstaff writers. Publishes 30 freelance submissions yearly; 50% by unpublished writers, 50% by authors who are new to the magazine. Receives 50 queries and unsolicited mss yearly.

Submissions
Query or send complete ms. Prefers email submissions to articles@pedsforparents.com. Accepts hard copy. SASE. Response time varies.
Articles: 750–1,500 words. Informational articles. Topics include prevention, fitness, medical advancements, new treatments, wellness, and pregnancy.
Depts/columns: Word lengths vary. New product information and article reprints.

Sample Issue
12 pages (no advertising): 10 articles; 2 depts/columns. Sample copy, $3. Guidelines available.
- "The New 'Super Staph'—MRSA." Article provides information about a new "superbug" version of the staph virus and how to avoid infection.
- "Amblyopia." Article describes a condition in which one eye has reduced or dim vision but is otherwise healthy.
- Sample dept/column: "Perspectives on Parenting" talks about the use of pacifiers and security blankets to soothe children.

Rights and Payment
First rights. Written material, to $25. Pays on publication. Provides 3 contributor's copies and a 1-year subscription.

Editor's Comments
We publish medically accurate articles that are useful to parents of children from prenatal to the early teens. Articles by non-medical authorities must be original, well-researched, and factual. We're not interested in "first-person" pieces unless they contain a large amount of useful information.

Piedmont Parent

P.O. Box 11740
Winston-Salem, NC 27116

Editor: Leigh Ann McDonald Woodruff

Description and Interests
Piedmont Parent offers regional news and information pertinent to families in Guilford and Forsyth counties in North Carolina.
- **Audience:** Parents
- **Frequency:** Monthly
- **Distribution:** 100% newsstand
- **Circulation:** 34,000
- **Website: www.piedmontparent.com**

Freelance Potential
50% written by nonstaff writers. Publishes 36–40 freelance submissions yearly; 25% by unpublished writers, 50% by authors who are new to the magazine. Receives 1,000+ queries and unsolicited mss yearly.

Submissions
Query or send complete ms. Accepts email submissions to editor@piedmontparent.com (Microsoft Word) and simultaneous submissions if identified. Responds in 2 months.
Articles: 500–1,200 words. Informational and how-to articles; and interviews. Topics include child development, day care, summer camps, gifted and special education, local and regional news, science, social issues, sports, popular culture, health, and travel.
Depts/columns: 600–900 words. Parent news and health updates.
Other: Family games and activities.

Sample Issue
36 pages (47% advertising): 6 articles; 4 depts/columns; 1 directory. Sample copy, free with 9x12 SASE ($1.50 postage). Writers' guidelines and theme list available.
- "Wacky Watermelons." Article covers the many ways to cut and serve this delicious summer fruit.
- "Determining Your Child's Learning Ability and Style." Article provides information on the different learning styles that children can have.
- Sample dept/column: "Family Health Notes" offers reviews on products to help keep families safe.

Rights and Payment
One-time rights. Written material, payment rates vary. Pays on publication. Provides 1 tearsheet.

Editor's Comments
Prospective authors should review our theme list prior to submitting material. Our feature articles require thorough research with a minimum of three sources.

Pikes Peak Parent

30 South Prospect Street
Colorado Springs, CO 80903

Editor: Lisa Carpenter

Description and Interests
This tabloid mixes information about local events and regional resources with profiles of local personalities and general articles on family issues and raising children. It is distributed free throughout the Colorado Springs area.
- **Audience:** Parents
- **Frequency:** Monthly
- **Distribution:** Unavailable
- **Circulation:** 30,000
- **Website:** www.pikespeakparent.com

Freelance Potential
5% written by nonstaff writers. Publishes 4 freelance submissions yearly; 2% by authors who are new to the magazine. Receives 60 queries yearly.

Submissions
Query with writing samples. No unsolicited mss. Accepts hard copy and email queries to parent@gazette.com. SASE. Response time varies.
Articles: 800–1,500 words. Informational and how-to articles. Topics include regional news, local resources, parenting, family life, sports, travel, social issues, and recreation.
Depts/columns: Word lengths vary. Health, fatherhood, family destinations, news.

Sample Issue
46 pages (50% advertising): 8 articles; 9 depts/columns; 1 camp guide; 1 calendar; 4 directories. Sample copy, free with 9x12 SASE.
- "Fun Father's Day Ideas." Article features offbeat ideas for activities to do with dad.
- "Keeping Fit for Baby." Articles details a safe, effective exercise program for pregnant women.
- Sample dept/column: "Moms at the Wheel" reviews family-friendly cars.

Rights and Payment
Buys all rights on original content when assigned, and second rights. Written material, payment rates vary. Pays on publication. Provides 1 contributor's copy.

Editor's Comments
Articles that demonstrate thorough research and an excellent writing ability will have the best chance for publication. We want pieces that have a local slant and include quotes from local experts and references to local resources. Please don't send personal essays about parenting; we receive too many.

Pittsburgh Parent

P.O. Box 374
Bakerstown, PA 15007

Editor: Pat Poshard

Description and Interests
Articles about parenting children of all ages appear in this magazine for Pittsburgh-area residents. It fills its pages with advice, information, tips, reviews, and updates on local events.
- **Audience:** Parents
- **Frequency:** Monthly
- **Distribution:** Subscription; newsstand; schools
- **Circulation:** 65,000
- **Website:** www.pittsburghparent.com

Freelance Potential
90% written by nonstaff writers. Publishes 50 freelance submissions yearly; 20% by authors who are new to the magazine. Receives 1,500 queries and unsolicited mss yearly.

Submissions
Query or send complete ms. Accepts hard copy, email submissions to editor@pittsburghparent.com, and simultaneous submissions if identified. SASE. Response time varies.
Articles: Cover story, 2,500–2,750 words. Other material, 400–900 words. Informational articles; profiles; and interviews. Topics include family issues, parenting, education, science, fitness, health, nature, the environment, college, computers, and multicultural subjects.
Depts/columns: Word lengths vary. Humor; education issues; book reviews; teen issues.
Other: Submit seasonal material 3 months in advance.

Sample Issue
44 pages (65% advertising): 7 articles; 4 depts/columns. Sample copy, free. Guidelines and editorial calendar available.
- "Taking the Lead in Sportsmanship." Article discusses the importance of parent role models in organized sports for kids.
- Sample dept/column: "Books" explores ways to entice reluctant readers.

Rights and Payment
First serial rights. All material, payment rates vary. Pays 45 days after publication. Provides 1 tearsheet.

Editor's Comments
All submissions must either be specific to this region or include information about local resources. We will consider personal stories from parents.

Plays

P.O. Box 600160
Newton, MA 02460

Editor: Elizabeth Preston

Description and Interests
Eight to ten easy-to-perform one-act plays are featured in each issue of *Plays*, a magazine that provides wholesome and entertaining dramatic material for students in elementary school through high school.
- **Audience:** 6–17 years
- **Frequency:** 7 times each school year
- **Distribution:** 100% subscription
- **Circulation:** 5,300
- **Website: www.playsmag.com**

Freelance Potential
100% written by nonstaff writers. Publishes 40–45 freelance submissions yearly; 25% by unpublished writers, 50% by authors who are new to the magazine. Receives 240–264 queries and unsolicited mss yearly.

Submissions
Query for adaptations of classics and folktales. Send complete ms for other material. Accepts hard copy. SASE. Responds to queries in 2 weeks, to mss in 1 month.
Fiction: One-act plays for high school, to 5,000 words; for middle school, to 3,750 words; for elementary school, to 2,500 words. Also publishes skits, monologues, and dramatized classics. Genres include patriotic, historical, and biographical drama; mystery; melodrama; comedy; and farce.
Other: Submit material for seasonal school holidays 4 months in advance.

Sample Issue
64 pages (5% advertising): 9 plays. Sample copy, free. Guidelines available.
- "For Love of Ginny." Play for the upper grades centers around a selfish high school senior who learns about compassion when his sister becomes ill.
- "Chronicles of Numeria." Skit uses puns, jokes, and music to make math come alive for young students.
- "A Twist of Fate." Play retells the Aesop's fable in which a slave's life is spared because of his kindness to a lion.

Rights and Payment
All rights. Written material, payment rates vary. Pays on acceptance. Provides 1 contributor's copy.

Editor's Comments
Please request our manuscript specification sheet and sample manuscript before submitting your play.

Pockets

The Upper Room
1908 Grand Avenue
P.O. Box 340004
Nashville, TN 37203-0004

Editor: Lynn W. Gilliam

Description and Interests
Stories, poems, activities, and prayers that help to foster a relationship with God are featured in this Christian magazine for children.
- **Audience:** 6–11 years
- **Frequency:** 11 times each year
- **Distribution:** 100% subscription
- **Circulation:** 98,000
- **Website: www.pockets.org**

Freelance Potential
98% written by nonstaff writers. Publishes 220 freelance submissions yearly; 40% by unpublished writers, 20% by authors who are new to the magazine. Receives 2,000 unsolicited mss yearly.

Submissions
Send complete ms. Accepts hard copy. Availability of artwork improves chance of acceptance. SASE. Responds in 6 weeks.
Articles: 400–1,000 words. Informational articles; profiles; and personal experience. Topics include multicultural and community issues; persons whose lives reflect their Christian commitment.
Fiction: 600–1,400 words. Stories that demonstrate Christian values.
Depts/columns: Word lengths vary. Recipes and Scripture readings.
Artwork: Color prints; 2–4 photos per submission for nonfiction submissions.
Other: Puzzles, activities, games, and poetry.

Sample Issue
48 pages (no advertising): 2 articles; 6 stories; 7 depts/columns; 2 activities; 3 poems. Sample copy, free with 9x12 SASE (4 first-class stamps). Guidelines and theme list available at website.
- "Through the Valley." Story tells of a young girl who turns to God to help her overcome her fear.
- Sample dept/column: "Peacemakers at Work" takes a look at an after-school Bible study and community service club in Kansas.

Rights and Payment
First and second rights. Written material, $.14 per word. Poetry, $2 per line. Games, $25–$50. Pays on acceptance. Provides 3–5 contributor's copies.

Editor's Comments
We are seeking articles on children involved in environmental, community, and peacemaking efforts.

Pointe

110 William Street, 23rd Floor
New York, NY 10038

Managing Editor: Jocelyn Anderson

Description and Interests
Dedicated to covering the world of ballet, this glossy magazine is read by students, fans, and leaders in the field. It provides informative and practical articles, photos, profiles, news, tips, and coverage of events.
- **Audience:** 10–18 years
- **Frequency:** 6 times each year
- **Distribution:** Unavailable
- **Circulation:** 40,000
- **Website:** www.pointemagazine.com

Freelance Potential
75% written by nonstaff writers. Publishes 5 freelance submissions yearly; 10% by unpublished writers, 25% by authors who are new to the magazine. Receives 25 unsolicited mss yearly.

Submissions
Query. Accepts hard copy. SASE. Responds in 2 months.
Articles: 1,200 words. Informational articles; personal experience pieces; photo-essays; profiles; and interviews. Topics include ballet news, events, places, people, and trends.
Depts/columns: 800–1,000 words. Happenings, premieres, opinions, performance information, equipment, and costumes.
Artwork: B/W and color prints or transparencies. Line art. Digital photos.

Sample Issue
168 pages (50% advertising): 5 articles; 21 depts/columns. Sample copy available.
- "America's Training Ground." Article takes a look at what's behind the Mid-States Regional Dance America Festival.
- "Summer Intensive Spotlight." Article explores three summer dance programs offered in Massachusetts.
- Sample dept/column: "Body Watch" offers activities to help de-stress after a class or performance.

Rights and Payment
All rights. Written material, payment rates vary. Pays on acceptance. Provides 2 contributor's copies.

Editor's Comments
We are seeking new approaches that explore trends in ballet. Articles should be written in a journalistic style that is easy-to-read. Please note that we do not cover negative issues. Short profiles of ballet companies provide the best opportunities for new writers.

Positive Teens

SATCH Publishing
P.O. Box 301126
Boston, MA 02130-0010

Publisher: Susan Manning

Description and Interests
Positive Teens provides an opportunity for teens and young adults around the world to express their views, real experiences, and creativity.
- **Audience:** 12–21 years
- **Frequency:** 6 times each year
- **Distribution:** Subscription; newsstand; other
- **Circulation:** 30,000
- **Website:** www.positiveteensmag.com

Freelance Potential
85% written by nonstaff writers. Publishes 150–200 freelance submissions yearly; 70% by unpublished writers, 80% by authors who are new to the magazine. Receives 480–600 queries and mss yearly.

Submissions
Query or send complete ms. Accepts hard copy, disk submissions, fax submissions to 617-522-2961, and email submissions to info@positiveteensmag.com. SASE. Responds in 2–3 months.
Articles: To 1,000 words. Informational articles; personal experience pieces; and opinion pieces. Topics include education, friendship, social issues, youth activism, health, fitness, current events, relationships, and humor.
Fiction: 800–1,000 words. Genres include contemporary fiction.
Depts/columns: Word lengths vary. Sports, commentaries, arts and entertainment, and book reviews.
Artwork: 8½x11 B/W or color prints. Line art.
Other: Poetry.

Sample Issue
28 pages (4% advertising): 5 articles; 2 stories; 46 poems; 11 depts/columns. Sample copy, $4.50 with 9x12 SASE. Guidelines available.
- "Big Dreams." Article discusses the importance of teens knowing what career choices are available.
- Sample dept/column: "Having Our Say" presents two personal essays on the difficulties of being a teen.

Rights and Payment
Permissions for exclusive use for 18 months only. Written material, $5–$30. Artwork, payment rates vary. Payment policy varies.

Editor's Comments
We feature real stories by teens everywhere. We would like to see nonfiction articles relevant to issues that affect youth and their future.

Potluck Children's Literary Magazine

P.O. Box 546
Deerfield, IL 60015-0546

Editor-in-Chief: Susan Napoli Picchietti

Description and Interests
This digest-sized literary magazine is written by and for young writers. It includes a mix of short fiction, poetry, and book reviews. Its "Creative Corner" section features articles that enhance writing skills and teach young authors about their craft.
• **Audience:** All ages
• **Frequency:** Quarterly
• **Distribution:** Unavailable
• **Circulation:** Unavailable
• **Website:** www.potluckmagazine.org

Freelance Potential
99% written by nonstaff writers. Publishes 2,400+ freelance submissions yearly; 95% by unpublished writers, 95% by authors who are new to the magazine. Receives 2,400 unsolicited mss yearly.

Submissions
Send complete ms. Accepts hard copy and email submissions to submissions@potluckmagazine.org. No simultaneous submissions. SASE. Response time varies.
Articles: Word lengths vary. Informational and how-to articles. Topics include writing, grammar, and character and story development.
Fiction: To 1,500 words. Genres include contemporary and science fiction, mystery, folktales, and fantasy.
Artwork: 8½x11 color photocopies.
Other: Book reviews, to 250 words. Poetry, to 30 lines.

Sample Issue
48 pages (no advertising): 1 article; 6 stories; 19 poems; 2 book reviews. Sample copy, $5.80. Guidelines available with SASE, at website, and in each issue.
• "The Knight and His Ladies." Story features Sir Lancelot and his encounter with three ladies as he rests beneath a tree.
• "The Zebra With No Stripes." Folktale tells about a white zebra and other animals who are lacking the marks other animals like them usually have.

Rights and Payment
First rights. Provides 1 contributor's copy in lieu of payment.

Editor's Comments
Our purpose is to let young readers express themselves creatively and prepare them for adult markets.

Prehistoric Times

145 Bayline Circle
Folsom, CA 95630-8077

Editor: Mike Fredericks

Description and Interests
Targeting an audience of teens and adults who share an enthusiasm for dinosaurs and other creatures from prehistory, this magazine offers informational articles about paleontology, as well as updates on related art and collectibles.
• **Audience:** YA–Adult
• **Frequency:** Quarterly
• **Distribution:** Subscription; other
• **Circulation:** Unavailable
• **Website:** www.prehistorictimes.com

Freelance Potential
40% written by nonstaff writers. Publishes 12 freelance submissions yearly; 60% by unpublished writers, 40% by authors who are new to the magazine. Receives 24+ unsolicited mss yearly.

Submissions
Send complete ms. Accepts email submissions to pretimes@comcast.net (attach file). Response time varies.
Articles: 1,500–2,000 words. Informational articles. Topics include dinosaurs, paleontology, prehistoric life, drawing dinosaurs, and dinosaur-related collectibles.
Depts/columns: Word lengths vary. Field news, dinosaur models, media reviews, interviews, and in-depth descriptions of dinosaurs and other prehistoric species.

Sample Issue
58 pages (30% advertising): 12 articles; 6 depts/columns. Sample copy, $7. Guidelines available via email to pretimes@comcast.net.
• "Dinosaur Dynasty." Article reports on a new exhibit from China on display in Chicago.
• "Prehistoric Cephalopods." Article presents information and drawings of invertebrates who lived in ancient seas.
• Sample dept/column: "How to Draw Dinosaurs" offers ideas for adding vegetation and other animals to dinosaur scenes.

Rights and Payment
All rights. Written material, payment rates vary. Payment policy varies. Provides contributor's copies.

Editor's Comments
Interviews with scientists are always needed. We also welcome articles about dinosaur collectibles from freelance writers.

Prep Traveler

621 Plainfield Road, Suite 406
Willowbrook, IL 60527

Editorial Coordinator: Kelley Thompson

Description and Interests
Launched in 2005, this digest addresses the growing demand of youth and performance groups and amateur sports and event travel markets. Information is provided on destinations, performance facilities, and issues pertinent to youth group coordinators.
• **Audience:** Youth travel planners
• **Frequency:** Twice each year
• **Distribution:** Unavailable
• **Circulation:** 26,000
• **Website:** www.preptraveler.com

Freelance Potential
5% written by nonstaff writers. Publishes 2–3 freelance submissions yearly; 5% by unpublished writers, 5% by authors who are new to the magazine. Receives 5 queries yearly.

Submissions
Query with résumé and field expertise. Accepts email submissions to kelley@ptmgroups.com (no attachments; copy within email text). Responds in 1 week.
Articles: Word lengths vary. Informational articles and how-to articles and profiles. Topics include travel destinations, music, and health and fitness.
Depts/columns: 700–2,000 words. Information related to youth travel planning.
Other: Submit seasonal material 6 months in advance.

Sample Issue
62 pages (40% advertising): 4 articles; 2 depts/columns. Guidelines and theme list available.
• "Fundraising 101B: Getting Organized." Article gives specific pointers on how to have a successful fundraiser for your group.
• "Dealing with Overbearing Parents." Article suggests ways a youth coordinator can deal positively with a child's parents.
• Sample dept/column: "Destination Showcase" highlights several group destinations with information on lodging, arenas, and activities.

Rights and Payment
All rights. Payment rates vary. Pays on publication. Provides contributor's copies.

Editor's Comments
Our publication looks for advice from experts on student sports and performance markets. The writing style is straightforward with little filler. The column section is most open for editorials from new writers.

Preschool Playhouse

Urban Ministries
P.O. Box 436987
Chicago, IL 60409

Editor: Judith St. Clair Hull, Ph.D.

Description and Interests
This Christian publication is written for young children living in urban areas. Its goal is to provide Christian solutions to real-life problems.
• **Audience:** Preschool children
• **Frequency:** Quarterly
• **Distribution:** 100% religious instruction
• **Circulation:** 50,000
• **Website:** www.urbanministries.com

Freelance Potential
25% written by nonstaff writers. Publishes 12 freelance submissions yearly; 10% by unpublished writers, 25% by authors who are new to the magazine. Receives 50+ unsolicited mss yearly.

Submissions
Send résumé with clips or writing samples. SASE. All material written on assignment. Response time varies.
Articles: Word lengths vary. Informational articles; how-to and personal experience pieces; photo-essays; and Bible stories. Topics include animals, crafts, hobbies, African American history, multicultural and social issues, nature, the environment, and religion.
Depts/columns: Word lengths vary. Games, puzzles, and filler.
Artwork: B/W or color prints or transparencies.

Sample Issue
4 pages: 1 Bible story; 1 contemporary story; 2 activities. Sample copy, $2.99. Guidelines available.
• "Shaquille." Short profile tells of a little boy who learns that when he helps other people, he is serving God.
• "God Makes Us Strong." Bible story based on a verse from Timothy explains how God helps people keep their bodies and minds strong.
• Sample dept/column: "Dear Parents" is an activity page that helps young readers realize their strength comes from the Lord.

Rights and Payment
All rights. Written material, payment rates vary. Pays on publication. Provides 1 contributor's copy.

Editor's Comments
Although all work is done on assignment, we look for writers who have the potential to present age-appropriate information to our readers. We look for Bible stories and activities that reinforce weekly Bible lessons and Scripture passages.

Primary Street

Urban Ministries
1551 Regency Court
Calumet City, IL 60409

Senior Editor: Judith St. Clair Hull, Ph.D.

Description and Interests
Primary Street targets religious education students living in urban areas. Each issue focuses on a Christian theme and includes three months' worth of Scripture lessons, Bible stories, and activities.
- **Audience:** 6–8 years
- **Frequency:** Quarterly
- **Distribution:** Subscription; other
- **Circulation:** 30,000
- **Website: www.urbanministries.com**

Freelance Potential
25% written by nonstaff writers. Publishes 15 freelance submissions yearly; 25% by unpublished writers, 25% by authors who are new to the magazine. Receives 180 queries yearly.

Submissions
Query with résumé or writing samples. All material is by assignment only. SASE. Response time varies.
Articles: Word lengths vary. Informational and how-to articles; personal experience pieces; photo-essays; and Bible stories. Topics include nature, the environment, animals, pets, crafts, hobbies, African history, multicultural and ethnic subjects, regional news, and social issues and concerns.
Depts/columns: Word lengths vary.
Artwork: B/W and color prints or transparencies.
Other: Puzzles, games, activities, and jokes.

Sample Issue
4 pages (no advertising): 1 story; 1 Bible story; 2 activities. Sample copy, $2.99 through website. Writers' guidelines available.
- "Kevin." Short story illustrates how taking turns is a fair way to play.
- "Let's Be Fair!" Bible story based on a passage from Isaiah teaches that God wants us to do what is fair.
- Sample dept/column: "Be Smart" is a word game that reinforces fair play.

Rights and Payment
All rights. Written material, payment rates vary. Pays on publication. Provides 1 contributor's copy.

Editor's Comments
Our Scripture material is based on international Sunday school lessons. We look for material that supports our mission to help children to follow the teachings of Jesus. Remember that all material is written on assignment; we will contact you if we are interested.

Primary Treasure

Pacific Press Publishing
P.O. Box 5353
Nampa, ID 83653-5353

Editor: Aileen Andres Sox

Description and Interests
The Seventh-day Adventist Church publishes this take-home paper for elementary school students who attend Sabbath school. It is filled with true-life, problem-solving stories that teach Christian values and practices.
- **Audience:** 6–9 years
- **Frequency:** Weekly
- **Distribution:** 100% religious instruction
- **Circulation:** 30,000
- **Website: www.primarytreasure.com**

Freelance Potential
10% written by nonstaff writers. Publishes 52 freelance submissions yearly; 10% by unpublished writers, 30% by authors who are new to the magazine. Receives 240 unsolicited mss yearly.

Submissions
Query for serials. Send complete ms for other submissions. Accepts hard copy, email submissions to ailsox@pacificpress.com, and simultaneous submissions if identified. SASE. Responds in 4 months.
Articles: 600–1,000 words. Features true stories about children in Christian settings and true, problem-solving pieces that help children learn about themselves in relation to God and others. All material must be consistent with Seventh-day Adventist beliefs and practices.
Other: Submit seasonal material 7 months in advance.

Sample Issue
16 pages (no advertising): 5 true-life stories; 2 Bible lessons; 1 puzzle. Sample copy, free with 9x12 SASE (2 first-class stamps). Guidelines available.
- "To Give or Not to Give." Story tells about an eight-year-old boy who gives his birthday money to the church paving fund.
- "Gina's Mission." Story features a girl who misses her American friends when she goes with her parents on a mission to Paraguay.

Rights and Payment
One-time rights. Written material, $25–$50. Pays on acceptance. Provides 3 contributor's copies.

Editor's Comments
We look for age-appropriate writing that conveys a positive Christian message that young children can relate to.

Principal

1615 Duke Street
Alexandria, VA 22314

Director of Publications: Lee Greene

Description and Interests
Articles on school administration and policies, health issues, teacher morale, and other topics that are of interest to elementary and middle school principals can be found in this resourceful magazine.
- **Audience:** K–8 school administrators
- **Frequency:** 5 times each year
- **Distribution:** 100% controlled
- **Circulation:** 36,000
- **Website:** www.naesp.org

Freelance Potential
90% written by nonstaff writers. Publishes 20 freelance submissions yearly; 80% by authors who are new to the magazine. Receives 84 unsolicited mss each year.

Submissions
Query or send complete ms. Accepts hard copy and email submissions to publications@naesp.org. SASE. Responds in 1 month.
Articles: 1,000–1,800 words. Informational and instructional articles; profiles; and opinion and personal experience pieces. Topics include elementary education, gifted and special education, parenting, mentoring, science, and computers.
Depts/columns: 750–1,500 words. Classroom management issues, legal issues, and technology.

Sample Issue
64 pages (25% advertising): 12 articles; 12 depts/columns. Sample copy, $8. Writers' guidelines and theme list available.
- "Curbing Childhood Obesity: Physical Activity Can Make a Difference." Article offers examples on how principals and schools can help promote exercise.
- "The Ideal Beverage." Article discusses how schools can improve milk consumption by offering new flavors and packaging.
- Sample dept/column: "Practitioner's Corner" takes a look at ways to plan a successful fundraiser.

Rights and Payment
All North American serial rights. No payment. Provides 3 contributor's copies.

Editor's Comments
Feel free to use quotes, data, and pertinent anecdotes from any source, including your personal experience, but please avoid excessive documentation and technical terms. Articles on innovative ideas are welcome.

Puget Sound Parent

211 2nd Avenue West
Seattle, WA 98119

Editor: Wenda Reed

Description and Interests
Parents of children in the Puget Sound region receive this magazine at no cost and benefit from the timely and informative articles on childcare, education, health, and family entertainment.
- **Audience:** Parents
- **Frequency:** Monthly
- **Distribution:** 100% newsstand
- **Circulation:** 20,000
- **Website:** www.pugetsoundparent.com

Freelance Potential
75% written by nonstaff writers. Publishes 24 freelance submissions yearly; 15% by unpublished writers, 25% by authors who are new to the magazine. Receives 240 queries yearly.

Submissions
Query with outline. Send queries for local stories to above. Send queries on national interest stories to Editor, United Parenting Publications, 15400 Knoll Trail, Suite 400, Dallas, TX 75248. Accepts hard copy and simultaneous submissions if identified. SASE. Responds in 2 weeks.
Articles: Word lengths vary. Informational, and how-to articles; and personal experience pieces. Topics include family and parenting issues, health, fitness, gifted and special education, regional news, travel, and social issues.
Depts/columns: Word lengths vary. Profiles, essays, and media reviews.

Sample Issue
40 pages (30% advertising): 2 articles; 8 depts/columns. Sample copy, $3. Writers' guidelines and theme list available.
- "Destination Play!" Article looks at nine great play spaces for the family to explore in summer.
- Sample dept/column: "Health Notes" looks at the importance of teaching children how to properly wash their hands.

Rights and Payment
Rights vary. Written material, $100–$450. Pays on acceptance. Provides 2 contributor's copies.

Editor's Comments
We are interested in seeing more pieces on education and fascinating people who are enriching the lives of children. Articles should have wide application to the majority of our readers, rather than a narrow focus.

Queens Parent

350 Fifth Avenue, Suite 2420
New York, NY 10118

Executive Editor: Helen Freedman

Description and Interests
Queens Parent offers its readers informative articles on family matters, raising children, and regional news. Local services and events in the metropolitan area are covered in each issue of this parenting publication. Parents and families in Queens, New York, read this tabloid for its useful and informative articles.
- **Audience:** Parents
- **Frequency:** Monthly
- **Distribution:** 100% controlled
- **Circulation:** 68,000
- **Website:** www.parentsknow.com

Freelance Potential
10% written by nonstaff writers. Publishes 20 freelance submissions yearly; 25% by authors who are new to the magazine. Receives 300 queries yearly.

Submissions
Query or send complete ms. Prefers email submissions to hellonwheels@parentsknow.com. Accepts hard copy. SASE. Responds to queries in 1 week.
Articles: 800–1,000 words. Informational and how-to articles; profiles; interviews; humor; and personal experience pieces. Topics include family issues, health, fitness, humor, nature, current events, gifted and special education, nutrition, crafts, and regional news.
Depts/columns: 750 words. News and reviews.
Other: Submit seasonal material 4 months in advance.

Sample Issue
64 pages (60% advertising): 6 articles; 5 depts/columns; 1 party guide; 1 calendar of events. Sample copy, free. Guidelines available.
- "Pregnancy Preparedness." Article lists important steps in getting ready for baby and the benefits of planning ahead.
- Sample dept/column: "Family Health Update" discusses the latest research on the dangers of overexposure to the sun.

Rights and Payment
First New York area rights. No payment.

Editor's Comments
We are very open to new writers. Understand that we are news-oriented and we always try to keep a New York City focus. Material should be timely with new spins on intelligent approaches. Currently we are not reading work on travel or general child-raising topics.

Ranger Rick

National Wildlife Federation
1100 Wildlife Center Drive
Reston, VA 20190-5362

Editor: Gerald Bishop

Description and Interests
Published by the National Wildlife Federation, *Ranger Rick* provides young readers with stories, articles, photo-essays, puzzles, games, and activities related to nature and the environment.
- **Audience:** 7–12 years
- **Frequency:** Monthly
- **Distribution:** 100% subscription
- **Circulation:** 560,000
- **Website:** www.nwf.org/gowild

Freelance Potential
10% written by nonstaff writers. Publishes 1–2 freelance submissions yearly; 1% by authors who are new to the magazine. Receives 1,200 queries yearly.

Submissions
Query with outline and sample paragraph. Accepts hard copy. SASE. Response time varies.
Articles: 900 words. Informational articles. Topics include nature, animals, crafts, the environment, outdoor adventure, dinosaurs, oceanography, and insects.
Fiction: 900 words. Genres include mystery, adventure, fantasy, fables, and stories about nature.
Depts/columns: Staff written.
Artwork: 35mm color prints or illustrations.
Other: Puzzles on topics related to nature. Submit seasonal material 1 month in advance.

Sample Issue
40 pages (no advertising): 6 articles; 1 story; 2 depts/columns; 1 poem. Guidelines available.
- "Walking on Water." Article explains how some animals—both big and small—are able to walk or run across the surface of water without sinking.
- "Parrot Pair-Ups." Article tells about a German woman who works to match up parrots so they won't lead lonely lives in captivity.

Rights and Payment
Rights vary. All material, payment rates vary. Pays on acceptance. Provides 2 contributor's copies.

Editor's Comments
Our writers have a strong appreciation and knowledge of nature, wildlife, and the outdoors, and they write about these topics with passion and a keen sense for what excites young readers. We need stories that have such flair and conviction that even reluctant readers are motivated to read them.

The Reading Teacher

International Reading Association
800 Barksdale Road
P.O. Box 8139
Newark, DE 19714-8139

Assistant Editor: Christina Lambert

Description and Interests
Subscribers to this peer-reviewed professional journal are involved in the literary education of children up to the age of 12. Its content focuses on effective classroom techniques, reading research, and the role of educational technology in the teaching of literacy.
- **Audience:** Educators
- **Frequency:** 8 times each year
- **Distribution:** 100% subscription
- **Circulation:** 57,500
- **Website:** www.reading.org

Freelance Potential
99% written by nonstaff writers. Publishes 50 freelance submissions yearly; 20% by unpublished writers, 30% by authors who are new to the magazine. Receives 348 unsolicited mss yearly.

Submissions
Submit manuscripts online by creating an account at http://mc.manuscriptcentral.com/ira. Responds in 1–2 months.
Articles: To 6,000 words. Informational and how-to articles; profiles; and personal experience pieces. Topics include literacy, reading education, instructional techniques, classroom strategies, reading research, and educational technology.
Depts/columns: 1,500–2,500 words. Reviews of children's books, teaching tips, and material on cultural diversity.

Sample Issue
102 pages (17% advertising): 6 articles; 4 depts/columns. Sample copy, $10. Guidelines available.
- "The Family Stories Project: Using Funds of Knowledge for Writing." Article reports on how students in a fourth-grade bi-literacy class wrote and translated family stories to improve skills in both languages.
- Sample dept/column: "International Voices" provides details on the Programme for International Student Assessment.

Rights and Payment
All rights. No payment. Provides 5 contributor's copies for articles, 2 copies for depts/columns.

Editor's Comments
We're looking for practices, research, and trends in literacy education and related fields. We need both full-length articles and shorter pieces that offer effective teaching tips.

Reading Today

International Reading Association
800 Barksdale Road
P.O. Box 8139
Newark, DE 19714-8139

Editor-in-Chief: John Micklos, Jr.

Description and Interests
This newspaper addresses the needs and interests of an international audience involved in reading education at all levels, from preschool through adult education.
- **Audience:** IRA members
- **Frequency:** 6 times each year
- **Distribution:** 100% subscription
- **Circulation:** 88,000
- **Website:** www.reading.org

Freelance Potential
30% written by nonstaff writers. Publishes 25 freelance submissions yearly; 10% by unpublished writers, 25% by authors who are new to the magazine. Receives 180 queries and unsolicited mss yearly.

Submissions
Prefers query; accepts complete ms. Accepts hard copy and simultaneous submissions if identified. SASE. Responds in 1 month.
Articles: 500–1,000 words. Informational and factual articles; and interviews. Topics include community programs, staffing, assessment, funding, censorship, and reading education.
Depts/columns: To 750 words. Classroom ideas and anecdotes, ideas for administrators, and tips for parents and children reading together.
Artwork: B/W and color prints. Line art.
Other: Puzzles, activities, and poetry,

Sample Issue
40 pages (30% advertising): 3 articles; 12 depts/columns. Sample copy, $6. Guidelines available.
- "The Right Direction." Article discusses the early days of E. B. White's writing career.
- Sample dept/column: "Interview with Claude Goldenberg" presents the views of the executive director of the Center for Language Minority Education and Research.

Rights and Payment
One-time rights. Written material, $.20–$.30 per word. Pays on publication. Provides 3 contributor's copies.

Editor's Comments
We invite readers to submit articles on a broad variety of topics relating to reading and reading education. We're looking for information on innovative reading programs and coverage of important conferences. Anything that will help reading professionals can be a potential article.

Real Sports

P.O. Box 8204
San Jose, CA 95155

Submissions Editor: Brian Styers

Description and Interests
Currently published exclusively online, *Real Sports* aims to increase media coverage of women's sports by generating more enthusiasm and increasing audience numbers. To encourage readers to give more attention to these sports, articles are written in a lively tone and cover the latest in women's sports.
- **Audience:** 9–18 years; Adults
- **Frequency:** Monthly
- **Distribution:** 100% Internet
- **Hits per month:** Unavailable
- **Website:** www.realsportsmag.com

Freelance Potential
75% written by nonstaff writers. Publishes 40 freelance submissions yearly; 5% by unpublished writers, 50% by authors who are new to the magazine. Receives 24 queries yearly.

Submissions
Query with brief summary. No unsolicited mss. Accepts email queries to info2@realsportsmag.com.
Articles: 1,500–2,000 words. Informational and how-to articles; profiles; and interviews. Topics include training, tennis, track and field, basketball, baseball, skating, golf, skiing, soccer, and sports personalities.
Depts/columns: 750–1,000 words. Opinion pieces, book reviews, news, and profiles.

Sample Issue
Guidelines available online.
- "Milestones Approaching." Article reviews the 2005 women's basketball season.
- "Surprises: Swoopes and Portland, College Hoops & Your Call – Best Athlete, Most Important Moments." Article follows the changes occurring in women's basketball and what they portend.
- "College Hoops, Lifestyle Tensions, TV Viewing, Eyes on the Strips and WNBA Off-Season Moves." Article provides short commentary on many aspects of women's basketball.

Rights and Payment
First rights. Written material, payment rates vary. Pays on publication.

Editor's Comments
Our aim is to remain on the cutting edge of women's sports coverage, keep our attitude, and bring about more media coverage. We're looking for compelling writing that communicates the excitement of the game.

Resource

6401 The Paseo
Kansas City, MO 64131

Managing Editor: Shirley Smith

Description and Interests
This denominational magazine includes ideas and fresh applications and suggestions for teaching and equipping Sunday school leaders, teachers, and workers with the inspiration and tools they need to help them in their ministries. It targets teachers who use the WordAction curriculum.
- **Audience:** Sunday school teachers
- **Frequency:** Quarterly
- **Distribution:** 100% subscription
- **Circulation:** 30,000
- **Website:** www.nazarene.org

Freelance Potential
90–95% written by nonstaff writers. Publishes 100 freelance submissions yearly; 5–10% by unpublished writers, 5–10% by authors who are new to the magazine. Receives 144+ unsolicited mss yearly.

Submissions
Send complete ms. Accepts hard copy and email submissions to ssmith@nazarene.org. SASE. Responds in 5 days.
Articles: 800 words. Informational, how-to, and self-help articles; and personal experience pieces. Topics include religion, education, and Sunday school programs and curricula.

Sample Issue
24 pages (no advertising): 20 articles. Sample copy, free with 9x12 SASE. Guidelines available.
- "Fun on the Floor." Article describes simple and inexpensive ideas for helping babies have fun while exploring on the floor.
- "Creating a Resource Room." Article offers suggestions for setting up a resource room.
- "Let's Get Organized." Article explains ways to get and keep classrooms in order.

Rights and Payment
All and second rights. Written material, $.05 per word. Pays on publication. Provides 1 contributor's copy.

Editor's Comments
We look for practical articles that will help equip Sunday school teachers as they strive to maximize spiritual growth in young adults. We're also interested in articles that support outreach efforts, as well as those that explore ways to build and strengthen community involvement. Be sure to offer how-to's, examples, and illustrations. Seasonal themes are welcome.

Richmond Parents Monthly

5511 Staples Mill Road, Suite 103
Richmond, VA 23228

Editor: Angela Lehman-Rios

Description and Interests
Families new to the Richmond area as well as long-time residents turn to this tabloid for information on community news and events. Discussions of general parenting issues appear along with party planning tips, camp information, and Q&As.
- **Audience:** Parents
- **Frequency:** Monthly
- **Distribution:** 100% controlled
- **Circulation:** 30,000
- **Website:** www.richmondparents.com

Freelance Potential
90% written by nonstaff writers. Publishes 70–90 freelance submissions yearly; 5% by authors who are new to the magazine. Receives 600 queries yearly.

Submissions
Query. Accepts email queries to mail@richmondpublishing.com. Availability of artwork improves chance of acceptance. Responds in 1–3 weeks.
Articles: 600–1,000 words. Informational and self-help articles. Topics include the arts, camps for children, pets, home and garden, birthday parties, school, education, women's health, and holidays.
Depts/columns: Word lengths vary. Family-related news, media reviews, technology.
Artwork: Color prints and transparencies.

Sample Issue
40 pages (15% advertising): 7 articles; 5 depts/columns; 1 calendar. Sample copy, free. Editorial calendar available.
- "Number 2 Pencils, Anyone?" Article discusses issues related to private schools and standardized testing.
- "Parties with Purpose." Article profiles children who have decided to have "present-less" parties to benefit local charities.

Rights and Payment
One-time rights. Written material, $.12 per word. Pays on publication.

Editor's Comments
For the coming year, we would like to see more articles about schools and educational issues. These pieces should have a local slant. We prefer to work with writers who are from Virginia and are familiar with issues important to the families who live here.

The Rock

Cook Communications Ministries
4050 Lee Vance View
Colorado Springs, CO 80918

Editor: Gail Rohlfing

Description and Interests
Designed for middle school children, *The Rock* is a tool used in Sunday school classes. This paper is published by Cook Communications Ministries and features Bible stories, daily devotions, and activities, all of which are intended to help children develop their relationship with God.
- **Audience:** 10–14 years
- **Frequency:** Weekly during the school year
- **Distribution:** 100% religious instruction
- **Circulation:** 65,000
- **Website:** www.cookministries.com

Freelance Potential
10% written by nonstaff writers. Publishes 2–3 freelance submissions yearly; 20% by unpublished writers.

Submissions
Query with résumé or writing samples. SASE. Response time varies.
Articles: Word lengths vary. Informational articles; personal experience pieces; profiles; and interviews. Also publishes meditations, allegories, and Bible lessons.
Fiction: Word lengths vary. Genres include inspirational, contemporary, and historical fiction; adventure; and real-life and problem-solving stories.
Other: Puzzles, quizzes, activities, and poetry.

Sample Issue
8 pages (no advertising): 1 article; 1 Bible study; 2 depts/columns. Guidelines available at website.
- "Precious in His Sight." Article shares the story of a pastor who learned of his value to God.
- "Custom Made." Bible story features the Scripture of Jeremiah.
- Sample dept/column: "Known Best, Loved Best" offers daily devotions for each day of the week.

Rights and Payment
Rights negotiable. All material, payment rates vary. Pays on acceptance. Provides 1 contributor's copy.

Editor's Comments
Our goal is to help children understand the messages of the Bible and develop a relationship with God. Based entirely on Scripture, the contents of *The Rock* correlate with the Sunday school curriculum. At this time, we are not accepting unsolicited manuscripts. If you have an idea that teaches and reinforces the truth of the Bible, send us a query for consideration.

Sacramento/Sierra Parent

457 Grass Valley Highway, Suite 5
Auburn, CA 95603

Editor-in-Chief: Shelly Bokman

Description and Interests
Distributed free to parents throughout the Sacramento and Sierra Foothills of California, this magazine features articles on topics such as family issues, health, fitness, finances, education, and child development.
- **Audience:** Parents and grandparents
- **Frequency:** Monthly
- **Distribution:** 70% newsstand; 27% schools; 3% subscription
- **Circulation:** 50,000
- **Website: www.ssparent.com**

Freelance Potential
75% written by nonstaff writers. Publishes 75 freelance submissions yearly; 5–10% by unpublished writers, 70% by authors who are new to the magazine. Receives 780 queries yearly.

Submissions
Query with list of topics and writing samples. Accepts email queries to ssparent@pacbell.net. Response time varies.
Articles: 700–1,000 words. Informational and how-to articles; personal experience pieces; and humor. Topics include fitness, family finance, alternative education, family travel, learning disabilities, grandparenting, sports, adoption, and regional news.
Depts/columns: 400–500 words. Child development, opinions, and hometown highlights.
Other: Activities and filler. Submit seasonal material 2–3 months in advance.

Sample Issue
50 pages (50% advertising): 4 articles; 13 depts/columns. Sample copy, free with 9x12 SASE ($1.29 postage). Writers' guidelines and theme list/editorial calendar available.
- "Swim Lessons: Whose Decision Is It?" Article discusses the importance of leaving the decision of whether to take swimming lessons to parents.
- Sample dept/column: "Let's Play" explores gardening with children.

Rights and Payment
Second rights. Articles, $50+. Depts/columns, $25–$40. Pays on publication. Provides author's copies.

Editor's Comments
We try to balance articles so that every age group is covered in each issue, and seek material that is informative, readable, and free of technical jargon.

St. Louis Parent

P.O. Box 190287
St. Louis, MO 63119

Editor: Barb MacRobie

Description and Interests
This free publication is distributed in the St. Louis, Missouri, area for parents and caregivers. Each issue offers information on family health, child-rearing, education, camps, and local services.
- **Audience:** Parents
- **Frequency:** 10 times each year
- **Distribution:** Newsstands; hospitals; schools
- **Circulation:** 45,000

Freelance Potential
90% written by nonstaff writers. Publishes 30–50 freelance submissions yearly; 5% by unpublished writers, 25% by authors who are new to the magazine. Receives 60 queries yearly.

Submissions
Query with résumé, outline/synopsis, and clips or writing samples. Accepts hard copy and simultaneous submissions if identified. SASE. Response time varies.
Articles: 700 words. Informational and how-to articles. Topics include education; family health; safety; nutrition; child care; personal finances; and regional resources, services, and events.
Other: Submit seasonal material 6 months in advance.

Sample Issue
18 pages (40% advertising): 5 articles; 1 summer camp directory. Sample copy, free with 9x12 SASE ($1 postage). Writer's guidelines and editorial calendar available.
- "A Loving Home Is Crucial." Article emphasizes the importance of creating a loving environment for a child's well being.
- "Like Family—The Au Pair Childcare Difference." Article shares a family's positive experience in choosing an au pair to help care for their children.
- "Local Author's Book Helps Children Say 'Hello' to People with Disabilities." Article discusses a book written to help children understand disabilities.

Rights and Payment
All rights. Articles, $50. Other material, payment rates vary. Pays on acceptance. Provides 2 author's copies.

Editor's Comments
Topics of interest to parents, especially hot topics with a local slant, are what we look for. We seek well-researched articles on education, local schools, and technology. Writers with knowledge of the region should query first with their article ideas.

San Diego Family Magazine

P.O. Box 23960
San Diego, CA 92193

Publisher & Editor: Sharon Bay

Description and Interests
This regional magazine is chock-full of informative articles on topics related to positive parenting. In addition, it includes information on regional resources and events. It is read by parents and families living in the San Diego area.
- **Audience:** Parents
- **Frequency:** Monthly
- **Distribution:** 99% controlled; 1% other
- **Circulation:** 120,000
- **Website:** www.sandiegofamily.com

Freelance Potential
90% written by nonstaff writers. Publishes 50 freelance submissions yearly; 50% by unpublished writers. Receives 360–600 queries and unsolicited mss yearly.

Submissions
Query or send complete ms with sample clip. Accepts hard copy, disk submissions (Microsoft Word), and email submissions to family@sandiegofamily.com. SASE. Responds to queries in 6–8 weeks, to mss in 2–3 months.
Articles: 750–1,000 words. Informational, how-to and self-help articles. Topics include parenting, gifted and special education, family issues, travel, health, fitness, sports, and multicultural issues. Also publishes humorous articles.
Depts/columns: Word lengths vary. Book reviews, restaurant reviews, advice, health, and the home.
Artwork: 3x5 or 5x7 B/W glossy prints.

Sample Issue
164 pages (60% advertising): 16 articles; 18 depts/columns. Sample copy, $4 with 9x12 SASE ($1 postage). Guidelines available.
- "The Family-Friendly Backyard." Article explains how to transform a backyard into a safe play area.
- "Teen Blogs." Article takes a look at why it is important for parents to read teen blogs.
- Sample dept/column: "Web Watch" offers websites with repair, safety, and house cleaning information.

Rights and Payment
First or second rights and all regional rights. Written material, $1.25 per published column inch. Pays on publication. Provides 1 contributor's copy.

Editor's Comments
We are looking for uplifting articles that stress how important and rewarding the job of parenting is.

Scholastic Choices

Scholastic Inc.
557 Broadway
New York, NY 10012-3999

Editor: Bob Hugel

Description and Interests
This classroom magazine focuses on life skills development for teens. All articles published conform to national standards for character education and for health, family, and consumer sciences education.
- **Audience:** 12–18 years
- **Frequency:** 6 times each year
- **Distribution:** 100% schools
- **Circulation:** 200,000
- **Website:** www.scholastic.com

Freelance Potential
90% written by nonstaff writers. Publishes 30–40 freelance submissions yearly; 10% by unpublished writers. Receives 60 queries, 60 unsolicited mss yearly.

Submissions
Query or send complete ms. Accepts hard copy and email submissions to choicesmag@scholastic.com. SASE. Responds to queries in 2 months, to mss in 3 months.
Articles: 500–1,000 words. Informational and self-help articles and personal experience pieces. Topics include health, fitness, personal development, relationships, safety, social issues, consumer and resource management, careers, sports, the environment, nature, popular culture, nutrition, and substance abuse prevention.
Depts/columns: Staff written.

Sample Issue
36 pages (20% advertising): 5 articles; 7 depts/columns. Sample copy, free with 9x12 SASE. Guidelines and editorial calendar available.
- "The Language of Fat." Article helps teens understand how they can turn their negative words about their bodies into positive language that can help them.
- "The High Road." Article tells of a teen's unfortunate decision to drive under the influence of marijuana.
- "Hooked on Fish." Article profiles a teen who saved a brook trout habitat in her community.

Rights and Payment
All rights. Written material, payment rates vary. Pays on publication. Provides 10 contributor's copies.

Editor's Comments
Query us if you can write a lively article that will help our teen readers develop good decision-making skills relevant to family life, consumer issues, or personal responsibility.

Scholastic DynaMath

Scholastic Inc.
557 Broadway, Room 4052
New York, NY 10012-3999

Editor: Matt Friedman

Description and Interests
Teachers distribute this take-home paper to their math students, who find nonfiction and fiction-based exercises that help teach math, articles that connect math concepts to the real world, and interactive activities that build math skills.
- **Audience:** 8–11 years
- **Frequency:** 8 times each year
- **Distribution:** 100% schools
- **Circulation:** 200,000
- **Website:** www.scholastic.com

Freelance Potential
10% written by nonstaff writers. Publishes 5 freelance submissions yearly; 25% by unpublished writers, 25% by authors who are new to the magazine. Receives 48 queries and unsolicited mss yearly.

Submissions
Query with outline and synopsis; or send complete ms. Accepts hard copy and simultaneous submissions if identified. SASE. Responds in 1–2 months.
Articles: To 600 words. Informational articles about math skills. Topics include critical thinking, chart and graph reading, measurement, addition, subtraction, fractions, division, decimals, problem solving, interdisciplinary issues, popular culture, sports, consumer awareness, geography, nature, and the media.
Other: Filler, puzzles, games, and jokes. Submit holiday material 4–6 months in advance.

Sample Issue
16 pages (no advertising): 3 articles; 8 activities. Sample copy, $4 with 9x12 SASE. Guidelines and editorial calendar available.
- "Hail to the Chef!" Article profiles the White House chef and provides activities that help kids learn how a cook expands a recipe to accommodate a crowd.
- "Baseball by the Numbers." Article explains how to use equivalent fractions and decimals to understand batting averages.

Rights and Payment
All rights. Articles, $250–$400. Puzzles, $25–$50. Pays on acceptance. Provides 3 contributor's copies.

Editor's Comments
We look for lively features that will make math concepts fun and easy for kids to grasp. Topics recently covered include solving two-step problems, probability, reading a line graph, and finding a pattern.

Scholastic Math Magazine

Scholastic Inc.
557 Broadway
New York, NY 10012-3999

Editor: Jack Silbert

Description and Interests
Students in grades six through nine find entertaining, creative ways to learn math in this take-home paper, which is distributed in classrooms. Regular features include sections on pre-algebra, geometry, and statistics; practice tests; and theme-related activities.
- **Audience:** 11–14 years
- **Frequency:** Monthly
- **Distribution:** 100% school subscription
- **Circulation:** 200,000
- **Website:** www.scholastic.com/classmags

Freelance Potential
30% written by nonstaff writers. Publishes 3 freelance submissions yearly; 5% by unpublished writers. Receives 24 queries yearly.

Submissions
Query. Accepts hard copy. SASE. Responds in 2–3 months.
Articles: 600 words. Articles focus on real-world math, consumer math, math-related news, and sports math. Topics include teen issues, sports celebrities, TV, music, movies, and current events—all with a connection to math.
Depts/columns: 140 words. Skill-building exercises, quizzes, and practice tests.
Other: Puzzles, activities, comic strips, Q&As, and mystery photos.

Sample Issue
16 pages (no advertising): 4 articles; 3 depts/columns; 1 comic strip; 4 activities. Sample copy, free with 9x12 SASE (3 first-class stamps). Guidelines and editorial calendar available.
- "Percents Top the Charts." Article explains how *Billboard* magazine uses percent of change to measure a CD's success.
- "A Bit Less Than the Sum of Its Parts." Article shows how a lawyer used the Pythagorean theorem to send a drug dealer to prison.
- Sample dept/column: "Year-End Skills Review" uses a *Jeopardy* format to test skills in five math categories.

Rights and Payment
All rights. Articles, $300+. Depts/columns, $35. Pays on publication.

Editor's Comments
Query us if you have an idea for an article or activity that will help middle-school kids grasp math concepts.

Scholastic Parent & Child

Scholastic Inc.
557 Broadway
New York, NY 10012-3999

Editor-in-Chief: Pam Abrams

Description and Interests
Child development pertinent to home and school is the focus of this publication from Scholastic Publishing. Information comes from teachers, parents, and experts in the field of child development. Information includes product recommendations, relationships, learning skills, personal development, and health.
• **Audience:** Parents
• **Frequency:** 7 times each year
• **Distribution:** Subscription
• **Circulation:** 1.2 million
• **Website:** www.parentandchildonline.com

Freelance Potential
90% written by nonstaff writers. Publishes 20 freelance submissions yearly; 90% by unpublished writers, 10% by authors who are new to the magazine. Receives 144 queries and unsolicited mss yearly.

Submissions
Query or send complete ms. Accepts hard copy. SASE. Responds to queries in 3 months, to mss in 2 months.
Articles: 500–1,000 words. Informational articles. Topics include child development and education.
Depts/columns: Word lengths vary. Literacy, health, parent/teacher relationships, arts and crafts, child development, and family issues.

Sample Issue
92 pages (33% advertising): 16 articles; 4 depts/columns. Sample copy, $2.95. Guidelines available.
• "Visit the World with Your Child." Article demonstrates how opening a child's mind to accept different cultures can start at home.
• "Learning Right From Wrong." Article stresses that character building is important from the start.
• Sample dept/column: "Parent and Teacher Exchange" offers ideas for activities and child care.

Rights and Payment
All rights. Written material, payment rates vary. Pays on publication. Provides contributor's copies.

Editor's Comments
As a learning link between home and school, our publication likes to see submissions that help children segue between the two settings. We welcome material that is reflective of today's issues, and that is inspiring and original. It should be relevant to the development of preschool and school aged children.

Scholastic Scope

Scholastic Inc.
557 Broadway
New York, NY 10012-3999

Associate Editor: Lisa Feder-Feitel

Description and Interests
A classroom magazine, *Scholastic Scope* offers its audience of teen readers high-interest nonfiction to sharpen reading comprehension skills; writing activities and prompts; and first-person, true teen stories.
• **Audience:** 12–18 years
• **Frequency:** 17 times each year
• **Distribution:** 99% schools; 1% other
• **Circulation:** 550,000
• **Website: www.scholastic.com/scope**

Freelance Potential
30% written by nonstaff writers. Publishes few freelance submissions yearly; 2% by unpublished writers, 10% by authors who are new to the magazine. Receives 200–300 queries yearly.

Submissions
Query with résumé, outline/synopsis, and clips. Accepts hard copy. SASE. Response time varies.
Articles: 1,000 words. News and features that appeal to teens and profiles of young adults who have overcome obstacles, performed heroic acts, or had interesting experiences.
Fiction: 1,500 words. Realistic stories about relationships and family problems, school issues, and other teen concerns. Also accepts science fiction.
Depts/columns: Staff written.
Other: Crossword puzzles and word activities. Submit seasonal material 4 months in advance.

Sample Issue
24 pages (8% advertising): 4 articles; 3 depts/columns; 1 play. Sample copy, $1.75 with 9x12 SASE (2 first-class stamps).
• "Aquamarine." Play features a mermaid who grants the wishes of two best friends in exchange for a favor.
• "Ahoy, Ye Landlubbers!" Article spotlights a new pirate movie and discusses why pirate stories have always been popular.
• "Strokes of Luck." True story relates how a teen helped his grandmother recover from a stroke.

Rights and Payment
Rights negotiable. Written material, $100+. Pays on acceptance. Provides contributor's copies on request.

Editor's Comments
True teen stories are a popular feature of our magazine, and we continue to look for these first-person narratives that relate noteworthy experiences.

SchoolArts

Davis Publications
2223 Parkside Drive
Denton, TX 76201

Editor: Nancy Walkup

Description and Interests
Since 1901, *SchoolArts* has published practical ideas
for art educators. Innovative lessons, successful teach-
ing units, and hands-on classroom activities appear in
each issue of this resourceful publication.
- **Audience:** Teachers, grades K–12
- **Frequency:** 9 times each year
- **Distribution:** 100% subscription
- **Circulation:** 20,000
- **Website: www.davisart.com**

Freelance Potential
90% written by nonstaff writers. Publishes 120 freelance submissions yearly; 60% by unpublished writers,
60% by authors who are new to the magazine.
Receives 396 unsolicited mss yearly.

Submissions
Send complete ms with artwork. Accepts hard copy.
SASE. Responds in 6 weeks.
Articles: 300–1,000 words. Informational, how-to,
and self-help articles. Topics include teaching art,
techniques, art history, projects and activities, curriculum development, and art programs for the gifted,
handicapped, and learning disabled.
Depts/columns: Word lengths vary. Media reviews,
news, and technology updates.
Artwork: B/W prints or 35mm color slides. B/W
line art.

Sample Issue
78 pages (40% advertising): 12 articles; 8 depts/
columns; 5 ready-to-use resources. Sample copy, $3.
Guidelines and editorial calendar available.
- "Magical Chinese Dragons." Article describes how
  visual arts helped a kindergarten class learn about
  the Chinese culture.
- "Paper Marbling." Article summarizes a lesson that
  taught a middle school class about the American
  Arts and Crafts Movement.
- Sample dept/column: "New Products" spotlights a
  variety of new art supplies.

Rights and Payment
First serial rights. Written material, $25–$150. Other
material, payment rates vary. Pays on acceptance.
Provides 3 contributor's copies.

Editor's Comments
We seek practical lessons using new technologies and
interdisciplinary approaches to teaching art.

The School Librarian's Workshop

1 Deerfield Court
Basking Ridge, NJ 07920

Editor: Ruth Toor

Description and Interests
An informative resource for librarians and other educa-
tional professionals, this publication offers new ideas for
research, library displays, literary themes, book reviews,
media, and professional development. It also provides
news on Web and Internet innovations.
- **Audience:** School librarians
- **Frequency:** 6 times each year
- **Distribution:** 99% subscription; 1% other
- **Circulation:** 7,000
- **Website: www.school-librarians-workshop.com**

Freelance Potential
25% written by nonstaff writers. Publishes 20 freelance submissions yearly; 2% by unpublished writers,
2% by authors who are new to the magazine. Receives
240 unsolicited mss yearly.

Submissions
Send 2 copies of complete ms. Prefers disk submissions (Microsoft Word); accepts hard copy. No simultaneous submissions. SASE. Responds in 3 weeks.
Articles: To 1,000 words. Informational, how-to, and
practical application articles; profiles; and interviews.
Topics include librarianship, special education, ethnic
studies, computers, technology, social and multicultural issues, and the environment.
Artwork: Line art.
Other: Submit seasonal material 8 months in
advance.

Sample Issue
24 pages (no advertising): 15 articles; 3 book reviews.
Sample copy, free with 9x12 SASE. Guidelines and
theme list available.
- "The LOC Connection." Article extols the wealth
  of material available at the Library of Congress
  website.
- "Professionally Speaking." Article explains that a new
  trend in education will establish new literacy standards for kindergarten through grade two.
- "Tech Talk." Article takes a look at the changes that
  are coming to the Internet in the near future.

Rights and Payment
First rights. No payment. Provides 3 author's copies.

Editor's Comments
As a practical resource, we like to see articles that provide information that is useful for all grades. We particularly like lists of books that tie into the article.

School Library Journal

360 Park Avenue
New York, NY 10010

News & Features Editor: Rick Margolis

Description and Interests
This magazine provides school librarians and media specialists with the latest news in technology and trends in library services and management. It includes articles and reviews of websites, children's literature, equipment, and technology.
- **Audience:** Librarians
- **Frequency:** Monthly
- **Distribution:** 100% subscription
- **Circulation:** 34,500
- **Website: www.slj.com**

Freelance Potential
80% written by nonstaff writers. Publishes 25 freelance submissions yearly; 60% by unpublished writers, 60% by authors who are new to the magazine. Receives 48–72 unsolicited mss yearly.

Submissions
Query or send complete ms. Accepts disk submissions (ASCII or Microsoft Word) and email submissions to rmargolis@reedbusiness.com. SASE. Responds to queries in 1 month, to mss in 3 months.
Articles: 1,500–2,500 words. Informational articles and interviews. Topics include children's and young adult literature, school library management, and library careers.
Depts/columns: 1,500–2,500 words. Book and media reviews; descriptions of successful library programs; and opinion pieces.
Artwork: Color prints, tables, charts, and cartoons.

Sample Issue
140 pages (25% advertising): 6 articles; 11 depts/columns; 1 review section. Sample copy, $6.75. Guidelines available at website.
- "Stop the Presses!" Article discusses a new after-school homework and writing center for kids.
- "Parents: Internet Is a Double-Edged Sword." Article reports on a study that says the Internet is more dangerous for kids than television.
- Sample dept/column: "The Buzz" highlights several new technological tools and gadgets.

Rights and Payment
First rights. Articles, $400. Depts/columns, $100–$200. Pays on publication. Provides 4 contributor's copies.

Editor's Comments
We look for features written in an easily accessible, conversational tone. Please avoid technical jargon.

School Library Media Activities Monthly

3401 Stockwell Street
Lincoln, NE 68506

Managing Editor: Deborah Levitov

Description and Interests
This publication is designed specifically to help school library media specialists in their teaching roles. Its teaching strategies and tips are appropriate for use at the elementary and junior high school levels.
- **Audience:** School library and media specialists, grades K–8
- **Frequency:** 10 times each year
- **Distribution:** 100% subscription
- **Circulation:** 12,000
- **Website: www.schoollibrarymedia.com**

Freelance Potential
80% written by nonstaff writers. Publishes 30 freelance submissions yearly; 15% by unpublished writers, 25% by authors who are new to the magazine. Receives 48 queries and unsolicited mss yearly.

Submissions
Query or send complete ms. Accepts hard copy and disk submissions. SASE. Responds in 2 months.
Articles: 1,000–1,500 words. Informational and factual articles. Topics include media education, information technology, integrating curriculum materials, and library management.
Depts/columns: "Activities Almanac" features short descriptions of media activities. "Into the Curriculum" uses lesson plans. Also publishes media reviews and short articles on media production.
Artwork: B/W transparencies and prints. Line art.

Sample Issue
60 pages (no advertising): 2 articles; 15 depts/columns. Guidelines available.
- "The 'Write' Links in the Library Media Center." Article discusses a variety of ways to integrate the teaching of writing into media center activities.
- "Inquiry and Living History." Article looks into the life of Phillis Wheatley, the first published African American poet.
- Sample dept/column: "Thematic Journeys" reports on books and movies about aliens.

Rights and Payment
All rights. All material, payment rates vary. Pays on publication. Provides 3+ contributor's copies.

Editor's Comments
We're interested in any article that will help school library media specialists in their expanding and changing roles as teachers.

The School Magazine

P.O. Box 1928
Macquarie Centre
New South Wales 2113
Australia

Editor: Tohby Riddle

Description and Interests
This literary magazine offers stories, poems, articles, and plays for elementary school children. Each issue includes four publications for students at different reading levels.
- **Audience:** 8–12 years
- **Frequency:** 10 times each year
- **Distribution:** 100% subscription
- **Circulation:** 150,000
- **Website:** www.schools.nsw.edu.au/school libraries/magazine

Freelance Potential
85% written by nonstaff writers. Publishes 100 freelance submissions yearly; 20% by unpublished writers, 30% by authors who are new to the magazine. Receives 50 unsolicited mss yearly.

Submissions
Send complete ms. Accepts hard copy. SAE/IRC. Responds in 6–8 weeks.
Articles: 800–2,000 words. Informational and factual articles. Topics include nature, pets, the environment, history, biography, science, technology, and multicultural and ethnic issues.
Fiction: 800–2,000 words. Adventure; humor; fantasy; science fiction; horror; mystery; folktales; problem-solving and real-life stories; and contemporary, multicultural, and historical fiction.
Depts/columns: Staff written.

Sample Issue
30 pages (no advertising): 1 article; 4 stories; 3 poems; 4 depts/columns. Sample copy, free with IRC ($2 Australian postage). Guidelines available.
- "The Stamp Story." Article presents the history and background of postage stamps and tells how to develop a stamp collection.
- "The Watcher." Story portrays the ordeal of survivors of a space expedition that are held captive on their native planet.

Rights and Payment
One-time serial rights. Written material, $226 (Australian) per 1,000 words. Poetry, payment rates vary. Pays on acceptance. Provides 2 author's copies.

Editor's Comments
We seek original and educational writing that appeals to children's imaginations. We discourage submissions that have an overt message or holiday theme.

Science Activities

Heldref Publications
1319 18th Street NW
Washington, DC 20036-1802

Managing Editor: Christine Polcino

Description and Interests
This science education journal offers teacher-tested projects, experiments, and curriculum ideas for kindergarten through twelfth grade science teachers.
- **Audience:** Science teachers
- **Frequency:** Quarterly
- **Distribution:** Subscription; schools; libraries
- **Circulation:** 1,200
- **Website:** www.heldref.org

Freelance Potential
80% written by nonstaff writers. Publishes 15 freelance submissions yearly; 25% by unpublished writers, 75% by authors who are new to the magazine. Receives 420 queries and unsolicited mss yearly.

Submissions
Query or send 2 copies of complete ms. Accepts hard copy and disk submissions. SASE. Responds in 3 months.
Articles: Word lengths vary. Informational and how-to articles. Topics include nature, science, technology, and computers.
Depts/columns: Word lengths vary. Book reviews, computer news, and classroom aids.
Artwork: B/W photos, prints, and slides. Line art and diagrams.

Sample Issue
48 pages (1% advertising): 5 articles; 4 depts/columns. Sample copy, $6 with 9x12 SASE. Writers' guidelines available.
- "Summary Frames: Language Acquisition for Special Education and ELL Students." Article discusses note taking and summarization skills of students at different levels.
- "A Long Walk to the Water's Edge." Article provides a discussion and activity to teach students about the Great Lakes region and its changing water levels in relation to climactic changes.
- Sample dept/column: "Classroom Aids" offers information on literacy teaching booklets and videos.

Rights and Payment
All rights. No payment. Provides 2 author's copies.

Editor's Comments
We need more articles on math, forensics, the Internet, and science, as well as more high school activities. We love to receive innovative manuscripts about any and all topics related to science.

Science and Children

National Science Teachers Association
1840 Wilson Boulevard
Arlington, VA 22201-3000

Managing Editor: Monica Zerry

Description and Interests
Science and Children is a preschool through middle level science teaching journal. Its content reflects the needs and interests of educators, administrators, and parents. Practical activities and instructional approaches are included in each issue.
- **Audience:** Science teachers, preK–grade 8
- **Frequency:** 9 times each year
- **Distribution:** 100% subscription
- **Circulation:** 23,000
- **Website:** www.nsta.org/elementaryschool#journal

Freelance Potential
99% written by nonstaff writers. Publishes 25 freelance submissions yearly; 95% by unpublished writers, 95% by authors who are new to the magazine. Receives 360 unsolicited mss yearly.

Submissions
Accepts submissions from practicing educators only. Send complete ms. Accepts email submissions to msrs.nsta.org. Responds in 6 months.
Articles: To 1,500 words. Informational and how-to articles; personal experience pieces; profiles; interviews; and reviews. Topics include science education, teacher training and techniques, staff development, classroom activities, astronomy, biology, chemistry, physics, and earth science.
Depts/columns: To 1,500 words. "Helpful Hints" and "In the Schools," to 500 words.
Other: Submit seasonal material 1 year in advance.

Sample Issue
76 pages (2% advertising): 16 articles; 5 depts/columns. Sample copy, free. Guidelines available.
- "The Early Years." Article presents fun ways for students to explore physical science concepts.
- "Science 101." Article explains the cause of lightning and thunder.
- Sample dept/column: "Every Day Science" offers a calendar of daily facts and challenges for the science explorer.

Rights and Payment
All rights. No payment. Provides 5 author's copies.

Editor's Comments
We seek articles discussing current issues in the elementary science classroom. We're always interested in successful classroom activities and experiences that are original, inspiring, and creative.

The Science Teacher

National Science Teachers Association
1840 Wilson Boulevard
Arlington, VA 22201-3000

Managing Editor: Jennifer Henderson

Description and Interests
High school science teachers read this magazine for its articles on scientific research, teaching techniques, and hands-on activities. It is published by the National Science Teachers Association.
- **Audience:** Science educators, grades 7–12
- **Frequency:** 9 times each year
- **Distribution:** 100% controlled
- **Circulation:** 29,000
- **Website:** www.nsta.org/highschool

Freelance Potential
100% written by nonstaff writers. Of the freelance submissions published yearly, 70% are by unpublished writers and 50% are by authors who are new to the magazine. Receives 360 unsolicited mss yearly.

Submissions
Send complete ms. Accepts email submissions to authors.nsta.org. Responds in 1 month.
Articles: 2,000 words. Informational articles; classroom projects; and experiments. Topics include science education, biology, earth science, computers, social issues, space, technology, and sports medicine.
Depts/columns: 500 words. Science updates, association news, and science careers.
Artwork: 5x7 or larger B/W glossy prints. Tables, diagrams, and line drawings.

Sample Issue
92 pages (40% advertising): 7 articles; 8 depts/columns. Sample copy, $4.25. Guidelines available.
- "Teaching Science to Students with Learning Disabilities." Article outlines basic educational principles that support the learning needs of students with disabilities.
- "Attitudes in Education." Article reports on a survey that evaluated teachers' use of accommodations that facilitate learning disabled student inclusion, as well as teacher attitudes about inclusion.
- Sample dept/column: "Idea Bank" takes a look at a wilderness search and rescue activity.

Rights and Payment
First rights. No payment. Provides author's copies.

Editor's Comments
We are looking for creative teaching activities from science teachers. Be sure to include assessment techniques, the approximate grade level you are targeting, and any safety considerations.

Science Weekly

2141 Industrial Parkway, Suite 202
Silver Springs, MD 20904

Publisher: Dr. Claude Mayberry

Description and Interests
Each issue of this educational classroom newsletter is published in seven grade-appropriate editions for students in kindergarten through grade eight. *Science Weekly* covers a different theme in each weekly issue, and includes related articles and activities for home or classroom use.
- **Audience:** Grades K–6
- **Frequency:** 14 times each year
- **Distribution:** Subscription; schools
- **Circulation:** 200,000
- **Website:** www.scienceweekly.com

Freelance Potential
100% written by nonstaff writers. Of the material published, 80% is by unpublished writers, 25% is by authors who are new to the magazine.

Submissions
Query with résumé only. No unsolicited mss. All work is assigned to writers in the District of Columbia, Maryland, or Virginia. SASE. Response time varies.
Articles: Word length varies. Informational and factual articles. Topics include space exploration, ecology, the environment, nature, biology, the human body, meteorology, ocean science, navigation, nutrition, photography, physical science, roller coasters, and secret codes.
Other: Theme-related puzzles, games, and activities.

Sample Issue
4 pages (no advertising): 1 article; 6 activities. Sample copy and theme list available.
- "Coral Reefs." Short article explains what coral reefs are and where they can be found.
- "Math." Short activity combines math facts with sea creature facts.
- "Bringing It Home." Activity suggests how to make a coral reef diorama.

Rights and Payment
All rights. All material, payment rates vary. Pays on publication.

Editor's Comments
Our publication is designed to promote student interest in science and the scientific process. Many of the articles and activities can be used across the curriculum to develop thinking skills. If you live in the Washington, DC, metropolitan area and have an idea that will work for us, let us know.

Scouting

Boy Scouts of America
1325 West Walnut Hill Lane
P.O. Box 152079
Irving, TX 75015-2079

Editor: Jon C. Halter

Description and Interests
Scouting has a dual purpose: to provide scout leaders with information about successful activities and programs, and to provide parents with ideas for creating positive family environments.
- **Audience:** Scout leaders and parents
- **Frequency:** 6 times each year
- **Distribution:** 100% subscription
- **Circulation:** 1 million
- **Website:** www.scoutingmagazine.org

Freelance Potential
80% written by nonstaff writers. Publishes 2–3 freelance submissions yearly; 2% by unpublished writers, 10% by authors who are new to the magazine. Receives 180+ queries yearly.

Submissions
Query with synopsis or outline and clips; or send complete ms. Responds in 3 weeks.
Articles: 500–1,200 words. Informational and how-to articles; personal experience pieces; profiles; interviews; and humor. Topics include scout programs, leadership, volunteering, nature, social issues, and trends, and history.
Depts/columns: 500–700 words. Scouting and family events, anecdotes, and scouting history.
Other: Puzzles.

Sample Issue
50 pages (33% advertising): 6 articles; 6 depts/columns. Sample copy, $2.50 with 9x12 SASE. Guidelines available.
- "A Helping Hand From Coast to Coast to Coast." Article conveys scout efforts to help after hurricanes.
- "It's a Winter Romp." Article considers all the cold-weather activities available in two states.
- Sample dept/column: "Outdoor Smarts" clears up misconceptions about living out of doors.

Rights and Payment
First North American serial rights. Written material, $300–$800. Pays on acceptance. Provides 2 contributor's copies.

Editor's Comments
We rely heavily on regional writers to cover an event or activity in a particular part of the country. In addition to scouting issues, we occasionally include general interest articles on nature, social issues and trends, or history geared to our adult audience.

Seattle's Child

511 2nd Avenue West
Seattle, WA 98119

Editor: Wenda Reed

Description and Interests
Distributed free to parents living in the greater Seattle area, this magazine features articles on parenting topics, health, fitness, education, and travel. Information on local resources and events is also included.
- **Audience:** Parents
- **Frequency:** Monthly
- **Distribution:** 100% newsstand
- **Circulation:** 70,000
- **Website:** www.seattleschild.com

Freelance Potential
80% written by nonstaff writers. Publishes 30 freelance submissions yearly; 10% by unpublished writers, 25% by authors who are new to the magazine. Receives 120+ queries yearly.

Submissions
Query with outline. Accepts hard copy, email queries to nweditor@seattleschild.com, and simultaneous submissions if identified. SASE. Responds in 1 month.
Articles: Word lengths vary. Informational and how-to articles; and personal experience pieces. Topics include family and parenting issues, health, fitness, regional news, travel, and social issues.
Depts/columns: Word lengths vary. Profiles, cooking, and media reviews.

Sample Issue
46 pages (30% advertising): 4 articles; 6 depts/columns, 1 calendar. Sample copy, $3. Guidelines and theme list available.
- "Can You Dig It?" Article offers great ways to share hands-on geology adventures with children.
- "Go West." Article takes a look at ways to enjoy a family trip to the Kitsap Peninsula.
- Sample dept/column: "Your Parenting Coach" discusses the use of cell phones by children.

Rights and Payment
Rights vary. Written material, $100–$450. Pays on acceptance. Provides 2 contributor's copies.

Editor's Comments
We look for well-written articles on fresh topics. Information on parenting resources and family events continue to be of interest to us. We welcome new writers who know the region, but ask that they include clips with their queries. Please note that since we are no longer part of United Parenting Publications, we are not in the market for national stories.

Seek

Standard Publishing Company
8121 Hamilton Avenue
Cincinnati, OH 45231

Editor: Margaret K. Williams

Description and Interests
The inspirational stories and Bible lessons that appear in this Sunday school pamphlet target young adult and adult readers. It offers a Christian perspective on contemporary issues and everyday challenges.
- **Audience:** YA–Adult
- **Frequency:** Weekly
- **Distribution:** 100% religious education
- **Circulation:** 27,000
- **Website:** www.standardpub.com

Freelance Potential
85% written by nonstaff writers. Publishes 150–200 freelance submissions yearly; 80% by authors who are new to the magazine.

Submissions
Send complete ms that relates to an upcoming theme. Prefers email to seek@standardpub.com. Responds in 3–6 months.
Articles: 500–1,200 words. Inspirational, devotional, and personal experience pieces. Topics include religious and contemporary issues, Christian living, moral and ethical dilemmas, and controversial subjects.
Fiction: 500–1,200 words. Stories about Christian living, moral and ethical problems, controversial topics, and coping with contemporary issues.
Other: Submit seasonal material 1 year in advance.

Sample Issue
8 pages (no advertising): 2 articles; 1 story; 2 Bible lessons. Sample copy, free with 6x9 SASE. Guidelines and theme list available at website.
- "Partners." Personal experience piece compares a woman's relationship with God to her relationship with a walking partner.
- "Women Mentoring Women." Article discusses how Christian women can benefit from the experiences of older women in the church.

Rights and Payment
First and second rights. Written material, $.05–$.07 per word. Artwork, $50. Pays on acceptance. Provides 5 contributor's copies.

Editor's Comments
Please remember to check our website for information about our theme list before contacting us with your idea. We always need first-person viewpoints of Christian life and true-to-life happenings. Material must be wholesome, vibrant, and relevant.

Seventeen

300 West 57th Street
New York, NY 10019

Submissions: Zandile Blay

Description and Interests
Articles on fashion, beauty, family, relationships, health and fitness, celebrities, and social issues make up the pages of this popular teen magazine.
- **Audience:** 13–21 years
- **Frequency:** Monthly
- **Distribution:** 70% subscription; 30% newsstand
- **Circulation:** 2 million
- **Website: www.seventeen.com**

Freelance Potential
20% written by nonstaff writers. Publishes 20 freelance submissions yearly; 5% by unpublished writers, 40% by authors who are new to the magazine. Receives 46 queries, 200 unsolicited mss yearly.

Submissions
Query with outline and clips or writing samples for nonfiction. Send complete ms for fiction. Accepts hard copy and simultaneous submissions if identified. SASE. Response time varies.
Articles: 650–3,000 words. Informational and self-help articles; personal experience pieces; and profiles. Topics include relationships, dating, family issues, current events, social concerns, friendship, and popular culture.
Fiction: 1,000–3,000 words. Stories that feature female teenage experiences.
Depts/columns: 500–1,000 words. Fashion, beauty, health, and fitness.
Other: Submit seasonal material 6 months in advance.

Sample Issue
214 pages (50% advertising): 6 articles; 42 depts/columns. Sample copy, $3.99 at newsstands. Guidelines available.
- "The Best Way to Get Rid of Acne." Article discusses the latest methods to achieve clear skin, as well as what really causes breakouts.
- Sample dept/column: "Lifestyle" offers tips on how to create a great looking, elegant bouquet.

Rights and Payment
First rights. Written material, $1–$1.50 per word. Pays on acceptance.

Editor's Comments
We'd like to review more original, real girl stories that focus on personal decisions and relationships as well as more "newsy material."

Sharing the Victory

Fellowship of Christian Athletes
8701 Leeds Road
Kansas City, MO 64129

Editor: Jill Ewert

Description and Interests
Inspirational accounts of Christian athletes fill the pages of this magazine for players and coaches. Rather than emphasize winning, it focuses on life lessons learned through sports participation.
- **Audience:** Athletes and coaches, grades 7 and up
- **Frequency:** 9 times each year
- **Distribution:** 95% subscription; 5% other
- **Circulation:** 80,000
- **Website: www.fca.org**

Freelance Potential
30% written by nonstaff writers. Publishes 20 freelance submissions yearly; 25% by unpublished writers, 10% by authors who are new to the magazine. Receives 48 queries and unsolicited mss yearly.

Submissions
Query with outline/synopsis and clips or writing samples; or send complete ms. Accepts hard copy and IBM disk submissions. Availability of artwork improves chance of acceptance. SASE. Response time varies.
Articles: To 1,200 words. Informational articles; profiles; interviews; and personal experience pieces. Topics include sports, competition, training, and Christian education.
Depts/columns: Staff written.
Artwork: Color prints.
Other: Submit seasonal material 3–4 months in advance.

Sample Issue
40 pages (30% advertising): 7 articles; 11 depts/columns. Sample copy, $1 with 9x12 SASE (3 first-class stamps). Guidelines available.
- "Side by Side." Article describes the wonderful friendship that developed between two sisters.
- "Walk-On Wonder." Article tells how a mediocre basketball player makes a big difference in every game he plays and inspires other players.
- "Victory Road." Article relates how three champions demonstrate that success isn't just about winning.

Rights and Payment
First serial rights. Articles, $150–$400. Pays on publication.

Editor's Comments
We would like to see more articles about female athletes in the Fellowship of Christian Athletes. The featured athlete can be anyone with a positive story.

SheKnows.com

7944 East Beck Lane, Suite 230
Scottsdale, AZ 85260

Editors: Nancy Price & Betsey Bailey

Description and Interests
Information and expert advice for women—on everything from pregnancy to parenting, health to hobbies, and home decor to family finances—appear on this online network for women. It strives to help readers improve and enjoy their lives.
- **Audience:** Mothers
- **Frequency:** Weekly
- **Distribution:** 100% Internet
- **Hits per month:** Unavailable
- **Website:** www.sheknows.com

Freelance Potential
50% written by nonstaff writers. Publishes 80–100 freelance submissions yearly. Receives 240 queries, 48 unsolicited mss yearly.

Submissions
Query or send complete ms. Accepts submissions through website and email submissions to content@coincide.com. Responds in 2 months.
Articles: 500–1,200 words. Informational, how-to, and factual articles; profiles; interviews; and personal experience pieces. Topics include parenting, fertility, pregnancy, maternity fashion trends, birth stories, pain management, depression, infants, toddlers, family issues, relationships, romance, entertainment, celebrities, work, health, hobbies, home decor, and money management.

Sample Issue
Sample copy and guidelines available at website.
- "How To Nurture Compassion." Article discusses ways to help kids feel more comfortable around children with disabilities and special needs.
- "Is It Butterflies? Feeling the Baby Move." Article helps pregnant women sort out the different feelings they have during the second trimester.
- "The Hapless Homemaker—Not a Perfect 10." Humorous piece tells how the author always manages to get injured when cooking.

Rights and Payment
First electronic rights. Features, $25–$50. First-person pieces, $10. Pays on publication.

Editor's Comments
If she wants to know it, we want to cover it! Originality, creativity, and interactive twists on more usual topics are encouraged. How-to pieces are welcome, as are checklists and step-by-step guides.

Shine Brightly

P.O. Box 7259
Grand Rapids, MI 49510

Managing Editor: Christina Malone

Description and Interests
This magazine is the official publication of GEMS Girls' Clubs. It offers a mix of inspirational stories and articles that stress a relationship with Jesus Christ.
- **Audience:** 9–14 years
- **Frequency:** 9 times each year
- **Distribution:** 100% subscription
- **Circulation:** 15,500
- **Website:** www.gemsgc.org

Freelance Potential
60% written by nonstaff writers. Publishes 35 freelance submissions yearly; 15% by unpublished writers, 90% by authors who are new to the magazine. Receives 780 unsolicited mss yearly.

Submissions
Send complete ms. Accepts hard copy and simultaneous submissions if identified. No email submissions. SASE. Responds in 1 month.
Articles: 50–500 words. Informational and how-to articles; personal experience pieces; profiles; and humor. Topics include community service, stewardship, contemporary social issues, family and friend relationships, and peer pressure.
Fiction: 400–900 words. Genres include contemporary fiction, romance, mystery, science fiction, and adventure. Also publishes stories about nature, animals, and sports.
Depts/columns: Staff written.
Artwork: 5x7 or larger B/W and color prints.
Other: Puzzles, activities, and cartoons.

Sample Issue
24 pages (no advertising): 1 article; 2 stories; 2 depts/columns; 1 activity. Sample copy, $1 with 9x12 SASE ($.75 postage). Guidelines available.
- "The Four Failures of Fiona Franklin." Story features a girl who turns her shortcomings into successes.
- "My Great Wall Adventure." Story reveals how a trip to China changed the way the author solved problems in her life.

Rights and Payment
First, second, and simultaneous rights. Articles and fiction, $.02–$.05 per word. Other material, payment rates vary. Pays on publication. Provides 2 copies.

Editor's Comments
We're looking for material that will help young readers see how Christian beliefs apply to their daily lives.

Single Mother

A Support Group in Your Hands

National Organization of Single Mothers
P.O. Box 68
Midland, NC 28107-0068

Editor: Andrea Engber

Description and Interests
Single Mother is a newsletter filled with practical articles that help single women face the daily challenges of parenting. It is published by a nonprofit group.
- **Audience:** Single mothers
- **Frequency:** Quarterly
- **Distribution:** Subscription; membership
- **Circulation:** 3,000–5,000
- **Website:** www.singlemothers.org

Freelance Potential
10% written by nonstaff writers. Publishes 6 freelance submissions yearly. Receives 12–24 queries and unsolicited mss yearly.

Submissions
Query or send complete ms. Prefers email submissions to singlemother@singlemothers.org. Accepts hard copy. Availability of artwork improves chance of acceptance. SASE. Response time varies.
Articles: Word lengths vary. Informational articles. Topics include parenting, money and time management, absent dads, dating, death, handling ex-families, pregnancy and childbirth, adoption, donor insemination, child support, paternity, custody, and visitation rights.
Depts/columns: Word lengths vary. News, book reviews, advice.

Sample Issue
16 pages (no advertising): 6 articles; 5 depts/columns. Sample copy, $2.95 with 9x12 SASE.
- "When the Carriage Comes First: Why More Single Women Are Choosing Motherhood before Marriage." Article explains why raising a family is important for many women who cannot find a partner.
- "Helping a Shy Child Make Friends." Article offers advice for parents of children with social anxiety.
- Sample dept/column: "Balancing Self and Motherhood" reports on a new photo service for busy moms.

Rights and Payment
Rights vary. Written material, payment rates vary. Payment policy varies.

Editor's Comments
Research-based, positive information that offers constructive solutions to the problems faced by single mothers is needed. Profiles of successful single mothers are always welcome.

Skating

United States Figure Skating Association
20 First Street
Colorado Springs, CO 80906

Director of Publications

Description and Interests
This magazine looks at the world of figure skating from all angles. It features event coverage, technical articles, and profiles of skaters for an audience that includes skating enthusiasts of all ages.
- **Audience:** 5 years–Adult
- **Frequency:** 10 times each year
- **Distribution:** Subscription; other
- **Circulation:** 45,000
- **Website:** www.usfigureskating.org

Freelance Potential
70% written by nonstaff writers. Publishes 15 freelance submissions yearly; 10% by unpublished writers, 20% by authors who are new to the magazine. Receives 72 queries and unsolicited mss yearly.

Submissions
Query with résumé, clips or writing samples, and photo ideas; or send complete ms with photos or art ideas. Accepts hard copy, Macintosh Zip disk submissions, and email to skatingmagazine@usfigureskating.org. SASE. Responds in 1 month.
Articles: 750–2,000 words. Informational articles; profiles; and interviews. Topics include association news, competitions, techniques, personalities, and training.
Depts/columns: 600–800 words. Competition results, profiles of skaters and coaches, sports medicine, fitness, and technique tips.
Artwork: B/W and color prints, slides, or transparencies. Electronic images at 300 dpi.

Sample Issue
52 pages: 4 articles; 8 depts/columns. Sample copy, $3 with 9x12 SASE. Guidelines available.
- "Success at Marshalls SkateFest in Detroit." Article reports on an event at which two Olympic silver medalists performed.
- "American Idol." Article profiles Kimmie Meissner, the new World Figure Skating champion.

Rights and Payment
First serial rights. Articles, $75–$150. Depts/columns, $75. Artwork, payment rates vary. Pays on publication. Provides 5–10 contributor's copies.

Editor's Comments
If you have connections in the world of figure skating and can write exciting skater profiles and event reports, we want to hear from you.

Skipping Stones

P.O. Box 3939
Eugene, OR 97403-0939

Editor: Arun N. Toké

Description and Interests
Exchanging meaningful multicultural ideas and experiences is the goal of this publication, which serves as a world forum for young people.
- **Audience:** 7–17 years; teachers; parents
- **Frequency:** 5 times each year
- **Distribution:** Subscription; schools; libraries; newsstand
- **Circulation:** 2,500
- **Website:** www.skippingstones.org

Freelance Potential
90% written by nonstaff writers. Publishes 175–200 freelance submissions yearly; 60% by unpublished writers, 75% by authors who are new to the magazine. Receives 2,400 unsolicited mss yearly.

Submissions
Send complete ms with cover letter. Accepts hard copy. Macintosh disk submissions, simultaneous submissions, and email submissions to editor@skippingstones.org. Artwork improves chance of acceptance. SASE. Responds in 3–4 months.
Articles: To 800 words. Essays and contemporary nonfiction. Topics include community service, family relationships, technology, problem-solving, sustainable living, disabilities, role models, and living abroad.
Fiction: To 800 words. Genres include multicultural, inspirational, and historical fiction; and folktales.
Depts/columns: 100–200 words. News, book reviews, opinion pieces, community action, and proverbs.
Artwork: 8x10 B/W and color prints. Line art.
Other: Puzzles, activities, games, and jokes. Poetry. Submit seasonal material 3 months in advance.

Sample Issue
36 pages (no advertising): 11 articles; 8 stories; 21 poems; 10 depts/columns. Sample copy, $5 with 9x12 SASE ($1 postage). Guidelines available.
- "Beyond the Veil: Women in Iran." Article goes behind the scenes in Iran to show women's lives.
- "Sunday Scoff." Story illustrates the maxim that honesty brings its own rewards.

Rights and Payment
First and nonexclusive reprint rights. No payment. Provides 4 copies and 25% discount on extra copies.

Editor's Comments
We encourage creative and informational stories about the writer's culture rather than pure fiction.

Slap

High Speed Productions
1303 Underwood Avenue
San Francisco, CA 94124

Editor: Mark Whiteley

Description and Interests
Skateboarding techniques, personalities, and events are covered in this magazine for teens. It also reports on the world of hip-hop, rap, and rock music.
- **Audience:** YA
- **Frequency:** Monthly
- **Distribution:** 50% newsstand; 10% subscription; 40% other
- **Circulation:** 130,000
- **Website:** www.slapmagazine.com

Freelance Potential
20% written by nonstaff writers. Publishes 25+ freelance submissions yearly.

Submissions
Send complete ms. Accepts hard copy, IBM or Macintosh disk submissions, and simultaneous submissions if identified. Availability of artwork improves chance of acceptance. SASE. Responds in 2 months.
Articles: Word lengths vary. Informational and how-to articles; interviews; and personal experience pieces. Topics include skateboarding, contest reports and statistics, skateboard equipment, music, and recreation.
Depts/columns: Word lengths vary. Skateboarding news, music news, and skateboarding tricks.
Artwork: 35mm B/W negatives; color prints and transparencies. B/W and color line art.
Other: Cartoons and comics about skateboarding and popular music.

Sample Issue
178 pages (40% advertising): 9 articles; 10 depts/columns. Sample copy, free with 9x12 SASE ($1.95 postage). Guidelines and editorial calendar available.
- "Zoodallo." Article portrays a filming and photo trip to Medellín, Colombia, led by the new Zoo York team manager, Don La.
- Sample dept/column: "Gossip" features updates on the lives and careers of skateboarding and music personalities.

Rights and Payment
First rights. All material, payment rates vary. Pays on publication. Provides 1 contributor's copy.

Editor's Comments
Most of our writers are immersed in the world of skateboarding and music—they know the lingo and they know what's hot on the hip-hop scene. Good photos are very important.

Social Studies and the Young Learner

321 M Townsend Hall
University of Missouri
Columbia, MO 65211-2400

Editor: Dr. Linda Bennett

Description and Interests
Published by the National Council for the Social Studies for kindergarten through sixth-grade educators, this magazine features articles about teaching history, geography, archaeology, political science, and other related humanities.
- **Audience:** Teachers
- **Frequency:** Quarterly
- **Distribution:** Subscription; newsstand
- **Circulation:** 10,000
- **Website: www.socialstudies.org**

Freelance Potential
95% written by nonstaff writers. Publishes 32 freelance submissions yearly; 30% by unpublished writers, 50% by authors who are new to the magazine. Receives 60 unsolicited mss yearly.

Submissions
Send complete ms. Accepts email submissions to ssyl@missouri.edu. Responds in 6 months.
Articles: To 2,000 words. Informational articles; profiles; and personal experience pieces. Topics include current events, gifted and special education, multicultural and ethnic issues, social issues, history, and the humanities.
Fiction: Word lengths vary. Folktales; folklore; and multicultural, ethnic, and historical fiction.
Depts/columns: To 500 words. Classroom resources and perspectives on topics related to social studies.
Artwork: B/W and color prints and transparencies. Line art.
Other: Filler, puzzles, and activities.

Sample Issue
32 pages: 6 articles; 2 depts/columns. Sample copy, $7.50. Writers' guidelines, theme list, and editorial calendar available.
- "American Indians: Hands-On Lessons." Article presents ideas for motivating students to learn about Native Americans.
- Sample dept/column: "Children's Literature" looks at books about the era of Christopher Columbus.

Rights and Payment
All rights. No payment.

Editor's Comments
We consider substantive articles, viewpoints, analyses, and ideas and techniques for strengthening social studies education in kindergarten through sixth grade.

South Florida Parenting

6501 Nob Hill Road
Tamarac, FL 33321

Managing Editor: Vicki McCash Brennan

Description and Interests
A potpourri of information relevant to families residing in Florida's Miami-Dade, Broward, and Palm Beach counties is found in this publication. Topics are service oriented and cover area events, parenting issues, travel ideas and experiences, media and book reviews, personal relationships, and issues facing children of all ages.
- **Audience:** Parents
- **Frequency:** Monthly
- **Distribution:** Controlled; schools; other
- **Circulation:** 110,000
- **Website: www.sfparenting.com**

Freelance Potential
85% written by nonstaff writers. Publishes 90 freelance submissions yearly; 10% by authors who are new to the magazine. Receives 996 unsolicited mss each year.

Submissions
Prefers complete ms; will accept queries. Accepts hard copy and email submissions to vmccash@sfparenting.com. SASE. Responds in 2–3 months.
Articles: 800–2,000 words. Informational and how-to articles; profiles; interviews; and personal experience pieces. Topics include family life, travel, parenting, education, leisure, music, health, and regional events.
Depts/columns: To 750 words. Family finance, health, nutrition, and advice on infants and preteens.

Sample Issue
154 pages (60% advertising): 4 articles; 19 depts/columns. Guidelines available.
- "Celebrating Milestones." Article presents creative ways to mark special birthdays.
- "Three Generations in Italy." Article documents grandparents, parents, and young children on a trip.
- Sample dept/column: "Family Matters" gives pointers on how parents can ease kids' nerves before a test.

Rights and Payment
One-time regional rights. Written material, $100–$300. Pays on publication. Provides contributor's copies upon request.

Editor's Comments
Our feature articles use writers, sources, and settings from the south Florida area. We will also consider insightful, captivating essays and well-sourced, well-researched submissions on universal themes.

Sparkle

P.O. Box 7259
Grand Rapids, MI 49510

Editor: Sarah Vanderaa

Description and Interests
This exciting Christian magazine for young girls offers articles, stories, and activities that teach readers about salvation and Jesus, and inspires them to apply God's Word to their life.
- **Audience:** Girls, 6–9 years
- **Frequency:** 3 times each year
- **Distribution:** Unavailable
- **Circulation:** 2,700
- **Website:** www.gemsgc.org

Freelance Potential
85% written by nonstaff writers. Publishes 9 freelance submissions yearly; 50% by unpublished writers, 50% by authors who are new to the magazine. Receives 240 unsolicited mss yearly.

Submissions
Send complete ms. SASE. Responds in 4–6 weeks.
Articles: 100–400 words. Informational articles. Topics include animals, sports, music, musicians, famous people, interaction with family and friends, service projects, and dealing with schoolwork.
Fiction: 100–400 words. Genres include adventure, mystery, and contemporary fiction. Also publishes stories about animals.
Other: Puzzles, games, recipes, party ideas, short humorous pieces, cartoons, and inexpensive craft ideas.

Sample Issue
14 pages (no advertising): 1 article; 2 stories; 4 activities; 1 cartoon, 1 Bible lesson. Sample copy, free with 9x12 SASE. Guidelines and theme list available.
- "Sitting Down with Connie Kendall!" Article offers an interview with a worker at Whit's End, a place where children have fun and learn about God.
- "Practice Again!?" Story tells of a girl who learns that practicing will help develop the talents God gave her.
- "May Day Mystery." Story unfolds around a basket full of goodies that mysteriously appears on a doorstep.

Rights and Payment
Rights vary. Articles, $20. Other material, payment rates vary. Pays on publication. Provides 2 contributor's copies.

Editor's Comments
We are looking for more articles that cover our animal theme. Also, we are in need of games and recipes. Material must be age appropriate.

Spider
The Magazine for Children

Cricket Magazine Group
315 Fifth Street, P.O. Box 300
Peru, IL 61354

Submissions Editor

Description and Interests
This fun-filled magazine includes lively stories, poetry, articles, illustrations, and challenging activities. It targets beginning readers.
- **Audience:** 6–9 years
- **Frequency:** Monthly
- **Distribution:** Subscription; newsstand
- **Circulation:** 60,000
- **Website:** www.cricketmag.com

Freelance Potential
97% written by nonstaff writers. Publishes 50 freelance submissions yearly; 30% by unpublished writers, 50% by authors who are new to the magazine. Receives 3,600 unsolicited mss yearly.

Submissions
Send complete ms; include bibliography for nonfiction. Accepts hard copy and simultaneous submissions if identified. Availability of artwork improves chance of acceptance. SASE. Responds in 6 months.
Articles: 300–800 words. Informational and how-to articles; profiles; and interviews. Topics include nature, animals, science, technology, history, multicultural issues, foreign cultures, and the environment.
Fiction: 300–1,000 words. Easy-to-read stories. Genres include humor, fantasy, fairy tales, folktales, realistic and historical fiction, and science fiction.
Other: Recipes, crafts, puzzles, games, brainteasers, and math and word activities. Poetry, to 20 lines.

Sample Issue
34 pages (no advertising): 1 article; 3 stories; 2 depts/columns; 2 activities; 1 poem. Sample copy, $5 with 9x12 SASE. Guidelines available at website.
- "Frost Crayons." Article discusses the wonders of frost and the two main types of frost.
- "Mattias's Crossing." Story tells how a young boy saves his ill mother.
- "The Danderfield Twins: Too Much Snow." Story describes how friends spend the day playing fun snow games.

Rights and Payment
All rights. Articles and fiction, $.25 per word. Poetry, to $3 per line. Other material, payment rates vary. Pays on publication. Provides 2 contributor's copies.

Editor's Comments
We are looking for articles and photos that will capture the hearts and minds of young readers.

SportingKid

3650 Brookside Parkway, Suite 300
Alpharetta, GA 30022

Editor: Michael J. Pallerino

Description and Interests
Articles that focus on the value of children being physically active can be found in this magazine. It covers a variety of sports, as well as information on coaching, training, health, and fitness. Profiles of players are also featured.
- **Audience:** Parents
- **Frequency:** 6 times each year
- **Distribution:** Subscription; newsstand
- **Circulation:** 400,000
- **Website:** www.sportingkid.com

Freelance Potential
20–30% written by nonstaff writers. Publishes 10 freelance submissions yearly; 10% by authors who are new to the magazine. Receives 600 queries yearly.

Submissions
Query or send complete ms. Accepts email submissions to editor@sportingkid.com. Queries must be pasted into the email message; manuscripts must be attached in a Microsoft Word document. Responds in 1 month.
Articles: Word lengths vary. Informational and how-to articles and personal experience pieces. Topics include all sports played by children, coaching, and training.
Depts/columns: Word lengths vary. The culture of youth sports, new product information, profiles of prominent sports figures, and essays from a parent's perspective.

Sample Issue
40 pages: 7 articles; 9 depts/columns. Sample copy and guidelines available at website.
- "Leader of the Pack." Article examines why New York Jets' player Curtis Martin plays football.
- "Are You Ready For Some Football?" Article discusses teaching kids basic skill progressions.
- Sample dept/column: "Excellence in Youth Sports" profiles St. Andrew's Parks' youth programs.

Rights and Payment
First and electronic rights. All material, payment rates vary. Pays on publication.

Editor's Comments
If you have a interesting story on how youth sports impacted your life, send it to us. We're also interested in articles and tips on topics such as fundraising, health, and coaching, as well as family fitness ideas.

Sports Illustrated Kids

Time & Life Building
1271 Avenue of the Americas
New York, NY 10020

Managing Editor: Bob Der

Description and Interests
This magazine shines the spotlight on up-and-coming young athletes while also profiling well-known professional and college players. Sports news and event coverage is also included. Its readership consists primarily of teens and pre-teens.
- **Audience:** 8–14 years
- **Frequency:** Monthly
- **Distribution:** 71% subscription; 27% controlled; 2% newsstand
- **Circulation:** 1.1 million
- **Website:** www.sikids.com

Freelance Potential
10–15% written by nonstaff writers. Publishes 20 freelance submissions yearly. Receives 204 queries each year.

Submissions
Query or send ms. Send for guidelines to determine which department your material should be sent to. Accepts hard copy. SASE. Responds in 2 months.
Articles: Lead articles and profiles, 500–700 words. Short features, 500–600 words. Topics include professional and aspiring athletes, fitness, health, safety, sports tips, hobbies, science, technology, and multicultural issues.
Depts/columns: Word lengths vary. Events coverage, team profiles, and humor.
Other: Poetry and drawings created by kids. Puzzles, games, and trivia.

Sample Issue
62 pages (24% advertising): 10 articles; 6 depts/columns; 1 game; 1 comic; 1 poster. Sample copy, $3.50 with 9x12 SASE to *Sports Illustrated Kids*, P.O. Box 830609, Birmingham, AL 35283. Writers' guidelines available.
- "Hidden Treasures of the Baseball Hall of Fame." Article showcases some of the items the museum stores but does not display.
- "Escape Artist." Article profiles Ohio State quarterback Troy Smith.

Rights and Payment
All rights. Articles, $100–$1,500. Depts/columns, payment rates vary. Pays on acceptance. Provides copies.

Editor's Comments
Unfortunately, we are accepting very, very few freelance submissions at this time.

Stone Soup

The Magazine by Young Writers & Artists

P.O. Box 83
Santa Cruz, CA 95063

Editor: Gerry Mandel

Description and Interests
The work of young writers and artists appears in each issue of this literary magazine. It offers a mix of stories, poems, book reviews, and artwork, all by children under the age of 14.
- **Audience:** 8–14 years
- **Frequency:** 6 times each year
- **Distribution:** 50% subscription; 25% newsstand; 25% schools
- **Circulation:** 20,000
- **Website:** www.stonesoup.com

Freelance Potential
100% written by nonstaff writers. Publishes 65 freelance submissions yearly; 90% by unpublished writers, 90% by authors who are new to the magazine. Receives 14,400 unsolicited mss yearly.

Submissions
Send complete ms. Accepts submissions by writers under 14 years of age. No simultaneous submissions. SASE. Responds in 6 weeks only if interested.
Fiction: To 2,500 words. Genres include multicultural, ethnic, and historical fiction; adventure; mystery; suspense; and science fiction.
Depts/columns: Book reviews, word length varies.
Other: Poetry, line length varies.

Sample Issue
48 pages (no advertising): 8 stories; 2 poems; 2 book reviews. Sample copy, $5.75. Guidelines available.
- "The Snowflake Lady." Short story explores the friendship that develops between a young girl and an elderly Cherokee woman.
- "The Swim Test." Short story relates the tale of a camp swim test in freezing lake water.
- Sample dept/column: "Book Review" examines a new fiction title for young adults about a would-be teen musician.

Rights and Payment
All rights. Written material, $40. Artwork, $25. Pays on publication. Provides 2 contributor's copies.

Editor's Comments
Send us stories and poems about the things you feel most strongly! Read a few copies of our magazine to get an idea of the type of stories and poems we publish. Prospective book reviewers, please tell us why you want to write reviews for us, and what type of books you enjoy reading.

Story Mates

Christian Light Publications
P.O. Box 1212
Harrisonburg, VA 22803-1212

Editor: Crystal Shank

Description and Interests
Young Mennonite children receive *Story Mates* in their Sunday school classrooms. Theme-based, the take-home paper offers stories that depict children learning how to live in ways that please God. Craft ideas, activities, and poems are other regular features.
- **Audience:** 4–8 years
- **Frequency:** Monthly
- **Distribution:** Subscription; religious instruction
- **Circulation:** 6,192
- **Website:** www.clp.org

Freelance Potential
90% written by nonstaff writers. Publishes 200 freelance submissions yearly. Receives 600 unsolicited mss yearly.

Submissions
Send complete ms. Accepts hard copy and email submissions to storymates@clp.org. SASE. Responds in 6 weeks.
Fiction: Stories related to Sunday school lessons and true-to-life stories; to 800 words. Picture stories; 120–150 words.
Other: Bible puzzles, crafts, and activities. Poetry, word length varies. Submit seasonal material 6 months in advance.

Sample Issue
4 pages (no advertising): 2 stories; 2 poems; 2 activities. Sample copy, free with 9x12 SASE ($.87 postage). Guidelines and theme list available.
- "Trip to the Nursing Home." Story tells of a young girl who finds joy in helping the sick as Jesus did.
- "Food for the Hungry." Story illustrates how a girl came to understand that God wants people who have plenty to share with those who have little.
- "Others." Activity features a verse to decode.

Rights and Payment
First, reprint, or multiple-use rights. Fiction, $.03–$.05 per word. Poetry, $.35–$.75 per line. Other material, payment rates vary. Pays on acceptance. Provides 1 contributor's copy.

Editor's Comments
The purpose of our take-home paper is to build Christian character, promote godly living, and warn of the dangers and deceptions of the world. Everything we print is intended to impress children with the joy of serving Christ.

Storytelling Magazine

National Storytelling Network
132 Boone Street, Suite 5
Jonesborough, TN 37659

Managing Editor: Grace Hawthorne

Description and Interests
Published by the National Storytelling Network, *Storytelling Magazine* features news and applications on oral storytelling tradition as well as read-aloud stories. Professional storytellers, librarians, and teachers are the target audience of this publication.
- **Audience:** Adults
- **Frequency:** 6 times each year
- **Distribution:** 90% controlled; 10% newsstand
- **Circulation:** 6,000
- **Website:** www.storynet.org

Freelance Potential
50% written by nonstaff writers. Publishes 100 freelance submissions yearly. Receives 48 unsolicited mss each year.

Submissions
Query. No unsolicited mss. Accepts email queries to ghawthorne@mindspring.com. Response time varies.
Articles: 1,000–2,000 words. Informational and how-to articles; and personal experience pieces. Topics include storytelling research and analysis, story origins, and multicultural and ethnic issues.
Depts/columns: 500 words. Noteworthy storytelling projects, resources, and reports on activities and events.

Sample Issue
46 pages (25% advertising): 11 articles; 5 stories; 10 depts/columns. Sample copy, $6 (includes postage).
- "Charging Your Worth." Article offers tips for artists on setting and negotiating fees.
- "New Profession Emerges." Article discusses a new academic field called Transformative Language Arts and describes this emerging profession.
- Sample dept/column: "Storytelling World" features the 2006 winners and honors of the Storytelling World Resource Awards.

Rights and Payment
First North American serial rights. No payment. Provides 2 contributor's copies.

Editor's Comments
We will consider queries from experienced storytellers who can provide us with something new. We seek new ideas and innovative applications of oral storytelling to be used for storytelling sessions. Reports on specific projects and events by their organizers are also of interest to us.

Student Assistance Journal

1270 Rankin Drive, Suite F
Troy, MI 48083

Editor: Erin Bell

Description and Interests
This publication provides comprehensive and specialized information to student assistance professionals and youth workers. Articles range from enhancement of core programs to current challenges related to student welfare.
- **Audience:** Student assistance personnel, K–12
- **Frequency:** Quarterly
- **Distribution:** Unavailable
- **Circulation:** 15,000
- **Website:** www.prponline.net

Freelance Potential
90% written by nonstaff writers. Publishes 12 freelance submissions yearly; 50% by unpublished writers. Receives 36 queries yearly.

Submissions
Query if outside the field. Professionals should send complete ms. Accepts hard copy, IBM DOS-compatible disk submissions (WordPerfect), and simultaneous submissions if identified. SASE. Responds only if interested.
Articles: 1,500 words. Informational and how-to articles; and personal experience pieces. Topics include high-risk students, special education programs, drug testing, substance abuse prevention, school violence, legal issues, federal funding, and staff development.
Depts/columns: 750–800 words. Book reviews, events, commentaries, short news items, legal issues, media resources, and related research.

Sample Issue
34 pages (20% advertising): 3 articles; 6 depts/columns. Sample copy, free. Guidelines available.
- "Click to Inflict: A Look at Cyber-Bullying." Article shows how kids use cyberspace to hurt peers.
- Sample dept/column: "News You Can Use" discusses psychological effects of natural disasters and the increased demand for student assistant services in the aftermath of the recent hurricanes.

Rights and Payment
First rights. No payment. Provides 5 author's copies.

Editor's Comments
We look for articles that contain in-depth information about innovative programs, evaluation of existing programs, and federally funded initiatives, as well as personal experiences that can be useful for other professionals.

Student Leader

Oxendine Publishing
412 Northwest 16th Avenue
Gainesville, FL 32604-2097

Editor: Anna Campitelli

Description and Interests

As the official publication of the American Student Government Association (ASGA), this magazine helps students and their advisors be more effective and influential leaders. It targets both high school and college students.
- **Audience:** High school and college students
- **Frequency:** 3 times each year
- **Distribution:** Schools; subscription
- **Circulation:** 130,000
- **Website:** www.studentleader.com

Freelance Potential

10% written by nonstaff writers. Publishes 10 freelance submissions yearly; 50% by unpublished writers, 80% by authors who are new to the magazine. Receives 60 queries yearly.

Submissions

Query only. Accepts hard copy, email queries to info@studentleader.com, and simultaneous submissions. Availability of artwork improves chance of acceptance. SASE. Responds in 6 weeks.
Articles: 1,000 words. Informational articles. Topics include organizational management, service projects, fundraising, student motivation, interpersonal skills, promoting special events, editorial standards, communication, and volunteerism.
Depts/columns: 250 words. ASGA updates.
Artwork: Color prints and 35mm slides.

Sample Issue

14 pages (50% advertising): 4 articles; 1 dept/column. Sample copy, $3.50 with 9x12 SASE ($1.07 postage). Guidelines and editorial calendar available.
- "Making Waves." Article describes projects conducted by the student government association at Salisbury University.
- "Moving On." Article tells students how to leave an orderly legacy when transitioning out of a student leadership post.

Rights and Payment

All rights. All material, payment rates vary. Pays on publication. Provides 1 contributor's copy.

Editor's Comments

We promote the vital importance of an effective and autonomous student governance organization on any campus. Our articles come from advisors, higher-education experts, and professional freelancers.

SuperScience

Scholastic Inc.
557 Broadway
New York, NY 10012-3999

Editor: Nancy Honovich

Description and Interests

Striving to make learning science fun and exciting, this magazine includes fascinating science news stories and photos, as well as hands-on activities. Published by Scholastic, it is distributed in classrooms and includes a teachers' guide.
- **Audience:** Grades 3–6
- **Frequency:** 8 times each year
- **Distribution:** 100% schools
- **Circulation:** 200,000
- **Website:** www.scholastic.com/superscience

Freelance Potential

75% written by nonstaff writers. Of the freelance submissions published yearly, 50% are by authors who are new to the magazine. Receives 60–120 queries yearly.

Submissions

Query with résumé and clips. No unsolicited mss. Accepts hard copy. SASE. Response time varies.
Articles: 300–1,000 words. Informational and how-to articles; profiles; interviews; and personal experience pieces. Topics include earth, physical, and life science; health; technology; chemistry; nature; and the environment.
Depts/columns: Word lengths vary. Science news.
Artwork: 8x10 B/W or color prints. Line art.
Other: Puzzles and activities.

Sample Issue

16 pages (no advertising): 2 articles; 1 story; 5 depts/columns. Sample copy, free with 9x12 SASE. Guidelines and editorial calendar available.
- "The Case of the Tongue Zapper." Story tells how students learn about electricity by using lemons.
- "America's Least Wanted." Article takes a look at some exotic animals and plants that pose a threat to wildlife.
- Sample dept/column: "Hands On" offers a test to find out if wind can transport seeds.

Rights and Payment

First rights. Articles, $75–$600. Other material, payment rates vary. Pays on acceptance. Provides 2 contributor's copies.

Editor's Comments

All of our work is assigned. Check our editorial calendar and send us a query outlining your exciting idea along with samples of your writing.

SW Florida Parent & Child

2442 Dr. Martin Luther King, Jr., Boulevard
Fort Myers, FL 33901

Editor: Pamela Smith Hayford

Description and Interests

Distributed free to parents residing in southwest
Florida, this publication includes articles on parenting
issues, education, health, family, and travel. It also
covers regional events, activities, and resources.
- **Audience:** Parents
- **Frequency:** Monthly
- **Distribution:** 100% controlled
- **Circulation:** 25,000
- **Website: www.swflparentchild.com**

Freelance Potential

75% written by nonstaff writers. Publishes 160 freelance submissions yearly; 5% by unpublished writers,
25% by authors who are new to the magazine.
Receives 275 queries and mss yearly.

Submissions

Query or send complete ms. Prefers email submissions to pamela@swflparentchild.com. Accepts hard
copy. SASE. Response time varies.
Articles: To 500 words. Informational articles;
profiles; and personal experience pieces. Topics
include family issues, parenting, education, travel,
sports, health, fitness, computers, and social and
regional issues.
Depts/columns: To 500 words. Dining, travel, parenting, education, and nutrition.

Sample Issue

84 pages (50% advertising): 4 articles; 21 depts/
columns. Guidelines available.
- "School Registration." Article offers information from
  different counties in southern Florida on the school
  registration process.
- "Fighting Prejudice." Article takes a look at Black
  History Month and activities that can encourage children to respect all cultures.
- Sample dept/column: "Health" discusses how to
  keep kids' mouths cavity free.

Rights and Payment

All rights. Written material, $25–$200. Pays on
publication.

Editor's Comments

We are looking for articles that will provide readers
with positive parenting information, strategies, and
resources. Send us something new and informative
that covers a hot parenting topic. We are receiving a
high volume of personal experience pieces.

Swimming World and Junior Swimmer

90 Bell Rock Plaza, Suite 200
Sedona, AZ 86351

Editor

Description and Interests

This magazine keeps competitive swimmers informed
of the latest happenings in the world of swimming. It
includes meet results; articles on training techniques,
nutrition, and fitness; and medical advice; as well as
inspirational stories and profiles.
- **Audience:** All ages
- **Frequency:** Monthly
- **Distribution:** 90% subscription; 10% newsstand
- **Circulation:** 59,000
- **Website: www.swimmingworldmagazine.com**

Freelance Potential

75% written by nonstaff writers. Publishes 5–10 freelance submissions yearly; 5% by unpublished writers,
25% by authors who are new to the magazine.
Receives 192+ queries yearly.

Submissions

Query. Accepts hard copy and email queries to
editorial@swimmingworldmagazine.com. SASE.
Responds in 1 month.
Articles: 500–3,500 words. Informational and how-to
articles; profiles; and personal experience pieces.
Topics include swimming, training, competition, medical advice, swim drills, nutrition, dryland exercise,
exercise physiology, and fitness.
Depts/columns: 500–750 words. Swimming news,
new product reviews, and nutrition advice.
Artwork: Color prints and transparencies. Line art.
Other: Activities, games, and jokes. Submit seasonal
material 1–2 months in advance.

Sample Issue

62 pages (30% advertising): 5 articles; 15 depts/
columns; 1 calendar. Sample copy, $4.50 with 9x12
SASE ($1.80 postage). Guidelines available.
- "Still Kicking." Article profiles Melissa Belote, a
  swimmer who won three gold medals at the
  1972 Olympics.
- Sample dept/column: "Aquatic Lifestyle" describes
  how a quadriplegic created a scholarship.

Rights and Payment

All rights. Written material, $.12 per word. Artwork,
payment rates vary. Pays on publication. Provides
2–5 contributor's copies.

Editor's Comments

We're looking for kid-oriented stories as well as features on some aspect of competitive swimming.

Synapse

25 Beacon Street
Boston, MA 02108

Editor

Description and Interests
Creative work by teens is showcased in *Synapse*.
Published both online and in print, it is the magazine
of the Young Religious Unitarian Universalists, the
youth organization of the Unitarian Universalist
Association. It also features youth group projects.
• **Audience:** 14–21 years
• **Frequency:** 3 times each year online/1 time print
• **Distribution:** Subscription; Internet
• **Circulation:** 2,500
• **Website:** www.uua.org/yruu/synapse

Freelance Potential
85% written by nonstaff writers. Of the freelance
submissions published yearly, 90% are by unpublished writers.

Submissions
Send complete ms with contact information. Accepts
disk submissions (Quark) and email submissions to
YRUU@uua.org. Responds in 1 month.
Articles: Word lengths vary. Informational articles;
personal experience pieces; and opinion pieces.
Topics include current events, social issues, popular
culture, regional events, youth programs, history, and
ethnic and multicultural issues.
Depts/columns: Word lengths vary. Social action
news, readings by Unitarian Universalist youth, sermons, homilies, and religious and spiritual reflections.
Other: Puzzles, activities, games, jokes, and poetry
related to Unitarian Universalism.

Sample Issue
40 pages (7% advertising): 7 articles; 10 depts/
columns; 1 event calendar. Sample copy and guidelines available at website.
• "What Does It Mean to Be Hot?" Article reports
  on the work of Unitarian Universalists regarding
  global warming.
• "Change the World: You Can, You Should, and You
  Will!" First-person piece describes one teen's work
  on social justice issues.

Rights and Payment
All rights. No payment.

Editor's Comments
We accept creative work and articles year-round. We
want to see strong, articulate, and beautiful work by
UU youth. We also want to hear about amazing projects your youth group is doing.

Syracuse Parent

5910 Firestone Drive
Syracuse, NY 13206

Editor: Brittany Jared

Description and Interests
This free parenting tabloid provides families living in
central New York with information on regional events
and resources while also covering more general top-
ics, such as child care, health, education, and family
entertainment.
• **Audience:** Parents
• **Frequency:** Monthly
• **Distribution:** 70% controlled; 20% schools;
   10% subscription
• **Circulation:** 26,500
• **Website:** www.syracuseparent.net

Freelance Potential
40% written by nonstaff writers. Publishes 15 freelance submissions yearly; 25% by unpublished writers,
10% by authors who are new to the magazine.
Receives 96 queries yearly.

Submissions
Query. Accepts hard copy. SASE. Responds in
4–6 weeks.
Articles: 800–1,000 words. Informational and
how-to articles; personal experience and practical
application pieces; profiles; interviews; and humor.
Topics include parenting, family issues, animals, pets,
education, health, current events, regional news,
social issues, nature, the environment, computers,
music, travel, and sports.
Depts/columns: Staff written.
Other: Submit seasonal and holiday material 3–4
months in advance.

Sample Issue
24 pages (50% advertising): 3 articles; 3 depts/
columns; 1 child-care guide; 1 events calendar.
Sample copy, guidelines, and editorial calendar, $1
with 9x12 SASE.
• "Local Psychologists Offer Alternative to ADHD
  Drugs." Article reports on an ADHD treatment
  program that uses a mix of discipline, structure,
  and counseling.
• "Tuna Best in Moderation." Article provides facts
  about mercury levels in canned tuna.

Rights and Payment
First rights. Articles, $25–$30. Pays on publication.

Editor's Comments
We strongly prefer articles with a local angle, featuring
local resources and quotes from local experts.

Take Five Plus

The General Council of the Assemblies of God
1445 North Boonville Avenue
Springfield, MO 65802-1894

Editor: James Meredith

Description and Interests
Young adult members of Assemblies of God congregations receive daily devotionals based on Scripture readings in this religious publication. Questions intended to stimulate thoughtful reflection are also part of *Take Five Plus*. It is designed to encourage teens to strengthen their relationship with God.
- **Audience:** 12–19 years
- **Frequency:** Quarterly
- **Distribution:** 90% religious instruction; 10% subscription
- **Circulation:** 20,000
- **Website: www.gospelpublishing.com**

Freelance Potential
98% written by nonstaff writers. Of the freelance submissions published yearly, 10% are by authors who are new to the magazine.

Submissions
All material is assigned. Send letter of introduction with résumé, church background, and clips or writing samples. Accepts hard copy. SASE. Responds in 3 months.
Articles: 200–235 words. Daily devotionals based on Scripture readings.
Artwork: Accepts material from teenagers only. 8x10 B/W prints and 35 mm color slides. 8x10 or smaller color line art.
Other: Poetry by teens, to 20 lines.

Sample Issue
126 pages (no advertising): 90 devotionals; 2 poems. Guidelines and sample devotional available on request for sample assignment.
- "Showing Kindness." Devotional based on Samuel emphasizes that showing kindness takes effort, but that it is worth the effort in God's eyes.
- "Unconditional Love." Devotional based on Solomon reminds us that real love is the most powerful force on earth because God created it.

Rights and Payment
First rights. Written material, $.05 per word. Artwork, payment rates vary. Pays on publication. Provides 2 contributor's copies.

Editor's Comments
Devotionals with connections to contemporary issues that teens face are of interest to us. Interested writers should contact us for guidelines and assignments.

Tar Heel Junior Historian

North Carolina Museum of History
4650 Mail Service Center
Raleigh, NC 27699-4650

Editor: Lisa Costen Hall

Description and Interests
Published by the state of North Carolina, this magazine corresponds to the curricula in the state's middle schools and high schools. It includes illustrated articles on history, geography, and government that are accompanied by educational activities.
- **Audience:** 9–18 years
- **Frequency:** Twice each year
- **Distribution:** 100% North Carolina schools
- **Circulation:** 9,000
- **Website: http://ncmuseumofhistory.org**

Freelance Potential
50% written by nonstaff writers. Publishes 15 freelance submissions yearly; 40% by unpublished writers, 20% by authors who are new to the magazine.

Submissions
Query. No unsolicited mss. SASE. Response time varies.
Articles: 700–1,000 words. Informational articles; profiles; interviews; and personal experience pieces. Topics include regional history; geography; government; and social, multicultural, and ethnic issues.
Fiction: Word lengths vary. Genres include historical, ethnic, and multicultural fiction; folktales; and folklore.
Artwork: B/W and color prints or transparencies. Line art.
Other: Puzzles, activities, and word games.

Sample Issue
38 pages (no advertising): 14 articles; 4 activities. Sample copy, $4 with 9x12 SASE ($2 postage). Guidelines and theme list available.
- "The Great Philadelphia Wagon Road." Article takes readers along a road that was used by immigrants in the 1700s to settle much of the interior back country of North Carolina.
- "A Forced Migration." Article traces the journey of slaves who came from Africa to North Carolina's plantations.

Rights and Payment
All rights. No payment. Provides 10 contributor's copies.

Editor's Comments
Most of our contributors are scholars or educators who have a deep knowledge of our state's history and heritage. All issues are theme-based, and the themes are determined two to three years in advance.

Teacher Librarian

15200 NBN Way
Blue Ridge Summit, PA 17214

Managing Editor: Kim Tabor

Description and Interests
This educational journal identifies and responds to the challenges faced by school library professionals. It provides thought-provoking articles to encourage continual learning.
- **Audience:** Professional school librarians; educators
- **Frequency:** 5 times each year
- **Distribution:** 100% subscription
- **Circulation:** 10,000
- **Website: www.teacherlibrarian.com**

Freelance Potential
60% written by nonstaff writers. Publishes 10 freelance submissions yearly; 25% by unpublished writers, 5% by authors who are new to the magazine. Receives 6 queries and unsolicited mss yearly.

Submissions
Query or send complete ms with résumé, abstract, or bibliography. Accepts hard copy, disk submissions, and email to editor@teacherlibrarian.com. SASE. Responds in 2 months.
Articles: 2,000+ words. Informational and analytical articles; and profiles. Topics include library funding, technology, leadership, library management, audio/visual materials, cooperative teaching, and young adult services.
Depts/columns: Staff written.

Sample Issue
72 pages (20% advertising): 5 articles; 20 depts/columns; 12 reviews. Guidelines and editorial calendar available.
- "The Internet and Student Research." Article stresses the importance of teaching critical evaluation skills to students to apply to Internet research.
- "Boys Are People Too." Article discusses the truths and misconceptions about the reading habits of young and young adult boys.

Rights and Payment
All rights. Written material, $100. Pays on publication. Provides 2 contributor's copies.

Editor's Comments
We strive to present challenging articles about strategies for effective advocacy and critical analysis of management and programming issues. We welcome material on all aspects of library services for children and young adults that contribute to excellence in programs and improved support for their delivery.

Teacher Magazine

Editorial Projects in Education
6935 Arlington Road, Suite 100
Bethesda, MD 20814

Managing Editor: Scott Cech

Description and Interests
Striving to give educators resourceful information for innovative teaching, this magazine includes research and commentaries, opinion pieces, book reviews, and news. It is read by teachers of kindergarten through grade twelve.
- **Audience:** Teachers
- **Frequency:** 6 times each year
- **Distribution:** Subscription; controlled
- **Circulation:** 120,000
- **Website: www.teachermagazine.com**

Freelance Potential
40% written by nonstaff writers. Publishes 35–40 freelance submissions yearly; 80% by unpublished writers, 20% by authors who are new to the magazine. Receives 480 unsolicited mss yearly.

Submissions
Send complete ms. Accepts hard copy. SASE. Responds in 3 months.
Articles: To 3,000 words. Educational articles; commentary; opinion pieces; and personal experience pieces. Topics include K–12 education, professional development, classroom teaching, literacy, technology, and bilingual education.
Depts/columns: 1,000–1,250 words. "Viewpoints" features opinion pieces on precollegiate education. "First Person" offers school-related personal experience pieces.

Sample Issue
60 pages: 5 articles; 7 depts/columns. Sample copy, $4. Guidelines available.
- "Exit Strategy." Article takes a look at investment options for retirement plans.
- "Back to the Future." Article describes an educational experiment in Virginia during the 1980s where students were given computers to use in the classroom.
- Sample dept/column: "Classroom Tech" discusses the future of technology in the classroom.

Rights and Payment
First rights. Written material, payment rates vary. Pays on publication. Provides 3 contributor's copies.

Editor's Comments
Freelancers have a better chance of acceptance if they submit a column or an opinion piece. Most of our articles are written in-house, but we will consider top-notch articles covering innovative educational ideas.

Teachers & Writers

520 Eighth Avenue, Suite 2020
New York, NY 10018

Publication Director: Amy Swauger

Description and Interests
This magazine provides teachers and other educators with practical ideas and strategies for teaching the art of creative and expository writing to students in kindergarten through college.
- **Audience:** Teachers
- **Frequency:** Quarterly
- **Distribution:** 100% subscription
- **Circulation:** 3,000
- **Website:** www.twc.org

Freelance Potential
70% written by nonstaff writers. Publishes 25 freelance submissions yearly; 5% by unpublished writers, 50% by authors who are new to the magazine. Receives 120 unsolicited mss yearly.

Submissions
Send complete ms. Accepts hard copy and simultaneous submissions if identified. No email submissions. SASE. Response time varies.
Articles: 700–5,000 words. Practical and theoretical articles featuring innovative teaching ideas; and fresh approaches to familiar teaching methods. Topics include teaching writing in conjunction with the visual arts; teaching oral history; and teaching writing to senior citizens. Also publishes translations.
Depts/columns: Word lengths vary. Information on events; book reviews.
Other: Submit seasonal material 6 months in advance.

Sample Issue
32 pages (no advertising): 4 articles. Sample copy, $4. Guidelines available.
- "Structure and Surprise." Article examines a new approach in categorizing poetry.
- "A Quarrel with Itself." Excerpt from a forthcoming book looks at the ironic structure in poetry.

Rights and Payment
First serial rights. Written material, $20 per printed column. Pays on publication. Provides 10 contributor's copies.

Editor's Comments
We are looking for submissions that tackle new and innovative ways of teaching creative writing. Our readers are smart and enthusiastic teachers who are looking for practical and theoretically-based teaching strategies.

Teachers Interaction

Concordia Publishing House
3558 South Jefferson Avenue
St. Louis, MO 63118-3698

Editor: Thomas A. Nummela

Description and Interests
Innovative strategies for teaching Sunday school are showcased in *Teachers Interaction*. It targets religious educators and administrators working with students in preschool through sixth grade.
- **Audience:** Sunday school teachers
- **Frequency:** Quarterly
- **Distribution:** 70% subscription; 30% churches
- **Circulation:** 12,000
- **Website:** www.cph.org

Freelance Potential
95% written by nonstaff writers. Publishes 20 freelance submissions yearly; 10% by unpublished writers, 20% by authors who are new to the magazine. Receives 48 unsolicited mss yearly.

Submissions
Query or send complete ms; include Social Security number. Prefers email submissions to tom.nummela@cph.org. Accepts hard copy. SASE. Responds in 3 months.
Articles: To 1,100 words. How-to articles and personal experience pieces. Topics include education, theology, teaching methods, and child development.
Depts/columns: 400 words. Humor, teaching tips, and classroom strategies.
Other: Practical ideas for teachers, 100–200 words. Submit seasonal material 10 months in advance.

Sample Issue
30 pages (no advertising): 5 articles; 10 depts/columns. Sample copy, $4.99. Guidelines available.
- "Technology: Toys or Tools?" Article asks whether technology has a place in today's Sunday school.
- "Making the Most of the Holidays." Article explains how holidays can be used to encourage family worship and to thank God for his work.
- Sample dept/column: "The Adaptive Teacher" talks about why it is important for teachers to get to know their students.

Rights and Payment
All rights. Articles, $55–$110. "The Teachers Toolbox," $20–$40. Pays on publication. Provides 1 contributor's copy.

Editor's Comments
The best way to break into our magazine is to send an original, creative, and practical idea for Sunday school classroom use.

Teachers of Vision

Christian Educators Association International
P.O. Box 41300
Pasadena, CA 91114

Contributing Editor: Judy Turpen

Description and Interests
The emphasis in this publication is on practical and inspiring teaching ideas for Christian educators.
- **Audience:** Christian teachers
- **Frequency:** 6 times each year
- **Distribution:** 90% controlled; 10% newsstand
- **Circulation:** 10,000
- **Website:** www.ceai.org

Freelance Potential
65% written by nonstaff writers. Publishes 30–40 freelance submissions yearly; 5% by unpublished writers, 30% by authors who are new to the magazine. Receives 80–100 unsolicited mss yearly.

Submissions
Send complete ms with brief biography. Prefers email submissions to judy@ceai.org (RTF files). Accepts letter-quality hard copy and disk submissions (RTF files or Microsoft Word) with hard copy. SASE. Responds in 2–3 months.
Articles: 400–1,000 words. How-to articles; personal experience pieces; and documented reports, 800–1,000 words. Topics include education issues, educational philosophy, and methodology. Interviews with noted Christian educators, 500–800 words. Teaching techniques, news, and special events, 400–500 words.
Depts/columns: 100–200 words. Reviews of books, videos, curricula, games, and other curricula resources for K–12 teachers.
Other: Submit seasonal material 4 months in advance.

Sample Issue
16 pages (1% advertising): 9 articles; 1 story; 7 depts/columns. Sample copy, free with 9x12 SASE (5 first-class stamps). Guidelines available.
- "Making the Case for Diversity Education." Article advocates having a range of cultures in a classroom.
- "God is Changing China." Article relates a firsthand account of a teacher's experience in China.
- Sample dept/column: "Color Blindness" equates a child's color blindness to accepting racial diversity.

Rights and Payment
First and electronic rights. Articles, $20–$40. Reviews, $5. Pays on publication. Provides 3 author's copies.

Editor's Comments
We need submissions featuring current issues pertinent to higher education and college classroom situations.

Teaching Elementary Physical Education

Human Kinetics Publishers
P.O. Box 5076
Champaign, IL 61825-5076

Senior Editor: Steve Stork

Description and Interests
Practical information that helps physical education teachers stay on top of their profession can be found in this magazine. It includes articles, tips, and reviews.
- **Audience:** Physical education teachers
- **Frequency:** 6 times each year
- **Distribution:** 95% subscription; 5% other
- **Circulation:** 4,000+
- **Website:** www.humankinetics.com

Freelance Potential
100% written by nonstaff writers. Publishes 76 freelance submissions yearly; 20% by unpublished writers, 30% by authors who are new to the magazine. Receives 96 unsolicited mss yearly.

Submissions
Query with clips; or send complete ms. Accepts hard copy. SASE. Responds in 1–4 weeks.
Articles: 2–12 double-spaced pages. Informational, how-to, personal experience, and self-help articles. Topics include health, fitness, physical education, liability, accountability, motivation, and public relations.
Depts/columns: 200–500 words. Early childhood issues, book reviews, and technology tips.
Artwork: B/W or color glossy prints; digital photos, 300 dpi minimum.

Sample Issue
40 pages (25% advertising): 5 articles; 5 depts/columns. Sample copy, $4 with 9x12 SASE. Guidelines available.
- "Squaring to the Rap!" Article discusses using rap music to teach students how to square dance.
- "Where the Rubber Meets the Road: Practical Tips for Behavior Management." Article offers classroom management strategies that guide students and engage them in their own problem-solving.
- Sample dept/column: "Active Healthy Lifestyles" takes a look at developmentally appropriate physical activities for elementary students.

Rights and Payment
First or one-time rights. No payment. Provides 1 contributor's copy.

Editor's Comments
We're looking for new ideas for fitness activities that are exciting, challenging, and fun. Authors are highly encouraged to submit artwork with their articles. Readers enjoy seeing interesting pictures.

Teaching PreK–8

40 Richards Avenue
Norwalk, CT 06854

Submissions Editor: Katherine Pierpont

Description and Interests
This magazine for professional teacher development offers proven classroom strategies, projects, and activities for elementary and middle-grade teachers.
• **Audience:** Teachers, preK–grade 8
• **Frequency:** 8 times each year
• **Distribution:** 100% subscription
• **Circulation:** 130,000
• **Website: www.teachingk-8.com**

Freelance Potential
80% written by nonstaff writers. Publishes 30–32 freelance submissions yearly; 95–98% by unpublished writers, 95% by authors who are new to the magazine. Receives 2,000 unsolicited mss yearly.

Submissions
Send complete ms. Accepts hard copy. No simultaneous submissions. SASE. Responds in 1 month.
Articles: To 1,000 words. Informational and how-to articles; and personal experience pieces. Topics include curriculum development, classroom management, gifted and special education, character education, teaching methods, early childhood education, homework strategies, math, social studies, science, and language arts.
Depts/columns: Staff written.
Artwork: Color prints. No digital images.

Sample Issue
72 pages (50% advertising): 8 articles; 19 depts/columns. Sample copy, $4.50 with 9x12 SASE (10 first-class stamps). Guidelines and theme list available.
• "All the President's Math." Article looks at the administrative goals of Francis "Skip" Fennell, president of the NCTM.
• "A String of Beads." Article details how to make a fun math activity for the 100th day of school.

Rights and Payment
All North American serial rights. Written material, $20–$50. Artwork, payment rate varies. Pays on publication. Provides 2 contributor's copies.

Editor's Comments
We continue to seek creative, proven classroom management ideas. Our focus is on hands-on activities that can be applied across the curriculum in preschool through grade eight. We are not interested in broad overviews of current educational programs, nor reports on general educational theory.

Teaching Theatre

2343 Auburn Avenue
Cincinnati, OH 45219

Editor: James Palmarini

Description and Interests
Established in 1989, this educational theatre journal is read by middle and high school theatre teachers, as well as others interested in teaching theatre. It includes articles on curriculum development, technical production advice, play suggestions, and classroom exercises.
• **Audience:** Theatre teachers
• **Frequency:** Quarterly
• **Distribution:** 80% controlled; 20% other
• **Circulation:** 4,500
• **Website: www.edta.org**

Freelance Potential
70% written by nonstaff writers. Publishes 15 freelance submissions yearly; 30% by unpublished writers, 50% by authors who are new to the magazine. Receives 75 queries yearly.

Submissions
Query with outline. Accepts hard copy. SASE. Responds in 1 month.
Articles: 1,000–3,000 words. Informational articles and personal experience pieces. Topics include theatre education, the arts, and curriculum materials.
Depts/columns: Word lengths vary. "Promptbook" features classroom exercises, ideas, technical advice, and textbook or play suggestions.

Sample Issue
32 pages (3–5% advertising): 3 articles; 11 depts/columns. Sample copy, $2 with 9x12 SASE ($2 postage). Guidelines available.
• "A Vicious Ballet." Article discusses methods developed by educators to make stage violence a positive part of their teaching repertoire.
• "Writing the Music, Singing the Songs." Article offers a step-by-step approach to leading a class through the composition of their first musical plays.
• Sample dept/column: "Prompt Book" takes a look at the use of t-shirts as costumes.

Rights and Payment
One time rights. Written material, payment rate varies. Pays on publication. Provides 5 contributor's copies.

Editor's Comments
We are looking for material on technology, directions, assessment, and middle school, all as they relate to teaching theatre. Also, profiles of exemplary theatre education programs are of interest to us.

Teach Kids!

P.O. Box 348
Warrenton, MO 63383-0348

Editor: Elsie Lippy

Description and Interests
Acting as a handy resource for Christian educators of children ages 4 to 11, this publication is filled with a mixture of teaching aids and ideas, as well as perspectives from children in that age range.
- **Audience:** Christian educators
- **Frequency:** 6 times each year
- **Distribution:** 75% subscription; 25% other
- **Circulation:** 12,000
- **Website:** www.teachkidsmag.com

Freelance Potential
75% written by nonstaff writers. Publishes 50 freelance submissions yearly; 5% by unpublished writers, 20% by authors who are new to the magazine.

Submissions
Query with outline; or send complete ms. Accepts hard copy and email submissions to editor@ teachkidsmag.com. SASE. Responds to queries in 1 month, to mss in 2 months.
Articles: 800–900 words. How-to, factual, and idea pieces. Topics include Christian education, religion, teaching techniques, and understanding children.
Fiction: 800–900 words for stories written at the third- and fourth-grade level. Features contemporary stories with scriptural solutions to problems faced by today's children.
Depts/columns: "Easy Ideas" offers creative teaching ideas teachers can use with children ages 4–11, 200–300 words.

Sample Issue
54 pages (25% advertising): 4 articles; 9 depts/columns; 4 teaching tools; 4 reproducibles. Sample copy, $3. Guidelines available.
- "Great Leaders Honor God." Article helps children learn to respect God's leaders.
- Sample dept/column: "Easy Ideas" presents several teaching aids for evangelizing and discipling kids.

Rights and Payment
All, first, one-time, or electronic rights. Written material, payment rates vary. Pays within 60 days of acceptance. Provides 1 contributor's copy.

Editor's Comments
We need hands-on, theme-related teaching ideas for preschool children. Short ideas including missions, review games, and object lessons are also needed for children up to age 11.

Tech Directions

Prakken Publications
832 Phoenix Drive
P.O. Box 8623
Ann Arbor, MI 48107

Managing Editor: Susanne Peckham

Description and Interests
Keeping readers up to date on technological advancements as they apply to education and careers is the goal of this publication, read by professionals involved in teaching this subject.
- **Audience:** Teachers; administrators
- **Frequency:** 10 times each year
- **Distribution:** 98% controlled; 2% subscription
- **Circulation:** 43,000
- **Website:** www.techdirections.com

Freelance Potential
80% written by nonstaff writers. Publishes 40 freelance submissions yearly; 50% by unpublished writers, 50% by authors who are new to the magazine. Receives 192 unsolicited mss yearly.

Submissions
Query or send complete ms. Accepts hard copy and Macintosh compatible email to susanne@ techdirections.com. SASE. Responds to queries in 1 week, to mss in 1 month.
Articles: To 3,000 words. Informational and how-to articles; and new product information. Topics include vocational and technical career education, technology, electronics, graphics, industrial arts, manufacturing, and computers.
Depts/columns: Word lengths vary. Legislative news, tool reviews, and new product information.

Sample Issue
36 pages (40% advertising): 5 articles; 8 depts/columns. Sample copy, $5 with 9x12 SASE (2 first-class stamps). Writers' guidelines and editorial calendar available.
- "Water Delivery—It's All About Pressure." Article explains water delivery systems.
- "Small Engine Mechanic." Article provides information on the necessary education for that career.
- Sample dept/column: "Technology Today" tackles the technology behind manipulating photos.

Rights and Payment
All rights. Articles, $50 for the first page, $25 for each additional page. Depts/columns, to $25. Pays on publication. Provides 3 contributor's copies.

Editor's Comments
We are interested in projects that provide students with practical hands-on experience that will further their knowledge and help them in their career pursuits.

Techniques

Connecting Education and Careers

1410 King Street
Alexandria, VA 22314

Editor: Susan Reese

Description and Interests
Issues related to technical education and careers fill the pages of this magazine published by the Association for Career and Technical Education. It features articles on a variety of topics including college, current events, computers, and careers.
- **Audience:** Educators
- **Frequency:** 8 times each year
- **Distribution:** 80% membership; 15% schools; 5% subscription
- **Circulation:** 35,000
- **Website: www.acteonline.org**

Freelance Potential
50% written by nonstaff writers. Publishes 10–20 freelance submissions yearly; 15% by unpublished writers, 30% by authors who are new to the magazine. Receives 96 unsolicited mss yearly.

Submissions
Query or send complete ms. Prefers email submissions to susan@printmanagementinc.com. Accepts hard copy and disk submissions (Microsoft Word). SASE. Responds in 4 months.
Articles: To 2,000 words. Informational and how-to articles; profiles; and reviews. Topics include careers, technology, education, computers, college, current events, science, math, and social studies.
Depts/columns: 500–850 words. Organizational news, opinion pieces, and legislative updates.
Artwork: Color prints and transparencies. Line art.
Other: Submit material about the end of the school year in March.

Sample Issue
62 pages (30% advertising): 9 articles; 12 depts/columns. Writers' guidelines and theme list available at website.
- "A Vision of the 21st Century." Article discusses strategies to improve technical and career education in America's high schools.
- Sample dept/column: "Classroom Connection" offers suggestions on coping with end-of-the-year maladies.

Rights and Payment
All and Internet rights. Articles, payment rates vary. Depts/columns, $500. Pays on publication.

Editor's Comments
We seek topics related to technology from writers who use a conversational style while relaying information.

Technology & Learning

CMP Media, Inc.
600 Harrison Street
San Francisco, CA 94107

Managing Editor: Mark Smith

Description and Interests
The use of technology in educational settings is the focus of this magazine. In addition to teaching ideas and strategies, it offers product, software, and website reviews. It also covers professional development topics for technology educators.
- **Audience:** Education and technology coordinators
- **Frequency:** Monthly
- **Distribution:** 70% subscription; 30% newsstand
- **Circulation:** 85,000
- **Website: www.techlearning.com**

Freelance Potential
50–60% written by nonstaff writers. Publishes 50 freelance submissions yearly; 5% by authors who are new to the magazine. Receives 60–96 queries yearly.

Submissions
Query with outline and clips or writing samples. Accepts hard copy. SASE. Responds in 3 months.
Articles: 1,200–2,500 words. Informational and how-to articles. Topics include technology, education, research, teaching, and controversial issues in education and technology. Also publishes reviews of software used in education.
Depts/columns: To 600 words. News, trends, opinions, the Internet, and emerging technologies.
Other: Submit material about the end of the school year in March.

Sample Issue
44 pages (40% advertising): 5 articles; 6 depts/columns. Sample copy, $3 with 9x12 SASE ($3 postage). Guidelines and editorial calendar available.
- "Staff Development 2.0." Article reports on why school districts must keep on the edge of professional development in the field of technology.
- "Remote Control." Article takes a look at classroom management software.
- Sample dept/column: "Open for Business" explains how open-source software can save schools money.

Rights and Payment
First rights. Articles, $400–$600. Software reviews, $150. Depts/columns, payment rates vary. Pays on publication. Provides 1 contributor's copy.

Editor's Comments
We often suggest that new writers begin by submitting to a department. Most of our contributors have extensive experience using technology in schools.

Teen

3000 Ocean Park Boulevard, Suite 3048
Santa Monica, CA 90405

Editor: Jane Fort

Description and Interests
This glossy magazine for pre-teen and teenage girls
is filled with articles on topics popular with this
age group: fashion and beauty, dating, health, and
teenage celebrities.
- **Audience:** 12–16 years
- **Frequency:** Quarterly
- **Distribution:** 100% newsstand
- **Circulation:** 650,000
- **Website:** www.teenmag.com

Freelance Potential
60% written by nonstaff writers. Of the freelance submissions published yearly, 5% are by authors who are
new to the magazine. Receives 120 queries yearly.

Submissions
Query for nonfiction. Send complete ms for fiction.
Accepts hard copy and simultaneous submissions if
identified. SASE. Responds in 2 months.
Articles: 800 words. Informational and how-to
articles and personal experience pieces. Topics
include relationships, beauty, fashion, music, popular
culture, recreation, the arts, crafts, current events, and
social issues.
Fiction: 1,000 words. Genres include romance and
inspirational fiction.
Depts/columns: Word lengths vary. Advice.

Sample Issue
106 pages (10% advertising): 7 articles; 2 stories;
25 depts/columns; 2 quizzes. Sample copy, $3.99
at newsstands.
- "Your Body Works." Article explains how hiccups,
  yawns, and other bodily reactions work.
- "Zac & Ashley." Article profiles two of Hollywood's
  hottest teenage stars.
- Sample dept/column: "Real-Life Stories" features
  readers' true tales about themselves.

Rights and Payment
All rights. Written material, payment rates vary. Pays
on publication. Provides 2 contributor's copies.

Editor's Comments
Our audience is primarily young teen girls.
Submissions should be of interest to our readers
(dating, beauty, celebrities), written in a style that is
fun and incorporates a young person's voice. Your
work must demonstrate that you are familiar with
the "teen scene."

Teenage Christian Magazine

Box 10750
Searcy, AR 72149

Editor: Renee Lewis

Description and Interests
Now available in print form, this former online maga-
zine features articles on topics of interest to Christian
teens. It presents uplifting material that centers on
having faith in Jesus Christ and living by His Word.
- **Audience:** 14–18 years
- **Frequency:** Quarterly
- **Distribution:** Subscription
- **Circulation:** Unavailable
- **Website:** www.tcmagazine.org

Freelance Potential
35% written by nonstaff writers. Publishes 5–10 freelance submissions yearly. Receives 60 queries, 60
unsolicited mss yearly.

Submissions
Query or send complete ms. Accepts email submissions to info@tcmagazine.org. Response time varies.
Articles: 450–700 words. Informational articles;
profiles; interviews; photo-essays; and personal
experience pieces. Topics include health, fitness,
multicultural and ethnic topics, music, popular
culture, religion, and social issues.
Depts/columns: Word lengths vary. Advice, sports,
and music.

Sample Issue
40 pages: 5 articles; 8 depts/ columns. Sample copy,
$3.95. Guidelines available at website.
- "Spotlight: By the Lawn." Article describes how a
  Georgia church youth group spent their spring break
  helping hurricane victims clean up in Mississippi.
- "River Raves." Article explores some of the best rafting spots across the country and includes tips for
  making the rafting experience a good one.
- Sample dept/column: "College Life" offers tips for
  making a search for scholarships a successful one.

Rights and Payment
All rights. Written material, payment rates vary.
Payment policy varies.

Editor's Comments
We're looking for articles that cover the challenging
issues that today's Christian teens are facing. Writing
should focus on spiritual growth, and be inspirational
and supportive. If you are itching to give us a story
idea, send that idea our way. Chances are we probably
need and want it. Also, we are currently open to ideas
for first-person columns.

Teen Graffiti

P.O. Box 452721
Garland, TX 75045-2721

Publisher: Sharon Jones-Scaife

Description and Interests
Launched by a nonprofit organization based in the Dallas/Fort Worth area, this magazine seeks to be a voice for teenagers across the nation. It focuses on addressing teen concerns, ideas, talents, achievements, and community involvement.
- **Audience:** 12–19 years
- **Frequency:** 6 times each year
- **Distribution:** 100% subscription
- **Circulation:** 10,000
- **Website:** www.teengraffiti.com

Freelance Potential
70% written by nonstaff writers. Publishes 30–40 freelance submissions yearly.

Submissions
Query or send complete ms. Prefers email submissions to publish@teengraffiti.com. Accepts hard copy. SASE. Response time varies.
Articles: 250 words. Informational articles; personal experience pieces; opinion pieces; and essays. Topics include college, careers, current events, popular culture, health, and social issues.
Depts/columns: 100–200 words. Advice and resource information from teachers. Teen-to-teen advice and book, music, and movie reviews.
Artwork: B/W and color prints accepted from teens only.
Other: Poetry written by teens.

Sample Issue
30 pages (3% advertising): 4 articles; 9 depts/columns; 2 poems. Sample copy, $2.75. Guidelines included in each issue.
- "What Most Teens and Parents Need to Know About MySpace.com." Article explains how this website works and its potential dangers to teens.
- "High School and Beyond." Article explains that the college scholarship and application process begins in middle school.
- Sample dept/column: "TeenSpeaks" features profiles of single moms written by their teen children.

Rights and Payment
One-time rights. No payment.

Editor's Comments
Most of the writing that appears in our magazine is written by either teachers who are members of our council or teens themselves.

Teen Light

6118 Bend of River Road
Dunn, NC 28334

Publisher: Annette Dammer

Description and Interests
Teen Light is written by teens for teens to help and inspire each other with personal accounts of true-life successes and failure. A Christian arts magazine, its content includes devotionals, timely essays, testimonials, short stories, art, and poetry.
- **Audience:** 10–21 years
- **Frequency:** Weekly
- **Distribution:** 100% Internet
- **Hits per month:** Unavailable
- **Website:** www.teenlight.org

Freelance Potential
50% written by nonstaff writers. Publishes 24 freelance submissions yearly; 75% by unpublished writers, 50% by authors who are new to the magazine. Receives 240 queries yearly.

Submissions
Query with brief introduction. Accepts email queries to publisher@teenlight.org (no attachments). SASE. Responds in 2 weeks.
Articles: To 500 words. Informational and self-help articles; profiles; devotionals; testimonials; photoessays; and personal experience pieces. Topics include the arts, college, popular culture, and social issues.
Fiction: 500 words. Contemporary fiction.
Artwork: Color JPG files.
Other: Poetry. Submit seasonal material 6 months in advance.

Sample Issue
Sample copy available online. Guidelines available.
- "Cymophobia." Book excerpt poses the question, "What Am I doing here?" and the writer hopes to get an answer before she does something stupid.
- "Pieces of Me." Poem shares the lyrics of a song written by the bass guitarist for the band, UnbrokenPromises.

Rights and Payment
Non-exclusive rights. No payment.

Editor's Comments
Our Christian writers are exclusively between 10 and 22 years of age. We would like to see more poetry, but we also accept journal entries, short stories, testimonials, views of global issues, poetry, art, and devotions. If you would like to be considered for a staff position, please let us know that in your query.

Teen Times

1910 Association Drive
Reston, VA 20191

Director of Communications: Bana Yahnke

Description and Interests
Teen Times is the national magazine for Family, Career and Community Leaders of America (FCCLA), a career and technical student organization. Articles focus on leadership skills, education, and careers. Member profiles are also included.
- **Audience:** 10–18 years
- **Frequency:** Quarterly
- **Distribution:** 98% schools; 2% other
- **Circulation:** 220,000
- **Website:** www.fcclainc.org

Freelance Potential
50% written by nonstaff writers. Publishes 20 freelance submissions yearly; 100% by unpublished writers.

Submissions
Query or send complete ms. Accepts hard copy. Availability of artwork improves chance of acceptance. SASE. Response time varies.
Articles: Word lengths vary. Informational and how-to articles; profiles; and photo-essays. Topics include careers, health, fitness, recreation, regional news, and member information.
Depts/columns: Word lengths vary. Leader profiles, event coverage, issues for action, news, and updates.
Artwork: Color prints and transparencies.
Other: Puzzles, activities, and games.

Sample Issue
22 pages (12% advertising): 6 articles; 8 depts/columns. Sample copy available with 9x12 SASE. Editorial calendar available.
- "Managing Chapter Conflicts Constructively." Article provides tips for resolving member conflicts.
- "Getting Good Press." Article offers ideas for getting local media coverage for chapter events.
- Sample dept/column: "The Council's Counsel" offers advice for managing aggression.

Rights and Payment
All rights. No payment. Provides contributor's copies upon request.

Editor's Comments
We are interested in articles that address family, career, and leadership activities and success stories that are relevant to our members. Our primary focus is on FCCLA activities and news from around the country. Writing should be targeted to middle school and high school students.

Teen Tribute

71 Barber Greene Road
Dons Mills, Ontario M3C 2A2
Canada

Submissions: Robin Stevenson

Description and Interests
This entertainment magazine is packed with music and movie updates, celebrity profiles and interviews, and tips on fashion and beauty. Its content appeals to Canadian teens.
- **Audience:** 14–18 years
- **Frequency:** Quarterly
- **Distribution:** 90% newsstand; 10% subscription
- **Circulation:** 310,000
- **Website:** www.tribute.ca

Freelance Potential
10% written by nonstaff writers. Publishes 5–10 freelance submissions yearly; 1% by authors who are new to the magazine. Receives 24 queries yearly.

Submissions
Query with clips or writing samples. No unsolicited mss. Availability of artwork improves chance of acceptance. SAE/IRC. Responds in 1–2 months.
Articles: 400–500 words. Informational articles; profiles; interviews; and personal experience pieces. Also publishes photo-essays. Topics include movies, the film industry, entertainment, the arts, music, popular culture, and social issues.
Depts/columns: Word lengths vary. Music, DVD, and game reviews.
Artwork: Color prints or transparencies.

Sample Issue
38 pages (50% advertising): 8 articles; 9 depts/columns. Sample copy, $1.95 Canadian with 9x12 SASE ($.86 Canadian postage).
- "So Much Moore." Article profiles the actress Mandy Moore and her role in the movie *American Dreamz*.
- "Here Kitty, Kitty." Article looks at the career of the Halifax-born actress Ellen Page, who appears in *X-Men: The Last Stand*.
- Sample dept/column: "Gaming" features reviews of top electronic games.

Rights and Payment
First serial rights. Written material, $75–$100 Canadian. Artwork, payment rates vary. Pays on publication. Provides 1 contributor's copy.

Editor's Comments
We're interested in hearing from writers who can get inside information about the movies, music, and celebrities that teens are interested in. Our greatest need is for celebrity profiles.

Teen Voices

P.O. Box 120-027
Boston, MA 02112-0027

Editor-in-Chief: Ellyn Ruthstrom

Description and Interests
Any topic that is important to a teen or young woman is accepted by this publication. It believes in empowering its audience members by listening to them.
- **Audience:** YA
- **Frequency:** Twice each year
- **Distribution:** Newsstand; other
- **Circulation:** 55,000
- **Website:** www.teenvoices.com

Freelance Potential
95% written by nonstaff writers. Publishes 100 freelance submissions yearly; 95% by unpublished writers, 95% by authors who are new to the magazine. Receives 2,000 unsolicited mss yearly.

Submissions
Accepts articles written by teenage girls only. Send complete ms. Response time varies.
Articles: Word lengths vary. Informational and self-help articles. Topics include family relationships, teen motherhood, the arts, popular culture, the media, surviving sexual assault, coping with disabilities and chronic illness, and experiences from teens around the world.
Fiction: Word lengths vary. Humorous, inspirational, contemporary, ethnic, and multicultural fiction.
Depts/columns: 500 words. News of interest to teens.
Artwork: B/W and color prints. Line art. Various art for features, as assigned.
Other: Poetry.

Sample Issue
57 pages (8% advertising): 8 articles; 1 short story; 8 depts/columns. Sample copy, $5. Guidelines and editorial calendar available.
- "Finding Your Voice After an Assault." Article urges teens to speak up after a sexual assault.
- "Flying Without Oxygen: My Trip Around the Milky Way." Story depicts a fantastic journey.
- Sample dept/column: "Good Reading" showcases poems submitted by readers.

Rights and Payment
First or one-time rights. No payment. Provides 5 contributor's copies.

Editor's Comments
Our feeling is if you want to talk about it, someone wants to read about it. We would particularly like to see more stories of community activism by teens.

Teenwire.com

434 West 33rd Street
New York, NY 10001

Editor: Susan Yudt

Description and Interests
This award-winning sexual health website for teens is committed to presenting the facts teens need to make responsible choices. It covers a wide range of topics, including sex and sexual health, the body, relationships, teen activism, and global issues.
- **Audience:** 13–21 years
- **Frequency:** Unavailable
- **Distribution:** 100% Internet
- **Hits per month:** 600,000
- **Website:** www.teenwire.com

Freelance Potential
90% written by nonstaff writers. Publishes 100–156 freelance submissions yearly; 10% by unpublished writers, 25% by authors who are new to the magazine.

Submissions
Query with brief biography and clips or writing samples. Accepts email queries to twstaff@ppfa.org (include "Write for Teenwire" in subject line). Responds in 1 week.
Articles: 500 words. Informational and factual articles; profiles; interviews; and Spanish pieces. Topics include teen relationships, sexual health, birth control, pregnancy, sexually transmitted diseases, teen activism, international youth issues, the arts, colleges, careers, current events, music, popular culture, recreation, substance abuse, social concerns, and multicultural and ethnic issues.
Other: Puzzles, games, and quizzes.

Sample Issue
Sample copy and guidelines available at website.
- "Writing for Their Lives." Article describes a young women's writing group that provides a place for girls to talk with peers and counselors.
- "Are You Sexually Healthy?" Article discusses ways to develop healthy sexuality.
- "Talking to Parents About Sex." Article offers suggestions for approaching a parent to discuss sex and sexual health.

Rights and Payment
All rights. Articles, $.50 per word, to $250. Pays on acceptance.

Editor's Comments
We welcome inquiries from freelance writers who are interested in writing for a teen audience. Send us a pitch for something we haven't done before.

Texas Child Care

P.O. Box 162881
Austin, TX 78716-2881

Editor: Louise Parks

Description and Interests
Persons involved with child care find informative support to advance their professional careers and to improve their skills in child-building. Contents include articles on the physical, cognitive, social, and emotional development in children, and how-to articles for administrative and business management.
- **Audience:** Child-care workers and parents
- **Frequency:** Quarterly
- **Distribution:** 80% controlled; 20% subscription
- **Circulation:** 32,000
- **Website:** www.childcarequarterly.com

Freelance Potential
50% written by nonstaff writers. Publishes 12–15 freelance submissions yearly; 10% by unpublished writers, 50% by authors who are new to the magazine. Receives 24–36 unsolicited mss yearly.

Submissions
Send complete ms. Accepts email submissions to editor@childcarequarterly.com. Responds in 3 weeks.
Articles: 2,500 words. Informational articles. Topics include child care, education, program administration, infant care, professional development, and issues and activities relating to school-age children.
Depts/columns: Word lengths vary. News and updates about child care, parenting, and licensing information.
Other: Submit seasonal material 6 months in advance.

Sample Issue
44 pages (no advertising): 6 articles; 5 depts/columns. Sample copy, $6.25. Guidelines available at website.
- "Dramatic Play: Every Day." Article shows how to develop learning skills through dramatic play.
- "Early Literacy: The Essentials." Article lists the types of books that encourage listening in children.
- Sample dept/column: "Building Business" tackles the importance of productive meetings.

Rights and Payment
All rights. No payment. Provides 3 contributor's copies and a 1-year gift subscription.

Editor's Comments
When selecting a topic for an article, narrow the subject to focus on specific information. We'd like to receive more articles on math, science, and infant care; we have enough on outdoor play and alphabet activities.

Theory Into Practice

122 Ramseyer Hall
29 West Woodruff Avenue
Ohio State University
Columbus, OH 43210

Editor: Anita Woolfolk Hoy

Description and Interests
This thematic, refereed journal is devoted to exploring educational topics through its engaging articles, which offer scholarly presentations of practical and theoretical information.
- **Audience:** Educators
- **Frequency:** Quarterly
- **Distribution:** 65% schools/libraries; 35% other
- **Circulation:** 2,000
- **Website:** www.coe.ohio-state.edu/tip

Freelance Potential
100% written by nonstaff writers. Publishes 2 freelance submissions yearly; 10% by unpublished writers, 90% by authors who are new to the magazine. Receives 24 queries and unsolicited mss yearly.

Submissions
Query or send 2 copies of complete ms. Accepts hard copy. SASE. Responds in 1–2 months.
Articles: 3,000–4,000 words. Factual and informational articles. Topics include educational technology, cultural diversity, literary theory, teacher quality, cooperative learning, children's literature, mentoring, classroom communication, foreign languages, community service, and curriculum theory.

Sample Issue
101 pages (3% advertising): 11 articles. Sample copy, $12. Guidelines and theme list available.
- "Essential Components of Peace Education." Article discusses essential elements needed in building a lasting peace through education.
- "School-Based Peace Building in Sierra Leone." Article describes a peace-building project in western Africa that links schools and the community.
- "Conflict, Contact, and Education in Northern Ireland." Article takes a look at research about the impact of educational responses to conflict in Northern Ireland on children and young people.

Rights and Payment
All rights. No payment. Provides 1 contributor's copy.

Editor's Comments
We welcome engaging articles that fit in with our theme schedule. Authors should focus their writing on concepts and ideas rather than on specific research or case studies. Themes must be broad enough to fit a range of articles, but narrow enough to be clear and focused. Please avoid technical writing.

Thrasher

1303 Underwood Avenue
San Francisco, CA 94121

Editor: Jake Phelps

Description and Interests
Teen boys read *Thrasher* to get the latest information
from the world of skateboarding and snowboarding.
Events and personalities are covered, often using
graphic language. It also reports on the music scene.
- **Audience:** Boys, 12–20 years
- **Frequency:** Monthly
- **Distribution:** 30% subscription; 30% newsstand;
  40% other
- **Circulation:** 200,000
- **Website:** www.thrashermagazine.com

Freelance Potential
20% written by nonstaff writers. Publishes 20 freelance submissions yearly; 100% by unpublished
writers. Receives 72–120 unsolicited mss yearly.

Submissions
Send complete ms. Prefers email submissions to
ryan@thrashermagazine.com (Macintosh compatible
Microsoft Word attachments). Accepts hard copy, disk
submissions, and simultaneous submissions if identified. Availability of artwork improves chance of acceptance. SASE. Responds in 1 month.
Articles: To 1,500 words. Informational articles; profiles; and interviews. Topics include skateboarding,
snowboarding, sports, and music.
Fiction: To 2,500 words. Stories with skateboarding
and snowboarding themes.
Depts/columns: 750–1,000 words. News, tips.
Artwork: Color prints or transparencies; 35mm B/W
negatives. B/W or color line art.

Sample Issue
236 pages (45% advertising): 12 articles; 8 depts/
columns. Sample copy, $3.99. Guidelines available.
- "Washington Street." Article visits a skatepark in
  southern California that gives skateboarders more
  freedom than typical skateparks.
- Sample dept/column: "'Zine Thing" features reviews
  of e-zines of interest to skateboarders.

Rights and Payment
First North American serial rights. Written material,
$.15 per word. Artwork, payment rates vary. Pays on
publication. Provides 2 contributor's copies.

Editor's Comments
Our readers are passionate about their sport and have
a little bit of an attitude. You must understand this
scene to write for us.

Three Leaping Frogs

P.O. Box 2205
Carson City, NV 89702

Publisher: Ellen Hopkins

Description and Interests
Dedicated to increasing literacy among the at-risk chil-
dren in grades three through six in northern Nevada,
this newspaper provides information on history, sci-
ence, math, sports, and recreation, as well as games,
crafts, puzzles, and profiles of children. It also pro-
vides a venue for publication of exceptional works.
- **Audience:** 7–12 years
- **Frequency:** 6 times each year
- **Distribution:** 100% schools
- **Circulation:** 35,000
- **Website:** www.goshawkroad.org

Freelance Potential
70% written by nonstaff writers. Publishes 50 freelance submissions yearly; 50% by unpublished
writers, 60% by authors who are new to the magazine.
Receives 192–480 unsolicited mss yearly.

Submissions
Send complete ms. Prefers email submissions to
goshawkroad@goshawkroad.org. Accepts hard copy.
SASE. Responds in 3 months.
Articles: 500 words. Informational articles; profiles;
and interviews. Topics include animals, nature, math,
fitness, hobbies, and history. Also publishes biographies and regional news.
Fiction: 1,000 words. Genres include mystery, adventure, historical and multicultural fiction, and science
fiction.
Depts/columns: 300 words. Science experiments
and advice.
Other: Puzzles, activities, games, and jokes. Poetry.
Submit seasonal material 6 months in advance.

Sample Issue
8 pages (no advertising): 7 articles; 2 poems; 2
quizzes. Sample copy, $1 with 9x12 SASE ($.57
postage). Guidelines and theme list available.
- "The Forgotten Holidays." Article discusses why holidays like President's Day are not just a day off.
- "A Bit of Blarney." Article examines the life of St.
  Patrick as well as why we celebrate St. Patrick's Day.

Rights and Payment
First rights. No payment. Provides 5 contributor's
copies.

Editor's Comments
Keep articles relatively short—around 500 words.
Also, our fiction is authored by our young readers.

Tidewater Parent

258 Granby Street
Norfolk, VA 23510

Editor: Jennifer O'Donnell

Description and Interests
This publication serves families living in Norfolk, Virginia, and the surrounding Tidewater region. Distributed through schools, child-care centers, hospitals, doctors' offices, and libraries, it includes articles on general parenting and child development issues, as well as local resource information and event updates.
- **Audience:** Parents
- **Frequency:** Monthly
- **Distribution:** 50% schools; 50% other
- **Circulation:** 48,000
- **Website:** www.tidewaterparent.com

Freelance Potential
90% written by nonstaff writers. Publishes 40 freelance submissions yearly; 10% by unpublished writers, 50% by authors who are new to the magazine. Receives 72 unsolicited mss yearly.

Submissions
Send complete ms. Will accept previously published mss that can be reprinted. Accepts hard copy. SASE. Response time varies.
Articles: 800–1,200 words. Informational and how-to articles. Topics include parenting, education, child health and development, family travel, and safety.
Depts/columns: Staff written.
Other: Submit seasonal material 2–3 months in advance.

Sample Issue
36 pages (50% advertising): 2 articles; 8 depts/columns; 1 events calendar. Sample copy, $2. Guidelines and theme list available.
- "Not Just the Baby Blues." Article explains that clinical depression can strike mothers at any time, not just during the postpartum period.
- "Good Work Is Hard to Find. Or Is It?" Article reports that work for teens is plentiful in the Hampton Roads area.
- "How Do You Make That?" Article features craft recipes for summer fun.

Rights and Payment
Rights vary. Written material, $25. Kill fee, 50%. Pays on publication. Provides 1 contributor's copy.

Editor's Comments
We are the primary source for local parenting information in our region. In addition to parents, we serve educators, and day-care and healthcare providers.

Tiger Beat

6430 Sunset Boulevard, Suite 700
Hollywood, CA 90028

Editor: Leesa Coble

Description and Interests
Who's hot in the teen media world is the focus of this publication. It dishes out the known and unknown facts on all the celebrities that interest today's tweens. The tone is upbeat with short, snappy copy that incorporates current slang expressions. Material includes interviews, news, fashion, and ever-changing celebrity trends.
- **Audience:** 10–16 years
- **Frequency:** Monthly
- **Distribution:** 90% newsstand; 10% subscription
- **Circulation:** 200,000
- **Website:** www.tigerbeatmag.com

Freelance Potential
1% written by nonstaff writers. Publishes 2 freelance submissions yearly; 50% by authors who are new to the magazine. Receives 96 queries yearly.

Submissions
Query with résumé and clips for celebrity angles only. Accepts hard copy and simultaneous submissions if identified. SASE. Responds in 3 months.
Articles: To 700 words. Interviews and profiles. Topics include celebrities in the film, television, and recording industries.
Depts/columns: Staff written.
Artwork: Color digital.
Other: Short updates on young celebrities. Submit seasonal material 3 months in advance.

Sample Issue
84 pages (12% advertising): 20 articles; 5 quizzes; 15 depts/columns; 20 posters. Sample copy, $3.99 at newsstands.
- "Kelly's in Control." Article profiles Kelly Clarkson, who has mastered the art of ignoring printed rumors.
- "Parental OMGs!" Article reveals teen stars' most embarrassing moments involving their parents.
- Sample dept/column: "Hear It" shares secrets of recording stars, The Veronicas.

Rights and Payment
All rights. Written material, payment rates vary. Pays on publication. Provides 2 contributor's copies.

Editor's Comments
We are always interested in new information about young media celebrities. Submissions can be interviews and profiles, or behind-the-scenes and on-the-street news items that interest our readers.

Time for Kids

Time-Life Building
1271 Avenue of the Americas, 22nd Floor
New York, NY 10020

Editor: Martha Pickerill

Description and Interests
Time for Kids provides cutting-edge current events information in a format children find engaging. This version of the well-known newsmagazine is distributed through schools and targets students in the elementary and middle school grades.
• **Audience:** 5–12 years
• **Frequency:** Weekly
• **Distribution:** 100% schools
• **Circulation:** 4.1 million
• **Website:** www.timeforkids.com

Freelance Potential
4% written by nonstaff writers. Publishes 4 freelance submissions yearly. Receives many queries and unsolicited mss yearly.

Submissions
Send résumé only. No unsolicited mss.
Articles: Word lengths vary. Informational and biographical articles. Topics include world news, current events, animals, education, health, fitness, science, technology, math, social studies, geography, multicultural and ethnic issues, music, popular culture, recreation, regional news, sports, travel, and social issues.
Depts/columns: Word lengths vary. Profiles and short news items.
Artwork: Color prints and transparencies.
Other: Theme-related activities.

Sample Issue
8 pages (no advertising): 3 articles; 4 depts/columns. Subscription, $3.95.
• "Crisis in the Middle East." Article reports on the increased violence in the conflict between Israel and Hizballah rebels in Lebanon.
• "Tsunami Relief Arrives in Indonesia." Article tells how the world is working together to help victims of a tsunami that struck Java Island, killing 531.
• "A Sad Day in India." Article recounts the reaction to terrorist bombings of trains in Mumbai, India.

Rights and Payment
All rights. Written material, payment rates vary. Pays on publication.

Editor's Comments
All of the articles we publish that are written by nonstaff writers are done on contract. We will only consider résumés from qualified writers before making assignments.

Today's Catholic Teacher

2621 Dryden Road, Suite 300
Dayton, OH 45439

Editor-in-Chief: Mary Noschang

Description and Interests
Read by professionals associated with education, this publication focuses on issues in private education in general, and Catholic education in particular.
• **Audience:** Educators, grades K–8
• **Frequency:** 6 times each year
• **Distribution:** 90% schools; 10% religious instruction
• **Circulation:** 50,000
• **Website:** www.peterli.com

Freelance Potential
95% written by nonstaff writers. Publishes 20 freelance submissions yearly; 50% by authors who are new to the magazine. Receives 192+ queries and unsolicited mss yearly.

Submissions
Query or send complete ms. Accepts hard copy, disk submissions with hard copy, email submissions to mnoschang@peterli.com, and simultaneous submissions if identified. SASE. Responds to queries in 1 month, to mss in 3 months.
Articles: 600–1,500 words. Informational, how-to, and self-help articles. Topics include technology, fundraising, character education, classroom management, curriculum development, administration, and educational issues and trends.
Depts/columns: Word lengths vary. Opinions, news items, software, and teaching tools.
Artwork: 8x10 B/W or color slides, prints, or transparencies.
Other: Classroom-ready reproducible activity pages.

Sample Issue
62 pages (45% advertising): 5 articles; 10 depts/columns. Sample copy, $5. Guidelines available.
• "Transforming the Reluctant Reader." Article suggests several steps to help a child enjoy reading.
• "Stories to Live and Learn By." Article investigates ways to find books that provide life lessons.
• Sample dept/column: "When Students Ask" delves into information about Vatican II.

Rights and Payment
All rights. Written material, $100–$250. Pays on publication. Provides contributor's copies.

Editor's Comments
The writing style we prefer is informal rather than scholarly. It's direct, concise, informative, and accurate without the use of educational jargon.

Today's Christian Woman

465 Gundersen Drive
Carol Stream, IL 60188

Associate Editor: Lisa Ann Cockrel

Description and Interests
Christian women in their 20s through 40s are the audience for this publication, which helps them deal with contemporary issues that impact their lives and to view their lives and relationships from a biblical perspective.
• **Audience:** Women
• **Frequency:** 6 times each year
• **Distribution:** Subscription; newsstand
• **Circulation:** 250,000
• **Website:** www.todayschristianwoman.com

Freelance Potential
75% written by nonstaff writers. Publishes 30–50 freelance submissions yearly; 25% by authors who are new to the magazine. Receives 1,200 queries yearly.

Submissions
Query with résumé and summary. Accepts hard copy. No simultaneous submissions. SASE. Responds in 2 months.
Articles: 1,000–2,000 words. Informational and self-help articles; personal experience pieces; and humor. Topics include parenting, family issues, spiritual living, contemporary women's concerns, and turning points in life.
Depts/columns: 100–300 words. Reviews, faith, parenting, and first-person narratives.

Sample Issue
66 pages (25% advertising): 8 articles; 9 depts/columns. Sample copy, $5 with 9x12 SASE ($3.19 postage). Guidelines available.
• "Purpose-Driven Wife." Article profiles AIDS activist and mom Kay Warren.
• "For the Birds." Humorous piece describes a mom's unfulfilling Mother's Day and what it taught her.
• Sample dept/column: "Reader to Reader" offers suggestions and solutions to women's problems from other women.

Rights and Payment
First rights. Written material, $.20 per word. Pays on publication. Provides 2 contributor's copies.

Editor's Comments
Articles should be practical and contain a distinct evangelical Christian perspective. Submissions should be personal in tone and utilize real-life anecdotes as well as quotes and advice from noted Christian professionals.

Today's Parent

1 Mount Pleasant Road, 8th Floor
Toronto, Ontario M4Y 2Y5
Canada

Managing Editor: Sarah Moore

Description and Interests
This Canadian magazine combines straightforward service articles with more philosophical, issue-oriented pieces. It covers topics of relevance to parents of children up to age 14.
• **Audience:** Parents
• **Frequency:** Monthly
• **Distribution:** Subscription; newsstand; other
• **Circulation:** 215,000
• **Website:** www.todaysparent.com

Freelance Potential
Of the freelance submissions published yearly, many are by unpublished writers and authors who are new to the magazine. Receives many queries yearly.

Submissions
Query with clips or writing samples; include information on article length. No unsolicited mss. Accepts hard copy. SAE/IRC. Response time varies.
Articles: 1,800–2,500 words. Informational, how-to, and self-help articles. Topics include parenting, family life, child development, health, nutrition, pregnancy, and childbirth.
Depts/columns: First-person forum for parents, 800 words; women's health and well-being, 1,200 words; education, 1,200–1,500 words; humor, 500 words.

Sample Issue
146 pages (15% advertising): 6 articles; 1 children's story; 13 depts/columns. Sample copy, $4.50 Canadian at newsstands. Guidelines available at website.
• "They've Seen It All and They Know Your Kids." Article features time-honored advice from children's camp directors.
• "Should You Give Your Child Time Outs?" Article evaluates the pros and cons of this popular form of discipline.
• Sample dept/column: "Your Turn" describes one mother's experience with "mommy meltdown."

Rights and Payment
All North American serial rights. Articles, $700–$1,500. Depts/columns, payment rates vary. Pays on publication. Provides 2 contributor's copies.

Editor's Comments
We embrace a gentle, nurturing parenting style that respects each child's unique personality, and we respect parents' abilities to understand their children and make good parenting decisions.

Today's Playground Magazine ☆

360 B Street
Idaho Falls, ID 83402

Editor: Shannon Amy

Description and Interests
Play structures are the focus of this magazine. It covers playground equipment and design, water play equipment, climbing walls, skate parks, and other structures for an audience that includes parks and recreation directors, educators, early childhood caregivers, and school administrators.
- **Audience:** Adults
- **Frequency:** 7 times each year
- **Distribution:** Subscription; other
- **Circulation:** 35,000
- **Website: www.todaysplayground.com**

Freelance Potential
40% written by nonstaff writers. Publishes 14–20 freelance submissions yearly; 40% by authors who are new to the magazine.

Submissions
Query or send complete ms. Accepts hard copy and email to shannon@todaysplayground.com. SASE. Responds in 1–2 months.
Articles: 800–1,200 words. Informational and how-to articles. Topics include play structures and amenities and industry trends.
Depts/columns: Word lengths vary. News, industry events, landscaping and design, legal issues.

Sample Issue
62 pages: 8 articles; 8 depts/columns. Sample copy, $5. Guidelines available.
- "More Than Just a Playground: It's a Center of Learning." Article visits a new playground in Tempe, Arizona, that is integrated with the Tempe Beach Park.
- "What's Cool with Aquatic Play." Article reports on the various aquatic play design components, including sprays, slides, and splash play areas.
- Sample dept/column: "Installer's Insights" focuses on jobsite safety.

Rights and Payment
First North American serial rights. Articles, $100–$300. Depts/columns, $50–$175. Payment policy varies.

Editor's Comments
Queries should include one or two paragraphs that briefly outline your idea. Tell us why your story is timely, unique, new, or of special interest. Our tone is informative, as this is a trade publication primarily for parks and recreation professionals.

Toledo Area Parent News

1120 Adams Street
Toledo, OH 43624

Editor: Lisa Laskey

Description and Interests
This parenting newspaper is distributed free throughout the Toledo, Ohio, area. Parents read it for coverage of current events and local resources, as well as for its informative articles on parenting issues. Each issue includes articles on topics of concern to parents such as education, health, and social issues.
- **Audience:** Parents
- **Frequency:** Monthly
- **Distribution:** 100% controlled
- **Circulation:** 81,000
- **Website: www.toledoparent.com**

Freelance Potential
75% written by nonstaff writers. Publishes 12–15 freelance submissions yearly; 10% by unpublished writers, 20% by authors who are new to the magazine. Receives 48 queries and unsolicited mss yearly.

Submissions
Query with clips; or send complete ms. Prefers email submissions to llaskey@toledoparent.com. Accepts hard copy. SASE. Responds in 1 month.
Articles: 700–2,000 words. Informational articles; profiles; and interviews. Topics include family issues, parenting, teen issues, education, social issues, health, and fitness.
Depts/columns: Word lengths vary. Brief news items related to family, and opinion essays.

Sample Issue
40 pages (60% advertising): 1 article; 7 depts/columns; 1 calendar. For sample copy, email kdevol@toledocitypaper.com. Guidelines available.
- "Family Favorites." Article lists descriptions of the best who, what, where, and the ever-mysterious other, in the Toledo area.
- Sample dept/column: "Dad's Notepad" shares an idea for the best Mother's Day present a husband can give to his wife.

Rights and Payment
All North American serial rights. Written material, $30–$200. Pays on publication.

Editor's Comments
We are always looking for advice on how to parent better. Our goal is to keep parents informed on all aspects of raising kids today. We also seek more hard-hitting news stories related to children living in the local area.

Transitions Abroad

P.O. Box 745
Bennington, VT 05201

Editor/Publisher: Sherry Schwarz

Description and Interests
Readers of this magazine find practical information and ideas that will help them plan a cultural immersion trip abroad. Much of the material is based on personal experience, often including work or study periods. Articles are mainly short and to the point.
- **Audience:** YA–Adult
- **Frequency:** 6 times each year
- **Distribution:** 75% subscription; 25% newsstand
- **Circulation:** 12,000
- **Website:** www.transitionsabroad.com

Freelance Potential
90% written by nonstaff writers. Publishes 150–180 freelance submissions yearly; 70% by unpublished writers, 90% by authors who are new to the magazine. Receives 300–420 queries and unsolicited mss yearly.

Submissions
Prefers query with outline; accepts complete ms with bibliography. Prefers email submissions to editor@ transitionsabroad.com. Accepts hard copy. SASE. Responds in 1–2 months.
Articles: To 1,500 words. Informational and how-to articles. Topics include overseas travel for teens, families, and seniors, as well as overseas study and employment programs.
Depts/columns: Word lengths vary. Responsible travel, budget travel, and volunteer travel.

Sample Issue
96 pages (50% advertising): 46 articles; 1 interview; 5 depts/columns. Sample copy, $4.95. Guidelines and editorial calendar available at website.
- "Moving to Middle Earth." Article follows the efforts of a couple who wanted to move to New Zealand.
- "Jules Maidoff: Painter." Interview features the artist who founded the Studio Arts Center International.
- Sample dept/column: "Traveler's Almanac" lists events happening around the world.

Rights and Payment
First rights. Written material, $2 per column inch; minimum $25. Artwork, payment rates vary. Pays on publication. Provides 2 contributor's copies.

Editor's Comments
Include practical information in your articles that will be of value to readers who are planning to work, study, volunteer, or travel responsibly. Well-researched supporting material increases the likelihood of acceptance.

Treasure Valley Family Magazine

13191 West Scotfield Street
Boise, ID 83713-0899

Publisher: Liz Buckingham

Description and Interests
This free parenting and family magazine is distributed through 500 sites in the cities of Boise, Meridian, Eagle, and Nampa, Idaho. It focuses on education, family fun, and parent involvement for families with children under the age of 12.
- **Audience:** Parents
- **Frequency:** 10 times each year
- **Distribution:** 100% controlled
- **Circulation:** 19,500
- **Website: www.treasurevalleyfamily.com**

Freelance Potential
100% written by nonstaff writers. Publishes 20 freelance submissions yearly; 5% by authors who are new to the magazine. Receives 204 unsolicited mss yearly.

Submissions
Send complete ms. Accepts email submissions to magazine@treasurevalleyfamily.com. Responds in 3–4 months.
Articles: To 1,500 words. How-to articles and personal experience pieces. Topics include regional news, education, gifted and special education, health, travel, fitness, crafts, hobbies, the arts, and recreation.
Fiction: Word lengths vary. Inspirational and historical fiction.
Depts/columns: 700–800 words. Book reviews, regional news, fatherhood.
Artwork: Color prints and transparencies. Line art.
Other: Activities, games, and filler on health and safety topics. Submit seasonal material 6 months in advance.

Sample Issue
66 pages (45% advertising): 10 articles; 4 depts/ columns; 1 event calendar. Sample copy, $1.50 with 9x12 SASE. Guidelines available.
- "Geocaching: Hi-Tech Gadgetry Meets Outdoor Fun." Article describes a family activity that combines technology, adventure, and the outdoors.
- "Fun Bicycle Stops on the Greenbelt." Article reports on a bicycle path in Boise.

Rights and Payment
First rights. All material, payment rates vary. Pays on publication. Provides 2 contributor's copies.

Editor's Comments
We want informative reporting on local issues and events of concern to parents in Idaho.

Tulsa Kids Magazine

1820 South Boulder Avenue, Suite 100
Tulsa, OK 74119-4409

Editor: Betty Casey

Description and Interests
Informative and entertaining articles on issues of interest to parents living in Tulsa, Oklahoma, can be found in this regional magazine. It covers topics such as health, education, social issues, and entertainment.
- **Audience:** Families
- **Frequency:** Monthly
- **Distribution:** 80% newsstand; 16% schools; 2% religious instruction; 2% subscription
- **Circulation:** 20,000
- **Website:** www.tulsakids.com

Freelance Potential
99% written by nonstaff writers. Publishes 100+ freelance submissions yearly; 5% by unpublished writers, 1% by authors who are new to the magazine. Receives 1,200 unsolicited mss yearly.

Submissions
Send complete ms. Accepts hard copy, disk submissions, and simultaneous submissions if identified. SASE. Responds in 2–3 months.
Articles: 500–800 words. Informational articles; profiles; interviews; humor; and personal experience pieces. Topics include family life, education, parenting, recreation, entertainment, college, health, fitness, careers, crafts, and social issues.
Depts/columns: 100–300 words. News, book reviews, safety, and family cooking.

Sample Issue
52 pages (50% advertising): 2 articles; 11 depts/columns; 1 calendar. Sample copy, free with 10x13 SASE ($.75 postage). Guidelines available.
- "Profile: Chasing Independence Through TSHA." Article profiles a hearing-impaired boy who gets help from the Tulsa Speech and Hearing Association.
- "Community: KABOOM! A Playground in a Day!" Article describes how a community came together to build a safe and exciting place to play.
- Sample dept/column: "Safety" discusses Safe Kids Week with a focus on pool safety.

Rights and Payment
One-time rights. Written material, $25–$100. Payment policy varies. Provides 1 contributor's copy.

Editor's Comments
We look for practical articles for parents on topics such as safety, social issues, and health. Information on family-friendly activities is welcome.

Turtle

Children's Better Health Institute
1100 Waterway Boulevard
P.O. Box 567
Indianapolis, IN 46206-0567

Editor: Terry Harshman

Description and Interests
Turtle magazine educates and entertains preschool children with stories, articles, and activities. Each issue contains fiction and nonfiction pieces encouraging children to live a healthy lifestyle while combining fun with learning. This magazine is published by the Children's Better Health Institute and is a sister publication to *Children's Playmate*.
- **Audience:** 2–5 years
- **Frequency:** 6 times each year
- **Distribution:** 100% subscription
- **Circulation:** 382,000
- **Website:** www.turtlemag.org

Freelance Potential
20% written by nonstaff writers. Publishes 20 freelance submissions yearly.

Submissions
Send complete ms. Accepts hard copy. SASE. Responds in 2–3 months.
Articles: To 500 words. Informational articles. Topics include science, health, fitness, and medicine.
Fiction: To 100 words for rebus stories. Genres include mystery; adventure; fantasy; humor; problem-solving stories; and contemporary, ethnic, and multicultural fiction.
Other: Puzzles, activities, and games. Poetry.

Sample Issue
36 pages (6% advertising): 1 article; 2 stories; 12 activities; 1 rebus; 1 recipe; 1 book review. Sample copy, $1.75 with 9x12 SASE. Guidelines available.
- "High Dive." Story tells of a turtle's unique idea for jumping off the diving board with his frog friends.
- "Three to Get Ready." Story features three animals working together to get across a pond.
- Sample dept/column: "Simple Science" offers an experiment showing how water passes through cracks, relating it to how caves are formed.

Rights and Payment
All rights. Articles and fiction, $.22 per word. Other material, payment rates vary. Pays on publication. Provides up to 10 contributor's copies.

Editor's Comments
We seek fun and lively articles that entertain while educating our preschool audience. Submissions relating to our central theme of healthy living are of interest. Material must be age-appropriate.

Twins

11211 East Arapahoe Road, Suite 101
Centennial, CO 80112

Editor-in-Chief: Susan Alt

Description and Interests
Parents of twins and triplets turn to this magazine for useful and helpful articles on child development issues, health, and baby care. It also includes traveling tips, book reviews, and support information.
- **Audience:** Parents
- **Frequency:** 6 times each year
- **Distribution:** 60% subscription; 37% controlled; 3% newsstand
- **Circulation:** 40,000
- **Website:** www.twinsmagazine.com

Freelance Potential
80% written by nonstaff writers. Publishes 60 freelance submissions yearly; 25% by unpublished writers, 25% by authors who are new to the magazine. Receives 252 queries and unsolicited mss yearly.

Submissions
Query. Accepts email queries to twins.editor@businessword.com. Responds in 3 months.
Articles: 800–1,300 words. Informational and how-to articles; profiles; and personal experience pieces. Topics include parenting, family life, health, fitness, education, music, the arts, house and home, nutrition, diet, sports, social issues, crafts, and hobbies.
Depts/columns: To 800 words. News, new product information, opinion pieces, and short items on child development.

Sample Issue
62 pages (30% advertising): 8 articles; 14 depts/columns. Sample copy, $5.50. Writers' guidelines available at website.
- "Keep Your Twins Together in School." Article discusses why it is important to keep twins in the same classes in school.
- "Camping with Twins." Article offers suggestions for organizing successful family camping trips.
- Sample dept/column: "The First Year" offers an essay on dealing with the sniffles.

Rights and Payment
All rights. All material, payment rates vary. Pays on publication. Provides 2 contributor's copies.

Editor's Comments
Be sure to check our website for complete guidelines before submitting. Please note we only accept material from parents of twins, triplets, and other multiples, and very rarely twins themselves.

Twist

270 Sylvan Avenue
Englewood Cliffs, NJ 07632

Assistant Editor: Robin Monheit

Description and Interests
Teens who like to stay up to date on celebrities and popular culture read this magazine, now in its tenth year. *Twist* features celebrity gossip, entertainment news, and fashion and beauty updates, as well as articles about relationships.
- **Audience:** 14–19 years
- **Frequency:** 10 times each year
- **Distribution:** Subscription; newsstand
- **Circulation:** 250,000
- **Website:** www.twistmagazine.com

Freelance Potential
5% written by nonstaff writers. Publishes 10 freelance submissions yearly; 5% by unpublished writers, 5% by authors who are new to the magazine. Receives 240 unsolicited mss yearly.

Submissions
Query. Accepts hard copy. SASE. Responds in 2–3 weeks.
Articles: Word lengths vary. Informational articles and humor. Topics include popular culture, music, celebrities, fashion favorites, beauty tips, health, fitness, nutrition, sex, and relationships.
Depts/columns: Word lengths vary. Advice, horoscopes, new fashion and beauty products, and embarrassing moments.

Sample Issue
86 pages (25% advertising): 12 articles; 31 depts/columns; 1 quiz; 6 posters. Sample copy, $2.99 with 9x12 SASE. Guidelines available.
- "Your Freaky Dreams Explained." Article decodes the meanings of several common dreams.
- "Is He a Summer Fling or the Real Thing?" Quiz helps readers determine whether a summer romance might turn into a lasting relationship.
- Sample dept/column: "Look 4 Less" tells how to put together a budget-priced version of an outfit worn by Katie Cassidy.

Rights and Payment
First North American serial rights. Written material, payment rates vary. Pays on acceptance. Provides 2 contributor's copies.

Editor's Comments
Celebrity interviews are in demand here. We also need original quizzes that deal with hip, upbeat topics that interest teens.

U Mag

United Services Automobile Association
9800 Fredericksburg Road
San Antonio, TX 78288-0264

Editor: Shari Biediger

Description and Interests
This publication is mailed free of charge to the children of members of the United Services Automobile Association. Published in thematic issues, it strives to help its readers grow up to be responsible adults while enjoying healthy lifestyles.
- **Audience:** 8–12 years
- **Frequency:** Quarterly
- **Distribution:** 99% controlled; 1% other
- **Circulation:** 440,000
- **Website: www.usaa.com**

Freelance Potential
90% written by nonstaff writers. Publishes 20 freelance submissions yearly; 1% by unpublished writers, 5% by authors who are new to the magazine. Receives 120 queries yearly.

Submissions
Query with résumé and clips or writing samples. Accepts hard copy. SASE. Responds in 6 weeks.
Articles: Word lengths vary. Informational, how-to, and self-help articles; profiles; interviews; and personal experience pieces. Topics include hobbies, history, mathematics, music, popular culture, current events, science, technology, social issues, the arts, travel, money management, and safety issues.
Other: Puzzles, games, activities, and jokes.

Sample Issue
16 pages (no advertising): 4 articles; 3 activities. Sample copy, free with 9x12 SASE ($2 postage). Guidelines and theme list available.
- "The Profiler: Do I Know You?" Article provides short profiles of some pre-teens and asks readers to complete a profile quiz.
- "Pilots and Their Call Signs." Article explains what pilot call signs are and how they are used in military and civilian aviation.
- "What's in Your Pocket?" Article talks about what you should and shouldn't carry in your pocket.

Rights and Payment
All rights. Written material, payment rates vary. Pays on acceptance. Provides 3–5 contributor's copies.

Editor's Comments
Our magazine teaches readers to think, laugh, learn, and interact with parents and others. We look for material that will nurture healthy, self-confident, and forward-thinking minds.

The Universe in the Classroom

Astronomical Society of the Pacific
390 Ashton Avenue
San Francisco, CA 94112

Editor: Anna Hurst

Description and Interests
Developed by the Astronomical Society of the Pacific, this free online newsletter targets elementary and secondary school educators. Each issue focuses on providing astronomical information and includes articles and hands-on classroom activities that help keep the excitement of astronomy alive in the classroom.
- **Audience:** Teachers
- **Frequency:** Quarterly
- **Distribution:** 100% Internet
- **Hits per month:** 10,000
- **Website: www.astrosociety.org**

Freelance Potential
90% written by nonstaff writers. Publishes 4 freelance submissions yearly; 50% by unpublished writers, 75% by authors who are new to the magazine. Receives 12 queries yearly.

Submissions
Query with outline. Accepts hard copy. Availability of artwork improves chance of acceptance. SASE. Responds in 1 month.
Articles: 3,000 words. Informational articles. Topics include astronomy, teaching methods, and astrobiology.
Artwork: Color prints and transparencies.
Other: Classroom activities.

Sample Issue
Sample copy available at website.
- "Our Solar Connection: A Themed Set of Activities for Grades 5–12." Article offers a summary of seven activities for classroom use with a theme centered on the sun.
- "The Music of the New Spheres?" Article discusses the Doppler-shift data that measures variations in planets, and how this data yields a waveform that resembles a musical octave.

Rights and Payment
One-time rights. No payment.

Editor's Comments
We strive to make learning astronomy easy and exciting for students. If you have an idea for something interesting, send us a query. We look for astronomical topics accompanied by one or two hands-on activities that will make the topic come alive for students, and stir their curiosity. Articles by authors who know the field, including teachers and other professionals, are welcome. Artwork is a plus.

USA Gymnastics

Pan American Plaza
201 South Capitol Avenue, Suite 300
Indianapolis, IN 46225

Editor: Luan Peszek

Description and Interests
Covering the sport of gymnastics, this magazine includes articles, competition reports, and interviews. Topics include men's, women's, and rhythmic gymnastics, and trampoline tumbling. It targets youth who compete as well as observers of the sport.
• **Audience:** 10+ years
• **Frequency:** 6 times each year
• **Distribution:** Subscription; newsstand
• **Circulation:** 98,000
• **Website:** www.usa-gymastics.org

Freelance Potential
5% written by nonstaff writers. Publishes 5–10 freelance submissions yearly; 5% by experts.

Submissions
Query or send complete ms. Accepts email submissions to lpeszek@usa-gymnastics.org. Responds in 1–2 months.
Articles: To 1,000 words. Informational articles; profiles; and personal experience pieces. Topics include all aspects of gymnastics, as well as nutrition and sports psychology.
Depts/columns: Word lengths vary. Event schedules and results, gym updates.

Sample Issue
50 pages (35% advertising): 6 articles; 5 depts/columns. Sample copy, $3.95. Guidelines available.
• "Thornton Triumphs at Visa Championships." Article spotlights the top winners of the men's national titles in the Visa National Championships.
• "Olga Karmansky Wins Rhythmic Title." Article spotlights the winner of the rhythmic all-around title at the Visa National Championships in Indianapolis.
• Sample dept/column: "Gym Update" takes a look at the winner of a gold medal in women's tumbling at the Trampoline and Tumbling World Cup in Belgium.

Rights and Payment
All rights. Written material, payment rates vary. Pays on publication.

Editor's Comments
We are currently looking for nutritional information and articles covering sports psychology. Writers must be experts in the field they are writing about. In addition, we are interested in up-to-date competition coverage, interviews with award-winning gymnasts, and information on the latest in gear and fashion.

U*S* Kids

Children's Better Health Institute
1100 Waterway Boulevard
P.O. Box 567
Indianapolis, IN 46206–0567

Editor: Daniel Lee

Description and Interests
This magazine uses kid-friendly articles, games, and activities to promote good health and improve the well-being of children.
• **Audience:** 6–8 years
• **Frequency:** 6 times each year
• **Distribution:** 100% subscription
• **Circulation:** 230,000
• **Website:** www.uskidsmag.org

Freelance Potential
10% written by nonstaff writers. Publishes 6 freelance submissions yearly; 10% by unpublished writers, 10% by authors who are new to the magazine. Receives 696 unsolicited mss yearly.

Submissions
Send complete ms. Accepts hard copy. SASE. Responds in 3 months.
Articles: 400 words. Factual and informational articles. Topics include health, exercise, nutrition, safety, hygiene, and drug education.
Fiction: 300–400 words. Genres include historical and contemporary fiction, mystery, fantasy, adventure, and folktales.
Depts/columns: Staff written.
Other: Activities and puzzles. Poetry, to 24 lines. Submit seasonal material 6 months in advance.

Sample Issue
36 pages (3% advertising): 5 articles; 4 depts/columns; 4 games; 1 recipe; 2 poems; 1 contest. Sample copy, $2.95 with 9x12 SASE (2 first-class stamps). Guidelines available.
• "Join the Pasta Patrol." Article discusses how pasta is made, its many forms, and its nutritional value.
• "Krilling Time." Article explores the eating habits of killer whales.
• "The Trade." Story depicts the consequences a bully faces when he swipes another kid's lunch.

Rights and Payment
All rights. Articles and fiction, $.17 per word. Other material, payment rates vary. Pays on publication. Provides 5 contributor's copies.

Editor's Comments
While we mostly use in-house material, we are committed to publishing information that promotes good health and fitness, and encourages a child's curiosity in the natural sciences.

U-Turn Magazine

U.25 Magazine

9800 Fredericksburg Road
San Antonio, TX 78288

Senior Editor: Shari L. Biediger

Description and Interests

Distributed to teens whose parents are members of the United Services Automobile Association, this magazine focuses on driving, finances, relationships, safety, and college and career planning.
- **Audience:** 13–17 years
- **Frequency:** Quarterly
- **Distribution:** 100% controlled
- **Circulation:** 540,000
- **Website: www.usaa.com**

Freelance Potential

80% written by nonstaff writers. Publishes 5 freelance submissions yearly; 5% by unpublished writers, 10% by authors who are new to the magazine. Receives 20 queries yearly.

Submissions

Query with clips. Accepts hard copy and email submissions to shari.biediger@usaa.com. SASE. Responds in 6 weeks.
Articles: Word lengths vary. Informational articles; profiles; interviews; and personal experience pieces. Topics include the arts, college, careers, crafts, hobbies, current events, history, music, popular culture, recreation, science, technology, social issues, sports, travel, teen driving, money, safety, and relationships.
Other: Activities, filler, games, jokes, puzzles, Q&As, and quizzes.

Sample Issue

30 pages: 5 articles; 2 activities. Sample copy, free with 9x12 SASE ($1.80 postage). Guidelines available.
- "Art Cause: Gone to Ghana." Article chronicles one teen's semester traveling in West Africa and how she used art to relate to the people of that region.
- "Roommate Files." Article features teens' personal experiences about learning to live with college and camp roommates.

Rights and Payment

All rights. Written material, payment rates vary. Pays on acceptance. Provides 3–5 contributor's copies.

Editor's Comments

Our mission is to educate USAA's young members about the topics that interest them now and will affect them in the future. We want to strengthen the character and knowledge of our readers. If you have an article idea that fits that description, we encourage you to contact us.

9800 Fredericksburg Road
San Antonio, TX 78288

Editor: Carol Barnes

Description and Interests

Striving to educate readers and help them prepare to become responsible adults, this four-color magazine includes articles on topics such as careers, education, finance, driving, and lifestyles. Its readers include young members of the United Services Automobile Association (USAA).
- **Audience:** 18–24 years
- **Frequency:** Quarterly
- **Distribution:** 100% controlled
- **Circulation:** 500,000
- **Website: www.usaa.com**

Freelance Potential

90% written by nonstaff writers. Publishes 10–15 freelance submissions yearly. Receives 60 queries yearly.

Submissions

Query with résumé and clips for feature articles. Send complete ms for shorter pieces. Accepts hard copy. Mss are not returned. Responds in 6–8 weeks.
Articles: 1,000 words. Shorter pieces, 300 words. Informational and how-to articles; profiles; interviews; and personal experience pieces. Topics include college, careers, saving and investing money, driving, and lifestyle issues.
Depts/columns: Word lengths vary. Short news items, USAA programs, and driving information.
Other: Activities, games.

Sample Issue

32 pages: 4 articles; 6 depts/columns. Sample copy, free with 9x12 SASE ($1.80 postage). Writers' guidelines available.
- "Tips on Tipping." Article takes a look at who, how much, and when to tip service providers, and how to receive better tips.
- "The Write Stuff." Article suggests ways to create a résumé that will attract attention.
- Sample dept/column: "Dollar Sense" offers guidance on handling credit wisely.

Rights and Payment

All rights. Feature articles, $500–$1,000. Other material, payment rates vary. Kill fee varies. Pays on acceptance.

Editor's Comments

Article ideas are welcome and encouraged. We use different styles of writing and are looking for features, profiles, and short news items.

Vegetarian Baby & Child

47565 323rd Avenue
Cass Lake, MN 56633

Editor: Melanie Wilson

Description and Interests
Targeting families living a vegetarian or vegan lifestyle, this online publication includes articles, recipes, interviews, and product reviews. It also includes networking resources.
• **Audience:** Parents
• **Frequency:** Quarterly
• **Distribution:** 100% Internet
• **Hits per month:** 90,000
• **Website:** www.vegetarianbaby.com

Freelance Potential
95% written by nonstaff writers. Publishes 25 freelance submissions yearly. Receives 24 queries, 12–24 unsolicited mss yearly.

Submissions
Query or send complete ms. Accepts hard copy and email submissions to melanie@vegetarianbaby.com (Microsoft Word attachment). SASE. Response time varies.
Articles: 350–1,500 words. Informational and how-to articles; profiles; interviews; and personal experience pieces. Topics include general nutrition, vegetarian pregnancy, dealing with friends and family, living with non-vegetarians, health, child care, activism, and support networks.
Depts/columns: Word lengths vary. Q&As, recipes, and book and new product reviews.
Other: Activities, games, and crafts for children.

Sample Issue
Sample copy and guidelines available at website.
• "Who Put the Graham in Graham Crackers?" Article explores the life of Sylvester Graham.
• "Applesauce Pancake Surprise." Story tells how a man makes his mother's special pancake recipe for his family.
• "A-Maize-ing Corn." Article takes a look at the history of corn, and how it is grown today.

Rights and Payment
First rights. Articles, $15. Pays on publication.

Editor's Comments
We're looking for articles that would be of interest to parents of vegetarian/vegan children and that fit into one of the current categories at our website. Articles should be balanced and fair. Any scientific claims about diet must be backed up by verifiable sources. Material should be well referenced if quotes are used.

Vegetarianteen.com

47565 323rd Avenue
Cass Lake, MN 56633

Editor: Melanie Wilson

Description and Interests
Written for teens, this supportive online publication explores topics related to living a vegetarian or vegan lifestyle. It includes articles, interviews, and recipes.
• **Audience:** YA–Adult
• **Frequency:** Quarterly
• **Distribution:** 100% Internet
• **Hits per month:** Unavailable
• **Website:** www.vegetarianteen.com

Freelance Potential
95% written by nonstaff writers. Publishes 10 freelance submissions yearly; 50% by authors who are new to the magazine. Receives 12–60 queries, 12–24 unsolicited mss yearly.

Submissions
Query or send complete ms. Accepts hard copy and email submissions to melanie@vegetarianbaby.com (Microsoft Word attachment). SASE. Response time varies.
Articles: 350–1,200 words. Informational and how-to articles; profiles; interviews; and personal experience pieces. Topics include health, food, fitness, family issues, animal activism, and nutrition.
Depts/columns: Word lengths vary. Recipes and book and product reviews.

Sample Issue
Sample copy and guidelines available at website.
• "Animals." Article reveals what teens are saying about animal cruelty and offers advice for living in a meat-eating world.
• "How I Went Veg." Personal experience piece tells how one teen became a vegetarian and changed her life for the better.
• "Wildlife Is in Danger." Article explores why people hunt and suggests ways to help save wildlife.

Rights and Payment
Rights vary. No payment.

Editor's Comments
We look for philosophical articles that tell it as it is when it comes to taking a stand and making a difference in the world. We're also interested in personal experience pieces that tell us about a day in the life of a veggie teen, how to make it through a holiday meal with meat-eating relatives, or dealing with social situations with non-vegetarian friends. Recipes are welcome.

VegFamily

9436 Deer Lodge Lane
Las Vegas, NV 89129

Editor: Erin Pavlina

Description and Interests
Parents who live a vegan lifestyle and are looking for ideas for preparing vegan meals for their families read this e-zine for recipes and articles on health, nutrition, and raising vegan children.
- **Audience:** YA–Adult
- **Frequency:** Monthly
- **Distribution:** 100% Internet
- **Hits per month:** 90,000
- **Website:** www.vegfamily.com

Freelance Potential
50% written by nonstaff writers. Publishes 40 freelance submissions yearly; 90% by unpublished writers, 50% by authors who are new to the magazine. Receives 60 queries yearly.

Submissions
Query. Accepts email queries to contact@vegfamily.com. Responds in 2 weeks.
Articles: 500–1,500 words. Informational, self-help, and how-to articles; profiles; and personal experience pieces. Topics include vegan pregnancy, babies and toddlers, vegan children and teens, health, nutrition, cooking, and parenting issues.
Fiction: 500–2,000 words. Genres include inspirational fiction, animal stories, and stories with nature and environmental themes.
Depts/columns: Word lengths vary. Recipes and book and product reviews.
Artwork: JPEG and GIF files.
Other: Activities. Submit seasonal material 2 months in advance.

Sample Issue
Sample copy and guidelines available at website.
- "Dealing with Doctors During Your Vegan Pregnancy." Article offers a first-person account of how one woman found resistance within the medical community to her vegan diet during her pregnancy.
- "College Vegetarianism 101." Article talks about the difficulties of being a vegetarian on campus.

Rights and Payment
All electronic rights. Articles, $20. Pays on publication.

Editor's Comments
We need original articles on a variety of subjects that will help parents successfully and confidently raise vegan children. Inspirational stories and practical pieces are both welcome.

Ventura County Parent Magazine

3477-D Old Conejo Road, Suite O
Newbury Park, CA 91320

Editor & Publisher: Jean Sutton

Description and Interests
Parents residing in and around Ventura County read this magazine for its articles, resources, new product information, profiles, news, and event listings.
- **Audience:** Parents
- **Frequency:** Monthly
- **Distribution:** 89% subscription; 11% subscription
- **Circulation:** 42,000
- **Website:** www.vcparent.com

Freelance Potential
50% written by nonstaff writers. Publishes 50 freelance submissions yearly; 10% by unpublished writers, 10% by authors who are new to the magazine. Receives 100+ queries, 50–75 unsolicited mss yearly.

Submissions
Query with sample paragraph; or send complete ms. Accepts disk submissions (Macintosh compatible) and email submissions to info@vcparent.com. SASE. Responds to queries in 2 months, to mss in 6 weeks.
Articles: 1,000–1,500 words. Informational articles and personal experience pieces. Topics include animals, crafts, hobbies, pets, the arts, computers, current events, education, health, fitness, social issues, popular culture, and news.
Fiction: 1,000–1,500 words. Publishes real-life and problem-solving fiction.
Depts/columns: 600 words. Health and safety news, media reviews, and Internet tips.
Artwork: B/W or color prints. Line art.
Other: Activities and filler on local topics.

Sample Issue
38 pages (44% advertising): 7 articles; 7 depts/columns. Sample copy, free with 12x14 SASE. Guidelines and theme list available.
- "PreK Education Offers a Variety of Health Benefits." Article discusses how children benefit from attending quality preschool programs.
- Sample dept/column: "Family Man" offers a dad's perspective on balancing work and family.

Rights and Payment
Exclusive regional rights. Written material, $35–$100. Artwork, payment rates vary. Pays on publication. Provides 1 contributor's copy.

Editor's Comments
We look for articles that will be supportive and enriching to parents. Parenting topics are welcome.

The Village Family

501 40th Street S
Fargo, ND 58103

Editor: Laurie Neill

Description and Interests
Published by the Village Family Service Center, this magazine is the only local publication for parents in the Fargo, North Dakota–Moorhead, Minnesota, area. The magazine offers positive, upbeat articles for parents of toddlers to teens.
• **Audience:** Parents, 25–50 years
• **Frequency:** 6 times each year
• **Distribution:** Subscription; other
• **Circulation:** 25,000
• **Website:** www.thevillagefamily.org

Freelance Potential
70% written by nonstaff writers. Publishes 30 freelance submissions yearly. Receives 1,200 queries and unsolicited mss yearly.

Submissions
Query or send complete ms with author bio. Accepts hard copy and email submissions to magazine@ thevillagefamily.org. SASE. Response time varies.
Articles: To 1,500 words. Informational, self-help, and how-to articles; profiles; interviews; and personal experience pieces. Topics include current events, health, fitness, recreation, regional news, social issues, sports, and travel.
Depts/columns: Word lengths vary. Medical updates, media reviews, humorous essays, crafts, recipes, money matters, and family issues.

Sample Issue
46 pages (15% advertising): 2 articles; 8 depts/ columns; 1 calendar of events. Guidelines available.
• "Celebrating Local Youth." Article discusses the positive attitudes and contributions of local youth.
• "Should Parents Pay Attention to Video Game Ratings?" Article explores the value of the video game rating system and how parents can make informed decisions for their families.

Rights and Payment
First and electronic rights. Written material, $.07–$.10 per word. Reprints, $30–$50. Pays on publication.

Editor's Comments
Our mission is to improve the quality of people's lives through articles and features that educate and encourage families to develop and maintain positive, constructive relationships. Since we receive a large number of unsolicited manuscripts, a reply is not always possible. We'll contact you if we're interested.

Voice of Youth Advocates

4501 Forbes Boulevard, Suite 200
Lanham, MD 20706

Editor-in-Chief: Cathi Dunn MacRae

Description and Interests
Targeting librarians and teachers who work with teens, this magazine offers articles, book reviews, and book lists. It covers young adult literature, contemporary authors, and library programs.
• **Audience:** Professionals who work with youth
• **Frequency:** 6 times each year
• **Distribution:** 90% subscription; 10% other
• **Circulation:** 6,500
• **Website:** www.voya.com

Freelance Potential
85% written by nonstaff writers. Publishes 50 freelance submissions yearly; 70% by unpublished writers, 60% by authors who are new to the magazine. Receives 60 queries yearly.

Submissions
Query with résumé, synopsis, and market analysis. Accepts hard copy and email queries to cmacrae@ voya.com. Availability of artwork improves chance of acceptance. SASE. Responds in 2–4 months.
Articles: 800–3,000 words. Informational and how-to articles; book reviews; and book lists. Prints one book list annually. Topics include young adult literature, contemporary authors, and library programs.
Other: Submit seasonal material 1 year in advance.

Sample Issue
90 pages (20% advertising): 12 articles; 164 book reviews. Sample copy, free with 9x12 SASE. Guidelines available with SASE and at website.
• "My Bennington Summer." Article by a young author shares the experience of attending the National Book Foundation's Summer Writing Camp.
• "From Kerosene to Computers." Article describes how a library in Millersburg, Ohio, meets the different needs of the local Amish and Mennonite communities.
• "Amazing, Astounding, and Absolutely A+." Article showcases a list of unique audiobooks that exhibit excellence for teens.

Rights and Payment
All rights. Articles, $50–$100. Pays on publication. Provides 3 contributor's copies.

Editor's Comments
We prefer non-scholarly, lively, how-to pieces, as well as book reviews and book lists for teens and professionals who work with teens.

Voices from the Middle

National Council of Teachers of English
1111 West Kenyon Road
Urbana, IL 61801-1096

Production Editor: Carol Schanche

Description and Interests
This professional journal is aimed at middle school teachers of language arts. Each issue has a central theme and includes theory-based articles with practical applications, classroom exercises, book reviews, and professional announcements.
• **Audience:** Teachers
• **Frequency:** Quarterly
• **Distribution:** 90% subscription; 10% other
• **Circulation:** 11,000
• **Website:** www.ncte.org

Freelance Potential
70% written by nonstaff writers. Publishes 20 freelance submissions yearly; 60% by unpublished writers, 85% by authors who are new to the magazine. Receives 150 unsolicited mss yearly.

Submissions
Send 3 copies of complete ms. Accepts hard copy and email submissions to cschanche@ncte.org (indicate issue for which you are submitting in the subject line). SASE. Responds in 3–5 months.
Articles: 2,500–4,000 words. Educational articles and personal experience pieces related to the issue's theme. Topics include middle school language arts and English instruction.
Depts/columns: Staff written.
Artwork: B/W prints or transparencies.

Sample Issue
64 pages (9% advertising): 8 articles; 12 depts/columns. Sample copy, $6. Writers' guidelines and theme list available.
• "Stories in Our Classrooms: Diverse Human Lives, as Narrated by Standardizing Policies." Article argues for a radical change in literacy education that embraces the learning skills of individual students.
• "We Often Miss This Point: Diversity Always Brings Vitality." Article maintains that teaching multiculturalism cultivates a student's ability to recognize and respect differences among people.

Rights and Payment
First and second rights. No payment. Provides 2 contributor's copies.

Editor's Comments
Each issue has a central theme. Upcoming themes and calls for manuscripts are available in the journal. Articles should include sources and references.

Washington Family Magazine

485 Spring Park Place, Suite 550
Herndon, VA 20170

Managing Editor: Marae Leggs

Description and Interests
In print for over 15 years, this magazine for families residing in the Washington, DC, area is full of informative articles on parenting topics, regional resources, and events and activities in and around the area.
• **Audience:** Parents
• **Frequency:** Monthly
• **Distribution:** 100% controlled
• **Circulation:** 100,000
• **Website:** www.washingtonfamily.com

Freelance Potential
75% written by nonstaff writers. Publishes 90 freelance submissions yearly; 50% by unpublished writers, 50% by authors who are new to the magazine. Receives 1,200 queries and unsolicited mss yearly.

Submissions
Query or send complete ms. Accepts Macintosh disk submissions and email submissions to editor@thefamilymagazine.com. SASE. Response time varies.
Articles: 500–700 words. How-to and self-help articles and personal experience pieces. Topics include parenting, family life, relationships, fitness, crafts, hobbies, the arts, gifted and special education, music, multicultural and ethnic issues, social issues, music, recreation, and travel.
Depts/columns: Word lengths vary. Travel, health, and news of interest to families.
Artwork: B/W prints or transparencies. Line art.
Other: Submit seasonal material 6 months in advance.

Sample Issue
126 pages (50% advertising): 14 articles; 11 depts/columns; 4 resource guides; 1 special section. Sample copy, $4 with 9x12 SASE. Guidelines and editorial calendar available.
• "Getting Fit after Pregnancy." Article offers an exercise plan for new moms.
• Sample dept/column: "Hands-on Kids!" offers instructions for making sun prints.

Rights and Payment
Regional rights. Articles, $35–$50. Depts/columns, payment rates vary. Pays on publication. Provides 1 contributor's copy.

Editor's Comments
We are interested in articles on pregnancy, adoption, health, relationships, and fine arts for children.

Washington Parent

4701 Sangamore Road, Suite N720
Bethesda, MD 20186

Editor: Margaret Hut

Description and Interests
This local tabloid gives updates on events and information for Washington, DC, parents. It includes general interest articles on family and parenting topics.
- **Audience:** Families
- **Frequency:** Monthly
- **Distribution:** 93% controlled; 7% subscription
- **Circulation:** 75,000
- **Website:** www.washingtonparent.com

Freelance Potential
98% written by nonstaff writers. Publishes 20 freelance submissions yearly. Receives 1,200 queries each year.

Submissions
Query. Accepts email queries to contactus@ washingtonparent.net (Microsoft Word or WordPerfect attachments). SASE. Response time varies.
Articles: 1,000–2,000 words. Informational and how-to articles. Topics include regional news and events, parenting, family issues, local entertainment, gifted and special education, child development, health, fitness, the environment, and multicultural and ethnic issues.
Depts/columns: Word lengths vary. Family travel, book and media reviews, education, topics relating to children with special needs, and short news items.

Sample Issue
130 pages (63% advertising): 8 articles; 8 depts/columns. Sample copy, guidelines, and editorial calendar available.
- "Kindergarten Readiness." Article offers guidelines for evaluating a child's readiness for kindergarten.
- "Childhood Cavities on the Rise." Article discusses ways to teach children about good dental hygiene.
- Sample dept/column: "Parenting 911" suggests strategies and responses when a child wants to stop music lessons.

Rights and Payment
First rights. Written material, payment rates vary. Pays on publication. Provides 3 contributor's copies.

Editor's Comments
Our goal is to offer readers a broad spectrum of family-oriented information. Articles are geared to support and educate local parents with material on health, education, child care, recreation, and current events.

Weatherwise

1319 Eighteenth Street NW
Washington, DC 20036

Assistant Editor: Meghan Joyce

Description and Interests
The features and photography published in *Weatherwise* provide information on the latest discoveries and hottest issues in meteorology for weather enthusiasts and weather professionals alike.
- **Audience:** YA–Adult
- **Frequency:** 6 times each year
- **Distribution:** 100% subscription
- **Circulation:** 8,000
- **Website:** www.weatherwise.org

Freelance Potential
50% written by nonstaff writers. Publishes 20 freelance submissions yearly; 5% by unpublished writers, 15% by authors who are new to the magazine. Receives 240 queries yearly.

Submissions
Query with résumé and clips. Accepts email queries to ww@heldref.org. Availability of artwork improves chance of acceptance. Responds in 2 months.
Articles: Word lengths vary. Informational articles; photo-essays; and reviews. Topics include storms, storm tracking, safety issues, and other topics related to the weather—all with a scientific basis.
Depts/columns: Word lengths vary. Book reviews and resources, weather highlights, forecasts, history, and Q&As about types of weather.
Artwork: Color prints or transparencies.

Sample Issue
82 pages: 6 articles; 1 story; 8 depts/columns. Guidelines available.
- "Blown Away: The 2005 Atlantic Hurricane Season." Article discusses the most active hurricane season on record.
- "Back in Business." Article reveals that the U.S. Congress may establish a committee to study the possibility of modifying weather for human benefit.
- Sample dept/column: "Weatherscapes" examines the changeable weather patterns of Navarino, Chile.

Rights and Payment
All rights. All material, payment rates vary. Pays on publication.

Editor's Comments
We get too many queries proposing broad-brush articles. Send us a focused query—look for the story within the story, and emphasize the human element. Describe the connections weather has to our lives.

Wee Ones

P.O. Box 226
Darlington, MD 21034

Editor: Jennifer Reed

Description and Interests
This website features short stories, articles, puzzles, activities, artwork, and age-appropriate web links that parents and children can read and explore together.
- **Audience:** 5–10 years
- **Frequency:** 6 times each year
- **Distribution:** 100% Internet
- **Hits per month:** 40,000+
- **Website:** www.weeonesmag.com

Freelance Potential
100% written by nonstaff writers. Publishes 200 freelance submissions yearly; 50% by unpublished writers, 50% by authors who are new to the magazine. Receives 960 unsolicited mss yearly.

Submissions
Send complete ms. Accepts email submissions only to submissions@weeonesmag.com (attach artwork). Responds in 1–4 weeks.
Articles: 500 words. Informational and how-to articles. Topics include animals, pets, the arts, crafts, hobbies, current events, health, fitness, history, music, multicultural and ethnic issues, nature, the environment, sports, travel, and recreation. Also publishes biographical articles.
Fiction: 500 words. Genres include contemporary, historical, and multicultural fiction; adventure; mystery; and suspense. Also publishes humor, sports stories, and read-along stories.
Artwork: Line art.
Other: Submit seasonal material 6 months in advance.

Sample Issue
Sample copy and guidelines available at website.
- "The Wonderful Things About Tigger." Article highlights the life of the late Paul Winchell, the voice of Tigger in the Winnie the Pooh cartoons.
- "Kaila's Beatballs." Humorous story tells of a young girl with a cold who brings a treat to her class for International Feast Day.

Rights and Payment
Non-exclusive worldwide, electronic, and reprint rights. Written material, $.05 per word. Pays on publication.

Editor's Comments
We need character-driven stories with themes that children can relate to. Nonfiction articles may include activities, arts and crafts, recipes, or puzzles. Our new section of kid-friendly poetry opens this year.

Westchester Family

7 Purdy Street, Suite 201
Harrison, NY 10528

Editor: Jean Sheff

Description and Interests
Locally relevant, insightful, and useful information for parents living in Westchester County, New York, can be found in this magazine. In addition to parenting topics, it covers education, recreation, and women's issues. Each issue also spotlights local dining and entertainment establishments.
- **Audience:** Parents
- **Frequency:** Monthly
- **Distribution:** 96% controlled; 4% subscription
- **Circulation:** 59,000
- **Website:** www.westchesterfamily.com

Freelance Potential
80% written by nonstaff writers. Publishes 40 freelance submissions yearly; 10% by unpublished writers, 30% by authors who are new to the magazine. Receives 600 queries yearly.

Submissions
Query with clips. Accepts hard copy. SASE. Response time varies.
Articles: 800–1,200 words. Informational articles; humor; profiles; interviews; photo-essays; and personal experience pieces. Topics include gifted education, music, recreation, regional news, social issues, special education, travel, and women's issues.
Depts/columns: 400–800 words. News and reviews.

Sample Issue
62 pages (52% advertising): 1 article; 7 depts/columns. Sample copy, free with 9x12 SASE. Guidelines available.
- "The Best Tools for Parents." Article takes a look at the National Publication Awards for outstanding parenting resources.
- Sample dept/column: "Mom Notes" offers information on the dangers of high-fructose corn syrup and reports on a new line of makeup.

Rights and Payment
First rights. Written material, $25–$200. Pays on publication. Provides 1 contributor's copy.

Editor's Comments
We're looking for ideas for engaging articles that offer solutions and support for parents, as well as information on local events and family-friendly places to visit. If you have an idea for something that hasn't been done before, send us a detailed query. It is important that writers know the Westchester area.

Westchester Parent

350 Fifth Avenue, Suite 2420
New York, NY 10118

Editor: Reneé Cho

Description and Interests
Child development, health issues, family matters, and regional news are covered in this parenting publication. Residents in Westchester and Rockland counties in New York, as well as the towns of Greenwich and Stamford in Connecticut, read this tabloid for information on child care and local news and events.
- **Audience:** Parents
- **Frequency:** Monthly
- **Distribution:** 100% controlled
- **Circulation:** 66,000
- **Website:** www.parentsknow.com

Freelance Potential
10% written by nonstaff writers. Publishes 20 freelance submissions yearly; 5% by unpublished writers, 20% by authors who are new to the magazine. Receives 300 queries and unsolicited mss yearly.

Submissions
Query or send complete ms. Accepts hard copy and email submissions to renee@parentsknow.com. SASE. Response time varies.
Articles: 800–1,000 words. Informational, self-help, and how-to articles; profiles; interviews; and personal experience pieces. Topics include parenting, family life, child development, animals, pets, the arts, computers, crafts, hobbies, current events, gifted and special education, health, fitness, recreation, regional news, and travel.
Depts/columns: 750 words. Short news items, family travel pieces, and media reviews.
Other: Submit seasonal material 4 months in advance.

Sample Issue
76 pages: 5 articles; 6 depts/columns; 1 calendar of events. Sample copy, free with 10x13 SASE. Guidelines available via email.
- "Motherhood." Article discusses the true feelings of some mothers about the pressures of motherhood.
- Sample dept/column: "Weaning Children Naturally" discusses the benefits of breast milk and breastfeeding children longer.

Rights and Payment
First New York area rights. No payment.

Editor's Comments
Local writers with experience in writing about family matters are welcome to submit their work. We look for well-written pieces on timely issues.

West Coast Families

224-280 Nelson Street
Vancouver, British Columbia V6B 2E2
Canada

Editor: Michelle Froese

Description and Interests
West Coast Families informs families living in Vancouver and all of British Columbia about regional events and activities. Distributed free of charge, it also covers education issues, the arts, health, family finances and travel, and women's issues.
- **Audience:** Families
- **Frequency:** 8 times each year
- **Distribution:** 93% controlled; 5% schools; 2% subscription
- **Circulation:** 50,000
- **Website:** www.westcoastfamilies.com

Freelance Potential
70% written by nonstaff writers. Publishes 25–50 freelance submissions yearly; 25% by authors who are new to the magazine. Receives 300 queries yearly.

Submissions
Query. Accepts hard copy and email queries to info@westcoastfamilies.com. SAE/IRC. Response time varies.
Articles: 600–800 words. Informational, self-help, and how-to articles; and personal experience pieces. Topics include family life, parenting, recreation, travel, religion, current events, health, fitness, education, sports, hobbies, science, technology, nature, animals, and pets.
Depts/columns: Staff written.
Other: Puzzles, activities, jokes, and games. Submit seasonal material 3 months in advance.

Sample Issue
44 pages (8% advertising): 15 articles; 7 depts/columns; 1 events calendar. Sample copy, free with 9x12 SASE ($1.45 Canadian postage). Guidelines and editorial calendar available.
- "Struggling to Conceive." Article examines the causes of infertility and several treatments available, including naturopathic treatments.
- "An Entertaining Idea." Article presents a number of unusual party ideas.

Rights and Payment
Rights vary. Written material, payment rates vary. Pays on acceptance or publication. Provides contributor's copies upon request.

Editor's Comments
Target your writing to an educated middle- to upper-income audience that is devoted to their families.

Western New York Family

3147 Delaware Avenue, Suite B
Buffalo, NY 14217

Editor: Michelle Miller

Description and Interests
Families residing in the Buffalo, New York, metropolitan region read this publication for articles and tips on topics related to parenting. In addition, it includes information on local resources and events.
• **Audience:** Parents
• **Frequency:** Monthly
• **Distribution:** 80% controlled; 10% subscription; 10% other
• **Circulation:** 26,500
• **Website: www.wnyfamilymagazine.com**

Freelance Potential
50% written by nonstaff writers. Publishes 100 freelance submissions yearly; 30% by unpublished writers, 30% by authors who are new to the magazine. Receives 1,200 unsolicited mss yearly.

Submissions
Send complete ms with short biography. Accepts email submissions to michelle@wnyfamilymagazine.com.
Articles: 750–1,000 words. Informational and how-to articles; creative nonfiction; humor; and self-help and personal experience pieces. Topics include family, parenting, health, fitness, education, seniors, travel, and leisure. Humorous stories; 750 words.
Depts/columns: 750–1,000 words. Family travel, single parenting, book reviews, and restaurant reviews.
Other: Hard news, factual pieces; 2,000 words.

Sample Issue
70 pages (40% advertising): 11 articles; 14 depts/columns. Sample copy, $2.50 with 9x12 SASE ($1.79 postage). Guidelines and theme list available.
• "Splash into Summer with Fun Websites." Article explores kid-friendly, parent-tested websites for children of all ages.
• "Family Travel: Tips For a Smooth Flight When Kids Fly Alone." Article discusses when it's safe for kids to travel alone and how to prepare for their flight.
• Sample dept/column: "The Newbie Dad" offers an essay on how dads-to-be need attention, too.

Rights and Payment
First or second rights. Written material, $40+. Pays on publication. Provides 1 contributor's copy.

Editor's Comments
We are looking for fresh articles written by dads on topics related to fathering or family life, as well as articles covering family-friendly travel destinations.

What If?

19 Lynwood Place
Guelph, Ontario N1G 2V9
Canada

Managing Editor: Mike Leslie

Description and Interests
Fiction, opinion pieces, and poetry written by young Canadian writers for their contemporaries comprise the content of this magazine.
• **Audience:** 12–19 years
• **Frequency:** 5 times each year
• **Distribution:** 60% schools; 20% subscription; 20% newsstands
• **Circulation:** 3,000
• **Website: www.whatifmagazine.com**

Freelance Potential
90% written by nonstaff writers. Publishes 100 freelance submissions yearly; 90% by unpublished writers, 90% by authors who are new to the magazine. Receives 2,400 unsolicited mss yearly.

Submissions
Send complete ms with résumé. Accepts hard copy, email to editor@whatifmagazine.com (Microsoft Word attachments), and simultaneous submissions if identified. Availability of artwork improves chance of acceptance. SAE/IRC. Responds in 3 months.
Articles: To 1,000 words. Opinion pieces and editorials.
Fiction: To 3,000 words. Genres include mystery; suspense; fantasy; humor; and contemporary, inspirational, real life, and science fiction.
Artwork: Full color prints. Line art.
Other: Poetry, to 20 lines.

Sample Issue
48 pages (3% advertising): 3 articles; 7 stories; 3 depts/columns; 1 interview; 8 poems. Sample copy, $7.50 with 9x12 SAE. Guidelines available.
• "Pleasing Your Publisher." Article focuses on a writer's responsibilities after acceptance of material.
• "Landmine Scars." Story examines a first meeting between two people acquainted through emails.
• "The Person We All Hate." Story goes inside the narrator to reveal an uncertain self image.

Rights and Payment
First rights. No payment. Provides 3 author's copies.

Editor's Comments
We are currently accepting material from young Canadian writers and illustrators only. We are particularly in need of mystery, adventure, and science fiction. Submissions are welcome from new as well as previously published writers.

What's Hers

03-212 Henderson Way, Suite 328
Winnipeg, Manitoba R2L 1L8
Canada

Editor: Twila Dreidger

Description and Interests
Teenage girls living in Canada turn to this magazine for updates on popular culture and the latest news from the fashion and beauty scene. It also publishes serious articles on world events.
- **Audience:** 14–18 years
- **Frequency:** Quarterly
- **Distribution:** 100% schools
- **Circulation:** 180,000
- **Website:** www.whatshers.com

Freelance Potential
40–45% written by nonstaff writers. Publishes 15–20 freelance submissions yearly; 5% by unpublished writers, 20% by authors who are new to the magazine. Receives 240 queries yearly.

Submissions
Query with clips. No unsolicited mss. Accepts email queries to letters@whatshers.com. Response time varies.
Articles: 300–1,700 words. Informational and factual articles; profiles; interviews; and humor. Topics include current events, popular culture, entertainment, health, social issues, and relationships.
Depts/columns: 300–1,700 words. Trends, entertainment, and celebrity news.
Artwork: Color prints or transparencies.

Sample Issue
24 pages (60% advertising): 7 articles; 4 depts/columns. Sample copy, $1.42 Canadian with 9x12 SAE/IRC. Guidelines available.
- "Work Wonders." Article features eight innovative and exciting job opportunities to cash in on this summer.
- "Suicidal Tendencies." Article discusses what to do if a friend threatens to commit suicide.
- Sample dept/column: "HERSay" features news of interest to teenage girls.

Rights and Payment
First rights. Written material, to $500. Pays 30 days after publication. Provides 2 contributor's copies.

Editor's Comments
While we use a light conversational writing style and an attention-grabbing format, we often address serious subjects that teens need to know about. Take a down-to-earth approach that makes the topic understandable to teen readers.

What's Up Kids Family Magazine

496 Metler Road
Ridgeville, Ontario L0S 1M0
Canada

Editor-in-Chief: Susan Pennell-Sebekos

Description and Interests
Formerly listed as *What's Up Kids?*, this informative and entertaining Canadian magazine has something for the whole family. Each issue includes articles on health, learning, travel, family life, entertainment, crafts, activities, and new product information.
- **Audience:** Parents and children
- **Frequency:** 6 times each year
- **Distribution:** Subscription; newsstand
- **Circulation:** 200,000
- **Website:** www.whatsupkids.com

Freelance Potential
80% written by nonstaff writers. Publishes 30 freelance submissions yearly; 60% by authors who are new to the magazine. Receives 348 queries yearly.

Submissions
Canadian authors only. Query. Accepts email queries only to susan@whatsupkids.com. Response time varies.
Articles: Word lengths vary. Informational articles. Topics include education, family issues, travel, fitness, nutrition, and health.
Depts/columns: Word lengths vary. Brief informational items on fathers, health, finance, and news.

Sample Issue
82 pages (15% advertising): 2 articles; 14 depts/columns; 1 kids' section.
- "Redecorate Your Child's Room." Article offers inexpensive design principles and creative ideas for children's décor.
- "Moving Day." Article suggests ways to keep stress levels low when uprooting the family and moving to a new home.
- Sample dept/column: "Family Tips" offers suggestions for picking a great hockey camp for boys and girls.

Rights and Payment
All rights. Written material, payment rates and payment policy vary. Provides contributor's copies.

Editor's Comments
We're looking for fresh ideas for articles on topics relating to family life issues. Material must be well written and offer practical solutions. In addition, we are always looking for educational and fun activities and interesting articles on animals for our kids' section. Keep in mind that we target children up to the age of 13 and work with Canadian writers only.

Winner

55 West Oak Ridge Drive
Hagerstown, MD 21740

Editor: Jan Schleifer

Description and Interests
This magazine's mission is to help middle school students say "no" to drugs and "yes" to life. *Winner* fills its pages with articles, stories, and activities that provide facts about drug and alcohol abuse, while also teaching life skills.
- **Audience:** 9–13 years
- **Frequency:** 9 times each year
- **Distribution:** 80% subscription; 20% other
- **Circulation:** 10,000
- **Website:** www.winnermagazine.org

Freelance Potential
25% written by nonstaff writers. Publishes 10–15 freelance submissions yearly; 5% by unpublished writers, 20% by authors who are new to the magazine. Receives 96 queries yearly.

Submissions
Send complete ms. Accepts email submissions to jschleifer@rhpa.org. Responds in 1 month.
Articles: 500–600 words. Informational, how-to, and self-help articles; and profiles. Topics include family issues; sports; peer pressure; tobacco, drug and alcohol abuse; life skills; social issues; and personal relationships.
Fiction: 600 words. True-life and problem-solving stories that focus on positive lifestyles.
Artwork: Color prints and transparencies. Line art.
Other: Puzzles, games, and filler.

Sample Issue
16 pages (no advertising): 4 articles; 1 story; 4 activities; 1 comic. Sample copy, $2 with 9x12 SASE (2 first-class stamps). Guidelines available at website.
- "One Day Closer." Story features two boys who live with their aunt while their father works overseas.
- "Crowning Touch." Article profiles the current Miss North Carolina Teen USA.
- "The Choice Is Yours." Article reports on the dangers of drinking and driving.

Rights and Payment
First rights. Articles, $80. Pays on acceptance. Provides 3 contributor's copies.

Editor's Comments
We're interested in fact-based articles and profiles of role models. Each article includes two or three thought questions and a pencil activity. Be sure to include those with your submission.

Wire Tap Magazine

c/o Independent Media Institute
77 Federal Street
San Francisco, CA 94107

Associate Editor: Kristina Rizga

Description and Interests
Wire Tap Magazine provides an online forum for young adults who wish to express their perspectives on social and political issues. It includes news articles, opinion pieces, and poems that address current events and contemporary culture.
- **Audience:** 18–30 years
- **Frequency:** Updated daily
- **Distribution:** 100% Internet
- **Hits per month:** 60,000
- **Website:** www.wiretapmag.org

Freelance Potential
95% written by nonstaff writers. Publishes 120 freelance submissions yearly. Receives 360 queries each year.

Submissions
Query. Accepts email queries only to k.rizga@wiretapmag.org (no attachments). Response time varies.
Articles: Word lengths vary. Informational articles; profiles; interviews; and personal experience pieces. Topics include social issues, politics, and culture.
Depts/columns: Word lengths vary. Reviews, politics, and news.
Other: Poetry.

Sample Issue
Guidelines available at website.
- "Know Your Rights: Skipping School to Protest." Article reports on the abuse of students who skip school to engage in political activism and exercise their constitutional right to free speech.
- "Downscaling the Dreams of Youth." Article describes the barriers to obtaining a college degree and the challenges many students face when trying to complete their education.

Rights and Payment
Electronic rights. Written material, $50–$400 for assigned pieces. No payment for unsolicited submissions. Payment policy varies.

Editor's Comments
We're always looking for new writers, activists, and artists to contribute to our site. We are most likely to publish writing that is respectful and socially responsible, with an activist or "what are you going to DO about it?" spin. We like to include the writing of those who have not traditionally had a voice.

Wondertime

Writers' Journal

244 Main Street
Northampton, MA 01060

Editor: Lisa Stiepock

Description and Interests
This new magazine from the editors of *FamilyFun* targets parents of children up to the age of six. It devotes its pages to the simple joys of raising a child and celebrating the love of learning in young children.
• **Audience:** Parents
• **Frequency:** 6 times each year
• **Distribution:** Subscription; newsstand
• **Circulation:** 400,000
• **Website:** www.wondertime.com

Freelance Potential
90% written by nonstaff writers. Publishes many freelance submissions yearly; 100% by authors who are new to the magazine.

Submissions
Query with clips. Accepts email queries to wondertime.editors@disney.com. Response time varies.
Articles: Word lengths vary. Informational articles. Topics include the social, physical, intellectual, creative, and emotional aspects of child development; parenting; family issues; and family activities.
Depts/columns: Word lengths vary. Food, new products, outdoor activities, and book reviews.

Sample Issue
144 pages: 7 articles; 12 depts/columns. Sample copy, $2.95 at newsstands. Guidelines available at website.
• "In So Many Words." Article chronicles one family's experiences in trying to get their child with Alfi's Syndrome to learn to speak.
• "Imaginary Friends Revealed." Article examines the real reasons why kids have imaginary friends.
• Sample dept/column: "The Great Outdoors" offers advice for parents of children who are afraid of the water.

Rights and Payment
Exclusive worldwide first periodical rights. Written material, $1+ per word. Payment policy varies.

Editor's Comments
Our writers and photographers are smart, funny, inquisitive moms and dads. We go beyond potty training, colic, and tantrums to help parents understand all the amazing things kids learn and do every day. Keep in mind that our audience is parents of children from birth through kindergarten and first grade.

P.O. Box 394
Perham, MN 56573

Editor: Leon Ogroske

Description and Interests
Positive, practical articles about writing are found in this publication. It focuses on skills and techniques for writing both fiction and nonfiction, while also covering the business aspects of publishing.
• **Audience:** YA–Adult
• **Frequency:** 6 times each year
• **Distribution:** 90% newsstand; 10% subscription
• **Circulation:** 23,000
• **Website:** www.writersjournal.com

Freelance Potential
90% written by nonstaff writers. Publishes 60 freelance submissions yearly; 50% by unpublished writers, 70% by authors who are new to the magazine. Receives 16 queries and unsolicited mss yearly.

Submissions
Query or send complete ms. Accepts hard copy. SASE. Responds in 2–6 months.
Articles: 1,000–2,000 words. Informational and how-to articles; profiles; and interviews. Topics include fiction writing, travel writing, technical writing, business writing, writing skills, interviewing, research, record keeping, and finances.
Depts/columns: Software reviews, 500–750 words. Marketing ideas and photography tips, 1,200–2,000 words.
Other: Poetry. Fiction contest, various genres.

Sample Issue
64 pages (10% advertising): 6 articles; 4 stories; 10 depts/columns; 2 poetry critiques. Sample copy, $5 with 9x12 SASE. Guidelines available.
• "Turn Your Family History into Historical Fiction." Article tells how you can add fictional elements to your family history to create winning stories.
• "A Man of Letters." Personal experience piece talks about a Scrabble club that builds vocabulary.
• Sample dept/column: "For Beginners Only" explains how to use plot diagrams to structure a novel.

Rights and Payment
One-time rights. Written material, $20 plus a 1-year subscription. Pays on publication. Provides 2 contributor's copies upon request.

Editor's Comments
We like ideas for unique and unusual ways for writers to produce income, such as technical writing, writing for websites, or writing church or business histories.

Yes Mag

501-3960 Quadra Street
Victoria, British Columbia V8X 4A3
Canada

Managing Editor: Jude Isabella

Description and Interests
This award-winning publication offers articles and activities that make learning science, technology, and mathematics exciting and fun. Each issue includes in-depth articles, projects, news, environmental updates, and information about new technology.
- **Audience:** 9–14 years
- **Frequency:** 6 times each year
- **Distribution:** 85% subscription; 15% newsstand
- **Circulation:** 23,000
- **Website: www.yesmag.ca**

Freelance Potential
70% written by nonstaff writers. Publishes 30 freelance submissions yearly; 5% by unpublished writers, 15% by authors who are new to the magazine. Receives 300 queries yearly.

Submissions
Query. Accepts email queries to editor@yesmag.ca. Response time varies.
Articles: Features, 300–800 words. Short, theme-related articles, 300–600 words. Informational articles, 250 words. Topics include astronomy, engineering, math, science, technology, plants and animals, and the environment.
Depts/columns: 250 words. Short items on current science, technology, and environmental events.

Sample Issue
32 pages (no advertising): 6 articles; 6 depts/columns. Sample copy, $4.50 with SAE/IRC. Guidelines and theme list available.
- "The Shadow Over Shoppers." Article reports on a study that shows why people spend more money on brand name items when shopping.
- "The Dark Side of Science." Article explains how caves are formed.
- Sample dept/column: "Eye on the Sky" takes a look at Mars and Saturn.

Rights and Payment
First rights. Written material, $.25 per word. Other material, payment rates vary. Pays on publication. Provides 1 contributor's copy.

Editor's Comments
We are interested in receiving exciting articles on topics such as physics, math, and chemistry. Our department, "Science and Technology Watch," is the best place for new writers to start.

Young Adult Today

P.O. Box 436987
Chicago, IL 60643-6987

Editor: Aja Carr

Description and Interests
Urban Ministries, Inc., an African American owned Christian media company, produces this Bible study guide for young adults who are enrolled in religious education classes.
- **Audience:** 18–24 years
- **Frequency:** Quarterly
- **Distribution:** 100% subscription
- **Circulation:** 25,000
- **Website: www.urbanministries.com**

Freelance Potential
95% written by nonstaff writers. Publishes 52 freelance submissions yearly; 50% by unpublished writers, 50% by authors who are new to the magazine. Receives 240 queries yearly.

Submissions
Query with résumé. No unsolicited mss. All articles and Bible lessons are assigned. SASE. Responds in 2 months.
Articles: To 400 words. Lessons consist of discussion pieces, questions, devotional readings, and Bible study guides that explain how to apply the lessons learned from Scripture to modern life.

Sample Issue
80 pages (4% advertising): 1 article; 13 discussion pieces; 13 corresponding Bible study guides. Sample copy, $2.25 with 9x12 SASE ($.87 postage). Guidelines provided on assignment.
- "Community: Living and Working Together." Article acknowledges the various forms of communities and examines how God uses members of communities to minister to each other.
- "Relay Race." Discussion piece explains that all believers possess one or more of the nine spiritual gifts and that each gift is vital to the building up of God's kingdom.
- "Called to the Common Good." Bible study teaches that all believers have an obligation to use their spiritual gifts as the Holy Spirit directs.

Rights and Payment
Rights negotiable. Written material, $150 per lesson. Pays on publication.

Editor's Comments
If you're experienced in Christian education and can write in a way that appeals to black urban youth, send us your résumé and a letter of introduction.

Young Adult Today Leader

P.O. Box 436987
Chicago, IL 60643-6987

Editor: Aja Carr

Description and Interests
Bible commentary, lesson plans, and other aids for religious education teachers appear in this publication from Urban Ministries, which was established to reach out primarily to African American Christians.
- **Audience:** Teachers
- **Frequency:** Quarterly
- **Distribution:** Unavailable
- **Circulation:** 15,000
- **Website:** www.youngadulttoday.com

Freelance Potential
95% written by nonstaff writers. Publishes 52 freelance submissions yearly; 50% by unpublished writers, 50% by authors who are new to the magazine. Receives 240 queries yearly.

Submissions
Query with résumé. All work is done on assignment. No unsolicited mss. SASE. Responds in 2 months.
Articles: Devotionals, 400 words. Topics include current events and social issues as they relate to Christianity and the Bible.

Sample Issue
80 pages (no advertising): 1 article; 13 discussion pieces; 13 corresponding Bible study guides. Sample copy, $2.25 with 9x12 SASE ($.87 postage). Guidelines available.
- "Thanking the People That Matter." Teaching plan explains how to encourage students to gratefully acknowledge the contributions others have made to their spiritual lives.
- "Apostles, Leaders, and Everybody Else." Teaching plan aims to help students understand the biblical description of apostles and apostolic ministry.
- "I Love Him, But . . ." Teaching plan covers the challenges Christian students will face in their relationships with believers as well as unbelievers.

Rights and Payment
Rights negotiable. Written material, $150. Pays on publication.

Editor's Comments
Our lessons are specifically designed to support African American young adults as they strive to live as faithful Christians. We will consider offering you an assignment if you are an experienced religious education teacher who can speak from the African American experience.

Young People's Press

374 Fraser Street
North Bay, ON P1B 3W7
Canada

Chief Executive Officer: Don Curry

Description and Interests
Young People's Press empowers a large network of youth and young adult writers to have a voice in the mainstream media. It acts as a showcase for issues that today's young people care about, and presents these concerns in their own voices.
- **Audience:** 14–24 years
- **Frequency:** Daily
- **Distribution:** 100% Internet
- **Hits per month:** 4,000
- **Website:** www.ypp.net

Freelance Potential
90% written by nonstaff writers. Publishes 100 freelance submissions yearly; 70% by unpublished writers, 70% by authors who are new to the magazine. Receives 600 queries, 600 unsolicited mss yearly.

Submissions
Prefers complete ms with contact information; accepts queries. Accepts email submissions to doncurry@ontera.net (Microsoft Word attachments). Availability of electronic artwork improves chance of acceptance. Responds to mss in 1 week.
Articles: 400–1,000 words. Informational articles; profiles; reviews; and personal experience pieces. Topics include music and the arts, current events, multicultural and social issues, popular culture, and self-help.
Depts/columns: Word lengths vary. Reviews of movies, CDs, and websites.
Artwork: Electronic images only.
Other: Submit seasonal material 1 month in advance.

Sample Issue
Guidelines available at website.
- "Where Is Pop Music Going?" Article traces the influence that music has had on pre-teens and teens.
- "We Are All Equal." Article asks readers to reassess their views on predetermined prejudices of people based on race and creed.
- "Decent Eats on Campus: Kitchen vs. Caf." Article considers the meal options on a Canadian campus.

Rights and Payment
Rights vary. No payment.

Editor's Comments
We would like to see more stories and submissions on political issues. Articles should have a national or international theme. Our editors will work with you.

Young Rider

P.O. Box 8237
Lexington, KY 40533

Editor: Lesley Ward

Description and Interests

Young equestrians find practical and fun articles in the pages of this magazine. It includes information on horse grooming and riding techniques, as well as profiles of well-known riders.
• **Audience:** 6–14 years
• **Frequency:** 6 times each year
• **Distribution:** 70% subscription; 30% newsstand
• **Circulation:** 92,000
• **Website:** www.youngrider.com

Freelance Potential

20% written by nonstaff writers. Publishes 20 freelance submissions yearly; 10% by unpublished writers, 10% by authors who are new to the magazine. Receives 60 queries yearly.

Submissions

Query. Prefers email to yreditor@bowtieinc.com (Microsoft Word attachments). Responds in 2 weeks.
Articles: Word lengths vary. Informational and how-to articles and profiles. Topics include horseback riding, training, techniques, careers, and general horse grooming and care.
Fiction: 1,200 words. Stories that feature horses and youth themes.
Artwork: Color prints, transparencies, and high-resolution digital images.

Sample Issue

64 pages (28% advertising): 10 articles; 1 story; 4 depts/columns; 1 contest. Sample copy, $3.99 with 9x12 SASE ($1 postage). Guidelines and editorial calendar available.
• "Learn How to Fit a Blanket." Article details how to measure your horse to get the perfect blanket.
• "Afleet Alex Amazes Everyone!" Article profiles a horse that almost won the Triple Crown.
• "Are You Safe in the Saddle?" Article discusses appropriate riding attire and accessories.

Rights and Payment

First serial rights. Written material, $.10 per word. Artwork, payment rates vary. Pays on publication. Provides 2 contributor's copies.

Editor's Comments

We need more good short stories with horse themes and "horsey interest" articles that will appeal to kids all over the country. We don't usually use freelance pieces about horse care or riding tips.

Young Salvationist

The Salvation Army
615 Slaters Lane
Alexandria, VA 22314

Editor: Major Curtiss A. Hartley

Description and Interests

The purpose of this magazine is to help young Salvationists develop a mature faith, personal ministry, and a Christian perspective on everyday life.
• **Audience:** 13–21 years
• **Frequency:** 10 times each year
• **Distribution:** 80% controlled; 20% subscription
• **Circulation:** 43,000

Freelance Potential

95% written by nonstaff writers. Publishes 60 freelance submissions yearly; 5% by unpublished writers, 10% by authors who are new to the magazine. Receives 480 unsolicited mss yearly.

Submissions

Send complete ms. Accepts hard copy, simultaneous submissions, and email submissions to ys@ usn.salvationarmy.org. SASE. Responds in 2 months.
Articles: 1,000–1,500 words. How-to, inspirational, and personal experience pieces; profiles; interviews; and humor. Topics include religion and issues of relevance to teens.
Fiction: 500–1,200 words. Genres include adventure, fantasy, romance, humor, and religious and science fiction—all written from a Christian perspective.
Other: Submit seasonal material 6 months in advance.

Sample Issue

24 pages (no advertising): 9 articles; 1 story; 1 contest. Sample copy, free with 9x12 SASE (3 first-class stamps). Guidelines and theme list available with #10 SASE.
• "Strike or Hold?" Article examines how biblical figures have dealt with conflict and whether they sought revenge or turned the other cheek.
• "Hooked on Sports." Story depicts a teenage boy who threw himself into sports and discovered that his success was empty without God in his life.

Rights and Payment

First and second rights. Written material, $.15 per word for reprint rights. Pays on acceptance. Provides 4 contributor's copies.

Editor's Comments

A good way to break in is by submitting short (350–600 words) evangelistic pieces aimed at teens, which communicate the Gospel through everyday examples rather than theology.

Youth & Christian Education Leadership

1080 Montgomery Avenue
Cleveland, TN 37311

Editor: Wanda Griffith

Description and Interests
The pages of this resourceful magazine are filled with articles and essays on topics of interest to Christian educators. Its content focuses on intentional acts of Christian education in the home, the classroom, or the sanctuary, or wherever they might occur.
- **Audience:** Adults
- **Frequency:** Quarterly
- **Distribution:** 100% subscription
- **Circulation:** 13,000
- **Website:** www.pathwaypress.org

Freelance Potential
10% written by nonstaff writers. Publishes 10 freelance submissions yearly; 90% by unpublished writers, 10% by authors who are new to the magazine. Receives 30–35 queries, 20–25 unsolicited mss each year.

Submissions
Prefers complete ms with author biography. Accepts queries. Accepts disk submissions (Microsoft Word or WordPerfect), and email to Wanda_Griffith@ pathwaypress.org. SASE. Responds in 3 weeks.
Articles: 500–1,000 words. Informational and how-to articles; profiles; interviews; and personal experience pieces. Topics include current events, humor, music, religion, social issues, psychology, parenting, and multicultural and ethnic subjects.
Depts/columns: Staff written.

Sample Issue
30 pages (2% advertising): 12 articles; 5 depts/columns. Sample copy, $1 with 9x12 SASE (2 first-class stamps). Guidelines available at website.
- "Love the Ones God Sends." Article discusses the importance of reaching all children with God's Word, even those who seem unlovable.
- "Juggling Smarts for Pre-teens." Article suggests using juggling to help tweens build their self-esteem and their faith in God.

Rights and Payment
First rights. Written material, $25–$50. Kill fee, 50%. Pays on publication. Provides 1–10 author's copies.

Editor's Comments
We're looking for testimonials about the impact of giving or receiving Christian education. We want to inspire our readers who are teachers and leaders. Practical how-to's are also of interest to us.

Youth Today

1200 17th Street NW, 4th Floor
Washington, DC 20036

Editor: Patrick Boyle

Description and Interests
Professionals in the child and youth services field read this nationally distributed tabloid for its informative articles and resources. Topics include adolescent health, gang and violence prevention, youth development, and job training. Each issue includes contact information, listings of grant awards, calendars of workshops, and book and video reviews.
- **Audience:** Youth workers
- **Frequency:** 10 times each year
- **Distribution:** 75% subscription; 25% controlled
- **Circulation:** 12,000
- **Website:** www.youthtoday.org

Freelance Potential
50% written by nonstaff writers. Publishes 25 freelance submissions yearly; 10% by authors who are new to the magazine. Receives 36 queries yearly.

Submissions
Query with résumé and clips. Responds in 3 months.
Articles: 1,000–2,500 words. Informational articles; news and research reports; profiles of youth workers and youth programs; and business features. Topics include foster care, child abuse, youth program management, violence, adolescent health, juvenile justice, job training and school-to-work programs, after-school programs and mentoring, and other social issues related to youth development.
Depts/columns: Book and video reviews; news briefs; opinion pieces; and people in the news.

Sample Issue
40 pages (50% advertising): 13 articles; 14 depts/columns. Sample copy, $5. Guidelines available.
- "Standardized Math Classes Helped Me Learn." Article shares a high school student's math education experience.
- "Are You My Mentor?" Article discusses the meaning of mentoring.
- Sample dept/column: "Youth Employment" looks at summer job opportunities for teens.

Rights and Payment
First and Internet rights. Written material, $.50–$.75 per word. Pays on acceptance. Provides 2 copies.

Editor's Comments
Every aspect of youth services is covered in *Youth Today*. We seek information on successful programs and resources that have proved to be effective.

YouthWorker

104 Woodmont Boulevard, Suite 300
Nashville, TN 37205

Editor: Steve Rabey

Description and Interests

For more than 20 years, *YouthWorker* has served as a source of inspiration for individuals who minister to Christian youth. Its purpose is to help them become more effective in teaching young people to know, love, and serve Jesus Christ.
- **Audience:** Adults who work with youth
- **Frequency:** 6 times each year
- **Distribution:** 100% subscription
- **Circulation:** 20,000
- **Website:** www.youthworker.com

Freelance Potential

75% written by nonstaff writers. Publishes 35 freelance submissions yearly; 10% by unpublished writers. Receives 720 queries yearly.

Submissions

Query with short biography. Prefers email queries to steve@youthworker.com (include "Query" in subject line). Accepts hard copy and faxes to 615-385-4412. SASE. Responds in 6–8 weeks.
Articles: Word lengths vary. Informational and practical application articles; personal experience pieces; and reviews. Topics include youth ministry, theology, helping youth, student worship, family ministry, popular culture, education, family issues, the media, and volunteering.
Depts/columns: Word lengths vary. National and regional trends, quotes from youth workers.

Sample Issue

64 pages (30% advertising): 5 articles; 11 depts/columns. Sample copy, $8. Guidelines and theme list available at website.
- "Deep Ministry in a Shallow World." Article offers a plan for teaching that goes beyond the superficial.
- "What Makes a Great Teacher?" Article pays tribute to favorite teachers.
- Sample dept/column: "Tech Talk" describes the ways technology has influenced our culture and our lives.

Rights and Payment

All rights. Written material, $15–$300. Pays on publication. Provides 1 contributor's copy.

Editor's Comments

Please be sure to check our upcoming themes, then read our writers' guidelines for detailed submission information before you send us your query.

Yu-Gi-Oh

Beckett Media
15850 Dallas Parkway
Dallas, TX 75248

Editorial Director: Doug Kale

Description and Interests

Yu-Gi-Oh collectors and enthusiasts are the target audience for this Beckett Media publication. It includes updates and information on cards, games, memorabilia, and other Yu-Gi-Oh products.
- **Audience:** YA–Adult
- **Frequency:** 6 times each year
- **Distribution:** 80% newsstand; 20% subscription
- **Circulation:** 250,000
- **Website:** www.beckettyugioh.com

Freelance Potential

50% written by nonstaff writers. Publishes 15–20 freelance submissions yearly; 10% by unpublished writers, 1% by authors who are new to the magazine.

Submissions

Prefers query with outline and clips. Accepts complete ms. Accepts hard copy. SASE. Responds in 1–2 months.
Articles: 500–1,200 words. Informational articles; profiles; and reviews. Topics include Yu-Gi-Oh cards, games, cheat codes, characters, episodes, collectors, and memorabilia.
Fiction: Word lengths vary. Stories about Yu-Gi-Oh.
Depts/columns: 500–750 words. Product news, tournament information, price guides.

Sample Issue

88 pages: 8 articles; 7 depts/columns; 2 special sections; 2 contests. Sample copy, $9.99. Writers' guidelines available.
- "Tech in the New Advanced." Article looks at cards that benefited from a format change, including older monsters, spells, and traps.
- "Jaden Vs. Yugi." Article compares the heroes of *King of Games* and *GX*.
- Sample dept/column: "News Update!" features the latest product and event information.

Rights and Payment

First North American serial rights. Articles and fiction, $100–$250. Depts/columns, $50–$200. Pays on acceptance. Provides 2 contributor's copies.

Editor's Comments

We're always interested in articles on rare cards, as well as tips for buying, selling, and collecting cards and memorabilia. You must be familiar with the world of Yu-Gi-Oh and the interests of its fans to successfully submit to us.

Additional Listings

Additional Listings

We have selected the following magazines to offer you additional publishing opportunities. These magazines range from general-interest publications to women's magazines to craft and hobby magazines. While children, young adults, parents, or teachers are not their primary target audience, these publications do publish a limited amount of children's-related material.

As you review the listings that follow, use the Description and Interests section as your guide to the particular needs of each magazine. This section offers general information about the magazine and its readers' interests, as well as the type of material it usually publishes. The Freelance Potential section will provide information about the publication's receptivity to freelance manuscripts.

After you survey the listings to determine if your work meets the magazine's specifications, be sure to read a recent sample copy and the current writers' guidelines before submitting your material.

Adventures

6401 The Paseo
Kansas City, MO 64131

Submissions: Denise Willemin

Description and Interests
Adventures is written specifically for early elementary children and correlates with the WordAction Sunday school curriculum. It is a weekly, full-color take-home paper for children in first and second grade. *Adventures* connects Sunday school learning with daily experiences and growth of the child. Circ: Unavailable.
Website: www.wordaction.com

Freelance Potential
50% written by nonstaff writers. Publishes 15 freelance submissions yearly; 10% by unpublished writers, 10% by authors who are new to the magazine. Receives 300 queries yearly.
Submissions and Payment: Guidelines and theme list available. Query. Accepts hard copy. SASE. Responds in 4–6 weeks. All North American serial rights. Articles, word lengths and payment rates vary. Pays on acceptance. Provides 2 contributor's copies.

AKC Family Dog

American Kennel Club
260 Madison Avenue
New York, NY 10016

Managing Editor: Erika Mansourian

Description and Interests
This publication seeks to inform and educate pet-owning Americans about their purebred dogs. Published six times each year, it features articles on pet grooming, training, health care, and behavior. Circ: 140,000.
Website: www.akc.org

Freelance Potential
90% written by nonstaff writers. Publishes 50 freelance submissions yearly; 2% by unpublished writers, 10% by authors who are new to the magazine. Receives 60–120 queries yearly.
Submissions and Payment: Sample copy and guidelines, free with 9x12 SASE. Query with outline. Accepts hard copy and email to familydog@akc.org (Microsoft Word attachments). SASE. Responds in 1–2 months. First North American serial rights. Articles, 1,000–2,000 words; $125–$500. Depts/columns, staff written. Pays on publication.

The ALAN Review

College of Liberal Arts & Sciences
Department of English
Arizona State University
P.O. Box 87032
Tempe, AZ 85287

Editor: Dr. James Blasingame

Description and Interests

Published three times each year, this magazine focuses on young adult literature and features interviews with authors and reports on publishing trends. Circ: 2,500.
Website: www.alan-ya.org

Freelance Potential

84% written by nonstaff writers. Publishes 38 freelance submissions yearly; 5% by unpublished writers, 65% by authors who are new to the magazine. Receives 90 unsolicited mss yearly.
Submissions and Payment: Guidelines available in magazine. Sample copy, free. Send 3 copies of complete ms with disk (ASCII or Microsoft Word 5.1 or higher). Accepts simultaneous submissions if identified. Availability of artwork improves chance of acceptance. SASE. Responds in 2 months. All rights. Articles, to 3,000 words. Depts/columns, word lengths vary. No payment. Provides 2 contributor's copies.

All About Kids
Parenting Magazine

1071 Celestial Street, Suite 1104
Cincinnati, OH 45202

Editor: Tom Wynne

Description and Interests

For more than 18 years, *All About Kids Parenting Magazine* has provided parents in the greater Cincinnati area with information and tips about children. The monthly publication is filled with articles from local writers who cover topics such as education, health, national news, local events, and family life. Circ: 120,000.
Website: www.aakmagazine.com

Freelance Potential

100% written by nonstaff writers. Publishes 30 freelance submissions yearly.
Submissions and Payment: Guidelines available at website. Send complete ms. Accepts disk submissions and email submissions (text files only; hard copy must be submitted by mail). SASE. Response time varies. Rights vary. Articles and depts/columns, word lengths and payment rates vary. Payment policy varies. Provides 1 contributor's copy.

Amazing Kids!

PMB 485
1158 26th Street
Santa Monica, CA 90403

Editor: Alyse Rome

Description and Interests

The works of children and teens are showcased in this e-zine that strives to inspire excellence in children. The website of *Amazing Kids!*, a nonprofit educational organization, seeks adult volunteers who are interested in writing stories for its section that spotlights kids of the month. Hits per month: 640,000.
Website: www.amazing-kids.org

Freelance Potential

40% written by nonstaff writers. Publishes 70 freelance submissions yearly; 90% by unpublished writers, 70% by authors who are new to the magazine. Receives 3,000 queries and unsolicited mss yearly.
Submissions and Payment: Sample copy available at website. Query or send complete ms. Accepts email submissions to info@amazing-kids.org. Response time varies. All rights. Articles, word lengths vary. No payment.

American History

Weider History Magazine Group
741 Miller Drive SE, Suite D2
Leesburg, VA 20175

Editorial Director: Roger Vance

Description and Interests

History enthusiasts read *American History* magazine for its entertaining and educational articles. Appearing six times each year, this publication also appeals to a general audience with its feature articles on the people, places, and events that have influenced our nation. Circ: 100,000.
Website: www.thehistorynet.com

Freelance Potential

80% written by nonstaff writers. Publishes 30 freelance submissions yearly; 50% by authors who are new to the magazine. Receives 1,200 queries yearly.
Submissions and Payment: Sample copy and guidelines, $6 with return label. Query with 1–2 page proposal. Accepts hard copy. SASE. Responds in 10 weeks. All rights. Articles, 2,000–4,000 words; $.20 per word. Depts/columns, word lengths vary; $75. Pays on acceptance. Provides 5 contributor's copies.

American School Board Journal ☆

1680 Duke Street
Alexandria, VA 22314

Editor-in-Chief: Sally Zakariya

Description and Interests
In print for over 115 years, this publication explores up-and-coming trends in education. Published monthly, it covers topics such as leadership, management, and social issues. Readers include educators, school board members, and other leaders in the field. Articles should provide facts and figures. Circ: 31,000.
Website: www.asbj.com

Freelance Potential
50% written by nonstaff writers. Publishes 35 freelance submissions yearly. Receives 360 queries yearly.
Submissions and Payment: Sample copy, $5. Prefers query with clips. Accepts complete ms. Accepts hard copy. SASE. Responds in 2 months. All rights. Articles, 2,200–2,500 words. Depts/columns, 1,000–1,200 words. Solicited articles, $800. Unsolicited articles and dept/columns, no payment. Pays on publication. Provides 3 contributor's copies.

The Apprentice Writer

Susquehanna University, Box GG
Selinsgrove, PA 17870-1001

Writers' Institute Director: Gary Fincke

Description and Interests
This tabloid showcases the best in creative writing and artwork by high school students from around the country. *The Apprentice Writer* is published once each year. Circ: 10,500.
Website: www.susqu.edu/writers (click on High School Students)

Freelance Potential
100% written by nonstaff writers. Publishes 80 freelance submissions yearly; 95% by unpublished writers, 95% by authors who are new to the magazine. Receives 5,000 unsolicited mss yearly.
Submissions and Payment: Sample copy, $3 with 9x12 SASE ($1.17 postage). Send complete ms. Accepts hard copy and simultaneous submissions if identified. SASE. Responds during the month of May. First rights. Articles and fiction, 7,000 words. Poetry, no line limits. No payment. Provides 2 author's copies.

Art Jewelry

21027 Crossroads Circle
Waukesha, WI 53187

Editorial Associate: Amy Robleski

Description and Interests
Beginner, intermediate, and advanced jewelry-making projects are showcased in this magazine, published six times each year. It needs more submissions for its "Beyond Jewelry" department. Circ: Unavailable.
Website: www.artjewelrymag.com

Freelance Potential
50% written by nonstaff writers. Publishes 54 freelance submissions yearly; 30% by unpublished writers, 50% by authors who are new to the magazine. Receives 350 queries yearly.
Submissions and Payment: Guidelines available. Sample copy, $5.95. Query with jewelry samples or photos. Accepts hard copy and email queries with JPEG images to editor@artjewelrymag.com. SASE. Responds in 1–2 months. All rights. Written material, word lengths vary; payment rates vary. Pays on acceptance. Provides 2 contributor's copies.

Athens Parent

P.O. Box 1251
Athens, GA 30603

Editor-in-Chief: Shannon Walsh Howell

Description and Interests
Athens Parent magazine is a local resource published eight times each year for families in the Athens area of Georgia. Each issue features original articles on topics such as health, teens, single parenting, dads' perspectives, discipline, and family life. Parents, grandparents, educators, and others interested in the well-being of children and families read this publication for informative and well-written articles. Circ: Unavailable.
Website: www.athensparent.com

Freelance Potential
85% written by nonstaff writers. Publishes 40 freelance submissions yearly. Receives 500 queries yearly.
Submissions and Payment: Query. Accepts hard copy and email queries to mail@metromags.com. SASE. Response time varies. First rights. Articles and depts/columns, word lengths and payment rates vary. Payment policy varies.

Autism Asperger's Digest

P.O. Box 337
Little Falls, NY 13365

Editor: Veronica Zysk

Description and Interests
This national magazine is devoted to autism spectrum disorders for parents, education professionals, and service providers. Published quarterly, it seeks articles that offer practical, hands-on ideas and strategies to help meet the real-life challenges of living with or working with a spectrum individual. Circ: 120,000.
Website: www.autismdigest.com

Freelance Potential
95% written by nonstaff writers. Publishes 80 freelance submissions yearly; 70% by unpublished writers, 50% by authors who are new to the magazine.
Submissions and Payment: Writers' guidelines available at website. Query. Accepts hard copy and email queries to editor@autismdigest.com. SASE. Responds in 6 weeks. First rights. Articles and depts/columns, word lengths vary. No payment. Provides a 1-year subscription.

Beta Journal

National Beta Club
151 Beta Club Way
Spartanburg, SC 29306–3012

Editor: Lori Guthrie

Description and Interests
Beta Journal is the official magazine of the National Beta Club, a leadership service club for students in the elementary grades through high school. Offered five times each year, it focuses on the challenges and accomplishments of its members. Circ: 300,000.
Website: www.betaclub.org

Freelance Potential
50% written by nonstaff writers. Publishes 2–4 freelance submissions yearly; 80% by unpublished writers. Receives 12 unsolicited mss yearly.
Submissions and Payment: Send complete ms. Accepts hard copy and email submissions to lguthrie@ betaclub.org. Availability of artwork improves chance of acceptance. SASE. Responds in 2 months. Rights vary. Articles, 700–1,000 words; $25–$50. B/W prints, transparencies, and line art; payment rates vary. Pays on publication. Provides 10 contributor's copies.

Baton Rouge Parents Magazine

11831 Wentling Avenue
Baton Rouge, LA 70816-6055

Editor: Amy Foreman-Plaisance

Description and Interests
This monthly magazine serves the families of Baton Rouge and the surrounding metro area. It provides locally oriented articles and information on topics related to raising healthy children. Circ: 55,000.
Website: www.brparents.com

Freelance Potential
95% written by nonstaff writers. Publishes 50+ freelance submissions yearly; 15% by unpublished writers, 30% by authors who are new to the magazine.
Submissions and Payment: Guidelines available via email request to brpm@brparents.com. Query with outline, list of potential sources, brief author bio, and two writing samples. Accepts hard copy and email queries to brpm@brparents.com. SASE. Response time varies. First North American serial rights. Written material, word lengths vary; $25–$70. Kill fee, $10. Pays on publication. Provides 2 contributor's copies.

Beyond Centauri

P.O. Box 782
Cedar Rapids, IA 52406

Editor: Tyree Campbell

Description and Interests
Published quarterly, *Beyond Centauri* is a science fiction and fantasy magazine for readers ages nine to fifteen. It features stories, poems, and illustrations from adults and younger readers. Circ: Unavailable.
Website: www.samsdotpublishing.com

Freelance Potential
100% written by nonstaff writers. Publishes 35–50 freelance submissions yearly.
Submissions and Payment: Sample copy and guidelines, $6. Query or send complete ms. Accepts hard copy and email submissions to beyondcentauri@ samsdotpublishing.com (RTF attachments). SASE. Responds to queries in 2 weeks, to mss in 2–3 months. First North American serial rights. Articles, to 500 words; $1. Fiction, to 2,000 words; $5. Poetry, to 50 lines; $2 per poem. B/W illustrations; $5. Pays on publication.

The Big Country Peacock Chronicle

RR 1 Box 89K-112
Aspermont, TX 79502

Editor-in-Chief: Audrey Yoeckel

Description and Interests
The Big Country Peacock Chronicle is an interactive e-zine dedicated to the preservation of community values and folk cultures. Traditional arts and crafts, artists, writers, information, resource links, and mutual support are the focus of this publication. It publishes material from both new and experienced authors. Hits per month: Unavailable.
Website: www.peacockchronicle.com

Freelance Potential
25% written by nonstaff writers. Publishes 10–12 freelance submissions yearly; 80% by authors who are new to the magazine.
Submissions and Payment: Sample copy available at website. Query or send complete ms. Accepts email submissions to audrey@peacockchronicle.com. Response time varies. Electronic rights. Articles, word lengths vary. No payment.

Bird Times

7-L Dundas Circle
Greensboro, NC 27407

Executive Editor: Rita Davis

Description and Interests
Informative, authoritative articles about pet birds are illustrated with high-quality photographs in this magazine. Published six times each year, it offers features on bird care, breeds, and training, as well as book and video reviews, advice columns, humor pieces, and Q&As. Circ: 20,000.
Website: www.birdtimes.com

Freelance Potential
90% written by nonstaff writers. Publishes 30–40 freelance submissions yearly; 10% by unpublished writers, 50% by authors who are new to the magazine.
Submissions and Payment: Sample copy, $5 with 9x12 SASE (4 first-class stamps). Query or send complete ms. SASE. Responds in 1 month. All rights. Articles, 1,200–2,000 words. Depts/columns, 600–800 words. Written material, $.10 per word. Pays on publication. Provides 1 contributor's copy.

Biography Today

615 Griswold Street
Detroit, MI 48226

Managing Editor: Cherie D. Abbey

Description and Interests
This magazine is written for young readers, as well as teachers and librarians, and provides abbreviated biographies of celebrities and personalities who are of interest to young people. Published six times each year, it includes the life stories of entertainers, athletes, politicians, scientists, activists, artists, writers, and business leaders. Circ: 9,000.
Website: www.biographytoday.com

Freelance Potential
50% written by nonstaff writers. Publishes several freelance submissions yearly. Receives 12 queries yearly.
Submissions and Payment: Sample copy and guidelines available with 9x12 SASE. Query with résumé. SASE. Responds in 2 months. All rights. Articles, 2,000–5,000 words; payment rates vary according to author's experience. Payment policy varies. Provides 2 contributor's copies.

Black Woman and Child

P.O. Box 47045
300 Borough Drive
Toronto, Ontario M1P 4P0
Canada

Editor: Nicole Osbourne James

Description and Interests
Appearing six times each year, *Black Woman and Child* presents pregnancy and parenting information strongly rooted in African culture for women of African descent. The undeniable spirit and knowledge of African mothers is the foundation of this magazine. Circ: Unavailable.
Website: www.blackwomanandchild.com

Freelance Potential
75% written by nonstaff writers. Publishes 25–40 freelance submissions yearly. Receives 75–100 queries, 30 unsolicited mss yearly.
Submissions and Payment: Guidelines available. Query or send complete ms. Accepts hard copy and email submissions to bwac@nubeing.com (text files). No simultaneous submissions. SAE/IRC. Response time varies. Rights vary. Articles, 750–1,500 words. Depts/columns, word lengths vary. Written material, payment rates vary. Pays on publication.

B'nai B'rith Magazine

2020 K Street NW, 7th Floor
Washington, DC 20006

Managing Editor

Description and Interests
Published quarterly, *B'nai B'rith Magazine* features articles focusing on Judaism and Jewish concerns. Issues relating to Jewish life in Israel and North America are covered in each issue. Circ: 100,000.
Website: www.bnaibrith.org

Freelance Potential
50% written by nonstaff writers. Publishes 12–15 freelance submissions yearly; 10% by unpublished writers, 50% by new authors. Receives 120 queries yearly.
Submissions and Payment: Sample copy and guidelines, $3 with 9x12 SASE (3 first-class stamps). Query with clips. Accepts hard copy and email to bbm@bnaibrith.org. SASE. Responds in 2–4 weeks. First North American serial rights. Articles, 1,000–3,000 words. Depts/columns, word lengths vary. Written material, payment rates vary. Pays on publication. Provides 2 contributor's copies.

Brain, Child

P.O. Box 5566
Charlottesville, VA 22905

Editors: Jennifer Niesslein & Stephanie Wilkinson

Description and Interests
Brain, Child, unlike the typical parenting publication, favors motherhood reflections over parenting advice. A quarterly published magazine, it portrays modern motherhood as it really is. It offers words from women in the field: mothers who are also great writers. Each issue includes essays, humor, reviews, fiction, art, and cartoons. Circ: 30,000+.
Website: www.brainchildmag.com

Freelance Potential
Publishes many freelance submissions yearly.
Submissions and Payment: Sample copy and guidelines, $5. Query or send complete ms. Accepts hard copy, simultaneous submissions, and email to editor@brainchildmag.com. SASE. Responds in 2 months. Electronic rights. Features, 3,000 words. Personal essays, 800–4,500 words. Fiction, 1,500–4,500 words. Written material, payment rates vary. Pays on publication.

Byronchild

P.O. Box 971
Mullumbimby, New South Wales 2482
Australia

Editor: Kali Wendorf
U.S. Editorial Contact: Lisa Reagan

Description and Interests
This quarterly magazine for parents seeks to "support families in changing times." It focuses on personal growth and social and political awareness. This year, it would like to see articles on fathering, men's issues, gay couples, and Muslim issues. Circ: Unavailable.
Website: www.byronchild.com

Freelance Potential
95% written by nonstaff writers. Publishes 20 freelance submissions yearly; 50% by unpublished writers, 95% by authors who are new to the magazine. Receives 100 queries and unsolicited mss yearly.
Submissions and Payment: Sample copy and guidelines available. Query or send complete ms with list of references and sources. Accepts email submissions to kali@byronchild.com (Microsoft Word documents). Response time varies. First rights. Articles, word lengths vary. No payment.

Caledonia Times

Box 278
Prince Rupert, British Columbia V8J 3P6
Canada

Editor: Debby Shaw

Description and Interests
Ten times each year, *Caledonia Times* is published for an audience of Christian young adult and adult readers. The small Canadian paper features fiction, nonfiction, and poetry—all with religious themes. Topics covered include regional news and social issues. Inspirational and problem-solving short stories also appear. Writers whose material focuses on religious issues and Christian life are welcome. Circ: 1,259.

Freelance Potential
90% written by nonstaff writers. Publishes 10 freelance submissions yearly. Receives many unsolicited mss each year.
Submissions and Payment: Send complete ms. Accepts hard copy. SAE/IRC. Responds in 2–4 weeks. All rights. Articles and fiction, 500–750 words. Depts/columns, word lengths vary. No payment. Provides 5 contributor's copies.

Canoe & Kayak Magazine

10526 NE 68th Street, Suite 3
Kirkland, WA 98033

Editor

Description and Interests
Subtitled "The #1 Paddlesports Resource," *Canoe & Kayak* features informative articles covering both white-water and flatwater boating. This publication appears seven times each year. Circ: 63,000.
Website: www.canoekayak.com

Freelance Potential
90% written by nonstaff writers. Publishes 25 freelance submissions yearly; 5% by unpublished writers, 25% by authors who are new to the magazine. Receives 240 queries and unsolicited mss yearly.
Submissions and Payment: Sample copy and guidelines, free with 9x12 SASE (7 first-class stamps). Query or send complete ms. Prefers email submissions to editor@canoekayak.com. Responds in 6–8 weeks. All rights. Articles, 400–2,000 words. Depts/columns, 150–750 words. Written material, $.15–$.50 per word. Pays within 30 days after publication. Provides 1 copy.

Cat Fancy

3 Burroughs
Irvine, CA 92618

Managing Editor: Sandy Meyer

Description and Interests
This monthly magazine for feline enthusiasts is interested in articles on the health, nutrition, and behavior of cats, and cat culture. Circ: 290,000.
Website: www.catchannel.com

Freelance Potential
95% written by nonstaff writers. Publishes 150 freelance submissions yearly; 10% by unpublished writers, 70% by authors who are new to the magazine. Receives 500+ queries yearly.
Submissions and Payment: Guidelines available. Query with clips between January 1 and May 1 only. Accepts email queries to query@catfancy.com. Availability of artwork improves chance of acceptance. Responds by August. First rights. Articles, 600–1,000 words. Depts/columns, 600 words. 35mm slides or high resolution digital photos with contact sheets. All material, payment rates vary. Pays on publication. Provides 2 copies.

Catalyst Chicago
Independent Reporting on Urban Schools

332 South Michigan Avenue, Suite 500
Chicago, IL 60604

Editorial Contact: Veronica Anderson

Description and Interests
This magazine zeroes in on educational reform issues in Chicago's urban school districts. Published nine times each year, *Catalyst Chicago* offers teachers and administrators current information on the problems and politics associated with the region's public education system at all levels, from elementary school through high school. Circ: 7,000.
Website: www.catalyst-chicago.org

Freelance Potential
25% written by nonstaff writers. Publishes 45 freelance submissions yearly; 20% by authors who are new to the magazine. Receives 45 queries yearly.
Submissions and Payment: Sample copy and guidelines, $2. Query or send letter of introduction. Accepts hard copy. SASE. Response time varies. All rights. Articles, to 2,300 words; $1,700. Pays on acceptance. Provides 1 contributor's copy.

Challenge

Pearson Education Australia
P.O. Box 1024
South Melbourne VIC 3205
Australia

Magazines Coordinator

Description and Interests
Independent and older readers between the ages of 11 and 14 are the target audience for *Challenge*. Each quarterly issue of this Australian magazine offers fiction in a variety of genres, nonfiction, book reviews, and activities. Circ: 20,000.
Website: www.pearsoned.com.au/magazines

Freelance Potential
100% written by nonstaff writers. Publishes 15 freelance submissions yearly. Receives 500 unsolicited mss yearly.
Submissions and Payment: Guidelines available. Send complete ms. Accepts hard copy, simultaneous submissions if identified, and email submissions to magazines@pearsoned.com.au. SAE/IRC. Responds in 3 months. First Australian serial rights. Articles, 200–600 words. Fiction, 400–1,000 words. Written material, $80–$200. Pays on publication.

Chickadee

Bayard Press Canada
10 Lower Spadina Avenue, Suite 400
Toronto, Ontario M4V 2V2
Canada

Submissions Editor

Description and Interests
Chickadee is a theme-based magazine published ten times each year for beginning readers. Each issue includes articles, stories, science experiments, crafts, activities, and puzzles. Exciting and informative articles about animals, science, social studies, and sports fill the pages of this publication. Circ: 85,000.
Website: www.owlkids.com

Freelance Potential
5% written by nonstaff writers. Publishes 1 freelance submission yearly; 5% by unpublished writers, 20% by authors who are new to the magazine. Receives 996 unsolicited mss yearly.
Submissions and Payment: Sample copy, $4. Guidelines and theme list available. All material is assigned. Query. SAE/IRC. Responds in 6 weeks. All rights. Fiction, 650–700 words; $250. Pays on acceptance. Provides 2 contributor's copies.

Child Life

Children's Better Health Institute
P.O. Box 567
Indianapolis, IN 46206-0567

Editor: Jack Gramling

Description and Interests
Appearing nine times each year for children ages nine to eleven, *Child Life* focuses on good health and physical fitness. Each issue features stories, book reviews, activities, recipes, poetry, and health-related articles. Designed to educate and entertain readers, this publication also includes puzzles, quizzes, and word games—all health-related. Currently this magazine consists mostly of reprints, however, its editors are interested in receiving poetry and limericks related to health and fitness, written by children. Circ: 20,000.
Website: www.childlifemag.org

Freelance Potential
25% written by nonstaff writers. Publishes several freelance submissions yearly.
Submissions and Payment: Sample copy, $2.95 with 9x12 SASE (4 first-class stamps). Currently not accepting submissions for articles and stories.

Childbirth Magazine

110 Fifth Avenue, 14th Floor
New York, NY 10011

Managing Editor: Kate Kelly

Description and Interests
Focusing on childbirth, this magazine from the publishers of *American Baby* offers a complete guide to the third trimester, as well as labor, delivery, and recovery. Published annually, it also includes information on childcare and parenting. Articles on the emotional and physical changes associated with pregnancy and labor are of interest. All writing is done on assignment. No unsolicited mss. Circ: 230,000.
Website: www.americanbaby.com

Freelance Potential
55% written by nonstaff writers. Publishes 10 freelance submissions yearly.
Submissions and Payment: Query. Accepts hard copy. SASE. Responds in 6 weeks. First serial rights. Articles, 1,000–2,000 words. Depts/columns, word lengths vary. Written material, payment rates vary. Pays on acceptance. Provides 5 contributor's copies.

Chirp

Bayard Press Canada
10 Lower Spadina Avenue, Suite 400
Toronto, Ontario M4V 2V2
Canada

Submissions Editor

Description and Interests
Children ages two through six are introduced to the relationship between words and pictures in this interactive magazine. Published nine times each year, *Chirp* teaches its readers about numbers, letters, nature, and animals. Stories, activities, puzzles, recipes, and games fill the pages of this "see and do, laugh and learn" publication. Circ: 60,000.
Website: www.owlkids.com

Freelance Potential
10% written by nonstaff writers. Publishes 1–3 freelance submissions yearly; 1% by unpublished writers, 10% by authors who are new to the magazine.
Submissions and Payment: Sample copy, $3.50. Guidelines available. All material is assigned. Query. SAE with $2 IRC. Response time varies. First and second rights. Written material, 300–400 words; payment rates vary. Pays on publication.

Cincinnati Family

4555 Lake Forest Drive, Suite 650
Cincinnati, OH 45242

Editor-in-Chief: Susan Brooke Day

Description and Interests
This monthly magazine serves families in the Cincinnati area by providing informative articles on parenting. It informs families of local resources, events, and other child-friendly activities, and offers advice that helps make childrearing easier. Popular topics include current events, careers, college, crafts, music, popular culture, travel, sports, and recreation. Circ: 75,000.
Website: www.cincinnatifamilymagazine.com

Freelance Potential
75% written by nonstaff writers. Publishes 36 freelance submissions yearly. Receives 240–300 queries and unsolicited mss yearly.
Submissions and Payment: Query or send ms. Accepts hard copy and email submissions to sherryh@daycommail.com. SASE. Response time varies. First rights. Articles and depts/columns, word lengths and payment rates vary. Pays 30 days after publication.

Clubhouse

P.O. Box 15
Berrien Springs, MI 49103

President/Editor: Elaine Trumbo

Description and Interests
Fiction in a variety of genres appears along with activities and nonfiction about nature, hobbies, crafts, the environment, animals, and pets in this magazine for children ages nine to twelve. Published monthly, *Clubhouse* emphasizes biblical principals. It is not accepting submissions of new material at this time. Circ: 500.
Website: www.yourstoryhour.org/clubhouse

Freelance Potential
85% written by nonstaff writers. Publishes several freelance submissions yearly; 75% by unpublished writers, 95% by authors who are new to the magazine.
Submissions and Payment: Sample copy, free with 6x9 SASE (2 first-class stamps). Send complete ms. Accepts hard copy. SASE. Response time varies. All rights. Articles and fiction, 1,500 words. B/W line art. All material, payment rates vary. Pays after publication.

Classic Toy Trains

21027 Crossroads Circle
Waukesha, WI 53187

Editor: Neil Besougloff

Description and Interests
Published nine times each year, this magazine targets the train enthusiast with how-to articles, display ideas, Q&As, and reviews. Circ: 68,000.
Website: www.classictoytrains.com

Freelance Potential
60% written by nonstaff writers. Publishes 40–50 freelance submissions yearly; 20% by unpublished writers, 20% by authors who are new to the magazine. Receives 96 queries, 60 unsolicited mss yearly.
Submissions and Payment: Sample copy, $4.95 ($3 postage). Prefers query. Accepts complete ms. Accepts hard copy, disk submissions (Microsoft Word), and email submissions to editor@classictoytrains.com. SASE. Responds in 3 months. Articles, 500–5,000 words; $75 per page. Depts/columns, word lengths and payment rates vary. Pays on acceptance. All rights. Provides 1 contributor's copy.

Coastal Family Magazine

340 Eisenhower Drive, Suite 240
Savannah, GA 31406

Managing Editor: Laura Gray

Description and Interests
Residents of the Savannah area of Georgia read this monthly publication for information on families and children. Published by the Coastal Empire Media, *Coastal Family Magazine* covers a variety of topics including child development, education, travel, books, family finances, and the media. Each issue also offers how-to's, profiles, and interviews. Circ: Unavailable.
Website: www.coastalfamily.com

Freelance Potential
5% written by nonstaff writers. Publishes 24–36 freelance submissions yearly. Receives 100–150 queries each year.
Submissions and Payment: Guidelines available. Query. Accepts hard copy and email queries to editor@coastalfamily.com. SASE. Response time varies. All rights. Articles and depts/columns, word lengths and payment rates vary. Payment policy varies.

Coins

700 East State Street
Iola, WI 54990

Editor: Robert Van Ryzin

Description and Interests
The pages of this magazine are full of articles on topics related to coin collecting. In addition, it features up-to-date coin news and coin buying information. It is read by beginner, intermediate, and expert collectors. Published monthly, it is interested in articles that offer information on buying opportunities. Writers must know the market. Circ: 60,000.
Website: www.collect.com

Freelance Potential
40% written by nonstaff writers. Publishes 70 freelance submissions yearly; 5% by authors who are new to the magazine. Receives 36–60 queries yearly.
Submissions and Payment: Sample copy and guidelines, free. Query. Accepts hard copy. SASE. Responds in 1–2 months. All rights. Articles, 1,500–2,500 words; $.04 per word. Work for hire. Pays on publication. Provides contributor's copies upon request.

College and Junior Tennis

Port Washington Tennis Academy
100 Harbor Road
Port Washington, NY 11050

Webmaster: Marcia Frost

Description and Interests
For over three decades *College and Junior Tennis* has provided its readers with in-depth coverage of the national and international junior tennis circuit. As an online publication, it brings the latest scores, rankings, and results to its readers. This e-zine also provides a comprehensive directory of every college in the U.S. with a tennis program. Hits per month: 500,000.
Website: www.collegeandjuniortennis.com

Freelance Potential
10% written by nonstaff writers. Publishes 5 freelance submissions yearly; 1% by authors who are new to the magazine. Receives 24 unsolicited mss yearly.
Submissions and Payment: Sample copy available at website. Send complete ms. Accepts email submissions to marcia@collegeandjuniortennis.com. Responds in 2–14 days. One-time rights. Articles, to 700 words. Games and 1-page puzzles. Written material, $25–$50.

Comet

Pearson Education Australia
P.O. Box 1024
South Melbourne V1C 3205
Australia

Magazines Coordinator

Description and Interests
The goal of *Comet* is to promote literacy in the early grades. Published quarterly, this magazine offers stories, articles, illustrations, and activities that are meant to appeal to Australian children between the ages of five and seven. Circ: 20,000.
Website: www.pearsoned.com.au/magazines

Freelance Potential
100% written by nonstaff writers. Publishes 15 freelance submissions yearly. Receives 500 unsolicited mss yearly.
Submissions and Payment: Guidelines available. Send complete ms. Accepts hard copy, simultaneous submissions if identified, and email submissions to magazines@pearsoned.com.au. SAE/IRC. Responds in 3 months. First Australian serial rights. Articles, 200–600 words. Fiction, 400–1,000 words. Written material, $80–$220. Pays on publication.

Community Education Journal

3929 Old Lee Highway, Suite 91-A
Fairfax, VA 22030

Editor: Valerie A. Romney

Description and Interests
Published quarterly, *Community Education Journal* is a forum for the exchange of ideas and practices in community education. It covers issues related to adult education, after-school programs, and summer educational programs. Circ: 2,500.
Website: www.ncea.com

Freelance Potential
98% written by nonstaff writers. Publishes 24 freelance submissions yearly; 30% by unpublished writers, 60% by authors who are new to the magazine. Receives 12–24 unsolicited mss yearly.
Submissions and Payment: Sample copy, guidelines, and theme list, $5. Send 5 copies of complete ms. Accepts hard copy and email submissions to varomney@hotmail.com. SASE. Responds in 1–2 months. All rights. Articles, 1,500–2,000 words. No payment. Provides 5 contributor's copies.

Cookie

750 Third Avenue
New York, NY 10017

Acquisitions: Mireille Hyde

Description and Interests
Published six times each year, this magazine targets busy, sophisticated parents of children from birth through age six. It covers topics such as health, fitness, child development, travel destinations, juggling work and family life, nutrition, beauty, fashion, decorating, and other lifestyle topics. In addition, it includes reviews and profiles. It seeks exercise pieces for women on the go. Writers are welcome to query with article organizational plan. Circ: 300,000.
Website: www.cookiemag.com

Freelance Potential
50% written by nonstaff writers. Receives 600–1,200 queries yearly.
Submissions and Payment: Query. Accepts hard copy. SASE. Response time varies. Rights vary. Articles, word lengths and payment rates vary. Pays on publication.

Creative Child Magazine

2505 Anthem Village Drive, Suite E619
Henderson, NV 89052

Editor

Description and Interests
Devoted to helping parents nurture their children's creativity, *Creative Child Magazine* features helpful tips for raising well-balanced children. It appears every other month and includes articles about health, safety, family activities, and gifted and special education. Circ: 50,000.
Website: www.creativechildonline.com

Freelance Potential
25% written by nonstaff writers. Publishes 20 freelance submissions yearly.
Submissions and Payment: Sample copy available with 9x12 SASE (4 first-class stamps). Query. Accepts hard copy and email queries to info@ creativechildonline.com. SASE. Responds in 1–3 months. First and electronic rights. Articles and depts/columns, word lengths and payment rates vary. Provides contributor's copies.

Curriculum Review

Paperclip Communications
125 Patterson Avenue
Little Falls, NJ 07424

Editor: Frank Sennett

Description and Interests
Appearing nine times each year, this newsletter includes articles, curriculum ideas, and reviews on topics relating to education. Read by teachers and school administrators, it welcomes practical, hands-on material from freelance writers experienced in the field of education. Circ: 5,000.
Website: www.curriculumreview.com or www.paper-clip.com

Freelance Potential
2% written by nonstaff writers. Publishes 10 freelance submissions yearly. Receives 24 queries yearly.
Submissions and Payment: Sample copy, free with 9x12 SASE (2 first-class stamps). Query. SASE. Responds in 1 month. One-time rights. Articles, to 4,000 words. Depts/columns, word lengths vary. Written material, payment rates vary. Payment policy varies. Provides contributor's copies.

Cyberteens Zeen

Able Minds, Inc.
1750-1 30th Street #170
Boulder, CO 80301

Editor

Description and Interests
Showcasing the works of teens from around the world, this e-zine features poetry, short stories, articles, personal experience pieces, and reviews. Stories with illustrations and upbeat articles have the best chance at publication. Circ: Unavailable.
Website: www.cyberteens.com

Freelance Potential
100% written by nonstaff writers. Publishes 30 freelance submissions yearly. Receives many unsolicited mss yearly.
Submissions and Payment: Sample copy available at website. Query or send complete ms. Accepts hard copy and email submissions to editor@cyberteens.com (no attachments). Availability of artwork improves chance of acceptance. SASE. Response time varies. All rights. Written material, to 10 pages. Artwork, TIFF or JPEG format. No payment.

Discoveries

WordAction Publishing Company
6401 The Paseo
Kansas City, MO 64131

Editorial Assistant: Sarah Weatherwax

Description and Interests
Discoveries is designed to correlate directly with the Sunday school curriculum developed by WordAction Publishing for children between the ages of eight and ten. Used by Evangelical Christian churches, it is a full-color story paper offering fiction, nonfiction, activities, and puzzles that relate to Scripture passages. Its editors urge writers to avoid trite, overly didactic summaries of scriptural themes. They look for stories that reflect the real world and feature true-to-life characters. Circ: 35,000.

Freelance Potential
70% written by nonstaff writers.
Submissions and Payment: Query or send complete ms. Accepts hard copy. SASE. Responds in 6–8 weeks. Multiple-use rights. Articles, 150 words; $15. Stories, to 500 words; $.05 per word. Pays on publication. Provides 4 contributor's copies.

Disney Magazine

114 Fifth Avenue
New York, NY 10011-5690

Managing Editor: Martha Jenkins

Description and Interests
This quarterly magazine is for fans who love Disney. Each issue offers readers a behind-the-scenes guide to Disney family entertainment and travel. It is looking for short, behind-the-scenes pieces on upcoming films, television programs, and direct-to-video movies written with an insider tone. Writers are encouraged to include photographs with their submissions. Circ: 500,000.
Website: http://disney.go.com/disneymagazine/index.html

Freelance Potential
10% written by nonstaff writers. Publishes few freelance submissions yearly.
Submissions and Payment: Sample copy, $3. Query with clips. Accepts hard copy. SASE. Responds in 2 months. All rights. Articles and depts/columns, 500–1,200 words. Written material, $.50–$1 per word. Pays on publication.

Discovery Girls

4300 Stevens Creek Boulevard, Suite 190
San Jose, CA 95129

Editor: Catherine Lee

Description and Interests
Created by and for girls ages seven to twelve, this award-winning magazine strives to empower young girls to take control of their destinies. It includes informational and how-to articles, personal experience pieces, profiles, and reviews. Topics include careers, crafts and hobbies, health, fitness, popular culture, self-help issues, fashion, volunteering, and sports. Appearing six times each year, it seeks positive, up-beat articles on topics of interest to pre-teens. Circ: 120,000.
Website: www.discoverygirls.com

Freelance Potential
75% written by nonstaff writers. Publishes 30 freelance submissions yearly.
Submissions and Payment: Query or send complete ms. Accepts hard copy. SASE. Response time varies. Rights vary. Articles and depts/columns, word lengths vary. No payment.

Dog Fancy

BowTie, Inc.
P.O. Box 6050
Mission Viejo, CA 92690-6050

Managing Editor: Hazel Barrowman

Description and Interests
Dog Fancy is published each month for dog trainers and breeders, and individuals interested in the general care of their dogs. Each issue offers practical information on the breeding, training, behavior, and health of purebred dogs and mixed breeds. Circ: 270,000.
Website: www.dogfancy.com

Freelance Potential
80% written by nonstaff writers. Publishes 20–25 freelance submissions yearly; 25% by authors who are new to the magazine. Receives 1,200 queries yearly.
Submissions and Payment: Guidelines available. Sample copy, $4.50 at newsstands. Query with résumé, outline, and writing samples. No unsolicited mss. Responds in 6–8 weeks. First North American serial rights. Articles, 1,200–1,800 words. Depts/columns, 650 words. All material, payment rates vary. Pays on publication. Provides 2 contributor's copies.

Dollhouse Miniatures

420 Boylston Street, 5th Floor
Boston, MA 02116

Editor-in-Chief: Terrence Lynch

Description and Interests
Collectors, crafters, and artisans of small-scale reproductions read this monthly. *Dollhouse Miniatures* is currently interested in extraordinary collections and profiles of minority miniaturists. Circ: 25,000.
Website: www.dhminiatures.com

Freelance Potential
90% written by nonstaff writers. Publishes 190 freelance submissions yearly; 10% by unpublished writers, 30% by authors who are new to the magazine. Receives 60 queries yearly.
Submissions and Payment: Guidelines available. Sample copy, $4.95 with 9x12 SASE ($1.95 postage). Query with outline. Accepts hard copy and email queries to editor@dhminiatures.com. SASE. Responds in 2 months. All rights. Articles and depts/columns, word lengths and payment rates vary. Pays on publication. Provides 1 contributor's copy.

Early Years

3035 Valley Avenue, Suite 103
Winchester, VA 22601

Submissions: Jennifer Hutchinson

Description and Interests
Nine times throughout the school year, parents of preschool and kindergarten children receive this informative newsletter, which is designed to provide busy families with quick and easy access to the latest news about raising young children and helping them adjust to school. Circ: 60,000.
Website: www.rfeonline.com

Freelance Potential
100% written by nonstaff writers. Publishes 80 freelance submissions yearly; 28% by unpublished writers. Receives 36 queries yearly.
Submissions and Payment: Sample copy, free with 9x12 SASE ($.77 postage). Query with résumé and clips. Accepts hard copy. SASE. Responds in 1 month. All rights. Articles, 225–300 words. Depts/columns, 175–200 words. Written material, $.60 per word. Pays on acceptance. Provides 5 contributor's copies.

Dyslexia Online Magazine ☆

P.O. Box 111, Guilford
Surrey GU1 9EH
England

Editor: John Bradford

Description and Interests
This resourceful e-zine features articles on topics related to dyslexia. Its readers include parents, teachers, dyslexic students, and dyslexic adults. It is interested in articles covering dyslexia testing for children and adults, and dyslexia programs. In addition, it seeks up-to-date information on available resources. Hits per month: 47,460.
Website: www.dyslexia-magazine.com

Freelance Potential
80% written by nonstaff writers. Publishes 10 freelance submissions yearly; 50% by unpublished writers, 80% by authors who are new to the magazine.
Submissions and Payment: Guidelines available at website. Send complete ms. Prefers email submissions to dyslextest@aol.com (no attachments). Accepts hard copy. SASE. Response time varies. All rights. Articles, word lengths vary. No payment. Provides 2 copies.

Earthwatch Institute Journal

3 Clock Tower Place, Suite 100
Maynard, MA 01754-0075

Editor: Philip Johansson

Description and Interests
Published three times each year, this member publication of the Earthwatch Institute engages people worldwide in scientific field research and education to promote the understanding and action necessary for a sustainable environment. It offers news, interviews, and human interest articles that provide readers with a broader perspective of the world. Circ: 25,000.
Website: www.earthwatch.org

Freelance Potential
30% written by nonstaff writers. Publishes 2–3 freelance submissions yearly. Receives 60 queries, 36 unsolicited mss yearly.
Submissions and Payment: Sample copy and guidelines available. Query or send complete ms. Prefers email submissions to pjohansson@earthwatch.org. Accepts hard copy. SASE. Response time varies. First rights. Articles, $500–$1,000. Pays on publication.

The Education Revolution

417 Roslyn Road
Roslyn Heights, NY 11577

Executive Director: Jerry Mintz

Description and Interests
Focusing on the latest news and developments in alternative education, this quarterly magazine from the Alternative Education Resource Organization features articles and information on available resources and job opportunities. Readers include educators, parents, students, and organizations interested in exploring the choices in alternative education. It is interested in personal essays from freelance writers with backgrounds in education. Circ: 1,500.
Website: www.educationrevolution.org

Freelance Potential
20% written by nonstaff writers. Publishes 10 freelance submissions yearly; 40% by authors who are new to the magazine. Receives 180 queries yearly.
Submissions and Payment: Query. SASE. Responds in 1 month. Rights vary. Written material, word lengths vary. No payment.

The Elementary School Journal

University of Missouri, College of Education
211-F Townsend Hall
Columbia, MO 65211-1150

Managing Editor

Description and Interests
The Elementary School Journal is a peer-reviewed academic journal that publishes articles on both education theory and research and their implications for teaching practice. It prefers studies that contain data about school and classroom processes in elementary and middle schools. Published five times each year, most of its material is written by college professors. Its readership is made up primarily of researchers, teacher educators, and practitioners. Circ: 2,200.
Website: www.journals.uchicago.edu/ESJ

Freelance Potential
Publishes several freelance submissions yearly.
Submissions and Payment: Sample copy, $13.50. Guidelines available at website. Send 4 copies of ms with an abstract of 100–150 words. Accepts hard copy. SASE. Response time varies. Rights vary. Articles, word lengths, payment rates, and payment policy vary.

EFCA Today

901 East 78th Street
Minneapolis, MN 55420

Editor: Diane McDougall

Description and Interests
EFCA Today aims to unify church leaders around the overall mission of the EFCA by bringing its stories and vision to life. It is read by pastors, elders, Sunday school teachers, and ministry volunteers. Topics pertinent to faith and life are covered in each quarterly issue. Circ: 30,000.
Website: www.efca.org/magazine

Freelance Potential
90% written by nonstaff writers. Publishes several freelance submissions yearly.
Submissions and Payment: Sample copy and guidelines, $1 with 9x12 SASE (5 first-class stamps). Query. Accepts hard copy and email queries to dianemc@ journeygroup.com. SASE. Response time varies. First rights. Articles, 200–700 words. Cover theme articles, 300–1,000 words. Written material, $.23 per word. Pays on acceptance.

Encyclopedia of Youth Studies

130 Essex Street
South Hamilton, MA 01982

Editor: Dean Borgman

Description and Interests
This online encyclopedia features information on all topics pertaining to youth culture. Individuals who work with, minister to, or care about youth and culture find information of interest, research articles, profiles, interviews, and personal experience essays at this Internet resource. Hits per month: Unavailable.
Website: www.centerforyouth.org

Freelance Potential
5–10% written by nonstaff writers. Publishes 5–10 freelance submissions yearly; 85% by unpublished writers, 85% by authors who are new to the magazine. Receives 48 queries, 12 unsolicited mss yearly.
Submissions and Payment: Sample copy and guidelines available at website. Query or send complete ms. Accepts email submissions to cys@centerforyouth.org. Responds to queries in 1 week, to mss in 1 month. All rights. Articles, 600 words. No payment.

301

Entertainment Magazine

P.O. Box 3355
Tucson, AZ 85722

Publisher: Robert Zucker

Description and Interests
Entertainment Magazine is a family-oriented e-zine that serves the Tucson area by providing daily updates about community activities. Topics covered include health and fitness, music, recreation, regional news, college and career information, and music. This e-zine provides journalists with an opportunity to be published and is currently accepting entertainment-related material. Hits per month: 30,000.
Website: www.entertainmentmagazine.net

Freelance Potential
100% written by nonstaff writers. Receives 1,000+ queries yearly.
Submissions and Payment: Guidelines and sample copy available at website. Query. Accepts email queries to publisher@emol.org. Responds in 1–2 days. Author retains rights. Articles, to 1,000 words. B/W digital prints. No payment.

Families on the Go ☆

Life Media
P.O. Box 55445
St. Petersburg, FL 33732

Editor: Pete CanCo

Description and Interests
This magazine for families in Florida's Pinellas and Hillsborough Counties is published six times each year. It offers articles, parenting tips, and information that empowers families to nurture positive relationships. Circ: 120,000.
Website: www.familiesonthego.org

Freelance Potential
85% written by nonstaff writers. Publishes 40 freelance submissions yearly; 25% by unpublished writers, 25% by authors who are new to the magazine.
Submissions and Payment: Sample copy, free with 9x12 SASE (4 first-class stamps). Query or send complete ms. Accepts hard copy and email submissions to info@familiesonthego.org. SASE. Response time varies. Regional rights. Articles and depts/columns, word lengths and payment rates vary. Pays on publication. Provides 2 contributor's copies.

Explore Magazine

Pearson Education Australia
P.O. Box 1024
South Melbourne V1C 3205
Australia

Magazines Coordinator

Description and Interests
This magazine for children between the ages of eight and ten encourages readers to explore the world around them. Each quarterly issue offers stories, articles, and activities that serve as a literacy resource for middle-grade readers. Circ: 20,000.
Website: www.pearsoned.com.au/magazines

Freelance Potential
100% written by nonstaff writers. Publishes 15 freelance submissions yearly. Receives 500 unsolicited mss yearly.
Submissions and Payment: Guidelines available at website. Query or send complete ms. Accepts hard copy, simultaneous submissions if identified, and email submissions to magazines@pearsoned.com.au. SAE/IRC. Responds in 1–3 months. First Australian rights. Articles, to 500 words; $100–$220. Fiction, to 800 words; $80–$200. Pays on publication.

Family Energy

P.O. Box 1780
Evanston, IL 60204

Submissions Editor

Description and Interests
Family Energy is published six times each year by iParenting Media, the leading producer of parenting information in magazine, newspaper, Internet, and radio formats. This entertaining and educational magazine features articles from experienced parents and experts. Contents include essays, news, articles, interviews, and how-to pieces focusing on family health, fitness, and fun. Circ: Unavailable.
Website: www.familyenergy.com

Freelance Potential
Publishes several freelance submissions yearly.
Submissions and Payment: Sample copy available at newsstands. Guidelines available at website. Query with list of sources to be interviewed. Accepts email queries to editors@iparenting.com (no attachments). Response time varies. All rights. Articles, 600–1,200 words; payment rates vary. Pays 30 days after acceptance.

Family-Life Magazine

100 Professional Center Drive, Suite 104
Rohnert Park, CA 94928

Editor

Description and Interests
This local family and parenting publication is distributed in Sonoma, Mendocino, and Lake Counties in California. It includes how-to articles, parenting advice, and humorous pieces. Calendars of events and activities in the local area and resource guides are other regular features. Circ: 28,000.
Website: www.family-life.us

Freelance Potential
40% written by nonstaff writers. Publishes 24–36 freelance submissions yearly; 10% by unpublished writers. Receives 120+ unsolicited mss yearly.
Submissions and Payment: Guidelines and editorial calendar available. Send complete ms. Accepts email submissions to katie@family-life.us (text only attachments). Response time varies. One-time rights. Articles and depts/columns, word lengths and payment rates vary. Pays on publication.

FamilyRapp.com

P.O. Box 117
Oxted RH8 OFN
United Kingdom

Submissions: Cathy Baillie & Jane Rouse

Description and Interests
This e-zine for parents features a wide range of informative articles that cover topics such as education, health, the holidays, family excursions, and social issues. Freelance submissions on these topics are needed to fill each issue of the e-zine, which is updated weekly. *FamilyRapp.com* also provides helpful links and a parenting resource list. Hits per month: Unavailable.
Website: www.familyrapp.com

Freelance Potential
75% written by nonstaff writers. Publishes 100 freelance submissions yearly. Receives 52 unsolicited mss each year.
Submissions and Payment: Sample copy and guidelines available at website. Send complete ms. Accepts email submissions to info@familyrapp.com. Response time varies. One-time and electronic rights. Articles, 500–1,000 words. No payment.

Family Safety & Health

1121 Spring Lake Drive
Itasca, IL 60143

Editor: Tim Hodson

Description and Interests
Appearing four times each year, *Family Safety & Health* features articles and tips on home, recreational, and traffic safety. Published by the National Safety Council, it presents information in a reader-friendly format. Experienced writers who submit résumés may be considered for assignments. Circ: 225,000.
Website: www.nsc.org

Freelance Potential
5% written by nonstaff writers. Publishes 5 freelance submissions yearly; 20% by new authors.
Submissions and Payment: Sample copy, $4 with 9x12 SASE ($.77 postage). No queries or unsolicited mss. All writing is done on a work-for-hire basis. Send résumé via email to hodsont@nsc.org. Response time varies. All rights. Articles, 1,200 words. Written material, payment rates vary. Pays on acceptance. Provides 2 contributor's copies.

Fantastic Stories of the Imagination

P.O. Box 329
Brightwaters, NY 11718

Editor-in-Chief: Edward J. McFadden

Description and Interests
Science fiction and fantasy are the focus of this magazine published four times each year. It also features stories of mixed genres such as science fiction and mystery. Due to an overload of material, new submissions will not be accepted until 2008. Circ: 7,000.
Website: www.dnapublications.com

Freelance Potential
100% written by nonstaff writers. Publishes 50 freelance submissions yearly; 10% by unpublished writers. Receives 5,400 unsolicited mss yearly.
Submissions and Payment: Sample copy, $5 with 9x12 SASE. Send complete ms. Accepts hard copy. SASE. Responds in 1–8 weeks. First North American serial rights. Fiction, 2,000–15,000 words. Depts/columns, word lengths vary. Poetry, no line limits. Written material, $.01–$.05 per word. Payment policy varies. Provides 1 contributor's copy.

Farm & Ranch Living

5925 Country Lane
Greendale, WI 53129

Editor: Nick Pabst

Description and Interests
This lifestyle magazine for and about farmers and ranchers is published six times each year. Its focus is on stories about people, not the technical aspects of farming. Circ: 350,000.
Website: www.farmandranchliving.com

Freelance Potential
90% written by nonstaff writers. Publishes 36 freelance submissions yearly; 50% by unpublished writers, 50% by authors who are new to the magazine. Receives 120 queries and unsolicited mss yearly.
Submissions and Payment: Sample copy, $2. Query or send complete ms. Accepts hard copy and email submissions to editors@farmandranchliving.com. Photos improve chance of acceptance. SASE. Responds in 6 weeks. One-time rights. Articles, 1,200 words. Depts/columns, 350 words. Written material, $10–$150. Pays on publication. Provides 1 author's copy.

Father Magazine

P.O. Box 231891
Houston, TX 77223

Managing Editor: John Gill

Description and Interests
Focusing on all aspects of fatherhood, this e-zine includes articles, tips, and short stories covering topics such as child care, discipline, health, education, travel with kids, and other parenting topics. It seeks thought-provoking and exciting articles on topics related to the importance and joys of fatherhood. Hits per month: 1 million.
Website: www.fathermag.com

Freelance Potential
95% written by nonstaff writers. Publishes 50 freelance submissions yearly; 50% by authors who are new to the magazine.
Submissions and Payment: Sample copy and writers' guidelines available at website. Query. Accepts email queries to jgill@fathermag.com. Response time varies. One-time rights. Articles and fiction, word lengths vary. No payment.

Fido Friendly

P.O. Box 10219
Costa Mesa, CA 92627

Editor: Nick Svelosky

Description and Interests
Subtitled "The Travel Magazine for You and Your Dog," *Fido Friendly* is written for people who take their dogs on long trips. Each quarterly issue features information on destinations throughout the U.S. and Canada that welcome canines. Circ: 30,000.
Website: www.fidofriendly.com

Freelance Potential
100% written by nonstaff writers. Publishes 4 freelance submissions yearly; 10% by unpublished writers, 60% by authors who are new to the magazine. Receives 120 queries yearly.
Submissions and Payment: Sample copy and guidelines, $4.95. Query with sample paragraph. Accepts email queries to nick@fidofriendly.com. SASE. Responds in 1 month. First rights. Articles, 800–1,200 words; $.10 per word. Pays on publication. Provides 1 contributor's copy.

FineScale Modeler

21027 Crossroads Circle
P.O. Box 1612
Waukesha, WI 53187

Editor: Matthew Usher

Description and Interests
Subtitled "The essential tool for model builders," this magazine provides detailed how-to articles for modelers of planes, cars, boats, and military vehicles. It appears 10 times each year. Circ: 60,000.
Website: www.finescale.com

Freelance Potential
85% written by nonstaff writers. Publishes 40 freelance submissions yearly; 20% by authors who are new to the magazine. Receives 120–240 unsolicited mss yearly.
Submissions and Payment: Sample copy, $4.95 with 9x12 SASE. Query or send complete ms. Accepts hard copy, disk submissions with hard copy, and email submissions to editor@finescale.com. SASE. Responds in 1–4 months. All rights. Articles, 750–3,000 words. Depts/columns, word lengths vary. Written material, $60–$75 per page. Pays on acceptance. Provides 1 contributor's copy.

Gay Parent Magazine

P.O. Box 750852
Forest Hills, NY 11375-0852

Editor: Angeline Acain

Description and Interests
Gay and lesbian parents turn to this magazine for information on gay-friendly camps, schools, and activities for their children. Published six times each year, it also includes discussions of gay, lesbian, bisexual, and transgender specific issues. Circ: 10,000.
Website: www.gayparentmag.com

Freelance Potential
3% written by nonstaff writers. Publishes 6 freelance submissions yearly; 1% by authors who are new to the magazine. Receives 75 unsolicited mss yearly.
Submissions and Payment: Sample copy and guidelines, $3.50. Send complete ms. Prefers email submissions to acain@gis.net. Artwork improves chance of acceptance. SASE. Response time varies. One-time rights. Articles, 500–1,000 words; $.10 per word. Color prints or electronic files. Pays on publication. Provides contributor's copies upon request.

Good Housekeeping

Hearst Corporation
300 West 57th Street
New York, NY 10019-5288

Executive Editor: Judith Coyne

Description and Interests
Married women with children are the target audience of this monthly. Submissions with a fresh angle, appropriately researched, and tailored to *Good Housekeeping* readers are most successful. Circ: 6 million.
Website: www.goodhousekeeping.com

Freelance Potential
80% written by nonstaff writers. Publishes 50+ freelance submissions yearly. Receives 18,000–24,000 queries yearly.
Submissions and Payment: Guidelines available. Sample copy, $2.50 at newsstands. Query with résumé and clips for nonfiction; SASE. Send complete ms for fiction; mss not returned. Accepts hard copy. Responds in 4–6 weeks. All rights for nonfiction; first North American serial rights for fiction. Articles, 750–2,500 words; to $2,000. Essays, to 1,000 words; to $750. Pays on acceptance. Provides 1 contributor's copy.

Girlfriend Magazine

35-51 Mitchell Street
McMahons Point, New South Wales 2060
Australia

Editorial Coordinator: Belinda Frizza

Description and Interests
This monthly magazine keeps teenage girls up to date with the latest in fashion, news, and celebrity gossip. It also includes articles on topics such as beauty, relationships, careers, and social issues. Circ: 112,000.
Website: www.girlfriend.com.au

Freelance Potential
30% written by nonstaff writers. Publishes 36 freelance submissions yearly; 25% by unpublished writers, 15% by authors who are new to the magazine.
Submissions and Payment: Sample copy, $4.50. Send complete ms. Accepts hard copy and email submissions to girlfriendonline@pacpubs.com.au. SAE/IRC. Responds in 3 weeks. Exclusive rights. Articles, 1,500–2,000 words. Fiction, 2,000 words. Depts/columns, 500 words. Color prints or transparencies. All material, payment rates vary. Pays on publication. Provides 3 contributor's copies.

Grandparents Magazine

281 Rosedale Avenue
Wayne, PA 19087

Editor: Katrina Hayday Wester

Description and Interests
This online publication targets grandparents seeking fun ways to interact with their grandchildren and enhance their relationships with them. Updated each month, it features informational articles on child development, reviews of new products and literature, personal experience pieces, profiles, and interviews. Topics include recreation, travel, life lessons, social issues, religion, relationships, and health and fitness. Hits per month: Unavailable.
Website: www.grandparentsmagazine.net

Freelance Potential
Publishes several freelance submissions yearly.
Submissions and Payment: Sample copy and guidelines available at website. Query. SASE. Accepts email queries to content@grandparentsmagazine.net. Response time varies. Electronic rights. Articles, word lengths vary. No payment.

Grand Rapids Family

549 Ottawa Avenue NW, Suite 201
Grand Rapids, MI 49503

Editor: Carole Valade

Description and Interests
Families living in western Michigan turn to this monthly award-winning magazine for informative articles and essays on topics such as family issues, education, and child care. In addition, it includes news and reviews, travel ideas, family-friendly events, and profiles of outstanding children from the region. It seeks articles on adoption, and other family-related pieces. Circ: 30,000.
Website: www.grfamily.com

Freelance Potential
20% written by nonstaff writers. Publishes 15 freelance submissions yearly.
Submissions and Payment: Guidelines available with #10 SASE. Query or send complete ms. Accepts hard copy. SASE. Responds to queries in 2 months, to mss in 6 months. All rights. Articles and depts/columns, word lengths and payment rates vary. B/W or color prints; $25. Kill fee, $25. Pays on publication.

Harford County Kids

P.O. Box 1666
Bel Air, MD 21014

Publisher: Joan Fernandez

Description and Interests
Parents residing in Bel Air and other Harford County, Maryland, communities are the target audience of this monthly magazine. It includes how-to and informational articles on topics such as health, education, family issues, and finances, and profiles of local families. In addition, it also reports on family-friendly events and local resources. Circ: 28,500.
Website: www.harfordcountykids.com

Freelance Potential
100% written by nonstaff writers. Publishes 20 freelance submissions yearly.
Submissions and Payment: Guidelines available. Query. Accepts hard copy and email to joanf@ aboutdelta.com. Response time varies. First electronic rights. Articles and depts/columns, word lengths and payment rates vary. Pays on publication. Provides 1 contributor's copy.

High School Years

3035 Valley Avenue, Suite 103
Winchester, VA 22601

Submissions Editor

Description and Interests
Covering topics of interest to parents of high school students, this monthly newsletter includes practical articles and tips on how to encourage school success. It seeks queries for short pieces on parenting issues, after-school jobs, career choices, peer pressure, and homework. Circ: 300,000.
Website: www.rfeonline.com

Freelance Potential
100% written by nonstaff writers. Publishes 80 freelance submissions yearly; 28% by unpublished writers. Receives 36 unsolicited mss yearly.
Submissions and Payment: Sample copy, guidelines, and editorial calendar, free with 9x12 SASE. Query with résumé and clips. SASE. Responds in 1 month. All rights. Articles, 225–300 words. Depts/columns, 175–200 words. Written material, $.60 per word. Pays on acceptance. Provides 5 contributor's copies.

Home & School Connection

3035 Valley Avenue, Suite 103
Winchester, VA 22601

Submissions: Jennifer Hutchinson

Description and Interests
Home & School Connection is published monthly for distribution in elementary schools. Its purpose is to provide parents with brief articles that support their children's efforts in school. Topics such as education, communication skills, special needs, parenting, and family issues are discussed. This newsletter is not reviewing queries or manuscripts at the present time. Circ: 3 million.
Website: www.rfeonline.com

Freelance Potential
100% written by nonstaff writers. Publishes 80 freelance submissions yearly; 28% by unpublished writers, 14% by authors who are new to the magazine. Receives 36 unsolicited mss yearly.
Submissions and Payment: Sample copy, free with 9x12 SASE ($.77 postage). Do not submit queries or manuscripts at this time.

Home Times Family Newspaper

3676 Collin Drive, Suite 16
West Palm Beach, FL 33406

Editor: Dennis Lombard

Description and Interests
Current events and vital issues of the day, including parenting, family, and education topics, are addressed from a biblical world view in *Home Times Family Newspaper*. Published monthly, it is seeking creative nonfiction, historical pieces, and humor. Circ: 6,000.
Website: www.hometimes.org

Freelance Potential
80% written by nonstaff writers. Publishes 20 freelance submissions yearly; 75% by authors who are new to the magazine. Receives 360 unsolicited mss yearly.
Submissions and Payment: Sample copy, $3. Send complete ms. Accepts hard copy and simultaneous submissions if identified. SASE. Responds in 1 month. One-time and electronic rights. Articles and fiction, 500–750 words. Depts/columns, word lengths vary. Written material, payment rates vary. Pays on publication. Provides contributor's copies upon request.

Hot Rod

6420 Wilshire Boulevard
Los Angeles, CA 90048

Editor: David Freiburger

Description and Interests
Covering technical information, industry commentary, and new trends, *Hot Rod* is the largest monthly magazine dedicated to high performance cars. Written for hot rod enthusiasts of all ages, it also includes race event coverage, driver profiles, and nostalgia pieces. Circ: 680,000.
Website: www.hotrod.com

Freelance Potential
15% written by nonstaff writers. Publishes 24 freelance submissions yearly. Receives 288 queries yearly.
Submissions and Payment: Sample copy, $3.50 at newsstands. Guidelines available. Query. SASE. Response time varies. All rights. Articles, 3,000 characters per page; $250–$300 per page. Depts/columns, word lengths vary; $100 per page. B/W and color prints and 35mm color transparencies; payment rates vary. Pays on publication.

I.D.

Cook Communications Ministries
4050 Lee Vance View
Colorado Springs, CO 80918

Editor: Gail Rohlfing

Description and Interests
I.D. is a weekly Sunday school paper distributed to students ages 15 to 17. It features stories related to Bible studies and biblical concepts. Profiles and interviews, personal experience pieces, and how-to articles are also included. Freelancers wishing to write for this market may submit a letter of inquiry, résumé, and list of publishing credits to the editor. Circ: 61,000.
Website: www.cookministries.org

Freelance Potential
30% written by nonstaff writers.
Submissions and Payment: Guidelines available. Query with résumé. No unsolicited mss. All articles are assigned. Accepts hard copy. SASE. Responds in 6 months. Rights vary. Articles, 600–1,200 words; $50–$300 depending on experience. B/W and color prints; payment rates vary. Pays on acceptance. Provides 1 contributor's copy.

I Love Cats

16 Meadow Hill Lane
Armonk, NY 10504

Editor: Lisa Allmendinger

Description and Interests
Appearing six times each year, *I Love Cats* features stories and articles about cats and their owners. Each issue includes tips for cat owners, reports of unusual cat happenings, interesting stories, and information on feline health and behavior. Circ: 25,000.
Website: www.iluvcats.com

Freelance Potential
95% written by nonstaff writers. Publishes 100 freelance submissions yearly; 50% by unpublished writers, 75% by authors who are new to the magazine. Receives 6,000 queries and unsolicited mss yearly.
Submissions and Payment: Sample copy and guidelines, $5 with 9x12 SASE. Query or send complete ms. Accepts hard copy and email to ilovecatseditor@sbcglobal.net. SASE. Responds in 1–2 months. All rights. Articles and fiction, 500–1,000 words; $25–$100. Pays on publication. Provides 1 author's copy.

Indian Life Newspaper

P.O. Box 3765
Redwood Post Office, Redwood Centre
Winnipeg, Manitoba R2L 1L6
Canada

Editor: Jim Uttley

Description and Interests
This Christian tabloid, published six times each year, is an evangelical tool designed to assist the North American Indian church address the social, cultural, and spiritual needs of its people. Circ: 20,000.
Website: www.indianlife.org

Freelance Potential
80% written by nonstaff writers. Publishes 10 freelance submissions yearly; 2% by unpublished writers, 25% by authors who are new to the magazine. Receives 276 unsolicited mss yearly.
Submissions and Payment: Sample copy, $2.50 with #9 SAE. Prefers query. Accepts complete ms. Accepts hard copy, disk submissions, and email submissions to iln.editor@indianlife.org. SAE/IRC. Responds in 1 month. First rights. Articles, 250–2,000 words. Written material, $25–$100. Pays on publication. Provides 15 contributor's copies.

Inside Kung-Fu

Action Pursuit Group
265 South Anita Drive, Suite 120
Orange, CA 92868–3310

Editor: Dave Cater

Description and Interests
Inside Kung-Fu provides information on all aspects of the martial arts for practitioners and enthusiasts of all ages. Published monthly, it provides current news on the sport, articles about technique, and profiles of masters and grandmasters. Circ: 110,000.
Website: www.apg-media.com

Freelance Potential
80% written by nonstaff writers. Publishes 100 freelance submissions yearly; 50% by unpublished writers, 50% by authors who are new to the magazine. Receives 504 queries yearly.
Submissions and Payment: Sample copy and guidelines, $2.95 with 9x12 SASE. Query. Accepts hard copy and email queries to dave.cater@apg-media.com. SASE. Responds in 4–6 weeks. First rights. Articles, 1,500 words. Depts/columns, 750 words. Written material, payment rates vary. Pays on publication.

Junior Storyteller

P.O. Box 205
Masonville, CO 80541

Editor: Vivian Dubrovin

Description and Interests
A quarterly publication, *Junior Storyteller* targets elementary through junior high school students who are interested in the art and craft of storytelling. It includes complete storytelling projects, as well as nonfiction pieces related to storytelling programs. Circ: 500.
Website: www.storycraft.com

Freelance Potential
30% written by nonstaff writers. Receives several queries and unsolicited mss yearly.
Submissions and Payment: Guidelines available at website. Sample copy, $3.50 with 6x9 SASE. Query. Accepts hard copy and email to jrstoryteller@direcway.com. Availability of artwork may improve chance of acceptance. SASE. Response time varies. First rights. Articles and fiction, 500–1,000 words; $50–$125. Pays on acceptance. Provides 10 contributor's copies.

Kahani

P.O. Box 590155
Newton Centre, MA 02459

Editor: Monika Jain

Description and Interests
Kahani is a literary magazine dedicated to empowering, educating, and entertaining children of South Asian descent living in North America. An alternative publication, it strives to reflect the unique life experiences of South Asian children through fictional stories, nonfiction on subcontinent issues, profiles of South Asian role models, reviews of current literature with a similar theme, puzzles, and other interactive activities. It is published quarterly. Circ: Unavailable.
Website: www.kahani.com

Freelance Potential
Publishes several freelance submissions yearly.
Submissions and Payment: Guidelines available at website. Send complete ms. Accepts email submissions to writers@kahani.com. Response time varies. Rights vary. Articles and fiction, word lengths vary. No payment.

Kansas 4-H Journal

116 Umberger Hall
KSU
Manhattan, KS 66506-3417

Editor: Rhonda Atkinson

Description and Interests
Members of 4-H clubs, their leaders, and their parents
read this journal appearing ten times each year. *Kansas
4-H Journal* reports on regional activities and events. It
also features how-to articles, photo-essays, and personal
experience pieces. Only writers involved in 4-H clubs or
youth groups may submit their work. All sections of this
journal are open to submissions. Circ: 14,000.

Freelance Potential
60% written by nonstaff writers. Publishes 100 freelance submissions yearly; 10% by unpublished writers,
20% by authors who are new to the magazine. Receives
696 queries and unsolicited mss yearly.
Submissions and Payment: Sample copy and editorial
calendar, $5. Query or send complete ms. Accepts hard
copy. SASE. Response time varies. Rights negotiable.
Articles, 500 words; payment rates vary. Payment policy
varies.

Keyboard

2800 Campus Drive
San Mateo, CA 94403

Editor-in-Chief: Ernie Rideout

Description and Interests
Keyboard is published for amateur and professional
musicians dedicated to improving their musical abilities. Technical and how-to articles are included in each
monthly issue. Circ: 61,000.
Website: www.keyboardmag.com

Freelance Potential
25–35% written by nonstaff writers. Publishes 120 freelance submissions yearly; 35% by unpublished writers,
55% by authors who are new to the magazine. Receives
60–120 unsolicited mss yearly.
Submissions and Payment: Sample copy and guidelines available via email. Send complete ms with
résumé. Accepts hard copy and email submissions
to keyboard@musicplayer.com. SASE. Responds in
3 months. All rights. Articles, 500–3,000 words. Depts/
columns, 400–800 words. All material, payment rates
vary. Pays on publication. Provides 5 author's copies.

Kids

341 East Lancaster Avenue
Downingtown, PA 19335

Editor: Bob Ludwick

Description and Interests
Chester County, Pennsylvania, families and educators
read this monthly newspaper for information on local
elementary and middle schools. Regular features
include reports on local school events, successful programs, profiles of outstanding teachers, and announcements of notable student accomplishments. Upbeat stories about Chester County teachers, students, and programs are always of interest. Circ: 45,000.

Freelance Potential
90% written by nonstaff writers. Publishes 120 freelance submissions yearly; 20% by unpublished writers.
Receives several queries yearly.
Submissions and Payment: Sample copy and editorial
calendar, free with 9x12 SASE. Query with résumé.
Accepts hard copy. SASE. Responds in 1 week. All
rights. Articles and depts/columns, to 500 words. No
payment. Provides 2 contributor's copies.

Kidsandkaboodle.com

1169 Mount Rushmore Way
Lexington, KY 40515

Editor: Jennifer Anderson

Description and Interests
Families in central Kentucky receive valuable information on parenting, safety, and child development from
this regional e-zine. Many of its articles have helpful
links and associated attachments. *Kidsandkaboodle.com*
is currently seeking articles on health, fitness, and pregnancy. Well-researched articles on health issues for children are also of interest. Hits per month: 50,000.
Website: www.kidsandkaboodle.com

Freelance Potential
20% written by nonstaff writers. Publishes 20 freelance
submissions yearly; 50% by unpublished writers, 50%
by authors who are new to the magazine. Receives
36–48 queries and unsolicited mss yearly.
Submissions and Payment: Sample copy available at
website. Send complete ms. Accepts email submissions
to editor@kidsandkaboodle.com. Response time varies.
All rights. Articles, word lengths vary. No payment.

The Kids Storytelling Club

Editor: Vivian Dubrovin

Description and Interests
This online magazine presents three-part storytelling projects for children that include: a story a child can tell; a craft the child can make to help the tale; and tips for storytelling. The site also includes a Parent-Teacher-Leader page with ideas on how adults can help in the storytelling process. Hits per month: 4,000+.
Website: www.storycraft.com

Freelance Potential
70% written by nonstaff writers. Publishes many freelance submissions yearly; many by unpublished writers, most by authors who are new to the magazine.
Submissions and Payment: Guidelines and sample copy available at website. Query. Accepts hard copy and email to jrstoryteller@direcway.com. SASE. Response time varies. First rights. Articles, 500 words. Fiction, 250–500 words. Written material, $25. Pays on acceptance.

Kiwibox.com

330 West 38th Street, Suite 1602
New York, NY 10018

Submissions Editor: Jasmine Kurjakovic

Description and Interests
This website was built for teens by teens in order to create a teen community on the Internet. The editorial content of the site is contributed exclusively by high school and college students. Any subject that would be of interest to young people is considered, including technology, dating, sports, music, fashion, films, and social issues. Hundreds of freelance submissions are published at this website, which is updated every three weeks. Hits per month: 10 million.
Website: www.kiwibox.com

Freelance Potential
90% written by nonstaff writers.
Submissions and Payment: Sample copy available at website. Send complete ms. Accepts email submissions to editor@kiwibox.net or mike@kiwibox.net. Responds in 2 weeks. All rights. Articles, 350 words. Fiction, word lengths vary. No payment.

Knucklebones

N7450 Aanstad Road
P.O. Box 5000
Iola, WI 54945-5000

Editor: Sarah Gloystein Peterson

Description and Interests
Knucklebones, published six times each year, focuses exclusively on games, including board games, card games, puzzles, and brainteasers. It offers reviews of new games as well as articles that encourage readers to get more involved in gaming. Submissions from freelancers are welcome. Circ: Unavailable.
Website: www.kbones.com

Freelance Potential
90% written by nonstaff writers. Publishes 150–175 freelance submissions yearly; 5% by unpublished writers, 10% by authors who are new to the magazine.
Submissions and Payment: Guidelines available with SASE or by email. Prefers query; accepts complete ms. Accepts hard copy and email submissions to editor@ kbones.com. SASE. Response time varies. First and electronic rights. Articles and depts/columns, word lengths and payment rates vary. Pays on publication.

Little Rock Family

122 East Second Street
Little Rock, AR 72201

Submissions Editor

Description and Interests
Little Rock Family is an award-winning parenting publication appearing monthly and distributed free of charge in central Arkansas. Each issue provides parents with information on local events and activities and articles about health care, education, and family relationships. A special section with a public school guide, private school guide, after-school activity guide, family favorites guide, and summer camp guide is included in each issue. Circ: 20,000.
Website: www.littlerockfamily.com

Freelance Potential
100% written by nonstaff writers. Publishes many freelance submissions yearly.
Submissions and Payment: Query. Accepts hard copy. SASE. Response time varies. First rights. Articles and depts/columns, word lengths and payment rates vary. Payment policy varies.

Metro Augusta Parent

700 Broad Street
Augusta, GA 30901

Editor: Amy Christian

Description and Interests
Metro Augusta Parent is a free monthly magazine for parents. A comprehensive calendar, which lists local events, classes, after-school programs, sports sign-ups, and support groups and activities for children and their parents, is included in each issue. The publication also provides information on local entertainment and camps, resources for parents, family dining guides, and party guides. Circ: Unavailable.
Website: www.augustaparent.com

Freelance Potential
100% written by nonstaff writers. Publishes 10 freelance submissions yearly.
Submissions and Payment: Query. Accepts hard copy and email queries to editor@augustaparent.com. SASE. Response time varies. First rights. Articles and depts/columns, word lengths and payment rates vary. Payment policy varies. Provides 1 author's copy.

Metro Parent

P.O. Box 13660
Portland, OR 97213

Editor: Marie Sherlock

Description and Interests
Families, teachers, and service providers in the Portland area read this monthly tabloid of resourceful information. Each issue provides articles of interest to parents and includes a calendar of local activities and events. Its editors will review queries from local writers only. Circ: 36,000.
Website: www.metro-parent.com

Freelance Potential
75% written by nonstaff writers. Publishes 50 freelance submissions yearly; 5% by unpublished writers. Receives 240 queries yearly.
Submissions and Payment: Sample copy and theme list, $2. Query with outline. Accepts hard copy, simultaneous submissions, and email queries to editor@metro-parent.com. SASE. Responds in 1 month. Rights vary. Articles and depts/columns, word lengths and payment rates vary. Pays on publication.

MetroFamily

306 South Bryant, Suite C-152
Edmond, OK 73034

Editor: Denise Springer

Description and Interests
This monthly tabloid that serves families in central Oklahoma features resource information and factual articles. It seeks truly funny, clean humor. Circ: 25,000.
Website: www.metrofamilymagazine.com

Freelance Potential
60% written by nonstaff writers. Publishes 60 freelance submissions yearly; 10% by unpublished writers, 10% by authors who are new to the magazine. Receives 300 queries and unsolicited mss yearly.
Submissions and Payment: Sample copy and guidelines, free with 10x13 SASE. Query or send complete ms. Accepts email submissions only to editor@metrofamilymagazine.com. Responds to queries in 3 weeks, to mss in 1 month. First North American serial rights. Articles, 300–600 words; $25–$50. Depts/columns, 600 words; $25–$35. Kill fee, 100%. Pays on publication. Provides 1 contributor's copy.

Middle Years

3035 Valley Avenue, Suite 104
Winchester, VA 22601

Submissions Editor: Jennifer Hutchinson

Description and Interests
In print since 1996, this resourceful newsletter for parents of middle-grade students features articles and tips on topics related to parenting and education. Appearing monthly, it seeks queries for short informational articles on parental involvement in education, and practical parenting tips. Circ: 1 million.
Website: www.rfeonline.com

Freelance Potential
100% written by nonstaff writers. Publishes 80 freelance submissions yearly. Receives 36 queries yearly.
Submissions and Payment: Sample copy and guidelines, free with 9x12 SASE ($.77 postage). Query with résumé and 3 clips. Accepts hard copy. SASE. Responds in 1 month. All rights. Articles, 225–300 words. Depts/columns, 175–200 words. Written material, $.60 per word. Pays on acceptance. Provides 5 contributor's copies.

311

Minnesota Parent

1115 Hennepin Avenue South
Minneapolis, MN 55403

Editor: Tricia Cornell

Description and Interests
Dedicated to educating and informing Minnesota parents of children from birth through school age, this magazine is published monthly. It offers parenting tips and ideas, interviews, expert advice, and product reviews, as well as news of regional family events. Our "ParentPages" section is particularly open to working with new writers. Circ: 80,000.
Website: www.mnparent.com

Freelance Potential
50% written by nonstaff writers. Publishes 50 freelance submissions yearly.
Submissions and Payment: Query only. Accepts hard copy and email submissions to tcornell@mnpubs.com. SASE. Response time varies. First serial and electronic rights. Articles and depts/columns, word lengths vary; $50–$350. Pays on publication. Provides 2 contributor's copies.

Mysteries Magazine

P.O. Box 490
Walpole, NH 03608

Editor: Kim Guarnaccia

Description and Interests
Factual articles and columns that explore the mysterious world and beyond can be found in this quarterly magazine. It seeks science related articles and game reviews. Circ: 16,000.
Website: www.mysteriesmagazine.com

Freelance Potential
30% written by nonstaff writers. Publishes 10 freelance submissions yearly; 20% by new authors. Receives 240 queries, 120 unsolicited mss yearly.
Submissions and Payment: Sample copy, $8. Guidelines available at website. Query or send complete ms. Accepts hard copy and email submissions to editor@mysteriesmagazine.com. SASE. Responds in 1 month. First North American serial rights. Articles, 3,000–5,000 words. Depts/columns, 1,200–1,500 words. Book reviews, 200–500 words. Written material, $.05 per word. Pays on publication. Provides 2 copies.

Model Airplane News

Air Age Publishing
100 East Ridge Road
Ridgefield, CT 06877-4606

Editor-in-Chief: Debra Cleghorn

Description and Interests
This monthly magazine for model airplane enthusiasts features articles on building techniques, tips on flying, and reviews of kits and the latest technology. *Model Airplane News* includes how-to articles and covers all aspects of aeromodeling. Circ: 95,000.
Website: www.modelairplanenews.com

Freelance Potential
90% written by nonstaff writers. Publishes 100 freelance submissions yearly; 33% by authors who are new to the magazine. Receives 144–288 queries yearly.
Submissions and Payment: Sample copy and guidelines, $3.50 with 9x12 SASE. Query with outline and biography describing model experience. Accepts hard copy. Availability of artwork improves chance of acceptance. SASE. Responds in 6 weeks. All North American serial rights. Articles, 1,700–2,000 words; $175–$600. Pays on publication. Provides up to 6 author's copies.

National PAL CopsNKids Chronicles

National Association of Police Athletic Leagues
658 West Indiantown Road
Jupiter, FL 33458

Creative Services Editor

Description and Interests
Teaching young people alternatives to crime and violence and improving their quality of life is the focus of this quarterly-published magazine. Professionals working for Police Athletic Leagues across the U. S. are the target audience of this publication. Regular features include articles on crime, violence prevention, and social and ethnic topics; ideas for games and competitions; and reports on successful programs and events. Circ: 21,000.
Website: www.nationalpal.org

Freelance Potential
75% written by nonstaff writers.
Submissions and Payment: Sample copy, free. Query or send complete ms. Accepts hard copy and email submissions to copnkid@nationalpal.org. SASE. Response time varies. All North American serial rights. Articles, word lengths vary. No payment.

Natural Jewish Parenting

P.O. Box 466
Sharon, MA 02067

Editor: Yael Resnick

Description and Interests
This quarterly family magazine focuses on Jewish
spirituality and natural family living. It features articles
related to the physical, emotional, and spiritual health
of Jewish families. Circ: 5,000.
Website: www.naturaljewishparenting.com

Freelance Potential
90% written by nonstaff writers. Publishes 40 freelance
submissions yearly; 50% by unpublished writers, 80%
by new authors. Receives 96 unsolicited mss yearly.
Submissions and Payment: Guidelines available.
Sample copy, $5 with 9x12 SASE ($1.65 postage). Send
complete ms. Accepts hard copy and email submissions
to njpmail@mindspring.com. SASE. Responds in 1–2
months. First and second rights. Articles, 1,000–3,000
words. Depts/columns, 500–1,500 words. Written material, $.04–$.05 per word. Pays on publication. Provides
1 contributor's copy.

Neapolitan Family Magazine

P.O. Box 110656
Naples, FL 34109

Editor: Andrea Breznay

Description and Interests
This monthly family and parenting publication is read by
families and educators residing in Naples and Collier
Counties in Florida. *Neapolitan Family Magazine* features articles on education, parenting, family issues,
travel, and local events and resources. Circ: 10,000.
Website: www.neafamily.com

Freelance Potential
80% written by nonstaff writers. Publishes 12–15 freelance submissions yearly. Receives 60 queries, 100
unsolicited mss yearly.
Submissions and Payment: Guidelines and editorial
calendar available at website. Sample copy, free with
9x12 SASE. Query or send complete ms. Prefers email
submissions to NeapolitanFamily@aol.com. Accepts
hard copy. SASE. Responds in 1 month. Rights vary.
Articles and depts/columns, word lengths and payment
rates vary. Pays on publication.

North State Parent

P.O. Box 1602
Mount Shasta, CA 96067

Editorial Department

Description and Interests
Editorial that promotes a developmentally appropriate,
healthy, and peaceful environment for children is of
special interest to this monthly publication. Formerly
listed as *Shasta Parent*, it strives to remain respectful
of cultural diversity and includes articles of interest
to families with a variety of lifestyles and beliefs.
Circ: Unavailable.
Website: www.northstateparent.com

Freelance Potential
90% written by nonstaff writers. Publishes 20 freelance
submissions yearly.
Submissions and Payment: Guidelines available at
website. Send complete ms. Accepts hard copy and
email submissions to pn@northstateparent.com. SASE.
Response time varies. First rights. Articles, 700–1,000
words. Depts/columns, 300–500 words. Written material,
$40–$70. Pays on publication.

The Numismatist

American Numismatist Association
818 North Cascade Avenue
Colorado Springs, CO 80903–3279

Editor-in-Chief: Barbara J. Gregory

Description and Interests
This monthly magazine of the American Numismatic
Association is read by collectors of coins, medals,
tokens, and paper money. Circ: 30,500.
Website: www.money.org

Freelance Potential
60% written by nonstaff writers. Publishes 36 freelance
submissions yearly; 20% by unpublished writers, 10%
by authors who are new to the magazine. Receives
48 unsolicited mss yearly.
Submissions and Payment: Sample copy and guidelines, free with 9x12 SASE ($2.50 postage). Send
complete ms with biography. Prefers email submissions
to magazine@money.org. Accepts hard copy and
disk submissions. SASE. Responds in 8–10 weeks.
Perpetual non-exclusive rights. Articles, to 3,500 words;
$.10 per word. Pays on publication. Provides 5 contrib-
utor's copies.

Our Little Friend

Pacific Press Publishing
P.O. Box 5353
Nampa, ID 83653-5353

Editor: Aileen Andres Sox

Description and Interests
This spiritually focused, weekly magazine is for children who attend beginner or kindergarten Sabbath school at a Seventh-day Adventist Church. It offers Bible lessons and stories teaching Christian values. Circ: 40,000.
Website: www.ourlittlefriend.com

Freelance Potential
20% written by nonstaff writers. Publishes 52 freelance submissions yearly; 10% by unpublished writers, 10% by authors who are new to the magazine. Receives 240 unsolicited mss yearly.
Submissions and Payment: Sample copy and guidelines, free with 9x12 SASE (2 first-class stamps). Send complete ms. Accepts hard copy, simultaneous submissions if identified, and email submissions to ailsox@pacificpress.com. SASE. Responds in 4 months. One-time rights. Articles and fiction, 500–650 words; $25–$50. Pays on acceptance. Provides 3 author's copies.

Owl

Bayard Press Canada
10 Lower Spadina Avenue, Suite 400
Toronto, Ontario M4V 2V2
Canada

Submissions Editor

Description and Interests
Appearing nine times each year, *Owl* magazine entertains and informs children ages eight and up with interesting and informative articles about their world. Topics include animals, people, and science. Circ: 104,000.
Website: www.owlkids.com

Freelance Potential
60% written by nonstaff writers. Publishes 1–3 freelance submissions yearly; 5% by unpublished writers, 10% by authors who are new to the magazine. Receives 600 queries yearly.
Submissions and Payment: Sample copy, $4.28. All material is assigned. Query with résumé, outline, and clips or writing samples. Accepts hard copy. Include $1.50 IRC for reply. Responds in 2–3 months. Rights vary. Articles, 500–1,000 words; $200–$500 Canadian. Depts/columns, word lengths and payment rates vary. Payment policy varies. Provides 1 contributor's copy.

Parenting for High Potential

4921 Ringwood Meadow
Sarasota, FL 34235

Editor: Dr. Donald Treffinger

Description and Interests
Parenting for High Potential is a magazine for parents who want to develop their children's gifts and talents. Each issue includes special features, expert advice columns, software and book reviews, ideas from parents, and a pullout children's section. Published quarterly, this magazine currently seeks pieces written for parents of high-ability children. Circ: Unavailable.
Website: www.nagc.org

Freelance Potential
100% written by nonstaff writers. Publishes 10–12 freelance submissions yearly; 50% by authors who are new to the magazine. Receives 20–30 mss yearly.
Submissions and Payment: Guidelines available. Send complete ms. Accepts email submissions to don@creativelearning.com. Responds in 6–8 weeks. First rights. Articles and depts/columns, word lengths vary. No payment.

ParentingHumor.com

P.O. Box 2128
Weaverville, NC 28787

Editor

Description and Interests
The lighter side of parenting is the focus of this weekly-updated online publication. It features humorous articles on parenting issues, pregnancy, relationships, child development, fashion, health, beauty, and cooking. New and established writers are invited to share their funny stories and advice related to topics of interest to parents and caregivers. Hits per month: Unavailable.
Website: www.parentinghumor.com

Freelance Potential
98% written by nonstaff writers. Publishes 350 freelance submissions yearly. Receives 300 queries yearly.
Submissions and Payment: Sample copy, guidelines, and submission form available at website. Query. Accepts email queries to staff@parentinghumor.com. Response time varies. One-time electronic rights. Articles, word lengths vary. No payment. Offers an author's biography and a link to the author's website.

Parents' Choice

Parents' Choice Foundation
201 West Padonia Road, Suite 303
Timonium, MD 21093

Editor: Claire Green

Description and Interests
This online publication is updated each month and printed in newsletter format twice each year. Targeting parents seeking information about products available for their children, it highlights those that are safe, age-appropriate, and socially sound. *Parents' Choice* also features reviews of children's books, videos, magazines, software, and television shows. Hits per month: 1 million+.
Website: www.parentschoice.org

Freelance Potential
80% written by nonstaff writers. Publishes many freelance submissions yearly.
Submissions and Payment: Sample copy available at website. Query or send complete ms. Accepts hard copy and simultaneous submissions if identified. SASE. Response time varies. All rights. Articles, to 1,500 words; payment rates vary. Pays on acceptance.

Parents

Gruner & Jahr
375 Lexington Avenue
New York, NY 10017

Editor

Description and Interests
Parents from diverse backgrounds read this monthly publication for its broad spectrum of informative articles. Topics include parenting information, child care, behavior, education, health, fitness, pregnancy, gifted and special education, and social issues. Personal experience articles and professional advice are also included. Circ: Unavailable.
Website: www.parents.com

Freelance Potential
50% written by nonstaff writers. Publishes 50 freelance submissions yearly. Receives 1,200 queries yearly.
Submissions and Payment: Sample copy, $3.50 with 9x12 SASE (4 first-class stamps). Query with clips. Accepts hard copy. SASE. Responds in 6 weeks. Rights vary. Articles and depts/columns, word lengths and payment rates vary. Pays on publication. Provides 2 contributor's copies.

Parents Express
Pennsylvania Edition

290 Commerce Drive
Fort Washington, PA 19034

Submissions Editor: Daniel Sean Kaye

Description and Interests
This monthly published magazine serves families in the Philadelphia and southern New Jersey areas. Parenting issues, regional resources, and local event coverage appear in each issue. Circ: 49,000.
Website: www.parents-express.net

Freelance Potential
30% written by nonstaff writers. Publishes 25–35 freelance submissions yearly; 25% by unpublished writers, 75% by new authors. Receives many queries yearly.
Submissions and Payment: Sample copy, free with 10x13 SASE ($2.14 postage). Query with clips or writing samples. Accepts hard copy and email to dkaye@ montgomerynews.com. Availability of artwork improves chance of acceptance. SASE. Responds in 1 month. One-time rights. Articles, 300–1,000 words; $35–$200. Depts/columns, 600–800 words; payment rates vary. Pays on publication. Provides contributor's copies.

Passport

WordAction Publishing
2923 Troost Avenue
Kansas City, MO 64109

Editorial Assistant: Kimberly Adams

Description and Interests
Passport is a weekly published paper used in religious education programs for pre-teens. The content of each issue supplements the lesson of the day and conforms to the teachings of the Church of the Nazarene. Circ: 55,000.
Website: www.nazarene.org

Freelance Potential
90% written by nonstaff writers. Publishes 30 freelance submissions yearly; 20% by unpublished writers, 20% by authors who are new to the magazine. Receives 240 queries and unsolicited mss yearly.
Submissions and Payment: Sample copy, free with 5x7 SASE. Query with author information; or send complete ms. Accepts hard copy. SASE. Responds in 4–6 weeks. Rights vary. Articles, 400–500 words. Fiction, 600–800 words. Written material, $15–$25. Pays on publication. Provides 2 contributor's copies.

Paws, Claws, Hooves & All ☆

P.O. Box 25
Dover, PA 17315

Editor: Margo Caskey

Description and Interests
Each issue of this monthly magazine highlights a variety of pets and pet-related topics. It includes humorous fiction, entertaining and informative articles, personal experience pieces, and interviews. It seeks well-written material by authors who love and care about the well-being of all animals. Circ: 15,000.
Website: www.meadowbrookpublications.com

Freelance Potential
75% written by nonstaff writers. Publishes 25–30 freelance submissions yearly.
Submissions and Payment: Sample copy available at website. Send ms. Accepts hard copy and email submissions to mcaskey@meadowbrookpublications.com (Microsoft Word attachment). SASE. Response time varies. All rights. Articles, 1,200–1,400 words; $100. Depts/columns, 1,200–1,400 words; payment rates vary. Pays on publication.

Pogo Stick

1300 Kicker Road
Tuscaloosa, AL 35404

Editor: Lillian Kopaska-Merkel

Description and Interests
Pogo Stick is a magazine written by children, for children. Appearing quarterly, it accepts work from writers up to the age of seventeen. It publishes fiction in a variety of genres, including adventure stories and multicultural and ethnic fiction. The editors would like to see more mystery stories, poetry, jokes, and riddles. It is overstocked with realistic fiction and fantasy at this time. Circ: Unavailable.

Freelance Potential
100% written by nonstaff writers. Publishes 40–60 freelance submissions yearly; 99% by authors who are new to the magazine. Receives 50–70 unsolicited mss yearly.
Submissions and Payment: Sample copy and guidelines, $3. Send complete ms; accepts 3 manuscripts per child per issue. Accepts hard copy. SASE. Responds in 1 month. All rights. Written material, to 2,000 words. No payment. Provides 1 contributor's copy.

Plum Magazine

100 Park Avenue, Suite 1600
New York, NY 10017

Submissions: Mary Jane Horton

Description and Interests
Appearing twice each year, *Plum Magazine* is published by The American College of Obstetricians and Gynecologists for pregnant women over the age of 35. It features informative articles on all topics related to older mothers, such as fertility and conception, prenatal testing, and postpartum health. Circ: Unavailable.
Website: www.plummagazine.com

Freelance Potential
90% written by nonstaff writers. Of the freelance submissions published yearly, 100% are by authors who are new to the magazine. Receives 100 queries yearly.
Submissions and Payment: Guidelines available at website. Query or send complete ms. Accepts email submissions to editor@plummagazine.com. Response time varies. All rights. Articles and depts/columns, word lengths and payment rates vary. Pays on publication. Provides 1 contributor's copy.

Popcorn Magazine for Children

8320 Brookfield Road
Richmond, VA 23227

Editor: Charlene Warner Coleman

Description and Interests
This magazine is designed for children ages 5 to 13. Its goal is to encourage an interest in reading and the arts while nourishing the creative and inquisitive nature that most children have. Appearing six times each year, it is being re-launched in the form of a hard copy magazine, a website, and a television program. It seeks material on topics such as sports, art, science, travel, fashion, and cooking. Building projects and movie and CD reviews are also needed. Circ: 100,000.

Freelance Potential
75% written by nonstaff writers. Publishes 500+ freelance submissions yearly.
Submissions and Payment: Send complete ms. Accepts hard copy and email submissions to cwcoleman1@comcast.net. SASE. Response time varies. Rights vary. Articles and depts/columns, word lengths vary. No payment.

Prairie Messenger

Box 190, 100 College Drive
Muenster, Saskatchewan S0K 2Y0
Canada

Associate Editor: Maureen Weber

Description and Interests
This weekly tabloid for Catholics living in Saskatchewan and Manitoba addresses political, social, and economic issues from the framework of the Gospel. It is currently seeking articles about youth concerns. Circ: 7,100.
Website: www.stpeters.ks.ca/prairie_messenger

Freelance Potential
60% written by nonstaff writers. Publishes 10 freelance submissions yearly. Receives 30 queries and unsolicited mss yearly.
Submissions and Payment: Sample copy and guidelines, $1 with 9x12 SAE/IRC. Query or send complete ms. Accepts email submissions to pm.canadian@stpeters.sk.ca. Responds in 1 month. First rights. Articles, 700 words; payment rates vary. Depts/columns, 700 words; $50 Canadian. Color prints or transparencies or line art, payment rates vary. Pays at the end of each month.

Racquetball

1685 West Uintah
Colorado Springs, CO 80904

Executive Assistant: Heather Fender

Description and Interests
Published six times each year by the United States Racquetball Association, this magazine is read by racquetball players, coaches, tournament directors, and fans. Each issue features informative articles on strategies and techniques. It also includes the latest national and local tournament coverage as well as profiles of outstanding players. Circ: 40,000.
Website: www.usaracquetball.com

Freelance Potential
50% written by nonstaff writers. Publishes 50 freelance submissions yearly.
Submissions and Payment: Sample copy and guidelines, $4. Prefers query; accepts complete ms. Accepts hard copy. SASE. Responds in 9 weeks. One-time rights. Articles, 1,500–2,000 words. Depts/columns, 500–1,000 words. Written material, $.03–$.07 per word. Pays on publication.

PTO Today

100 Stonewall Boulevard, Suite 3
Wrentham, MA 02093

Editor-in-Chief: Craig Bystrinski

Description and Interests
Published six times each year, this magazine helps elementary and middle school PTO/PTA leaders run their groups more efficiently and serve their schools more effectively. All stories must have a strong parent group angle. It currently seeks articles that provide expert advice on issues such as recruiting and keeping parent volunteers, and on starting parent-teacher organizations. Circ: 80,000.
Website: www.ptotoday.com

Freelance Potential
80% written by nonstaff writers. Publishes 60 freelance submissions yearly. Receives 100–150 queries yearly.
Submissions and Payment: Guidelines available. Query. Accepts email queries to craigb@ptotoday.com. Responds in 2 months. Articles, word lengths vary; payment rates vary. Pays on publication. First and electronic rights. Provides 1 contributor's copy.

Radio Control Boat Modeler

Air Age Publishing
100 East Ridge Road
Ridgefield, CT 06877-4606

Executive Editor: Matt Higgins

Description and Interests
Published four times each year for the remote control boating enthusiast, this magazine covers every facet of the hobby. Features include building and racing articles, event coverage, and boat reviews. Circ: 55,000.
Website: www.rcboatmodeler.com

Freelance Potential
70% written by nonstaff writers. Publishes 20–25 freelance submissions yearly; 75% by unpublished writers. Receives 180 queries yearly.
Submissions and Payment: Sample copy and guidelines, free with 9x12 SASE. Query with outline and brief biography. Accepts hard copy and email queries to rcboatmodeler@airage.com. Availability of artwork improves chance of acceptance. B/W prints and 35mm slides. SASE. Responds in 1–3 months. All rights. Articles, 1,000–2,000 words; $50–$500. Pays on publication. Provides 2 contributor's copies.

Radio Control Car Action

Air Age Publishing
100 East Ridge Road
Ridgefield, CT 06877-4606

Executive Editor: Peter Vieira

Description and Interests
Published monthly since 1985, this magazine caters to the RC enthusiast—from racing to ready-to-runs, from kits to custom creations—with expert advice, comparison tests, race coverage, technical tips, painting and detailing articles, and in-depth product reviews. Circ: 140,000.
Website: www.rccaraction.com

Freelance Potential
30% written by nonstaff writers. Publishes 50 freelance submissions yearly. Receives 410 unsolicited mss each year.
Submissions and Payment: Sample copy and guidelines available. Send complete ms with available artwork. Accepts hard copy and disk submissions (ASCII). SASE. Response time varies. Articles, word lengths and payment rates vary. 35mm color slides. Pays on acceptance. All rights. Provides 2 contributor's copies.

Rainbow Kids

P.O. Box 202
Harvey, LA 70059

Editor: Martha Osborne

Description and Interests
Published online each month and updated weekly, this is the largest e-zine dedicated to helping families before, during, and after adoption. Its editor is particularly interested in personal stories about adoption and parenting children with special needs. Hits per month: 1.5 million.
Website: www.rainbowkids.com

Freelance Potential
80% written by nonstaff writers. Publishes 40 freelance submissions yearly; 50% by authors who are new to the magazine.
Submissions and Payment: Sample copy and guidelines available at website. Query or send ms. Accepts email submissions to martha@rainbowkids.com. Availability of artwork improves chance of acceptance. Responds in 2–3 days. Electronic rights. Articles, word lengths vary. No payment.

Read

Weekly Reader
200 First Stamford Place
Stamford, CT 06912

Managing Editor: Debra Dolan Nevins

Description and Interests
Read is published 18 times each year for middle school and high school students. Its content is designed to promote classroom discussion. This Weekly Reader publication is currently not reviewing unsolicited manuscripts. Circ: 180,000.
Website: www.weeklyreader.com

Freelance Potential
60% written by nonstaff writers. Publishes 8–10 freelance submissions yearly; 10% by authors who are new to the magazine. Receives 900 queries yearly.
Submissions and Payment: Query with résumé. Accepts hard copy, simultaneous submissions if identified, and email to read@weeklyreader.com. SASE. Responds in 1–2 months. First North American and electronic one-time user rights. Articles, 1,000–2,000 words; payment rates vary. Pays on acceptance. Provides 5 contributor's copies.

Read, America!

3900 Glenwood Avenue
Golden Valley, MN 55422

Editor & Publisher: Roger Hammer

Description and Interests
Leaders of reading programs such as Reading is Fundamental, Head Start, and Migrant Education, as well as schools, libraries, and book suppliers, receive this newsletter. It features informational articles for adults and poetry and short stories for children. Reading, literacy, and comprehension are the focus of this quarterly. Circ: 10,000.

Freelance Potential
50% written by nonstaff writers. Publishes 40 freelance submissions yearly; 100% by unpublished writers, 100% by authors who are new to the magazine. Receives 1,500 unsolicited mss yearly.
Submissions and Payment: Sample copy and guidelines, $7.50. Send complete ms. No simultaneous submissions. SASE. Responds in 2–3 months. All rights. Articles and fiction, to 1,000 words. Written material, $50. Pays on acceptance.

Redbook

Hearst Corporation
224 West 57th Street
New York, NY 10019

Articles Department

Description and Interests
Redbook is published monthly and is targeted to young women between the ages of 25 and 44. Each issue is a provocative mix of features geared to entertain and inform its readers with news, essays, articles, and reports. Topics include social issues, pivotal moments in a woman's life, marriage, health, parenting, and popular trends. Circ: 2.3 million.
Website: www.redbookmag.com

Freelance Potential
5% written by nonstaff writers. Publishes 10 freelance submissions yearly; 2% by unpublished writers. Receives 9,960+ queries yearly.
Submissions and Payment: Sample copy, $2.99 at newsstands. Query with clips. Accepts hard copy. SASE. Responds in 3–4 months. All rights. Articles, 1,000–3,000 words; $.75–$1 per word. Depts/columns, 1,000–1,500 words; payment rates vary. Pays on acceptance.

Research in Middle Level Education

College of Education
Southwest Missouri State University
Springfield, MO 65804

Editor: David Hough

Description and Interests
This online journal is read by university professors, public school teachers, and administrators. Peer-reviewed and updated twice each year by the National Middle School Association, this e-zine covers a variety of topics related to the middle grades. Hits per month: 30,000.
Website: www.nmsa.org

Freelance Potential
95% written by nonstaff writers. Publishes 10 freelance submissions yearly; 90% by unpublished writers, 50% by authors who are new to the magazine. Receives 72 unsolicited mss yearly.
Submissions and Payment: Sample copy, $20. Send 5 full-binded copies of complete ms including title and 150–200 word abstract. Accepts hard copy. SASE. Responds in 1 week. All rights. Articles, 1,500–2,500 words. No payment. Provides 1 contributor's copy.

Reptiles

P.O. Box 6050
Mission Viejo, CA 92690

Editor: Russ Case

Description and Interests
This monthly magazine offers the latest information on the care and keeping of reptiles and amphibians for professionals such as veterinarians, and beginner through advanced reptile owners. Circ: 50,000.
Website: www.reptilesmagazine.com

Freelance Potential
60% written by nonstaff writers. Publishes 55 freelance submissions yearly; 50% by unpublished writers, 40% by authors who are new to the magazine. Receives 120 queries yearly.
Submissions and Payment: Sample copy, $4.50 at newsstands. Query or send complete ms. Accepts hard copy. No simultaneous submissions. SASE. Responds in 2–3 months. First North American serial rights. Articles and depts/columns, word lengths and payment rates vary. Payment policy varies. Provides 2 contributor's copies.

Rugby Magazine

459 Columbus Avenue, Suite 1200
New York, NY 10024

Editor: Ed Hagerty

Description and Interests
This monthly magazine focuses on the sport of rugby in the U.S. It covers national and international games and provides reports on rugby news worldwide, as well as profiles of men and women actively involved in rugby. Circ: 10,500.
Website: www.rugbymag.com

Freelance Potential
50% written by nonstaff writers. Publishes 50 freelance submissions yearly; 75% by unpublished writers, 75% by authors who are new to the magazine. Receives 2,400 unsolicited mss yearly.
Submissions and Payment: Sample copy and guidelines, $4 with 9x12 SASE ($1.70 postage). Query or send complete ms. Accepts hard copy and disk submissions. SASE. Responds in 2 weeks. Written material, word lengths and payment rates vary. Pays on publication. All rights. Provides 3 contributor's copies.

Scholastic News

Scholastic Inc.
557 Broadway
New York, NY 10012

Submissions Editor, Editions 1–3: Janis Behrens
Submissions Editor, Editions 4–6: Lee Baier

Description and Interests
Scholastic News is distributed weekly in classrooms across the country. Each issue provides elementary school children with informative articles on current events and people in the news, along with interactive components that test their knowledge of world issues. There is one edition for each grade from one through six. Circ: 1 million+.
Website: www.scholastic.com

Freelance Potential
5% written by nonstaff writers.
Submissions and Payment: Query or send complete ms with résumé. Accepts hard copy and simultaneous submissions if identified. Availability of artwork improves chance of acceptance. SASE. Responds in 1–3 months. All rights. Articles, to 500 words; $75–$500. Pays on publication. Provides 3+ contributor's copies.

Scholastic News English/Español

557 Broadway
New York, NY 10012

Editor: Graciela Vidal

Description and Interests
This new monthly bilingual publication from Scholastic has a flip format that allows Spanish-speaking students to read in their native language and then turn the magazine over to get the same content in English. It is written for elementary school children in grades one through three. Circ: 40,000.
Website: www.scholastic.com

Freelance Potential
10% written by staff writers. Publishes several freelance submissions yearly. Receives many unsolicited mss each year.
Submissions and Payment: Sample copy and editorial calendar available at website. Query or send complete ms with résumé. Accepts hard copy and simultaneous submissions if identified. Responds in 1–3 months. All rights. Articles, to 500 words; $75–$500. Pays on publication. Provides 3+ contributor's copies.

Science World

Scholastic Inc.
557 Broadway
New York, NY 10012-3999

Editor: Patricia Janes

Description and Interests
Exploring the exciting world of science, this magazine includes articles for junior and high school students. Appearing 14 times each year, it seeks interesting articles on topics relating to physical science, earth science, and life science. Circ: 400,000.
Website: www.scholastic.com

Freelance Potential
50% written by nonstaff writers. Publishes 2 freelance submissions yearly; 10% by authors who are new to the magazine. Receives 120 queries yearly.
Submissions and Payment: Sample copy and guidelines, free with 9x12 SASE. All articles are assigned. Query with list of publishing credits and clips or writing samples. Accepts hard copy. SASE. Responds in 2 months. All rights. Articles, to 750 words; $200–$650. Depts/columns, 200 words; $100–$125. Pays on publication. Provides 2 contributor's copies.

Scott Stamp Monthly

Scott Publishing Company
P.O. Box 828
Sidney, OH 45365

Editor: Michael Baadke

Description and Interests
Every month, stamp collectors, from beginners to advanced, turn to this magazine for informative feature articles covering all aspects of this hobby, including new stamp issue listings. Circ: 25,000.
Website: www.scottonline.com

Freelance Potential
75% written by nonstaff writers. Publishes 120 freelance submissions yearly; 10% by unpublished writers, 15% by authors who are new to the magazine. Receives 180 queries and unsolicited mss yearly.
Submissions and Payment: Sample copy and guidelines, $3.50 with 9x12 SASE ($1.95 postage). Prefers query. Accepts ms. Accepts hard copy and disk submissions (Microsoft Word). SASE. Responds in 1 month. First rights. Articles, 1,200–2,000 words; $75–$150. Depts/columns, word lengths and payment rates vary. Pays on publication. Provides 1 contributor's copy.

Scuola Calcio Soccer Coaching Magazine ☆

P.O. Box 15669
Wilmington, NC 28408

Editor: Scuola Calcio

Description and Interests
Soccer youth coaches and players are the target audience of this magazine that brings the Italian method perspective to training and development. Published nine times each year, it seeks informational and how-to articles and tips on coaching responsibilities and duties, technical training, youth development, scoring development, and techniques and drills. Circ: 350+.
Website: www.soccercoachingmagazine.com

Freelance Potential
10% written by nonstaff writers. Publishes 10 freelance submissions yearly.
Submissions and Payment: Guidelines available at website. Query. Accepts hard copy and email queries to magazine@soccercoachingmagazine.com (Microsoft Word document). SASE. Response time varies. World rights. Articles and depts/columns, word lengths and payment rates vary. Payment policy varies.

Sesame Street Magazine

Sesame Workshop
One Lincoln Plaza
New York, NY 10023

Editor: Rebecca Herman

Description and Interests
Striving to make learning fun and educational, this popular magazine targets children ages two through five. Each issue includes funny stories, interesting nonfiction on topics such as animals, health, and art, and activities. Published by the Parenting Group, Inc., it appears 11 times each year. While it does not accept unsolicited manuscripts, freelancers may submit a query or résumé detailing their qualifications. Circ: 650,000.
Website: www.sesamestreet.com

Freelance Potential
Publishes few freelance submissions. Receives 48 queries yearly.
Submissions and Payment: Query or send résumé only. No unsolicited mss. Accepts hard copy. SASE. Response time varies. All rights. Written material, word lengths and payment rates vary. Pays on publication. Provides contributor's copies.

Shameless

360A Bloor Street W
P.O. Box 68548
Toronto, Ontario M5S 1X1
Canada

Editor: Nicole Cohen

Description and Interests
Shameless is Canada's independent voice for young women. Appearing three times each year, this grassroots magazine is published for teenage girls looking for an alternative to the typical teen magazine. Regular features include profiles of amazing women; discussions of hot topics, the latest technology, health, sexuality, nutrition, and sports; and do-it-yourself guides to crafty activities. Circ: Unavailable.
Website: www.shamelessmag.com

Freelance Potential
30% written by nonstaff writers. Publishes 25 freelance submissions yearly.
Submissions and Payment: Guidelines available at website. Query with clips. Prefers email to submit@ shamelessmag.com. Accepts hard copy. SAE/IRC. Response time varies. First and electronic rights. Articles, 650–2,000 words. Profiles, 300–500 words. No payment.

Simply You Magazine

P.O. Box 284
Phillips, WI 54555-0284

Editor

Description and Interests
Simply You Magazine is an online publication focusing on enhancing the body, mind, and spirit of young adults. Updated six times each year, it is especially interested in true-life teen and young adult stories and documentaries. It also offers personal advice, poetry, and message boards. Hits per month: 10,000.
Website: www.simplyyoumagazine.com

Freelance Potential
25% written by nonstaff writers. Publishes 20 freelance submissions yearly; 25% by unpublished writers, 50% by authors who are new to the magazine. Receives 100 unsolicited mss yearly.
Submissions and Payment: Sample copy and guidelines, free with #10 SASE. Send complete ms. Accepts email to lynne@simplyyoumagazine.com. Responds in 1–2 months. All rights. Articles, word lengths vary. No payment. Provides 1 contributor's copy.

Skiing

929 Pearl Street, Suite 200
Boulder, CO 80302

Editor-in-Chief: Marc Peruzzi

Description and Interests
This sports magazine is published seven times each year for skiing enthusiasts of all skill levels. It features articles, news, and information on this popular winter sport. Circ: 400,000.
Website: www.skiingmag.com

Freelance Potential
60% written by nonstaff writers. Publishes 50 freelance submissions yearly; 2% by unpublished writers, 5% by authors who are new to the magazine. Receives 180 queries yearly.
Submissions and Payment: Sample copy and guidelines, $2.50 with 9x12 SASE ($1 postage). Query with clips or writing samples. No simultaneous submissions. Accepts hard copy. SASE. Responds in 2–4 months. First universal and all media rights. Articles and depts/columns, word lengths vary; $.75 per word. Pays on acceptance. Provides contributor's copies.

Softball Youth ☆

P.O. Box 983
Morehead, KY 40351

President: Scott Hacker

Description and Interests
This quarterly magazine targets girls interested in softball. It includes informational and how-to articles, personal experience pieces, photo-essays, interviews, and reviews. Through its articles, it strives to inspire and motivate readers to play softball and hopes to re-energize the sport. It seeks training tips and interviews with players and coaches. Prospective writers must know the sport. Circ: Unavailable.
Website: www.softballyouth.com

Freelance Potential
80% written by nonstaff writers. Publishes 25–30 freelance submissions yearly.
Submissions and Payment: Query or send complete ms. Accepts email submissions to mailbox@baseballyouth.com. Response time varies. Exclusive rights. Written material, word lengths and payment rates vary. Pays on publication.

Small Town Life Magazine

1046 Barnett Hill Road
Punxsutawney, PA 15767

Editor: Jennifer Forrest

Description and Interests
This upbeat family magazine provides features, recipes, puzzles, and other feel-good articles that are suitable for all ages. It also prides itself on providing new writers with an opportunity to get their work published. *Small Town Life* is available at newsstands in Pennsylvania six times per year. Circ: 5,000.
Website: www.smalltownlifemagazine.com

Freelance Potential
80% written by nonstaff writers. Publishes 60 freelance submissions yearly; 10% by unpublished writers, 25% by authors who are new to the magazine.
Submissions and Payment: Sample copy, $5. Guidelines available at website. Query or send complete ms. Accepts disk submissions and email submissions to editor@smalltownlifemagazine.com. SASE. Response time varies. First rights. Articles, 3–4 pages. Depts/columns, 500–700 words. No payment.

Spirit

Sisters of St. Joseph of Carondelet
1884 Randolph Avenue
St. Paul, MN 55105-1700

Editor: Joan Mitchell

Description and Interests
Spirit is published 28 times each year for religious education classes. This take-home paper for teens reflects the theme found in each weekly Gospel. Suggestions for ways to build a Christian community and coping solutions for teens appear in each issue. Circ: 25,000.
Website: www.goodgroundpress.com

Freelance Potential
50% written by nonstaff writers. Publishes 6–10 freelance submissions yearly; 50% by unpublished writers. Receives 192 queries and unsolicited mss yearly.
Submissions and Payment: Sample copy, free. Guidelines available. Query or send complete ms. Accepts hard copy and simultaneous submissions if identified. SASE. Responds to queries in 1 month, to mss in 6 months. All rights. Articles and fiction, to 1,200 words; $200. Pays on publication. Provides 5–10 contributor's copies.

Start

321 North Pine
Lansing, MI 48933

Editor: Sheryl James

Description and Interests
Previously published as *Wonder Years*, *Start* is a free publication that seeks to help parents, guardians, and caregivers increase their children's chances for success from birth through college. Features most open to free-lancers include skill building activities and journal-style stories that share lessons learned as a parent. The magazine is a publication of Partnership for Learning. Circ: 60,000.
Website: www.partnershipforlearning.org

Freelance Potential
85% written by nonstaff writers.
Submissions and Payment: Guidelines available at website. Sample copy, free with 9x12 SASE. Query. Accepts hard copy and email queries to info@ partnershipforlearning.org. Response time varies. Rights vary. Articles, 150–800 words; $75–$150. Pays on publication.

Surfing

950 Calle Amanecer, Suite C
San Clemente, CA 92673

Editor: Evan Slater

Description and Interests
Young surfers enjoy this monthly magazine for its arti-cles on skill building and living the surfing lifestyle. Its departments are most open to new writers. Circ: 105,000.
Website: www.surfingthemag.com

Freelance Potential
35% written by nonstaff writers. Publishes 15 freelance submissions yearly; 50% by unpublished writers. Receives 72 unsolicited mss yearly.
Submissions and Payment: Sample copy, $3.99 at newsstands. Guidelines available. Query or send com-plete ms. Prefers email submissions to surfing@ primedia.com. Accepts hard copy, disk submissions (QuarkXPress or Microsoft Word), and simultaneous sub-missions if identified. SASE. Responds in 1 month. One-time rights. Articles, 2,000–3,000 words. Depts/ columns, 35–500 words. Written material, $.10–$.25 per word. Pays on publication. Provides 2 copies.

Supertwins

P.O. Box 306
East Islip, NY 11730

Editor: Maureen D. Boyle

Description and Interests
Supertwins magazine is published quarterly by Mothers of Supertwins (MOST) for families with children in diapers as well as elementary school. It features informative articles, an in-depth Q&A section, birth announcements, and pictures of multiples and their families. Circ: Unavailable.
Website: www.MOSTonline.org

Freelance Potential
100% written by nonstaff writers. Publishes 16 free-lance submissions yearly. Receives 100 queries yearly.
Submissions and Payment: Sample copy, $5 with 9x12 SASE. Query or send complete ms. Accepts hard copy and email to info@mostonline.org. No simultane-ous submissions. SASE. Response time varies. Rights vary. Articles and depts/columns, word lengths and payment rates vary. Pays on publication. Provides 2 con-tributor's copies.

Synchro Swimming USA ☆

201 South Capitol Avenue, Suite 901
Indianapolis, IN 46225

Editor: Taylor D. Payne

Description and Interests
This quarterly magazine is published as an incentive to members of U.S. Synchronized Swimming. The majority of its readers are coaches, athletes, or judges of the sport of synchronized swimming. In addition to articles on teams, members, and coaches, it also includes com-petition results and gear information. It seeks articles from writers who can provide up-to-date information on the sport. Circ: 7,000.
Website: www.usasynchro.org

Freelance Potential
50% written by nonstaff writers. Publishes 15–18 free-lance submissions yearly; 35% by unpublished writers, 50% by authors who are new to the magazine.
Submissions and Payment: Query or send complete ms. Accepts hard copy. SASE. Response time varies. First North American serial rights. Articles and depts/ columns, word lengths vary. No payment.

TAP: The Autism Perspective

10153½ Riverside Drive, Suite 243
Toluca, CA 91602

Publisher: Nicki Fisher

Description and Interests

The purpose of this quarterly magazine is to present options and perspectives that provide the readership hands-on experiences, useful therapies, and cutting-edge interventions or techniques that can improve life for people with autism and those who care for them. It seeks articles, research findings, and first-person accounts that reflect its focus. Circ: Unavailable.
Website: www.theautismperspective.org

Freelance Potential

100% written by nonstaff writers. Publishes 120–140 freelance submissions yearly. Receives 360 queries yearly.
Submissions and Payment: Guidelines available at website. Query. Accepts hard copy and email queries to submissions@theautismperspective.org. SASE. Response time varies. All rights. Articles, 800–1,000 words. Depts/columns, 1,200 words. Written material, payment rates and payment policy vary. Provides 1 contributor's copy.

Teen People

Time Life Building, 35th Floor
Rockefeller Center
New York, NY 10020-1393

Managing Editor: Lori Majewski

Description and Interests

Pre-teens and teens enjoy this magazine for its articles and photos covering popular young celebrities. In addition, it includes articles on topics such as health and beauty, fashion, relationships, and the music scene. Spotlights of ordinary teens doing extraordinary things are also featured. While the majority of its content is created in-house, it will consider queries addressed to the appropriate editor on the masthead from experienced magazine writers. It is published ten times each year. Circ: 1.6 million.
Website: www.teenpeople.com

Freelance Potential

Publishes few freelance submissions.
Submissions and Payment: Sample copy, $3.99 at newsstands. Query. SASE. Response time varies. All rights. Articles and depts/columns, word lengths and payment rates vary. Pays on acceptance.

Think & Discover

P.O. Box 408
Fort Madison, IA 52627

Editor: Donna Borst

Description and Interests

Appearing five times each year for students in grades one through four, this classroom magazine strives to challenge readers with hands-on activities such as puzzles, creative writing exercises, and problem-solving scenarios. In addition, it includes enrichment activities for the core curriculum. It is looking for creative, thought-provoking activities such as logic puzzles and unique worksheets. Circ: 1,200.
Website: www.menageriepublishing.com

Freelance Potential

99% written by nonstaff writers. Publishes 60–100 freelance submissions yearly.
Submissions and Payment: Guidelines available. Query. Accepts email queries to donna@ menageriepublishing.com. Response time varies. First rights. Articles and activities, word lengths and payment rates vary. Pays on publication. Provides 1 author's copy.

Tiny Tummies

P.O. Box 5756
Napa, CA 94581

Editor: Sanna Delmonico

Description and Interests

Tiny Tummies is used by dieticians, pediatricians, Head Start, WIC programs, day care providers, mother's groups, and teachers to educate parents. Articles such as "Learning to Like Vegetables," "Starting Solids," and "Feeding Toddlers" appear in this magazine published six times each year. Circ: 10,000.
Website: www.tinytummies.com

Freelance Potential

30% written by nonstaff writers. Publishes 10 freelance submissions yearly; 15% by authors who are new to the magazine. Receives 36 queries and unsolicited mss each year.
Submissions and Payment: Sample copy, $1; also available at website. Query or send complete ms. SASE. Response time varies. Rights vary. Articles and depts/columns, word lengths and payment rates vary. Payment policy varies.

Today's Christian

465 Gundersen Drive
Carol Stream, IL 60188

Editorial Coordinator: Cynthia Thomas

Description and Interests
People from all walks of life and Christians of every church affiliation read this digest-sized magazine, published six times each year. It primarily accepts inspirational, first-person pieces. Circ: 125,000.
Website: www.todays-christian.com

Freelance Potential
40% written by nonstaff writers. Publishes 25–30 freelance submissions yearly; 10% by unpublished writers,10% by authors who are new to the magazine. Receives 1,800 unsolicited mss yearly.
Submissions and Payment: Sample copy, free with 6x9 SASE (4 first-class stamps). Send complete ms. Accepts hard copy and email submissions to tceditor@todays-christian.com. SASE. Responds in 2 months. First serial rights. Articles, 700–2,800 words. Depts/columns, word lengths vary. Written material, $.15–$.25 per word. Pays on acceptance. Provides 2 copies.

Total Reader

3214 50th Street Court NW, Suite 200
Gig Harbor, WA 98335

Editor

Description and Interests
This online resource for educators, teachers, and students in grades three through twelve offers help in improving and measuring a student's reading level. It offers tools for meeting students' needs, monitoring and assessing reading levels, and directing appropriate curriculum to improve reading skills. It uses high interest/low reading level material on science and history, and science fiction, fantasy, and contemporary fiction. This e-zine is not reviewing queries or unsolicited manuscripts at the present time. Check the website for updates to its submission policy. Circ: Unavailable.
Website: www.totalreader.com

Freelance Potential
25% written by nonstaff writers. Publishes 20 freelance submissions yearly.
Submissions and Payment: Currently not accepting submissions. Check website for updates.

Toy Farmer

7496 106th Avenue SE
LaMoure, ND 58458–9404

Editorial Assistant: Cheryl Hegvik

Description and Interests
This monthly magazine for farm toy collectors includes articles about farm toys; toy histories; manufacturer profiles; personal stories; and information on new farm toys, current shows, and events. Circ: 27,000.
Website: www.toyfarmer.com

Freelance Potential
80% written by nonstaff writers. Publishes 50 freelance submissions yearly; 20% by unpublished writers, 20% by authors who are new to the magazine. Receives numerous queries yearly.
Submissions and Payment: Sample copy, guidelines, and editorial calendar, $5 with 9x12 SASE. Query with writing samples. Accepts hard copy. SASE. Responds in 1 month. First rights. Articles, 1,500 words. Depts/columns, 800 words. Written material, $.10 per word. Pays on publication. Provides 2 contributor's copies.

True Girl!

P.O. Box 874
LaPorte, IN 46352

Editor: Brandi Lee

Description and Interests
Written for Catholic teens, this magazine strives to positively encourage girls in their love of God and of the church. It seeks articles that provide practical advice on relationships and real world skills, profiles of positive Catholic role models, and fashion that focuses on healthy bodies. *True Girl* is published six times each year. Circulation: Unavailable.
Website: www.truegirlonline.com

Freelance Potential
50% written by nonstaff writers. Publishes 25 freelance submissions yearly.
Submissions and Payment: Guidelines available at website. Query or send complete ms. Accepts hard copy and email to brandi@truegirlonline.com. Responds in 4–6 weeks. First North American serial rights and electronic rights for 3 months. Written material, 800–1,200 words; $.15–$.20 per word. Pays on acceptance.

Turtle Trails

P.O. Box 19623
Reno, NV 89502

Editor: Virginia Castleman

Description and Interests
Turtle Trails is a new multicultural magazine for children ages six through twelve. Each issue has a thematic focus that promotes tolerance and understanding. It seeks stories written in short sentences—using foreign words and an active voice—on topics such as friendship, courage, traditions, faith, and generosity. Nonfiction pieces provide the best opportunities for new writers. Submit seasonal material six months in advance. Circ: 20,000+.

Freelance Potential
55% written by nonstaff writers.
Submissions and Payment: Sample copy, $3.50 with 6x9 SASE. Guidelines and theme list available. Send complete ms. Accepts email submissions to vcastleman@sbcglobal.net. Responds in 3 months. First rights. Articles and fiction, 500–800 words; $25. Pays on publication. Provides 1 contributor's copy.

Vegetarian Journal

P.O. Box 1463
Baltimore, MD 21205

Managing Editor: Debra Wasserman

Description and Interests
Recipes made without animal products appear along with articles on nutrition, fitness, and natural foods in this quarterly. The editors of *Vegetarian Journal* recognize and cater to the growing number of vegetarian kids and teens. Circ: 20,000.
Website: www.vrg.org

Freelance Potential
50% written by nonstaff writers. Publishes 12 freelance submissions yearly; 5% by unpublished writers, 15% by authors who are new to the magazine. Receives 96–120 queries and unsolicited mss yearly.
Submissions and Payment: Guidelines available. Query or send complete ms. Accepts hard copy. SASE. Response time varies. First rights. Articles, 1,200–2,000 words. Depts/columns, 600–800 words. All material, payment rates vary. Pays on acceptance. Provides 2 contributor's copies.

Tuscaloosa Christian Family

P.O. Box 66
Northport, AL 35476

Editor: Craig Threlkeld

Description and Interests
This regional Christian lifestyles magazine provides resources for Christian and non-Christian families on topics such as parenting, money, music, movies, and books for all age segments of the population. It is published monthly. Circ: 10,000.
Website: www.tuscaloosachristianfamily.com

Freelance Potential
60–70% written by nonstaff writers. Publishes 26 freelance submissions yearly; 5% by unpublished writers. Receives 96 queries yearly.
Submissions and Payment: Sample copy, free with 9x12 SASE ($3 postage). Query with photos if applicable. Accepts hard copy and email queries to editorial@tuscaloosachristianfamily.com. SASE. Responds in 2 months. Rights vary. Articles and fiction, 500 words. Depts/columns, 500 words. No payment. Provides 1 contributor's copy.

Vertical Thought

555 Technecenter Drive
Milford, OH 45150

Editor: David Treybig

Description and Interests
This magazine strives to serve up relevant content to help young adults and teens discover and live God's way of life. Published quarterly, it seeks material that helps readers not only think about, but act on, the things from God that are most important in life. All articles must conform to the teachings and doctrines of the United Church of God. It will consider all contributions consistent with it values. Circ: 24,000.
Website: www.verticalthought.org

Freelance Potential
5% written by nonstaff writers. Publishes 3–4 freelance submissions yearly; 20% by unpublished writers.
Submissions and Payment: Send complete ms. Accepts hard copy and email submissions to info@verticalthought.org. SASE. Response time varies. One-time rights. Written material, word lengths vary. No payment.

VerveGirl

401 Richmond Street West, Suite 245
Toronto, Ontario M5V 1X3
Canada

Editor-in-Chief: Jaishree Drepaul

Description and Interests
Young women ages 14 to 18 read this magazine for informational articles, profiles, and interviews on topics such as health, fashion, nutrition, the environment, education, recreation, careers, beauty, music, and social issues. Published eight times each year by Youth Culture Group, it seeks profiles of teen heroes who have made a difference in their communities, as well as how-to articles and humorous pieces. Circ: 150,000 English; 30,000 French.
Website: www.vervegirl.com

Freelance Potential
15% written by nonstaff writers. Publishes 10–20 freelance submissions yearly.
Submissions and Payment: Query. Accepts hard copy. SAE/IRC. Response time varies. Rights vary. Articles and depts/columns, word lengths and payment rates vary. Pays on publication.

Virtue Magazine ☆

107 Crestview Drive
Morgantown, WV 26505

Editor: Theresa Moss

Description and Interests
Virtue is an online conservative magazine created by high school students aimed at no specific audience. Updated every two weeks, this e-zine is a place for young people to express commentary on political issues both nationally and internationally, along with other popular cultural topics of interest. Topics include book reviews, music, current events, social issues, and essays. Hits per month: 7,100
Website: www.virtuemag.org

Freelance Potential
3% written by nonstaff writers. Receives 10 unsolicited mss yearly.
Submissions and Payment: Guidelines available. Send complete ms with short biography and photo. Accepts email submissions to editor@virtuemag.org. Response time varies. All rights. Articles, 400–500 words. No payment.

Vibrant Life

55 West Oak Ridge Drive
Hagerstown, MD 21740

Editor: Charles Mills

Description and Interests
Adult men and women are the target audience of this health magazine published six times each year. *Vibrant Life* promotes physical health, mental clarity, and spiritual balance from a Christian perspective. Circ: 28,500.
Website: www.vibrantlife.com

Freelance Potential
95% written by nonstaff writers. Publishes 18 freelance submissions yearly; 50% by unpublished writers, 50% by authors who are new to the magazine. Receives 480 unsolicited mss yearly.
Submissions and Payment: Sample copy and guidelines, $1 with 9x12 SASE (3 first-class stamps). Prefers complete ms; accepts queries. Accepts hard copy. SASE. Responds in 1 month. First world and reprint rights. Articles, 1,000 words. Depts/columns, word lengths vary. Written material, $50–$400. Pays on acceptance. Provides 3 contributor's copies.

Volta Voices

Alexander Graham Bell Association
for the Deaf and Hard of Hearing
3417 Volta Place NW
Washington, DC 20007-2778

Editor

Description and Interests
This award-winning publication focuses on hearing loss and spoken language education. Published six times each year, it covers a variety of topics including hearing aids and cochlear implants, early intervention and education, professional guidance, legislative updates, and perspectives from individuals across the U.S. and around the world. Circ: 5,500.
Website: www.agbell.org

Freelance Potential
90% written by nonstaff writers. Publishes 6–8 freelance submissions yearly; 50% by unpublished writers. Receives 24 unsolicited mss yearly.
Submissions and Payment: Sample copy available at website. Send complete ms. Accepts email submissions to editor@agbell.org (Microsoft Word). Responds in 1–3 months. All rights. Articles, 500–2,000 words. No payment. Provides 3 contributor's copies.

Wanna Bet?

North American Training Institute
314 West Superior Street, Suite 508
Duluth, MN 55802

Submissions

Description and Interests
Wanna Bet? is an online publication for kids concerned about gambling. Its focus is to provide education about the downside of gambling. Updated monthly, it features age-appropriate articles about the problems gambling can lead to, alternatives to gambling, and how a parent's gambling addiction affects the family. It also covers topics of current interest, such as the rising popularity of poker playing among middle school kids. Hits per month: 60,000.
Website: www.wannabet.org

Freelance Potential
25% written by nonstaff writers. Publishes 12–15 freelance submissions yearly.
Submissions and Payment: Sample copy available at website. Query or send ms. Accepts email submissions to info@wannabet.org. Response time varies. Electronic rights. Articles, word lengths vary. No payment.

The Water Skier

USA Water Ski
1251 Holy Cow Road
Polk City, FL 33868-8200

Editor: Scott Atkinson

Description and Interests
Self-described as the "world's number one information source for water skiers," this magazine first appeared in 1951. Nine times each year it offers profiles of water skiing teams and athletes, along with well-illustrated features on water skiing tournaments, training, and techniques. Circ: 35,000.
Website: www.usawaterski.org

Freelance Potential
25% written by nonstaff writers. Publishes 3–5 freelance submissions yearly; 60% by authors who are new to the magazine. Receives 12 queries yearly.
Submissions and Payment: Sample copy, $1.25 with 9x12 SASE. Query. Accepts email queries only to usawsmagazine@usawaterski.org. Responds in 1 month. All rights. Articles, 1,000 words. Fiction, 500–1,000 words. Written material, payment rates vary. Pays on publication. Provides 1 contributor's copy.

Waterski

460 North Orlando Avenue, Suite 200
Winter Park, FL 32789

Editor: Todd Ristorcelli

Description and Interests
Appearing 10 times each year, *Waterski* magazine features information on boating and skiing techniques. It also includes articles on destinations, new products, training, and water safety. Circ: 320,000.
Website: www.waterskimag.com

Freelance Potential
10% written by nonstaff writers. Publishes 6–10 freelance submissions yearly; 10% by unpublished writers. Receives 12 queries, 12 unsolicited mss yearly.
Submissions and Payment: Sample copy and guidelines, $3 with 9x12 SASE. Query with résumé, outline, and clips; or send complete ms. Accepts hard copy and IBM disk submissions. SASE. Responds in 2 months. First or one-time rights. Articles, 1,000–2,500 words; $300–$500. Depts/columns, 650–850 words; payment rates vary. Artwork, $75–$500. Kill fee, 50%. Pays on publication. Provides 10 contributor's copies.

West Tennessee Parent & Family

245 West Lafayette Street
Jackson, TN 38301

Editor: Jacque Hillman

Description and Interests
Parents in the western Tennessee region find informational and how-to articles on parenting issues, travel, health and fitness, recreation, education, nutrition, pets, and social issues in this monthly magazine. In addition, it includes profiles, photo-essays, reviews, and information about local events and resources. Keep in mind that it accepts material from local contributors only. Articles spotlighting family-friendly destinations are welcome. Circ: Unavailable.
Website: www.wtnparent.com

Freelance Potential
100% written by nonstaff writers. Publishes 25 freelance submissions yearly.
Submissions and Payment: Query or send complete ms. SASE. Response time varies. All rights. Articles and depts/columns, word lengths and payment rates vary. Payment policy varies.

Wild West

Primedia History Group
741 Miller Drive SE, Suite D-2
Leesburg, VA 20175

Editor: Greg Lalire

Description and Interests

The American frontier and its settlement are the focus of this magazine. Published six times each year, it looks for historically accurate articles that include action and quotes. *Wild West* appeals to history enthusiasts, and is often used by high school teachers. Circ: 80,000.
Website: www.thehistorynet.com

Freelance Potential

90% written by nonstaff writers. Publishes 60 freelance submissions yearly; 10% by unpublished writers, 20% by authors who are new to the magazine. Receives 250 queries yearly.
Submissions and Payment: Sample copy and guidelines, $6. Query with résumé, outline, illustration ideas, source lists, and clips or writing samples. Accepts hard copy. SASE. Responds in 4–6 months. All rights. Articles, to 3,500 words; $300. Depts/columns, to 2,000 words; $150. Pays on publication.

With

The Magazine for Radical Christian Youth

722 Main Street
P.O. Box 347
Newton, KS 67114

Editor: Carol Duerksen

Description and Interests

This magazine for Mennonite teens, published six times per year, tackles tough social issues and current events. Articles include first-person accounts, reviews, and inspirational stories. Circ: 4,000.
Website: www.withonline.org

Freelance Potential

100% written by nonstaff writers. Publishes 60 freelance submissions yearly; 5% by unpublished writers, 5% by new authors. Receives 960 queries and mss yearly.
Submissions and Payment: Sample copy, guidelines, and theme list, free with 9x12 SASE (4 first-class stamps). Query with clips or writing samples for how-to and first-person stories. Send complete ms for other material. Accepts hard copy and simultaneous submissions if identified. SASE. Responds to queries in 1 month. Simultaneous and reprint rights. All material, word lengths and payment rates vary. Pays on publication.

Women Today Magazine ☆

Box 300 STN "A"
Vancouver, BC V6C 2X3
Canada

Senior Editor: Claire Colvin

Description and Interests

This online magazine speaks to the whole woman: physically, emotionally, and spiritually. Updated monthly, it is seeking articles on relationships and first-person experiences that appeal to active, modern women. Hits per month: Unavailable.
Website: www.womentodaymagazine.com

Freelance Potential

60% written by nonstaff writers. Publishes 20–30 freelance submissions yearly; 10% by unpublished writers, 25% by authors who are new to the magazine. Receives 200 unsolicited mss yearly.
Submissions and Payment: Sample copy available at website. Send complete ms. Accepts email submissions only to info@womentodaymagazine.com. Responds in 4–6 weeks. One-time rights. Articles, 1,000–1,500 words. Depts/columns, 700–1,000 words. No payment.

World Around You

#6 Kendall School
Gallaudet University
800 Florida Avenue NE
Washington, DC 20002

Editor: Cathryn Caroll

Description and Interests

World Around You is an online publication for students who are deaf or hard of hearing. Published by the only university for undergraduate students who are deaf or hearing impaired and updated five times each year, this e-zine provides information on careers, reports on the achievement of the hearing impaired, and personal experience pieces. Hits per month: Unavailable
Website: www.gallaudet.edu/worldaroundyou/

Freelance Potential

10% written by nonstaff writers. Publishes 3–5 freelance submissions yearly. Receives 48 queries yearly.
Submissions and Payment: Sample copy, $2 with 9x12 SASE. Query. Accepts hard copy and simultaneous submissions if identified. SASE. Responds in 1 month. Rights negotiable. Written material, word lengths and payment rates vary. Pays on publication. Provides 5 contributor's copies.

World Pulse Magazine

2823 North Killingsworth Street
Portland, OR 97217

Editor

Description and Interests
Exploring the world through the eyes of women and children, this magazine features cutting-edge international articles and analysis, as well as poetry and essays. Appearing six times each year, it seeks material covering international issues. Circ: Unavailable.
Website: www.worldpulsemagazine.com

Freelance Potential
15% written by nonstaff writers. Publishes 15–20 freelance submissions yearly.
Submissions and Payment: Guidelines available. Query with brief author biography and 2–4 clips. Accepts email queries to editor@worldpulsemagazine.com. Responds in 3 months. Rights vary. Articles, 1,000–2,500 words. Fiction and poetry, word lengths vary. Depts/columns, 200–1,200 words. All material, payment rates and payment policy vary. Provides 1 contributor's copy and a 1-year subscription.

Your Child

155 Fifth Avenue
New York, NY 10010-6802

Editor: Kay E. Pomerantz

Description and Interests
This newsletter for Jewish parents includes media reviews, personal experiences, and informational articles on parenting, family, religion, social issues, music, popular culture, and recreation. *Your Child* is published three times each year by the United Synagogue of Conservative Judaism and the Commission on Jewish Education. Circ: 3,000.
Website: www.uscj.org

Freelance Potential
Of the freelance submissions published yearly, 50% are by unpublished writers.
Submissions and Payment: Sample copy, free with 9x12 SASE ($.55 postage). Send complete ms. Accepts hard copy. Availability of artwork improves chance of acceptance. SASE. Response time varies. All rights. Articles, word lengths vary. 8x10 B/W transparencies; line art. No payment. Provides 1 contributor's copy.

Young Expressions Magazine

810 East Jackson Boulevard, Suite B-2
Jackson, MO 63755

Editor: Lisa Cooley

Description and Interests
Young Expressions encourages self-realization, self-confidence, and self-expression for young people ages 10 to 16 with its interesting and educational material. Appearing six times each year online, this e-zine features articles on health, beauty, fashion, and lifestyles, and reviews of games, music, and television programs. Teens are welcome to submit stories, articles, essays, and artwork. Hits per month: Unavailable.
Website: www.youngexpressions.com

Freelance Potential
50% written by nonstaff writers. Publishes 20–25 freelance submissions yearly.
Submissions and Payment: Guidelines available at website. Send complete ms. Accepts email submissions to submit@young-expressions.com. Response time varies. Rights vary. Articles, 500–2,000 words. No payment.

ZooGoer

Friends of the National Zoo Communications Office
National Zoological Park
3001 Connecticut Avenue NW
Washington, DC 20008

Associate Editor: Shannon Lyons

Description and Interests
Published six times each year, *ZooGoer* features factual articles about wildlife, biology, conservation, and natural history. It accepts no fiction or poetry. Circ: 30,000.
Website: www.fonz.org/zoogoer.htm

Freelance Potential
70% written by nonstaff writers. Publishes 25 freelance submissions yearly; 15% by unpublished writers, 25% by authors who are new to the magazine. Receives 15 queries and unsolicited mss yearly.
Submissions and Payment: Guidelines available. Query with synopsis and clips or writing sample; or send complete ms. Accepts hard copy, disk submissions (Microsoft Word), and email submissions to shannon@fonz.org. SASE. Responds in 1–2 months. First rights. Articles, 2,500–3,000 words. Depts/columns, 800–1,500 words. Written material, $.50 per word. Pays on publication. Provides 5 author's copies.

Contests and Awards

Selected Contests and Awards

Entering a writing contest will provide you with a chance to have your work read by established writers and qualified editors. Winning or placing in a contest or an award program can open the door to publication and recognition of your writing. If you don't win, try to read the winning entry if it is published; doing so will give you some insight into how your work compares with its competition.

For both editors and writers, contests generate excitement. For editors, contests are a source to discover new writers. Entries are more focused because of the contest guidelines, and therefore more closely target an editor's current needs.

For writers, every contest entry is read, often by more than one editor, as opposed to unsolicited submissions that are often relegated to a slush pile.

And you don't have to be the grand-prize winner to benefit—non-winning manuscripts are often purchased by the publication for future issues.

To be considered for the contests and awards that follow, your entry must fulfill all of the requirements mentioned. Most are looking for unpublished article or story manuscripts, while a few require published works. Note special entry requirements, such as whether or not you can submit the material yourself, need to be a member of an organization, or are limited in the number of entries you can send. Also, be sure to submit your article or story in the standard manuscript submission format.

For each listing, we've included the address, the contact, a description, the entry requirements, the deadline, and the prize. In some cases, the 2007 deadlines were not available at press time. We recommend that you write to the addresses provided or visit the websites to request an entry form and the contest guidelines, which usually specify the current deadline.

Amy Writing Awards

The Amy Foundation
P.O. Box 16091
Lansing, MI 48901

Description
These annual awards recognize creative writing that presents the biblical position on issues affecting the world today in a sensitive, thought-provoking manner. The competition is open to all writers and eligible entries will have been published in a secular, non-religious publication, but must contain Scripture.
Website: www.amyfound.org
Length: No length requirements.
Requirements: No entry fee. All entries must contain quotes from the Bible. Send an SASE or visit the website for complete guidelines.
Prizes: First-place winner receives a cash award of $10,000.
Deadline: December 31.

Isaac Asimov Award

University of South Florida
School of Mass Communications
4202 East Fowler
Tampa, FL 33620

Description
Open to undergraduate students, this annual award looks to promote and encourage the writing of high-quality science fiction and fantasy. It accepts previously unpublished entries only.
Website: www.asimovs.com
Length: 1,000–10,000 words.
Requirements: Open to full-time college students only. Entry fee, $10. Limit three entries per competition. Entries should include a cover sheet with author's name, address, and university. Author's name should not appear on the entry itself.
Prizes: Winner receives a cash prize of $500 and will be considered for publication in *Asimov's Science Fiction Magazine*.
Deadline: December 15.

AuthorMania.com Writing Contests

Cindy Thomas
AuthorMania.com
Rt. 4 Box 201-A
Buna, TX 77612

Description
The contests sponsored by AuthorMania.com are open to writers living in the U.S. and look for original, unpublished material. Entries must be written in English and may be on any subject, but must not include violence or hate.
Website: www.authormania.com
Length: Fiction, to 5,000 words. Poetry, no length limits.
Requirements: Entry fee, $20. Multiple entries will be accepted provided each is accompanied by a separate entry fee. Accepts photocopies and computer printouts. Manuscripts will not be returned. Send an SASE or visit the website for complete guidelines.
Prizes: Fiction contest winner receives a cash award of $1,000. Poetry contest winner receives a cash award of $400.
Deadline: May 31.

AWA Contests

Appalachian Writers Association
Dept. of English
1350 King College Road
Bristol, TN 37620-2699

Description
These contests, sponsored by the Appalachian Writers Association, offer several different awards in categories that include short story, essay, and playwriting. The competition is open to members of AWA and accepts previously unpublished material only.
Website: www.king.edu/awa
Length: Lengths vary for each award category.
Requirements: No entry fee. Entrants may submit up to 3 entries per category. Accepts photocopies and computer printouts. Submit two copies of each entry. Manuscripts will not be returned.
Prizes: First-place winners in each award category receive a cash award of $100. Second- and third-place winners receive cash awards of $50 and $25, respectively.
Deadline: June 1.

Baker's Plays High School Playwriting Contest

Baker's Plays
P.O. Box 699222
Quincy, MA 02269-9222

Description

Accepting submissions from high school students only, this contest looks to acknowledge playwrights at the high school level and to insure the future of American theater. It is recommended that each entry receive a public reading or production prior to submission.
Website: www.bakersplays.com
Length: No length requirements.
Requirements: No entry fee. Plays must be accompanied by the signature of a sponsoring high school English teacher. Accepts photocopies and computer printouts. Include an SASE for return of manuscript. Visit the website or send an SASE for complete guidelines and entry form.
Prizes: First-place winner receives a cash award of $500 with a royalty-earning contract from Baker's Plays. Second- and third-place winners also receive cash prizes.

Waldo M. and Grace C. Bonderman Youth Theatre Playwriting Competition

Indiana Repertory Theatre
140 West Washington Street
Indianapolis, IN 46204

Description

This competition for well-written plays looks to encourage writers to create theatrical scripts for young audiences. Each playwright receives constructive criticism on their entry.
Website: www.indianarep.com/Bonderman
Length: 45-minute running time.
Requirements: No entry fee. Limit one entry per competition. Accepts photocopies and computer printouts. For dramatizations or adaptations, written proof is required that the original work is in the public domain or that permission has been granted by the copyright holder. Send an SASE or visit the website for more details.
Prizes: Awards will be presented to 10 finalists. Four cash awards of $1,000 are also awarded to the playwrights whose plays are selected for development.
Deadline: September 1.

ByLine Magazine Contests

Contests, *ByLine* Magazine
P.O. Box 5240
Edmond, OK 73083-5240

Description

The contests sponsored by *ByLine* are presented in several different categories each month. Past categories include short story, juvenile short story, inspirational article, and poetry.
Website: www.bylinemag.com/contests.asp
Length: Lengths vary according to category.
Requirements: Fees vary according to category but range from $3 to $5. Multiple entries are accepted. Accepts photocopies and computer printouts. Send an SASE or visit the website for complete category information and further guidelines.
Prizes: Cash prizes ranging from $10 to $70 are presented to the winners. Runners-up also receive cash awards in each category. Winning entries for the Annual Literary Awards are published in *ByLine,* and receive a cash award of $250.
Deadline: Deadlines vary according to category.

Calliope Fiction Contest

Calliope
P.O. Box 466
Moraga, CA 94556-0466

Description

Sponsored by *Calliope,* this contest accepts entries of short fiction that display creativity, good storytelling, and appropriate use of language for the target audience.
Length: To 2,500 words.
Requirements: Entry fee, $2 per story for non-subscribers; first entry is free for subscribers. Limit 5 entries per competition. Accepts photocopies and computer printouts. Manuscript will not be returned. Enclose an SASE for winners' list.
Prizes: First-place winner receives a cash award of $75. Second- and third-place winners receive $25 and $10, respectively. All winners are published in *Calliope* (requires one-time rights). Winners also receive certificates and a 1-year subscription to *Calliope.*
Deadline: Entries are accepted between April 15 and September 30.

Canadian Writer's Journal Short Fiction Contest

Canadian Writer's Journal
Box 1178
New Liskeard, Ontario P0J 1P0
Canada

Description
This semi-annual contest accepts original, unpublished stories in any genre. It is sponsored by *Canadian Writer's Journal*.
Website: www.cwj.ca
Length: To 1,200 words.
Requirements: Entry fee, $5. Multiple entries are accepted. Accepts photocopies and computer printouts. Author's name should not appear on manuscript. Include a cover sheet with author's name, address, and title of entry. Manuscript will not be returned. Send an SASE or visit the website for further guidelines.
Prizes: First-place winners receive a cash prize of $100. Second- and third-place winners receive cash prizes of $50 and $25, respectively.
Deadline: September 30 or March 31.

CAPA Competition

c/o Daniel Uitti
Connecticut Authors and Publishers
223 Buckingham Street
Oakville, CT 06779

Description
Open to residents of Connecticut, this competition accepts previously unpublished entries in the categories of children's story, short story, personal essay, and poetry.
Website: http://aboutcapa.com
Length: Children's stories and short stories, to 2,000 words. Personal essays, to 1,500 words. Poetry, to 30 lines.
Requirements: Entry fee, $10 for 1 story or essay or up to 3 poems. Multiple entries are accepted. Submit four copies of manuscript. Manuscripts will not be returned. Visit the website or send an SASE for complete guidelines.
Prizes: First-place winner in each category receives a cash prize of $100. Second-place winners receive a cash award of $50.
Deadline: May 31.

Children's Writer Contests

Children's Writer
95 Long Ridge Road
West Redding, CT 06896-1124

Description
Children's Writer sponsors two contests each year with different themes for original, unpublished fiction and nonfiction. Upcoming themes for 2007 are YA personal experience and middle-grade adventure.
Website: www.childrenswriter.com
Length: Requirements vary for each contest; usually 500–1,000 words.
Requirements: Entry fee, $10 for non-subscribers (entry fee includes an 8-month subscription); no entry fee for subscribers. Multiple entries are accepted. Manuscripts are not returned. Visit the website or send an SASE for current themes and further requirements.
Prizes: Cash prizes vary per contest. Winning entries are published in *Children's Writer*.
Deadline: February and October of each year.

CNW/FFWA Florida State Writing Competition

CNW/FFWA
P.O. Box A
North Stratford, NH 03590

Description
Open to all writers, this annual competition presents awards in several categories including children's literature short story, children's nonfiction, novel chapter, nonfiction book chapter, and poetry.
Website: www.writers-editors.com
Length: Vary according to category.
Requirements: Entry fees vary for each category. Multiple entries are accepted, as long as each entry is accompanied by an entry fee. Use paper clips only. Author's name must not appear on manuscript. Send an SASE or visit the website for complete contest guidelines, specific category information, and official entry form.
Prizes: First- through third-place winners will be awarded in each category. Winners receive cash awards ranging from $50 to $100.
Deadline: March 15.

Shubert Fendrich Memorial Playwriting Contest

Pioneer Drama Service, Inc.
P.O. Box 4267
Englewood, CO 80155-4267

Description

This annual playwriting contest honors its winners with publication and a royalty advance. Plays may be on any subject that is appropriate for family viewing.
Website: www.pioneerdrama.com
Length: Running time, 20 to 90 minutes.
Requirements: No entry fee. Cover letter must accompany all submissions. Include title, synopsis, cast list breakdown, proof of production, number of sets and scenes, and, if applicable, musical score and tape. Any writers currently published by Pioneer Drama Service are not eligible. Send SASE for contest guidelines and information.
Prizes: Winner receives $1,000 royalty advance in addition to publication.
Deadline: March 1. Winners will be announced in June.

Focus on Writers Contest

3rd Floor
828 I Street
Sacramento, CA 95814

Description

This competition is open to residents of California and offers writers the opportunity to test their writing talents against other writers. It looks for high-quality, unpublished submissions of short stories, articles, books/articles for children, and first chapter of a young adult novel.
Website: www.saclib.org
Length: Length limits vary for each category.
Requirements: Entry fee, $10. Limit 5 entries per competition. Accepts hard copy. Author's name should not be included on manuscript. Include a 3x5 index card with author's name, address, and title of entry. Send an SASE or visit the website for contest guidelines.
Prizes: First-place winners in each category receive $200. Second- and third-place winners receive $100 and $50, respectively.

Foster City International Writing Contest

Foster City Recreation Dept.
650 Shell Boulevard
Foster City, CA 94404

Description

The Foster City International Writing Contest accepts original, unpublished entries in the categories of children's story, fiction, humor, poetry, and personal essay.
Website: www.geocities.com/fostercity_writers/
Length: Children's stories and fiction, to 3,000 words. Humor and personal experience pieces, to 2,000 words. Poetry, to 500 words.
Requirements: Entry fee, $12. Multiple entries are accepted. Accepts hard copy and email submissions to fostercity_writers@yahoo.com (RTF or Microsoft Word attachments). Check website for further category information.
Prizes: First-place winners in each category receive a cash award of $100.
Deadline: December 30.

Friends of the Library Writing Contest

130 North Franklin
Decatur, IL 62523

Description

Held annually, this contest accepts material in the categories of fiction, juvenile fiction, essay, and poetry (both rhymed and unrhymed). It is co-sponsored by Hutton Publications and the Decatur Public Library.
Website: www.decatur.lib.il.us
Length: Fiction and juvenile fiction, to 3,000 words. Essay, to 2,000 words. Poetry, to 40 lines.
Requirements: Entry fee, $3 per piece. Limit 5 entries per competition. Accepts hard copy. Include an SASE for winners' list. Send an SASE or visit the website for complete contest guidelines and category information.
Prizes: Winners in each category receive cash prizes ranging from $20 to $50.
Deadline: September 25.

John Gardner Memorial Prize for Fiction

Harpur Palate
English Department, Binghamton University
Box 6000
Binghamton, NY 13902-6000

Description
Honoring John Gardner for his dedication to the creative writing program at Binghamton University, this competition welcomes the submission of previously unpublished short stories in any genre.
Website: http://harpurpalate.binghamton.edu
Length: To 8,000 words.
Requirements: Entry fee, $10 (checks should be made out to *Harpur Palate*). Multiple entries are accepted under separate cover only. Include a cover letter with name, address, phone number, email address, and title. Manuscripts will not be returned. Send an SASE or visit the website for further information.
Prizes: Winner receives a cash award of $500 and publication in *Harpur Palate*.
Deadline: March 31.

Paul Gillette Writing Contest

Pikes Peak Writers
P.O. Box 63114
Colorado Springs, CO 80962

Description
This annual contest accepts manuscripts from unpublished writers in several different categories including children's, young adult, mystery, historical fiction, and creative nonfiction.
Website: www.ppwc.net
Length: Lengths vary for each category.
Requirements: Entry fee, $25 ($40 entry fee includes a manuscript critique). Accepts hard copy. All entries must be accompanied by an entry form, cover letter, and two copies of manuscript. Guidelines are available with an SASE or at the website.
Prizes: First-place winner in each category receives a cash prize of $100. Second-place winners receive a cash award of $50.
Deadline: November 1.

Lorian Hemingway Short Story Competition

P.O. Box 993
Key West, FL 33041

Description
The Lorian Hemingway Short Story Competition is open to all writers and has a goal of helping writers who have not yet achieved major success in the world of publishing. All themes will be considered.
Website: www.shortstorycompetition.com
Length: To 3,000 words.
Requirements: Entry fee, $10 postmarked by May 1; $15 per submission postmarked between May 1 and May 15. Multiple entries are accepted. Accepts photocopies and computer printouts. Send an SASE for complete guidelines and further information.
Prizes: First-place winner receives a cash award of $1,000. Second- and third-place winners each receive a cash award of $500.
Deadline: May 15.

Highlights for Children Fiction Contest

Fiction Contest
803 Church Street
Honesdale, PA 18431

Description
This annual contest has a commitment to raise the quality of writing for children. It looks for well-written short stories for children ages two through twelve. Stories should not contain violence, crime, or derogatory humor.
Website: www.highlights.com
Length: To 500 words.
Requirements: No entry fee. Multiple entries accepted. Accepts photocopies and computer printouts. Include SASE for manuscript return. Send SASE for further guidelines.
Prizes: Winners receive a cash award of $1,000 and publication in *Highlights for Children* (requires all rights).
Deadline: Entries must be postmarked between January 1 and February 28.

Insight Writing Contest

Insight Magazine
55 West Oak Ridge Drive
Hagerstown, MD 21740-7390

Description
The *Insight* Writing Contest puts value on the mechanics of good writing, particularly that with a spiritual message. It accepts entries of short nonfiction and poetry that is of interest to young people ages 14 to 22.
Website: www.insightmagazine.org
Length: From 1,500 to 2,000 words (no longer than seven pages).
Requirements: No entry fee. Accepts hard copy and email submissions to insight@rhpa.org. Author's name must not be included on the manuscript. Include cover letter with title, category, name, address, phone number, and Social Security number. Multiple submissions accepted. Include SASE for return of entry.
Prizes: Winners receive cash awards ranging from $150 to $250 and publication in *Insight*. All other entries will be considered for purchase.
Deadline: June 1.

Milkweed Fiction Prize

Milkweed Editions
Suite 400
430 First Avenue North
Minneapolis, MN 55401-1473

Description
This prize is awarded to the best fiction manuscripts received by Milkweed during each calendar year. Manuscripts can be a collection of short stories or individual stories previously published in magazines or anthologies.
Website: www.milkweed.org
Length: No length requirement.
Requirements: No entry fee. Manuscripts previously submitted to Milkweed Editions should not be resubmitted. Individual stories previously published in magazines or anthologies are eligible.
Prizes: Winner receives a $10,000 cash advance.
Deadline: Ongoing.

Magazine Merit Awards

The Society of Children's Book Writers & Illustrators
8271 Beverly Boulevard
Los Angeles, CA 90048

Description
These awards look to honor previously published fiction and nonfiction. The purpose of these awards is to recognize outstanding original magazine work for young people published during that calendar year.
Website: www.scbwi.org
Length: No length requirements.
Requirements: No entry fee. SCBWI members only. Submit 4 copies of the published work showing proof of publication date. Include 4 cover sheets with member's name as listed by SCBWI, mailing address, phone number, entry title, category, name of publication, and date of issue.
Prizes: Winners in each category receive a plaque. Honor certificates are also awarded.
Deadline: Entries are accepted between January 31 and December 15 of each year.

NWA Nonfiction Contest

National Writers Association
10940 S. Parker Rd, #508
Parker, CO 80134

Description
Sponsored by the National Writers Association, this contest encourages the writing of nonfiction and recognizes those who excel in this field. The competition is open to all writers.
Website: www.nationalwriters.com
Length: To 5,000 words.
Requirements: Entry fee, $18. Multiple entries are accepted under separate cover. Accepts photocopies and computer printouts. All entries must be accompanied by an entry form (available with an SASE or at the website).
Prizes: First-place winner receives $200. Second- and third-place winners receive $100 and $50, respectively.
Deadline: December 31.

NWA Short Story Contest

National Writers Association
10940 S. Parker Rd, #508
Parker, CO 80134

Description
This annual contest accepts previously unpublished manuscripts and looks to encourage the development of creative skills, and recognize and reward outstanding ability in this field.
Website: www.nationalwriters.com
Length: To 5,000 words.
Requirements: Entry fee, $15. Multiple entries are accepted under separate cover. Accepts photocopies and computer printouts. All entries must be accompanied by an entry form (available with an SASE or at the website).
Prizes: First-place winner receives $250. Second- and third-place winners receive $100 and $50, respectively.
Deadline: July 1.

Pacific Northwest Writers Association Literary Contest

P.O. Box 2016
Edmonds, WA 98020-9516

Description
Presenting awards in 11 categories, including juvenile short story or picture book, nonfiction/memoir, young adult novel, and screenwriting, this annual contest is sponsored by the Pacific Northwest Writers Association.
Website: www.pnwa.org
Length: Length limits vary for each category.
Requirements: Entry fee, $35 for members; $45 for non-members. Limit one entry per category. Accepts hard copy. Send two copies of manuscript. Author's name should not appear on manuscript. Include a 3x5 index card with author's name, address, and title of entry. Send an SASE or visit the website for guidelines and specific category information.
Prizes: Winners in each category receive a cash prize of $1,000 and publication of their entry.
Deadline: February 28.

Pockets Annual Fiction Contest

Attn. Lynn Gilliam
Box 340004
1908 Grand Avenue
Nashville, TN 37203-0004

Description
This annual contest accepts fiction entries in all categories except historical and biblical fiction. It is open to all writers.
Website: www.pockets.org
Length: From 1,000 to 1,600 words.
Requirements: No entry fee. Multiple entries are accepted. Accepts hard copy. Manuscripts must list accurate word count on cover sheet. Entries not adhering to the contest word lengths will be disqualified. Send an SASE for return of manuscript. Visit the website or send an SASE for complete competition guidelines.
Prizes: Winner receives a cash award of $1,000 and publication in *Pockets Magazine*.
Deadline: Submissions must be postmarked between March 1 and August 15.

Seventeen Magazine Fiction Contest

Seventeen Magazine
13th Floor
1440 Broadway
New York, NY 10018

Description
Sponsored by *Seventeen Magazine,* this contest is open to writers between the ages of 13 and 21. It accepts original short story entries that exemplify creativity, originality, and writing ability.
Website: www.seventeen.com
Length: To 2,000 words.
Requirements: No entry fee. Multiple entries are accepted. Accepts hard copy. Send an SASE or visit the website for complete guidelines.
Prizes: Grand-prize winner receives a cash prize of $1,000 and publication in *Seventeen Magazine*. Cash prizes and possible publication are awarded to second- and third-place winners.
Deadline: December 31.

Skipping Stones Awards

Skipping Stones
P.O. Box 3939
Eugene, OR 97403

Description
These awards look to cultivate awareness of our multi-cultural world without perpetuating stereotypes or biases. Entries should promote cooperation, non-violence, and an appreciation of nature. Entries may be published magazine articles, books, or educational videos.
Website: www.efn.org/~skipping
Length: No length requirements.
Requirements: Entry fee, $3. Send 4 copies of each entry. Only entries produced in the preceding year are eligible. Send an SASE, visit the website, or send email to editor@SkippingStones.org for complete guidelines.
Prizes: Cash prizes are awarded to first- through fourth-place winners. Winners are announced in April and reviewed in the summer issue of *Skipping Stones.*
Deadline: January 20.

Southwest Writers Contests

Southwest Writers Workshop
3721 Morris NE
Albuquerque, NM 87111

Description
These annual contests present awards in several categories including middle-grade short story, children's picture book, screenplay, genre story, and young adult short story. The competition accepts unpublished material only.
Website: www.southwestwriters.org
Length: Length limits vary for each category.
Requirements: Entry fee, $25 for members; $45 for non-members. Accepts hard copy. Multiple entries are accepted under separate cover. Author's name should only appear on entry form (available at website or with an SASE). Send an SASE or visit the website for complete category information and further guidelines.
Prizes: Winners receive cash awards ranging from $75 to $150.
Deadline: May 1.

Sweet 16 Scholarship Contest

Guideposts Sweet 16
16 East 34th Street
New York, NY 10016

Description
In its first year, this scholarship contest is presented by *Guideposts Sweet 16* and accepts true, first-person stories from writers between the ages of 13 and 18. Entries should reflect a life-changing experience.
Website: www.sweet16mag.com
Length: To 1,600 words.
Requirements: No entry fee. Accepts hard copy and email submissions to scholarship@sweet16mag.com. Visit the website or send an SASE for complete details.
Prizes: First-place winner receives a $16,000 scholarship. Second-place winner receives a $10,000 scholarship. Third- and fourth-place winners receive scholarships valued at $5,000 and $2,500, respectively.
Deadline: November 1.

Sydney Taylor Manuscript Competition

Association of Jewish Libraries
c/o Rachel Glasser
315 Maitland Avenue
Teaneck, NJ 07666

Description
The Sydney Taylor Manuscript Competition was established to encourage aspiring writers of Jewish children's books. It looks for fiction manuscripts of interest to children ages 8 to 11. Entries must have a universal appeal and should reveal positive aspects of Jewish life.
Website: www.jewishlibraries.org
Length: From 64 to 200 pages.
Requirements: No entry fee. Limit one entry per competition. Accepts hard copy. Send an SASE or visit the website for complete guidelines and submission information.
Prizes: Winner receives a cash award of $1,000 and possible publication.
Deadline: December 31.

Utah Original Writing Competition

617 E. South Temple
Salt Lake City, UT 84102

Description
This competition looks to promote and reward excellence from Utah's finest writers. The competition presents awards in several categories including juvenile book, juvenile essay, short story, biography, and general nonfiction. It accepts previously unpublished work from Utah writers only.
Website: http://arts.utah.gov/literature/comprules.html
Length: Varies for each category.
Requirements: No entry fee. Limit one entry per category. Accepts hard copy. Manuscripts will not be returned. Send an SASE or visit the website for complete category guidelines.
Prizes: Winners receive cash prizes ranging from $300 to $5,000.
Deadline: June 24. Winners are notified in September.

Tennessee Williams One-Act Play Competition

Tennessee Williams New Orleans Literary Festival
938 Lafayette Street, Suite 514
New Orleans, LA 70113

Description
This competition looks to celebrate and honor previously unpublished playwrights. Entries should be one-act plays that feature small casts and minimal technical support.
Website: www.tennesseewilliams.net
Length: One act; 1 hour in length.
Requirements: Entry fee, $25 per piece. Accepts photocopies, computer printouts, and multiple submissions. All entries must be typed and must include an entry form, available with an SASE or at the website. Send an SASE or visit the website for guidelines.
Prizes: Winner receives a cash prize of $1,000 and a staged reading of their winning entry.
Deadline: Entries are accepted between September 1 and December 15.

Vegetarian Essay Contest

The Vegetarian Resource Group
P.O. Box 1463
Baltimore, MD 21203

Description
The Vegetarian Resource Group sponsors this competition that awards prizes in three age categories: 14–18; 9–13; and 8 and under. Entrants should base their submissions on interviews, research, or personal opinion. Entrants need not be vegetarian to enter.
Website: www.vrg.org
Length: 2–3 pages.
Requirements: No entry fee. Limit one entry per competition. Accepts photocopies, computer printouts, and handwritten entries. Send an SASE or visit the website for complete guidelines.
Prizes: Winners in each category receive a $50 savings bond and publication in the *Vegetarian Journal* (requires all rights).
Deadline: May 1. Winners are announced at the end of the year.

Paul A. Witty Short Story Award

International Reading Association
P.O. Box 8139
Newark, DE 19714-8139

Description
This award is presented annually to the author of an original short story published for the first time during the current calendar year. Entries should serve as a literary standard that encourages young readers to read periodicals.
Website: www.reading.org
Length: No length requirements.
Requirements: No entry fee. Accepts photocopies accompanied by a copy of the periodical. No more than three entries per magazine. Publishers or authors may nominate a short story and send it to the designated Paul A. Witty Award Subcommittee Chair. For additional information and award guidelines, send an SASE, or email exec@reading.org.
Prizes: $1,000 awarded to winner at the annual IRA Convention.
Deadline: December 1.

Writers at Work Fellowship Competition

P.O. Box 540370
North Salt Lake, UT 84054-0370

Description
The Writers at Work Fellowship Competition is open to emerging writers in the genres of fiction, nonfiction, and poetry. It is open to previously unpublished entries only.
Website: www.writersatwork.org
Length: Fiction and nonfiction, to 5,000 words. Poetry, to 10 pages (up to 6 poems).
Requirements: Entry fee, $15. Accepts photocopies and computer printouts. Multiple entries are accepted under separate cover only. Indicate contest category on outside envelope. Manuscripts will not be returned. Visit the website or send an SASE for complete guidelines.
Prizes: Winners in each category receive a cash prize of $1,500 and publication in *Quarterly West.* Honorable mentions are also awarded.
Deadline: March 1.

Writer's Digest Annual Writing Competition

4700 East Galbraith Road
Cincinnati, OH 45236

Description
This annual competition accepts works in several categories including children's fiction, feature article, genre short story, memoir/personal essay, and stage play script.
Website: www.writersdigest.com
Length: Children's fiction, to 2,000 words. Other categories, word lengths vary.
Requirements: Entry fee, $10. Multiple submissions are accepted under separate cover. Accepts hard copy. Author's name, address, phone number, and category should appear in the upper left corner of the first page. Manuscripts are not returned. Visit the website or send an SASE for complete category list and guidelines.
Prizes: Winners will be published in a short story collection by Outskirts Press.
Deadline: June 1.

The Writing Conference, Inc. Writing Contests

P.O. Box 664
Ottawa, KS 66067-0664

Description
These contests are open to children and young adults and accept entries of short stories, short nonfiction, and poetry. The goal of these contests is to encourage a love of writing among young people.
Website: www.writingconference.com
Length: No length requirements.
Requirements: No entry fee. Limit one entry per competition. Accepts photocopies and computer printouts. Visit the website or send an SASE for further information.
Prizes: Winners in each category receive publication in *The Writers' Slate.*
Deadline: January.

Writing for Children Competition

Writers' Union of Canada
90 Richmond Street, Suite 200
Toronto, Ontario M5C 1P1
Canada

Description
The Writing for Children Competition looks to discover, encourage, and promote new and emerging writers. It is open to Canadian residents and entries must target children, and may be either fiction or nonfiction.
Website: www.writersunion.ca
Length: To 1,500 words.
Requirements: Entry fee, $15 per piece. Multiple entries are accepted. Accepts hard copy. Send an SASE or visit the website for complete competition guidelines.
Prizes: Winner receives a cash prize of $1,500 and the Writers' Union of Canada will submit the winning entry to several children's publishers.
Deadline: April 24.

Indexes

2007 Market News

New Listings ☆

Ad Astra
African American Family
AIM Magazine
American School Board Journal
Autism Asperger's Digest
Baseball Youth
Baton Rouge Parents Magazine
The Blue Review
Cheat Codes Magazine
Chess Life for Kids
Childbirth Magazine
Curious Parents
Discovery Girls
Disney Magazine
Dyslexia Online Magazine
Families on the Go
The Family Digest
Father Magazine
FLW Outdoor Magazine
Fuel
Paul Gillette Memorial Writing Contest
Ignite Your Faith
Jakes Magazine
Junior Baseball
Kaleidoscope
Kids' Ministry Ideas

Kids on Wheels
Kids' Rooms Etc.
Know
L.A. Parent Magazine
Learning Through History
Lifted Magazine
Loud Magazine
The Magazine
Massive Online Gamer
Middle Years
Minnesota Conservation Volunteer
Minnesota Parent
M: The Magazine for Montessori Families
Mysteries Magazine
New Jersey Suburban Parent
North State Parent
North Texas Teens
Parenting
Park & Pipe
Paws, Claws, Hooves and All
Popcorn Magazine for Children
Prep Traveler
Ranger Rick
Scholastic News English/Espanol

Scuola Calcio Soccer Coaching Magazine
Softball Youth
Start
Sweet 16 Scholarship Contest
Synchro Swimming USA
Today's Playground Magazine
True Girl!
Turtle Trails
USA-Gymnastics
U-Turn Magazine
Vertical Thought
Virtue Magazine
Western New York Family Magazine
Women Today Magazine
Wondertime
Young People's Press

2007 Market News (cont.)

Deletions and Name Changes

Becoming Family: Unable to locate

Boutique Magazine: Ceased publication

Busy Family Network: Ceased publication

Catholic Parent: Ceased publication

Christian Parenting Today: Ceased publication

Connect: Removed per editor's request

Cool! Magazine: Unable to locate

Drink Smart: Ceased publication

The Edge: Ceased publication

Education in Focus: Ceased publication

ePregnancy: Ceased publication

The Family Digest (IN): Unable to contact

57 Story Lane: Ceased publication

Florida Leader: Ceased publication

Footsteps: Ceased publication

Go-Girl: No longer using freelance material

Great Lakes Family Magazine: On hiatus

Grrr!: Ceased publication

Guideposts for Kids Online: Ceased publication

Healthy Beginnings: No longer using freelance material

Healthy Choices: No longer using freelance material

Healthy Growing: No longer using freelance material

Imperial Valley Family: Ceased publication

Inspirationstation Magazine: Ceased publication

Iowa Parent: Unable to contact

Jam Rag: Unable to contact

Kentuckiana Parent: Ceased publication

Kickoff Magazine: Ceased publication

Kid's Directory: Removed per editor's request

Long Island Mothers Journal: Ceased publication

Mentoring Bigtime: Ceased publication

Middle Years: Unable to contact

Mommy Too! Magazine: No longer using freelance material

Nashville Christian Family: Unable to locate

Neopets: Future uncertain

On the Line: Ceased publication

Parents and Children Together Online: Future uncertain

Realiteen Magazine: Unable to contact

Recreational Ice Skating: No longer using freelance material

Reunions Magazine: Unable to contact

Riot: Publication suspended

RTJ: The Magazine for Catechist Formation: No longer using freelance material

The Saturday Evening Post: Unable to contact

SchoolNet Magazine: Ceased publication

SG Magazine: Ceased publication

Shasta Parent: See listing for **North State Parent**

Story Friends: Ceased publication

Student Leadership: Ceased publication

Suburban Parent: See listing for **New Jersey Suburban Parent**

Toy Tips Magazine: Unable to contact

True Love: Unable to contact

What's His: Ceased publication

Young & Alive: Ceased publication

Fifty+ Freelance

You can improve your chances of selling by submitting to magazines that fill their pages with freelance material. Of the 632 freelance markets listed in this directory, we have listed 169 markets that buy at least 50% of their freelance material from writers who are new to the magazine. Of course, there are no guarantees; but if you approach these magazines with well-written manuscripts targeted to their subject, age range, and word-limit requirements, you can increase your publication odds.

Abilities
Adoptalk
Adoptive Families
AIM Magazine
The ALAN Review
Alateen Talk
Amazing Journeys
    Magazine
Amazing Kids!
American Libraries
American Secondary
    Education
American String Teacher
The Apprentice Writer
Austin Family
Autism Asperger's
    Digest
Babybug
Bay Area Baby
Bay State Parent
Big Country Peacock
    Chronicle
Bop
Boston Parents Paper
Bread for God's Children
Brilliant Star
Brio and Beyond
Byronchild
Camping Magazine
Canadian Guider
Cappers
Cat Fancy
Characters
Cheat Codes Magazine
ChemMatters
Child Care Information
    Exchange
Childhood Education
Children and Families
Children's Digest
Children's Playmate
Child Welfare Report
Circle K
The Claremont Review
The Clearing House
Club Connection
Clubhouse
CollegeBound Teen
    Magazine
College Outlook

Community Education
    Journal
Creative Kids
Cricket
The Dabbling Mum
Davey and Goliath
Devo'Zine
Dig
Dimensions
Dimensions of Early
    Childhood
Dovetail
Dramatics
Early Childhood Today
East of the Web
Educational Horizons
Education Forum
Education Week
Eduguide
Elementary School
    Writer
Encyclopedia of Youth
    Studies
Exceptional Parent
Fido Friendly
Fort Myers Magazine
Fuel
Gifted Education Press
    Quarterly
Green Teacher
Grit
Group
Guideposts Sweet 16
The High School Journal
High School Writer
    (Junior High Edition)
High School Writer
    (Senior High Edition)
Hit Parader
Homes Times Family
    Newspaper
The Illuminata
Insight
Instructor
Inteen
Inteen Teacher
Jack And Jill
Jakes Magazine
Journal of School Health
Juco Review
Justine Magazine

Kaleidoscope
Kansas School Naturalist
Keys for Kids
Know
The Lamp-Post
Leadership for Student
    Activities
Leading Edge
Learning and Leading
    with Technology
Live
Look-Look Magazine
The Magazine
Momentum
Moo-Cow Fan Club
Mothering
Mother Verse Magazine
Mr. Marquis' Museletter
My Friend
Natural Jewish Parenting
New Expression
Northern Michigan Family
    Magazine
The Old Schoolhouse
    Magazine
Our Children
Parent and Preschooler
    Newsletter
Parentguide News
Parenting New
    Hampshire
Parents & Kids
Park & Pipe
Pediatrics for Parents
Piedmont Parent
Plays
Plum Magazine
Pogo Stick
Positive Teens
Potluck Children's
    Literary Magazine
Principal
Read, America!
Real Sports
Rugby Magazine
Sacramento/Sierra
    Parent
San Diego Family
SchoolArts
School Library Journal
Science Activities

Science and Children
The Science Teacher
Seek
Shine Brightly
Simply You Magazine
Skipping Stones
Sparkle
Spider
Stone Soup
Student Assistance
    Journal
Student Leader
SuperScience
Synchro Swimming USA
Teachers and Writers
Teachers of Vision
Teaching PreK–8
Teaching Theatre
Teen Light
Teen Voices
Texas Childcare
Theory Into Practice
Thrasher
Three Leaping Frogs
Tidewater Parent
Tiger Beat
Today's Catholic
    Teacher
Transitions Abroad
The Universe in the
    Classroom
Vegetarianteen.com
Voice of Youth
    Advocates
Voices from the Middle
The Water Skier
Wee Ones
What If?
What's Up Kids Family
    Magazine
Wondertime
Writers' Journal
Young Adult Today
Young Adult Today
    Leader
Young People's
    Press

Category Index

To help you find the appropriate market for your manuscript or query letter, we have compiled a category and subject index listing magazines according to their primary editorial interests. Pay close attention to the markets that overlap. For example, when searching for a market for your rock-climbing adventure story for 8- to 12-year-old readers, you might look under the categories "Adventure Stories" and "Middle-grade (Fiction)." If you have an idea for an article about blue herons for early readers, look under the categories "Animals/Pets" and "Early Reader (Nonfiction)" to find possible markets. Always check the magazine's listing for explanations of specific needs.

For your convenience, we have listed below all of the categories that are included in this index. If you don't find a category that exactly fits your material, try to find a broader term that covers your topic.

Adventure Stories
Animals (Fiction)
Animals/Pets (Nonfiction)
Audio/Video
Bilingual (Nonfiction)
Biography
Boys' Magazines
Canadian Magazines
Career/College
Child Care
Computers
Contemporary Fiction
Crafts/Hobbies
Current Events
Drama
Early Reader (Fiction)
Early Reader (Nonfiction)
Education/Classroom
Factual/Informational
Fairy Tales
Family/Parenting
Fantasy
Folktales/Folklore
Games/Puzzles/Activities
Geography
Gifted Education
Girls' Magazines
Health/Fitness

Historical Fiction
History
Horror
How-to
Humor (Fiction)
Humor (Nonfiction)
Inspirational Fiction
Language Arts
Mathematics
Middle-grade (Fiction)
Middle-grade (Nonfiction)
Multicultural/Ethnic
  (Fiction)
Multicultural/Ethnic
  (Nonfiction)
Music
Mystery/Suspense
Nature/Environment
  (Fiction)
Nature/Environment
  (Nonfiction)
Personal Experience
Photo-Essays
Popular Culture
Preschool (Fiction)
Preschool (Nonfiction)
Profile/Interview
Read-aloud Stories

Real-life/Problem-solving
Rebus
Recreation/Entertainment
Regional
Religious (Fiction)
Religious (Nonfiction)
Reviews
Romance
Science Fiction
Science/Technology
Self-help
Services/Clubs
Social Issues
Special Education
Sports (Fiction)
Sports (Nonfiction)
Travel
Western
Writing
Young Adult (Fiction)
Young Adult (Nonfiction)
Young Author (Fiction)
Young Author
  (Nonfiction)

353

Historical Fiction

History

Horror

How-to

Magazine and Contest Index

The following codes have been used to indicate each publication's readership: **YA**=Young adults, **A**=Adults, **E**=Educators (including librarians, teachers, administrators, student group leaders, and child-care professionals), **F**=Family (general interest), **P**=Parents. We have listed age ranges when specified by the editor.

If you do not find a particular magazine, turn to Market News on page 344.

★ indicates a newly listed magazine